Human Resource Management

THIRTEENTH EDITION

R. Wayne Mondy, SPHR

In collaboration with

Judy Bandy Mondy

PEARSON

Boston   Columbus   Indianapolis   New York   San Francisco   Upper Saddle River
Amsterdam   Cape Town   Dubai   London   Madrid   Milan   Munich   Paris   Montréal   Toronto
Delhi   Mexico City   São Paulo   Sydney   Hong Kong   Seoul   Singapore   Taipei   Tokyo

Editor in Chief: Stephanie Wall	Senior Art Director: Kenny Beck
Senior Acquisitions Editor: Kris Ellis-Levy	Cover Designer: Laura C. Ierardi
Director of Editorial Services: Ashley Santora	Interior Designer: Laura C. Ierardi
Editorial Project Manager: Sarah Holle	Cover Photo/Art: Shutterstock/ design36
Editorial Assistant: Bernard Ollila	Senior Media Project Manager, Editorial: Denise Vaughn
Director of Marketing: Maggie Moylan	MyLab Product Manager: Joan Waxman
Marketing Assistant: Gianna Sandri	Media Project Manager, Production: Lisa Rinaldi
Senior Managing Editor: Judy Leale	Full-Service Project Management and Composition: Element LLC
Production Project Manager: Ilene Kahn	Printer/Binder: Courier/Kendallville
Operations Specialist: Cathleen Petersen	Cover Printer: Lehigh-Phoenix Color/Hagerstown
Creative Director: Blair Brown	Text Font: Times LT Std Roman

Credits and acknowledgments borrowed from other sources and reproduced, with permission, in this textbook appear on the appropriate page within text.

Library of Congress Cataloging-in-Publication Data

Mondy, R. Wayne
  Human resource management / R. Wayne Mondy. – 13th ed.
  p. cm.
  Includes index.
  ISBN 978-0-13-304354-9
  1. Personnel management–United States.   2. Personnel management.   I. Title.
  HF5549.2.U5M66 2013
  658.3–dc23

                                                      2012023843

10 9 8 7 6 5 4 3

V011

  ISBN 10: 0-13-304354-1
ISBN 13: 978-0-13-304354-9

To two great grandkids, Madison and Matthew Wallace

Brief Contents

Contents

PART FIVE   Compensation 221

Chapter 9   **Direct Financial Compensation 222**

Preface

Overview of the 13th Edition of HRM

Human resource management is arguably the most exciting area in business. Much has changed in the world since the writing of the 12th edition. Certainly the 2012 national elections and the continuing uncertainty of the economy affected many aspects of human resource management. Major technological changes appear to be increasing geometrically with no end in sight. These changes have dramatically affected how the work of the HR professional is performed such as with mobile recruiting and learning. Social media tools such as wikis, blogs, LinkedIn, Facebook, and Twitter have become an integral part of the world of the HR professional. National disasters continue to have an effect on how HR is applied. Each edition seems to provide new examples to be discussed. The need for companies to operate in the global environment continues to expand. The interrelationship of the human resource management functions and the increasing utilization of technology is reflected throughout this book.

The 13th edition of *Human Resource Management* reveals HR as strategically important to management in a practical, realistic manner yet maintains a balance of pragmatism and theoretical concepts. As will be noted throughout the 13th edition, much continues to be done regarding who performs the human resource tasks. HR outsourcing, HR shared service centers, professional employer organizations, and line managers now assist in the accomplishment of human resource activities. As a shift is made in the allocation of those who perform the human resource function, many HR departments continue to get smaller. This shift should permit HR to shed its administrative image and focus on strategic and mission-oriented activities.

Features of the Book

- **HRM in Action** features are provided at the beginning of each chapter and present current topics in human resource management that set the tone for a discussion of major topics included within the chapter.
- **Trends & Innovations** that highlight current developments in the field of human resource management are included in each chapter.
- **A Global Perspective** that highlights HRM in the global environment is included in all but the last chapter. In addition to the Global Perspectives, new global information is provided in virtually all chapters.
- **Social media** topics are examined prominently throughout the text.
- **End-of-chapter exercises** have been added as a new feature to the 13th edition. These exercises provide in-depth, thought-provoking questions to the material covered in the text.
- **The recently passed Dodd–Frank Wall Street Reform and Consumer Protection Act** affects many aspects of HR and is discussed in various sections of the text.
- **The importance of technology** is emphasized throughout the text.
- **The impact of corporate culture** on many of the HR activities is reflected throughout the text.
- **Small business and HR** provides an additional focus for the 13th edition. Five major sections are provided in addition to small business information provided in every chapter.

New or Substantially Updated Topics by Chapter

I especially appreciate the efforts of the professionals who reviewed and provided valuable suggestions for this edition. Many of the changes listed below are based on their suggestions. For example, I have added new sections relating to HR and small business management. In addition, a new section entitled "Exercises" has been added at the end of each chapter to provide students with thought-provoking assignments.

Chapter 1

Mobile HR: Is the Cloud the Limit?; Human Resource Management in Small Businesses; Recruitment Process Outsourcing; Corporate Culture and Employer Branding; Country Culture as a Possible Barrier to Global Business; and Corporate Culture as a Major Internal Environment Factor.

Chapter 2

Pay for Whistleblowing; Corporate Sustainability; Not Everyone Is on Board with Corporate Social Responsibility; Can Corporate Social Responsibility Succeed in the Global Environment?; and Creating an Ethical Culture.

Chapter 3

Lesbian, Gay, Bisexual, and Transgender Employees as a Protected Class?; Employee Retaliation; HR Laws and Executive Orders Affecting Small Businesses; Avoiding EEO Litigation; Global Sexual Harassment; Baby Boomers, Gen X, Gen Y, and Gen Z; and the Vietnam Era Veterans' Readjustment Act of 1974, as Amended.

Chapter 4

Disaster Planning: From Natural Calamities to Human-made Crises; Small Business Succession Planning; Layoff Alternatives; and Global Talent Management.

Chapter 5

Outsourcing and Offshoring; Onshoring; Social Media Recruiting; Reshoring; .Jobs; and Will Contingent Workers Replace Full-Time Employees?

Chapter 6

Recruitment and Selection with LinkedIn; Video Interview; Background Investigation with Social Networking; Situational Interview; Biometrics for HR?; Integrity Tests; Employment Eligibility Verification (Form I-9); and Leadership Styles in the Global Environment.

Chapter 7

Mobile Learning; Informal Training through Social Networking; Shortage of Skilled Workers; Training Games; Executive Onboarding for External Hires; and Global Meetings through Telepresence.

Chapter 8

Can a Case Be Made for Getting Rid of Traditional Performance Appraisal?; Performance Appraisal for Telecommuters; Employee Engagement for a Committed Workforce; and Performance Appraisal versus a Country's Culture.

Chapter 9

Say on Pay, Golden Parachutes, and Clawback Policies; Executive Pay as a Lightning Rod for Criticism; and Executive Compensation in the Global Environment.

Chapter 10

Unique Employee Benefits; Results-Only Work Environment (ROWE); Domestic Partner Benefits; Smoke-free Workplaces and the Patient Protection and Affordable Care Act; and Global Customized Benefits.

Chapter 11

Resilience Training; Workplace Bullying; OSHA and the Small Business; OSHA and Whistleblowers; Musculoskeletal Disorders; Social Networking and Wellness; Evaluation of Safety Programs; and Health Care in the Global Environment.

Chapter 12

Project Labor Agreements (PLA); Revisiting the National Labor Relations Board; The Two-Tier Wage System Returns; and Labor Unrest in China.

Chapter 13

Worker Retention: Keeping Your Top Performers; Emotional Intelligence Needed in Disciplinary Action; and Administering Disciplinary Action in the Global Environment.

Chapter 14

Globalization for Small to Medium-sized Businesses; Recruiting Host-country Nationals; Global Issues Confronting Women; and Global Bribery, the Conviction List Grows.

Approach to the Writing of This HRM Book

I approach the study of human resource management in a realistic, practical, interesting, and stimulating manner. I focus on showing how HRM is practiced in the real world. Throughout the book, you will see examples of how organizations practice human resource management. In explaining a concept, I often quote HR professionals, yet all HR discussion is based on sound theoretical concepts. Throughout this book, the strategic role of HR is apparent in the discussion of each major HRM function. In addition, I show how HR topics are related to other HR topics. For instance, a firm that emphasizes recruiting top-quality candidates but neglects to provide satisfactory compensation is wasting time, effort, and money. A firm's compensation system will be inadequate unless employees are provided a safe and healthy work environment. If a firm's compensation system pays below-market wages, the firm will always be hiring and training new employees only to see the best leave for a competitor's higher wages. This interrelationship will become more obvious as these topics are addressed throughout the book. These interrelationships are also shown to be important as organizations work within the global environment.

Course Prerequisite

This book is designed primarily for the first undergraduate course in human resource management. It is intended primarily for students who are being exposed to human resource management for the first time. It is designed to put them in touch with the field through the use of numerous examples and company material and will reinforce the notion that, by definition, all managers are necessarily involved with human resources. The book provides helpful insights for those students who aspire to management positions. A recommended but not required prerequisite is an introduction to management course.

Instructor Supplements

Instructor's Manual

A comprehensive Instructor's Manual (IM) prepared by the author is available with the 13th edition. In the IM, chapter objectives are first identified; key terms used in each chapter are defined; a comprehensive lecture outline is prepared for each chapter; ethical dilemmas provided in each chapter are analyzed; answers to review questions are provided; possible answers to each of the HRM Incidents presented in the text are provided. Possible answers to the new Chapter Exercises are also provided.

MyManagementLab® (mymanagementlab.com) is an easy-to-use online tool that personalizes course content and provides robust assessment and reporting to measure student and class performance. All the resources you need for course success are in one place—flexible and easily adapted for your course experience. Some of the resources include an eBook version of all chapters, quizzes, video clips, and PowerPoint presentations that engage students while helping them study independently.

PowerPoint Slides

The author prepared comprehensive PowerPoint slides for both instructor and students. The Instructor's version includes text boxes to assist in providing additional information to students. The Student version is black and white and contains no text boxes.

Test Item File/TestGenerator

An extensive set of questions is available for download from the Instructor's resource center. Each chapter contains approximately 100 multiple-choice, 40 true–false, and 10 essay questions for use in assessing your students' knowledge.

Video Library

Videos illustrating the most important subject topics are available in two formats:

DVD—available for in classroom use by instructors, includes videos mapped to Pearson textbooks.

MyLab—available for instructors and students, provides round the clock instant access to videos and corresponding assessment and simulations for Pearson textbooks.

Contact your local Pearson representative to request access to either format.

Acknowledgments

As with the previous editions, the support and encouragement of many practicing HRM professionals has helped to make this book possible. The reviewers for this edition were especially valuable. These individuals are:

Angela Boston
University of Texas at Arlington

Clare Francis
University of North Dakota

Cynthia Cordes
University of Miami

Debbie Mackey
University of Tennessee

Ellen Mullen
Iowa State University

Eileen Kaplan
Montclair University

Jon Bryan
Bridgewater State University

Lee Weyant
Kutztown University

Lydia Anderson
Fresno City College

About R. Wayne Mondy

I have always had a strong interest in business practices as evidenced by my many years of academic and professional experience. I believe that managing people is the crucial side of business because a firm's human resources are the foundation upon which everything is accomplished. Prior to entering academics, I had business experience with such companies as Peat, Marwick, Mitchell, and Co. (now KPMG), General Electric Corporation, Gulf South Research Institute, and Houston Data Center. In addition, I served in the United States Air Force as a management analysis officer. Several examples in your text relate to my business experience.

I received my DBA from Louisiana Tech University and have enjoyed many years of teaching and administration, having served as professor, department head of the Department of Management & Marketing, and Dean of the College of Business. I have authored or co-authored seven college textbooks in a total of thirty-one editions, fifty-four articles, and twenty papers. The textbooks are *Management: Concepts, Practices, and Skills* (eighth edition); *Human Resource Management* (thirteenth edition); *Personal Selling: Function, Theory and Practice* (fourth edition); *Supervision* (third edition); *Management Concepts and Canadian Practices* (second edition); *Staffing the Contemporary Organization*; and *Management and Organizational Behavior*. In addition to the 13th edition of *Human Resource Management,* the HR book has been translated into Spanish (*Administracin de Recursos Humanos,* Prentice Hall, 1997, 2001, and 2005), and Chinese (Prentice Hall, 1998, 2002, 2005, and 2011). A special 2008 two-part international edition of the 10th edition was prepared for India, Bangladesh, Bhutan, Pakistan, Nepal, Sri Lanka, and the Maldives. In addition, a Pearson International Edition was prepared for the 10th edition. A 2010 international edition was prepared for the 11th edition. Articles have been published in such journals as *Business Journal, Journal of Education for Business, HR Magazine,* and *The Journal of Business Ethics.*

I am also Life Certified as a Senior Professional in Human Resources (SPHR) by the Human Resource Certification Institute. During my career at various universities, I have had the opportunity to charter three student chapters of the Society for Human Resource Management. In one instance, about 20 students wanted to take the certification examination. I was excited about their enthusiasm until they informed me, "Dr. Mondy, you have to take it, too." I have never studied so hard but we all were successful in achieving our objectives. That is how I received my SPHR designation; I earned it.

R. Wayne Mondy, SPHR

Part One
Introduction

Chapter 1
Strategic Human
Resource Management:
An Overview

1 Strategic Human Resource Management: An Overview

HRM in Action | Corporate Culture and Employer Branding

employer branding

Firm's corporate image or culture created to attract and retain the type of employees the firm is seeking.

Corporate culture is the system of shared values, beliefs, and habits within an organization that interacts with the formal structure to produce behavioral norms. Throughout this text the importance of various topics related to *corporate culture* will be described with *employer branding* discussed first.

I remember as a child that my mother would always buy a certain brand of canned fruit even though it was more expensive. The brand name itself caused her to buy a product that while higher priced was, I suspect, the same or similar quality as less expensive brands. The company had created a positive image that made her want to use the product. As with the canned fruit my mother purchased, companies want a brand that will entice individuals to join and remain with the firm. Employer branding is an extension of product or business branding. **Employer branding** is the firm's corporate image or culture created to attract and retain the type of employees the firm is seeking. It is what the company stands for in the public eye.[1] As such, the focus on employer branding has become increasingly important for organizations.[2]

Jeffrey St. Amour, national practice leader for PricewaterhouseCoopers' HR Services strategic communication group said, "They're both trying to create the same thing, which is product loyalty or a feeling that this is a high-quality company."[3] Employer branding has become a major recruitment and retention strategy and everyone in the company works to promote the image of the firm.[4]

Brands imply what employees will get from working there, and why working for the company is a career and not just a job. Organizations such as Southwest Airlines believe that their employment brand is a key strategic advantage and sees it as a key contributor to its success.[5] As more Gen Yers enter the workforce, firms may need to alter their brand in order to attract and retain these young people who view having fun in an engaging work environment as important as a good

CHAPTER OBJECTIVES   After completing this chapter, students should be able to:

1. Describe employer branding and define *human resource management*.
2. Identify the human resource management functions.
3. Identify the external environmental factors that affect human resource management and describe the trend for increased mobility of tasks performed by HR professionals.
4. Explain why corporate culture is a major internal environment factor.
5. Explain who performs human resource management tasks.
6. Describe how human resource management activities may be different for small businesses.
7. Describe the various human resource classifications, including executives, generalists, and specialists.
8. Describe the evolution of human resource management and explain the evolving HR organization.
9. Describe the professionalization of human resource management.
10. Explain the possible hurdles of managing human resources across different countries' cultures.

salary. A well-paying job that is boring will not keep them for long. They want an organization that is "cool."[6] Gen Yers tend to be choosier and seek companies that match their personal standards as well as identity.[7]

An employer brand embodies the values and standards that guide people's behavior. Through employer branding, people get to know what the company stands for, the people it hires, the fit between jobs and people, and the results it recognizes and rewards. Every company has a brand, which could be the company of choice or one of last resort. A robust employment brand attracts people and makes them want to stay. In fact, most workers want to belong to an organization that embraces the ideas and principles they share.[8] Employer branding has become a driving force to engage and retain the firm's most valuable employees.[9] As the economy moves out of the recent recession and firms begin hiring again, employer branding is attracting more attention.

Achieving acknowledgment by an external source is a good way for a brand to be recognized. Being listed on *Fortune* magazine's 100 Best Companies to Work For is so desirable that some organizations try to change their culture and philosophies to get on the list. Think about how being on the following lists might assist in a company's recruitment and retention programs:

- *Working Mother* list of 100 best companies
- *Fortune* magazine list of 100 fastest-growing companies in the United States
- *Money* magazine list of 100 best places to live
- *Business Ethics* magazine list of 100 Best Corporate Citizens
- *Computerworld* list of Best Places to Work
- *Black Enterprise* list of Best Companies for Diversity

OBJECTIVE **1.2**
Identify the human resource management functions.

human resource management (HRM)
Utilization of individuals to achieve organizational objectives.

staffing
Process through which an organization ensures that it always has the proper number of employees with the appropriate skills in the right jobs, at the right time, to achieve organizational objectives.

Human Resource Management

Human resource management (HRM) is the utilization of individuals to achieve organizational objectives. Basically, all managers get things done through the efforts of others. Consequently, managers at every level must concern themselves with HRM. Individuals dealing with human resource matters face a multitude of challenges, ranging from a constantly changing workforce to ever-present government regulations, a technological revolution, and the economy of the United States and the world. Furthermore, global competition has forced both large and small organizations to be more conscious of costs and productivity. Because of the critical nature of human resource issues, these matters must receive major attention from upper management.

Human Resource Management Functions

People who are engaged in the management of human resources develop and work through an integrated HRM system. As Figure 1-1 shows, five functional areas are associated with effective HRM: staffing, human resource development, compensation, safety and health, and employee and labor relations. These functions are discussed next.

Staffing

Staffing is the process through which an organization ensures that it always has the proper number of employees with the appropriate skills in the right jobs, at the right time, to achieve organizational objectives. Staffing involves job analysis, human resource planning, recruitment, and selection, all of which are discussed in this text.[10]

Job analysis is the systematic process of determining the skills, duties, and knowledge required for performing jobs in an organization. It impacts virtually every aspect of HRM, including planning, recruitment, and selection. *Human resource planning* is the systematic process of matching the internal and external supply of people with job openings anticipated in the organization over a specified period. The data provided set the stage for recruitment or other HR actions. *Recruitment* is the process of attracting individuals on a timely basis, in sufficient numbers, and with appropriate qualifications, to apply for jobs with an organization. *Selection* is the process of choosing from a group of applicants the individual best suited for a particular position and the organization. Successful accomplishment of the staffing function is vital if the organization is to effectively accomplish its mission. These topics are collectively often referred to as staffing.

Human Resource Development

Human resource development is a major HRM function consisting not only of training and development but also of career planning and development activities, organization development,

FIGURE 1-1

**Human Resource
Management Functions**

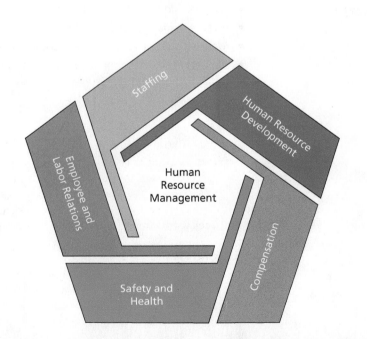

human resource development (HRD)
Major HRM function consisting not only of training and development but also of individual career planning and development activities, organization development, and performance management and appraisal.

and performance management and appraisal. *Training* is designed to provide learners with the knowledge and skills needed for their present jobs. *Development* involves learning that goes beyond today's job and has a more long-term focus.

Organization development (OD) is planned and systematic attempts to change the organization (corporate culture), typically to a more behavioral environment. OD applies to an entire system, such as a company or a plant. A number of OD methods are discussed that serve to improve a firm's performance.

Career planning is an ongoing process whereby an individual sets career goals and identifies the means to achieve them. According to the Bureau of Labor Statistics, today's employees will work for approximately nine companies during their careers. A survey conducted by NYU's School of Continuing and Professional Studies showed that on average, individuals will change careers (not merely "jobs") three times in their life.[11] Employee loyalty loses its meaning in this environment.

Career development is a formal approach used by the organization to ensure that people with the proper qualifications and experiences are available when needed. Individual careers and organizational needs are not separate and distinct. Organizations should assist employees in career planning so the needs of both can be satisfied.

Performance management is a goal-oriented process that is directed toward ensuring that organizational processes are in place to maximize the productivity of employees, teams, and ultimately, the organization. *Performance appraisal* is a formal system of review and evaluation of individual or team task performance. It affords employees the opportunity to capitalize on their strengths and overcome identified deficiencies, thereby helping them to become more satisfied and productive employees.

Compensation

The question of what constitutes a fair day's pay has plagued management, unions, and workers for a long time. A well-thought-out compensation system provides employees with adequate and equitable rewards for their contributions to meeting organizational goals. As used in this book, the term *compensation* includes the total of all rewards provided employees in return for their services. The rewards may be one or a combination of the following:

- **Direct Financial Compensation:** Pay that a person receives in the form of wages, salaries, commissions, and bonuses.
- **Indirect Financial Compensation (Benefits):** All financial rewards that are not included in direct compensation, such as paid vacations, sick leave, holidays, and medical insurance.
- **Nonfinancial Compensation:** Satisfaction that a person receives from the job itself or from the psychological and/or physical environment in which the person works.

Safety and Health

Safety involves protecting employees from injuries caused by work-related accidents. *Health* refers to the employees' freedom from physical or emotional illness. These aspects of the job are important because employees who work in a safe environment and enjoy good health are more likely to be productive and yield long-term benefits to the organization. Today, because of federal and state legislation that reflect societal concerns, most organizations have become attentive to their employees' safety and health needs.

Employee and Labor Relations

Businesses are required by law to recognize a union and bargain with it in good faith if the firm's employees want the union to represent them. In the past, this relationship was an accepted way of life for many employers, but most firms today would rather have a union-free environment. When a labor union represents a firm's employees, the human resource activity is often referred to as industrial relations, which handles the job of collective bargaining. Internal employee relations comprise the human resource management activities associated with the movement of employees within the organization such as promotions, demotion, termination, and resignation.

Human Resource Research

Although human resource research is not a distinct HRM function, it pervades all functional areas, and the researcher's laboratory is the entire work environment. For instance, a study related to recruitment may suggest the type of worker most likely to succeed in the culture of a particular firm. Research on job safety may identify the causes of certain work-related accidents.

The reasons for problems such as excessive absenteeism or excessive grievances may not be readily apparent. However, when such problems occur, human resource research can often find the causes and offer possible solutions. Human resource research is clearly an important key to developing the most productive and satisfied workforce possible.

Interrelationships of HRM Functions

All HRM functional areas are highly interrelated. Management must recognize that decisions in one area will affect other areas. For instance, a firm that emphasizes recruiting top-quality candidates but neglects to provide satisfactory compensation is wasting time, effort, and money. In addition, a firm's compensation system will be inadequate unless employees are provided a safe and healthy work environment. If a firm's compensation system pays below-market wages, the firm will always be hiring and training new employees only to see the best leave for a competitor's higher wages. The interrelationships among the HRM functional areas will become more obvious as these topics are addressed throughout the book.

OBJECTIVE **1.3**

Identify the external environmental factors that affect human resource management and describe the trend for increased mobility of tasks performed by HR professionals.

external environment

Factors outside an organization's boundaries that affect a firm's human resources makeup.

Dynamic Human Resource Management Environment

Many interrelated factors affect the five previously identified HRM functions. Factors outside an organization's boundaries that affect a firm's human resources make up the **external environment**.

The firm often has little, if any, control over how the external environment affects management of its human resources. As illustrated in Figure 1-2, external factors include the legal considerations, labor market, society, political parties, unions, shareholders, competition, customers, technology, the economy, and unanticipated events. Each factor, either separately or in combination with others, can place constraints on how HRM tasks are accomplished.

Legal Considerations

A significant external force affecting HRM relates to federal, state, and local legislation and the many court decisions interpreting this legislation. In addition, presidential executive orders have had a major impact on HRM. These legal considerations affect virtually the entire spectrum of human resource policies. Laws, court decisions, and executive orders affecting other HRM activities will be described in the appropriate chapters.

FIGURE 1-2

Environment of Human Resource Management

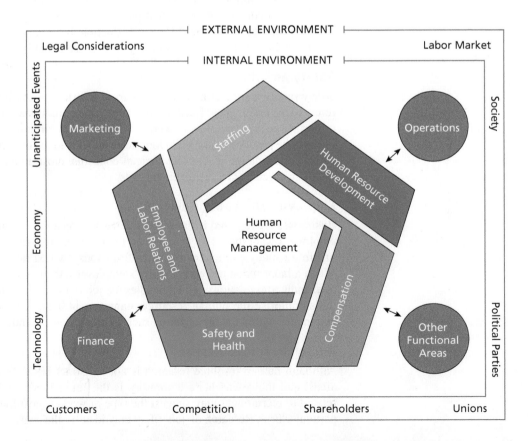

Labor Market

Potential employees located within the geographic area from which employees are normally recruited comprise the *labor market*. The capabilities of a firm's employees determine, to a large extent, how well the organization can perform its mission. Since new employees are hired from outside the firm, the labor market is considered an external environmental factor. The labor market is always changing, and these shifts inevitably cause changes in the workforce of an organization. In turn, changes in individuals within an organization affect the way management must deal with its workforce.

Society

Society may also exert pressure on HRM. The public is no longer content to accept, without question, the actions of business. To remain acceptable to the general public, a firm must accomplish its purpose while complying with societal norms.

 Ethics is the discipline dealing with what is good and bad, or right and wrong, or with moral duty and obligation. Corporate social responsibility (CSR) is closely related to ethics. *CSR* is the implied, enforced, or felt obligation of managers, acting in their official capacity, to serve or protect the interests of groups other than themselves.[12]

Political Parties

Closely related to society, but not the same, are political parties. There are two major political parties in the United States. These parties often have differing opinions on how human resource management should be accomplished. On a global perspective, countries change governments from time to time, which may affect how human resource management is practiced.

Unions

union
Employees who have joined together for the purpose of dealing with their employer.

Wage levels, benefits, and working conditions for millions of employees reflect decisions made jointly by unions and management. A **union** consists of employees who have joined together for the purpose of dealing with their employer. Unions are treated as an environmental factor because, essentially, they become a third party when dealing with the company. In a unionized organization, the union rather than the individual employee negotiates an agreement with management.

Shareholders

shareholders
Owners of a corporation.

The owners of a corporation are called **shareholders**. Because shareholders, or stockholders, have invested money in the firm, they may at times challenge programs considered by management to be beneficial to the organization. Stockholders are wielding increasing influence, and management may be forced to justify the merits of a particular program in terms of how it will affect future projects, costs, revenues, profits, and even benefits to society as a whole.[13] Considerable pressure has recently been exerted by shareholders and lawmakers to control the salaries of corporate executives.

Competition

Firms may face intense global competition for both their product or service and labor markets. Unless an organization is in the unusual position of monopolizing the market it serves, other firms will be producing similar products or services. A firm must also maintain a supply of competent employees if it is to succeed, grow, and prosper. But other organizations are also striving for that same objective. A firm's major task is to ensure that it obtains and retains a sufficient number of employees in various career fields to allow it to compete effectively. A bidding war often results when competitors attempt to fill certain critical positions in their firms. Even in a depressed economy, firms are sometimes forced to resort to unusual means to recruit and retain such employees.

Customers

The people who actually use a firm's goods and services also are part of its external environment. Because sales are crucial to the firm's survival, management has the task of ensuring that its employment practices do not antagonize the customers it serves. Customers constantly demand high-quality products and after-purchase service. Therefore, a firm's workforce should be capable of providing top-quality goods and services. These conditions relate directly to the skills, qualifications, and motivations of the organization's employees.

Mobile HR: Is the Cloud the Limit?

A rapidly developing trend is the increased mobility of tasks performed by HR professionals. Cloud computing and the use of mobile devices are changing the way HR work is performed, and the change is moving at an amazing pace.[14] Mobile products such as laptops and smartphones have been widely available for five to 10 years. Therefore, many workers, especially people in their 30s and 40s have become very accustomed to using mobile technology.[15] Mobile products gained rapid growth with the introduction of Apple's first iPhone. The development of other smartphones such as the BlackBerry, RAZR, and Palm Treo, among others, further allowed HR professionals to operate on the go. Now, virtually everyone has mobile HR capability.[16] Once mobile devices were available, apps could then be developed for them.[17] Terry Terhark, CEO and founder of The RightThing, said, "Like it or not, mobile technology is the future."[18]

Mobile applications have been adopted for recruitment and other HR functions such as scheduling, employee and manager self-service, performance reviews, and e-learning. Software developers are creating mobile HR applications, and human capital management vendors are making it possible for existing applications to be used on mobile devices. The list is sure to expand in the future. Julie Gebauer, global head of Talent & Rewards at Towers Watsons, said, "With so many professionals on the road these days, the need for instant access to the latest information on HR and employee benefit trends has never been greater."[19] J. Gerry Purdy, principal analyst at MobileTrax LLC, an Atlanta-based consulting firm, said, "Mobile devices are becoming strategic corporate assets. You keep the business process moving as a result of having good mobile systems."[20]

A major factor contributing to HR mobility is *cloud computing*, a means of providing software and data via the Internet.[21] With the cloud there is no more expensive, capital-intensive hardware and infrastructure and no more expensive, time-consuming, staff-intensive upgrades.[22] Cloud computing permits businesses to buy and use what they need, when they need it.[23] It allows large organizations to move away from managing their own computer centers and focus on the core competencies of the firm.[24] Cloud users have the ability to access the application securely from anywhere. A person can be at home, on a smartphone, on any operating system. HR professionals can be virtually anywhere and access the cloud, all through any standard Web.[25]

HR Technology

The world has never before seen such a rapid rate of technological change that is occurring today. The development of technology has created new roles for HR professionals but also places additional pressures on them to keep abreast of the technology. For example, advances in technology have made it easier to steal corporate information or harass other workers, and HR has to be able to use technology to identify and stop such actions, a field of study referred to as digital forensics.[26] The younger generation especially embraces the use of technology in their work. In a recent study, two-thirds of college students and more than half of young professionals identify a mobile device such as a laptop, smartphone, or tablet as the most important technology in their lives.[27] As more and more employees use their own smartphone or notepad at work, companies are looking for ways to secure sensitive company data on this dual-use technology.[28]

HR certainly needs to learn and embrace the ever-changing technology.[29] Those who do not support the emerging technology will be left behind in this rapidly changing HR environment.

human resource information system (HRIS)
Any organized approach for obtaining relevant and timely information on which to base human resource decisions.

With the increased technology sophistication has come the ability to design a more useful **human resource information system (HRIS)**, which is any organized approach for obtaining relevant and timely information on which to base human resource decisions. The HRIS brings under one encompassing technology system many human resource activities. Think of an HRIS as an umbrella for merging the various subsystems discussed throughout this text. Today, mainstay HR responsibilities such as planning, recruitment, selection, oversight of legal and regulatory compliance, benefits administration, and the safeguarding of confidential employee information cannot be carried out effectively without an HRIS. Throughout the text, topics will be highlighted that are part of an HRIS. In addition, all of the HRIS applications may be accessed through cloud computing.

Economy

The economy of the nation and world is a major environmental factor affecting HRM. As a generalization, when the economy is booming, it is more difficult to recruit qualified workers. On the other hand, when a downturn is experienced, more applicants are typically available. To complicate this situation even further, one segment of the country may be experiencing a downturn, another a slow recovery, and another a boom. A major challenge facing HR is working within this dynamic, ever-changing economic environment, as it impacts every aspect of human resource management.[30]

Unanticipated Events

Unanticipated events are occurrences in the external environment that cannot be foreseen. The recent oil spill off the Gulf Coast caused major modification in the performance of many of the human resource functions. Every disaster, whether human-made or natural, likely requires a tremendous amount of adjustment with regard to human resource management. On a global perspective, think of the many different ways HR was affected by the tsunami in Japan. Japanese automobile plants in the United States were forced to temporarily shut down because of a lack of parts produced in Japan. Other recent disasters, such as heat waves, earthquakes, tornadoes, floods, and fires, have created their own type of difficulty.

OBJECTIVE 1.4

Explain why corporate culture is a major internal environment factor.

corporate culture

System of shared values, beliefs, and habits within an organization that interacts with the formal structure to produce behavioral norms.

Corporate Culture as a Major Internal Environment Factor

As an internal environment factor affecting human resource management, corporate culture refers to the firm's social and psychological climate. **Corporate culture** is defined as the system of shared values, beliefs, and habits within an organization that interacts with the formal structure to produce behavioral norms. An infinite variety of cultures could exist, so we probably should view them as a continuum.

Culture gives people a sense of how to behave and what they ought to be doing. Each individual gradually forms such perceptions over a period of time as the person performs assigned activities under the general guidance of a superior and a set of organizational policies. The culture existing within a firm influences the employees' degree of satisfaction with the job, as well as the level and quality of their performance. The assessment of how desirable the organization's culture is may differ for each employee. One person may perceive the environment as bad, and another may see the same environment as positive. An employee may actually leave an organization in the hope of finding a more compatible culture.[31] Max Caldwell, a managing director at Towers Watson, said, "Maybe the best definition of company culture is what everyone does when no one is looking."[32] Topics related to corporate culture are presented throughout this text. Some corporate culture topics include the following:

- *Employer branding* is the firm's corporate image or culture created to attract and retain the type of employees the firm is seeking. It is what the company stands for in the public eye.
- A *country's culture* is the set of values, symbols, beliefs, languages, and norms that guide human behavior within the country. Cultural differences are often the biggest barrier to doing business in the world market.
- Corporate culture is a driving force when discussing business ethics and corporate social responsibility.
- Diversity management is about pursuing an inclusive corporate culture in which newcomers feel welcome and everyone sees the value of his or her job.
- Talent management is a strategic endeavor to optimize the use of human capital, which enables an organization to drive short- and long-term results by building culture, engagement, capability, and capacity through integrated talent acquisition, development, and deployment processes that are aligned to business goals.
- A good Web site should provide a feeling of the kind of corporate culture that exists within the company.
- *Organizational fit* refers to management's perception of the degree to which the prospective employee will fit in with the firm's culture or value system.
- New hire orientation reflects the firm's corporate culture by showing in effect, "How we do things around here."
- Organization development is a major means of achieving change in the corporate culture.
- Today's dynamic organizations increasingly use teams to perform jobs, and managers need to recognize overall team culture as well as individual contributions.
- Anything that the company provides an employee is included in compensation, from pay and benefits to the organization's culture and environment.

● Accident rates decline when the corporate culture encourages workers consciously or sub-consciously to think about safety.
● A corporate culture that does not consider the needs of employees as individuals makes the firm ripe for unionization.
● Retaining the best employees often rests with the corporate culture that exists within the organization.
● Many of the global topics discussed throughout your text are influenced by the issue of corporate culture or country culture.

How Human Resource Management is Practiced in the Real World

At the beginning of each chapter, there is an *HRM in Action* that focuses on an important topic related to the chapter. Features entitled *Ethical Dilemmas* are included in all but the first chapter to test how you would respond in an ethical situation. A *Trends & Innovations* feature is included in each section to highlight current developments and advances in the field of human resource management. *A Global Perspective* is included at the end of each chapter that highlights HRM in the global environment. *HRM Exercises* are provided at the end of each chapter to provide a hands-on approach to understanding HR. Two *HRM Incidents* are provided at the end of each chapter to highlight material covered in the chapter.

OBJECTIVE **1.5**

Explain who performs human resource management tasks.

HR's Changing Strategic Role: Who Performs the Human Resource Management Tasks?

The person or units who perform the HRM tasks have changed dramatically in recent years, and today there is no typical HR department. Many of these changes are being made so that HR professionals can accomplish a more strategic role. Also, the recent recession forced some HR departments to accomplish more with less, and some companies have downsized the HR department in order to keep production-oriented people. This restructuring often resulted in a shift in who carries out each function, not the elimination of the previously identified five HR functions. Some organizations continue to perform the majority of HR functions within the firm. However, as internal operations are reexamined, questions are raised, such as: Can some HR tasks be performed more efficiently by line managers or outside vendors? Can some HR tasks be centralized or eliminated altogether? Can technology improve the productivity of HR professionals? One apparent fact is that all functions within today's organizations are being scrutinized for cost cutting, including HR. All units must operate under a lean budget in this competitive global environment, and HR is no exception.

Evidence provided by The Hackett Group shows that the HR functions have been impacted more than other support functions with regard to reductions in staff and operating budgets.[33] In fact, the most efficient companies typically spend nearly 30 percent less per employee on HR and operate with 25 percent fewer HR employees.[34] Mobile HR, previously discussed, has been a major factor in this trend. Many HR departments continue to get smaller because others outside the HR department now perform certain functions. HR outsourcing, shared service centers, professional employer organizations, and line managers now assist in the accomplishment of many traditional human resource activities. Let us first look at the role of the traditional human resource manager.

Human Resource Manager

Historically, the human resource manager was responsible for each of the five HR functions. Traditionally, a **human resource manager** was an individual who normally acted in an advisory or staff capacity, working with other managers to help them deal with human resource matters. Often, large HR departments were created, with the central figure being the HR manager or executive. The human resource manager was primarily responsible for coordinating the management of human resources to help the organization achieve its goals. There was a shared responsibility between line managers and human resource professionals. Frequently, the line manager went to HR for guidance in topics such as selection, training, promotion, and taking disciplinary action. The traditional distinction between human resource management and the human resource manager is illustrated by the following account:

human resource manager
Individual who normally acts in an advisory or staff capacity, working with other managers to help them deal with human resource matters.

Bill Brown, the production supervisor for Ajax Manufacturing, has just learned that one of his machine operators has resigned. He immediately calls Sandra Williams, the human resource manager, and says, "Sandra, I just had a Class A machine operator quit down here. Can you find some qualified people for me to interview?" "Sure Bill," Sandra replies. "I'll send two or three down to you within the week, and you can select the one that best fits your needs."

In this instance, both Bill and Sandra are concerned with accomplishing organizational goals, but from different perspectives. As a human resource manager, Sandra identifies applicants who meet the criteria specified by Bill. Yet, Bill will make the final decision about hiring, because he is responsible for the machine operators' performance. His primary responsibility is production; hers is human resources. As a human resource manager, Sandra must constantly deal with the many problems related to human resources that Bill and the other managers face. Her job is to help them meet the human resource needs of the entire organization.

HR Outsourcing

HR outsourcing (HRO) is the process of hiring external HR professionals to do the HR work that was previously done internally. It is estimated that HRO is a $15 billion industry.[35] In the early days of HRO, cost savings was the primary driver in determining which activities to outsource. Today, outsourcing agreements are focusing more on quality of service and saving time, which is often more important than saving money. Ron Gier, vice president of human capital planning and employee relations for Sprint, said, "Outsourcing is about concentrating where you are going to put your energy, where you are going to build competency as a company and where you can use a partner to perform activities that are not core to your business."[36] This permits HR to focus on strategic organizational issues. As will be stressed throughout the text, strategic HR has become a major driver for HR professionals.

Discrete services outsourcing involves one element of a business process or a single set of high-volume repetitive functions to be outsourced. Benefits have often been the HR task most likely to be outsourced.[37] Dan Thomas, president of Trivalent Benefits Consulting Inc., said, "Benefits administration has become so complex that it really takes someone who works with it every single day to keep track of all of the different laws and changes that are going on."[38] For example, the Family and Medical Leave Act often has managers struggling to complete the required paperwork, which caused a drain on productivity.[39] One survey found that 65 percent of companies outsourced their health and welfare benefits.[40]

Business process outsourcing (BPO) is the transfer of the majority of HR services to a third party. Typically larger companies are involved with BPO, both as a provider and a user. A major HR outsourcer is IBM with over $96 billion in revenue.[41] Kraft Foods Inc. and IBM signed a multiyear BPO agreement in which IBM took over workforce administration, compensation, and performance reporting for all of Kraft's 98,000 employees spread across 72 countries.[42] Florida created a Web-based HR information system and outsourced administration of most HR functions for approximately 240,000 state employees and retirees. Outsourced services included recruiting, payroll, and HR administration services and benefits administration.[43]

As the recent recession wound slowly down and firms began to hire again, some companies realized that they had lost their recruiting skills. Many had not kept up with the rapidly changing technology that is currently needed to successfully recruit in this new environment. To fill this gap, *recruitment process outsourcing (RPO)* is being used. With RPO an employer uses an external service provider to perform all or part of its recruitment activities. The RPO market was projected to grow by as much as 30 percent in 2011, reaching $1.45 billion. Robert Schulte, president of myStaffingPro, a Lima, Ohio-based maker of applicant tracking software, said, "The RPO industry is all about being efficient and doing more work with less people."[44]

HR Shared Service Centers

A **shared service center (SSC)**, also known as a center of expertise, takes routine, transaction-based activities dispersed throughout the organization and consolidates them in one place. For example, a company with 20 strategic business units might consolidate routine HR tasks and perform them in one location. Shared service centers provide an alternative to HR outsourcing and can often provide the same cost savings and customer service.[45] Fewer HR professionals are needed when shared service centers are used, resulting in significant cost savings.[46] The most common HR

HR outsourcing
Process of hiring external HR professionals to do the HR work that was previously done internally.

shared service center (SSC)
A center that takes routine, transaction-based activities dispersed throughout the organization and consolidates them in one place.

functions that use SSCs are benefits and pension administration, payroll, relocation assistance and recruitment support, global training and development, succession planning, and talent retention.

The use of shared service centers takes on a different twist when activities such as human resources, accounts payable, and procurement for different organizations are centralized under a single department or service. This concept has been used effectively in the health care field. Hospitals that use administrative shared services centers have achieved a significantly greater level of efficiency.[47]

Professional Employer Organizations (Employee Leasing)

A **professional employer organization (PEO)** is a company that leases employees to other businesses. When a decision is made to use a PEO, the company releases its employees, who are then hired by the PEO. The PEO then manages the administrative needs associated with employees. It is the PEO that pays the employees' salaries; it also pays workers' compensation premiums, payroll-related taxes, and employee benefits. The PEO is responsible to the IRS if, for example, the payroll taxes go unpaid. The company reimburses the PEO, which typically charges a fee of from 2 to 7 percent of the customer's gross wages, with percentages based on the number of leased employees. Since the PEO is the employees' legal employer it has the right to hire, fire, discipline, and reassign an employee. However, the client company maintains enough control so it can run the day-to-day operations of its business. Although PEOs have been available since the early 1980s, they have recently become a multibillion dollar industry. In fact, there is an estimated two to three million U.S. workers employed under a PEO-type arrangement and that number is certain to grow.[48] PEOs permit business owners to focus on their core business while the PEO handles HR activities.[49] Companies using a PEO typically have a high level of benefits and greater HR expertise than they could possibly have had on their own. Today, more business owners may be reaching out to PEOs to help them sort through health care reform.[50]

PEOs also have advantages for employees. Because they provide workers for many companies, they often enjoy economies of scale that permit them to offer a wider selection of benefits at considerably lower cost. In addition, workers frequently have greater opportunities for job mobility. Some leasing firms operate throughout the nation. The relocation of one employed spouse in a dual-career family may be more satisfactory if the leasing company locates the other spouse a job in the new location too. In addition, if a client organization suffers a downturn, the leasing company offers job security. The PEO can transfer employees to another client, avoiding both layoffs and loss of seniority. Since smaller companies are less likely to have a dedicated human resources specialist, a PEO may provide an ideal means of handling compliance requirements of programs such as 401(k) programs.

A potential disadvantage to the client is erosion of employee loyalty because workers receive pay and benefits from the leasing company. Regardless of any shortcomings, use of employee leasing is growing.

Line Managers

Individuals directly involved in accomplishing the primary purpose of the organization are **line managers**. As the traditional work of HR managers declines, line managers are stepping up and performing some duties typically done by human resource professionals.[51] Automation has assisted greatly in this process. Managers are being assisted by manager self-service, the use of software, and the corporate network to automate paper-based human resource processes that require a manager's approval, recordkeeping or input, and processes that support the manager's job. Everything from recruitment, selection, and performance appraisal to employee development has been automated to assist line managers in performing traditional HR tasks.

Human Resource Management in Small Businesses

The Small Business Administration (SBA) defines a small business as one that is independently owned and operated, is organized for profit, and is not dominant in its field. The discussion throughout this text has historically focused primarily on how HR is practiced with major corporations. However, today, many college graduates obtain jobs in small businesses. In fact, growth of small business is often a primary driver for the economy. Therefore, the practice of HR as it is conducted in small businesses is discussed at various times in your text.

Typically the same HR functions previously identified must be accomplished by small business but the manner in which they are accomplished may be altered. Small businesses often do

executive

A top-level manager who reports directly to a corporation's chief executive officer or to the head of a major division.

generalist

A person who may be an executive and performs tasks in a variety of HR-related areas.

OBJECTIVE 1.7

Describe the various human resource classifications, including executives, generalists, and specialists.

specialist

An individual who may be a human resource executive, a human resource manager, or a nonmanager, and who is typically concerned with only one of the five functional areas of human resource management.

OBJECTIVE 1.8

Describe the evolution of human resource management and explain the evolving HR organization.

not have a formal HR unit or an HRM specialist. Rather, line managers often handle the HR functions. The focus of their activities is generally on hiring and retaining capable employees. Some aspects of HR functions may actually be more significant in smaller firms than in larger ones. For example, a staffing mistake in hiring an incompetent employee who alienates customers may cause the business to fail. In a larger firm, such an error might be much less harmful.

New small businesses are faced with a host of federal and state government regulatory requirements, tax laws, and compensation demands. The SBA has identified various compliance steps for new small businesses.[52] Before anyone is hired, an Employment Identification Number (EIN) should be obtained. EINs can be acquired online from the IRS and are needed to report taxes as well as information about new employees to state government. Then, procedures for withholding taxes should be made. The IRS requires that businesses keep records of employment taxes for at least four years. This includes employee wages, tips, and sickness records, as well as employee tax withholding certificates.

Verification of eligibility to work is required for new employees within three days of the hire date. An Employment Eligibility Verification Form I-9 must be completed. Also all employers are required to report newly hired and rehired employees to a state directory within 20 days of their hire or rehire date.

Workers' compensation insurance should then be obtained. Any business that hires employees must carry this insurance. A new business should also register for unemployment insurance tax. Small businesses may also be required to pay unemployment insurance tax. New companies should also check to see if they are required to purchase disability insurance. Some states require employers to provide partial wage replacement insurance coverage to eligible employees for non-work-related sickness or injury.

Laws also require that businesses prominently display posters that inform employees of their rights and the small businesses responsibilities to them under labor laws. New employers now have different and new federal and state tax filing requirements that apply. Once these tasks have been completed, new small businesses can focus on creating a fulfilling, safe, and fair workplace.

There are some further steps to take after hiring the first employees. Records should be kept ranging from tax and labor recordkeeping requirements to personnel performance and training records. In fact, according to the SBA, small business owners spend up to 25 percent of their time on employee-related paperwork. New firms must also stress providing a safe and healthy work environment. The Occupational Safety and Health Administration's Quick Start tool can tell small businesses what applies. Also, employee benefit plans must adhere to minimum standards. The small business may also be concerned with standards that protect employees' rights. The Equal Employment Opportunity Commission (EEOC) and Fair Labor Standards Act (FLSA) offer guidance on any required standards. As a final note, small businesses may choose to use a professional employer organization to handle many of the HR administrative tasks.

Human Resource Designations

Various designations are used within the human resource profession; among these are HR executives, generalists, and specialists. An **executive** is a top-level manager who reports directly to the corporation's chief executive officer (CEO) or to the head of a major division. A **generalist**, who may be an executive, performs tasks in a variety of HR-related areas. The generalist is involved in several, or all, of the five HRM functions. A **specialist** may be an HR executive, manager, or nonmanager who is typically concerned with only one of the five functional areas of HRM. Figure 1-3 helps clarify these distinctions.

The vice president of industrial relations, shown in Figure 1-3, specializes primarily in union-related matters. This person is both an executive and a specialist. An HR vice president is both an executive and a generalist, having responsibility for a wide variety of functions. The compensation manager is a specialist, as is the benefits analyst. Whereas a position level in the organization identifies an executive, the breadth of such positions distinguishes generalists and specialists.

Evolution of Human Resource Management

It seems appropriate, as the 13th edition of *Human Resource Management* is published, to see how HR management has evolved over the past 30-plus years. Traditionally, separate functions such as staffing, training and development, compensation, safety and health, and labor relations

FIGURE 1-3

**Human Resource
Executives, Generalists,
and Specialists**

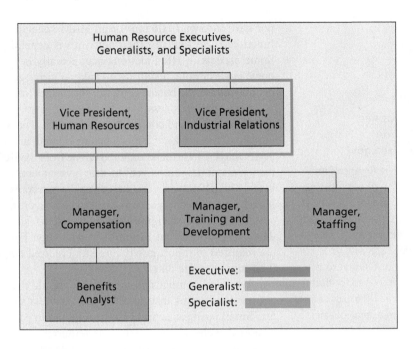

(if the firm was unionized) were created and placed under the direction of a human resource manager or executive (see Figure 1-4). Large firms might have had a manager and staff for each HR function that reported to the HR executive. The HR vice president worked closely with top management in formulating corporate policy.

The title of this textbook says much about the HR evolution. In the first edition, this text was titled *Personnel: The Management of Human Resources* and the focus was more on personnel as a staff or advisory function. By the fourth edition, the title of the book had changed to *Human Resource Management,* and a more general management focus was evolving. This was about the same time that the journal *Personnel Administrator* changed its name to *HR Magazine.* The journal entitled *Personnel* changed its name to *HR Focus,* and the journal entitled *Personnel Journal* changed its name to *Workforce Management.* Moving from the more narrow focus of personnel suggested the more important role that human resource management would play out in the business world.

We wrote in the first edition:

Not many decades ago, people engaged in human resource work had titles such as welfare secretary and employment clerk. Their duties were rather restrictive and often dealt only with

FIGURE 1-4

**Traditional Human
Resource Functions in a
Large Firm**

such items as workers' wages, minor medical problems, recreation, and housing. Personnel, as human resources was most commonly called, as a profession was generally held in low esteem, and its organizational position was typically near the bottom of the hierarchy. As one personnel director said, "the personnel executive was the 'glad hander' or 'back slapper' who kept morale up in a company by running the company picnic and making sure the recreation program went off well."

These days are over in many organizations. The personnel director's position is no longer a retirement position given to managers who cannot perform adequately anywhere else in the organization.

Today, HR tasks are often performed differently than they were even a decade ago. As more and more companies use alternative means to accomplish HR tasks, the role of the traditional HR manager has changed. HR is now involved more in strategic HR, focusing more on the bottom line of the organization and leaving the more administrative tasks to technology or others.[53] The American Society for Personnel Administration changed it name to Society for Human Resource Management (SHRM) in 1989 to better reflect the more strategic focus of the profession. SHRM is the world's largest association devoted to human resource management.

Evolving HR Organizations

In previous editions, the manner in which human resource tasks changed as the firm grew was presented. HR functions in small businesses, medium-sized businesses, and large firms were described. Describing the typical HR organization today is much more difficult. As previously discussed, line managers, HR outsourcing, HR shared service centers, and professional employer organizations are now handling many of the traditional HR tasks. In discussions with numerous human resource managers in organizations of various sizes, the conclusion was that there is no pattern for how human resource tasks are now achieved. The only certainty is that the five previously identified HR functions must still be accomplished. Each company must choose the appropriate vehicle for doing these tasks based on its specific needs and goals.

A possible example of an evolving HR organization is presented in Figure 1-5. Here, the company has outsourced training and development, a function previously performed in house by the Training & Development Department. The compensation function is now performed at a shared service center. Safety and health has been removed from HR and, because of its importance in this particular firm, reports directly to the CEO. Staffing activities remain under the strategic vice president for human resources but many activities have been automated and line managers are now more involved in the selection process. Since the firm is nonunion, there is no Industrial Relations Manager. In this example, as the title suggests, the HR vice president is now more concerned with the strategic human resource matters. Because of the many changes that have occurred in HR in recent years, it is not realistic to show a typical HR organization. The organization of HR in today's environment is truly a work in progress.

FIGURE 1-5

A Possible Example of an Evolving HR Organization

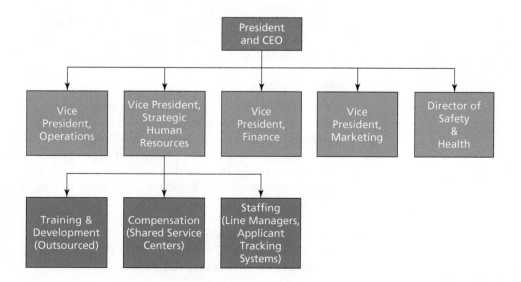

OBJECTIVE **1.9**

Describe the professionalization of human resource management.

profession
Vocation characterized by the existence of a common body of knowledge and a procedure for certifying members.

Professionalization of Human Resource Management

A **profession** is a vocation characterized by the existence of a common body of knowledge and a procedure for certifying members. Performance standards are established by members of the profession rather than by outsiders; that is, the profession is self-regulated. Most professions also have effective representative organizations that permit members to exchange ideas of mutual concern. These characteristics apply to the field of human resources, and several well-known organizations serve the profession. Among the more prominent is the Society for Human Resource Management, the Human Resource Certification Institute, the American Society for Training and Development, and WorldatWork.

Society for Human Resource Management

The largest national professional organization for individuals involved in all areas of human resource management is the Society for Human Resource Management (SHRM). The basic goals of the society include defining, maintaining, and improving standards of excellence in the practice of human resource management. Founded in 1948, SHRM presently represents nearly 260,000 individual members.[54] Members are from over 140 countries, with a network of more than 575 affiliated chapters in the United States, as well as offices in China and India.[55]

SHRM publishes a monthly journal, *HR Magazine*, and a monthly newspaper, *HR News*. A major subsidiary of SHRM, Staffing Management, offers in-depth information on issues addressing employment and retention issues, whereas SHRM offers a broader coverage of HR issues.[56]

Human Resource Certification Institute

HR Web Wisdom

Human Resource Certification Institute (HRCI)

http://www.hrci.org

The Professional Certification Program in HR Management is for individuals seeking to expand their formal HR training.

One of the more significant developments in the field of HRM has been the establishment of the Human Resource Certification Institute (HRCI), an affiliate of SHRM. Founded in 1976, HRCI's goal is to recognize human resource professionals through a certification program. HRCI offers three certifications for HR professionals—PHR (Professional in Human Resources), SPHR (Senior Professional in Human Resources), and GPHR (Global Professional in Human Resources). Today more than 115,000 HR professionals maintain their credentials.[57] Certification encourages human resource professionals to update their knowledge and skills continuously. It provides recognition to professionals who have met a stated level of training and work experience.

American Society for Training and Development

Founded in 1944, the American Society for Training and Development (ASTD) is the world's largest association dedicated to workplace learning and performance professionals. ASTD's members come from more than 100 countries and connect locally with 125 U.S. chapters and more than 20 international partners. Members work in thousands of organizations of all sizes, in government, as independent consultants, and as suppliers.[58] The ASTD Certification Institute has the Certified Professional in Learning and Performance (CPLP™) credential to provide a way for workplace learning and performance professionals to prove their value to employers and to be confident about their knowledge of the field.[59]

WorldatWork

WorldatWork is a professional association focused on compensation, benefits, work–life effectiveness and integrated total rewards—strategies to attract, motivate, and retain an engaged and productive workforce. WorldatWork was founded in 1955 as the American Compensation Association (ACA) and provides a network of more than 30,000 members and professionals in more than 100 countries with training, certification, research, conferences, and community. WorldatWork Society of Certified Professionals is an organization that certifies human resource professionals in the disciplines of compensation, benefits, and work–life. WorldatWork Society designations include Certified Compensation Professional (CCP), Certified Benefits Professional (CBP), Global Remuneration Professional (GRP), and Work–Life Certified Professional (WLCP), Certified Benefits Professional (CBP), and Global Remuneration Professional (GRP).[60]

OBJECTIVE 1.10

Explain the possible hurdles of managing human resources across different countries' cultures.

Scope of this Book

Effective HRM is crucial to the success of every organization. To be effective, managers must understand and competently practice HRM. This book was designed to give you the following:

- An appreciation of the impact of technology and global competition.
- An awareness of the importance of business ethics and corporate social responsibility.
- An insight into the role of strategic HRM in today's organizations and the strategic role of HR functions. An understanding of job analysis, human resource planning, recruitment, and selection.
- An awareness of the importance of human resource development, including training and developing, for employees at all levels.
- An understanding of performance appraisal and its role in performance management.
- An appreciation of how compensation programs are formulated and administered.
- An understanding of safety and health factors as they affect the firm's profitability.
- An opportunity to understand employee and labor relations.
- An appreciation of the global impact on HRM.

Students often question whether the content of a book corresponds to the realities of the business world. In writing and revising this book, the comments, observations, and experiences of HR practitioners are integrated throughout, along with extensive research efforts. HR practices of leading business organizations are provided to illustrate how theory can be applied in the real world. The intent is to enable you to experience human resource management in action.

This book is organized in eight parts, as shown in Figure 1-6; combined, they provide a comprehensive view of human resource management. As you read it, hopefully you will be stimulated to increase your knowledge in this rapidly changing and challenging field.

country's culture

Set of values, symbols, beliefs, language, and norms that guide human resource behavior within the country

FIGURE 1-6

Organization of This Book

HUMAN RESOURCE MANAGEMENT, 13TH EDITION

PART ONE. INTRODUCTION
Chapter 1: Strategic Human Resource Management: An Overview

PART TWO. ETHICS, SOCIAL, AND LEGAL CONSIDERATIONS
Chapter 2: Business Ethics and Corporate Social Responsibility
Chapter 3: Workforce Diversity, Equal Employment Opportunity, and Affirmative Action

PART THREE. STAFFING
Chapter 4: Job Analysis, Strategic Planning, and Human Resource Planning
Chapter 5: Recruitment
Chapter 6: Selection

PART FOUR. HUMAN RESOURCE DEVELOPMENT
Chapter 7: Training and Development
Chapter 8: Performance Management and Appraisal

PART FIVE. COMPENSATION
Chapter 9: Direct Financial Compensation
Chapter 10: Indirect Financial Compensation (Benefits) and Nonfinancial Compensation

PART SIX. SAFETY AND HEALTH
Chapter 11: A Safe and Healthy Work Environment

PART SEVEN. EMPLOYEE AND LABOR RELATIONS
Chapter 12: Labor Unions and Collective Bargaining
Chapter 13: Internal Employee Relations

PART EIGHT. OPERATING IN A GLOBAL ENVIRONMENT
Chapter 14: Global Human Resource Management

Country Culture as a Possible Barrier to Global Business

A **country's culture** is the set of values, symbols, beliefs, languages, and norms that guide human behavior within the country. It is learned behavior that develops as individuals grow from childhood to adulthood. As one goes from one side of this country to the other, a wide range of cultural differences will be experienced. The same can be said in traveling from north to south. Then think about the cultural differences that exist in going from this country to another. Even though the language may be the same, such as is the case with the United States and the United Kingdom, major cultural differences exist. Dean Foster, a New York–based consultant on intercultural business issues said, "The United Kingdom really is a foreign country—and HR departments that ignore that fact are at their peril. It's that expectation of similarity that throws everyone off."[61] A businessperson who travels from Switzerland to Italy goes from a country where meetings tend to be highly structured and expected to start on time to one where meetings can be more informal and punctuality is less important.[62]

Throughout this text, cultural differences between countries will be identified as a major factor influencing global business. This borderless world adds dramatically to the difficulty of managing human capital. Cultural differences reveal themselves in everything from the workplace environments to differences in the concept of time, space, and social interaction.[63] Companies operating in the global environment recognize that national cultures differ and that such differences cannot be ignored.[64]

Chrysler Corporation employees have gone through major cultural changes in the last several years. First, they were merged into a German firm, Daimler-Benz, then they were resold back to an American company, and they are now merged into Fiat, an Italian firm. Each ownership change brought new cultural rules with which employees had to deal. Certainly the Germans and Italians have two distinct, but different cultures.[65] InBev, based in Leuven, Belgium, purchased Anheuser-Busch several years ago, making it the leading global brewer and one of the world's top five consumer products companies. Merging two large corporate cultures after an acquisition is often not easy. In fact, InBev NV's purchase of Anheuser-Busch has been particularly difficult, even two-and-a-half years after the $52 billion deal closed.[66]

The cultural norms of Japan promote loyalty and teamwork. The work culture there is one where honesty and hard work are prized assets. In Japan, most managers tend to remain with the same company for life. In the United States, senior executives often change companies, but the Japanese believe strongly that leaving a job is to be avoided out of respect for the business team.[67]

Cultural misunderstandings are common, but they can be hazards to executives managing global workforces. Samuel Berner, head of HR of the private banking Asia Pacific division in Singapore for Credit Suisse AG said, "Things that are perfectly natural in one culture offend in another."[68] Eric Rozenberg, CMM, CMP, president, Ince&Tive, of Brussels, Belgium, stated, "Even though people are aware that there are cultural differences between various nationalities, they're still uncomfortable with it and are afraid of making mistakes."[69] Cultural barriers are not easily overcome.

MyManagementLab

Go to **mymanagementlab.com** to complete the problems marked with this icon ⭐.

Summary

1. *Describe employer branding and define* **human resource management.** *Employer branding* is the firm's corporate image or culture created to attract and retain the type of employees the firm is seeking. It is what the company stands for in the public eye.

   Human resource management is the utilization of individuals to achieve organizational objectives. Consequently, all managers at every level must concern themselves with HRM.

2. *Identify the human resource management functions.* The HRM functions include staffing, human resource development, compensation, safety and health, and employee and labor relations.

3. *Identify the external environmental factors that affect human resource management and describe the trend*

   for increased mobility of tasks performed by HR professionals. External factors include legal considerations, the labor market, society, political parties, unions, shareholders, competition, customers, technology, economy, and unanticipated events.

   A rapidly developing trend is that HR tasks will be increasingly portable. Mobile use turned sharply upward with the introduction of Apple's first iPhone. Now, virtually everyone has mobile search capability.

4. *Explain why corporate culture is a major internal environment factor.* *Corporate culture* is the system of shared values, beliefs, and habits within an organization that interacts with the formal structure to produce behavioral norms. It affects job performance throughout the organization and consequently affects profitability.

5. *Explain who performs human resource management tasks.* *Human resource managers* are individuals who normally act in an advisory or staff capacity, working with other managers to help them deal with human resource matters.

   HR outsourcing is the process of hiring an external provider to do the work that was previously done internally.

   HR shared service centers take routine, transaction-based activities that are dispersed throughout the organization and consolidate them in one place.

   A *professional employer organization* is a company that leases employees to other businesses.

   Line managers in certain firms are being used more frequently than before to deliver HR services.

6. *Describe how human resource management activities may be different for small businesses.* Often the same HR functions previously identified must be accomplished by small business but the manner in which they are accomplished may be altered. Small businesses often do not have a formal HR unit or HRM specialists. Rather, other line managers in the company handle HR functions.

7. *Describe the various human resource classifications, including executives, generalists, and specialists.* *Executives* are top-level managers who report directly to the corporation's CEO or the head of a major division.

   Generalists (who are often executives) are persons who perform tasks in a wide variety of HR-related areas.

   A *specialist* may be a human resource executive, manager, or nonmanager who typically is concerned with only one of the functional areas of HRM.

8. *Describe the evolution of human resource management and explain the evolving HR organization.* The title of the book says much about the HR evolution. In the first edition, the book was titled *Personnel: The Management of Human Resources*, and the focus was more on personnel as a staff or advisory function. By the fourth edition, the title of the book had been changed to *Human Resource Management*, and a more general management focus was evolving.

   The HR organizational structure of firms changes as they outsource, use professional employer organizations and shared service centers, and involve line managers more in traditional HR tasks. Regardless of an organization's design, the five HR functions must still be accomplished.

9. *Describe the professionalization of human resource management.* Several well-known organizations serve the profession. Among the more prominent are the Society for Human Resource Management (SHRM), the Human Resource Certification Institute (HRCI), the American Society for Training and Development (ASTD), and WorldatWork (formerly the American Compensation Association).

10. *Explain the possible hurdles of managing human resources across different countries' cultures.* Cultural differences reveal themselves in everything from the workplace environments to differences in the concepts of time, space, and social interaction. Cultural differences are often the biggest barrier to doing business in the world market.

Key Terms

employer branding   2
human resource management
   (HRM)   4
staffing   4
human resource development (HRD)   4
external environment   6
union   7
shareholders   7

human resource information system
   (HRIS)   8
corporate culture   9
human resource manager   10
HR outsourcing (HRO)   11
shared service center (SSC)   11
professional employer organization
   (PEO)   12

line managers   12
executive   13
generalist   13
specialist   13
profession   16
country's culture   18

Exercises

1. Employer branding was discussed at the beginning of this chapter. On a scale of 1 (Poor) to 5 (Excellent), how valuable are the following brands? Why do you rate them low or high?
   a. Bank of America
   b. McDonald's
   c. BP Global
   d. Walmart

2. Review the employment classified ads in the *Wall Street Journal, HR Magazine*, and a Sunday edition of a large city newspaper. Make a list of the types of human resource management jobs, the companies offering employment,

and the qualifications needed to obtain the positions. What is your basic conclusion after this review in terms of the availability of human resource management positions and the necessary qualifications for obtaining a position?

3. The Trends & Innovations in the chapter entitled "Mobile HR: Is the Cloud the Limit?" paints a much different picture of how HR work was done in the past. Do you believe that mobile HR is truly the trend of the future? What might be the pros and cons of this trend?

4. The HR functions are highly interrelated. How would a change in one of the following affect the other HR functions?
   a. Paying the lowest wages in the industry

b. Being recognized as an industry leader in providing continuous training and development

c. Having a reputation for providing a work environment that is unhealthy

5. Corporate culture is discussed throughout your text as having a significant impact on HR tasks. How might the following cultures affect the five HR functions?

a. Employees generally believe that this is a fun place to work

b. Management generally has the attitude that "It's my way. Don't question me."

c. Rewards are available for productive, hardworking employees

Questions for Review

1. Define human resource management. What human resource management functions must be performed regardless of the organization's size?
2. What are the external environmental factors that affect human resource management? Describe each.
3. How might mobile HR affect the various HR functions?
4. Define *corporate culture*. Explain why corporate culture is a major internal environment factor.
5. This chapter describes HR's changing role in business. Describe each component that is involved in human resource management.

6. According to the Small Business Administration what does a small business need to do before hiring the first employee?
7. What are the various designations associated with human resource management?
8. What has been the evolution of human resource management?
9. Define *profession*. Do you believe that the field of human resource management is a profession? Explain your answer.

INCIDENT 1   HR after a Disaster

After Hurricane Rita struck Lake Charles, in southwest Louisiana, many businesses wondered if they would ever return to their former selves. Massive destruction was everywhere. Lake Charles, known for its large and beautiful oak and pine trees, now had the job of removing those downed trees from homes, businesses, and lots. You could see for miles through what used to be thick forests. Huge trucks designed for removing massive tree trunks were everywhere. While driving down a street, downed trees could be seen stacked two stories high, waiting to be picked up. The town grew rapidly in size because of the increased number of repair crews working on recovery operations. The noise created by their chain saws could be heard from daylight until dark. The sounds of hammers were everywhere as homeowners scrambled to get their roofs repaired. Often repair crews would just find an empty lot and set up tents for the night because all motels were full. Traffic was unbelievably slow, and it appeared as if everyone was attempting to get on the road at the same time. Just driving from Point A to Point B could often be quite an adventure. As might be expected in conditions such as these, accidents were numerous. Often police did not have the resources to ticket every fender bender, so unless there were injuries, insurance cards were exchanged and the police went on to the next accident.

Months after Hurricane Rita struck, large and small businesses were still frantically trying to find workers so they could start up again. It appeared that every business in the town had a "Help Wanted" sign out front. Individuals who wanted a job could get one and could command a premium salary. Walmart, known for remaining open 24 hours a day, could only stay open on an abbreviated schedule.

Employers often had to bus employees from locations not affected by the hurricane each morning and returned them at night because there were not enough workers available in the local area. Restaurants that normally remained open late into the evening closed at 6:00 p.m., if they opened at all. Compensation scales that were in use prior to the hurricanes had to be thrown out and new plans implemented. Minimum-wage jobs were nonexistent. Employees who earned minimum wage before the storm could now command $10 per hour just for being a flagger (a person who directs traffic). Fast-food restaurants that normally paid minimum wage now paid $10 or $11. Burger King was even offering a $1,500 bonus for entry-level workers. Upscale restaurants that normally paid minimum wage plus tips now paid premium rate plus tips. Restaurants that remained open often had a much younger staff and it was evident that the managers and assistant managers were working overtime to train these new workers. Restaurant patrons had to learn patience because there would be mistakes by these eager, but largely untrained workers.

Questions

1. Which external environment factor(s) did Hurricane Rita affect? Discuss.
2. How were the human resource functions affected by Hurricane Rita?
3. Do you believe the HR situations described regarding Hurricane Rita would be typical in a disaster? Explain.

INCIDENT 2 Downsizing

As the largest employer in Ouachita County, Arkansas, International Forest Products Company (IFP) is an important part of the local economy. Ouachita County is a mostly rural area in south central Arkansas. It employs almost 10 percent of the local workforce, and few alternative job opportunities are available in the area.

Scott Wheeler, the human resource director at IFP, tells of a difficult decision he once had to make. According to Scott, everything was going along pretty well despite the economic recession, but he knew that sooner or later the company would be affected. "I got the word at a private meeting with the president, Janet Deason, that we would have to cut the workforce by 30 percent on a crash basis. I was to get back to her within a week with a suggested plan. I knew that my plan would not be the final one, since the move was so major, but I knew that Ms. Deason was depending on me to provide at least a workable approach.

"First, I thought about how the union would react. Certainly, workers would have to be let go in order of seniority. The union would try to protect as many jobs as possible. I also knew that all of management's actions during this period would be intensely scrutinized. We had to make sure that we had our act together.

"Then there was the impact on the surrounding community to consider. The economy of Ouachita County had not been in good shape recently. Aside from the influence on the individual workers who were laid off, I knew that our cutbacks would further depress the area's economy. I knew that there would be a number of government officials and civic leaders who would want to know how we were trying to minimize the harm done to the public in the area.

"We really had no choice but to make the cuts, I believed. First of all, I had no choice because Ms. Deason said we were going to do it. Also, I had recently read a news account that one of our competitors,

Johns Manville Corporation in West Monroe, Louisiana, had laid off several hundred workers in a cost-cutting move. To keep our sales from being further depressed, we had to ensure that our costs were just as low as those of our competitors. The wood products market is very competitive and a cost advantage of even 2 or 3 percent would allow competitors to take many of our customers.

"Finally, a major reason for the cutbacks was to protect the interests of our shareholders. A few years ago a shareholder group disrupted our annual meeting to insist that IFP make certain antipollution changes. In general, though, the shareholders seem to be more concerned with the return on their investments than with social responsibility. At our meeting, the president reminded me that, just like every other manager in the company, I should place the shareholders' interests above all else. I really was quite overwhelmed as I began to work up a human resource plan that would balance all of these conflicting interests."

Questions

1. How might each HR function be affected by the reduction in force? Remember that all employees at IFP are not members of the union.
2. List the elements in the company's environment that will affect Scott's suggested plan. How legitimate is the interest of each of these?
3. Is it true that Scott should be concerned first and foremost with protecting the interests of shareholders? Discuss.
4. Corporate culture is discussed in this chapter as a major internal environmental factor affecting an organization. How might the downsizing of International Forest Products affect the corporate culture of the company?

MyManagementLab

Go to **mymanagementlab.com** for Auto-graded writing questions as well as the following Assisted-graded writing questions:

1-1. What is employer branding? How might employer branding affect a company's ability to recruit?

1-2. How might a country's culture be a barrier to global business?

1-3. Mymanagementlab Only – comprehensive writing assignment for this chapter.

Notes

1. Bob Duffy, "Rethinking Employer Brands," *Journal of Corporate Recruiting Leadership* 5 (June 2010): 10–15.
2. Paul Jacobs, "Emergence of Human Techsourcing," *Human Resources Magazine* 16 (February/March 2012): 14–15.
3. Soumya Gaddam, "Modeling Employer Branding Communication: The Softer Aspect of HR Marketing Management," *ICFAI Journal of Soft Skills* 2 (2008): 45–55.
4. Kelly Borth, "Live Your Brand," *Smart Business Columbus* 19 (March 2011): 6.
5. Joseph Shaheen, "Issues of Employment Branding and the Psychological Contract: A Discussion," *Journal of Corporate Recruiting Leadership* 5 (September 2010): 7–13.
6. Joanne G. Sujansky, "'Cool' Is the New Recruiting Tool," *Nonprofit World* 29 (May/June 2011): 19.
7. Cecilia Dahlstrom, "Matchmaking Employers with Employees: The Era of Personality Targeting: Employer Branding Now Means Finding and Attracting People Who Fit Your Culture," *Journal of Corporate Recruiting Leadership* 6 (March 2011): 10–12.
8. Ronald J. Alsop, "Cultural Awareness," *Workforce Management* 90 (July 2011): 42.
9. Brett Minchington, "Where to Next for Employer Branding?" *Human Resources Magazine* 16 (October/November 2011): 22.
10. R. Wayne Mondy, Robert M. Noe, and Robert E. Edwards, "What the Staffing Function Entails," *Personnel* 63 (April 1986): 55–58.

11. Mike Brennan and Andrew Gebavi, "Managing Career Paths: The Role of the CLO," *Chief Learning Officer* 7 (March 2008): 48–51.

12. Kenneth E. Goodpaster and John B. Matthews, Jr., "Can a Corporation Have a Conscience?" *Harvard Business Review* 60 (January–February 1982): 132–141.

13. Steve Bates, "Report: Prepare for Increased Shareholder Activism," *HR Magazine* 54 (June 2009): 32.

14. Bill Roberts, "The Grand Convergence," *HR Magazine* 56 (October 2011): 39–46.

15. Lawrence Cummer, "Office? I Don't Need an Office," *Backbone* (April 2011): 20–21.

16. John Zappe, "The New, Improved Social Job Boards," *Journal of Corporate Recruiting Leadership* 5 (September 2010): 3–6.

17. "Growing Use of Apps Expanding Operations of HR Professionals," *HR Focus* 87 (November 2010): 4–5.

18. Julie Bos, "Top Trends in Staffing: Is Your Organization Prepared for What Lies Ahead?" *Workforce Management* 90 (February 2011): 18–21.

19. "iPad HR App First for Towers Watson," *Corporate Adviser* (April 2011): 7.

20. Bill Roberts, "Mobile Workforce Management?" *HR Magazine* 56 (March 2011): 67–70.

21. Harry Katzan, Jr. "On An Ontological View Of Cloud Computing," *Journal of Service Science* 3 (2010): 1–6.

22. Jane Ward, "Structuring Your Selection Process," *Human Resources Magazine* 16 (February/March 2012): 22–23.

23. "Are You Using Cloud Computing?" *Backbone* (February/March 2011): 33–36.

24. Edward J. Giniat, "Cloud Computing: Innovating the Business of Health Care," *Healthcare Financial Management* 65 (May 2011): 130–131.

25. Ron Gill, "Why Cloud Computing Matters to Finance," *Strategic Finance* 92 (January 2011): 43–47.

26. Tamara Lytle, "Cybersleuthing," *HR Magazine* 57 (January 2012): 55–57.

27. "The Internet: A Fundamental Human Resource," *Journal of Financial Planning* (January/February 2012 Practice Solutions): 16.

28. Dave Zielinski, "Bring Your Own Device," *HR Magazine* 57 (February 2012): 71–74.

29. Kathy Gurchiek, "More U.S. Companies Investing in HR Technology," *HR Magazine* 56 (August 2011): 24.

30. "As Economy Recovers, HR Will Have More Opportunities to Show Value," *HR Focus* 89 (February 2012): 6.

31. R. Wayne Mondy and Shane R. Premeaux, *Management: Concepts, Practices, and Skills,* 7th ed. (Upper Saddle River, NJ: Prentice Hall, 1995), 473–475.

32. Lydell C. Bridgeford, "Blinding Them with Science," *Employee Benefit News* 25 (January 2011): 8–9.

33. Eric Krell, "Change Within," *HR Magazine* 56 (August 2011): 42–50.

34. "Despite Recession, World-Class HR Organizations Reduce Costs by 13 Percent," *Controller's Report* 2011 (August 2011): 1–19.

35. Donald L. Caruth and Gail D. Caruth, "Outsourcing Human Resource Activities: A Proposed Model," *Supervision* 71 (July 2010): 3–8.

36. Eric Krell, "Focus In to Farm Out," *HR Magazine* 56 (July 2011): 47–49.

37. Lynn Gresham, "Spring Thaw," *Employee Benefit News* 24 (April 2010): 1–18.

38. Joel Berg, "Employers Outsource HR Work in Recession," *Central Penn Business Journal* 25 (November 13, 2009): 17–21.

39. Diane Cadrain, "A Leave Law That Just Won't Go Away," *HR Magazine* 55 (July 2010): 49–52.

40. Lydell C. Bridgeford, "Are You In or Are You Out," *Employee Benefit News* 25 (April 2011): 26–29.

41. "End-to-End Large Market HR Outsourcing Providers," *Workforce Management* 89 (March 2010): 12.

42. Jessica Marquez, "Kraft-IBM Deal Could Signal HRO Rebound," *Workforce Management* 88 (February 16, 2009): 12–13.

43. Bill Leonard, "Salvage, Don't Scrap," *HR Magazine* 56 (June 2011): 74–77.

44. Susan G. Hauser, "Tech Turbo Boosters on Hyperdrive," *Workforce Management* 90 (August 2011): 24–26.

45. Denise Bedell, "Shared Value," *Global Finance* (September 2010): Supplement 17–18.

46. "HR Metrics: HR Labor Costs per Employee Average $798 at 1,000-employee Companies," *Controller's Report* 2009 (January 2009): 15.

47. Jim McDowell, "Shared Services Centers Can Drive Significant Savings," *Healthcare Financial Management* 65 (June 2011): 118–124.

48. Richard Hicks, "Engaging an Expert," *Smart Business Atlanta* 9 (January 2012): 14.

49. David Imbrogno, "The Outsourcing of HR," *Quality* 49 (December 2010): 34–35.

50. Dorothy L. Miraglia, "Sizing Up Health Care Reform: What Small and Midsize Companies Need to Know," *Benefits Magazine* 48 (February 2011): 30–35.

51. Jon Severs, "Supervisors on the Front Line," *PrintWeek* (January 21, 2011): 20–21.

52. Caron Beesley, "10 Regulatory Steps You Must Follow When Hiring Your First Employee," http://community.sba.gov/community

53. Edgar H. Schein, "The Role of Organization Development in the Human Resource Function," *OD Practitioner* 42 (Fall 2010): 6–11.

54. Henry G. Jackson, "A Great Year—With More in 2012," *HR Magazine* 57 (January 2012): 8.

55. About, The Society for Human Resource Management, http://www.shrm.org/about

56. SHRM Staffing Management Focus Area, http://www.shrm.org/hrdisciplines/staffingmanagement/

57. http://www.hrci.org

58. American Society for Training & Development, http://www.astd.org/ASTD/aboutus

59. Certified Professional in Learning and Performance (CPLP), http://www.astd.org/content/ASTDcertification

60. http://www.worldatwork.org/waw/home/html/home

61. DeeDee Doke, "Perfect Strangers," *HR Magazine* 49 (December 2004): 62–68.

62. Richard Miller, "Taste for Risk Varies Across Europe," *Business Insurance* 43 (September 28, 2009): 9–10.

63. Norm Kamikow, "Lost in Translation," *Chief Learning Officer* 8 (September 2009): 4.

64. Pankaj Ghemawat, "The Cosmopolitan Corporation," *Harvard Business Review* 89 (May 2011): 92–99.

65. John Freivalds, "Nokia Comes to the US: Cultural Differences," *MultiLingual* 20 (September 2009): 30–31.

66. David Kesmode, "Bitter Brew: The Continued Budweiser/InBev Culture Clash," *Wall Street Journal Online* (May 2, 2011).

67. Anumeha Chaturvedi, "Loving It in Tokyo," *Business Today* 20 (August 21, 2011): 127.

68. Kathryn Tyler, "What Are Global Cultural Competencies?" *HR Magazine* 56 (May 2011): 44–46.

69. Julie Barker, "The Cultural Divide," *Incentive* 182 (March 2008): 2–6.

Part Two
Ethical, Social, and Legal Considerations

2

Business Ethics and Corporate Social Responsibility

HRM in Action ## Pay for Whistleblowing

OBJECTIVE 2.1
Explain the purpose of paying whistleblowers.

In the legal use of the term, a *whistleblower* is someone who participates in an activity that is protected. The use of whistleblowers has been around since 1863 when President Lincoln signed into law the Federal False Claims Act, which was designed to protect the United States from purchases of fake gunpowder during the Civil War.[1] The number of whistleblower suits has increased dramatically in recent years under federal and state laws aimed at uncovering fraud and protecting the public. In 2011, the False Claims Act awarded whistleblowers $532 million, with the federal government collecting $3.3 billion.[2] Under the Internal Revenue Service's Informant Claims Program, the Internal Revenue Service (IRS) paid an unidentified CPA $4.5 million as the first award under a newly expanded whistleblower program.[3]

The whistleblower part of the Dodd–Frank Wall Street Reform and Consumer Protection Act is shaped after the successful IRS program. In passing the act, Congress believed that bounty programs were a good method to get people to provide fraud information to responsible law enforcement officials. The act requires the Securities and Exchange Commission to give an award to qualified whistleblowers between 10 and 30 percent of the total amount obtained if the information is voluntarily provided and leads to a successful enforcement or related action. The act also improves whistleblowers' retaliation protection from their employers through the expansion of the whistleblower protections of the Sarbanes-Oxley Act of 2002. This is important because often in the past whistleblowers were fired, demoted, blacklisted, or quit under duress. SEC Chair Mary L. Schapiro

After completing this chapter, students should be able to:

1 Explain the purpose of paying whistleblowers.

2 Define ethics and describe sources of ethical guidance.

3 Discuss attempts at legislating ethics.

4 Explain the importance of creating an ethical culture, describe a code of ethics, and support the importance of linking pay to ethical behavior.

5 Explain human resource ethics and describe ethics training.

6 Describe the concept of corporate social responsibility.

7 Explain why everyone is not on board with regard to corporate social responsibility.

8 Explain corporate sustainability.

9 Describe a social audit.

10 Describe possible difficulties for corporate social responsibility to succeed in the global environment.

---

said, "While the SEC has a history of receiving a high volume of tips and complaints, the quality of the tips we have received has been better since Dodd–Frank became law, and we expect this trend to continue."[4]

Many believe that information provided by whistleblowers is much more effective in uncovering wrongdoings than are external auditors. In testimony to the Senate Banking Committee, Certified Fraud Examiner Harry Markopolos stated that "whistleblower tips detected 54.1 percent of uncovered fraud schemes in public companies. External auditors detected a mere 4.1 percent of fraud schemes."[5]

Companies have some uneasiness regarding the whistleblower provision of the Dodd–Frank Act.[6] A recent survey of senior legal, compliance, and human resources executives at publicly traded or highly regulated companies found that 96 percent expressed either great concern or moderate concerns about potential whistleblower complaints.[7] The major concern is that the rules run counter to a firm's internal compliance efforts.[8] Companies are afraid that employees will not go through internal channels first and instead go directly to government authorities. Another fear is that an employee might have another grievance with the company and use the whistleblower provision to get back at the company.

OBJECTIVE 2.2

Define ethics and describe sources
of ethical guidance.

ethics
Discipline dealing with what is good
and bad, or right and wrong, or with
moral duty and obligation.

HR Web Wisdom

*International Business Ethics
Institute*

http://www.business-ethics.org

The Institute was founded in 1994
in response to the growing need
for transnational organizations in
the field of business ethics.

Ethics

Ethics is the discipline dealing with what is good and bad, or right and wrong, or with moral
duty and obligation.

Ethics at times may appear to be complicated because businesses are created to produce a
short-term profit, which could potentially conflict with ethical behavior.[9] Today, some companies and individuals behave unethically perhaps because ethics was moved to the back burner
while executives focus on what they believe to be more important concerns. The past corrupt
conduct of corporations such as WorldCom and Enron and the senior managers who led them
provides deplorable examples of just how far some ethical behavior had strayed. Lately, we for-
got to guard against the type of ethical abuses that ultimately bankrupted companies such as Bear
Stearns and Lehman Brothers. CEOs have to be clear that unethical behavior is not acceptable.
In one survey, 67 percent of investors said they would move their account if they discovered the
company was involved in unethical behavior.[10] Jeff Immelt, GE's CEO, begins and ends each
annual meeting of 220 officers and 600 senior managers by restating the company's fundamental
integrity principles: "GE's business success is built on our reputation with all stakeholders for
lawful and ethical behavior."[11] At GE, when it comes to integrity violations, it is one strike and
you are out. There are no second chances.[12] The focus should be on just doing the right thing.
The image of the business world would be in much better shape if this simple advice were followed. Hopefully ethical standards are improving.

Most of the 500 largest corporations in the United States now have a code of ethics, which
encompasses written conduct standards, internal education, and formal agreements on industry
standards, ethics offices, social accounting, and social projects. Even so, business ethics scandals
continue to be headline news. Lying on résumés, obstruction of justice, destruction of records,
stock price manipulation, cutting corners to meet Wall Street's expectations, fraud, waste, and
abuse, unfortunately, are occurring all too often when those in business go wrong ethically. Then,
there were the corporate executives that took home millions although their company failed and
employees were laid off. They evidently realized that they could make a quick profit through
their unethical behavior.[13]

However, business is not alone. There is virtually no occupation that has not had its own
painful ethical crises in recent years. There were the teachers who provided answers on standardized tests to improve their schools' performance scores. Doctors who make money by falsely
billing Medicare do not even make the headlines any more. But certainly a devastating blow to
society has been dealt by business, and ethical breaches in business continue today.

Compliance with the law sets the minimum standard for ethical behavior; ethics, however,
is much more. There must be leaders who are able and willing to instill ethics throughout the
culture of the organization. Ethics is about deciding whether an action is good or bad and what
to do about it if it is bad. Ethics is a philosophical discipline that describes and directs moral
conduct. Those in management make ethical (or unethical) decisions every day. Do you hire the
best-qualified person, who is a minority? Do you forget to tell a candidate about the dangerous
aspect of a certain job? Some ethical decisions are major and some are minor. But decisions in
small matters often set a pattern for the more important decisions a manager makes. Attitudes
such as "It's standard practice," "It's not a big deal," "It's not my responsibility," and "I want to
be loyal" are simply not acceptable.[14] The Roman philosopher Cicero echoed this situation when
he said, "It is a true saying that one falsehood leads easily to another."[15]

Sources of Ethical Guidance

The sources of ethical guidance should lead to our beliefs or a conviction about what is right or
wrong. Most would agree that people have a responsibility to avail themselves to these sources
of ethical guidance. In short, individuals should care about what is right and wrong and not just
be concerned with what is expedient. One might use a number of sources to determine what is
right or wrong, good or bad, moral or immoral. These sources include the Bible and other holy
books. They also include the small voice that many refer to as conscience. Many believe that
conscience is a gift of God or the voice of God. Others see it as a developed response based
on the internalization of societal mores. Another source of ethical guidance is the behavior and
advice of the people psychologists call "significant others"—our parents, friends, and role models and members of our churches, clubs, and associations. For most professionals, there are codes
of ethics that prescribe certain behavior. Without this conscience that has developed, it might be

A Selection Quandary

You are being promoted to a new assignment within your company, and your boss has asked you to nominate one of your subordinates as your replacement. The possible candidates are Randy Carlton, who is obviously more qualified, and James Mitchell, who, though not as experienced, is much better liked by the workers. If Randy is given the promotion, you are not certain the workers will accept him as their leader. James, on the other hand, is a hard worker and is well liked and respected by the others, including Randy. As you labor over the decision, you think about how unfair it would be to Randy if the feelings of the other workers kept him from getting a deserved promotion. At the same time, you feel that your primary responsibility should be to maintain the productivity of the work unit. If your former division fell apart after your departure, it would hurt your reputation, not to mention the company.

What would you do?
What factor(s) in this ethical dilemma might influence a person to make a less-than-ethical decision?

This is the only place in this text where I will recommend the ethical choice and also identify other factors that might make a person take a less-than-ethical stand. What would you have done if placed in a situation such as this?

Ethical Choice: Recommend Randy, who is the best-qualified employee.

Factors Influencing Another Decision: The department might fall apart if Randy is given the promotion. Other workers might not work for Randy and the workers would more readily accept James. Your reputation may be hurt if the department productivity declines. Besides, Randy can work with James.

---

easy to say, "Everyone does it," "Just this once won't hurt," or "No one will ever know." Some still believe that greed is acceptable as long as the SEC does not find out.[16]

Laws also offer guidance to ethical behavior, prohibiting acts that can be especially harmful to others. They codify what society has deemed to be unacceptable.[17] If a certain behavior is illegal, most would consider it to be unethical as well. There are exceptions, of course. For example, through the 1950s, laws in most southern states relegated blacks to the backs of buses and otherwise assigned them inferior status. Martin Luther King Jr. resisted such laws and, in fact, engaged in civil disobedience and other nonviolent forms of resistance to their enforcement. King won the Nobel Peace Prize for his efforts.

OBJECTIVE 2.3
Discuss attempts at legislating ethics.

Legislating Ethics

In 1907, Teddy Roosevelt said, "Men can never escape being governed. If from lawlessness or fickleness, from folly or self-indulgence, they refuse to govern themselves, then in the end they will be governed [by others]."[18] Many contend that ethics cannot be legislated. Although laws cannot mandate ethics, they may be able to identify the baseline separating what is good and what is bad. Much of the current legislation was passed because of business ethics breakdowns. There have been four attempts to legislate business ethics since the late 1980s.

Procurement Integrity Act

The Procurement Integrity Act of 1988 prohibits the release of source selection and contractor bid or proposal information. Also, a former employee who served in certain positions on a procurement action or contract in excess of $10 million is barred from receiving compensation as an employee or consultant from that contractor for one year. The act was passed after there were reports of military contracts for $500 toilet seats. There was also a $5,000 hammer.

Federal Sentencing Guidelines for Organizations Act

The second attempt occurred with the passage of the 1992 Federal Sentencing Guidelines for Organizations Act (FSGO), which outlined an effective ethics training program and explained the seven minimum requirements for an effective program to prevent and detect violations.[19] The FSGO promised softer punishments for wayward corporations that already had ethics programs in place. In the law were recommendations regarding standards, ethics training, and a system to anonymously report unacceptable conduct. Executives were supposed to be responsible for the misconduct of those lower in the organization. If executives were proactive in their efforts to prevent white-collar crime, it would lessen a judgment against them and reduce the liability. Organizations responded by creating ethics officer positions, installing ethics hotlines, and developing codes of ethics. But, it is one thing to have a code of ethics and quite another to have this code instilled in all employees from top to bottom.

Corporate and Auditing Accountability, Responsibility and Transparency Act

The third attempt at legislating business ethics was the Corporate and Auditing Accountability, Responsibility and Transparency Act of 2002, which criminalized many corporate acts that were previously relegated to various regulatory structures. Known as the Sarbanes–Oxley Act, its primary focus is to redress accounting and financial reporting abuses in the light of corporate scandals. The act contains broad employee whistleblower protections that subject corporations and their managerial personnel to significant civil and criminal penalties for retaliating, harassing, or discriminating against employees who report suspected corporate wrongdoing. The whistleblower protections of the act apply to corporations listed on U.S. stock exchanges; companies otherwise obligated to file reports under the Securities and Exchange Act; and officers, employees, contractors, subcontractors, and agents of those companies.

The act states that management may not discharge, demote, suspend, threaten, harass, or in any other manner discriminate against an employee protected by the act. It protects any employee who lawfully provides information to governmental authorities concerning conduct he or she reasonably believes constitutes mail, wire, or securities fraud; violations of any rule or regulation issued by the Securities and Exchange Commission (SEC); or violations of any other federal law relating to fraud against shareholders. The act evidently has teeth, because in the 2003 *Bechtel v Competitive Technologies Inc.* Supreme Court case involving wrongful termination under Sarbanes–Oxley's whistleblower-protection rule, the Court ruled that the company violated the act by firing two employees and ordered them reinstated. They were fired because during a meeting they had raised concerns about the company's decision not to report, on its SEC filing, an act they thought should have been disclosed.[20]

The law prohibits loans to executives and directors. It requires publicly traded companies to disclose whether or not they have adopted a code of ethics for senior officers. The act does not require SEC reporting banks and bank-holding companies to have a code of ethics, but if an SEC reporting company does not have one, it must explain why.[21] However, as former SEC Chairman Arthur Levitt said, "While the Sarbanes–Oxley Act has brought about significant change, the greatest change is being brought about not by regulation or legislation, but by humiliation and embarrassment and private rights of action."[22]

Dodd–Frank Wall Street Reform and Consumer Protection Act

The fourth, the Dodd–Frank Wall Street Reform and Consumer Protection Act, was signed into law in 2010. The act was brought on by the worst financial crisis since the Great Depression, which resulted in the loss of 8 million jobs, failed businesses, a drop in housing prices, and wiped out personal savings of many workers. As the financial crisis advanced, it became clear that executive compensation played a major role in the financial services sector as well as in the capital markets following the collapse of investment services firms as Lehman Brothers, Merrill Lynch, Bear Stearns, and AIG.[23] The whistleblowing aspect of the act was discussed in the HRM in Action at the beginning of the chapter. The major components of the act may be seen in Table 2-1.

OBJECTIVE 2.4

Explain the importance of creating an ethical culture, describe a code of ethics, and support the importance of linking pay to ethical behavior.

Creating an Ethical Culture

Mark Twain once said, "Always do right. This will gratify some people and astonish the rest."[24] This is certainly good advice for both employees and employers if the firm wants to create an ethical culture. Saying that a company has an ethical culture and actually having one may be two different things. For example, the Enron debacle was not supposed to happen. The Enron Code of Ethics was 62 pages long and had a foreword by Kenneth L. Lay, who was then the company's chairman, saying "Enron's reputation finally depends on its people, on you and me. Let's keep that reputation high."[25] Even with the ethical code, it is apparent that Enron's top management pursued business as usual.

One way for a firm to create and sustain an ethical culture is to audit ethics, much like a company audits its finances each year.[26] An ethics audit is simply a systematic, independent,

TABLE 2-1

Major Components of the Dodd-Frank Wall Street Reform and Consumer Protection Act

Transparency and Accountability: Eliminates loopholes that allow risky and abusive practices to go on unnoticed and unregulated.

Executive Compensation and Corporate Governance: Provides shareholders with a say on pay and corporate affairs with a non-binding vote on executive compensation and golden parachutes.

Consumer Protections with Authority and Independence: Creates a new independent overseer with the authority to ensure American consumers get the clear, accurate information they need to shop for mortgages, credit cards, and other financial products, and protect them from hidden fees, abusive terms, and deceptive practices.

Ends Too Big to Fail Bailouts: Ends the possibility that taxpayers will be asked to bail out financial firms that threaten the economy.

Advance Warning System: Creates a council to identify and address risks posed by large, companies, products, and activities before they threaten the stability of the economy.

Protects Investors: Provides tough new rules for transparency and accountability for credit rating agencies to protect investors and businesses.

Enforces Regulations on the Books: Strengthens oversight and empowers regulators to aggressively pursue financial fraud, conflicts of interest and manipulation of the system that benefits special interests at the expense of American families and businesses.

Source: Dodd-Frank Wall Street Reform and Consumer Protection Act

and documented process for obtaining evidence regarding the status of an organization's ethical culture. It takes a closer look at a firm's ethical culture instead of just allowing it to remain unexamined. An ethical culture is made up of factors such as ethical leadership, accountability, and values. The climate with top management is fundamental to a company's ethical culture.[27] Ethical leadership begins with the board of directors and CEO and continues to middle managers and supervisors. Building an ethical culture that lasts requires a foundation of practices that continue even when leaders change.[28]

According to the Corporate Executive Board in Arlington, Virginia, companies with weak ethical cultures experience 10 times more misconduct than companies with strong ethical cultures.[29] In strong ethical cultures, employees are at ease to speak up about their concerns without fear of retaliation. In workplaces with a strong ethical culture, only 4 percent of employees feel pressure to compromise standards and commit misconduct compared to 15 percent in a weaker culture.[30]

Code of Ethics

For organizations to grow and prosper, good people must be employed. Companies are also searching for new employees who have a sound ethical base because they have discovered that an ethical person tends to be more successful. Dov Seidman, a management guru who advocates corporate virtue to many companies, believes that companies that "outbehave" their competitors ethically will generally outperform them financially.[31] Further, the ethical—or unethical—behavior of an organization is a critical factor for new college graduates seeking jobs, according to the National Association of Colleges and Employers.[32]

By fostering a strong ethical culture, firms are better able to gain the confidence and loyalty of their employees and other stakeholders, which can result in reduced financial, legal, and reputation risks, as well as improvements in organizational performance. Organizations are redesigning their ethics programs to facilitate a broader and more consistent process that incorporates the analysis of outcomes and continual improvement. To build and sustain an ethical culture, organizations need a comprehensive framework that encompasses communication of behavior expectations, training on ethics and compliance issues, stakeholder input, resolution of reported matters, and analysis of the entire ethics program. To make it really work, involvement by top management is certainly necessary.

A distinction needs to be made between a code of conduct and a code of ethics; the former should tell employees what the rules of conduct are. The code of ethics helps employees know what to do when there is not a rule for something.[33] A broad-based participation of those subject to the code is important. For a company to behave ethically, it must live and breathe its code of ethics, train its personnel, and communicate its code through its vision statements. It cannot just print a manual that sits on a corporate shelf. The code is a statement of the values adopted by the company, its employees, and its directors, and sets the official tone of top management regarding expected behavior. Many industry associations adopt such codes, which are then recommended to members. There are many kinds of ethical codes. An excellent example of a code of ethics was developed by the Society for Human Resource Management (SHRM). Major provisions in the SHRM code of ethics include professional responsibility, professional development, ethical leadership, fairness and justice, conflicts of interest, and use of information.

Just what should be included in a code of ethics? Topics typically covered might be business conduct, fair competition, and workplace and HR issues. For example, employees in purchasing would be shown what constitutes a conflict of interest. The same would occur for sales. At Walmart, it is considered unethical to accept gifts from suppliers. Gifts are either destroyed or given to charity. Fidelity International recently fired two Hong Kong–based fund managers over breaches of its internal code of ethics. Fidelity said, "Our routine checks discovered a pattern of behavior that breached our internal policies."[34]

To keep the code on the front burner for employees, larger firms appoint an ethics officer. The ethics officer is the point person in guiding everyone in the company toward ethical actions. This individual should be a person who understands the work environment. To obtain the involvement of others within the organization, an ethics committee is often established.

There are reasons to encourage industry associations to develop and promote codes of ethics. It is difficult for a single firm to pioneer ethical practices if its competitors take advantage of unethical shortcuts. For example, U.S. companies must comply with the Foreign Corrupt Practices Act, which prohibits bribes of foreign government officials or business executives. Obviously, the law does not prevent foreign competitors from bribing government or business officials to get business and such practices are common in many countries. This sometimes puts U.S. companies at a disadvantage.

Even the criteria for winning the Malcolm Baldrige National Quality Award have changed, and an increased emphasis on ethics in leadership is now stressed. The criteria say senior leaders should serve as role models for the rest of their organizations. Baldrige applicants are asked questions about how senior leaders create an environment that fosters legal and ethical behavior. They need to show how the leaders address governance matters such as fiscal accountability and independence in audits.

Linking Pay to Ethical Behavior

The importance of linking pay to performance is an appropriate topic when discussing ethics. It is well known in the compensation world that "what you reward is what you get." If the statement is correct, then a problem exists because most companies do not link pay to ethical behavior but base pay on entitlement and custom.[35] A survey of 358 compliance and ethics professionals by the Society of Corporate Compliance and Ethics (SCCE) and Health Care Compliance Association found that only a few companies have made ethics and compliance a process for determining how employees are compensated, and only about one company in six ties employee bonuses and incentives to ethical performance.[36] In another survey, when asked how much impact the ethics and compliance function has on the compensation process for executives, just 34 percent of respondents said it had some or a great deal of impact. The majority indicated that compliance and ethics played very little (27 percent) or no role (29 percent), while the balance was unsure of the role of ethics and compliance.[37] CEO Roy Snell of SCCE said, "The net result is that there is more work to be done in aligning business practices with stated commitment to compliant, ethical behavior."[38] For example, ethical expectation could be made part of the performance review and the results tied to pay raises.[39] As one author recently stated, "When employees behave in undesirable ways, it's a good idea to look at what you're encouraging them to do."[40]

OBJECTIVE **2.5**
Explain human resource ethics and describe ethics training.

Human Resource Ethics

Human resource ethics is the application of ethical principles to human resource relationships and activities. It is vitally important that human resource professionals know those practices that are acceptable and unacceptable and work to ensure that organizational members also have this awareness in dealing with others.

human resource ethics
Application of ethical principles to human resource relationships and activities.

Some believe that those in human resources have a great deal to do with establishing an organization's conscience. In fact, according to a Society for Human Resource Management report, integrity and ethical behavior rank in the top five competencies needed for senior HR leaders.[41] Certainly ethics is a quality the HR professionals should possess. It is the duty of HR professionals to help create an ethical climate in their organization.[42]

HR professionals can help foster an ethical culture, but that means more than just hanging the ethics codes posters on walls. Instead, since the HR professionals' primary job is dealing with people, they must help to instill ethical practices into the corporate culture. Those values must be clearly communicated to all employees, early and often, beginning with the interview process, reinforced during employee orientation, and regularly recognized during performance reviews, public ceremonies, celebrations, and awards. They need to help establish an environment in which employees throughout the organization work to reduce ethical lapses. The ethical bearing of those in HR goes a long way toward establishing the credibility of the entire organization.

There are many topics through which HR professionals can have a major impact on ethics and, therefore, on creating an ethical corporate culture. Some ethical questions that might be considered include:

- Do you strive to create a diverse workforce?
- Do you insist that job descriptions are developed to accurately depict jobs that are dangerous or hazardous?
- Do you strive to recruit and select the best-qualified applicant for the job?
- Are your training initiatives geared so that everyone will have an opportunity to receive the best training and development possible?
- Is your performance management and appraisal system able to identify those who are indeed the best producers and rewarded accordingly?
- Is your compensation and benefit system developed so that employees will view it as fair and impartial?
- Does your organization make a sincere attempt to provide a safe and healthy work environment?
- Does your organization attempt to develop a work environment in which employees will not feel compelled to join a union?
- Are you fair and impartial when dealing with disciplinary action, promotion, transfer, demotion, resignation, discharge, layoff, and retirement?
- Does your firm adhere to ethical norms when operating in the global environment?

HR should review, develop, and enforce organizational policies to ensure a high level of ethics throughout the organization. All employees should know what is ethical and unethical in their specific area of operations. It is insufficient to say that everyone should be ethical. Dialogue should be developed so that workers in different areas know what is ethical.

Ethics Training

The Federal Sentencing Guidelines for Organizations Act outlined an effective ethics training program and explained the seven minimum requirements for an effective program to prevent and detect violations. The fourth requirement stated, "Educate employees in the company's standards and procedures through publications and training." Companies train employees on many topics, but ethics training is often not considered, which is a major oversight. Because of its inclusion within the FSGO, a brief discussion of ethics training will be provided in this chapter.

Companies that consistently rank high on the lists of best corporate citizens tend to make ethics training part of a company-wide initiative to promote integrity.[43] Ethics training should be part of a proactive, not reactive, strategy. Regular training builds awareness of common ethical issues and provides tools for effective problem solving.[44] Ethics training should begin at the top and continue through all levels in the organization. However, training should take into consideration the differences in these levels. While top management sets the ethical tone, middle managers are the ones who will likely be the first to receive reports of unethical behavior.

KPMG believes that there are three fundamental factors in handing ethics issues: provide multiple channels for raising alarms, eliminate fear of retaliation for those who raise questions, and ensure consistent investigation and resolution of all matters reported. Individuals who report potential ethics violations could be subject to retaliation, so KPMG monitors performance reviews and other metrics to proactively identify retaliatory behavior. The credibility of the program requires all reports to be consistently investigated and resolved.[45]

Cisco created a unique ethics training program that showcased cartoon contestants singing about various ethical workplace situations found in Cisco's Code of Business Conduct. Jeremy Wilson, manager, ethics office for Cisco Systems, Inc., said, "We wanted what was right for our employees, based upon our own risk analysis." When Cisco created its program, it invited input from more than 120 people from departments across the organization, including legal, human resources, IT security, and records management.[46]

Ethics training for global organizations is more complicated than preparing the training for U.S. employees. One must also train for the country in which the global company operates. Since 1994, LRN has helped 15 million people at 700 companies across the world simultaneously navigate legal and regulatory environments and foster ethical cultures.[47] A few of their customers include CBS, Dow Chemical, eBay, 3M, and Siemens. Chris Campbell, creative director at LRN, says, "Localization is as important as the accuracy of the translation process. Learners need to be able to connect in a way that is believable to them."[48]

OBJECTIVE 2.6

Describe the concept of corporate social responsibility.

corporate social responsibility (CSR)

Implied, enforced, or felt obligation of managers, acting in their official capacity, to serve or protect the interests of groups other than themselves.

Corporate Social Responsibility

Corporate social responsibility (CSR) is the implied, enforced, or felt obligation of managers, acting in their official capacity, to serve or protect the interests of groups other than themselves.

What do the following U.S. companies have in common: Johnson & Johnson, Intel Corp., General Electric Co., Agilent Technologies, Inc., Johnson Controls Inc., Weyerhaeuser Co., Prologis, Procter & Gamble Co., Kraft Foods, Inc., P G & E Corp., Hewlett-Packard Co., Coca-Cola Enterprises, and Baxter International, Inc.? They have been identified as having a commitment to excellence in the area of corporate social responsibility and are included in the 2011 Global 100 Most Sustainable Corporations in the World.[49] These companies have demonstrated the ability to manage the "triple bottom line" of social responsibility (society, environment, and economy).[50] They represent the top 5 percent of socially responsible companies.

Corporate social responsibility is the model in which economic, social, and environmental responsibilities are satisfied concurrently.[51] When a corporation behaves as if it has a conscience, it is said to be socially responsible. CSR considers the overall influence of corporations on society at large and goes beyond the interests of shareholders. It is how a company as a whole behaves toward society. In many companies, social responsibility has moved from nice-to-do to must-do. More and more companies are issuing corporate social responsibility reports that detail their environmental, labor, and corporate-giving practices. Some firms, such as Burger King, have created the position of director of corporate social responsibility.

Apparently, socially responsible behavior pays off on the bottom line. When GE CEO Jeffrey Immelt announced that the company would double its spending on green technology research, it was no grand attempt to save the planet; it was an example of astute business strategy. Immelt said, "We plan to make money doing it."[52] Social responsibility has also impacted the recruiting process. College graduates of today often seek out corporations that have a reputation for being socially responsible, which was not often the case in the past. In fact, job seekers tend to be more attracted to organizations known for corporate social responsibility.[53]

Procter & Gamble has long believed it has a responsibility for the long-term benefit of society as well as the company. Over the years, P&G has pursued programs to strengthen U.S. education, to encourage employment opportunities for minorities and women, to develop and implement environment-protection technology, and to encourage employee involvement in civic activities and the political process.

Deborah Leipziger, an Ethical Corporation Institute researcher, said, "The more credible efforts tend to be led by key players within a company."[54] An organization's top executives usually determine a corporation's approach to social responsibility. For example, when McDonald's began, it was Ray Kroc's philosophy to be a community-based business. His philosophy from the very beginning was to give back to the communities that McDonald's served.[55]

One of the best benchmarks for defining social responsibility in manufacturing is the one-page set of operating principles developed 60 years ago by Robert Wood Johnson, then Johnson & Johnson's chairman of the board. The document is still in use today and addresses supporting good works and charities.[56]

HR Web Wisdom

Business for Social Responsibility

http://www.bsr.org

This is a global organization that helps member companies achieve success in ways that respect ethical values, people, communities, and the environment.

Not Everyone Is on Board with Corporate Social Responsibility

Thus far only the virtues of corporate social responsibility have been provided. However, the question of whether businesses should promote corporate social responsibility is at times hotly debated and not all companies have embraced the concept.[57] Some have challenged the concept that doing well is doing good (DWDG). They believe that although appealing to some, DWDG is also profoundly wrong.[58] Milton Friedman was an American economist, statistician, academic, and author who taught at the University of Chicago for more than three decades and was a recipient of the Nobel Memorial Prize in Economic Sciences. In his book *Capitalism and Freedom,* he argued that the only social responsibility of business was to increase its profits. According to Friedman, as a firm creates wealth for its shareholders, society as a whole will also be benefited.[59] Friedman disciples continue to condemn CSR as a hotchpotch of "value-destroying nonsense."[60]

These days, more employers are publicly endorsing a culture of ethics and social responsibility. However, some believe that it is being done more as a public relations campaign. Long before the enormous oil spill in 2010, BP promoted itself as being eco-friendly. Its literature stated that BP stood for "Beyond Petroleum." BP marketed itself as a producer of alternative energies, an image that was seriously damaged by the devastating oil spill in the Gulf of Mexico.[61] Instead of spending billions on eco-friendly energy and building an employer brand campaign around it, many believe that BP would have been much better off if it had spent more time and effort in training its employees on its oil drilling platforms, establishing stronger safety protocols, and waiting until they were safe to operate. Even during this public relations campaign, BP had a history of safety violation. BP had been "fined more than $100 million for safety violations that led to deaths of workers, explosions of refineries, and leaking pipelines."[62]

Brighter Planet, a sustainability technology company, discovered in a recent survey that although more firms are engaging in green activities, the effectiveness of these efforts has declined.[63] Some believe that the problem with CSR is that it consists of a universal set of guidelines such as the "triple bottom line" (society, environment, and economy) mentioned earlier. To be "socially responsible," each firm has to follow the same guidelines instead of what would be the most appropriate strategy for each firm. Using this logic, it would be more logical for oil companies such as BP to focus on being profitable, yet be an environmentally conscious oil company. Fast-food restaurants such as McDonald's and retailers such as Walmart should each use a different set of rules to do the same thing in their own industries.

There are those who believe that all shareholders should not be required to be involved in CSR investments. They think that only investors who want to be involved should participate. These investors would do so with the understanding that the objective is not just to make money but also to do good. For example, an oil company such as Exxon could establish an alternative-energy subsidiary. Exxon would own a controlling stake, but funding would come from new investors who want to support alternative energy and thus be socially responsible. If the subsidiary was unsuccessful, the losses would be confined to the new investors. If it succeeded, the profits would be shared by all shareholders.[64]

OBJECTIVE 2.7

Explain why everyone is not on board with regard to corporate social responsibility.

OBJECTIVE 2.8

Explain corporate sustainability.

HR Web Wisdom

Deloitte Sustainability Are You Overlooking Opportunities?
http://www.deloitte.com /view/en_US/us/Insights/hot- topics/sustainability/index.htm

Many executives are turning to sustainability to help improve the bottom line.

During the Vietnam War, Dow Chemical gained a bad reputation for not being social responsibility because it produced the deadly chemical agent napalm. As a result Dow had difficulty recruiting the best scientists and other professionals. To overcome this image, Dow built a campaign that highlighted how Dow has benefitted agricultural production. Once people saw the positive side of Dow, its ability to recruit and retain the best chemists improved.[65]

Corporate Sustainability

Corporate sustainability has evolved from the more traditional view of corporate social responsibility. According to the World Commission on Environment and Sustainability, the narrow definition of sustainability is "meeting the needs of the present without compromising the ability of future generations to meet their own needs."[66] In recent years, sustainability has been expanded to include the social, economic, environmental, and cultural systems needed to support an organization. This type of organization is capable of continuing both now and in the future. Corporate sustainability may be thought of as being a business and investment approach that strives to use the best business practices to meet the needs of current and future shareholders. Today it relates to how an organization's decisions could affect society and the environment as a whole. Essentially it is about how a firm handles its business while understanding how these decisions may affect others. One could think of corporate sustainability in a business sense as providing long-term profitability. Thus, sustainability should be a fundamental part of business strategy, product development, talent development, and capital investment. Recently, some organizations have emphasized the importance of corporate sustainability by establishing the position of chief sustainability officer.[67] Others such as Johnson & Johnson prefer to see it developed into the overall culture of the firm. Tish Lascelle, Johnson & Johnson's senior director environment, said, "Sustainability is embedded in our culture. It's been a part of who we are for more than 65 years, long before the notion of sustainability became trendy."[68]

Numerous companies are working toward becoming eco-friendly. For example, Target's waste-reduction efforts have cut waste by 70 percent. Home Depot attempts to make sure that wood and lumber sold in its stores come from sustainable forests. Corporate environmental responsibility for McDonald's focuses on energy efficiency, sustainable packing and waste management, and green restaurant design.[69] McDonald's has eliminated the use of containers made with ozone-depleting chlorofluorocarbons, cut down on the amount and type of packaging it uses, and implemented a program of purchasing goods made from recycled materials. Walmart is working on sustainable initiatives. Solar panels are being installed in all of the retailer's super centers with unused energy being sold back into the energy grid, a cost-saving move for the community.[70]

Increasingly, environmentally sound and cost-cutting operating procedures are being included in firms' business plans not only for their own employees, products, and facilities, but also for suppliers and trade partners. Walmart Stores Inc. has initiated and promoted sustainability not only in its own stores and production facilities, but also for its U.S. and global suppliers.[71] Frito-Lay, which operates the world's seventh-largest private delivery fleet, has put 176 all-electric box trucks on the road in places such as California, Texas, and the Pacific Northwest. The trucks are expected to cut diesel consumption by 500,000 gallons a year while limiting greenhouse emissions by 75 percent over combustion engines. The trucks will also cut annual maintenance costs by as much as $700,000.[72]

Approximately 62 percent of large and medium-sized companies worldwide have an active sustainability program in place, and another 11 percent are developing one, according to a sustainability survey commissioned by consulting firm KPMG.[73] Corporate Knights, a Toronto-based media company and sustainability reporter, recently released its seventh annual report of the world's best sustainable corporations. The top five U.S. companies with the most green-friendly, sustainable practices were Johnson & Johnson, Intel Corp., General Electric Co., Agilent Technologies, Inc., and Johnson Controls Inc.[74]

PPG Industries recently issued a corporate sustainability report that provides information about the company's financial performance, environmental metrics such as greenhouse gas emissions and energy use, safety statistics, stakeholder engagement, philanthropic activities, and awards and recognition. In the report, Charles E. Bunch, PPG chairman and CEO, said, "Sustainability is business as usual at PPG. An underlying principle for the company since its founding in 1883, a commitment to sustainability has been crucial to our long-term success."[75] Dow Chemical's way of thinking regarding sustainability is, "If you can't do it better, why do it?" This philosophy is at the very heart of sustainability at Dow. Every decision is made with the future in mind.[76]

Institutional investors managing more than $1.6 trillion in assets are starting to put pressure on the world's 30 largest stock exchanges to force companies to improve their sustainability reporting. Twenty-four institutional shareholders said they want it to be easier to judge the environmental, social, and governance risks of the firms in which they invest.[77]

Sustainability has also become extremely popular for companies operating in the global environment. Recently, Danone's German division switched to a plastic made from plants (not oil) for its Activia yogurt packaging sold in Germany.[78] Coca-Cola Enterprises in Great Britain has cut its carbon emissions by 470,000t, which is about a third of its 2020 target. It is also recycling 99 percent of the factory waste it produces, with five out of six of its production sites sending zero waste to landfills.[79] Global polystyrene leader Styron LLC has more than 2,000 employees at 20 plants worldwide with annual sales of $5 billion. It begins each corporate meeting with the topic of sustainability. Employees' bonuses are tied in to meeting sustainability goals. Recently, Styron introduced a recycled-content grade of polycarbonate at the Chinaplas trade show in Guangzhou, China.[80] Renault partnershiped with Veolia Environment to build the world's first zero-emissions, 100-percent renewable energy-reliant car manufacturing plant in Morocco.[81]

| OBJECTIVE **2.9**
| Describe a social audit.

social audit
Systematic assessment of a company's activities in terms of its social impact.

Conducting a Social Audit

To overcome the negative publicity of corporate misdeeds and to restore trust, businesses are now conducting audits of their social responsibility activities, not just financial audits. A **social audit** is a systematic assessment of a company's activities in terms of its social impact.

A GLOBAL PERSPECTIVE

Can Corporate Social Responsibility Succeed in the Global Environment?

The global environment has traditionally judged management primarily on furthering the firm's bottom line. If this is so, it may be easier to be socially responsible in a prospering economy but more difficult when the economy is bad. Recently, some global firms appear to be questioning the wisdom of being socially responsible. The question being asked is, "Can firms competing in the global environment continue the lowest possible production costs while still being in compliance with national laws and also be socially responsible?"

Even before the recent recession began, corporations and their contractor manufacturers (often Korean, Taiwanese, and Hong Kong companies operating throughout the world) focused on obtaining the lowest production costs regardless of the accompanying social and environmental impacts. As labor costs have increased in China, companies quickly move their manufacturing to lower labor cost countries such as Cambodia, Laos, India, and Vietnam.[82] No consideration was made for the workers and families of the workers who were left behind.

Although some companies continue to say that they are fully committed to CSR, their less than socially responsible behavior speaks otherwise. A fire in a garment factory in Bangladesh killed 29 workers and hundreds were injured as they were suffocated, burned alive, trampled in stairwells, or leapt to their deaths from the 9th and 10th floors because four of seven exit doors were locked. After more than 15 years of corporate social responsibility programs, women garment workers continue to die making clothing for retailers such as Abercrombie & Fitch, Kenneth Cole, DKNY, Gap, Tommy Hilfiger, H&M, Izod, JC Penney, Calvin Klein, Kohl's, Lee, North Face, OshKosh, Sears, Target, Timberland, Wrangler, and Walmart. Moreover, Bangladesh's garment workers are among the worst paid in the world.[83]

There is a growing recognition among some leading global CSR organizations that the first 15 years of CSR efforts has not produced the desired results, and that significant changes will have to be made if CSR is to be anything more than an expensive exercise in "reputational management." Dan Rees, director of the UK's Ethical Trading Initiative, said, "CSR in general has become a bit of a victim of its own hype...we have to stop pretending that companies in and of themselves can on their own transform industrial relations in foreign lands."[84] However, a recent study does not fully support these conclusions. In the study on global CSR conducted during the economic breakdown, 44 percent believe that CSR policies will be applied more often as a result of the crisis, 28 percent think that the real meaning of CSR will change in the framework of the new conditions, and 22 percent believe that the crisis will have a negative impact on CSR.[85]

OBJECTIVE 2.10

Describe possible difficulties for corporate social responsibility to succeed in the global environment.

Some of the topics included in the audit focus on core values such as social responsibility, open communication, treatment of employees, confidentiality, and leadership. Firms are now acknowledging responsibilities to various stakeholder groups other than corporate owners.[86]

Some even set specific objectives in social areas. They are attempting to formally measure their contributions to various elements of society and to society as a whole. An increasing number of companies, as well as public and voluntary sector organizations, are trying to assess their social performance systematically. Three possible types of social audits are currently being used: (1) simple inventory of activities, (2) compilation of socially relevant expenditures, and (3) determination of social impact. The inventory is generally a good starting place. It consists of a listing of socially oriented activities undertaken by the firm. Here are some examples: minority employment and training, support of minority enterprises, pollution control, corporate giving, involvement in selected community projects by executives, and a hard-core unemployment program. The ideal social audit would go well beyond a simple listing and involve determining the true benefits to society of any socially oriented business activity.

Summary

1. *Explain the purpose of paying whistleblowers.* The Dodd–Frank Act offers whistleblowers financial rewards for their help in uncovering wrongdoing. In passing the act, Congress believed that bounty programs are an effective method to encourage people with information regarding violations of the law to come forward with the information to responsible law enforcement officials.

2. *Define ethics and describe sources of ethical guidance.* *Ethics* is the discipline dealing with what is good and bad, or right and wrong, or with moral duty and obligation.

   The sources of ethical guidance should lead to our beliefs or a conviction about what is right or wrong. Most would agree that people have a responsibility to avail themselves to these sources of ethical guidance. In short, individuals should care about what is right and wrong and not just be concerned with what is expedient. One might use a number of sources to determine what is right or wrong, good or bad, moral or immoral. These sources include the Bible and other holy books. They also include the small voice that many refer to as conscience. Many believe that conscience is a gift of God or the voice of God. Others see it as a developed response based on the internalization of societal mores. Another source of ethical guidance is the behavior and advice of the people psychologists call "significant others"—our parents, friends, and role models and members of our churches, clubs, and associations. For most professionals, there are codes of ethics that prescribe certain behavior. Without this conscience that has developed it might be easy to say, "Everyone does it," "Just this once won't hurt," or "No one will ever know." Some still believe that greed is acceptable as long as the SEC does not find out.

3. *Discuss attempts at legislating ethics.* There have been four attempts to legislate business ethics since the late 1980s, the Procurement Integrity Act, the Federal Sentencing Guidelines for Organizations, the Corporate and Auditing Accountability, Responsibility and Transparency Act, and the Dodd–Frank Wall Street Reform and Consumer Protection Act.

4. *Explain the importance of creating an ethical culture, describe a code of ethics, and support the importance of linking pay to ethical behavior.* An ethical culture is made up of factors such as ethical leadership, accountability, and values. The climate at the top is fundamental to a company's ethical culture. Ethical leadership begins with the board of directors and CEO and continues to middle managers and supervisors. Building an ethical culture that lasts requires a foundation of practices that continue even when leaders change.

   A *code of ethics* establishes the rules that the organization lives by. Only a few companies have made ethics and compliance a process for determining how employees are compensated.

   It is well known in the compensation world that "what you reward is what you get." If the statement is correct, then a problem exists with regard to compensation because most companies do not link pay to ethical behavior.

5. *Explain human resource ethics and describe ethics training.* *Human resource ethics* is the application of ethical principles to human resource relationships and activities.

   Ethics training is not merely for top-level managers; it should be for everyone from the bottom to the top. Companies that consistently rank high on the lists of best corporate citizens tend to make ethics training part of a company-wide initiative to promote integrity. Ethics training should be part of a proactive, not reactive, strategy. Regular training builds awareness of common ethical issues and provides tools for effective problem solving.

6. *Describe the concept of corporate social responsibility.* *Corporate social responsibility* is the implied, enforced, or felt obligation of managers, acting in their official capacity, to serve or protect the interests of groups other than themselves.

7. *Explain why everyone is not on board with regard to corporate social responsibility.* Milton Friedman was an American economist, statistician, academic, and author who taught at the University of Chicago for more than three decades and was a recipient of the Nobel Memorial Prize in Economic Sciences. In his book *Capitalism and Freedom,* he argued that the only social responsibility of business was to increase its profits. According to Friedman, as a firm creates wealth for its shareholders, society as a whole will also be benefited. Friedman disciples continue to condemn CSR.

8. *Explain corporate sustainability.* *Corporate sustainability* has evolved from the more traditional corporate social responsibility. According to the World Commission on Environment and Sustainability, the narrow definition of sustainability is "meeting the needs of the present without compromising the ability of future generations to meet their own needs." In recent years, sustainability has been expanded to include the social, economic, environmental, and cultural systems needed to support an organization. This type of organization is capable of continuing both now and in the future.

9. *Describe a social audit.* A *social audit* is a systematic assessment of a company's activities in terms of its social impact.

10. *Describe possible difficulties for corporate social responsibility to succeed in the global environment.* The global environment often judges management primarily on protecting the firm's bottom line. If this is so, it may be easy to be socially responsible in a prospering economy but more difficult when the economy is bad.

Key Terms

ethics 26
human resource ethics 30

corporate social responsibility
(CSR) 32

social audit 34

Exercises

⭐ 1. The HRM in Action at the beginning of the chapter entitled "Pay for Whistleblowing" creates a situation where an employee of a company who reports a wrongdoing by the firm to the government gets paid for this action. What might be some pros and cons of paying a whistleblower?

2. The Trends & Innovations in the chapter entitled "Not Everyone Is on Board with Corporate Social Responsibility" suggests that CSR is not as strongly advocated as this text suggests it is. Do you accept the argument for or against CSR? Defend your decision.

Questions for Review

1. Why does the government pay for whistleblowing?
2. What laws have been passed in an attempt to legislate ethics?
3. Why is it important to have a code of ethics?
4. With regard to business ethics, what does the statement "what you reward is what you get" mean?
5. What are human resource ethics?
6. What are the areas in which HR professionals can have a major impact on ethics?
7. What is corporate social responsibility?
8. What does corporate sustainability mean?
9. What is involved in conducting a social audit?
⭐10. Why might it be difficult for corporate social responsibility to succeed in the global environment?

INCIDENT 1   An Ethical Flaw

Amber Davis had recently graduated from college with a degree in general business. Amber was quite bright, although her grades did not reflect this. She had thoroughly enjoyed school, dating, playing tennis, and swimming, but found few stimulating academic endeavors. When she graduated, she had not found a job. Her dad was extremely upset when he discovered this, and he took it upon himself to see that Amber became employed.

Amber's father, Allen Davis, was executive vice president of a medium-sized manufacturing firm. One of the people he contacted in seeking employment for Amber was Bill Garbo, the president of another firm in the area. Mr. Davis purchased many of his firm's supplies from Garbo's company. After telling Bill his problem, Allen was told to send Amber to Bill's office for an interview. Amber went, as instructed by her father, and before she left Bill's firm, she was surprised to learn that she had a job in the accounting department. Amber may have been lazy, but she certainly was not stupid. She realized that Bill had hired her because he hoped that his action would lead to future business from her father's company. Although Amber's work was not challenging, it paid better than the other jobs in the accounting department.

It did not take long for the employees in the department to discover the reason she had been hired; Amber told them. When a difficult job was assigned to Amber, she normally got one of the other employees to do it, implying that Mr. Garbo would be pleased with that person if he or she helped her out. She developed a pattern of coming in late, taking long lunch breaks, and leaving early. When the department manager attempted to reprimand her for these unorthodox activities, Amber would bring up the close relationship that her father had with the president of the firm. The department manager was at the end of his rope.

Questions

1. From an ethical standpoint, how would you evaluate the merits of Mr. Garbo's employing Amber? Discuss.
2. Now that she is employed, what course would you follow to address her on-the-job behavior?
3. It may be that Mr. Garbo viewed the hiring of Amber as strictly a business decision that would ensure receiving continued business from Amber's father. What might be some negative results of this questionable ethical decision?

INCIDENT 2   "You Can't Fire Me"

Norman Blankenship came in the side door of the office at Consolidation Coal Company's Rowland mine, near Clear Creek, West Virginia. He told the mine dispatcher not to tell anyone he was there. Norman was general superintendent of the Rowland operation. He had been with Consolidation for 23 years, having started out as a mining machine operator.

Norman had heard that one of his section bosses, Tom Serinsky, had been sleeping on the job. Tom had been hired two months earlier and assigned to the Rowland mine by the regional personnel office. He had gone to work as section boss, working the midnight to 8:00 a.m. shift. Because of his age and experience, Serinsky was the senior person in the mine on his shift.

Norman took one of the battery-operated jeeps used to transport personnel and supplies in and out of the mine and went to the area where Tom was assigned. Upon arriving, he saw Tom lying on an emergency stretcher. Norman stopped his jeep a few yards away from where Tom was sleeping and approached him. "Hey, are you asleep?" Norman asked. Tom awakened with a start and said, "No, I wasn't sleeping."

Norman waited for Tom to collect his senses and then said, "I could tell that you were sleeping, but that's beside the point. You weren't at your workstation. You know that I have no choice but to fire you." After Tom had left, Norman called his mine foreman and asked him to come in and complete the remainder of Tom's shift.

The next morning, Norman had the mine HR manager officially terminate Tom. As part of the standard procedure, the mine HR manager notified the regional HR manager that Tom had been fired and gave the reasons for firing him. The regional HR manager asked the mine HR manager to get Norman on the line. The regional HR manager said, "Norm, you know Tom is Justus Frederick's brother-in-law, don't you?" Frederick was a regional vice president. "No, I didn't know that," replied Norman, "but it doesn't matter. The rules are clear. I wouldn't care if he was Frederick's son."

The next day, the regional human resource manager showed up at the mine just as Norman was getting ready to make a routine tour of the mine. "I guess you know what I'm here for," said the HR manager. "Yeah, you're here to take away my authority," replied Norman. "No, I'm just here to investigate," said the regional HR manager.

By the time Norman returned to the mine office after his tour, the regional HR manager had finished his interviews. He told Norman, "I think we're going to have to put Tom back to work. If we decide to do that, can you let him work for you?" "No, absolutely not," said Norman. "In fact, if he works here, I go." A week later, Norman learned that Tom had gone to work as section boss at another Consolidation coal mine in the region.

Questions

1. What would you do now if you were Norman?
2. Do you believe the regional HR manager handled the matter in an ethical manner? Explain.

MyManagementLab

Go to **mymanagementlab.com** for Auto-graded writing questions as well as the following Assisted-graded writing questions:

2-1. Why should a firm want to create an ethical culture?

2-2. Why is everyone not on board with regard to corporate social responsibility?

2-3. Mymanagementlab Only – comprehensive writing assignment for this chapter.

Notes

1. Jonathan Lawner and Denise Dickins, "Will There Be Whistleblowers?" *Regulation* 34 (Summer 2011): 36–40.
2. "Facts & Figures," *InsideCounsel* 23 (March 2012): 16.
3. "$4.5M Whistleblower Award for CPA," *Accounting Today* 25 (May 2011): 43.
4. Curtis C. Verschoor, "New Whistleblower Rules Broaden Opportunities," *Strategic Finance* 93 (September 2011): 13–69.
5. Anthony M. Alexis, Marcia E. Goodman, and Scott A. Clafee, "New Whistleblower Provisions Provide Bounty Incentives and Greatly Expanded Protections," *Insights: The Corporate & Securities Law Advisor* 24 (September 2010): 45–50.
6. "Companies Anticipate an Increase in Whistleblower Claims," *Corporate Board* 32 (January/February 2012): 28–29.
7. "Whistleblower Claims in Dodd–Frank Era Expected," *Financial Executive* 28 (January/February 2012): 11.
8. Jason C. Schwartz and Porter N. Wilkinson, "2011 Year-End Update on Dodd–Frank and SOX Employee Whistleblower Provisions," *Insights: The Corporate & Securities Law Advisor* 26 (January 2012): 15–22.
9. Kyle Scott, "Business Ethics: Do What's Right, or What's Right Now?" *Supervision* 72 (July 2011): 8–9.
10. "Investors Are Looking Closely at Corporate Ethics," *Corporate Board* 28 (September 2007): 28.
11. Ben W. Heineman, Jr., "Avoiding Integrity Land Mines," *Harvard Business Review* 85 (April 2007): 100–108.
12. Steve Steckler, "The Leadership Challenges Facing HR: Top CHROs Share Learnings and Advice on What's Next," *People & Strategy* 33 (2010): 14–21.
13. Kyle Scott, "Acting Ethically Is the Only Option," *Supervision* 73 (January 2012): 6–7.
14. Mary C. Gentile, "Keeping Your Colleagues Honest," *Harvard Business Review* 88 (March 2010): 114–17.
15. T. L. Stanley, "Ethics in Action," *Supervision* 69 (April 2008): 14–16.
16. Ikujiro Nonaka and Hirotaka Takeuchi, "The Wise Leader," *Harvard Business Review* 89 (May 2011): 58–67.
17. Bill Streeter, "Regulation Is Not Ethics," *ABA Banking Journal* 104 (January 2012): 6.
18. Kenneth D. Lewis, "The Responsibility of the CEO: Providing Ethical and Moral Leadership," *Vital Speeches of the Day* 69 (October 15, 2002): 6–9.
19. Joyce A. Ostrosky, Linda M. Leinicke, John Digenan, and W. Max Rexroad, "Assessing Elements of Corporate Governance: A Suggested Approach," *CPA Journal* 79 (February 2009): 70–72.
20. Cathleen Flahardy, "SOX Gives DOL Power to Reinstate Whistleblowers," *Corporate Legal Times* 15 (August 2005): 24–26.
21. Melissa Klein Aguilar, "Questions Arise on Timely Ethics Disclosure," *Compliance Week* 7 (March 2010): 58–59.
22. Howard Stock, "Ethics Trump Rules, Levitt Says," *Investor Relations Business* (April 7, 2003): 1.
23. Paul Schneider, "Dodd–Frank Financial Reform Legislation Addresses Executive Compensation," *Journal of Financial Service Professionals* 65 (January 2011): 27–31.
24. Shele Bannon, Kelly Ford, and Linda Meltzer, "How to Instill a Strong Ethical Culture," *CPA Journal* 80 (July 2010): 56–58.
25. Alec Wilkinson, "The Enron Example," *New Yorker* 81 (July 4, 2005): 30–31
26. Eric Krell, "How to Conduct an Ethics Audit," *HR Magazine* 55 (April 2010): 48–51.
27. Steve Watkins, "Build Top Ethical Culture," *Investor's Business Daily* (March 30, 2012): 3.
28. Patricia Harned, "Beyond Tone at the Top," *Boardroom Briefing* 7 (Fall 2010): 39–40.

29. Dori Meinert, "Strong Ethical Culture Helps Bottom Line," *HR Magazine* 55 (December 2010): 21.
30. Curtis C. Verschoor, "Top-Management Example and Peer Pressures Bring Benefits," *Strategic Finance* 92 (September 2010): 15–63.
31. Richard McGill Murphy, "Why Doing Good Is Good for Business," *Fortune* 161 (February 8, 2010): 90–95.
32. "Ethics as Recruiting Tool," *Journal of Accountancy* 207 (January 2009): 21.
33. Christopher Bauer, "Baking Ethics into Company Culture," *Financial Executive* 25 (May 2009): 18–21.
34. "Fidelity Fires Hong Kong Managers," *Fund Action* (February 22, 2010): 76.
35. Darnell Lattel, "The Slippery Slope," *T+D* 66 (March 2012): 22.
36. Sven Erik Holmes, "Under Pressure: Maintaining an Effective Ethics and Compliance Program," *Directorship* 35 (October/November 2009): 72.
37. "Few Tie Executive Pay or Bonuses to Compliance," *Compliance Week* 6 (July 2009): 10.
38. S. Steffee, "Weak Link between Business Ethics and Executive Compensation," *Internal Auditor* 66 (August 2009): 16.
39. Patricia J. Harned, "Encourage Ethical Behavior as Economy Recovers," *HR Specialist: Compensation & Benefits* 5 (January 2010): 5.
40. Max H. Bazerman and Ann E. Tenbrunsel, "Ethical Breakdowns," *Harvard Business Review* 89 (April 2011): 58–65.
41. "Competencies Senior HR Pros Need Now, in Five Years," *HR Focus* 87 (June 2010): 12–13.
42. Ken Sloan and Joanne H. Gavin, "Human Resource Management: Meeting the Ethical Obligations of the Function," *Business & Society Review* 115 (Spring 2010): 57–74.
43. Luis Ramos, "Outside-the-Box Ethics," *Leadership Excellence* 26 (April 2009): 19.
44. Marhta Perego, "Building an Ethical Culture," *Public Management* 93 (March 2011): 2–3.
45. Jerry Maginnis and Joseph P. Charles, "Build a Strong Ethical Culture," *Pennsylvania CPA Journal* 80 (Summer 2009): 1–2.
46. Cynthia Kincaid, "Corporate Ethics Training: The Right Stuff," *Training* 46 (May 2009): 35.
47. http://www.lrn.com/who-we-are February 21, 2012.
48. Ron Miller, "It's a Small World After All," *EContent* 31 (January/February 2008): 26–31.
49. http://www.global100.org/
50. Nguyen Thi Hong Ngoc, "Being Socially Responsible and Environmentally Friendly Improves the Corporate Competitiveness and Profitability?" *Advances in Management* 4 (March 2011): 21–25.
51. Paul Shum and Sharon Yam, "Ethics and Law: Guiding the Invisible Hand to Correct Corporate Social Responsibility Externalities," *Journal of Business Ethics* 98 (February 2011): 549–571.
52. Simon Zadek, "Responsibility Isn't a Blame Game," *Fortune (Europe)* 152 (October 3, 2005): 70–73.
53. David A. Jones, Chelesa R. Willness, and Sarah Madey, "Why Are Job Seekers Attracted to Socially Responsible Companies? Testing Underlying Mechanisms," *Academy of Management Annual Meeting Proceedings* (2010): 1–6.
54. John S. McClenahen, "Defining Social Responsibility," *Industry Week* 254 (March 2005): 64–65.
55. Wendy S. Becker, "Are You Leading a Socially Responsible and Sustainable Human Resource Function?" *People & Strategy* 34 (2011): 18–23.
56. Z. Jill Barclift, "Corporate Social Responsibility and Financial Institutions: Beyond Dodd–Frank," *Banking & Financial Services Policy Report* 31 (January 2012): 13–19.
57. V. Sivarama Krishnan, "In Defense of Social Responsibility of Business," *Journal of Business & Ethics* (2011): 31–37.
58. "Milton Friedman Goes on Tour," *Economist* 398 (January 29, 2011): 63.
59. Ronald J. Alsop "Cultural Awareness," *Workforce Management* 90 (July 2011): 42.
60. "Corporate Social Responsibility Heads for Oblivion," *Trends Magazine* 94 (February 2011): 10–14.
61. Steve Bates, "Report Questions Effectiveness of Employers' Green Initiatives," *HR Magazine* 57 (January 2012): 18.
62. Theo Vermaelen, "An Innovative Approach to Funding CSR Projects," *Harvard Business Review* 89 (June 2011): 28.
63. Adam Werbach, "Learning to Be Sustainable," *Chief Learning Officer* 10 (May 2011): 46–49.
64. Lilli Monolis, "Sustainability: It Will Change Your Business. . . If It Hasn't Already," *Plastics Technology* 58 (January 2012): 34–63.
65. Aneel Karnani, "Doing Well by Doing Good: The Grand Illusion," *California Management Review* 53 (Winter 2011): 69–86.
66. "Johnson & Johnson: Sustainability Is Mission-Critical," *Site Selection* 57 (January/February 2012): 42.
67. Nguyen Thi Hong Ngoc, "Profitability?" *Advances in Management* 4 (March 2011): 21–25.
68. Michael Laff, "Triple Bottom Line," *T+D* 63 (February 2009): 34–39.
69. Jaclyn Jaeger, "Choosing Among a Vast Array of CSR Initiatives," *Compliance Week* 6 (October 2009): 60–70.
70. "Social Responsibility: An Ongoing Mission for a Good Corporate Citizen," *Nation's Restaurant News* (April 11, 2005): 60–66.
71. Sean Milmo, "LCA Plays Key Role for Sustainability," *ICIS Chemical Business* 280 (October 3, 2011): 13.
72. "Institutional Investors Push for Increased Corporate Sustainability Reporting," *Business & the Environment with ISO 14000 Updates* 22 (April 2011): 5–6.
73. Scott Ladd, "Corporate 'Greening,'" *Financial Executive* 26 (March 2010): 36–41.
74. Duane Stanford, "Sustainability Meets the Profit Motive," *Bloomberg Businessweek* (April 4, 2011): 25–26.
75. "Corporate Sustainability," *Industry Week* 260 (February 2011): 49.
76. "Sustainability by the Numbers," *Business & the Environment with ISO 14000 Updates* 22 (July 2011): 13–14.
77. "PPG Issues 2010 Corporate Sustainability Report," *Paintindia* 61 (May 2011): 128–130.
78. Jim Carper, "Danone Uses Plant-based Packaging for Activia Yogurt in Germany," *Dairy Foods* 112 (August 2011): 10–11.
79. "Coca-Cola: Manufacturers Will Never Win the Battle of the Biodegradable Bottle," *Food Manufacture* 86 (August 2011): 7.
80. Frank Esposito, "Styron's Sustainability Goals, Progress Detailed in Report," *Plastics News* 23 (July 18, 2011): 4.
81. Ann Moline, "Not Your Father's Recycling Program," *Site Selection* 57 (January/February 2012): 41–45.
82. Bill Powell, "The End of Cheap Labor in China," *Time* 177 (June 27, 2011): 1–4.
83. Garrett Brown, "Corporate Social Responsibility: What Is It Good For?" *Industrial Safety & Hygiene News* 45 (May 2011): 34–36.
84. Garrett Brown, "Corporate Social Responsibility: The Moment of Truth Arrives," *Industrial Safety & Hygiene News* 43 (May 2009): 36.
85. M. Jothi, "CSR . . . in the Era of Global Economic Meltdown," *Global Management Review* 4 (2010): 93–97.
86. John Peloza, "Using Corporate Social Responsibility as Insurance for Financial Performance," *California Management Review* 48 (Winter 2006): 52–72.

3

Workforce Diversity, Equal Employment Opportunity, and Affirmative Action

HRM in Action

Lesbian, Gay, Bisexual, and Transgender Employees as a Protected Class?

OBJECTIVE 3.1

Discuss lesbian, gay, bisexual, and transgender employees as a protected class.

There has been an increased focus in the political and workforce arena with regard to lesbian, gay, bisexual, and transgender (LGBT) employees. In addressing the United Nations General Assembly, President Obama said, "No country should deny people their rights to freedom of speech and freedom of religion, but also no country should deny people their rights because of who they love, which is why we must stand up for the rights of gays and lesbians everywhere."[1] President Obama also decided that the 1996 Defense of Marriage Act that bars federal recognition of same-sex marriages was unconstitutional and told the Justice Department to stop defending the law in court, bringing harsh criticism from many congressional members.[2] In 2012, the president declared support for same-sex-marriages. The president also repealed the "don't ask, don't tell" rule barring the military from allowing gays to serve openly.

Polls show that the public tends to support equal rights for gay people, with the exception of the right to marry. Nearly 90 percent of Americans favor equality of opportunity in the workplace, and more than 60 percent favored overturning "don't ask, don't tell." But the public remains evenly divided on same-sex marriage. A few states also prohibit discrimination based on sexual orientation, but limit protection to public employees.[3] Sixteen states and at least 139 localities

CHAPTER OBJECTIVES   After completing this chapter, students should be able to:

1 Discuss lesbian, gay, bisexual, and transgender employees as a protected class.

2 Describe diversity and diversity management and explain the various components of the diverse workforce.

3 Identify the major laws affecting equal employment opportunity.

4 Describe the recent trend against employee retaliation.

5 Identify some of the major Supreme Court decisions that have had an impact on equal employment opportunity and affirmative action.

6 Describe the Equal Employment Opportunity Commission and explain the purpose of the *Uniform Guidelines on Employee Selection Procedures*.

7 Describe disparate treatment and adverse impact and explain the *Uniform Guidelines* related to sexual harassment, national origin, religion, and caregiver (family responsibility) discrimination.

8 Explain affirmative action as required by presidential Executive Orders 11246 and 11375 and describe affirmative action programs.

9 Describe sexual harassment in the global environment.

---

currently specifically prohibit employment discrimination on the basis of a person's gender identity.[4] Houston's mayor signed an executive order protecting LGBT city employees "at every level of municipal government" from discrimination and harassment based on their sexual orientation.[5]

Many companies have policies supporting LGBT employees perhaps due to legal requirements. Other firms have policies to recruit and retain qualified employees no matter their sexual orientation.[6] Over the last decade, corporations have increasingly created a more-welcoming environment for LGBT employees. An estimated 86 percent of Fortune 500 firms now ban discrimination on the basis of sexual orientation, up from 61 percent in 2002, and approximately 50 percent also ban discrimination against transsexuals, compared with 3 percent in 2002.[7] Nonetheless, surveys show that many LGBT employees still view their sexual orientation as a hindrance on the job, and approximately 48 percent of those surveyed remain "closeted" at work.[8]

Diversity and Diversity Management

Twenty-five years ago, diversity was primarily concerned with race and gender.[9] Today, the definition is quite different. **Diversity** refers to *any* perceived difference among people: age, race, religion, functional specialty, profession, sexual orientation, geographic origin, lifestyle, tenure with the organization or position, and any other perceived difference. Further, as companies have become more global, the work group itself has become more diverse.[10] The challenge for managers is to recognize that people with characteristics that are common but are different from those in the mainstream, often think, act, learn, and communicate differently. Diversity is more than equal employment and affirmative action (topics to be discussed later in this chapter); the actual definition is constantly changing and expanding.

Diversity management is ensuring that factors are in place to provide for and encourage the continued development of a diverse workforce by combining these actual and perceived differences among workers to achieve maximum productivity. Because every person, culture, and business situation is unique, there are no simple rules for managing diversity; but diversity experts say that employers need to develop patience, open-mindedness, acceptance, and cultural awareness. Diversity management focuses on the principle that all workers regardless of any factor are entitled to the same privileges and opportunities.[11] According to R. Roosevelt Thomas Jr., former president of the American Institute for Managing Diversity, "diversity and diversity management are about managing and engaging people who are different and similar, all for the benefit of the organization and its goals."[12] In his book *The Future and the Work Ahead of Us*, Harris Sussman writes, "Diversity is about our relatedness, our connectedness, our interactions, where the lines cross."[13]

If organizations want to remain competitive in the marketplace, diversity has to be a part of the strategic goal. New York–based accounting giant KPMG employs more than 23,000 people in the United States. It has a complex diversity program that includes a diversity advisory board, diversity networks, diversity recruiting, accountability mechanisms, scorecards, mandatory training, and a diversity officer. Kathy Hannan, national managing partner for diversity and corporate social responsibility with KPMG, reports directly to the CEO.[14] Programs that highlight a firm's diversity management program can be used to help attract desirable recruits.[15]

You will realize as you read the remainder of this chapter that diversity management and equal employment opportunity are different. Equal employment opportunity focuses on laws, court decisions, and executive orders. Diversity management is about pursuing an inclusive corporate culture in which newcomers feel welcome, and everyone sees the value of his or her job. It involves creating a supportive culture where all employees can be effective. In creating this culture, top management must strongly support workplace diversity as a company goal and include diversity initiatives in their companies' business strategies. It has grown out of the need for organizations to recognize the changing workforce and other social pressures that often result. Achieving diversity is more than being politically correct; it is about fostering a culture that values individuals and their wide array of needs and contributions.

Components of the Diverse Workforce

Components that combine to make up the diverse workforce will be discussed next.

Single Parents and Working Mothers

The number of single-parent households in the United States is growing. Although the divorce rate peaked in the early 1980s, the percentage of marriages ending in divorce remains around 50 percent. Often, children are involved. Of course, there are always widows and widowers who have children, and there are some men and women who choose to raise children outside of wedlock.

Managers need to be sensitive to the needs of working parents. Many women who formerly remained at home to care for children and the household now need and want to work outside the home. In fact, according to Bureau of Labor Statistics data, 77 percent of American women with school-age children work.[16] If this valuable segment of the workforce is to be effectively utilized, organizations must fully recognize the importance of addressing work–family issues. Businesses are seeing that providing child-care services and workplace flexibility may influence workers' choice of employers. Companies that were chosen in the top among *Working Mother* magazine's 100 best companies to work for placed greater emphasis on work–life balance, tele-commuting, and flextime.

Women in Business

Numerous factors have contributed to the growth and development of the U.S. labor force. However, nothing has been more prominent than the rise in the number of women in the labor force. More and more women are entering the labor force in high-paying, professional jobs and women dominate the health care sector, which is one of the fastest-growing categories. In 2010, for the first time ever, women made up the majority of the American workforce. Women-owned businesses now account for nearly one-third of all enterprises in the market today. The American Express Open State of Women-Owned Businesses Report shows the number of women-owned firms from 1997 to 2011 increased by 50 percent.[17]

Professional women are entering the workforce at the same rates as men. However, many opt out of the corporate life. Perhaps this is one of the reasons that women hold only 12 of the 500 CEO positions in Fortune's 2011 list of the largest U.S. companies, down from a peak of 20 in 2006.[18] But this does not mean that they are opting out of business careers. Instead, they are making their own career paths that allow them to combine work and life on their own terms. As a result, organizations are losing talented employees in whom they have made substantial investments. Numerous companies are working diligently keep professional women in the workforce although more work needs to be done.[19]

Mothers Returning to the Workforce

Today, more new mothers are leaving the labor force only to return later. To get them to return, companies are going beyond federal law and giving mothers a year or more for maternity leave. Other businesses are specifically trying to recruit them to return to the labor force.

While some companies are recruiting these women, other employers have programs that help their employees leave and later return. IBM has a program that allows employees to take up to three years off. Typically, working mothers who use the program take a year or more off, and then they use the remainder of their leave to re-enter work on a part-time basis. After the three years are up, they have the option of returning either full- or part-time. IBM surveyed employees who had taken the leave and found that 59 percent would have left the company if the program had not been available. "We didn't want a situation where women had to opt out," says Maria Ferris, manager of work–life and women's initiatives at IBM. "We've invested in them, trained them. We want to retain them."[20]

Dual-Career Families

dual-career family
A situation in which both husband and wife have jobs and family responsibilities.

The increasing number of **dual-career families** where both husband and wife have jobs and family responsibilities presents both challenges and opportunities for organizations. The majority of children growing up today have both parents working outside the home. Households consisting of male breadwinner married to a housewife were a majority in the United States in the 1950s, but in the 21st century the proportion of U.S. households with only a male wage earner is less than 20 percent.[21]

Today, employees have turned down relocations because of spouses' jobs and concerns about their children. Of the top three reasons employees turn down assignments, family or spouse's career is cited almost twice as often as concern with the employee's career or compensation.[22] As a result, firms are developing polices to assist the spouse of an employee who is transferred. Some are offering assistance in finding a position for the spouse of a transferred employee. However, companies may need to learn more about how to handle dual-career couples in a global environment. If companies make the willingness to locate globally a requirement for promotion, many in this group will reject the offer, thereby reducing the size of the labor pool.

Workers of Color

By 2016, according to the Bureau of Labor Statistics, 43 percent of new job applicants will be people of color. Workers of color (including Hispanics, African Americans, and Asians) are at times stereotyped. They may encounter misunderstandings and expectations based on ethnic or cultural differences. Members of ethnic or racial groups are socialized within their particular culture. People's attitudes are influenced by the ancestral and cultural experiences of their childhood. Many are socialized as members of two cultural groups, the dominant culture and their racial or ethnic culture. Ella Bell refers to this dual membership as *biculturalism*. In her study of African American women, Bell identifies the stress of coping with membership in two cultures simultaneously as bicultural stress. She indicates that role conflict (competing roles from two cultures) and role overload (too many expectations to comfortably fulfill) are common characteristics of bicultural stress. Although these issues can be applied to other minority groups, they are particularly intense for women of color, because this group experiences dynamics affecting both minorities and women.[23]

Socialization in one's culture of origin can lead to misunderstandings in the workplace. This is particularly true when the manager relies solely on the cultural norms of the majority group. According to norms within the American culture it is acceptable, even considered positive, to publicly praise an individual for a job well done. However, in cultures that place primary value on group harmony and collective achievement, this method of rewarding an employee may cause emotional discomfort. Some employees feel that, if praised publicly, they will lose face within their group.

Older Workers

During the past decade, the number of individuals ages 45 to 64 has increased 31.5 percent, from 62 million to 81.5 million.[24] In 2011, the first baby boomers turned 65, and approximately 10,000 more will continue to do so every day for the next 20 years. In recent years, many boomers deferred retirement because of a faltering economy. As the economy improves, plans must be in place to handle a rapid departure of boomers from the workforce.[25] Even so, many boomers will resist retirement, some because they feel healthy enough to continue work and others because their retirement income was hit hard by the economy. The U.S. Bureau of Labor Statistics estimates that 13.2 million workers 65 and over will be working in 2022, up from about 7.3 million today.[26]

Despite massive layoffs resulting from the recent recession, many companies try to keep the over 55 worker. This may be due, in part, to legal concerns based on the Age Discrimination in Employment Act, discussed later in this chapter, which protects workers 40 and older against discrimination. However, a large part of this movement is the desire to keep the experienced workers on board. "Seniority matters," says Marcie Pitt-Catsouphes, director of the Sloan Center on Aging & Work at Boston College.[27]

People with Disabilities

According to the U.S. Census Bureau, people with disabilities are the largest minority in the United States with an estimated 19.8 million working-age Americans. Common disabilities include limited hearing or sight, limited mobility, mental or emotional deficiencies, and various nerve disorders. Such disabilities limit the amount or kind of work a person can do or make its achievement unusually difficult. In jobs for which they are qualified, however, disabled workers do as well as unimpaired workers in terms of productivity, attendance, and average tenure. In fact, in certain high-turnover occupations, disabled workers have lower turnover rates. A Department of Labor survey found that a majority of large businesses are hiring people with disabilities and discovering that costs for accommodations differ very little from those for the general employee population. The survey also showed that once an employer hires one person with a disability, it is much more likely to hire other people with disabilities. Walgreens opened its second state-of-the-art distribution center in Windsor, Connecticut, designed specifically to employ people with disabilities. Its goal is to fill at least one-third of the available jobs with individuals with disabilities.[28]

Immigrants

Large numbers of immigrants from Asia and Latin America have settled in many parts of the United States. Some are highly skilled and well educated and others are only minimally qualified and have little education. They have one thing in common: an eagerness to work. They have brought with them attitudes, values, and mores particular to their home country cultures.

After the end of hostilities in Vietnam, Vietnamese immigrants settled along the Mississippi and Texas Gulf Coast. At about the same time, thousands of Thais fleeing the upheaval in Thailand came to the Boston area to work and live. New York's Puerto Rican community has long been an economic and political force there. Cubans who fled Castro's regime congregated in southern Florida, especially Miami. A flood of Mexicans and other Hispanics continues across the southern border of the United States. The Irish, the Poles, the Italians, and others who came here in past decades have long since assimilated into, and indeed became, the culture. Newer immigrants require time to adapt. Meanwhile, they generally take low-paying and menial jobs, live in substandard housing, and form enclaves where they cling to some semblance of the cultures they left.

Wherever they settle, members of these ethnic groups soon begin to become part of the regular workforce in certain occupations and break out of their isolation. They begin to adopt the English language and American customs. They learn new skills and adapt old skills to their new country. Managers can place these individuals in jobs appropriate to their skills, with excellent results for the organization. As corporations employ more foreign nationals in this country, managers must work to understand the different cultures of their employees.

Foreign Workers

The H-1B employment visa brings in approximately 115,000 skilled foreign workers annually, including some 30,000 researchers and academicians not subject to the annual visa cap set by Congress. Of those 115,000, 85,000 are distributed to employers through a lottery system each April held by U.S. Citizenship and Immigration Services, an arm of the U.S. Department of Homeland Security. However, the exact number of H-1B visa holders is difficult to determine. A three-year initial visa can be renewed for another three years, and if a worker is on track for a green card, H-1B status can be renewed annually.

Until the recent recession, demand far outpaced supply, and companies constantly encouraged Congress to raise the cap. Many employers say the H-1B visa program provided the only practical avenue for finding high-tech workers with cutting-edge skills. Others do not agree and there continues to be a debate regarding the hiring of foreign workers. Still, U.S. employers at both ends of the skills spectrum say they have no choice.

Young Persons, Some with Limited Education or Skills

A lower labor force participation rate for young people is being experienced for all those under 24 years of age and not merely young persons with limited education and skills, as was so often the case in the past. The recent recession denied many young workers the opportunity of entering the workforce, so a large number decided to gain additional education to be more competitive.[29]

The downturn was especially harsh for 16- to 19-year-olds when the unemployment rate was 27 percent, the highest recorded since the government began monitoring it in the 1940s.[30] Even so, each year, thousands of young, unskilled workers are hired, especially during peak periods, such as holiday buying seasons. These workers generally have limited education, sometimes even less than a high school diploma. Those who have completed high school often find that their education hardly fits the work they are expected to do. Many of these young adults and teenagers have poor work habits; they tend to be tardy or absent more often than experienced or better-educated workers.

Although the negative attributes of these workers at times seem to outweigh the positive ones, they are a permanent part of the workforce. Certainly, when teenagers are hired, an organization is not hiring maturity or experience; but young people possess many qualities, such as energy, enthusiasm, excitement, and eagerness to prove themselves. There are many jobs they can do well. More jobs can be de-skilled, making it possible for lower-skilled workers to do them. A well-known example of de-skilling is McDonald's use of pictures on its cash register keys. Managers should also look for ways to train unskilled workers and to further their formal education.

Baby Boomers, Gen X, Gen Y, and Gen Z

Never in the history of America have so many different generations with such different views and attitudes been asked to work together. There have been tremendous changes since the boomers first entered the workplace. Each generation has its unique culture that has shaped its nature. Although generalizations about a group are risky, the following discussion may provide additional insight into each group. The discussion begins with baby boomers fully realizing that there remain some members of the *Silent Generation* in the workforce, those born during the Great Depression and World War II.[31]

baby boomers
People born just after World War II
through the mid-1960s.

BABY BOOMERS Baby boomers were born just after World War II through the mid-1960s. Corporate downsizing in the 1980s and 1990s cast aside millions of baby boomers. Companies now want to keep the boomers. Employers seek out boomers because they bring a wealth of skills and experience to the workplace, as well as have low turnover rates and high engagement levels. Companies today place considerable value on their skill, experience, and a strong work ethic, characteristics that many boomers possess.[32] Retirees and laid-off boomers can quickly move into production with little or no training and are recognized as having a great work ethic and a solid attendance record.

Generation X
Label affixed to the 40 million
American workers born between the
mid-1960s and late 1970s.

GENERATION X Generation X is the label affixed to the approximately 41 million American workers born between the mid-1960s and late 1970s. Many organizations have a growing cadre of Generation X employees who possess lots of energy and promise. Ranjan Dutta, a director at PwC Saratoga said, "Gen X workers will be the largest part of the workforce for years to come, and increasingly make up senior leadership ranks in organizations."[33] They are one of the most widely misunderstood phenomena facing management today. Generation Xers differ from previous generations in some significant ways, including their natural affinity for technology and their entrepreneurial spirit. Job instability and the breakdown of traditional employer–employee relationships brought a realization to Generation Xers that it is necessary to approach the world of work differently from past generations.

Generation Xers recognize that their careers cannot be founded securely on a relationship with any one employer. They are very skeptical, particularly when it comes to the business world and job security. They worry about their jobs being outsourced and how they are going to pay for their children's education. They think of themselves more as free agents in a mobile workforce and expect to build career security, not job security, by acquiring marketable skills and expertise. Gen Xers are focused on gaining transferrable skills so that they can be ready if "the rug is pulled out from under them."[34] They are not afraid of changing jobs quite often. The surest way to gain Gen Xers' loyalty is to help them develop career security. When a company helps them expand their knowledge and skills, it is preparing them for the job market. Gen Xers will often want to stay on board to learn those very skills.

Generation Y
Comprises people born between the
late 1970s and mid-1990s.

GENERATION Y Generation Y comprises people born between the late 1970s and mid-1990s. Estimates are that by 2016 Gen Yers (or Millennials) will account for nearly half of all employees worldwide.[35] They have never wound a watch, dialed a rotary phone, or plunked the keys of a manual typewriter. But, without a thought, they download music from the Internet and insert pictures of events on Facebook. They cannot imagine how the world ever got along without computers. These individuals are the leading edge of a generation that promises to be the richest, smartest, and savviest ever. They are well educated, well versed in technology, and bursting with confidence.[36] Generation Yers—often referred to as the echo boomers, Millennials, and Nexters—are the coddled, confident offspring of post–World War II baby boomers. Generation Y individuals are a most privileged generation, who came of age during the hottest domestic economy in memory.

Gen Yers tend to have a strong sense of morality and civic-mindedness. They are more ethnically diverse than previous generations, and nearly one-third of them have been raised in single-parent households. They want a workplace that is both fun and rewarding. They want jobs where there is a balance between work and family. They want jobs that conform to their interests and do not accept the way things have been done in the past. Generation Y employees want flexible working hours, which is a benefit that they are very enthusiastic about. They also tend to have more of a sense of entitlement not found in other generation of workers. However, Gen Yers' childhoods have been short-lived, as they have been exposed to some of the worst things in life: schoolyard shootings, drug use, terrorism, sex scandals, and war.

Generation Z or Digital Natives
Internet-assimilated children born
between 1995 and 2009.

GENERATION Z OR DIGITAL NATIVES After Generation Y came **Generation Z or Digital Natives**, the Internet-assimilated children born between 1995 and 2009. Gen Zers are more worldly, high-tech, and confident in their ability to multitask; they tend to have short attention spans and desire speed over accuracy; and they enjoy media that provides live social interaction.[37] They tend to use social networks to avoid the complications of dealing with face-to-face situations. In a recent survey, almost 25 percent of respondents found their relationship with their significant other was over by first seeing it on Facebook.[38] Digital Natives do not trust politicians, social institutions, the media, or corporations. Rather, they rely largely on themselves and their peers to decide what to think, what to do, and what to buy. The main thrust of the book *2018: Digital Natives Grow Up and Rule The World* was that "Digital natives are protagonists for massive technology adoption and a consequent adaption of human behavior."[39] Two Gen Zer children sitting in the back seat of the family car may now be texting each other instead of speaking with each other.

GENERATION ALPHA Some have suggested that the next generation, born from 2010, will be called Generation Alpha. Although Generation Z is often referred to as the 21st-century generation, Generation Alpha will be the first true millennial generation, as they will be the first born into the 21st century.

Multigenerational Diversity

Four generations are now participating in the workforce and each has different defining characteristics and nicknames. The concept of generational differences as a legitimate workplace diversity issue has gained increasing recognition. Baby boomers are remaining on the job longer because of the economy and often find themselves working with Generation Y employees. Traditionally, discussions of workplace diversity tended to focus on topics of race, ethnicity, gender, sexual orientation, and disability. Shirley A. Davis, SHRM's director of diversity and inclusion initiatives, said, "In all parts of the world, there is another category of diversity that cannot be overlooked: multigenerational diversity."[40] Today, there are greater numbers of workers from each segment that bring both new opportunities and challenges. If organizations want to thrive in this competitive environment of global talent management, they need employees and managers who are aware of and skilled in dealing with the different generations that make up the workforce.

Equal Employment Opportunity: An Overview

As can be seen from the previous discussion, the workforce of today has become truly diverse. But, this was not the case in the early 1960s; in fact, little of the workforce of those days remotely resembled that of today. Then, few mainstream opportunities were available to women, minorities, and those with disabilities. If this were so today, our economy would certainly grind to a halt. But diversity did not just happen. Legislation (federal, state, and local), Supreme Court decisions, and executive orders have encouraged both public and private organizations to tap the abilities of a workforce that was largely underused before the mid-1960s. The concept of equal employment opportunity has undergone much modification and fine-tuning since the passage of the Equal Pay Act of 1963, the Civil Rights Act of 1964, and the Age Discrimination in Employment Act of 1967.

Numerous amendments to these acts have been passed, as well as other acts in response to oversights in the initial legislation. Major Supreme Court decisions interpreting the provisions of the acts have also been handed down. A presidential executive order was signed into law that provided for affirmative action. Five decades have passed since the introduction of the first legislation, and equal employment opportunity has become an integral part of the workplace.

Although equal employment opportunity has come a long way since the early 1960s, continuing efforts are required because some problems still exist. Although perfection is elusive, the majority of businesses today do attempt to make employment decisions based on who is the best qualified, as opposed to whether an individual is of a certain gender, race, religion, color, national origin, or age or is disabled. Throughout the remainder of this chapter, *hiring standards to avoid* will be identified based on some of the laws, executive orders, and Supreme Court decisions that have had a major impact in creating this diverse workforce.

OBJECTIVE **3.3**

Identify the major laws affecting equal employment opportunity.

Laws Affecting Equal Employment Opportunity

Numerous national laws have been passed that have had an impact on equal employment opportunity. The passage of these laws reflects society's attitude toward the changes that should be made to give everyone an equal opportunity for employment. The most significant of these laws will be described in the following sections.

Civil Rights Act of 1866

The oldest federal legislation affecting staffing is the Civil Rights Act of 1866, which is based on the Thirteenth Amendment to the U.S. Constitution. Specifically, this act provides that all citizens have the same right "as enjoyed by white citizens . . . to inherit, purchase . . . hold, and convey . . . property, [and that] all persons . . . shall have the same right to make and enforce contracts . . . as enjoyed by white citizens." As interpreted by the courts, employment, as well as membership in a union, is a contractual arrangement. Blacks and Hispanics are covered by this act if they are discriminated against on the basis of race. Until 1968, it was assumed that the act was applicable only when action by a state or state agency, and not by private parties, was involved. That year the Supreme Court overruled that assumption and broadened the interpretation of the act to cover all contractual arrangements. There is no statute of limitations to the act, as evidenced by the fact that it continues to be used today. For example, in 2008, the Supreme Court ruled 7–2 in the case of *CBOCS West Inc. v Humphries,* that there is an implied right to sue on a retaliation basis under the Civil Rights Act of 1866, even though that law does not explicitly include a cause of action for retaliation. A former African American Cracker Barrel assistant manager claimed he was fired for complaining to management about race discrimination.[41]

Equal Pay Act of 1963, Amended in 1972

Passed as an amendment to the Fair Labor Standards Act, the Equal Pay Act of 1963 (EPA) prohibits an employer from paying an employee of one gender less money than an employee of the opposite gender, if both employees do work that is substantially the same. The EPA was passed largely to overcome the outdated belief that a man should be paid more than a woman because he was the primary breadwinner. The EPA covers work within the same physical place of business. For example, an employer could pay a female more in San Francisco than a male working in the same position in Slippery Rock, Pennsylvania, even if the jobs were substantially the same, because of the cost-of-living difference. A key point to remember is that the pay difference must be substantial and that small pay differences might be acceptable. Once a prima facie case of gender discrimination under the EPA has been made, then liability may be avoided by showing one of the following affirmative defenses that allow unequal pay for equal work:

- Seniority system
- Merit system
- System that measures earnings by quantity or quality of production
- Any other factor other than sex

For the first nine years of the EPA, the requirement of equal pay for equal work did not extend to persons employed in an executive, administrative, or professional capacity, or as an outside salesperson. In 1972, Congress enacted the Educational Amendment of 1972, which now covers those individuals. One thing is certain, the Equal Pay Act has teeth and they will get sharper because the U.S. Department of Labor is aggressively enforcing the EPA and seeking harsher penalties against companies that violate it.

Lilly Ledbetter Fair Pay Act of 2009

Lilly Ledbetter worked as a supervisor for Goodyear Tire from 1979 until 1998. Just before retirement, she received information that compared her salary with salaries of male coworkers. She was earning $3,727 monthly compared with 15 male coworkers who earned between $4,286 and $5,236. She sued, claiming pay discrimination under Title VII of the Civil Rights Act of 1964 and the Equal Pay Act of 1963.[42] In the 2007 Supreme Court case of *Ledbetter v Goodyear Tire & Rubber Co., Inc.,* the Court said that discrimination charges must be filed within 180 days after the allegedly discriminatory pay decision. Lilly Ledbetter had worked for Goodyear for many years but she did not realize until she was close to retirement that she was being discriminated against because of pay. Since she did not file a discrimination charge within 180 day of her employment, the Supreme Court ruled against her. To reverse the Ledbetter decision, the Lilly Ledbetter Fair Pay Act was passed by Congress and signed into law in 2009. The law creates a rolling or open time frame for filing wage discrimination claims. Each paycheck that unfairly pays a worker less than it should is a discriminatory act. The act gives the worker a fresh 180-day period (300 days in some states) to file a charge of discrimination with the EEOC. As a result of the law, employers should keep records longer for performance appraisals that affect pay and job classification decisions.

Comparable Worth

comparable worth
Determination of the values of dissimilar jobs (such as company nurse and welder) by comparing them under some form of job evaluation, and the assignment of pay rates according to their evaluated worth.

Since the passage of the Equal Pay Act, there has been much discussion to expand its coverage to include the concept of comparable worth, or pay equity. **Comparable worth** requires determination of the values of dissimilar jobs (such as company nurse and welder) by comparing them under some form of job evaluation, and the assignment of pay rates according to their evaluated worth. Although the Equal Pay Act requires equal pay for equal work, comparable worth advocates prefer a broader interpretation of requiring equal pay for comparable worth, even if market rates vary and job duties are considerably different. Although the Supreme Court has ruled the law does not require comparable worth, a number of state and local governments, along with some jurisdictions in Canada, have passed legislation mandating this version of pay fairness.

Title VII of the Civil Rights Act of 1964, Amended in 1972

The statute that has had the greatest impact on equal employment opportunity is Title VII of the Civil Rights Act of 1964, as amended by the Equal Employment Act of 1972. Under Title VII, it is illegal for an employer to discriminate in hiring, firing, promoting, compensating, or in terms, conditions, or privileges of employment on the basis of race, color, sex, religion, or national origin. The act also forbids retaliation against an employee who has participated in an investigation, proceeding, or hearing.

Title VII covers employers engaged in or affecting interstate commerce who have 15 or more employees for each working day in each of 20 calendar weeks in the current or preceding calendar year. Also included in the definition of employers are state and local governments, schools, colleges, unions, and private employment agencies with 15 or more employees. All private employers who are subject to the Civil Rights Act of 1964 as amended with 100 employees or more must annually submit an EEO-1 (see Figure 3-1).

Three notable exceptions to discrimination as covered by Title VII are bona fide occupational qualifications (BFOQs), seniority and merit systems, and testing and educational requirements. According to the act it is not an unlawful employment practice for an employer to hire and employ employees on the basis of his religion, sex, or national origin in those certain instances where religion, sex, or national origin is a bona fide occupational qualification reasonably necessary to the normal operation of the particular business or enterprise. For example, religious institutions, such as churches or synagogues, may legally refuse to hire teachers whose religious conviction is different from that of the hiring institution. Likewise, a maximum-security correctional institution housing only male inmates may decline to hire females as security guards. The concept of bona fide occupational qualification was designed to be narrowly, not broadly, interpreted and has been so interpreted by the courts in a number of cases. For instance, historically women sales representative were barred from working in a male clothing store because it was thought that men would not purchase from them. This stereotype has certainly been overcome as men regularly see female salespersons working in men's clothing stores. The burden of proving the necessity for a BFOQ rests entirely on the employer.

The second exception to discrimination under Title VII is a bona fide seniority system such as the type normally contained in a union contract. Differences in employment conditions among workers are permitted, provided that such differences are not the result of an intention to discriminate because of race, color, religion, sex, or national origin. Even if a bona fide seniority system has an adverse impact on those individuals protected by Title VII (i.e., it affects a class or group), the system can be invalidated only by evidence that the actual motives of the parties to the agreement were to discriminate.

Finally, in the matter of testing and educational requirements, Title VII states that it is not "an unlawful employment practice for an employer to give, and to act upon, the results of any professionally developed ability test provided that such test, its administration, or action upon the results is not designed, intended or used to discriminate because of race, color, religion, sex, or national origin." Employment testing and educational requirements must be job related, and when adverse impact is shown, the burden of proof is on the employer to establish that a demonstrable relationship exists between actual job performance and the test or educational requirement.

Persons not covered by Title VII include aliens not authorized to work in the United States and members of the Communist party. Homosexuals are also not protected under Title VII. The courts have consistently ruled that where the term *sex* is used in any federal statute that term

FIGURE 3-1

Equal Employment Opportunity Employer Information Report

Joint Reporting Committee

- Equal Employment Opportunity Commission
- Office of Federal Contract Compliance Programs (Labor)

EQUAL EMPLOYMENT OPPORTUNITY

EMPLOYER INFORMATION REPORT EEO—1

Standard Form 100
(Rev. 4–92)
O.M.B. No. 3048–0007
EXPIRES 12/31/93
100-213

Section A—TYPE OF REPORT
Refer to instructions for number and types of reports to be filed.

1. Indicate by marking in the appropriate box the type of reporting unit for which this copy of the form is submitted (MARK ONLY ONE BOX).

   (1) ☐ Single-establishment Employer Report

   Multi-establishment Employer:
   (2) ☐ Consolidated Report (Required)
   (3) ☐ Headquarters Unit Report (Required)
   (4) ☐ Individual Establishment Report (submit one for each establishment with 50 or more employees)
   (5) ☐ Special Report

2. Total number of reports being filed by this Company (Answer on Consolidated Report only) _____

Section B—COMPANY IDENTIFICATION (To be answered by all employers)

OFFICE USE ONLY

1. Parent Company
   a. Name of parent company (owns or controls establishment in item 2) omit if same as label

   a.

   Address (Number and street)

   b.

   City or town | State | ZIP code

   c.

2. Establishment for which this report is filed. (Omit if same as label)
   a. Name of establishment

   d.

   Address (Number and street) | City or town | County | State | ZIP code

   e.

   b. Employer identification No. (IRS 9-DIGIT TAX NUMBER)

   f.

   Was an EEO–1 report filed for this establishment last year? ☐ Yes ☐ No

Section C—EMPLOYERS WHO ARE REQUIRED TO FILE (To be answered by all employers)

☐ Yes ☐ No   1. Does the entire company have at least 100 employees in the payroll period for which you are reporting?

☐ Yes ☐ No   2. Is your company affiliated through common ownership and/or centralized management with other entitles in an enterprise with a total employment of 100 or more?

☐ Yes ☐ No   3. Does the company or any of its establishments (1) have 50 or more employees AND (b) is not exempt as provided by 41 CFR 60–1.5, AND either (1) is a prime government contractor or first-tier subcontractor, and has a contract, subcontract, or purchase order amounting to $50,000 or more, or (2) serves as a depository for Government funds in any amount or is a financial institution which is an issuing and paying agent for U.S. Savings Bonds and Savings Notes?

   If the response to question C–3 is yes, please enter your Dun and Bradstreet Identification number (if you have one):

NOTE: If the answer is yes to questions 1, 2, or 3, complete the entire form, otherwise skip to Section G.

NSN 7540–00–180–6384

refers to biological gender and not to sexual preference. However, as suggested by the HRM in Action at the beginning of the chapter, changes may be on the way in this area.

The Civil Rights Act of 1964 also created the Equal Employment Opportunity Commission (EEOC) and assigned enforcement of Title VII to this agency. Consisting of five members appointed by the president, the EEOC is empowered to investigate, conciliate, and litigate charges of discrimination arising under provisions of Title VII. In addition, the commission has the responsibility of issuing procedural regulations and interpretations of Title VII and the other statutes it enforces. The most significant regulation issued by EEOC is the *Uniform Guidelines on Employee Selection Procedures*.

The act continues to be important. Chicago-based Ceisel Masonry settled a race and national-origin discrimination suit with the EEOC for $500,000. Recently, Talbert Builders agreed to settle a race discrimination suit with the EEOC for $80,000. The suit claimed that coworkers and supervisors had created a racially hostile work environment, and the EEOC also required the firm's supervisors and employees to undergo training on race-based harassment.

Section D—EMPLOYMENT DATA   SF 100—Page 2

Employment at this establishment—Report all permanent full- and part-time employees including apprentices and on-the-job trainees unless specifically excluded as set forth in the instructions. Enter the appropriate figures on all lines and in all columns. Blank spaces will be considered as zeros.

Job Categories	Number of Employees (Report employees in only one category)														
	Race/Ethnicity														Total Col A - N
	Hispanic or Latino		Not-Hispanic or Latino												
			Male						Female						
	Male	Female	White	Black or African American	Native Hawaiian or Other Pacific Islander	Asian	American Indian or Alaska Native	Two or more races	White	Black or African American	Native Hawaiian or Other Pacific Islander	Asian	American Indian or Alaska Native	Two or more races	
	A	B	C	D	E	F	G	H	I	J	K	L	M	N	O
Executive/Senior Level Officials and Managers 1.1															
First/Mid-Level Officials and Managers 1.2															
Professionals 2															
Technicians 3															
Sales Workers 4															
Administrative Support Workers 5															
Craft Workers 6															
Operatives 7															
Laborers and Helpers 8															
Service Workers 9															
TOTAL 10															
PREVIOUS YEAR TOTAL 11															

1. Date(s) of payroll period used: _____ (Omit on the Consolidated Report.)

Approval

O.M.B. No. 3046-0007
Revised 01/2006
Expires 1/2009

FIGURE 3-1
(Continued)

Pregnancy Discrimination Act of 1978

Passed as an amendment to Title VII of the Civil Rights Act, the Pregnancy Discrimination Act prohibits discrimination in employment based on pregnancy, childbirth, or related medical conditions. Questions regarding a woman's family and childbearing plans should not be asked. Similarly, questions relating to family plans, birth control techniques, and the like may be viewed as discriminatory because they are not asked of men. The basic principle of the act is that women affected by pregnancy and related conditions must be treated the same as other applicants and employees on the basis of their ability or inability to work. A woman is therefore protected against such practices as being fired or refused a job or promotion merely because she is pregnant or has had an abortion. She usually cannot be forced to take a leave of absence as long as she can work. If other employees on disability leave are entitled to return to their jobs when they are able to work again, so too are women who have been unable to work because of pregnancy. Also, limiting job advancement opportunities while a woman is pregnant may be a violation of the act.

The same principle applies in the benefits area, including disability benefits, sick leave, and health insurance. A woman unable to work for pregnancy-related reasons is entitled to disability benefits or sick leave on the same basis as employees unable to work for other medical reasons. Also, any health insurance provided must cover expenses for pregnancy-related conditions on the same basis as expenses for other medical conditions. However, health insurance for expenses arising from an abortion is not required except where the life of the mother would be endangered if the fetus were carried to term or when medical complications have arisen from an abortion.

In a class action suit originally filed in 1978, but not settled until 1991, American Telephone & Telegraph Company (AT&T) agreed to settle a pregnancy discrimination suit with the EEOC for $66 million. This suit was the largest cash recovery in the agency's history and involved more than 13,000 then-present and former female AT&T workers. The suit charged that Western Electric required pregnant workers to leave their jobs at the end of their sixth month of pregnancy, denied them seniority credit, and refused to guarantee them a job when they returned.

Pregnancy discrimination cases continue and pregnancy discrimination settlements are at an all-time high. The Kinston-based Britthaven nursing home and assisted-living chain settled a pregnancy discrimination claim with the EEOC for $300,000. The agreement settles a lawsuit brought by pregnant employees who claimed they were treated differently from other employees because the company required them to obtain full medical clearance as soon as it learned they were pregnant. As a result, even though the women were still capable of performing their jobs, they were forced to take leave or be terminated.[43] Recently Crothall Healthcare paid more than $88,000 to settle a pregnancy discrimination claim. The company fired a housekeeper at the Arkansas facility after it discovered she was pregnant.

Civil Rights Act of 1991

During 1988–1989, the Supreme Court rendered six employment discrimination decisions of such magnitude that a congressional response was required to overturn these decisions. The result was passage of the Civil Rights Act of 1991. The act amended five statutes: (1) the Civil Rights Act of 1866; (2) Title VII of the Civil Rights Act of 1964, as Amended; (3) the Age Discrimination in Employment Act of 1967, as Amended; (4) the Rehabilitation Act of 1973; and (5) the Americans with Disabilities Act of 1990.

The Civil Rights Act of 1991 had the following purposes:

- To provide appropriate remedies for intentional discrimination and unlawful harassment in the workplace.
- To codify the concepts of *business necessity* and *job-relatedness* pronounced by the Supreme Court in *Griggs v Duke Power Company*.
- To confirm statutory authority and provide statutory guidelines for the adjudication of disparate impacts under Title VII of the Civil Rights Act of 1964. Disparate impact occurs when certain actions in the employment process work to the disadvantage of members of protected groups. Disparate impact will be discussed below under the concept of *Adverse Impact*.
- To respond to decisions of the Supreme Court by expanding the scope of relevant civil rights statutes in order to provide adequate protection to victims of discrimination.

Under this act, a complaining party may recover punitive damages if the complaining party demonstrates that the company engaged in a discriminatory practice with malice or with reckless indifference to the law. However, the following limits, based on the number of people employed by the company, were placed on the amount of the award:

- Between 15 and 100 employees—$50,000
- Between 101 and 200 employees—$100,000
- Between 201 and 500 employees—$200,000
- More than 500 employees—$300,000

In each case, aggrieved employees must be with the firm for 20 or more calendar weeks in the current or preceding calendar year.

With regard to burden of proof, a complaining party must show that a particular employment practice causes a disparate impact on the basis of race, color, religion, sex, or national origin. It must also be shown that the company is unable to demonstrate that the challenged practice is job related for the position in question and consistent with business necessity. The act also extends the coverage of the Civil Rights Act of 1964 to extraterritorial employment. However, the act does not apply to U.S. companies operating in other countries if compliance "would cause such employer, or a corporation controlled by such employer, to violate the laws of the country in which such workplace is located."[44] The act also extends the nondiscrimination principles to Congress and other government agencies, such as the General Accounting Office and the Government Printing Office.

Also included in the Civil Rights Act of 1991 is the Glass Ceiling Act. The **glass ceiling** is the invisible barrier in organizations that impedes women and minorities from career advancement.

glass ceiling
Invisible barrier in organizations that impedes women and minorities from career advancement.

This act established a Glass Ceiling Commission to study the manner in which businesses fill management and decision-making positions, the developmental and skill-enhancing practices used to foster the necessary qualifications for advancement to such positions, and the compensation programs and reward structures currently used in the workplace. It was also to study the limited progress made by minorities and women. It established an annual award for excellence in promoting a more diverse skilled workforce at the management and decision-making levels in business. Yet, work remains to be done. According to a key finding in Calvert Investments' "Examining the Cracks in the Ceiling: A Survey of Corporate Diversity Practices of the S&P 100," women were underrepresented on corporate boards and in C-level positions. Of the companies surveyed, less than 10 percent of women were found to be highly paid officials, and less than 20 percent were listed as board members.[45]

Age Discrimination in Employment Act of 1967, Amended in 1978 and 1986

As originally enacted, the Age Discrimination in Employment Act (ADEA) prohibited employers from discriminating against individuals who were 40 to 65 years old. The 1978 amendment provided protection for individuals who were at least 40, but less than 70 years old. In a 1986 amendment, employer discrimination against anyone age 40 or older is illegal. Questions asked about an applicant's age or date of birth may be ill-advised. Even mentioning age as a factor in the selection process to a coworker may become evidence of discrimination. In the recent court decision *EEOC v City of Greensboro*, the city lost the case because the manager told a coworker that he did not want to hire the older, more qualified applicant because he might retire shortly, forcing the whole hiring process to start all over again.[46] Also, assuming that only younger applicants are more eager and ready to learn new technology may bring an age discrimination suit because people of any age may possess these qualities. However, a firm may ask for age information to comply with the child labor law. For example, the question could be asked, "Are you under the age of 18?" Nonetheless, questions about the ages of children, if any, could be potentially discriminatory because a close approximation of the applicant's age often is obtained through knowledge of the ages of the applicant's children. The EEOC is responsible for administering this act. The ADEA pertains to employers who have 20 or more employees for 20 or more calendar weeks (either in the current or preceding calendar year); unions with 25 or more members; employment agencies; and federal, state, and local government subunits.

Enforcement begins when a charge is filed, but the EEOC can review compliance even if no charge is filed. The Age Discrimination in Employment Act differs from Title VII of the Civil Rights Act because it provides for a trial by jury and carries possible criminal penalty for violation of the act. The trial-by-jury provision is important because juries are thought to have great sympathy for older people who may have been discriminated against. The criminal penalty provision means that a person may receive more than lost wages if discrimination is proved. The 1978 amendment also makes class action suits possible.

Automotive rubber parts manufacturer Freudenberg-NOK G.P. settled a discrimination suit filed on behalf of a man claiming he was denied a job with the company because of his age. The settlement brought by the EEOC provides $80,000 to Timothy Poh, an applicant for the controller position at Freudenberg-NOK's Bristol, New Hampshire, site. Poh interviewed for the job and was told that although he was well-qualified, the company was looking for a younger person with less experience. The firm eventually offered the position to two younger applicants and hired a younger, less-qualified person. Recently Metallic Products Corporation agreed to settle an EEOC suit because of an unlawful mandatory policy that required employees to retire when they reached age 70. When Jeronimo Vidals refused to retire at age 70, he was fired. He received $60,000 under the settlement terms, the policy had to be rescinded, and all former employees who may have been affected had to be notified of the decision.

Age Can Actually Be a Bona Fide Occupational Qualification

Age can actually be a bona fide occupational qualification when it is reasonably necessary to the essence of the business, and the employer has a rational or factual basis for believing that all, or substantially all, people within an age class would not be able to perform satisfactorily. Courts have continued to rule that the Federal Aviation Administration adequately explained its

HR Web Wisdom

*Office of Contract
Compliance Programs*
http://www.dol.gov/ofccp/

Home page for the OFCCP, the
agency responsible for ensuring
that employers doing business
with the federal government comply with the laws and regulations
requiring nondiscrimination and
affirmative action.

long-standing rule that it can force commercial pilots to retire at age 60. The age 60 rule was first imposed in 1959 and was long controversial. However, in 2007, the retirement age for commercial pilots was raised to 65.

This ruling supported the 1974 Seventh Circuit Court decision that Greyhound did not violate the ADEA when it refused to hire persons 35 years of age or older as intercity bus drivers. Again, the likelihood of risk or harm to its passengers was involved. Greyhound presented evidence concerning degenerative physical and sensory changes that humans undergo at about age 35 that have a detrimental effect on driving skills, and that the changes are not detectable by physical tests. These skills would gradually deteriorate with increased age.

Rehabilitation Act of 1973

The Rehabilitation Act prohibits discrimination against disabled workers who are employed by certain government contractors and subcontractors and organizations that receive federal grants in excess of $2,500. Individuals are considered disabled if they have a physical or mental impairment that substantially limits one or more major life activities or if they have a record of such impairment. Protected under the act are diseases and conditions such as epilepsy, cancer, cardiovascular disorders, AIDS, blindness, deafness, mental retardation, emotional disorders, and dyslexia.

There are two primary levels of the act. All federal contractors or subcontractors exceeding the $2,500 base are required to post notices that they agree to take affirmative action to recruit, employ, and promote qualified disabled individuals. If the contract or subcontract exceeds $50,000, or if the contractor has 50 or more employees, the employer must prepare a written affirmative action plan for review by the Office of Federal Contract Compliance Programs (OFCCP), which administers the act. In it, the contractor must specify that reasonable steps are being taken to hire and promote disabled persons.

In an interpretation of Section 8 of the Rehabilitation Act, federal technology buyers are forced to think about people who are blind, deaf, paralyzed, or have other disabilities before they buy software, computers, printers, copiers, fax machines, kiosks, telecommunications devices, or video and multimedia products. Federal employees with disabilities must have access to and use of information and data that is comparable to the access and use by federal employees who are not individuals with disabilities, unless an undue burden would be imposed on the agency.

Americans with Disabilities Act of 1990

The Americans with Disabilities Act (ADA) prohibits discrimination against qualified individuals with disabilities. The ADA prohibits discrimination in all employment practices, including job application procedures, hiring, firing, advancement, compensation, training, and other terms, conditions, and privileges of employment. It applies to recruitment, advertising, tenure, layoffs, leaves, benefits, and all other employment-related activities. The employment provisions apply to private employers, state and local governments, employment agencies, and labor unions. Persons discriminated against because they have a known association or relationship with a disabled individual are also protected. Employers with 15 or more employees are covered. The ADA defines an individual with a disability as a person who has, or is regarded as having, a physical or mental impairment that *substantially limits* one or more major life activities, and has a record of such an impairment, or is regarded as having such an impairment. The ADA prohibits discrimination in employment due to one's disability and requires that employers provide an employee or job applicant with a reasonable accommodation unless doing so would cause significant difficulty or expense for the employer. In 2011, UPS Supply Chain Solutions agreed to pay $95,000 to settle a disability discrimination lawsuit filed by the EEOC. The EEOC had charged that UPS unlawfully denied a reasonable accommodation to a deaf employee.

The EEOC guidelines on pre-employment inquiries and tests regarding disabilities prohibit inquiries and medical examinations intended to gain information about applicants' disabilities before a conditional job offer. In the Supreme Court case of *Leonel v American Airlines,* the Court ruled that the airline violated the ADA's required sequence for prehire medical inquiries/examinations by making medical inquiries and requiring individuals to take medical examinations before completing and making its hiring decisions.

The guiding principle is to ask only about potential employees' ability to do the job, and not about their disabilities. Lawful inquiries include those regarding performance of specific functions or possession of training appropriate to the job, whereas illegal inquiries include those that ask about previous medical conditions or extent of prior drug use. The ADA does not protect people currently using illegal drugs. It does protect those in rehabilitation programs who are not currently using illegal drugs, those who have been rehabilitated, and those erroneously labeled as drug users. Coverage under the ADA continues to evolve as evidenced with the passing of the American with Disabilities Act Amendments Act of 2008.

Americans with Disabilities Act Amendments Act of 2008

The Americans with Disabilities Act Amendments Act (ADAAA) brings millions more people within the ADA's protection. The ADAAA expands the definition of "disability," so that many more applicants and employees are eligible for reasonable accommodations.[47] The ADAAA broadened the ADA's definition of disability by expanding the term "major life activities," doing away with the "substantially limited" requirement (previously mentioned) for those regarded as having a disability, and overturning two U.S. Supreme Court decisions that interpreted the ADA's definition of disability narrowly.

According to the EEOC, one of the purposes of the ADAAA is the reinstatement of a broad scope of protection by expanding the definition of the term "disability." Congress found that persons with many types of impairments—including epilepsy, diabetes, multiple sclerosis, major depression, and bipolar disorder—had been unable to bring ADA claims because they were found not to meet the ADA's definition of disability. The ADA still covers only qualified individuals with disabilities and provides that to be disabled, an individual must have "a physical or mental impairment that substantially limits one or more major life activities," or must have a record of such an impairment, or must be regarded as having such an impairment. The ADAAA also defines and vastly expands the term "major life activities" as including caring for oneself, performing manual tasks, seeing, hearing, eating, sleeping, walking, standing, lifting, bending, speaking, breathing, learning, reading, concentrating, thinking, communicating, and working. The amendment states that major life activities include the operation of a major bodily function, such as functions of the immune system, normal cell growth, digestive, bowel, bladder, neurological, brain, respiratory, circulatory, endocrine, and reproductive functions. The only exception to this rule is that if a person's vision can be corrected with eyeglasses or contact lenses, he or she will not be considered disabled.

Immigration Reform and Control Act of 1986

The desire to stem illegal immigration prompted Congress to enact the Immigration Reform and Control Act (IRCA) of 1986. The IRCA granted amnesty to approximately 1.7 million long-term unauthorized workers in an effort to bring them out of the shadows and improve their labor market opportunities. It also established criminal and civil sanctions against employers who knowingly hire unauthorized aliens. The IRCA also makes unlawful the hiring of anyone unless the person's employment authorization and identity are verified. When dealing with the national origin provision of the Civil Rights Act, IRCA reduces the threshold coverage from 15 employees to 4.

The IRCA has toughened criminal sanctions for employers who hire illegal aliens, denied illegal aliens federally funded welfare benefits, and legitimized some aliens through an amnesty program. To comply with the IRCA, candidates for employment are not required to be U.S. citizens, but they must prove they are eligible to work in the United States. Employers must require all new employees to complete and sign a verification form, Form I-9, to certify their eligibility for employment.

The U.S. Immigration & Customs Enforcement Agency is aggressively pursuing violators of the IRCA, and employers are at the center of the crackdowns. The agency is targeting employers by pursuing effective worksite enforcement, which includes civil and criminal enforcement. Of recent, investigators have concentrated on building cases against businesses suspected of hiring undocumented immigrants before they raid workplaces and round up any illegal workers. The agency recently announced that a settlement for more than $1.04 million had been reached with Abercrombie & Fitch for violations. Also, the president of a California furniture manufacturer was charged with criminal violations stemming from an investigation into allegations that the company hired unauthorized workers.[48]

Illegal Immigration Reform and Immigrant Responsibility Act of 1996

The Illegal Immigration Reform and Immigrant Responsibility Act was passed partly in response to the fact that at least one of the terrorists who blew up the World Trade Center in 1993, killing six people and wounding 1,000, had legally entered the United States on a student visa. The law places severe limitations on persons who come to the United States and remain in the country longer than permitted by their visas and/or persons who violate their nonimmigrant status. Anyone unlawfully present in the United States for 180 days, but less than one year, is subject to a three-year ban for admission to the United States. Anyone unlawfully present in the United States for one year or more is subject to a 10-year ban from admission to the United States. There are certain exceptions, however, such as extreme hardship. However, since 9/11, the law has been enforced more rigorously.

Uniformed Services Employment and Reemployment Rights Act of 1994

The Uniformed Services Employment and Reemployment Rights Act (USERRA) provides protection to Reserve and National Guard members. Under the USERRA, those workers are entitled to return to their civilian employment after completing their military service. The USERRA is intended to eliminate or minimize employment disadvantages to civilian careers that can result from service in the uniformed services. The USERRA was enacted to protect the reemployment benefits and nondiscrimination rights of individuals who voluntarily or involuntarily take a leave of absence from employment to serve in the military. As a general rule, a returning employee is entitled to reemployment in the same job or position that he or she would have attained with reasonable certainty if not for the absence to serve in the military. Known as the *escalator principle*, this requirement is designed to ensure that a returning employee is not penalized (by losing a pay raise, promotion, etc.) for the time spent on active duty, not exceeding five years.[49] There are no special rights under USERRA for temporary workers or the new hires taking over the Reserve or National Guide members' jobs.

The Veterans Opportunity to Work (VOW) Act passed in 2011 amended the Uniformed Services Employment and Reemployment Rights Act. It is now easier for employees to sue employers based on hostile work environment claims related to an employee's military status. Estimates are that USERRA cases will increase based on the new law and the projected budget reduction at the Department of Defense.[50]

Vietnam Era Veterans' Readjustment Assistance Act of 1974, as Amended

As originally passed, the Vietnam Era Veterans' Readjustment Assistance Act (VEVRAA) only covered honorably discharged persons who served more than 18 days on active duty between August 5, 1964, and May 7, 1975. Now the definition of "protected" or "covered" veteran has been expanded to include those who have served in a campaign or expedition for which a campaign badge was issued.[51] This includes campaigns such as Desert Storm and the current engagements in the Middle East. Under VEVRAA, federal contractors and subcontractors are required to take affirmative action in hiring covered veterans. VEVRAA prohibits federal contractors from discriminating against specified categories of veterans and requires them to take affirmative action to recruit, employ, and promote protected veterans. Contractors with 50 or more employees (and $100,000 in federal contracts made on or after December 1, 2003) must maintain a written affirmative action plan.[52]

State and Local Laws

Numerous state and local laws also affect equal employment opportunity. A number of states and some cities have passed fair employment practice laws prohibiting discrimination on the basis of race, color, religion, sex, or national origin. Even prior to federal legislation, several states had antidiscrimination legislation relating to age and gender. For instance, New York protected individuals between the ages of 18 and 65 prior to the passing of the ADEA, and California had no upper limit on protected age. San Francisco has voted to ban weight discrimination. The Board of Supervisors added body size to city laws that already bar discrimination based on race, color, religion, age, ancestry, sex, sexual orientation, disability, place of birth, or gender identity. The State of California has a law that requires sexual harassment prevention training. Washington explicitly prohibits bias against transgender people. When EEOC regulations conflict with state or local civil rights regulations, the legislation more favorable

TRENDS & INNOVATIONS

Employee Retaliation

Retaliation against an employee who has participated in an investigation, proceeding, or hearing was prohibited in all the previously discussed acts. However, in recent years, there has been a significant increase in the number of employee retaliation charges made against employers. In fact, 37,334 retaliation charges, or 37.4 percent of all private-sector charges that EEOC received in fiscal 2011 related to employee retaliation.[53] Some HR professionals predicted that the U.S. Supreme Court's 2006 decision in *Burlington Northern & Santa Fe Railway Co. v White* would open the floodgates for retaliation charges and lawsuits. That case lowered the standard of proof for retaliation claims, making it much easier for employees to prove.[54] Typically, a retaliation claim is made if an employee is disciplined or treated in an adverse way because he or she engaged in an alleged protected activity. Then the employee claims that the discipline or adverse action was motivated because they brought a discrimination against an employer. To succeed, the employee need only show that retaliation was a motivating factor in the employer's later decision.[55] The ruling prohibits any employer action that might discourage a reasonable worker from making or supporting a discrimination charge.[56]

In another landmark decision involving *Thompson v North American Stainless L.P.U.S.*, the Supreme Court expanded the scope of who might bring a retaliation charge. The Court unanimously decided that an employee who was linked to a coworker who made a discrimination charge should also be protected from workplace retaliation. According to the ruling, Mr. Thompson, a metallurgical engineer, and Miriam Regalado, then his fiancée and later his wife, both worked for the Ghent, Kentucky–based North American Stainless. Ms. Regalado filed a sex discrimination claim against the company with the EEOC. Mr. Thompson was terminated three weeks later. He sued, alleging his termination was in retaliation for Ms. Regalado's complaint. The company said the firing was performance-related. The 6th U.S. Circuit Court of Appeals in Cincinnati overturned a three-judge panel's decision and ruled that only those who engaged in protected activity are protected against retaliation. The Supreme Court disagreed. Justice Scalia wrote in the unanimous opinion, "We have little difficulty concluding that if the facts alleged by Thompson are true, then his firing violated Title VII."[57] The court ruling cited the *Burlington Northern & Santa Fe Railway Co. v White* decision.

Many believe that the possibility of discrimination claims will now increase dramatically.[58] For example, suppose that a person who claims discrimination is also well-liked and has a lot of friends in the workplace. These friends may complain they are being retaliated against if any negative job action is taken against them. Although it may be difficult to prove a person was the victim of discrimination, it is a much easier to show that he or she was the victim of retaliation.

OBJECTIVE 3.4

Describe the recent trend against employee retaliation.

to women and minorities applies. Recently state laws have addressed drug and alcohol testing, equal employment opportunity, human trafficking, immigration, time off, wages paid, and worker privacy.[59]

OBJECTIVE 3.5

Identify some of the major Supreme Court decisions that have had an impact on equal employment opportunity and affirmative action.

Significant U.S. Supreme Court Decisions Affecting Equal Employment Opportunity

Knowledge of the law is obviously important for those involved with human resource management; however, the manner in which the courts interpret the law is also vital. Court interpretations continuously change, even though the law may not have been amended. Discussions of some of the more significant U.S. Supreme Court decisions affecting equal employment opportunity follow.

Griggs v Duke Power Company

A major decision affecting human resource management was rendered in 1971. A group of black employees at Duke Power Company had charged job discrimination under Title VII of the Civil Rights Act of 1964. Prior to Title VII, the Duke Power Company had two workforces, separated by race. After passage of the act, the company required applicants to have a high school diploma and pass a paper-and-pencil test to qualify for certain jobs. The plaintiff was able to demonstrate that, in the relevant labor market, 34 percent of the white males but only 12 percent of the black males had a high school education. The plaintiff was also able to show that people already in those jobs were performing successfully even though they did not have high school diplomas. No business necessity could be shown for this educational requirement. The *Griggs v Duke Power Company* case continues to be a benchmark case and an example of disparate impact in employment law.

What Was the Real Message?

You were recently hired as information technology manager, and one of your first tasks was to prescreen candidates for an IT position with a subsidiary. After interviewing 20 candidates, you recommend to upper management a minority person as the most qualified and he should be invited for a second interview. A day later, you are taken aside by a friend who suggested that you should not waste management's time by sending certain types for an interview. The intent of the message was clear: if you want to be accepted as a team player with this company, you had better get with the program.

What would you do?
What factor(s) in this ethical dilemma might influence a person to make a less-than-ethical decision?

In an 8–0 vote, the Supreme Court ruled against Duke Power Company and stated, "If an employment practice which operates to exclude Negroes cannot be shown to be related to job performance, the practice is prohibited." A major implication of the decision is that when human resource management practices eliminate substantial numbers of minority or women applicants (prima facie evidence), the burden of proof is on the employer to show that the practice is job related. This Court decision significantly affected the human resource practices of many firms. Questions in employment procedures that should be avoided if not job related include credit record, conviction record, garnishment record, and education. It should be noted that actually asking non-job-related questions is not illegal; it is how a hiring person uses the gained information that makes it illegal. For instance, asking a person his or her age is not in and of itself illegal. Using this information to systematically eliminate older workers from consideration is illegal. Stating that a job requires a college degree when it could be accomplished effectively by a high school graduate can also be potentially discriminatory.

Albemarle Paper Company v Moody

In 1966, a class action suit was brought against Albemarle Paper Company and the plant employees' labor union. A permanent injunction was requested against any policy, practice, custom, or usage at the plant that violated Title VII. In 1975, the Supreme Court, in *Albemarle Paper Company v Moody*, reaffirmed the idea that any test used in the selection process or in promotion decisions must be validated if it has an adverse impact on women and minorities. The employer has the burden of proof for showing that the test is valid. Subsequently, the employer must show that any selection or promotion device actually measures what it is supposed to measure.

Phillips v Martin Marietta Corporation

In 1971, the Court ruled that Martin Marietta had discriminated against a woman because she had young children. The company had a rule prohibiting the hiring of women with school-age children. The company argued that it did not preclude all women from job consideration, only those women with school-age children. Martin Marietta contended that this was a business requirement. The argument was obviously based on stereotypes and was rejected. A major implication of this decision is that a firm cannot impose standards for employment only on women. For example, a firm cannot reject women with school-age children if it does not also reject men with school-age children. Neither application forms nor interviews should contain questions for women that do not also apply to men. Examples of questions that should be avoided are: "Do you wish to be addressed as Ms., Miss, or Mrs.?" "Are you married?" "Do you have children?" "Do you plan on having any more children?" "Where does your husband work?"

Dothard v Rawlingson

At the time Rawlingson applied for a position as correctional counselor trainee, she was a 22-year-old college graduate whose major course of study had been correctional psychology. She was refused employment because she failed to meet the minimum height and weight requirements. In this 1977 case, the Supreme Court upheld the U.S. District Court's decision that Alabama's statutory minimum height requirement of five feet, two inches and minimum weight requirement of 120 pounds for the position of correctional counselor had a discriminatory impact on women applicants. The contention was that minimum height and weight requirements for the position of correctional counselor were job related. However, the Court stated that this argument does not rebut prima facie evidence showing these requirements have a discriminatory impact on women, whereas no evidence was produced correlating these requirements with a requisite amount of strength thought essential to good performance.

American Tobacco Company v Patterson

This 1982 Supreme Court decision allows seniority and promotion systems established since Title VII to stand, although they unintentionally hurt minority workers. Under *Griggs v Duke Power Co.*, a prima facie violation of Title VII may be established by policies or practices that are neutral on their face and in intent, but that nonetheless discriminate against a particular group. A seniority system would fall under the *Griggs* rationale if it were not for Section 703(h) of the Civil Rights Act, which provides:

> *Notwithstanding any other provision of this subchapter, it shall not be an unlawful employment practice for an employer to apply standards of compensation, or different terms, conditions, or privileges of employment pursuant to a bona fide seniority or merit system . . . provided that such differences are not the result of an intention to discriminate because of race, color, religion, sex, or national origin, nor shall it be an unlawful employment practice for an employer to give and to act upon the results of any professionally developed ability test provided that such test, its administration or action upon the results is not designed, intended or used to discriminate because of race, color, religion, sex, or national origin.*

Thus, the Court ruled that a seniority system adopted after Title VII may stand even though it has an unintended discriminatory impact.

O'Connor v Consolidated Coin Caterers Corp.

The U.S. Supreme Court unanimously ruled that an employee does not have to show that he or she was replaced by someone younger than 40 to bring suit under the ADEA. The Court declared that discrimination is illegal even when all the employees are members of the protected age group. The case began in 1990 when James O'Connor's job as a regional sales manager was eliminated. The company did not select O'Connor, age 56, to manage either of its two remaining sales territories. He later was fired. His replacement was 40 years old. O'Connor was evidently doing so well that he earned a bonus of $37,000 the previous year. Apparently, O'Connor's new boss told him "he was too damn old for the kind of work he was doing and that what the company needed was new blood."

Writing for the Court, Justice Scalia stated, "The ADEA does not ban discrimination against employees because they are aged 40; it bans discrimination against employees because of their age, but limits the protected class to those who are 40 or older." Thus, it is not relevant that one member in the protected class has lost out to another member in that class, so long as the person lost out because of his or her age. The Court also found that being replaced by someone substantially younger was a more reliable indicator of age discrimination than being replaced by someone outside the protected class.

Significant U.S. Supreme Court Decisions Affecting Affirmative Action

Discussed below are some of the more significant U.S. Supreme Court decisions affecting affirmative action.

University of California Regents v Bakke

University of California Regents v Bakke was an affirmative action case and was the first major test involving reverse discrimination. The University of California had reserved 16 places in each beginning medical school class for minorities. Allen Bakke, a white man, was denied admission even though he scored higher on the admission criteria than some minority applicants who were admitted. The Supreme Court ruled 5–4 in Bakke's favor. As a result, Bakke was admitted to the university and later received his degree. But, at the same time, the Court reaffirmed that race may be taken into account in admission decisions.

Grutter v Bollinger

The Supreme Court appeared to support the *Bakke* decision. In the case of *Grutter v Bollinger,* the Court ruled in a 5–4 decision that colleges and universities have a compelling interest in achieving diverse campuses. Schools may favor black, Hispanic, and other minority students in admissions as long as administrators take the time to assess each applicant's background and potential. Justice Sandra Day O'Connor, in writing for the majority opinion, said, "Effective participation by members of all racial and ethnic groups in the civic life of our nation is essential if the dream of one nation, indivisible, is to be realized."

Gratz v Bollinger

In the case involving *Gratz v Bollinger,* the Court, in a 6–3 decision, said that in trying to achieve diversity, colleges and universities could not use point systems that blindly give extra credit to minority applicants. The university used a point system to determine admissions criteria in its College of Literature, Science and the Arts, with minority applicants receiving bonus points. The Court determined that Michigan's 150-point index for screening applicants, which gave an automatic 20 points to minority applicants, was not the proper way to achieve racial diversity. The ruling in this decision was quite similar to the *Bakke* decision previously discussed.

Ricci v DeStefano

The City of New Haven, Connecticut, administered a test to determine which firefighters were qualified for promotion to fill vacant lieutenant and captain positions. The results of the tests showed that white candidates had outperformed minority candidates. Of the 43 whites, 19 blacks, and 15 Hispanics who took the lieutenant test, only 34 candidates passed: 25 whites, 6 blacks, and 3 Hispanics. The hiring authority needed to choose a candidate from among the top scorers, meaning that only the top candidates, all white, were eligible to fill the eight vacant lieutenant positions. Fearing lawsuits, the city threw out the results. The plaintiffs who passed the test but did not get promoted sued. The U.S. Supreme Court in a 5–4 decision reversed a Second Circuit decision and held that the city discriminated against white firefighters who likely would have been promoted to lieutenant or captain but for the city's decision to avoid risking disparate impact liability, by throwing out the results of examinations it otherwise would have used in considering the promotions. The evidence demonstrates that the city rejected the test results because the higher-scoring candidates were white. The majority held that the city had to show a "strong basis in evidence" that the tests were not job related or that another, less discriminatory test existed. Justice Anthony Kennedy, writing for the majority, stated that fear of litigation alone cannot justify an employer's reliance on race to the detriment of individuals who passed the examinations and qualified for promotions.[60]

OBJECTIVE 3.6

Describe the Equal Employment Opportunity Commission and explain the purpose of the *Uniform Guidelines on Employee Selection Procedures*.

Equal Employment Opportunity Commission

Title VII of the Civil Rights Act, as amended, created the Equal Employment Opportunity Commission, which is charged with administering the act. Under Title VII, filing a discrimination charge initiates EEOC action. The EEOC continually receives complaints. Recently U.S. employees filed 93,277 workplace discrimination charges with the Equal Employment Opportunity Commission. The EEOC obtained approximately $376 million in monetary relief for thousands of discrimination victims as well as significant nonmonetary remedies from employer.[61]

Charges may be filed by one of the presidentially appointed EEOC commissioners, by any aggrieved person, or by anyone acting on behalf of an aggrieved person. Charges must be filed within 180 days of the alleged act; however, the time is extended to 300 days if a state or local

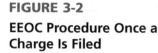

FIGURE 3-2

EEOC Procedure Once a Charge Is Filed

HR Web Wisdom

EEOC

http://www.eeoc.gov

The home page for the Equal Employment Opportunity Commission.

Steps in Handling a Discrimination Case

agency is involved in the case. Because of this time restriction, the Civil Rights Act of 1866 may be called into play because it has no statute of limitations.

Notice in Figure 3-2 that when a charge is filed, the EEOC first attempts a no-fault settlement. Essentially, the organization charged with the violation is invited to settle the case with no admission of guilt. Most charges are settled at this stage. Failing settlement, the EEOC investigates the charges. Once the employer is notified that an investigation will take place, no records relating to the charge may be destroyed. During the investigative process, the employer is permitted to present a position statement. After the investigation has been completed, the district director of the EEOC will issue a probable cause or a no probable cause statement.

In the event of a probable cause statement, the next step involves attempted conciliation. In the event this effort fails, the case will be reviewed for litigation potential. Some of the factors that determine whether the EEOC will pursue litigation are (1) the number of people affected by the alleged practice; (2) the amount of money involved in the charge; (3) other charges against the employer; and (4) the type of charge. Recommendations for litigation are then passed on to the general counsel of the EEOC. If the recommendation is against litigation, a right-to-sue notice will be issued to the charging party.

Uniform Guidelines on Employee Selection Procedures

Prior to 1978, employers were faced with complying with several different selection guidelines. In 1978, the Equal Employment Opportunity Commission, the Civil Service Commission, the Department of Justice, and the Department of Labor adopted the *Uniform Guidelines on Employee Selection Procedures*. These guidelines cover several federal equal employment opportunity statutes and executive orders, including Title VII of the Civil Rights Act, EO 11246, and the Equal Pay Act.

The *Uniform Guidelines* provide a single set of principles that were designed to assist employers, labor organizations, employment agencies, and licensing and certification boards in complying with federal prohibitions against employment practices that discriminate on the basis of race, color, religion, sex, and national origin. The *Uniform Guidelines* provide a framework for making legal employment decisions about hiring, promotion, demotion, referral, retention,

Uniform Guidelines
Provide a single set of principles that were designed to assist employers, labor organizations, employment agencies, and licensing and certification boards in complying with federal prohibitions against employment practices that discriminate on the basis of race, color, religion, sex, and national origin.

licensing and certification, the proper use of tests, and other selection procedures. Under the *Uniform Guidelines*, recruiting procedures are not considered selection procedures and therefore are not covered.

Regarding selection procedures, the *Uniform Guidelines* state that a test is

> *any measure, combination of measures, or procedures used as a basis for any employment decision. Selection procedures include the full range of assessment techniques from traditional paper-and-pencil tests, performance tests, testing programs or probationary periods, and physical, education, and work experience requirement through informal or casual interviews and unscored application forms.*

Using this definition, virtually any instrument or procedure used in the selection decision is considered a test.

OBJECTIVE 3.7

Describe disparate treatment and adverse impact and explain the *Uniform Guidelines* related to sexual harassment, national origin, religion, and caregiver (family responsibility) discrimination.

disparate treatment
Employer treats some people less favorably than others because of race, religion, color, sex, national origin, or age.

Concept of Disparate Treatment

Unlawful employment discrimination, as established through various Supreme Court decisions, can be divided into two broad categories: disparate treatment and adverse impact. **Disparate treatment** means that an employer treats some employees less favorably than others because of race, religion, color, sex, national origin, or age. It is the most easily understood form of discrimination.

For example, males are treated differently from females; whites are treated differently from blacks. The crux of disparate treatment is different treatment on the basis of some non-allowable criterion. It may be thought of as direct discrimination. Common forms of disparate treatment include selection rules with a racial, sexual, or other premise; prejudicial action; unequal treatment on an individual basis; and different hiring standards for different groups. *McDonald v Santa Fe Trail Transportation Company* offers an example of disparate treatment. Three of the company's employees, two whites and one black, had allegedly misappropriated 60 gallons of antifreeze. Santa Fe took disciplinary action against the workers by terminating the two whites, but not the black employee. The discharged white workers filed suit against the company, charging that their termination violated both Title VII and the Civil Rights Act of 1866. The Supreme Court agreed with the plaintiffs that they had been the recipients of unequal treatment on the basis of their race. Central to disparate treatment is the matter of proof. The plaintiff must first be able to establish a prima facie case, and, second, be able to establish that the employer was acting on the basis of a discriminatory motive.

Concept of Adverse Impact

Prior to the issuance of the *Uniform Guidelines*, the only way to prove job-relatedness was to validate each test. The *Uniform Guidelines* do not require validation in all cases. Essentially, it is required only in instances in which the test or other selection device produces an adverse impact on a minority group. **Adverse impact**, a concept established by the *Uniform Guidelines*, occurs if women and minorities are not hired at the rate of at least 80 percent of the best-achieving group.

adverse impact
Concept established by the *Uniform Guidelines*; it occurs if women and minorities are not hired at the rate of at least 80 percent of the best-achieving group.

Under the *Uniform Guidelines*, adverse impact has been described in terms of selection rates, the selection rate being the number of qualified applicants hired or promoted, divided by the total number of qualified applicants. This has also been called the four-fifths rule, which is actually a guideline subject to interpretation by the EEOC. The groups identified for analysis under the guidelines are (1) blacks, (2) Native Americans (including Alaskan natives), (3) Asians, (4) Hispanics, (5) women, and (6) men.

The following formula is used to compute adverse impact for hiring:

$$\frac{\text{Success rate for least-achieving group of applicants}}{\text{Success rate for best-achieving group of applicants}} = \text{Determination of adverse impact}$$

The success rate for the least-achieving group (often women and minority applicants) is determined by dividing the number of members of a specific group employed in a period by the number of qualified applicants in a period. The success rate of best-achieving group applicants is determined by dividing the number of people in the best-achieving group employed by the number of the best-achieving group applicants in a period.

Using the formula, let us determine whether there has been adverse impact in the following case. During 2013, 400 people were hired for a particular job. Of the total, 300 were white and 100 were black. There were 1,500 qualified applicants for these jobs, of whom 1,000 were white and 500 were black. Blacks were determined to be the least-achieving group because 100/500 = .2. Whites were determined to be the best-achieving group because 300/1000 = .3. Using the adverse formula, you have:

$$\frac{100/500}{300/1000} = \frac{0.2}{0.3} = 66.67\%$$

Thus, adverse impact exists.

Evidence of adverse impact involves more than the total number of minority workers employed. Also considered is the total number of qualified applicants. For instance, assume that 300 blacks and 300 whites were hired. But there were 1,500 qualified black applicants and 1,000 qualified white applicants. Blacks were determined to be the least-achieving group because 300/1500 = .2. Whites were determined to be the best-achieving group because 300/1000 = .3. Putting these figures into the adverse impact formula, it can be concluded that adverse impact still exists.

$$\frac{300/1500}{300/1000} = \frac{0.2}{0.3} = 66.67\%$$

Therefore, it is clear that firms must monitor their recruitment efforts very carefully. Obviously, firms should attempt to recruit qualified individuals because once in the applicant pool, they will be used in computing adverse impact.

Assuming that adverse impact is shown, employers have two avenues available to them if they still desire to use a particular selection standard. First, the employer may validate a selection device by showing that it is indeed a predictor of success. For instance, the employer may be able to show a strong relationship between the selection device and job performance, and that if it did not use this procedure, the firm's training costs would become prohibitive. If the device has proved to be a predictor of job performance, business necessity has been established.

The second avenue available to employers should adverse impact be shown is the bona fide occupational qualification (BFOQ) defense. The BFOQ defense means that only one group is capable of performing the job successfully. Courts have narrowly interpreted this defense because it almost always relates to sex discrimination. For instance, courts have rejected the concept that because most women cannot lift 100 pounds, all women should be eliminated from consideration for a job requiring heavy lifting.

Creators of the *Uniform Guidelines* adopted the bottom-line approach in assessing whether a firm's employment practices are discriminatory. For example, if a number of separate procedures are used in making a selection decision, the enforcement agencies will focus on the end result of these procedures to determine whether adverse impact has occurred. Essentially, the EEOC is more concerned with what is occurring than how it occurs. It admits that discriminatory employment practices that cannot be validated may exist; however, the net effect, or the bottom line, of the selection procedures is the focus of the EEOC attention.

Additional Guidelines on Employment Selection Procedures

Since the *Uniform Guidelines* were published in 1978, they have been modified several times. Some of these changes reflect Supreme Court decisions; others clarify implementation procedures. The four major changes discussed are the Guidelines on Sexual Harassment, Guidelines on Discrimination Because of National Origin, Guidelines on Discrimination Because of Religion, and Guidelines on Caregiver (Family Responsibility) Discrimination.

Guidelines on Sexual Harassment

As previously mentioned, Title VII of the Civil Rights Act generally prohibits discrimination in employment on the basis of gender. The EEOC has also issued guidelines that state that

TABLE 3-1

EEOC Definition of Sexual Harassment

Unwelcome sexual advances, requests for sexual favors, and verbal or physical conduct of a sexual nature that occur under any of the following situations:

1. When submission to such conduct is made either explicitly or implicitly a term or condition of an individual's employment

2. When submission to or rejection of such contact by an individual is used as the basis for employment decisions affecting such individual

3. When such conduct has the purpose or effect of unreasonably interfering with an individual's work performance or creating an intimidating, hostile, or offensive working environment

employers have a duty to maintain a workplace that is free from sexual harassment. The OFCCP has issued similar guidelines. Managers in both for-profit and not-for-profit organizations must be particularly alert to the issue of sexual harassment. The EEOC issued the guidelines because of the belief that sexual harassment was a widespread problem. Table 3-1 contains the EEOC's definition of sexual harassment. As you see, there are two distinct types of sexual harassment: (1) where a hostile work environment is created, and (2) when there is a quid pro quo, for example, an offer of promotion or pay raise in exchange for sex.

According to these guidelines, employers are totally liable for the acts of their supervisors, regardless of whether the employer is aware of the sexual harassment act. In *Faragher v City of Boca Raton* and *Burlington Industries, Inc. v Ellerth,* the Supreme Court held that an employer is strictly liable, meaning that it has absolutely no defense, when sexual harassment by a supervisor involves a tangible employment action. Courts expect employers to carefully train supervisors so they do not engage in any type of behavior that could be construed as sexual harassment. In addition, all employees should be trained so as to understand their rights and responsibilities.[62]

As with the Civil Rights Act of 1964, retaliation is forbidden against an employee who has participated in an investigation, proceeding, or hearing. Recently Blockbuster, Inc. entered into a consent judgment requiring it to pay over $2 million to settle an employment discrimination lawsuit filed by EEOC. The EEOC had charged Blockbuster with subjecting female temporary employees to sexual harassment, retaliating against them for resisting sexual advances and complaining, and subjecting Hispanic temporary employees to national origin and race harassment and other discrimination. "This case should act as a warning to all employers who use staffing agency personnel," said EEOC Philadelphia Regional Attorney Debra M. Lawrence, whose jurisdiction includes Maryland. "Employers who are customers of staffing agencies have a responsibility to protect their temporary workers from unlawful discrimination. Too frequently, such employers fail to create systems to prevent and detect abuse of temporary workers and fail to respond forcefully to it. Those employers do so at their peril."[63]

Where coworkers are concerned, the employer is responsible for such acts if the employer knew, or should have known, about them. The employer is not responsible when it can show that it took immediate and appropriate corrective action on learning of the problem. Another important aspect of these guidelines is that employers may be liable for acts committed by nonemployees in the workplace if the employer knew, or should have known, of the conduct and failed to take appropriate action.

Firms are responsible for developing programs and policies to prevent sexual harassment in the workplace. Managers must be trained to know what to do when there is a complaint. They must investigate all formal and informal complaints alleging sexual harassment.[64] Failure to do so constitutes a violation of Title VII, as interpreted by the EEOC. To prevail in court, companies must have clear procedures for handling sexual harassment complaints. If the sexual harassment complaint appears legitimate, the company must take immediate and appropriate action.[65] However, this does not mean that everyone who is guilty of sexual harassment must be fired. A single incident does not mean that sexual harassment exists unless the employer ignores the incident and lets the situation worsen.[66]

The first sexual harassment case to reach the U.S. Supreme Court was the case of *Meritor Savings Bank v Vinson* in 1986. In the *Vinson* decision, the Supreme Court recognized for the first time that Title VII could be used for offensive-environment claims. According to the EEOC, specific actions that could create a hostile workplace include a pattern of threatening, intimidating, or hostile acts and remarks, negative sexual stereotyping, or the display of written or graphic materials considered degrading. The 1993 Supreme Court decision in *Harris v Forklift Systems, Inc.* expanded the hostile-workplace concept and made it easier to win sexual harassment claims. In a unanimous decision, the Supreme Court held that "to be accountable as abusive work environment harassment, conduct need not seriously affect . . . the psychological well-being or lead the plaintiff to suffer injury." No longer does severe psychological injury have to be proved. Under this ruling, the plaintiff only needs to show that his or her employer allowed a hostile-to-abusive work environment to exist.

Duane Reade, the New York/New Jersey drug store chain, agreed to settle an EEOC lawsuit for $240,000 for allowing the work environment at one of its New York stores to become hostile. The store manager frequently made vulgar remarks about women's anatomy, sexually propositioned female employees, made lewd comments about them during pregnancies, assigned pregnant women the least desirable store tasks, and sometimes grabbed female employees' buttocks while they worked.[67] Unchecked sexual harassment can be financially crippling. In a recent case, a jury awarded the plaintiff $95 million, including $80 million in punitive damages.[68]

Males are not precluded from sexual harassment. From 1990 to 2009, the percentage of sexual harassment claims filed by male employees doubled from 8 to 16 percent.[69] Recently, the 9th U.S. Circuit Court of Appeals held that a female coworker's "relentless" pursuit of a male employee could form the basis of a sexually hostile environment claim, even without any physical conduct of a sexual nature. The 9th Circuit pointed out that under Title VII of the Civil Rights Act of 1964, "[b]oth sexes are protected from discrimination."[70]

For a long time, an unresolved question in employment law has been whether same-sex harassment (for example, males harassing males) is unlawful under Title VII of the Civil Rights Act of 1964. The Supreme Court, in the case of *Oncale v Sundowner Offshore Services*, held that same-sex sexual harassment may be unlawful under Title VII. The Supreme Court decided that a plaintiff could make a claim for sexual harassment as long as the harassing conduct was because of sex. The Court emphasized that Title VII does not prohibit all verbal or physical harassment in the workplace, only that which constitutes discrimination because of sex.

Guidelines on Discrimination Because of National Origin

Both EEOC and the courts have interpreted national origin protection under Title VII as extending far beyond discrimination against individuals who came from, or whose forebears came from, a particular country. National origin protection also covers (1) marriage or association with a person of a specific national origin; (2) membership in, or association with, an organization identified with, or seeking to promote the interests of national groups; (3) attendance at, or participation in, schools, churches, temples, or mosques generally used by persons of a national origin group; and (4) use of an individual's or spouse's name that is associated with a national origin group. As Table 3-2 shows, the EEOC has identified certain selection procedures that may be discriminatory.

Harassment on the basis of national origin is a violation of Title VII. Employers have a duty to maintain a working environment free from such harassment. Ethnic slurs and other verbal or physical conduct relating to an individual's national origin constitute harassment when this conduct (1) has the purpose or effect of creating an intimidating, hostile, or offensive working environment; (2) has the purpose or effect of unreasonably interfering with an individual's work performance; or (3) otherwise adversely affects an individual's employment opportunity.

TABLE 3-2

Selection Procedures That May Be Discriminatory with Regard to National Origin

1. Fluency in English requirements: One questionable practice involves denying employment opportunities because of an individual's foreign accent or inability to communicate well in English. When this practice is continually followed, the Commission will presume that such a rule violates Title VII and will study it closely. However, a firm may require that employees speak only in English at certain times if business necessity can be shown.

2. Training or education requirements: Denying employment opportunities to an individual because of his or her foreign training or education, or practices that require an individual to be foreign trained or educated may be discriminatory.

Of interest with regard to national origin is the English-only rule. Courts have generally ruled in the employer's favor if the rule would promote safety and product quality and stop harassment. For example, suppose a company has a rule that only English must be spoken except during breaks. That rule must be justified by a compelling business necessity. In *Garcia v Spun Steak,* the Ninth Circuit Court of Appeals (the Supreme Court refused to review) concluded that the rule did not necessarily violate Title VII. Spun Steak's management implemented the policy after some workers complained they were being harassed and insulted in a language they could not understand. The rule allowed workers to speak Spanish during breaks and lunch periods. A recent ruling supported the job-related aspect of the English-only rule. In *Montes v Vail Clinic, Inc.,* the tenth circuit court agreed with the English-only rule prohibiting housekeepers from speaking Spanish while working in the operating room. However, English-only policies that are not job related have been challenged and eliminated. The U.S. Equal Employment Opportunity Commission (EEOC) settled a Title VII lawsuit against a company that enforced an English-only rule solely against Hispanics. "What was strange was that the rule was only targeted at Hispanics. Tagalog, a Spanish language spoken in the Philippines, was openly spoken," said Anna Park, the EEOC's regional attorney in Los Angeles. "This was very troublesome."[71]

Guidelines on Discrimination Because of Religion

The number of religion-related discrimination complaints filed with the EEOC continues to increase. According to the Supreme Court's decision in *TWA v Hardison*, employers have an obligation to accommodate sincerely held religious practices as long as the requested accommodation does not create more than a minimum cost to the employer.[72] Courts generally do not require employers to hire additional employees just to cover for another employee who needs a religious accommodation. Consideration is given to identifiable costs in relation to the size and operating costs of the employer and the number of individuals who actually need the accommodation. These guidelines recognize that regular payment of premium wages constitutes undue hardship, whereas these payments on an infrequent or temporary basis do not. Undue hardship would also exist if an accommodation required a firm to vary from its bona fide seniority system.

The most common claims filed under the religious accommodation provisions involve employees objecting to either Sabbath employment or membership in or financial support of labor unions. These guidelines identify several means of accommodating religious practices that prohibit working on certain days. Some of the methods suggested included voluntary substitutes, flexible scheduling, lateral transfer, and change of job assignments. Some collective bargaining agreements include a provision that each employee must join the union or pay the union a sum equivalent to dues. When an employee's religious beliefs prevent compliance, the union should accommodate the employee by permitting that person to make an equivalent donation to a charitable organization.

Guidelines on Caregiver (Family Responsibility) Discrimination

caregiver (family responsibility) discrimination
Discrimination against employees based on their obligations to care for family members.

Caregiver (family responsibility) discrimination is discrimination against employees based on their obligations to care for family members. The EEOC has issued a technical assistance document titled "Employer Best Practices for Workers with Caregiving Responsibilities" on how employers of workers with caregiving responsibilities can avoid violations of Title VII of the 1964 Civil Rights Act and other fair employment laws and reduce the likelihood of discrimination complaints. This form of discrimination makes an assumption based on what a person assumes to be true about a group, including people with family responsibilities.

According to the EEOC, the guidance s not binding on employers but rather offers best practices that are proactive measures that go beyond federal nondiscrimination requirements. Federal law does not prohibit discrimination on the basis of "caregiver status" but rather it is concerned when workers with caregiving responsibilities are treated differently based on a characteristic that is protected by laws, such as gender, race, or association with an individual with a disability.

Caregiver discrimination has become the new battleground in employment claims.[73] Examples of possible caregiver discrimination violations include treating male caregivers more favorably than female caregivers; reassigning a woman to less desirable projects based on the assumption that, as a new mother, she will be less committed to her job; or lowering subjective evaluations of a female employee's work performance after she becomes the primary caregiver of her grandchildren, despite the absence of an actual decline in work performance.[74]

In recent years, employees have begun filing more and more caregiver discrimination lawsuits. Most cases share a common element—the employee alleges that the caregiving responsibilities cause the alleged discriminatory action by the employer. In EEO-related suits, plaintiffs win in only about 20 percent of cases alleging race, sex, or other more familiar types of discrimination. However, with caregiver discrimination, the win rate is twice that.[75] The challenge for employers is to develop the right mix of flexibility and fairness in work scheduling, leave policies, dependent-care assistance, and benefits. This will promote positive employee relations, recruit and retain a diverse and well-qualified workforce, address and resolve job-related issues, and defend against claims of unfair or unlawful conduct.

Avoiding EEO Litigation

Much has occurred since the first piece of EEO legislation was enacted approximately 50 years ago, and the basic hiring standards to avoid are largely understood by those in the workforce. In a perfect world, discrimination, retaliation, and harassment would not exist. However, despite a company's best efforts to treat employees fairly, suits are still brought and won because of mistakes in adherence to these standards.[76] Perhaps, it was only a temporary lapse where a manager knowingly decides to hire a less-qualified friend over a qualified member of a protected group. Or, the manager may sincerely believe that he or she has the best intention of abiding by the law but still makes a mistake perhaps because of some complexity in the law.

To limit the prospect of an EEO lawsuit, an organization can do a few things. First, and foremost, it must have and enforce a strong EEO policy against discrimination. This policy must begin with top management and filter down to everyone in the organization. This policy should clearly spell out what standards are to be avoided. It should also conspicuously describe the complaint procedure and the various avenues that can be followed if the person in charge is the cause of the complaint. Certainly, the policy should provide a strong anti-retaliation clause. Workers need to believe that a complaint will result in immediate and appropriate action.

Even with a policy such as the one described above, there may still be breakdowns. When they do occur, it becomes an opportunity to train employers how to handle an employee-relations problem better the next time. By taking the high road in the solution of a suit, it provides a means of reinforcing the seriousness of the nondiscrimination policy.

OBJECTIVE 3.8

Explain affirmative action as required by presidential Executive Orders 11246 and 11375 and describe affirmative action programs.

executive order (EO)

Directive issued by the president that has the force and effect of law enacted by Congress as it applies to federal agencies and federal contractors.

affirmative action

Stipulated by Executive Order 11246, it requires employers to take positive steps to ensure that employment of applicants and treatment of employees during employment are without regard to race, creed, color, or national origin.

Affirmative Action: Executive Order 11246, As Amended by Executive Order 11375

An **executive order (EO)** is a directive issued by the president and has the force and effect of a law enacted by Congress as it applies to federal agencies and federal contractors. Many believe that the concept of affirmative action got its beginning in 1948 when President Harry S. Truman officially ended racial segregation in all branches of the military by issuing Executive Order 9981.

However, officially it began in 1965 when President Lyndon B. Johnson signed EO 11246, which establishes the policy of the U.S. government as providing equal opportunity in federal employment for all qualified people. It prohibits discrimination in employment because of race, creed, color, or national origin. The order also requires promoting the full realization of equal employment opportunity through a positive, continuing program in each executive department and agency. The policy of equal opportunity applies to every aspect of federal employment policy and practice.

A major provision of EO 11246 requires adherence to a policy of nondiscrimination in employment as a condition for the approval of a grant, contract, loan, insurance, or guarantee. Every executive department and agency that administers a program involving federal financial assistance must include such language in its contracts. Contractors must agree not to discriminate in employment because of race, creed, color, or national origin during performance of a contract.

Affirmative action, stipulated by EO 11246, requires covered employers to take positive steps to ensure that employment of applicants and treatment of employees during employment are without regard to race, creed, color, or national origin. In 1968, EO 11375 changed the word "creed" to "religion" and added sex discrimination to the other prohibited items. These EOs are enforced by the Department of Labor through the Office of Federal Contract Compliance

Programs (OFCCP). Recently the Vietnam Era Veterans' Readjustment Assistance Act and the Rehabilitation Act have received additional attention from the OFCCP.[77]

Covered human resource practices relate to employment, upgrading, demotion, transfer, recruitment or recruitment advertising, layoffs or termination, rates of pay or other forms of compensation, and selection for training, including apprenticeships. Employers are required to post notices explaining these requirements in conspicuous places in the workplace. In the event of contractor noncompliance, contracts can be canceled, terminated, or suspended in whole or in part, and the contractor may be declared ineligible for future government contracts.

Affirmative Action Programs

affirmative action program (AAP)

Approach developed by organizations with government contracts to demonstrate that workers are employed in proportion to their representation in the firm's relevant labor market.

An **affirmative action program (AAP)** is an approach developed by organizations with government contracts to demonstrate that workers are employed in proportion to their representation in the firm's relevant labor market.

An affirmative action program may be voluntarily implemented by an organization. In such an event, goals are established and actions taken to hire and move minorities and women up in the organization. In other situations, an AAP may be mandated by the OFCCP. The degree of control the OFCCP will impose depends on the size of the contract, with contracts of $10,000 or less not covered. The first level of control involves contracts that exceed $10,000 but are less than $50,000. These contractors are governed by the equal opportunity clause, as shown in Table 3-3. The second level of control occurs if the contractor (1) has 50 or more employees; (2) has a contract of $50,000 or more; (3) has contracts that, in any 12-month period, total $50,000 or more or reasonably may be expected to total $50,000 or more; or (4) is a financial institution that serves as a depository for government funds in any amount, acts as an issuing or redeeming agent for U.S. savings bonds and savings notes in any amount, or subscribes to federal deposit or share insurance. Contractors meeting these criteria must develop a written AAP for each of their establishments and file an annual EEO-1 report. Note that the threshold is 50 employees here, but it is 100 with regard to those covered by the Civil Rights Act of 1964.

The third level of control on contractors is in effect when contracts exceed $1 million. All previously stated requirements must be met, and in addition, the OFCCP is authorized to conduct preaward compliance reviews. In determining whether to conduct a preaward review, the OFCCP may consider, for example, the items presented in Table 3-4. Alcoa Mill Products Inc. paid $484,656.19 in back wages to 37 Hispanics and African Americans as well as $35,516.88 to two women who were rejected for job positions at the company's Lancaster, Pennsylvania, plant. The OFCCP determined that the company had violated EO 11246 by failing to meet its obligations as a federal contractor. Alcoa holds contracts with the U.S. Army in excess of $50 million.

Recently every 25th supply and service federal contractor selected for a compliance evaluation by the OFCCP is subjected to a full compliance review that includes onsite visits by compliance officers, even though there are no indicators of potential discrimination or other violations. The "active case enforcement" directive also provides that the OFCCP will perform a full desk audit in every compliance evaluation to comprehensively analyze a contractor's written affirmative action plans.[78] Before this decision, only 25 compliance reviews were made per year.[79]

If an investigation indicates a violation, the OFCCP first tries to secure compliance through persuasion. If persuasion fails to resolve the issue, the OFCCP serves a notice to show cause or a notice of violation. A show cause notice contains a list of the violations, a statement of how the OFCCP proposes that corrections be made, a request for a written response to the findings, and a suggested date for a conciliation conference. The firm usually has 30 days to respond. Successful conciliation results in a written contract between the OFCCP and the contractor. In a conciliation agreement, the contractor agrees to take specific steps to remedy noncompliance with an EO. Firms that do not correct violations can be passed over in the awarding of future contracts. The procedures for developing affirmative action plans were published in the *Federal Register* of December 4, 1974. These regulations are referred to as Revised Order No. 4. Revised Order No. 4 is quite specific with regard to dissemination of a firm's EEO policy, both internally and externally. An executive should be appointed to manage the firm's equal employment opportunity program. This person should be given the necessary support by top management to accomplish the assignment. Revised Order No. 4 specifies the minimum level of responsibility associated with

TABLE 3-3

Equal Opportunity Clause—Government Contracts

1. The contractor will not discriminate against any employee or applicant for employment because of race, color, religion, sex, or national origin. The contractor will take affirmative action to ensure that applicants are employed, and that employees are treated during employment, without regard to their race, color, religion, sex, or national origin. Such action shall include, but not be limited to the following: employment, upgrading, demotions, or transfer; recruitment or recruitment advertising, layoff or termination; rates of pay or other forms of compensation; and selection for training, including apprenticeship. The contractor agrees to post in conspicuous places, available to employees and applicants for employment, notices to be provided by the contracting officer setting forth the provisions for this nondiscrimination clause.

2. The contractor will in all solicitations or advertisements for employees placed by or on behalf of the contractor, state that all qualified applicants will receive consideration for employment without regard to race, color, religion, sex, or national origin.

3. The contractor will send to each labor union or representative of workers with which he or she has a collective bargaining agreement or other contract or understanding, a notice to be provided by the agency contracting officer, advising the labor union or workers' representative of the contractor's commitments under section 202 of Executive Order 11246 of September 24, 1965, and shall post copies of the notice in conspicuous places available to employees and applicants for employment.

4. The contractor will comply with all provisions of Executive Order 11246 of September 24, 1965, and the rules, regulations, and relevant orders of the Secretary of Labor.

5. The contractor will furnish all information and reports required by Executive Order 11246 of September 24, 1965, and by the rules, regulations, and orders of the Secretary of Labor, or pursuant thereto, and will permit access to his or her books, records, and accounts by the contracting agency and the Secretary of Labor for purposes of investigation to ascertain compliance with such rules, regulations, and orders.

6. In the event of the contractor's noncompliance with the nondiscrimination clauses of this contract or with any of such rules, regulations, or orders, this contract may be canceled, terminated, or suspended in whole or in part and the contractor may be declared ineligible for further Government contracts in accordance with procedures authorized in Executive Order 11246 of September 24, 1965, or by rule, regulation, or order of the Secretary of State, or as otherwise provided by law.

7. The contractor will include the provisions of paragraphs (1) through (7) in every subcontract or purchase order unless exempted by rules, regulations, or orders of the Secretary of Labor issued pursuant to section 204 of Executive Order 11246 of September 24, 1965, so that such provisions will be binding upon each subcontractor or vendor. The contractor will take such action with respect to any subcontract or purchase order as may be directed by the Secretary of Labor as a means of enforcing such provisions including sanctions for noncompliance: Provided, however, that in the event the contractor becomes involved in, or is threatened with litigation with a subcontractor or vendor as a result of such direction, the contractor may request the United States to enter into such litigation to protect the interests of the United States.

Source: Federal Register, 45, no. 251 (Tuesday, December 30, 1980): 86230.

TABLE 3-4

Factors That the OFCCP May Consider in Conducting a Preaward Review

1. The past EEO performance of the contractor, including its current EEO profile and indications of underutilization.
2. The volume and nature of complaints filed by employees or applicants against the contractor.
3. Whether the contractor is in a growth industry.
4. The level of employment or promotional opportunities resulting from the expansion of, or turnover in, the contractor's workforce.
5. The employment opportunities likely to result from the contract in issue.
6. Whether resources are available to conduct the review.

the task of EEO manager. The OFCCP guide for compliance officers, outlining what to cover in a compliance review, is known as Order No. 14.

The OFCCP is very specific about what should be included in an AAP. A policy statement has to be developed that reflects the CEO's attitude regarding equal employment opportunity, assigns overall responsibility for preparing and implementing the AAP, and provides for reporting and monitoring procedures. The policy should state that the firm intends to recruit, hire, train, and promote persons in all job titles without regard to race, color, religion, gender, or national origin, except where gender is a bona fide occupational qualification (BFOQ). Recently protected military veterans and individuals with disabilities have been included in affirmative action. The policy should guarantee that all human resource actions involving areas such as compensation, benefits, transfers, layoffs, return from layoffs, company-sponsored training, education, tuition assistance, and social and recreational programs will be administered without regard to race, color, religion, gender, or national origin.

An acceptable AAP must include an analysis of deficiencies in the utilization of minority groups and women. The first step in conducting a utilization analysis is to make a workforce analysis. The second step involves an analysis of all major job groups. An explanation of the situation is required if members of protected groups are currently being underutilized. A *job group* is defined as one or more jobs having similar content, wage rates, and opportunities.

Underutilization is defined as having fewer minorities or women in a particular job group than would reasonably be expected by their availability. The utilization analysis is important because the calculations determine whether underutilization exists. For example, if the utilization analysis shows that the availability of blacks for a certain job group is 30 percent, the organization should have at least 30 percent black employment in that group. If actual employment is less than 30 percent, underutilization exists, and the firm should set a goal of 30 percent black employment for that job group. The goal of affirmative action is for a contractor's workforce to generally reflect the gender, racial, and ethnic profile of the labor pools from which the contractor recruits and selects.

The primary focus of any AAP is on goals and timetables, with the issue being how many and by when. Goals and timetables developed by the firm should cover its entire AAP, including correction of deficiencies. These goals and timetables should be attainable; that is, they should be based on results that the firm, making good-faith efforts, could reasonably expect to achieve. Goals should be significant and measurable, as well as attainable. Two types of goals must be established regarding underutilization: annual and ultimate. The annual goal is to move toward elimination of underutilization, whereas the ultimate goal is to correct all underutilization. Goals should be specific in terms of planned results, with timetables for completion. However, goals should not establish inflexible quotas that must be met. Rather, they should be targets that are reasonably attainable. Some techniques that can be used to improve recruitment and increase the flow of minority and women applicants are shown in Table 3-5.

HR Laws and Executive Orders Affecting Small Businesses

Small business managers usually do not have the HR resources that are available to large organizations. Often line managers are handling many HR-related tasks. However, all but the very small businesses fall under the coverage of federal and local laws and presidential executive orders. For example, the Equal Pay Act prohibits an employer from paying an employee of one gender less money than an employee of the opposite gender, if both employees do work that is substantially the same. Title VII covers employers engaged in or affecting interstate commerce who have 15 or more employees. Since the Pregnancy Discrimination Act is an amendment to the Civil Rights Act, the threshold coverage is also 15, as is the Civil Rights Act of 1991. The threshold coverall for the Age Discrimination in Employment Act is 20 employees. The threshold coverage for the Americans with Disabilities Act is 15. When dealing with the national origin provision of the Civil Rights Act, Immigration Reform and Control Act reduces the threshold coverage from 15 employees to 4. If a federal contract or subcontract exceeds $50,000, or if the contractor has 50 or more employees, the employer must prepare a written AAP for review by the OFCCP. The Occupational Safety and Health Act affects businesses with just one employee. Because small businesses usually do not have a person who is solely dedicated to handling government compliance, small businesses may be unduly affected.

TABLE 3-5

Techniques to Improve Recruitment of Minorities and Women

- Identify referral organizations for minorities and women.
- Hold formal briefing sessions with representatives of referral organizations.
- Encourage minority and women employees to refer applicants to the firm.
- Include minorities and women on the Personnel Relations staff.
- Permit minorities and women to participate in Career Days, Youth Motivation Programs, and related activities in their community.
- Actively participate in job fairs and give company representatives the authority to make on-the-spot commitments.
- Actively recruit at schools having predominant minority or female enrollments.
- Use special efforts to reach minorities and women during school recruitment drives.
- Undertake special employment programs whenever possible for women and minorities. These might include technical and nontechnical co-op programs, after-school and/or work-study jobs, summer jobs for underprivileged individuals, summer work-study programs, and motivation, training, and employment programs for the hardcore unemployed.
- Pictorially present minorities and women in recruiting brochures.
- Include the minority news media and women's interest media when expending help wanted advertising.

Source: Federal Register, 45, no. 251 (Tuesday December 30, 2008): 86243.

OBJECTIVE 3.9

Describe sexual harassment in the global environment.

A GLOBAL PERSPECTIVE

Global Sexual Harassment

Sexual harassment was discussed in this chapter only as it pertained to the United States, but it is also a global issue. When individuals from two different cultures interact, there is a potential for sexual harassment problems. Some behaviors that violate U.S. cultural norms may not be perceived as a problem in another culture. In many Mediterranean and Latin countries, physical contact and sensuality are a common part of socializing. The famous Cirque du Soleil, headquartered in Montreal, Canada, has had to adapt to the U.S. definition of sexual harassment when performing in the United States. While kissing good friends and coworkers on both cheeks is common in Montreal, such behavior could be considered a form of sexual harassment in the United States. Also, there are the seminude photos of Cirque performers hanging on the walls of the company's Montreal headquarters.[80] These would likely never be seen in the United States.

The level of enforcement against workplace sexual harassment varies considerably from country to country. Although 117 countries outlaw sexual harassment in the workplace, 311 million working-age women continue to live and work in countries without this legal protection.[81] In a recent study, 26 percent of the workers surveyed in India said they had been sexually harassed, whereas only 1 percent of Sweden's employees said that they had been sexually harassed. Chinese workers had the second highest rate of sexual harassment

victimization (18 percent), followed by Saudi Arabia (16 percent).[82] Sexual harassment remains a significant problem in Pakistan, and women must constantly be alert to protect themselves from problem situations. Lara Arif, 32, who sells fabric for women's dresses from her home in Karachi, avoids taxis when she visits clients. Instead, she favors crowded buses or rickshaws, which have no doors, making escape easier. "You have to be very reserved and remain alert all the time," Arif says.[83]

Australia, Canada, the Netherlands, Sweden, United States, and the United Kingdom have laws specifying prohibited conduct and allowing employees to seek individual remedies. Italy, the Philippines, Taiwan, and Venezuela define sexual harassment as a criminal offense, and penalties and remedies are provided in special statutory penal codes. In Germany, Spain, and Thailand, sexual discrimination laws allow employees to terminate their employment relationships due to discrimination or harassment. Employers are required to pay employees a substantial sum if the cause of their termination is due to discrimination or harassment.[84]

France considers quid pro quo as the only form of sexual harassment claims. The country does not recognize claims of a sexually hostile work environment. However, France considers the request for sexual favors for a job or promotion to be a criminal matter with the possibility of prison. In Thailand, quid pro quo is not recognized as sexual harassment because getting a work benefit such as promotion for having sexual relations is considered mutually beneficial. Sexual harassment is mainly defined as some type of sexual assault of a serious nature under criminal law.[85]

MyManagementLab

Go to **mymanagementlab.com** to complete the problems marked with this icon ⭐.

Summary

1. *Discuss lesbian, gay, bisexual, and transgender employees as a protected class.* There appears to be an increased focus in the political arena and workforce concerning lesbian, gay, bisexual, and transgender (LGBT) employees.

2. *Describe diversity and diversity management and explain the various components of the diverse workforce.*
   Diversity refers to any perceived difference among people: age, race, religion, functional specialty, profession, sexual orientation, geographic origin, lifestyle, tenure with the organization, or position, and any other perceived difference.

   Diversity management is ensuring that factors are in place to provide for and encourage the continued development of a diverse workforce by melding these actual and perceived differences among workers to achieve maximum productivity.

   The workforce may include single parents and working mothers, women in business, mothers returning to the workforce, dual-career families, workers of color, older workers, people with disabilities, immigrants, foreign workers, young persons (some with limited education or skills), and multigenerational workers.

3. *Identify the major laws affecting equal employment opportunity.* Major laws include the Civil Rights Act of 1866; Equal Pay Act of 1963, amended in 1972; Lilly Ledbetter Fair Pay Act of 2009; Title VII of the Civil Rights Act of 1964, amended in 1972; Pregnancy Discrimination Act of 1978; Civil Rights Act of 1991; Age Discrimination in Employment Act of 1967, amended in 1978 and 1986; Rehabilitation Act of 1973; Americans with Disabilities Act of 1990; Americans with Disabilities Act Amendments Act (ADAAA) of 2008; Immigration Reform and Control Act (IRCA) of 1986; Illegal Immigration Reform and Immigrant Responsibility Act of 1996; the Uniformed Services Employment and Reemployment Rights Act of 1994; and the Vietnam Era Veterans' Readjustment Assistance Act of 1974, as amended.

4. *Describe the recent trend against employee retaliation.* In recent years, there has been a significant increase in the number of employee retaliation charges made against employers. Some HR professionals have predicted that the U.S. Supreme Court's 2006 decision in *Burlington Northern & Santa Fe Railway Co. v White* would open the floodgates for retaliation charges and lawsuits. That case lowered the standard of proof for retaliation claims, making it much easier for employees to prove.

5. *Identify some of the major Supreme Court decisions that have had an impact on equal employment opportunity*

   and affirmative action. Major decisions include *Griggs v Duke Power Company, Albemarle Paper Company v Moody, Phillips v Martin Marietta Corporation, Dothard v Rawlingson, American Tobacco Company v Patterson, O'Connor v Consolidated Coin Caterers Corp., University of California Regents v Bakke, Grutter v Bollinger, Gratz v Bollinger,* and *Ricci v DeStefano.*

6. *Describe the Equal Employment Opportunity Commission and explain the purpose of the Uniform Guidelines on Employee Selection Procedures.* The Civil Rights Act of 1964 also created the Equal Employment Opportunity Commission (EEOC) and assigned enforcement of Title VII to this agency. Consisting of five members appointed by the president, the EEOC is empowered to investigate, conciliate, and litigate charges of discrimination arising under provisions of Title VII. In addition, the commission has the responsibility of issuing procedural regulations and interpretations of Title VII and the other statutes it enforces. The most significant regulation issued by EEOC is the *Uniform Guidelines on Employee Selection Procedures.*

   The *Uniform Guidelines* adopted a single set of principles that were designed to assist employers, labor organizations, employment agencies, and licensing and certification boards to comply with requirements of federal law prohibiting employment practices that discriminated on the basis of race, color, religion, sex, and national origin.

7. *Describe disparate treatment and adverse impact and explain the Uniform Guidelines related to sexual harassment, national origin, religion, and caregiver (family responsibility) discrimination.* With *disparate treatment,* an employer treats some people less favorably than others because of race, religion, sex, national origin, or age.

   Adverse impact occurs if women and minorities are not hired at the rate of at least 80 percent of the best-achieving group.

   Employers have an affirmative duty to maintain a workplace free from sexual harassment. Discrimination on the basis of national origin is the denial of equal employment opportunity because of an individual's ancestors or place of birth or because an individual has the physical, cultural, or linguistic characteristics of a national origin group. Employers have an obligation to accommodate religious practices unless they can demonstrate a resulting hardship. Caregiver (family responsibility) discrimination is discrimination against employees based on their obligations to care for family members.

8. *Explain affirmative action as required by presidential Executive Orders 11246 and 11375 and describe affirmative*

action programs. Affirmative action, stipulated by EO 11246, requires covered employers to take positive steps to ensure that employment of applicants and treatment of employees during employment is without regard to race, creed, color, or national origin. The order prohibited discrimination in employment because of race, creed, color, or national origin. EO 11375 changed the word "creed" to "religion" and added sex discrimination to the other prohibited items.

An *affirmative action program* is an approach that an organization with government contracts develops to demonstrate that women or minorities are employed in proportion to their representation in the firm's relevant labor market.

9. *Describe sexual harassment in the global environment.* Sexual harassment was discussed in this chapter only as it pertained to the United States, but it is also a global problem. When individuals from two different cultures interact, there is a potential for sexual harassment problems. Some behaviors that violate U.S. cultural norms may not be perceived as a problem in another culture.

Key Terms

diversity   42
diversity management   42
dual-career family   43
baby boomers   46
Generation X   46
Generation Y   46

Generation Z or Digital Natives   46
comparable worth   49
glass ceiling   52
Uniform Guidelines   61
disparate treatment   62
adverse impact   62

caregiver (family responsibility)
   discrimination   66
executive order (EO)   67
affirmative action   67
affirmative action program
   (AAP)   68

Exercises

1. Many laws, court decisions, and executive orders have had a profound effect on the composition of the workforce. It is highly likely that our economy would have ground to a halt without these additional workers. How might the demographic composition of your classroom be different if it was not for these laws, court decisions, and executive orders?

2. During 2013, 400 people were hired for a particular job. Of the total, 300 were white and 100 were black. There were 1,200 qualified applicants for these jobs, of whom 800 were white and 400 were black. Does adverse impact exist? If adverse impact exists, what does this mean?

3. You are a human resource manager with a large manufacturing firm that does a large portion of its business with the federal government with sales over $1,000,000.

Your application form asks the following questions: Marital Status, Height and Weight, Age, Sex, Occupation of Spouse, Education, Criminal Convictions, Plans to Have Children (if you are female), Handicaps, and Work Experience. Are any of these factors employment standards to avoid? Why? Discuss as appropriate.

4. You are the HR manager for a company that has recently received a federal contract in excess of $1 million. In conducting utilization analysis on your present workforce of operators you find that 10 percent of your workforce is black while 30 percent of the workforce in the relevant labor market is black. According to affirmative action guidelines, what must be done to correct this difference?

Questions for Review

1. What might be the reasons for companies to have policies in support of LGBT employees?
2. Define *diversity* and *diversity management*.
3. What are the components that combine to make up the present diverse workforce? Briefly describe each.
4. Briefly describe the following laws:
   (a) Civil Rights Act of 1866
   (b) Equal Pay Act of 1963
   (c) Lilly Ledbetter Fair Pay Act of 2009
   (d) Title VII of the Civil Rights Act of 1964, as amended in 1972
   (e) Pregnancy Discrimination Act of 1978
   (f) Civil Rights Act of 1991
   (g) Age Discrimination in Employment Act of 1967, as amended in 1978 and 1986
   (h) Rehabilitation Act of 1973

   (i) Americans with Disabilities Act of 1990
   (j) Americans with Disabilities Act Amendments Act (ADAAA) of 2008
   (k) Immigration Reform and Control Act (IRCA) of 1986
   (l) Illegal Immigration Reform and Immigrant Responsibility Act of 1996
   (m) Uniformed Services Employment and Reemployment Rights Act of 1994
   (n) Vietnam Era Veterans' Readjustment Assistance Act of 1974

5. Why have employee retaliation charges experienced a dramatic increase?

6. What are the significant U.S. Supreme Court decisions that have had an impact on equal employment opportunity? On affirmative action?

7. What are the steps that the EEOC uses once a charge is filed?
8. What is the purpose of the *Uniform Guidelines on Employee Selection Procedures?*
9. What is the difference between disparate treatment and adverse impact?
10. How does the EEOC define sexual harassment?
11. What has been the impact of the Supreme Court decisions of *Meritor Savings Bank v Vinson* and *Harris v Forklift Systems, Inc.?*
12. How does the EEOC interpret the national origin guidelines?
13. What are some guidelines to follow with regard to religion-related discrimination?
14. What is meant by the term *caregiver discrimination?*
15. What is a presidential executive order? Describe the major provisions of EO 11246, as amended by EO 11375.
16. What is the purpose of the Office of Federal Contract Compliance Programs?
17. What is an affirmative action program?
18. How do countries other than the United States view sexual harassment?

INCIDENT 1   I Feel Great

Les Partain, manager of the training and development department for Gazelle Corporation, was 64 years old and had been with the firm for over 30 years. For the past 12 years he had served as Gazelle's training and development manager and felt that he had been doing a good job. This belief was supported by the fact that during the past five years he had received excellent performance reports from his boss, LaConya Caesar, HR director.

Six months before Les's birthday, he and LaConya were enjoying a cup of coffee together. "Les," said LaConya, "I know that you're pleased with the progress our T&D section has made under your leadership. We're really going to miss you when you retire this year. You'll certainly live the good life because you'll receive the maximum retirement benefits. If I can be of any assistance to you in developing the paperwork for your retirement, please let me know."

"Gee, LaConya," said Les. "I really appreciate the good words, but I've never felt better in my life, and although our retirement plan is excellent, I figure that I have at least five more good years. There are many other things I would like to do for the department before I

retire. I have some excellent employees, and we can get many things done within the next five years."

After finishing their coffee, both returned to their work. As LaConya left, she was thinking, "My gosh, I had no idea that character intended to hang on. The only reason I gave him those good performance appraisals was to make him feel better before he retired. He was actually only an average worker and I was anxious to move a more aggressive person into that key job. We stand to lose several good people in that department if Les doesn't leave. From what they tell me, he's not doing too much of a job."

Questions

1. From a legal viewpoint, what do you believe LaConya can do regarding this situation? Discuss.
2. What actions should LaConya have taken in the past to avoid her current predicament?
3. What might occur if LaConya begins to evaluate Les in the manner she should likely have been doing all along?

INCIDENT 2   So, What's Affirmative Action?

Supreme Construction Company began as a small commercial builder located in Baytown, Texas. Until the early 2000s, Alex Boyd, Supreme's founder, concentrated his efforts on small, freestanding shops and offices. Up to that time, Alex had never employed more than 15 people.

In 2008, Alex's son Michael graduated from college with a degree in construction management and immediately joined the company full-time. Michael had worked on a variety of Supreme jobs while in school, and Alex felt his son was really cut out for the construction business. Michael was given increasing responsibility, and the company continued its success, although with a few more projects and a few more employees than before. In 2012, Michael approached his father with a proposition: "Let's get into some of the bigger projects now. We have the capital to expand and I really believe we can do it." Alex approved, and Supreme began doing small shopping centers and multistory office buildings in addition to work in its traditional area of specialization. Soon, the number of employees had grown to 75.

In 2013, the National Aeronautics and Space Administration (NASA) released construction specifications for two aircraft hangars

to be built southeast of Houston. Although Supreme had never done any construction work for the government, Michael and Alex considered the job within the company's capabilities. Michael worked up the $1,982,000 bid and submitted it to the NASA procurement office.

Several weeks later the bids were opened. Supreme had the low bid. However, the acceptance letter was contingent on submission of a satisfactory affirmative action program.

Questions

1. Explain why Supreme must submit an affirmative action program.
2. Generally, what should the program be designed to accomplish?
3. In conducting a utilization analysis, Michael discovers that although 30 percent of the general population of construction workers is black, only 10 percent of Supreme's employees are black. According to affirmative action, what is Supreme Construction required to do?

MyManagementLab

Go to **mymanagementlab.com** for Auto-graded writing questions as well as the following Assisted-graded writing questions:

3-1. What is the purpose of the Equal Employment Opportunity Commission?

3-2. How might HR law have a greater impact on small businesses?

3-3. Mymanagementlab Only – comprehensive writing assignment for this chapter.

Notes

1. "We Must Stand Up for the Rights of Gays and Lesbians Everywhere," Agency Group 09 *FDCH Regulatory Intelligence Database* (September 22, 2011).
2. Todd A. Solomon, Joseph S. Adams, and Brett R. Johnson, "How Conflicting Same-Sex Union Laws Are Impacting Employee Benefits," *Benefits Magazine* 49 (January 2012): 14–21.
3. James Walsh, "Gay Groups Refocus on Workplace," *Workforce Management* 90 (March 2011): 3–4.
4. "State Laws, Ruling on Bias Signal Employers to Address Issues," *HR Focus* 89 (February 2012): 12–14.
5. "Houston Issues Comprehensive LGBT Discrimination Order," *HR Specialist: Texas Employment Law* 5 (May 2010): 5.
6. Nadine Vogel, "Disability & LGBT—Similarities and Difference and How to Support Them in the Workplace," *Profiles in Diversity Journal* 13 (March/April 2011): 124.
7. "Of Companies and Closets," *Economist* 402 (February 11, 2012): 70.
8. Sylvia Ann Hewlett and Karen Sumberg, "For LGBT Workers, Being 'Out' Brings Advantages," *Harvard Business Review* 89 (July/August 2011): 28.
9. Marie Y. Philippe, "Corporate Diversity Training: Is Yours Meeting 21st Century Needs?" *Profiles in Diversity Journal* 12 (January/February 2010): 60.
10. Andrew L. Molinsky, Thomas H. Davenport, Bala Iyer, and Cathy Davidson, "3 Skills Every 21-Century Manager Needs," *Harvard Business Review* 90 (January/February 2012): 139–143.
11. Mike Brennan, "The Measuring Stick," *Chief Learning Officer* 10 (August 2011): 22–25.
12. "R. Roosevelt Thomas," *T+D* (May 2011): 66–67.
13. Pamela Arnold, "The Role of Diversity Management in the Global Talent Retention Race," *Profiles in Diversity Journal* 13 (May/June 2011): 16.
14. Fay Hansen, "Diversity of a Different Color," *Workforce Management* 89 (June 2010): 22–26.
15. Wendy S. Becker, "Are You Leading a Socially Responsible and Sustainable Human Resource Function?" *People & Strategy* 34 (2011): 18–23.
16. Lisa Miller, "Mommy Is Busy Right Now," *Newsweek* 157 (February 14, 2011): 9.
17. Alexis Jeffries, "Women-Owned Businesses on the Rise," *Black Enterprise* 41 (June 2011): 44.
18. Fay Hansen, "Women's Pay Gap Persists," *Workforce Management* 90 (June 2011): 30–31.
19. Saundra Stroope and Bonnie Hagemann, "Women, Water, + Leadership: Are We Making Progress?" *T+D* 65 (March 2011): 50–53.
20. Kelley M. Butler, "Today's Working Women Seek Mentors, Motherhood Transition," *Employee Benefit News* 20 (April 2006): 17–19.
21. Elizabeth Cabrera, "Fixing the Leaky Pipeline: Five Ways to Retain Female Talent," *People & Strategy* 32 (2009): 40–45.
22. Lorraine Bello and Galen Tinder, "Dual Career Implications on Workforce Mobility: The Evolution of the Relocating Spouse/Partner," *Benefits & Compensation Digest* 46 (September 2009): 36–39.
23. Ella Bell, "The Bicultural Life Experience of Career Oriented Black Women," *Journal of Organizational Behavior* 11 (November 1990): 459–478.
24. Don Meinert, "Census Data Reflect Older, More Diverse U.S. Workforce," *HR Magazine* 56 (July 2011): 18–19.
25. Robert R. Trumble and Jared Williams, "Implications of Baby Boomers' Retirement for Human Resources," *Benefits Magazine* 49 (January 2012): 44.
26. Colleen Leahey, "What—Me Retire?" *Fortune* 165 (January 16, 2012): 56.
27. Joseph Weber, "Employers Avoid Axing Oldies but Goodies," *Business Week Online* (January 22, 2009).
28. Susan J. Wells, "Counting on Workers with Disabilities," *HR Magazine* 53 (April 2008): 45–49.
29. Jennifer Schramm, "Planning for Population Shifts," *HR Magazine* 56 (February 2011): 80.
30. Stephen Gandel, "The Teen Job Chop," *Time* 175 (January 18, 2010): 38–43.
31. Beverly Kaye, "Four Generations," *Leadership Excellence* 29 (January 2012): 20.
32. Amy Bladen Shatto, "In Practice Two Sides of the Retention Dilemma," *Chief Learning Officer* 10 (August 2011): 34.
33. "Turnover, Globalization Among Emerging Challenges Facing HR," *HR Focus* 88 (September 2011): 10–11.
34. Adrienne Fox, "Talkin' Bout My Generation," *HR Magazine* 56 (May 2011): 26–27.
35. Megnan Casserly, "Millennials and Baby Boomers: At Odds or Peas in a Pod?" *Forbes.com* (January 19, 2012): 30.
36. "How 'Recession-Proof' Will Millennial Workers Be?" *HR Focus* 86 (March 2009): 6–7.
37. Sharon Williams, "Welcome to Generation Z," *B&T Magazine* 60 (December 10, 2010): 12.
38. Eric Lauzon, "Paradox: The Anti-social Generation," *Enterprise Innovation* 7 (February/March 2011): 44.
39. Jerry Selitto, "Anyone Up for Some Time Travel?" *Mortgage Banking* 71 (March 2011): 22–23.
40. "The Multigenerational Workforce: Opportunity for Competitive Success," *HR Magazine* 54 (March 2009): Special section 1–9.
41. "Retaliation Claims OK under Civil Rights Act," *HR Focus* 85 (July 2008): 2.
42. Dick Weaver, "How Is Lilly Ledbetter Helping You Sell EPLI," *National Underwriter* / P&C 115 (March 28, 2011): 26.

43. "Britthaven Nursing Home Settles Pregnancy Discrimination Claim," *HR Specialist: North Carolina Employment Law* 3 (June 2009): 5.

44. Tyler M. Paetkau, "When Does a Foreign Law Compel a U.S. Employer to Discriminate Against U.S. Expatriates?" A Modest Proposal for Reform," *Labor Law Journal* 60 (Summer 2009): 92–103.

45. Eileen McKeown, "Top Suite in Corporate America Still Eludes Women," *T+D* 65 (January 2011): 18.

46. "When Hiring, Never Mention Age—to Anyone," *HR Specialist: North Carolina Employment Law* 5 (February 2011): 1–2.

47. "EEOC's Views on Accommodation under Amended ADA Discussed," *HR Focus* 89 (January 2012): 3–6.

48. Stephenie Overman, "Avoiding Immigration Audits," *HR Magazine* 56 (January 2011): 57–59.

49. "Samuel Greencard, "When Johnny or Janey Comes Marching Home," *Workforce Management* 90 (June 2011): 3–4.

50. "As Economy Recovers, HR Will Have More Opportunities to Show Value," *HR Focus* 89 (February 2012): 1–6.

51. http://www.dol.gov/ofccp/regs/compliance/ca_vevraa.htm

52. "OFCCP Issues Proposed Revision of Veterans' Affirmative Action Rules," *HR Focus* 88 (June 2011): 12.

53. "Retaliation Charges Were Most Common in Record-Breaking FY 2011," *HR Focus* 89 (March 2012): 8–9.

54. David P. Twomey, "Employee Retaliation Claims under the Supreme Court's Burlington, Crawford and Thompson Decisions: Important Implications for Employers," *Labor Law Journal* 62 (Summer 2011): 57–66.

55. Barnett Brooks, Gail Farb, and Mandi Ballard, "The Future of Retaliation Claims," *HR Magazine* 56 (January 2011): 69–71.

56. Joanne Deschenaux, "Title VII Protects Third Parties from Retaliation," *HR Magazine* 56 (March 2011): 16.

57. Judy Greenwald, "High Court Broadens Grounds for Retaliation Claims," *Business Insurance* 45 (January 31, 2011): 1–20.

58. Judy Greenwald, "Court Rulings Protect Employees from Retaliation," *Business Insurance* 45 (September 19, 2011): 19.

59. "Measures Enacted in 2010 on Discrimination, Privacy, Other Issues," *HR Focus* 88 (March 2011): 13–15.

60. Stephen C. Muffler, Frank J. Cavico, and Bahaudin G. Mujtaba, "Diversity, Disparate Impact, and Ethics in Business: Implications of the New Haven Firefighters' Case and the Supreme Court's Ricci v DeStefano Decision," *SAM Advanced Management Journal* 75 (Summer 2010): 11–20.

61. "Employees Still Filing Job-discrimination Complaints in Near-record Numbers," *HR Specialist* 8 (February 2010): 8.

62. "Harassment: How to Stop It Before—and After—It Starts," *HR Specialist: Florida Employment Law* 7 (January 2012): 4.

63. http://www1.eeoc.gov/eeoc/newsroom/release/12-14-11b.cfm

64. "Preventing Workplace Sexual Harassment Should Be HR Priority, Attorney Tells Webinar," *HR Focus* 89 (March 2012): 16.

65. David B. Ritter and Mari Kaluza, "Lesson from Walmart: How to Cut Risk when a Co-worker Harasses," *HR Specialist: Illinois Employment Law* 5 (May 2011): 6.

66. "Delete Your Liability: Copy Xerox Response to Harassment Complaint," *HR Specialist: Employment Law* 40 (May 2011): 3.

67. "Duane Reade Settles Sex Harassment Lawsuit," *HR Specialist: New York Employment Law* 4 (August 2009): 5.

68. "Price of Supervisor Pleasuring Himself Over an Employee: $95 Million," *Legal Alert for Supervisors* 6 (June 24, 2011): 4.

69. "Men Now Filing One-sixth of All Sexual Harassment Claims," *HR Specialist: North Carolina Employment Law* 4 (April 2010): 1.

70. Maria Greco Danaher, "Men Entitled to Title VII Protection," *HR Magazine* 55 (December 2010): 93.

71. Allen Smith, "EEOC Settlement Reflects Challenges of English-Only Policies," *HR Magazine* 54 (June 2009): 26.

72. Tanya Marcum and Sandra J. Perry, "Dressed for Success: Can a Claim of Religious Discrimination Be Successful?" *Labor Law Journal* 61 (Winter 2010): 184–191.

73. Abigail Crouse, "Be Careful! Caregiver Discrimination Claims Are on the Rise," *HR Specialist: Minnesota Employment Law* 3 (April 2010): 6.

74. Gerald E. Calvasina, Richard V. Calvasina, and Eugene J. Calvasina, "Caregiver Responsibility Discrimination and the Equal Employment Opportunity Commission (EEOC) Guidelines: Policy Issues for Employers," *Journal of Legal, Ethical & Regulatory Issues* 13 (June 2010): 1–10.

75. Rita Zeidner, "Handle with Care," *HR Magazine* 54 (November 2009): 22–28.

76. Todd H. Girshon, "Jury or Nonjury Trials," *HR Magazine* 57 (February 2012): 79–85.

77. Alissa A. Horvitz and Lance E. Gibbons, "Federal Contractors Get New Scrutiny," *HR Magazine* 56 (November 2011): 71–82.

78. "New Directive Calls for More Full Compliance Evaluations," *HR Focus* 88 (April 2011): 4–5.

79. Nadine Vogel, "The OFCCP Ramps Up Enforcement," *Profiles in Diversity Journal* 13 (January/February 2011): 18.

80. Cindy Waxer, "Life's a Balancing Act for Cirque du Soleil's Human Resources Troupe," *Workforce Management* 84 (January 2005): 52–53.

81. Susan R. Heyman, "Working Women around the World Lack Basic Workplace Protections, United Nations Reports," *SHRM Online* (July 26, 2011).

82. "Global Workplace Violence: India Worst, Sweden Best," *Security Director's Report* 11 (January 2011): 8.

83. Naween Mangi, "Now on the Job in Pakistan: Women," *Bloomberg Businessweek* (September 12, 2011): 57–58.

84. Gerald L. Maatmann Jr., "Harassment, Discrimination Laws Go Global," *National Underwriter* 104 (September 11, 2000): 34–35.

85. Tom Tudor, "Global Issues of Sexual Harassment in the Workplace," *Franklin Business & Law Journal* (2010): 51–57.

Part Three
Staffing

4

Job Analysis, Strategic Planning, and Human Resource Planning

HRM in Action

Disaster Planning: From Natural Calamities to Human-made Crises

OBJECTIVE 4.1

Describe the importance of disaster planning, explain why job analysis is a basic human resource tool, and give the reasons for conducting job analysis.

In 2011, a total of 12 natural calamities killed 646 people and caused about $52 billion in damage.[1] Hopefully companies affected by these disasters had an effective disaster plan. A firm's disaster plans should focus on possible catastrophes that range from natural calamities such as hurricanes, earthquakes, and floods to smaller events such as a building fire, water leak, or computer crash. Even the recent financial crash would be a factor to consider in disaster planning.[2] Certainly the 2010 oil spill disaster on the Gulf Coast caused many companies along the coast to review and update their disaster plan. In fact, the environmental disaster in the Gulf of Mexico has brought into focus the danger of a disaster plan built on wishful thinking. BP's plan said it would be able to contain any leak. Conservative estimates suggest the company's actual recovery rate was less than three percent.[3]

When Hurricane Rita struck Lake Charles, Louisiana, the town in southwest Louisiana truly looked like a war zone. Businesses were not only damaged by wind but some also faced flood damage and destruction of their products. For a long time there was no electricity, mail service, or newspaper delivery. Employees were scattered across the country. Business owners often had to also contend with the destruction of their own homes. Where a dense forest once stood, one could now see clearly because trees lay broken and twisted on the ground or on top of homes. Houses that had withstood the wind often had the roof covered with a blue tarp, compliments of FEMA. Looking at the massive destruction, one might wonder if businesses in the area could ever recover. It quickly became evident that quite a few organizations had poorly designed disaster plans, or none at all. Many wished that they had devoted more time to disaster planning.

CHAPTER OBJECTIVES After completing this chapter, students should be able to:

1. Describe the importance of disaster planning, explain why job analysis is a basic human resource tool, and give the reasons for conducting job analysis.

2. Describe the types of information required for job analysis and describe the various job analysis methods.

3. Identify who conducts job analysis and describe the components of a job description.

4. Explain Standard Occupational Classification (SOC), O*NET, job analysis for team members, and describe how job analysis helps satisfy various legal requirements.

5. Describe the need for the human resource manager to be a strategic partner, explain the strategic planning process, and describe the human resource planning process.

6. Describe forecasting human resource requirements and availability and how databases can assist in matching internal employees to positions.

7. Identify what a firm can do when either a shortage or a surplus of workers exists and explain strategic succession planning in today's environment.

8. Describe manager and employee self-service and explain some job design concepts.

9. Describe the importance of global talent management.

Some businesses, however, had excellent disaster plans. Although the petroleum refineries in the area were hit hard, managers and workers knew precisely what their roles were. The plan called for a few critical workers to remain in safe havens within the refineries to be able to hasten the recovery after the hurricane passed. These individuals were able to tell returning individuals the extent of the damage and what resources were needed to begin repairs. Many predicted recovery would take years; but because of the detailed disaster planning, these companies were up and running in record time.

Despite the type of disaster, the result is usually the same. Business has been interrupted for an undetermined amount of time, there has been a loss of contact with consumers and clients, and the firm's financial situation has been harmed. When a disaster occurs, there are always significant human resource issues to address.[4] Management should not be surprised if employees choose to take care of their families first as opposed to concerning themselves with the company survival.[5]

Many consider disaster planning as the ability to handle big events such as the Gulf oil release or the tsunami that hit Japan. Bob Boyd, CEO of Agility Recovery Solutions, a disaster recovery provider, said, "People think about the big disasters. But well over 70 percent of the recoveries we make every year are isolated to just one business."[6] For example, what would happen if a fire destroyed critical irreplaceable documents? Another reason for having a well-thought-out disaster plan is because customers want assurance that the business can continue operation after a disaster. If a company cannot recover rapidly from a disaster, this also affects its customers. Technology such as cloud has been a boom in rapid recovery of computer-generated data. Disaster recovery using the cloud is much more cost effective and simpler than traditional disaster recovery solutions.[7]

Job Analysis: A Basic Human Resource Management Tool

Job analysis is the systematic process of determining the skills, duties, and knowledge required for performing jobs in an organization.

With job analysis, the tasks needed to perform the job are identified. Traditionally, it is an essential and pervasive human resource technique and the starting point for other human resource activities.[8] In today's rapidly changing work environment, the need for a sound job analysis system is critical. New jobs are being created, and old jobs are being redesigned or eliminated. A job analysis that was conducted only a few years ago may now be obsolete and must be redone. Some have even suggested that changes are occurring too fast to maintain an effective job analysis system.

A **job** consists of a group of tasks that must be performed for an organization to achieve its goals. A job may require the services of one person, such as that of the president, or the services of 75, as might be the case with machine operators in a large manufacturing firm. A **position** is the collection of tasks and responsibilities performed by *one* person; there is a position for every individual in an organization.

In a work group consisting of a supervisor, two senior analysts, and four analysts, there are three jobs and seven positions. A small company might have 25 jobs for its 75 employees, whereas in a large company 2,000 jobs may exist for 50,000 employees. In some firms, as few as 10 jobs may make up 90 percent of the workforce.

The purpose of job analysis is to obtain answers to six important questions:

1. What physical and mental tasks does the worker accomplish?
2. When is the job to be completed?
3. Where is the job to be accomplished?
4. How does the worker do the job?
5. Why is the job done?
6. What qualifications are needed to perform the job?

Job analysis provides a summary of a job's duties and responsibilities, its relationship to other jobs, the knowledge and skills required, and working conditions under which it is performed. Job facts are gathered, analyzed, and recorded, as the job exists, not as the job should exist.[9] Determining how the job should exist is most often assigned to industrial engineers, methods analysts, or others. Job analysis is conducted after the job has been designed, the worker has been trained, and the job is being performed.

Job analysis is performed on three occasions: (1) when the organization is founded and a job analysis program is initiated for the first time; (2) when new jobs are created; and (3) when jobs are changed significantly as a result of new technologies, methods, procedures, or systems. Jobs also change when there is increased emphasis on teamwork in organizations, empowerment of employees, or other managerial interventions such as quality management systems. Job analysis is most often performed because of changes in the nature of jobs. From job analysis information, both job descriptions and job specifications can be prepared.

The **job description** is a document that provides information regarding the essential tasks, duties, and responsibilities of the job. The minimum acceptable qualifications a person should possess in order to perform a particular job are contained in the **job specification**.[10] Both types of documents will be discussed in greater detail later in this chapter.

Reasons for Conducting Job Analysis

As Figure 4-1 shows, data derived from job analysis in the form of the job description/specification can have an impact on virtually every aspect of human resource management.[11] In practice, both the job description and job specification are combined into one document with the job specification presented after the job description.

Staffing

All areas of staffing would be haphazard if the organization did not know the qualifications needed to perform the various jobs. A major use of job analysis data is found in human resource planning (discussed later in this chapter). Merely knowing that the firm will need 1,000 new

---

job analysis
Systematic process of determining the skills, duties, and knowledge required for performing jobs in an organization.

job
Group of tasks that must be performed for an organization to achieve its goals.

position
Collection of tasks and responsibilities performed by one person.

job description
Document that provides information regarding the essential tasks, duties, and responsibilities of a job.

job specification
A document that outlines the minimum acceptable qualifications a person should possess to perform a particular job.

FIGURE 4-1

Job Analysis: A Basic Human Resource Management Tool

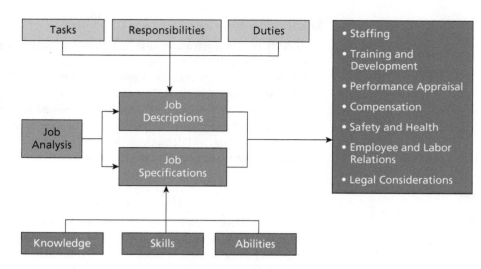

employees to produce goods or services to satisfy sales demand is insufficient. Each job requires different knowledge, skills, and ability levels. Obviously, effective human resource planning must take these job requirements into consideration. Also, lacking up-to-date job descriptions and specifications, a firm would have to recruit and select employees for jobs without having clear guidelines, a practice that could have disastrous consequences.[12]

Training and Development

Job description information often proves beneficial in identifying training and development needs. If it suggests that the job requires a particular knowledge, skill, or ability, and the person filling the position does not possess all the qualifications required, training and/or development are probably in order. Training should be directed at assisting workers in performing duties specified in their present job descriptions or at developing skills for broader responsibilities.

Performance Appraisal

Most workers want to know what they are supposed to accomplish and good job descriptions provide that. Then, employees should be evaluated in terms of how well they accomplish the duties specified in their job descriptions and any other specific goals that may have been established. A manager who evaluates an employee on factors not clearly predetermined is left open to allegations of discrimination.

Compensation

In the area of compensation, it is helpful to know the relative value of a particular job to the company before a dollar value is placed on it. Jobs that require greater knowledge, skills, and abilities should be worth more to the firm. For example, the relative value of a job calling for a master's degree normally would be higher than that of a job that requires a high school diploma. This might not be the case if the market value of the job requiring only a high school diploma was higher, however. Such a situation occurred in a major West Coast city a number of years ago. It came to light that city sanitation engineers (garbage collectors) were paid more than better-educated public schoolteachers.

Safety and Health

Information derived from job analysis is also valuable in identifying safety and health considerations. For example, employers are required to inform workers when a job is hazardous. The job description/specification should reflect this condition. In addition, in certain hazardous jobs, workers may need specific information about the hazards in order to perform their jobs safely.

Employee and Labor Relations

Job analysis information is also important in employee and labor relations. When employees are considered for promotion, transfer, or demotion, the job description provides a standard for evaluation and comparison of talent.[13] Information obtained through job analysis can often lead to more objective human resource decisions.

Legal Considerations

A properly prepared job analysis is particularly important for supporting the legality of employment practices. Prior to the equal employment opportunity movement in the early 1960s and 1970s, few firms had effective job analysis systems.[14] But, the need to validate basic job requirements hastened the growth in the use of job analysis to prepare job descriptions/specifications. The importance of job analysis is well documented in the *Uniform Guidelines on Employee Selection Procedures*.[15] Job analysis data are needed to defend decisions involving termination, promotion, transfers, and demotions. Job analysis provides the basis for tying the HR functions together and the foundation for developing a sound human resource program.

Types of Job Analysis Information

Considerable information is needed for the successful accomplishment of job analysis. The job analyst identifies the job's actual duties and responsibilities and gathers the other types of data such as work activities; worker-oriented activities; machines, tools, equipment, and work aids used; and personal requirements. This information is used to help determine the job skills needed. In addition, the job analyst looks at job-related tangibles and intangibles, such as the knowledge needed, the materials processed, and the goods made or services performed. Essential functions of the job are determined in this process.

Some job analysis systems identify job standards. Work measurement studies may be needed to determine how long it takes to perform a task. With regard to job content, the analyst studies the work schedule, financial and nonfinancial incentives, and physical working conditions. Specific education, training, and work experience pertinent to the job are identified. Because many jobs are often performed in conjunction with others, organizational and social contexts are also noted. Subjective skills required, such as strong interpersonal skills, should be identified if the job requires the jobholder to be personable.

Job Analysis Methods

Job analysis has traditionally been conducted in a number of different ways because organizational needs and resources for conducting job analysis differ. Selection of a specific method should be based on the purposes for which the information is to be used (job evaluation, pay increases, development, and so on) and the approach that is most feasible for a particular organization. The historically most common methods of job analysis are discussed in the following sections.

Questionnaires

Questionnaires are typically quick and economical to use. The job analyst may administer a structured questionnaire to employees, who identify the tasks they perform. However, in some cases, employees may lack verbal skills, a condition that makes this method less useful. Also, some employees may tend to exaggerate the significance of their tasks, suggesting more responsibility than actually exists.

Observation

When using the observation method, the job analyst watches the worker perform job tasks and records his or her observations. This method is used primarily to gather information on jobs emphasizing manual skills, such as those of a machine operator. It can also help the analyst identify interrelationships between physical and mental tasks. Observation alone is usually an insufficient means of conducting job analysis, however, particularly when mental skills are dominant in a job. Observing a financial analyst at work would not reveal much about the requirements of the job.

Interviews

An understanding of the job may also be gained through interviewing both the employee and the supervisor. Usually, the analyst interviews the employee first, helping him or her describe the duties performed. Then, the analyst normally contacts the supervisor for additional information, to check the accuracy of the information obtained from the employee, and to clarify certain points.

Employee Recording

In some instances, job analysis information is gathered by having employees describe their daily work activities in a diary or log. With this method, the problem of employees exaggerating job importance may have to be overcome. Even so, valuable understanding of highly specialized jobs, such as, recreational therapist, may be obtained in this way.

Combination of Methods

Usually an analyst does not use one job analysis method exclusively. A combination of methods is often more appropriate. In analyzing clerical and administrative jobs, the analyst might use questionnaires supported by interviews and limited observation. In studying production jobs, interviews supplemented by extensive work observations may provide the necessary data. Basically, the analyst should use the combination of techniques needed for accurate job descriptions/specifications.

Over the years, attempts have been made to provide more systematic methods of conducting job analysis. Several of these approaches are discussed in Table 4-1.

TABLE 4-1

Other Methods Available for Conducting Job Analysis

Department of Labor Job Analysis Schedule

The U.S. Department of Labor established a method of systematically studying jobs and occupations called the job analysis schedule (JAS). When the JAS method is used, a trained analyst gathers information. A major component of the JAS is the Work Performed Ratings section. Here, what workers do in performing a job with regard to data (D), people (P), and things (T) is evaluated. Each is viewed as a hierarchy of functions, with the items higher in the category being more difficult. The codes in the worker functions section represent the highest level of involvement in each of the three categories.

The JAS component "Worker Traits Ratings" relates primarily to job requirement data. The topics general education designation (GED), specific vocational preparation (SVP), aptitudes, temperaments, interests, physical demands, and environmental conditions are included. The Description of Tasks section provides a specific description of the work performed. Both routine tasks and occasionally performed tasks are included.

Functional Job Analysis

Functional job analysis (FJA) is a comprehensive job analysis approach that concentrates on the interactions among the work, the worker, and the organization. This approach is a modification of the job analysis schedule. It assesses specific job outputs and identifies job tasks in terms of task statements.

Position Analysis Questionnaire

The position analysis questionnaire (PAQ) is a structured job analysis questionnaire that uses a checklist approach to identify job elements. It focuses on general worker behaviors instead of tasks. Some 194 job descriptors relate to job-oriented elements. Advocates of the PAQ believe that its ability to identify job elements, behaviors required of job incumbents, and other job characteristics makes this procedure applicable to the analysis of virtually any type of job. Each job descriptor is evaluated on a specified scale such as extent of use, amount of time, importance of job, possibility of occurrence, and applicability.

Each job being studied is scored relative to the 32 job dimensions. The score derived represents a profile of the job; this can be compared with standard profiles to group jobs into known job families, that is, job of a similar nature. In essence, the PAQ identifies significant job behaviors and classifies jobs. Using the PAQ, job descriptions can be based on the relative importance and emphasis placed on various job elements. The PAQ has been called one of the most useful job analysis methods.

Management Position Description Questionnaire

The management position description questionnaire (MPDQ) is a method of job analysis designed for management positions; it uses a checklist to analyze jobs. The MPDQ has been used to determine the training needs of individuals who are slated to move into managerial positions. It has also been used to evaluate and set compensation rates for managerial jobs and to assign the jobs to job families.

Guidelines-Oriented Job Analysis

The guidelines-oriented job analysis (GOJA) responds to the legislation affecting staffing and involves a step-by-step procedure to define the work of a particular job classification. It is also used for developing selection tools, such as application forms, and for documenting compliance with various legal requirements. The GOJA obtains the following types of information: (1) machines, tools, and equipment; (2) supervision; (3) contacts; (4) duties; (5) knowledge, skills, and abilities; (6) physical and other requirements; and (7) differentiating requirements.

OBJECTIVE **4.3**

Identify who conducts job analysis and describe the components of a job description.

Conducting Job Analysis

The person who conducts job analysis is interested in gathering data on what is involved in performing a particular job. The people who participate in job analysis should include, at a minimum, the employee and the employee's immediate supervisor. Large organizations may have one or more job analysts, but in small organizations line supervisors may be responsible for the task. Organizations that lack the technical expertise may use outside consultants to perform job analysis.

Regardless of the approach taken, before conducting job analysis, the analyst should learn as much as possible about the job by reviewing organizational charts and talking with individuals acquainted with the jobs to be studied. Before beginning, the supervisor should introduce the analyst to the employees and explain the purpose of the job analysis. Upon completion of the job analysis, two basic human resource documents, job descriptions and job specifications, can be prepared. As previously mentioned, in practice, both the job description and job specification are combined into one document with the job specification presented after the job description.

Job Description

Information obtained through job analysis is crucial to the development of job descriptions. It is vitally important that job descriptions are both relevant and accurate.[16] They should provide concise statements of what employees are expected to do on the job, how they do it, and the conditions under which the duties are performed. Concise job descriptions put an end to the possibility of hearing "that's not my job." Among the items frequently included in a job description are these:

- Major duties performed
- Percentage of time devoted to each duty
- Performance standards to be achieved
- Working conditions and possible hazards
- Number of employees performing the job, and to whom they report
- The machines and equipment used on the job

Having accurate job descriptions is the starting point for most HR tasks. Table 4-2 provides some suggestions for the proper language to be used in job descriptions.

The contents of the job description vary somewhat with the purpose for which it will be used. The next sections address the parts of a job description.

TABLE 4-2

Proper Language in the Job Description

Keep each statement in the job description crisp and clear:

- Structure your sentences in classic verb/object and explanatory phrases. Since the occupant of the job is your sentences' implied subject, it may be eliminated. For example, a sentence pertaining to the description of a receptionist position might read: "Greets office visitors and personnel in a friendly and sincere manner."
- Always use the present tense of verbs.
- If necessary, use explanatory phrases telling why, how, where, or how often to add meaning and clarity. For example: "Collects all employee time sheets on a biweekly basis for payroll purposes."
- Omit any unnecessary articles such as "a," "an," "the," or other words for an easy-to-understand description. Using the above example, the statement could have read, "Greets all visitors and the office personnel to the building in a friendly and a sincere manner."
- Use unbiased terminology. For example, use the he/she approach or construct sentences in such a way that gender pronouns are not required.
- Avoid using words which are subject to differing interpretations. Try not to use words such as "frequently," "some," "complex," "occasional," and "several."

Source: http://www.sba.gov/content/writing-effective-job-descriptions

Job Identification

The job identification section includes the job title, the department, the reporting relationship, and a job number or code. A good title will closely approximate the nature of the work content and will distinguish that job from others. Unfortunately, job titles are often misleading. An executive assistant in one organization may be little more than a highly paid clerk, whereas a person with the same title in another firm may practically run the company. For instance, one former student's first job after graduation was with a major tire and rubber company as an *assistant district service manager*. Because the primary duties of the job were to unload tires from trucks, check tread wear, and stack tires in boxcars, a more appropriate title would probably have been *tire checker and stacker*.

Date of the Job Analysis

The job analysis date is placed on the job description to aid in identifying job changes that would make the description obsolete. Some firms have found it useful to place an expiration date on the document. This practice ensures periodic review of job content and minimizes the number of obsolete job descriptions.

Job Summary

The job summary provides a concise overview of the job. It is generally a short paragraph that states job content.

Duties Performed

The body of the job description delineates the major duties to be performed. Usually, one sentence beginning with an action verb (such as *receives, performs, establishes,* or *assembles*) adequately explains each duty. Essential functions may be shown in a separate section to aid in complying with the Americans with Disabilities Act. An example of a job description/specification of a records clerk is shown in Figure 4-2.

FIGURE 4-2

Job Description/ Specification Example

Administrative Information
Job Title: Records Clerk
Department: Loan Operations
Reports To: Loan Operation Manager
Job Number: 11

Date of Job Analysis
January 21, 2013

Expiration Date
January 2016

Job Summary
Returns all consumer paid loan documents to customers. Supervises the daily activities of two clerks.

Essential Functions Performed
Receives monthly files for accounts that have been paid in full and require the return of contracts, mortgage documents, auto titles, and other documents.
Answers telephone and e-mail inquiries from customers or loan officers concerning documents.
Maintains file on temporary automobile titles until permanent title is received.
Files permanent automobile titles, contracts, mortgage documents, and other documents in customer files on a daily basis.
Supervises two file clerks who maintain correspondence and other general files.
Performs file clerk duties as needed.
Performs other duties, as required, on a temporary basis, to maintain section or departmental operations and services.

Job Specifications
Education
High school diploma preferred, but not required
Experience
Six months or more in a financial institution and familiarity with various loan documents
Skills Required
Working knowledge of Microsoft Word and Excel
Ability to enter data at a rate of 35 words per minute

Job Specification

Job specifications should always reflect the minimum, not the ideal qualifications for a particular job. Several problems may result if specifications are inflated. First, if specifications are set too high, they might systematically eliminate minorities or women from consideration for jobs. Therefore, the organization runs the risk of being charged with discrimination. Second, compensation costs will increase because ideal candidates will have to be compensated more than candidates with lesser skills. Third, job vacancies will be harder to fill because ideal candidates are more difficult to find than minimally qualified candidates. Finally, including an unnecessary requirement in the job specification may actually keep really qualified applicants out of the selection pool.[17]

Determining the appropriate qualifications for a job is undoubtedly the most difficult part of job analysis. It requires a great deal of probing on the part of the job analyst as well as a broad understanding of the skills needed to perform varieties of work. Items typically included in the job specification are factors that are job related, such as educational requirements, experience, and job-related personality traits and physical abilities. As previously mentioned, in practice, job specifications are often included as a major section of job descriptions.

After jobs have been analyzed and the descriptions written, the results should be reviewed with the supervisor and the worker to ensure that they are accurate, clear, and understandable. The courtesy of reviewing results with employees also helps to gain their acceptance.

OBJECTIVE 4.4

Explain Standard Occupational Classification (SOC), O*NET, job analysis for team members, and describe how job analysis helps satisfy various legal requirements.

HR Web Wisdom

Standard Occupational Classification (SOC)

http://www.bls.gov/soc/2010/ soc_alph.htm

Provides an alphabetical list of SOC occupations.

Standard Occupational Classification (SOC)

The federal government updates job descriptions for all U.S. workers in more than 800 occupations every 10 years. The 2010 SOC replaced the 2000 system. The SOC's substantive structural changes are based on actual changes in the nature or organization of work activities being performed in the economy. The update also provides an opportunity for professional organizations and labor groups to seek recognition or a higher profile for their members' occupations by gaining a separate listing or reclassification. Most current occupations will be unaffected except perhaps for a change in the description's wording. Some representative SOC descriptions for HR professionals may be seen in Table 4-3.[18]

TABLE 4-3

Representative SOC Descriptions for HR Professionals

13-1071 Human Resources Specialists

Perform activities in the human resource area. Includes employment specialists who screen, recruit, interview, and place workers. Excludes "Compensation, Benefits, and Job Analysis Specialists" (13-1141) and "Training and Development Specialists" (13-1151).

Illustrative examples: *Staffing Coordinator, Personnel Recruiter, Human Resources Generalist*

11-3111 Compensation and Benefits Managers

Plan, direct, or coordinate compensation and benefits activities of an organization. Job analysis and position description managers are included in "Human Resource Managers" (11-3121).

Illustrative examples: *Wage and Salary Administrator, Employee Benefits Director, Compensation Director*

13-1141 Compensation, Benefits, and Job Analysis Specialists

Conduct programs of compensation and benefits and job analysis for employer. May specialize in specific areas, such as position classification and pension programs.

Illustrative examples: *Employee Benefits Specialist, Retirement Plan Specialist, Job Analyst*

11-3131 Training and Development Managers

Plan, direct, or coordinate the training and development activities and staff of an organization.

Illustrative examples: *Labor Training Manager, Employee Development Director, E-Learning Manager*

17-2111 Health and Safety Engineers, Except Mining Safety Engineers and Inspectors

Promote worksite or product safety by applying knowledge of industrial processes, mechanics, chemistry, psychology, and industrial health and safety laws. Includes industrial product safety engineers.

Illustrative examples: *Product Safety Engineer, Fire Protection Engineer, Industrial Safety Engineer*

Source: http://www.bls.gov/soc/2010/soc

O*NET, the Occupational Information Network

O*NET, the Occupational Information Network, is a comprehensive, government-developed database of worker attributes and job characteristics. It is the nation's primary source of occupational information. It is a flexible, easy-to-use database system that provides a common language for defining and describing occupations. Its flexible design also captures rapidly changing job requirements. It provides the essential foundation for facilitating career counseling, education, employment, and training activities by containing information about knowledge, skills, abilities; interests; general work activities; and work context.[19] Portions of the information included in an O*NET description for a Human Resources Specialists may be seen in Table 4-4.

HR Web Wisdom

*O*NET OnLine*

http://www.onetonline.org/

O*NET OnLine has detailed descriptions of the world of work for use by job seekers, workforce development and HR professionals, students, researchers, and more!

TABLE 4-4

Portions of Information Included in an O*NET Description for a Human Resources Specialist

TASKS

- Address employee relations issues, such as harassment allegations, work complaints, or other employee concerns.
- Analyze employment-related data and prepare required reports.
- Conduct exit interviews and ensure that necessary employment termination paperwork is completed.
- Conduct reference or background checks on job applicants.
- Confer with management to develop or implement personnel policies or procedures.
- Contact job applicants to inform them of the status of their applications.
- Develop or implement recruiting strategies to meet current or anticipated staffing needs.
- Hire employees and process hiring-related paperwork.
- Inform job applicants of details such as duties and responsibilities, compensation, benefits, schedules, working conditions, or promotion opportunities.
- Interpret and explain human resources policies, procedures, laws, standards, or regulations.

KNOWLEDGE

Personnel and Human Resources—Knowledge of principles and procedures for personnel recruitment, selection, training, compensation and benefits, labor relations and negotiation, and human resource information systems.

English Language—Knowledge of the structure and content of the English language including the meaning and spelling of words, rules of composition, and grammar.

Customer and Personal Service—Knowledge of principles and processes for providing customer and personal services. This includes customer needs assessment, meeting quality standards for services, and evaluation of customer satisfaction.

Administration and Management—Knowledge of business and management principles involved in strategic planning, resource allocation, human resources modeling, leadership technique, production methods, and coordination of people and resources.

Clerical—Knowledge of administrative and clerical procedures and systems such as word processing, managing files and records, stenography and transcription, designing forms, and other office procedures and terminology.

Sales and Marketing—Knowledge of principles and methods for showing, promoting, and selling products or services. This includes marketing strategy and tactics, product demonstration, sales techniques, and sales control systems.

Computers and Electronics—Knowledge of circuit boards, processors, chips, electronic equipment, and computer hardware and software, including applications and programming.

Law and Government—Knowledge of laws, legal codes, court procedures, precedents, government regulations, executive orders, agency rules, and the democratic political process.

Communications and Media—Knowledge of media production, communication, and dissemination techniques and methods. This includes alternative ways to inform and entertain via written, oral, and visual media.

Psychology—Knowledge of human behavior and performance; individual differences in ability, personality, and interests; learning and motivation; psychological research methods; and the assessment and treatment of behavioral and affective disorders.

(continued)

TABLE 4-4
(continued)

SKILLS

Speaking—Talking to others to convey information effectively.

Active Listening—Giving full attention to what other people are saying, taking time to understand the points being made, asking questions as appropriate, and not interrupting at inappropriate times.

Reading Comprehension—Understanding written sentences and paragraphs in work related documents.

Writing—Communicating effectively in writing as appropriate for the needs of the audience.

Social Perceptiveness—Being aware of others' reactions and understanding why they react as they do.

Service Orientation—Actively looking for ways to help people.

Critical Thinking—Using logic and reasoning to identify the strengths and weaknesses of alternative solutions, conclusions or approaches to problems.

Time Management—Managing one's own time and the time of others.

Judgment and Decision Making—Considering the relative costs and benefits of potential actions to choose the most appropriate one.

Coordination—Adjusting actions in relation to others' actions.

ABILITIES

Oral Comprehension—The ability to listen to and understand information and ideas presented through spoken words and sentences.

Oral Expression—The ability to communicate information and ideas in speaking so others will understand.

Speech Clarity—The ability to speak clearly so others can understand you.

Speech Recognition—The ability to identify and understand the speech of another person.

Written Comprehension—The ability to read and understand information and ideas presented in writing.

Written Expression—The ability to communicate information and ideas in writing so others will understand.

Near Vision—The ability to see details at close range (within a few feet of the observer).

Inductive Reasoning—The ability to combine pieces of information to form general rules or conclusions (includes finding a relationship among seemingly unrelated events).

Deductive Reasoning—The ability to apply general rules to specific problems to produce answers that make sense.

Problem Sensitivity—The ability to tell when something is wrong or is likely to go wrong. It does not involve solving the problem, only recognizing there is a problem.

WORK ACTIVITIES

Getting Information—Observing, receiving, and otherwise obtaining information from all relevant sources.

Communicating with Supervisors, Peers, or Subordinates—Providing information to supervisors, co-workers, and subordinates by telephone, in written form, e-mail, or in person.

Establishing and Maintaining Interpersonal Relationships—Developing constructive and cooperative working relationships with others, and maintaining them over time.

Staffing Organizational Units—Recruiting, interviewing, selecting, hiring, and promoting employees in an organization.

Communicating with Persons Outside Organization—Communicating with people outside the organization, representing the organization to customers, the public, government, and other external sources. This information can be exchanged in person, in writing, or by telephone or e-mail.

Judging the Qualities of Things, Services, or People—Assessing the value, importance, or quality of things or people.

Interacting With Computers—Using computers and computer systems (including hardware and software) to program, write software, set up functions, enter data, or process information.

Organizing, Planning, and Prioritizing Work—Developing specific goals and plans to prioritize, organize, and accomplish your work.

Documenting/Recording Information—Entering, transcribing, recording, storing, or maintaining information in written or electronic/magnetic form.

Making Decisions and Solving Problems—Analyzing information and evaluating results to choose the best solution and solve problems.

(continued)

JOB ZONE

Title Job Zone Four: Considerable Preparation Needed

Education Most of these occupations require a four-year bachelor's degree, but some do not.

Related Experience A considerable amount of work-related skill, knowledge, or experience is needed for these occupations. For example, an accountant must complete four years of college and work for several years in accounting to be considered qualified.

Job Training Employees in these occupations usually need several years of work-related experience, on-the-job training, and/or vocational training.

WORK STYLES

Dependability—Job requires being reliable, responsible, and dependable, and fulfilling obligations.

Integrity—Job requires being honest and ethical.

Self-Control—Job requires maintaining composure, keeping emotions in check, controlling anger, and avoiding aggressive behavior, even in very difficult situations.

Initiative—Job requires a willingness to take on responsibilities and challenges.

Adaptability/Flexibility—Job requires being open to change (positive or negative) and to considerable variety in the workplace.

Cooperation—Job requires being pleasant with others on the job and displaying a good-natured, cooperative attitude.

Stress Tolerance—Job requires accepting criticism and dealing calmly and effectively with high stress situations.

Attention to Detail—Job requires being careful about detail and thorough in completing work tasks.

Persistence—Job requires persistence in the face of obstacles.

Concern for Others—Job requires being sensitive to others' needs and feelings and being understanding and helpful on the job.

Source: http://online.onetcenter.org/

Job Analysis for Team Members

Historically, companies have established permanent jobs and filled these jobs with people who best fit the job description. The jobs then continued in effect for years to come. In many firms today, people are being hired as team members. Whenever someone asks a team member, "What is your job description?" the reply might well be "Whatever." What this means is that if a project has to be completed, individuals do what has to be done to complete the task.

With team design, there are no narrow job descriptions. Today, the work that departments do is often bundled into teams. The members of these teams have a far greater depth and breadth of skills than would have been required in traditional jobs. Formerly, there might have been 100 separate job classifications in a facility. With team design, there may be just 10 or fewer broadly defined roles of teams. Another dimension is added to job analysis when teams are considered: Job analysis may determine how important it is for employees to be team players and work well in group situations.

Jobs are changing by getting bigger and more complex. The last duty shown on the job description, "And any other duty that may be assigned," is increasingly becoming *the* job description. This enlarged, flexible, complex job changes the way many tasks are performed. Managers cannot simply look for individuals who possess narrow job skills. They must go deeper and seek competencies, intelligence, ability to adjust, and ability and willingness to work in teams. Today more than ever, people go from project to project and from team to team. Job definitions become blurred, and titles become almost meaningless as job descriptions have become even more all-encompassing. Basically, what matters is what you know and how well you apply it to the business.

Job Analysis and the Law

Effective job analysis is essential to sound human resource management as an organization recruits, selects, and promotes employees. Legislation requiring thorough job analysis includes the following acts:

- *Fair Labor Standards Act:* Employees are categorized as exempt or nonexempt, and job analysis is basic to this determination. Nonexempt workers must be paid time and a half when they work more than 40 hours per week. Overtime pay is not required for exempt employees.
- *Equal Pay Act:* If jobs are not substantially different, employees performing them must receive similar pay. When pay differences exist, job descriptions can be used to show whether jobs are substantially equal in terms of skill, effort, responsibility, and working conditions.
- *Civil Rights Act:* Human resource management has focused on job analysis because selection methods need to be clearly job related. Job descriptions may provide the basis for an equitable compensation system and an adequate defense against unfair discrimination charges in initial selection, promotion, and all other areas of human resource administration. When job analysis is not performed, defending certain qualifications established for the job is usually difficult. In the *Griggs v Duke Power Company* case, the company stated that supervisors must have a high school diploma. However, the company could show no business necessity for this standard. Placing a selection standard in the job specification without having determined its necessity through job analysis makes the firm vulnerable in discrimination suits.
- *Occupational Safety and Health Act:* Job descriptions are required to specify elements of the job that endanger health or are considered unsatisfactory or distasteful by the majority of the population. Showing the job description to the employee in advance is a good defense.
- *Americans with Disabilities Act (ADA)/ADA Amendments Act:* Employers are required to make reasonable accommodations for workers with disabilities who are able to perform the *essential functions* of a job and job analysis is needed to obtain this information. Key elements used to determine essential functions include physical skills, mental skills, job duties, and behavioral skills.[20] The EEOC defines *reasonable accommodation* as any modification or adjustment to a job, an employment practice, or the work environment that makes it possible for an individual with a disability to enjoy an equal employment opportunity. The ADA Amendments Act expands the definition of "disability" and many more applicants and employees are eligible for reasonable accommodations. Certainly stating that every task in a job is essential sends a red flag to the EEOC.[21]

HR as a Strategic Business Partner

OBJECTIVE 4.5

Describe the need for the human resource manager to be a strategic partner, explain the strategic planning process, and describe the human resource planning process.

Since the early 1960s, many laws, court cases, and executive orders have been passed that impact the HR environment. At the time these laws were passed, managers often did not know how to operate within this new compliance environment. They were bombarded with questions regarding what to do and what not to do in hiring, promoting, and even firing a person. There were so many myths that surfaced during this time such as "You can't fire that person because he or she is—black, a woman, disabled, etc." Someone was needed to restore calm and inform managers regarding what was fact and what was fiction. The growth of HR as a profession grew in number and importance as it moved into this administrative and compliance arena. There were forms to complete such as the EEO-1 and managers to educate as to hiring standards to avoid. Over time, the administrative role of HR has diminished, as equal employment opportunity became understood by the general workforce. Human Resource Services Inc. President William Zinke said, "There was a time when HR was seen as just an administrative function, the smile and file department, the paper pushers."[22]

Today, HR professions are increasingly taking on the role of being a strategic partner with upper management. In this role, HR professionals are able to focus on matters that are truly important to the company as a whole.[23] In moving from a transactional to a strategic model, HR professionals work toward solving strategic problems in the organization.[24] No longer is an administrative and compliance role appropriate as their primary jobs. HR executives today need to think like the CEO in order to become a strategic partner in achieving organizational plans and results.[25] In doing so, they understand the production side of the business and help to determine the strategic capabilities of the company's workforce, both today and in the future.[26] HR professionals need to be agile in their thinking as they adapt to the ebbs and flows of business. Therefore, HR executives are ensuring that human resources support the firm's mission.

HR professionals have changed the way they work. Working as a strategic business partner requires a much deeper and broader understanding of business issues.[27] What exactly strategically should HR be doing? Possible strategic tasks for HR include making workforce strategies fundamental to company strategies and goals; increasing HR's role in strategic planning, mergers, and acquisitions; developing awareness and/or an understanding of the business; and helping line managers achieve their goals.

Human resource professionals can give the CEO and CFO a powerful understanding of the role human capital plays in the organization and the way it combines with business processes to expand or shrink shareholder value. HR professionals are integrating the goals of HR with the goals of the organization and focusing on expanding its strategic and high-level corporate participation with an emphasis on adding value. In doing so, HR is demonstrating that it can produce a return on investment for its programs. It analyzes HR activities to determine whether they are maintaining acceptable profit margins. The CEO needs help in matters that human resource professionals are qualified to handle. HR professionals are the enablers; they are the ones who should know about change and develop strategies to make it work.

Strategic Planning Process

As noted in the previous discussion, HR executives are now focusing their attention on how human resources can help the organization achieve its strategic objectives. Thus, HR executives are highly involved in the strategic planning process. In the past they often waited until the strategic plan was formulated before beginning **strategic planning**, the process by which top management determines overall organizational purposes and objectives and how they are achieved.

strategic planning
Process by which top management determines overall organizational purposes and objectives and how they are achieved.

Strategic planning is an ongoing process that is constantly changing in order to find a competitive advantage.[28] At times an organization may see the need to diversify and increase the variety of the goods that are made or sold. At other times, downsizing may be required in response to the external environment. Or, the strategic plan may see integration, the unified control of a number of successive or similar operations, as their driving force. Strategic planning attempts to position the organization in terms of the external environment. For example, the recent recession showed weakness in the marketplace for some firms, which led to lower company valuations, increased business failures, and firms spinning out or selling off their noncore business units. Forward-thinking companies found opportunities that were not available when business was booming, such as expanding their company through acquisition.[29] Companies always need to look for ways to stay competitive, gain market share, and be the first to innovate a new product or service.

Strategic planning at all levels of the organization can be divided into four steps: (1) determination of the organizational mission, (2) assessment of the organization and its environment, (3) setting of specific objectives or direction, and (4) determination of strategies to accomplish those objectives (see Figure 4-3). The strategic planning process described here is basically a derivative of the SWOT (strengths, weaknesses, opportunities, and threats) framework that affects organizational performance, but it is less structured.

Mission Determination

mission
Unit's continuing purpose or reason for being.

The first step in the strategic planning process is to determine the corporate mission. The **mission** is a unit's continuing purpose or reason for being. The corporate mission is the sum total of the organization's ongoing purpose. Arriving at a mission statement should involve answering questions such as: What are we in management attempting to do for whom? Should we maximize profit so shareholders will receive higher dividends or so share price will increase? Or should we emphasize stability of earnings so employees will remain secure? Certainly, HR can provide valuable assistance in answering these questions.

There are many other mission possibilities. Mission determination also requires deciding on the principles on which management decisions will be based. Will the corporation be honorable or dishonorable, ruthless or considerate, devious or forthright in dealing with its various constituencies? The answers to these questions tend to become embedded in a corporate culture and help determine the organizational mission. Top management expects HR activities to be closely aligned to this mission and add value toward achieving these goals.

FIGURE 4-3
Strategic Planning Process

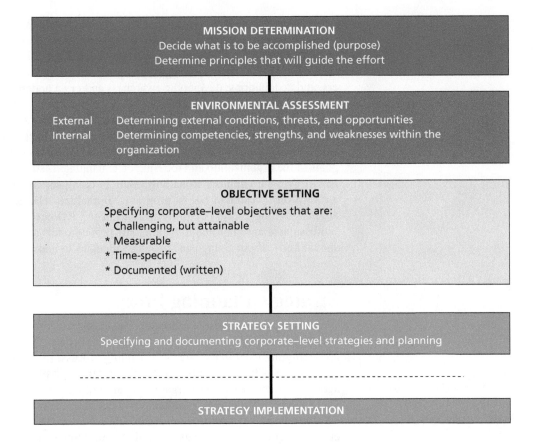

MISSION DETERMINATION
Decide what is to be accomplished (purpose)
Determine principles that will guide the effort

ENVIRONMENTAL ASSESSMENT
External — Determining external conditions, threats, and opportunities
Internal — Determining competencies, strengths, and weaknesses within the organization

OBJECTIVE SETTING
Specifying corporate–level objectives that are:
* Challenging, but attainable
* Measurable
* Time-specific
* Documented (written)

STRATEGY SETTING
Specifying and documenting corporate–level strategies and planning

STRATEGY IMPLEMENTATION

Environmental Assessment

Once the mission has been determined, the organization should assess its *strengths* and *weaknesses* in the internal environment and the *threats* and *opportunities* from the external environment (often referred as a SWOT analysis). Making strategic plans involves information flows from both the internal and the external environments. From inside comes information about organizational competencies, strengths, and weaknesses. Scanning the external environment allows organizational strategists to identify threats and opportunities, as well as constraints. In brief, the strategy would be to take advantage of the company's strengths and minimize its weaknesses in order to grasp opportunities and avoid threats.

HR professionals are in the best position to identify workforce strengths and weaknesses. Should the company be considering, for instance, a merger or acquisition, HR would be able to work with top management to determine whether the present workforce can be effectively integrated into the workforce of the merged company. For example, does the workforce of the merged company improve the overall value of the company, or is there only duplication of talent? Any reorganization affects people and HR professionals must be in the forefront of people-related matters.

Objective Setting

Objectives are the desired end results of any activity. Objectives should have four basic characteristics: (1) They should be expressed in writing, (2) they should be measurable, (3) they should be specific as to time, and (4) they should be challenging but attainable. Strategic objectives might be directed at factors such as profitability, customer satisfaction, financial returns, technological leadership, and operating efficiency. Objectives should be developed only after a cost–benefit analysis of each alternative is considered. Since HR professionals are in the people business, it is difficult to imagine any strategic objective that would not involve them in some manner.

Strategy Setting

Strategies can now be developed for accomplishing those objectives. Strategies should be developed to take advantage of the company's strengths and minimize its weaknesses in order to grasp opportunities and avoid threats. HR professionals should be highly involved in these activities, since the composition of the workforce will certainly influence the strategies chosen.

There has never been a more pressing time for HR professionals and leaders to develop a long-term workforce strategy for their organizations. The leading organizations will be the ones that are able to look beyond the current situation and identify the competencies they will need in the future. HR professionals and corporate leaders need to work together to define what their future workforce must look like. HR professionals need to lead corporations forward by developing a long-term workforce strategy.

Strategy Implementation

Once the strategic planning process is complete, the strategy must be implemented. Some people argue that strategy implementation is the most difficult and important part of strategic management. No matter how creative and well formulated the strategic plan, the organization will not benefit if it is incorrectly implemented. Strategy implementation requires changes in the organization's behavior, which can be brought about by changing one or more organizational dimensions, including management's leadership ability, organizational structure, information and control systems, production technology, and human resources.[30]

LEADERSHIP A leader is able to get others to do what he or she wants them to do. Managers must influence organization members to adopt the behaviors needed for strategy implementation. Top-level managers seeking to implement a new strategy may find it useful to build coalitions and persuade others to go along with the strategic plan and its implementation. HR must take the leadership role in dealing with human resource matters. Basically, leadership is used to encourage employees to adopt supportive behaviors and, when necessary, to accept the required new values and attitudes.

ORGANIZATIONAL STRUCTURE A company's organizational structure is typically illustrated by its organizational chart. The particular form of structure needed is determined by the needs of the firm. It may be informal and highly changeable in small, uncomplicated businesses. By contrast, large, diverse, and complex organizations usually have a highly formalized structure. But that should not mean the structure is so rigid that it does not change, perhaps even frequently. Newly formed high-tech companies are most likely to restructure or reorganize frequently, but even some of the largest *Fortune* 500 industrial firms such as General Motors and Chrysler have experienced major reorganizations. Many variations of organizational structures are available for use today. HR should be in a good position to recommend the most effective structure needed by the organization.

INFORMATION AND CONTROL SYSTEMS Among the information and control systems are reward systems; incentives; objectives-oriented systems; budgets for allocating resources; information systems; and the organization's rules, policies, and implementations. Certainly, HR should be a valuable asset in developing and working with these systems. A proper mix of information and control systems must be developed to support the implementation of the strategic plan.

TECHNOLOGY The knowledge, tools, and equipment used to accomplish an organization's assignments comprise its technology. The appropriate level of technology must be found for proper implementation of the strategic plan. Certainly, technology is revolutionizing how organizations operate today. This is definitely the case for HR professionals.

HUMAN RESOURCES The human resource functions must be properly aligned to successfully implement the strategic plan. HR will be central to understanding the future of an asset that is increasingly important to the organization—the intellectual and productive capacity of its workforce. In essence, a proper balance of human resources must be developed to support strategy implementation. Once strategic planning has taken place, human resource planning may be developed to help implement the strategic plan.

human resource planning
Systematic process of matching the internal and external supply of people with job openings anticipated in the organization over a specified period of time.

Human Resource Planning

Human resource planning (workforce planning) is the systematic process of matching the internal and external supply of people with job openings anticipated in the organization over a specific period of time. Workforce planning has evolved from a knee-jerk planning undertaking to a fundamental strategic function. It includes business plan, human resource data, and statistical interactions. It is also incorporated into the business and financial planning process, so it provides a foundation for a plan that is aligned with the business strategy.[31] As organizations exited the recent recession, there was evidence that they were becoming more focused on workforce planning. A recent poll found that 53 percent of the respondents conducted, or planned to conduct, a strategic workforce planning assessment to identify skills gaps.[32]

The human resource planning process is illustrated in Figure 4-4. Note that strategic planning precedes human resource planning. Human resource planning has two components: *requirements* and *availability*. A **requirements forecast** involves determining the number, skill, and location of employees the organization will need at future dates in order to meet its goals.

The determination of whether the firm will be able to secure employees with the necessary skills, and from what sources, is called an **availability forecast**.

When employee requirements and availability have been analyzed, the firm can determine whether it will have a surplus or shortage of employees. Ways must be found to reduce the number of employees if a surplus is projected. If a worker shortage is forecast, the firm must obtain the proper quantity and quality of workers from outside the organization. In this case, external recruitment and selection are required.

Because conditions in the external and internal environments can change quickly, the human resource planning process must be continuous. Changing conditions could affect the entire organization, thereby requiring extensive modification to the forecasts. The recent recession provided a major challenge for some firms as they raced to develop a downsizing strategy. And, as the economy improved, plans were made to increase the size of the workforce.

requirements forecast
Determining the number, skill, and location of employees the organization will need at future dates in order to meet its goals.

availability forecast
Determination of whether the firm will be able to secure employees with the necessary skills, and from what sources.

FIGURE 4-4

The Human Resource Planning Process

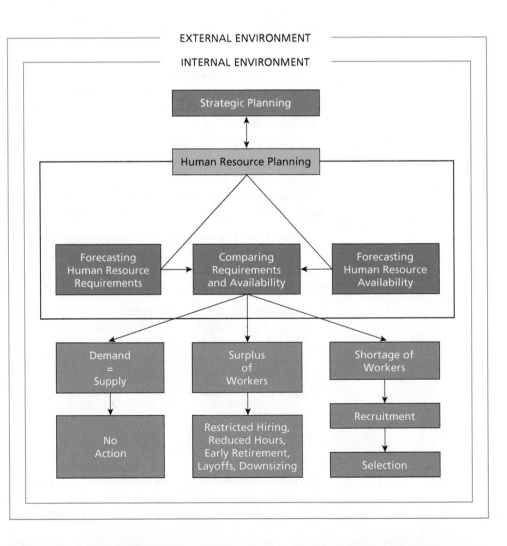

OBJECTIVE **4.6**

Describe forecasting human resource requirements and availability and how databases can assist in matching internal employees to positions.

HR Web Wisdom

HR Planning Organization
http://www.hrps.org

This is the Web site for the Human Resource Planning Society.

zero-base forecast
Forecasting method that uses the organization's current level of employment as the starting point for determining future staffing needs.

bottom-up forecast
Forecasting method in which each successive level in the organization, starting with the lowest, forecasts its requirements, ultimately providing an aggregate forecast of employees needed.

Forecasting Human Resource Requirements

Before human resource requirements can be projected, demand for the firm's goods or services must be forecasted. This forecast is then converted into people requirements for the activities necessary to meet this demand. For a firm that manufactures personal computers, activities might be stated in terms of the number of units to be produced, number of sales calls to be made, number of vouchers to be processed, or a variety of other activities. For example, manufacturing 1,000 laptop computers each week might require 10,000 hours of work by assemblers during a 40-hour week. Dividing the 10,000 hours by the 40 hours in the workweek gives 250 assembly workers needed. Similar calculations are performed for the other jobs needed to produce and market the computers.

Several techniques for forecasting human resource requirements are currently used. Some of the techniques are qualitative in nature, and others are quantitative.

Zero-Base Forecast

The **zero-base forecast** uses the organization's current level of employment as the starting point for determining future staffing needs.

Essentially, the same procedure is used for human resource planning as for zero-base budgeting, whereby each budget must be justified again each year. If an employee retires, is fired, or leaves the firm for any reason, the position is not automatically filled. Instead, an analysis is made to determine whether the firm can justify filling it. Equal concern is shown for creating new positions when they appear to be needed. The key to zero-base forecasting is a thorough analysis of human resource needs. Frequently, the position is not filled and the work is spread out among remaining employees, as often is the case with firms that downsize. Plans may also involve outsourcing or other approaches as an alternative to hiring.

Bottom-Up Forecast

In the **bottom-up forecast**, each successive level in the organization, starting with the lowest, forecasts its requirements, ultimately providing an aggregate forecast of employees needed.

It is based on the reasoning that the manager in each unit is most knowledgeable about employment requirements. Beginning with the lowest-level work units in the organization, each unit manager makes an estimate of personnel needs for the period of time encompassed by the planning cycle. As the process moves upward in the company, each successively higher level of management in turn makes its own estimates of needs, incorporating the input from each of the immediately preceding levels. The result, ultimately, is an aggregate forecast of needs for the entire organization. This process is often highly interactive in that estimated requirements from the previous level are discussed, negotiated, and reestimated with the next level of management as the forecast moves upward through the organization. The interactive aspect of managerial estimating is one of the advantages of this procedure because it forces managers to justify their anticipated staffing needs.

Relationship between Volume of Sales and Number of Workers Required

Historically, one of the most useful predictors of employment levels is sales volume. The relationship between demand and the number of employees needed is a positive one. As you can see in Figure 4-5, a firm's sales volume is depicted on the horizontal axis and the number of employees actually required is shown on the vertical axis. In this illustration, as sales decrease, so does the number of employees. Using such a method, managers can approximate the number of employees required at different demand levels. Quantitative methods such as regression analysis can be helpful in determining the number of workers needed.

Forecasting Human Resource Availability

To forecast availability, the human resource manager looks to both internal sources (current employees) and external sources (the labor market). The determination of whether the firm will be able to secure employees with the necessary skills, and from what sources, is an *availability forecast*. It helps

FIGURE 4-5

Relationship of Sales Volume to Number of Employees

to show whether the needed employees may be obtained from within the company, from outside the organization, or from a combination of the two sources. Another possibility is that the required skills are not immediately available from any feasible source. Consider the following example:

> *A large manufacturing firm on the West Coast was preparing to begin operations in a new plant. Analysts had already determined there was a large long-term demand for the new product. Financing was available and equipment was in place. But production did not begin for two years! Management had made a critical mistake: It had studied the demand side of human resources but not the supply side. There were not enough qualified workers in the local labor market to operate the new plant. New workers had to receive extensive training before they could move into the newly created jobs.*

This illustration provides one more instance of the importance of HR involvement in strategic planning.

Human Resource Databases

A *human resource database* contains employee information that permits management to make HR decisions. Information that might appear in such databases includes, but is not limited to, work history and experience, specific skills and knowledge, licenses or certifications held, organizational training completed, educational background, previous performance appraisal evaluations, assessment of strengths and weaknesses, developmental needs, promotion potential at present, and with further development, current job performance, field of specialization, job preferences, geographic preferences, career goals and aspirations, anticipated retirement date, and personal history, including psychological assessments. Employee information that is included in such databases can affect virtually any topic related to the management of human resources.

Many of the workers needed for future positions likely already work for the firm and are included in the database. However, information includes data regarding not only present workers but also former workers and prospective new members as they apply for jobs in the company. For example, former employees often desire to return to the company. And, as individuals make application with the firm, they too become part of the HR database.

Another benefit of an HR database is that it permits a firm to perform workforce analysis, which has become a priority in many organizations. Studying recruiting, performance, and turnover data can lead to insights such as the best sources of new candidates, the most effective training programs, and the most valuable employees to retain. Through regression analyses, organizations can determine the relative importance of different factors. Relationships may be virtually impossible to detect with the naked eye but make sense through statistical analysis.[33]

OBJECTIVE 4.7

Identify what a firm can do when either a shortage or a surplus of workers exists and explain strategic succession planning in today's environment.

Shortage of Workers Forecasted

When firms are faced with a shortage of workers, organizations will have to intensify their efforts to recruit the necessary people to meet the needs of the firm. Some possible actions will be discussed next.

Which "Thinker" Should Go?

Your company is a leading producer of advanced microchips. You are the chief researcher in your firm's *think tank*, which consists of eight people with various specialties. Your group has generated most of the ideas and product innovations that have kept the company an industry leader for 10 years. In fact, the think tank has been so successful that another one has been organized to support the company's newest manufacturing operation on the West Coast. The individuals included in the new think tank have already been selected, but your boss has just assigned you the task of deciding who from your group of thinkers will head the new organization.

The person best qualified for the job is Tim Matherson. Tim is an MIT graduate, the informal team leader, and the individual who personally spearheaded three of the team's five most successful product advancements. However, if Tim is given the promotion, the void created by his leaving will be difficult to fill. On the other hand, the boss forced his nephew, Robert Jones, into your group. He is a sharp graduate of the local state university, but he is not a team player and he is always trying to push you around. You can either recommend Tim, illustrating that those who produce the most benefit the most, or you can recommend Robert, making the boss happy, getting rid of a problem, and, most important of all, keeping your best performer.

What would you do?
What factor(s) in this ethical dilemma might influence a person to make a less-than-ethical decision?

Innovative Recruiting

A shortage of personnel often means that new approaches to recruiting must be used. The organization may have to recruit in different geographic areas than in the past, explore new methods, and seek different kinds of candidates. In using innovative recruiting, businesses must attempt to determine who their prospective employees are and what motivates them.

Compensation Incentives

Firms competing for workers in a high-demand situation may have to rely on compensation incentives. Premium pay is one obvious method; however, this approach may trigger a bidding war that the organization cannot sustain for an extended period. To offset the bidding war, some organizations use signing bonuses to entice individuals to join the firm. More subtle forms of rewards may be required to attract employees to a firm, such as four-day workweeks, flexible working hours, telecommuting, part-time employment, and child-care centers.

Training Programs

Special training programs may be needed to prepare previously unemployable individuals for positions with a firm. Remedial education and skills training are two types of programs that may help attract individuals to a particular company. For example, a small firm in Los Angeles expanded its market by hiring people with few, if any, qualifications. The firm was willing to spend the necessary time and money needed to provide even basic training.

Different Selection Standards

Another approach for dealing with shortages of workers is the lowering of employment standards. Selection criteria that screen out certain workers may have to be altered to ensure that enough people are available to fill jobs. Instead of desiring extensive work experience, a firm may be willing to hire an inexperienced worker and train the individual to do the job.

Surplus of Employees Forecasted

When a comparison of requirements and availability indicates that a worker surplus will result, most companies look to alternatives to layoffs but downsizing may ultimately be required.

Layoff Alternatives

At times, layoffs can be a necessary cost-cutting measure. However, there are counterproductive problems associated with layoffs, such as increased turnover, especially among the best, most productive workers, and the creation of anxiety among remaining staff, resulting in lower morale, reduced worker engagement, and decreased productivity. Therefore, firms need to look for alternatives to layoff and retain as many workers as possible.

One of the first alternatives to layoffs is to implement a restricted hiring policy that reduces the workforce by not replacing employees who leave. There are basically three forms of freezes. A *hard freeze* means that no new workers are hired to replace a vacated position. A *soft freeze* means that the company is only hiring to fill critical positions. New workers are hired only when the overall performance of the organization may be affected. A new term, *smart freeze* has entered HR vocabulary. HR and managers evaluate every position to determine the ones the company could not survive without and those that are difficult to fill and continue to hire them. Some companies might even lay off marginal workers in critical positions and seek more qualified workers to fill these positions.[34]

Early retirement is another way to reduce the number of workers. Some employees will be delighted to retire, but others will be somewhat reluctant. However, the latter may be willing to accept early retirement if the total retirement package is made sufficiently attractive. A tactic that is popular in the construction market is swapping employees. Some companies loan out staff to partner companies during slow times, while promising to hire back the workers when conditions improve. While the workers were away, they learned new skills and those left behind learned the skills to replace them.

Another alternative to layoffs is permitting an employee to go from full-time to 30 hours a week without losing health benefits.[35] Some companies may offer job-sharing arrangements. This arrangement can enable organizations to retain top talent in lieu of layoffs while having minimal impact on the overall labor budget. For example, employee benefits can be fairly managed on a per-employee basis, as two 20-hour-a-week part timers may have comparably pro-rated, scaled back benefits.[36] Other companies may reduce the workweek from five days to four thereby having a 20 percent reduction in wages. Some companies may offer an unpaid holiday option where instead of taking two weeks off, employees are being asked to take five, with three being unpaid.

The classic case of a firm that believes a no-layoff policy is best for continuous well-being of the firm is Cleveland's Lincoln Electric, a manufacturer of arc welding equipment. Since the 1930s, this $3 billion company has kept its promise to its American employees to never lay them off for economic reasons. For decades, wages were 20 to 30 percent above industry averages. The firm believes that a stable workforce provides a long-term competitive advantage. In difficult times, hours are reduced, people are reassigned, and white-collar salaries are cut. As long as workers meet the firm's performance standards, no one is laid off.[37]

Another example of a company with a no-layoff policy is Southeastern Freight Lines, a regional firm that prides itself as a less-than-truckload transportation services provider. When the recession began, Southeastern formed a "Keep Our People Working" task force to develop strategies for each unit with goals of keeping all employees working and maintaining all benefits and wage levels. Creative ways were found such as reducing costs for outsourced services and refurbishing trucks instead of buying new ones.[38]

Succession Planning: A Component of Strategic Planning

Succession planning is the process of ensuring that qualified persons are available to assume key managerial positions once the positions are vacant.

Nothing could be as important to the strategic well-being of a company as ensuring that a qualified person is in place to lead the company both now and in the future. This succession planning definition includes untimely deaths, resignations, terminations, or the orderly retirements of key managerial personnel.[39] The goal is to help ensure a smooth transition and operational efficiency, but the transition is often difficult. The Institute for Corporate Productivity (i4cp) paper "Succession Planning Highlight Report" found that succession planning will be among the top five challenges executives face in the future.[40] However, in another survey, over half of U.S. and Canadian companies surveyed could not immediately name a successor to their organization's chief executive officer. Evidently, boards of directors do not appear to be spending sufficient time with succession planning.[41]

General Electric (GE) provides an example of a company with an excellent succession plan. At GE the goal is same-day succession. When senior vice president Larry Johnston quit to become the CEO at Albertsons, the position was filled the same day. Bill Conaty, former senior vice president of HR at General Electric said, "We had candidates with two or three backups for all key positions—including the C-suite and all business units. And the board already knew who was lined up thanks to six-month reviews."[42] This process is in sharp contrast to the difficulty that Hewlett-Packard has experienced in the selection of a new CEO. HP has its third CEO in just over a year[43] and its eighth CEO since 1999. [44]None of the former CEOs at HP had implemented a succession plan that would have at least identified internal candidates who were qualified to take over should the need arise.[45] This form of disruption can be a serious drain on both morale and the financial well-being of the firm.

Because of the tremendous changes that will confront management this century, succession planning is taking on more importance than ever before.[46] Deaths are not the only challenges that have created an increased focus on succession planning. For example, the premature firing of CEOs is no longer a rare event. CEOs are being terminated more quickly than in the past.

In recent years, succession planning is going much deeper into the workforce. A firm might have a good succession plan for top-level positions but few plans for the levels where all the work is performed. There is a movement away from traditional succession planning, which was focused only on top executives of the company. Succession management is now involving middle managers, where they are developed to help ensure that key roles below the C-suite have ready replacements.[47] The succession plan needs to consider both external and internal candidates.

Small Business Succession Planning

Succession planning is often neglected in small businesses because it is generally thought of in terms of replacing CEOs and key executives within larger businesses. But, succession planning is just as, or more, important for small businesses. A problem, however, is that only 31 percent of small business owners say their businesses are extremely or very prepared for such an event.[48] Without proper succession planning, the company could face economic and tax disasters.[49] Often the small business owner's argument against succession planning may be "we're too small," "we're too new," "we have good people in place," or "I'm not going anywhere soon."[50] Many of today's small businesses will not survive to the next generation of same family ownership. In fact, it is estimated that only 30 percent of businesses make it to the second generation, and just 10 percent survive to the third generation.[51] Peter Handal, president, CEO, and chairman of Dale Carnegie Training, said, "The failure to establish a comprehensive succession plan is a leading cause of this phenomenon."[52]

Disaster stories are readily available about small business owners who did not have a succession plan. There was the factory tire store that went out of business after the owner died because no one in the family wanted to continue the business. In another story, the owner died at age 57 of a heart attack and left behind a company worth $2 million, but he did not have a succession plan. His will was not updated and it created issues between his ex-wife and his second wife. As a result, the firm ended up in the hands of creditors, and the owner's wife received nothing.[53] Another unpleasant situation that may need to be addressed is what would happen in the event of a divorce. Splitting up the business may actually force the business to close its doors or to sell to a third party with the proceeds being split.[54] In developing a succession plan, someone ranging anywhere from the owner to a nonfamily employee should be assigned the responsibility for preparation of the succession plan.

As a small business grows from strictly family to one that is more complex, going outside the family is often required. After more than 80 years, Kane Is Able, a family-owned and operated trucking and logistics business, went outside the family for a new president and chief operating officer. Chris Kane, chief customer officer and a grandson of Edward Kane, who founded the company in 1930s, said, "Within the last year, the board really challenged us to take advantage of the economy to invest for the future." The company recognized the importance of a management team with broad experience in the market where Kane Is Able plans to progress.[55]

OBJECTIVE **4.8**
Describe manager and employee self-service and explain some job design concepts.

manager self-service (MSS)
The use of software and the corporate network to automate paper-based human resource processes that require a manager's approval, record-keeping or input, and processes that support the manager's job.

Manager Self-Service

HR software is increasingly available to permit managers to perform tasks that were previously done by HR. **Manager self-service (MSS)** is the use of software and the corporate network to automate paper-based human resource processes that require a manager's approval, record-keeping or input, and processes that support the manager's job. MSS software can reduce the administrative workload for HR and give managers more control over HR processes. Manager self-service is increasingly using a mobile format to conduct performance reviews and e-learning. It is also used for recruiting and onboarding, performance management, succession planning, and career development.

Rita Harris, SPHR, director of HR for GreenbergFarrow, an architecture, planning, engineering, and development services firm headquartered in Atlanta, said, "The efficiency of self-service helps you move from more of a reactive role to a proactive one."[56] Tasks can now be done online that previously required the help of HR staff, often reducing the HR staff needed. It frees the remaining HR staff to perform higher-level tasks that produce value for the organization.

The decision to develop an MSS system may be easy, but implementation often has been difficult. At times, the culture of the organization has to change, and that takes time. There is the difficulty of getting people to accept a new way of doing things. Managers have gotten used to telling the HR department to handle the transactions that MSS now requires managers to perform. Some view an MSS as extra work placed on managers. Managers may complain, and ask, "Why am I doing HR's work?" When that happens, MSS has not been properly presented as beneficial to the organization.

Employee Self-Service

employee self-service (ESS)
Processes that automate transactions that previously were labor intensive for both employees and HR professionals.

Employee self-service (ESS) consists of processes that automate transactions that previously were labor intensive for both employees and HR professionals. ESS applications can free up valuable HR staff time, reducing administrative time and costs. Employee self-service systems are more popular than ever and widely accepted by employees and employers. They have become part of a larger movement toward automation and Web-enabled technology that is becoming a part of our daily lives. There are several types of self-service applications, including interactive voice response, Internet, and intranet. The systems create a single, secure repository for confidential payroll and human resources information and processes. Some of the areas that an ESS addresses include company administration, human resources, benefits, and payroll. Human resource tasks include maintenance of personal information, emergency contacts, maintenance of dependents and beneficiaries, job postings, and employee development.[57]

Job Design Concepts

job design
Process of determining the specific tasks to be performed, the methods used in performing these tasks, and how the job relates to other work in an organization.

We previously said that new jobs were being created at a rapid pace. If this is so, jobs have to be designed. **Job design** is the process of determining the specific tasks to be performed, the methods used in performing these tasks, and how the job relates to other work in the organization. Several concepts related to job design will be discussed next.

Job Enrichment

job enrichment
Changes in the content and level of responsibility of a job so as to provide greater challenges to the worker.

Strongly advocated by Frederick Herzberg, **job enrichment** consists of basic changes in the content and level of responsibility of a job so as to provide greater challenges to the worker. Job enrichment provides a vertical expansion of responsibilities.

The worker has the opportunity to derive a feeling of achievement, recognition, responsibility, and personal growth in performing the job. Although job enrichment programs do not always achieve positive results, they have often brought about improvements in job performance and in the level of worker satisfaction in many organizations. Today, job enrichment is moving toward the team level, as more teams become autonomous, or self-managed.

Job Enlargement

job enlargement
Increasing the number of tasks a worker performs, with all of the tasks at the same level of responsibility.

There is a clear distinction between job enrichment and job enlargement. **Job enlargement** is defined as increasing the number of tasks a worker performs, with all of the tasks at the same level of responsibility.

Job enlargement, sometimes called cross-training, involves providing greater variety to the worker. For example, instead of knowing how to operate only one machine, a person is taught to operate two or even three, but no higher level of responsibility is required. Workers with broad skills may become increasingly important as fewer workers are needed because of tight budgets. Some employers have found that providing job enlargement opportunities improves employee engagement and prevents stagnation.[58]

job rotation
Moves workers from one job to another to broaden their experience.

Job Rotation

Job rotation (cross-training) moves employees from one job to another to broaden their experience. Higher-level tasks often require this breadth of knowledge. Rotational training programs help employees understand a variety of jobs and their interrelationships, thereby improving

> **OBJECTIVE 4.9**
>
> Describe the importance of global talent management.

A GLOBAL PERSPECTIVE

Global Talent Management

Talent management is a strategic endeavor to optimize the use of human capital, which enables an organization to drive short- and long-term results by building culture, engagement, capability, and capacity through integrated talent acquisition, development, and deployment processes that are aligned to business goals. Roger Cude, senior vice president of global talent management at Walmart Stores Inc., said through talent management, "Our leaders know what they're getting reviewed on and how they're getting calibrated on what's important but also where the business is heading."[59] Six key components of talent management include recruitment, compensation and rewards, performance management, succession management, engagement and retention, and leadership development.[60] Talent management attempts to ensure that the right person is in the right job at the right time. A fully integrated talent management system helps answer many questions that a CEO may ask, such as "Do I have the executive talent to lead an initiative?" or "How long before we have enough knowledge and skills within the organization for the initiative to take hold?" CEOs want assurance that they have the workers available to achieve their business goals, both now and in the future.[61] A recent study found that high-performing organizations tend to integrate talent management components more than low-performing organizations.[62] Companies such as General Electric, Unilever, PepsiCo, and Shell are known for their painstaking attention to talent management. But these companies are typically not the norm.[63]

Heath Williams, Plateau Systems' vice president, international sales, said, "Good talent management systems start with careful analysis not just of HR functions, but of the organization itself, including existing processes, long and short-term goals, the organization's competitive position, culture and so on."[64] More and more companies are automating the talent management process into a single information system. At Chevron Corporation, Taryn Shawstad, general manager of global workforce development, works with a database of about 60,000 employees from approximately180 countries. She says, "In the past, we were siloed by country. Now, instead of looking at the United States or Indonesia or Nigeria, we can look across the globe at job families, capabilities, supply, and demand."[65]

According to an Ernst & Young report "Managing Today's Global Workforce," top-quality talent management is strongly associated with improved business performance. Companies that aligned talent management programs with their business strategy produced a return on investment (ROI) that was approximately 20 percent higher over a five-year period than companies without such an orientation. Companies that combined certain key elements of talent management such as succession planning and recruiting saw even more dramatic results. The ROI over a five-year period averaged being 38 percent higher than those that failed to integrate those capabilities.[66] Also a recent report from Bersin & Associates found that organizations in the United States with a mature, integrated talent management strategy enjoyed 17 percent lower voluntary turnover, 26 percent higher revenue-per-employee, and better business stability.[67] Basically, talent management exists to support company objectives. In today's dynamic international environment, talent management provides HR with a significant and demanding challenge. As Vic Speers, director of talent management at Hudson, a provider of talent management services worldwide, says, "The second war for talent is brewing. Young and talented employees are increasingly rare and firms are faced with an aging population where more people retire every year than join the workforce."[68] Organizations are finding it increasingly difficult to recruit quality talent because competitors want these same individuals.

The successful firms in this dynamic global environment will be the ones that have been successful at talent management.[69] Much has changed in the world today, and firms that move beyond the traditional approach to talent management will have the advantage.

talent management
Strategic endeavor to optimize the use of human capital, which enables an organization to drive short- and long-term results by building culture, engagement, capability, and capacity through integrated talent acquisition, development, and deployment processes that are aligned to business goals.

reengineering
Fundamental rethinking and radical redesign of business processes to achieve dramatic improvements in critical, contemporary measures of performance such as cost, quality, service, and speed.

productivity. Job rotation is often used by organizations to relieve boredom, stimulate better performance, reduce absenteeism, and provide additional flexibility in job assignments. Also, if the task to be accomplished is boring or distasteful, job rotation means that one person will not be stuck with it for all times.[70] Individuals who know how to accomplish more than one task are more valuable both to themselves and to the firm. Staffing then becomes more flexible and these multiskilled workers are then more insulated from layoffs.[71] If job rotation is to be effective, management must be sure to provide sufficient training so that each individual in the rotation can perform the task in a similar manner.[72]

Reengineering

Reengineering is "the fundamental rethinking and radical redesign of business processes to achieve dramatic improvements in critical contemporary measures of performance, such as cost, quality, service, and speed."[73]

Reengineering essentially involves the firm rethinking and redesigning its business system to become more competitive. It emphasizes the radical redesign of work in which companies organizes around process instead of by functional departments. Incremental change is not what is desired; instead, deep-seated changes are wanted that will alter entire operations at one time. Essentially, the firm must rethink and redesign its business system from the ground up.

Reengineering focuses on the overall aspects of job designs, organizational structures, and management systems. It stresses that work should be organized around outcomes as opposed to tasks or functions. Reengineering should never be confused with downsizing even though a workforce reduction often results from this strategy. Naturally, job design considerations are of paramount concern because as the process changes, so do essential elements of jobs. Through an initiative called Project Accelerate, Family Dollar reengineered its merchandising and supply chain processes to enable better performance by store teams. In doing so, it produced a new store layout that is easier and more convenient to shop.[74]

LG Electronics provides another example of how reengineering can work. LG management previously let each division deal with suppliers. That meant a procurement manager in Seoul did not know how much his counterpart at a flat-screen TV factory in Mexico paid for chips from the same company. Then Chief Executive Nam Yong decided to reengineer and rethink the company where managers seldom shared information. Today no one at LG can issue a purchase order without clearance from procurement engineering. By centralizing purchases, LG has cut more than $2 billion from its annual $30 billion purchases.[75]

MyManagementLab

Go to **mymanagementlab.com** to complete the problems marked with this icon ⭐.

Summary

1. *Describe the importance of disaster planning, explain why job analysis is a basic human resource tool, and give the reasons for conducting job analysis.* A firm's disaster plans should focus on possible catastrophes that range from natural calamities such as hurricanes, earthquakes, and floods to smaller events such as a building fire, water leak, or computer crash. Despite the type of disaster, the result is usually the same. Business has been interrupted for an undetermined amount of time, there has been a loss of contact with consumers and clients, and the firm's financial situation has been harmed.

Job analysis is the systematic process of determining the skills, duties, and knowledge required for performing jobs in an organization. It is an essential and pervasive human resource technique.

Without a properly conducted job analysis, it would be difficult, if not impossible, to satisfactorily perform the other human resource–related functions.

2. *Describe the types of information required for job analysis and describe the various job analysis methods.* Work activities, worker-oriented activities, and the types of machines, tools, equipment, and work aids used in the job

are important. This information is used to help determine the job skills needed. In addition, the job analyst looks at job-related tangibles and intangibles.

The job analyst may administer a structured questionnaire or witness the work being performed, or he or she may interview both the employee and the supervisor or ask them to describe their daily work activities in a diary or log. A combination of methods is often used.

3. *Identify who conducts job analysis and describe the components of a job description.* The people who participate in job analysis should include, at a minimum, the employee and the employee's immediate supervisor. Organizations that lack the technical expertise may use outside consultants to perform job analysis.

Components include the job identification section, which includes the job title, department, reporting relationship, and a job number or code; the job analysis date; the job summary; and the body of the job description that delineates the major duties to be performed.

4. *Explain Standard Occupational Classification (SOC), O*NET, job analysis for team members, and describe how job analysis helps satisfy various legal requirements.* The SOC's substantive structural changes are based on actual changes in the nature or organization of work activities being performed in the economy.

O*NET, the Occupational Information Network, is a comprehensive, government-developed database of worker attributes and job characteristics.

In many firms today, people are being hired as team members. Whenever someone asks a team member, "What is your job description?" the reply might well be "Whatever."

Legislation requiring thorough job analysis includes the following acts: Fair Labor Standards Act, Equal Pay Act, Civil Rights Act, Occupational Safety and Health Act, and the Americans with Disabilities Act (ADA)/ADA Amendments Act.

5. *Describe the need for the human resource manager to be a strategic partner, explain the strategic planning process, and describe the human resource planning process.* If HR is to be a strategic partner, HR executives must work with top management in achieving concrete plans and results.

Strategic planning is the process by which top management determines overall organizational purposes and objectives and how they will be achieved.

Strategic planning at all levels of the organization can be divided into four steps: (1) determination of the organizational mission, (2) assessment of the organization and its environment, (3) setting of specific objectives or direction, and (4) determination of strategies to accomplish those objectives.

Human resource planning (sometimes called workforce planning) is the systematic process of matching the internal and external supply of people with job openings anticipated in the organization over a specified period of time.

6. *Describe forecasting human resource requirements and availability and how databases can assist in matching internal employees to positions.* A *requirements forecast* is an estimate of the numbers and kinds of employees the organization will need at future dates in order to realize its goals. Determining whether the firm will be able to secure employees with the necessary skills and from what sources these individuals may be obtained is called an *availability forecast.*

Databases are being used by organizations to enable human resources to match people with positions.

7. *Identify what a firm can do when either a shortage or a surplus of workers exists and explain strategic succession planning in today's environment.* When a shortage of workers exists, creative recruiting, compensation incentives, training programs, and different selection standards are possible. When a worker surplus exists, most companies look for alternatives to layoffs, but downsizing may ultimately be required.

Succession planning is the process of ensuring that qualified persons are available to assume key managerial positions once the positions are vacant.

8. *Describe manager and employee self-service and explain some job design concepts.* *Manager self-service* is the use of software and the corporate network to automate paper-based human resource–related processes that require a manager's approval, record-keeping or input, and processes that support the manager's job.

Employee self-service consists of processes that automate transactions that used to be labor intensive for both employees and HR professionals.

Job design is the process of determining the specific tasks to be performed, the methods used in performing the tasks, and how the job relates to other work in the organization. *Job enrichment* consists of basic changes in the content and level of responsibility of a job so as to provide greater challenge to the worker. *Job enlargement* is increasing the number of tasks a worker performs, with all of the tasks at the same level of responsibility. *Job rotation* (sometimes called cross-training) moves employees from one job to another to broaden their experience. *Reengineering* is the fundamental rethinking and radical redesign of business processes to achieve dramatic improvements in critical contemporary measures of performance, such as cost, quality, service, and speed.

9. *Describe the importance of global talent management.* *Talent management* is a strategic endeavor to optimize the use of human capital, which enables an organization to drive short- and long-term results by building culture, engagement, capability, and capacity through integrated talent acquisition, development, and deployment processes that are aligned to business goals.

Key Terms

job analysis   80
job   80
position   80
job description   80
job specification   80
strategic planning   91
mission   91

human resource planning   93
requirements forecast   94
availability forecast   94
zero-base forecast   95
bottom-up forecast   95
succession planning   98
manager self-service (MSS)   100

employee self-service (ESS)   100
job design   100
job enrichment   100
job enlargement   101
job rotation   101
talent management   101
reengineering   102

Exercises

1. Prepare a job specification for each of the following jobs:
   a. social media recruiter
   b. automobile mechanic for Lexus dealership
   c. chef for an upscale restaurant
   d. cook at Burger King
2. The Trends & Innovations in the chapter entitled "Layoff Alternatives" suggests that layoffs should only be used as a last alternative. Do you agree that alternatives should only be used as a desperate measure? Be prepared to defend your decision.
3. The discussion of "Disaster Planning" suggests that major disasters such as hurricanes, earthquakes, and floods and smaller events such as a building fire, water leak, or computer crash are occurring all too often. It is likely that everyone has been involved in one, including you. Identify a disaster that you have been involved in and suggest how the various functions of HR were affected.

Questions for Review

1. Why is disaster planning important?
2. What is the distinction between a job and a position? Define job analysis.
3. When is job analysis performed?
4. What are the types of information required for job analysis?
5. What are the methods used to conduct job analysis? Describe each type.
6. What are the basic components of a job description? Briefly describe each.
7. What is the purpose of the O*NET, the Occupational Information Network, and the Standard Occupational Classification?
8. What is meant by the statement "With team design, there are no narrow jobs"?
9. Describe how effective job analysis can be used to satisfy each of the following statutes:
   (a) Fair Labor Standards Act
   (b) Equal Pay Act
   (c) Civil Rights Act
   (d) Occupational Safety and Health Act
   (e) Americans with Disabilities Act (ADA)/ADA Amendments Act
10. What are the steps involved in the strategic planning process?
11. What are the steps involved in the human resource planning process?
12. What are the human resource forecasting techniques?
13. Distinguish between forecasting human resource requirements and availability.
14. What are the purposes of human resource databases?
15. What actions could a firm take if it forecasted a shortage of workers?
16. What are some alternatives to layoffs?
17. Define succession planning. Why is it important?
18. What are manager and employee self-service?
19. Define each of the following:
   (a) job design
   (b) job enrichment
   (c) job enlargement
   (d) job rotation
   (e) reengineering
20. Why is the use of *talent management* so important in today's environment?

INCIDENT 1   A Degree for Meter Readers

Judy Anderson was assigned as a recruiter for South Illinois Electric Company (SIE), a small supplier of natural gas and electricity for Cairo, Illinois, and the surrounding area. The company had been expanding rapidly, and this growth was expected to continue. In January 2014, SIE purchased the utilities system serving neighboring Mitchell County. This expansion concerned Judy. The company workforce had increased by 30 percent the previous year, and Judy had struggled to recruit enough qualified job applicants. She knew that new expansion would intensify the problem.

Judy was particularly concerned about meter readers. The tasks required in meter reading are relatively simple. A person drives to homes served by the company, finds the gas or electric meter, and electronically records its current reading. If the meter has been tampered with, it is reported. Otherwise, no decision making of any consequence is associated with the job. The reader performs no calculations. The pay was $10.00 per hour, high for unskilled work in the area. Even so, Judy had been having considerable difficulty keeping the 37 meter reader positions filled.

Judy was thinking about how to attract more job applicants when she received a call from the human resource director, Sam McCord. "Judy," Sam said, "I'm unhappy with the job specification calling for only a high school education for meter readers. In planning for the future, we need better-educated people in the company. I've decided to change the education requirement for the meter reader job from a high school diploma to a college degree."

"But, Mr. McCord," protested Judy, "the company is growing rapidly. If we are to have enough people to fill those jobs we just can't insist that college graduates get paid to do such basic tasks. I don't see how we can meet our future needs for this job with such an unrealistic job qualification."

Sam terminated the conversation abruptly by saying, "No, I don't agree. We need to upgrade all the people in our organization. This is just part of a general effort to do that. Anyway, I cleared this with the president before I decided to do it."

Questions

1. Should there be a minimum education requirement for the meter reader job? Discuss.
2. What is your opinion of Sam's effort to upgrade the people in the organization?
3. What legal ramifications, if any, should Sam have considered?
4. Based on the information provided in this incident, what tasks would likely be included in the "Duties Performed" section? How would this affect the job specification section?

INCIDENT 2   Strategic HR?

Brian Charles, the vice president of marketing for Sharpco Manufacturing, commented at the weekly executive directors' meeting, "I have good news. We can get the large contract with Medord Corporation. All we have to do is complete the project in one year instead of two. I told them we could do it."

Charmagne Powell, vice president of human resources, brought Brian back to reality by reminding him, "Remember the strategic plan we were involved in developing and we all agreed to? Our present workers do not have the expertise required to produce the quality that Medord's particular specifications require. Under the two-year project timetable, we planned to retrain our present workers gradually. With this new time schedule, we will have to go into the job market and recruit workers who are already experienced in this process. We all need to study your proposal further. Human resource costs will rise considerably if we attempt to complete the project in one year instead of two. Sure, Brian, we can do it, but with these constraints, will the project be cost effective?"

Questions

1. Was Charmagne considering the strategic nature of human resource planning when she challenged Brian's "good news" forecast? Discuss.
2. How did the involvement in developing the corporate strategic plan assist Charmagne in challenging Brian?
3. Strategic planning at all levels of the organization can be divided into four steps. Which step in the strategic planning process did Brian violate?

MyManagementLab

Go to **mymanagementlab.com** for Auto-graded writing questions as well as the following Assisted-graded writing questions:

4-1. Why is job analysis considered to be a basic human resource tool?

4-2. Why does the human resource manager need to be a strategic partner with top management?

4-3. Mymanagementlab Only – comprehensive writing assignment for this chapter.

Notes

1. "U.S. Hit by Record 12 Weather Disasters, Costing $1 Billion Each in 2011," *Healthcare Purchasing News* 36 (January 2012): 36.
2. Leslie Stevens-Huffman, "Fast Relief," *Smart Business Philadelphia* 7 (July 2011): 26.
3. "How Do You Test the Readiness of a Disaster Plan Before Disaster?" *Security Director's Report* 10 (August 2010): 1–15.
4. Caroline McDonald, "How Sound Is Your Firm's Disaster Contingency Plan?" *National Underwriter/Property & Casualty Risk & Benefits Management* 114 (July 5, 2010): 23–25.
5. Cameron Sturdevant, "Updating Disaster Plans," *eWeek* 28 (March 21, 2011): 42.
6. Anne Rosso, "When Disaster Strikes," *Collector* 75 (June 2010): 26–31.
7. Eric Savitz and Werner Vogels, "How the Cloud Changes Businesses Big and Small," *Forbes.com* (February 16, 2012): 14.
8. Philip Bobko, Philip L. Roth, and Maury A. Buster, "A Systematic Approach for Assessing the Currency ("Up-to-Dateness") of Job-Analytic Information," *Public Personnel Management* 37 (Fall 2008): 261–277.
9. Deb Levine, Lesa Albright, and Margaret Fiester, "Investigation of Bullying, Job Analyses, Dual Career Ladders," HR Magazine 55 (November 2010): 20–21.
10. Jonathan A. Segal, "Hiring Days Are Here Again," *HR Magazine* 56 (July 2011): 58–60.
11. Jacqueline Berry and Donald Cable, "The Humble Position Description—Still a Valuable Resource," *Human Resources Magazine* 15 (June/July 2010): 16–17.
12. Marty Stanley, "Accountability: The New Normal," *Supervision* 71 (July 2010): 16–18.
13. "In All Promotion Notices, Include Specifics about Minimum Job Requirements," *HR Specialist: Employment Law* 40 (February 2010): 2.
14. Thomas A. Stetz, Scott B. Button, and W. Benjamin Poor, "New Tricks for an Old Dog: Visualizing Job Analysis Results," *Public Personnel Management* 38 (Spring 2009): 91–100.
15. *Uniform Guidelines on Employee Selection Procedures, Federal Register,* Friday, August 25, 1978, Part IV.
16. Laurie Burkhard, "Define Employees' Roles and Responsibilities," *Advisor Today* 104 (January 2009): 59–60.
17. Liz Ryan, "10 Ways to Fix Broken Corporate Recruiting Systems," *BusinessWeek.com* (July 13, 2011): 3.
18. http://www.bls.gov/soc/2010/soc_alph.htm
19. http://online.onetcenter.org/ December 26, 2011
20. "Get It in Writing: Creating Effective and Legal Job Descriptions," *HR Specialist: California Employment Law* 4 (November 2010): 4.
21. "Is Every Function Really Essential? Be Flexible about Disabled Employees' Duties," *HR Specialist: Illinois Employment Law* 6 (January 2012): 3.
22. "Survey Finds Major Companies Using HR to Address Broad Goals," *HR Focus* 89 (February 2012): 14.
23. Jill Fowler and Jeanette Savage, "Ask 'What,' Not 'How,'" *HR Magazine* 56 (August 2011): 85–86.
24. Philip Johnson and Vincent Milich, "Won't You Be My Partner?" *Chief Learning Officer* 10 (August 2011): 34–37.
25. "Attorney Urges HR Professionals to Think Like the CEO," *HR Focus* 89 (April 2012): 10.
26. Jathan Janove, "To Know the Business, Start in the Trenches," 57 *HR Magazine* (April 2012): 57.
27. Cam Caldwell, Do X. Truong, Pham T. Linh, and Anh Tuan, "Strategic Human Resource Management as Ethical Stewardship," *Journal of Business Ethics* 98 (January 2011): 171–182.
28. Mona Pearl, "Going Global: What Is Your Competitive Edge?" *Manufacturing Today* 10 (Winter 2010): 12–15.
29. Rory Cooper, "Smart HR Strategies in an Unpredictable Economy," *Maryland Banker* (Third Quarter 2009): 8.
30. J. R. Gallbraith and Robert K. Kazannian, Strategy Implementation: *Structure, Systems, and Process,* 2nd ed. (St. Paul, MN: West Publishing, 1986), 115.
31. Mitzi Jordan, "Breaking Out of the Crisis Mode," *Journal of Corporate Recruiting Leadership* 6 (February 2011): 7–11.
32. Jennifer Schramm, "Planning for Population Shifts," *HR Magazine* 56 (February 2011): 292–307.
33. Ed Frauenheim, "Personnel Precision," *Workforce Management* 90 (March 2011): 22–26.
34. Adrienne Fox, "The Big Chill," *HR Magazine* 54 (March 2009): 28–33.
35. Darryl Demos, "Flexible Staffing Meets Branch Needs," *CU360* 35 (July 7, 2009): 4–5.
36. Jennifer Schramm, "Work Turns Flexible," *HR Magazine* 54 (March 2009): 88.
37. Frank Koller, "Lay Off the Layoffs," *Corporate Knights Magazine* 9 (Winter 2011): 12.
38. Dean Smallwood, "Keeping 'em Working," *Commercial Carrier Journal* 168 (June 2011): 55–56.
39. William J. Rothwell, "The Future of Succession Planning," *T+D* 64 (September 2010): 50–54.
40. Robert Kleinsorge, "Expanding the Role of Succession Planning," *T+D* 64 (April 2010): 66–69.
41. Theresa Minton-Eversole, "Most Companies Unprepared for Succession at the Top," *HR Magazine* 55 (October 2010): 22.
42. Robert J. Grossman, "Rough Road to Succession," *HR Magazine* 56 (June 2011): 46–51.
43. Jeffrey Burt, "IBM, Apple, HP: Stark Contrasts in CEO Succession," *eWeek* 28 (November 7, 2011): 10.
44. "'HP Matters' Says Incoming CEO Meg Whitman," *Channel Insider* (September 23, 2011): 1-2.
45. A. G. Lafley and Noel M. Tichy, "The Art and Science of Finding the Right CEO," *Harvard Business Review* 89 (October 2011): 66–74.
46. Eileen McKeown, "Turbulent Times Highlight the Need for Succession Planning," *T+D* 64 (January 2010): 18–19.
47. Joe Shaheen, "Talent Acquisition as a Potent Tool of Succession Management," *Journal of Corporate Recruiting Leadership* 5 (November 2010): 9–12.
48. "Business Owners Fall Short on Contingency Planning," *North Western Financial Review* 196 (September 15, 2011): 22.
49. Irv Blackman, "A True Succession Planning Horror Story," *Contractor Magazine* 58 (July 2011): 38.
50. Sara LaForest and Tony Kubiac, "Understanding the Role of Succession Planning for Small Business Success," *Alaska Business Monthly* 27 (June 2011): 26–28.
51. David Harvey, "A Family Affair," *Commercial Motor* 216 (September 22, 2011): 48–49.
52. Joanne L. Stewart, "Train for the Future," *T+D* 65 (July 2011): 54–57.
53. Vera Linsalata, "Business Succession Plans," *Tire Business* 29 (April 11, 2011): 10–17.

54. Eric Savitz and Charley Moore, "Divorce Doesn't Have To Kill Your Family Business," *Forbes.com* (September 2, 2011): 4.

55. William B. Cassidy, "Not All in the Family," *Journal of Commerce* 12 (June 20, 2011): 27.

56. Drew Robb, "Making the Move to Manager Self-Service," *HR Magazine* 55 (November 2010): 67–70.

57. "Employee Self-Service Systems Starting to Grow in Popularity," *Payroll Manager's Report* 10 (July 2010): 1–5.

58. Yvette Lee, Shari Lau, and Patricia Graves, "Job Swapping, I-9 Forms, Travel Pay," *HR Magazine* 56 (April 2011): 24–25.

59. Natalie Morera, "Walmart: Your Global Neighborhood Store," *Chief Learning Officer* 10 (August 2011): 42–43.

60. Kevin Oakes and Pat Galagan, "Too Many Soloists; Not Enough Music," *T+D* 65 (May 2011): 44–47.

61. Larry Israelite, "Talent Management Is the New Buzzword," *T+D* 64 (February 2010): 14.

62. Michael Green, "Talent Management," *T+D* 65 (May 2011): 58–60.

63. Claudio Fernandez-Araoz, Boris Claudion, and Nitin Nohria, "How to Hang On to Your High Potentials," *Harvard Business Review* 89 (October 2011): 76–83.

64. Bob Little, "Best Practice Talent Management," *Training Journal* (November 2010): 45–49.

65. Lois Webster, "Leaving Nothing to Chance," *T+D* 63 (February 2009): 54–60.

66. Kim Girard, "A Talent for Talent," *CFO* 27 (May 2011): 27–28.

67. Jason Corsello, "Managing Talent in the Cloud," *Training Journal* (January 2012): 20–23.

68. Cushing Anderson, "Talent Management as Survival Skill," *Chief Learning Officer* 9 (March 2010): 46–48.

69. Phaedra Brotherton, "Improving Economy Boosts Talent Management Efforts," *T+D* 65 (January 2011): 16–17.

70. Wendi Everton, "Keeping Your Best & Brightest Workers," *Nonprofit World* 28 (November/December 2010): 12–13.

71. "Training Budgets Bounce Back: Where to Spend," *HR Specialist* 9 (March 2011): 1–5.

72. Jill Jusko, "When One Job Becomes Three," *Industry Week* 260 (July 2011): 16–17.

73. Michael Hammer and James Champy, *Reengineering the Corporation: A Manifesto for Business Revolution* (New York: Harper Collins Publishers, 1993), 32.

74. "Initiatives Pay Dividends for Family Dollar," *MMR* 28 (May 16, 2011): 94.

75. Moon Ihlaw and Kevin Cho, "Creative When No One's Looking," *BusinessWeek* (April 25, 2010): 37.

5

Recruitment

HRM in Action

Will Contingent Workers Replace Full-Time Employees?

OBJECTIVE 5.1

Describe the possibility of contingent workers replacing full-time employees.

contingent workers

Described as the "disposable American workforce" by a former secretary of labor, have a nontraditional relationship with the worksite employer, and work as part-timers, temporaries, or independent contractors.

Contingent workers, described as the "disposable American workforce" by a former secretary of labor, have a nontraditional relationship with the worksite employer and work as part-timers, temporaries, or independent contractors. The United States Government Accountability Office has estimated that so-called contingent workers make up nearly a third of the workforce. And forecasters believe that amount will rise.[1] Joyce Russell, who as president of Adecco Staffing oversees the placement of contingent workers in the United States, said, "We are super busy at Adecco. We are seeing sustained growth across all industries from pharmaceuticals to technology to consumer products to aerospace."[2] Although there are an estimated 10,000 temps in the United States, the five largest U.S. staffing companies, by revenue, are Allegis Group Services, Randstad, Adecco, Manpower, and Kelly Services.[3]

Contingent workers are the human equivalents of just-in-time inventory. These *disposable workers* permit maximum flexibility for the employer and lower labor costs. Historically, contingent workers have been called the bookends of recessions. They are the first to go when a recession begins and the last to be recalled when the economy gets better. However, toward the end of the recent recession, many companies were reversing this trend and following the strategy of holding off on the hiring of regular full-time employees and choosing instead to use contingent workers. Companies are now using contingent workers as a continuing strategy in both good and bad times.[4] In fact, the Bureau of Labor Statistics data suggest that between 2008 and 2018, staffing companies will add jobs at almost twice the rate of estimated job growth overall.

CHAPTER OBJECTIVES After completing this chapter, students should be able to:

1. Describe the possibility of contingent workers replacing full-time employees.
2. Define *recruitment* and explain alternatives to recruitment.
3. Explain the external environment of recruitment and describe how promotion policies influence recruitment.
4. Describe the recruitment process and explain internal recruitment methods.
5. Identify external recruitment sources.
6. Explain the impact of mobile HR recruiting.
7. Describe online recruitment methods and discuss the possibility of job search scams.
8. Identify traditional external recruitment methods.
9. Describe how recruitment methods and sources are tailored to each other.
10. Define *reshoring* and explain why some firms are rejecting outsourcing and returning the lost jobs to the United States.

The latest recession caused companies to rethink the way work gets done. This brought a refocus on the use of contingent workers, who can be added or cut as demand requires. In fact, the pace of contingent job growth suggests a shift toward more use of temporary labor at the expense of permanent jobs.[5] Garry Mathiason, vice chairman of Littler Mendelson in San Francisco, said, "In the future companies will likely make wider use of staffing methods similar to those practiced by the film industry. There, entire crews of contingent production workers are assembled for a movie then disbanded once it is finished."[6] A study by the Institute for Corporate Productivity (i4cp) found that high-performing organizations have increased their use of contingent workers from traditional administrative positions to technical support, operations, and high-skilled professional positions, including engineering, legal, and finance.[7] If the use of contingent workers is indeed the trend, the manner that human resource is practiced will experience considerable change.

Some businesses such as Hilton Worldwide are resisting the trend to increase the number of contingent workers. Hilton, for example, coordinates its staffing on a regional basis and sends full-time employees from one hotel to another nearby hotel to handle temporary increases in demand. Jim MacDonald, Hilton's vice president of human resources for the Americas, said, "This strategy not only makes efficient use of the hotel chain's staff but also helps develop an agile workforce."[8]

OBJECTIVE **5.2**

Define *recruitment* and explain alternatives to recruitment.

recruitment
Process of attracting individuals on a timely basis, in sufficient numbers, and with appropriate qualifications to apply for jobs with an organization.

Recruitment Defined

Recruitment is the process of attracting individuals on a timely basis, in sufficient numbers, and with appropriate qualifications to apply for jobs with an organization.

The firm may then select those applicants with qualifications most closely related to job descriptions. Finding the appropriate way of encouraging qualified candidates to apply for employment is extremely important, however, because recruiting costs can be expensive. Thus, a properly functioning recruiting program can have a major impact on the bottom line of a company.

The recruitment process is critical because employees quickly become either assets or liabilities based on how they contribute to the value of the company.[9] How many times have we heard CEOs state, "Our employees are our most important asset"? Instead they should be saying, "The right employees are our most important asset." Hiring the best people available has never been more critical than it is today, because of the economy and global competition. A company's ability to recruit and manage talent has become the measure for the overall health and longevity of the organization.[10] It is estimated that just the cost of replacing an employee alone when a bad decision is made is two to three times the employee's annual salary. Therefore, it is crucial to have a finely tuned recruitment process if the selection process is to function properly. However, before beginning the recruitment process, alternatives to recruitment need to be considered.

Alternatives to Recruitment

Even when HR planning indicates a need for additional employees, a firm may decide against increasing the size of its workforce. Recruitment and selection costs are significant when you consider all the related expenses. The cost of replacing a person making $50,000 per year can easily reach $75,000.[11] Therefore, a firm should consider alternatives carefully before engaging in recruitment. In addition to the alternatives discussed below, contingent workers (discussed in the HRM in Action at the beginning of the chapter) provide another significant alternative to recruiting.

outsourcing
Process of hiring an external provider to do the work that was previously done internally.

offshoring
Migration of all or a significant part of the development, maintenance, and delivery of services to a vendor located in another country.

Outsourcing and Offshoring

Outsourcing is the process of hiring an external provider to do the work that was previously done internally. Outsourcing has become a widespread and increasingly popular alternative involving virtually every business area and has been a common practice in industry for decades. An increasing number of businesses are looking to outsource noncore services such as IT, payroll services, and fleet management to a third-party specialist.[12]

Offshoring is the migration of all or a significant part of the development, maintenance, and delivery of services to a vendor located in another country. According to a recent study, 54 percent of global companies engaged in offshoring expect to expand their offshoring initiatives during the next three years. Traditionally, the reason given for offshoring is to reduce costs. Today, increased quality service is also being given as reasons for offshoring.[13] Offshoring growth concentrates in information technology, software development, and innovation services (product design, research and development, and engineering services).[14]

onshoring
Moving jobs not to another country but to lower-cost American cities.

Onshoring

Onshoring involves moving jobs not to another country but to lower-cost American cities. Some companies might like to offshore their jobs but the government may require onshore handling of certain financial, health, and defense data. This requirement often represents more than 15 percent of all IT service work. As an example, one global company opened a midwestern U.S. facility with more than 1,000 IT service employees. Wages at the facility were 35 percent lower than at headquarters, and the company also received $50 million in government incentives.[15]

Overtime

Perhaps the most commonly used alternative to recruitment, especially in meeting short-term fluctuations in work volume, is overtime. Overtime may help both employer and employee. The employer benefits by avoiding recruitment, selection, and training costs. The employees gain from increased income during the overtime period.

There are potential problems with overtime, however. Some managers believe that when employees work for unusually long periods, the company pays more and receives less in return. Employees may become fatigued and lack the energy to perform at a normal rate. Two additional possible problems relate to the use of prolonged overtime. Consciously or not, employees may pace themselves to ensure overtime. They may also become accustomed to the added income resulting from overtime pay. Employees may even elevate their standard of living to the level permitted by this additional income. Then, when a firm tightens its belt and overtime is limited, employee morale may deteriorate along with the pay.

OBJECTIVE 5.3

Explain the external environment of recruitment and describe how promotion policies influence recruitment.

External Environment of Recruitment

Like other human resource functions, the recruitment process does not occur in a vacuum. Factors external to the organization can significantly affect the firm's recruitment efforts.

Labor Market Conditions

Of particular importance to the success of recruitment is the demand for and supply of specific skills in the labor market. A firm's recruitment process is often simplified when the unemployment rate in an organization's labor market is high. The number of unsolicited applicants is usually greater, and the increased size of the labor pool provides a better opportunity for attracting qualified applicants. However, if demand for a particular skill is high relative to supply, an extraordinary recruiting effort may be required. Further, the area where recruitment takes place often impact the labor market conditions. Today, the labor market for many professional and technical positions is much broader and truly global. Even in a depressed economy, top-quality workers are in demand and forward-thinking organizations are looking to entice these individuals to join their firms.

Some companies are focusing on actively recruiting employees from competitors' most productive workers. This competition for specific skills has driven up pay for certain job skills. The specific type of job being recruited for can have a major impact on the recruiting process.[16] For example, recently, tech companies were aggressively recruiting engineers, designers, computer scientists, and executives who could compete and adapt to the rapid changes that are occurring in the industry.[17] The competition for qualified applicants was especially aggressive among workers involved in social media, mobile technology, and e-commerce even as others remain unemployed and the unemployment rate remained relatively high.

In the current market, there is even a high demand for laid off executives who have demonstrated that they know how to develop businesses. Korn Ferry recruiters estimate that currently about five to 10 percent of executive candidates are ending up with multiple job offers within three or four months of starting their search. Competition is aggressive for that group, and big signing bonuses are common.[18]

Possessing a college degree used to be the passport to secure a good job. However, in the present job market, the type of degree awarded may mean the difference between serving coffee or being a grocer stocker and obtaining a professional well-paying position. Also, many of the jobs available today do not require a college degree. Rather, skills to perform crafts such as welders, pipe fitters, painters, and machinists are needed. In fact, today there is a critical shortage of such skills in the United States.

According to a recent McKinsey Global Institute report, 40 percent of full-time job openings in companies planning to hire remain unfilled for six months or longer because they cannot find qualified applicants.[19] New technology may require that workers have a specialized degree even though one was unnecessary 10 years ago.[20] In fact, largely because of technology, the United States generates almost one-fourth more goods and services today than it did in 1999, while using almost the same number of workers.[21] There has been a "skill-based technology" change in the job market. Computers have automated many of the repetitive physical and mental tasks. Workers are now being recruited who can perform tasks that cannot be automated and are nonrepetitive and more sophisticated.[22]

active job seekers

Individuals committed to finding another job whether presently employed or not.

Active or Passive Job Seekers

The recruitment method that proves to be most successful will depend to an extent on whether the recruited individual is an active or passive job seeker. **Active job seekers** are individuals who are committed to finding another job whether presently employed or not. These individuals are usually easier to identify because their names have been placed in the job market. Their résumés are on job boards and friends, associates, or companies have been contacted directly to learn about job opportunities. **Passive job seekers**, on the other hand, are potential job candidates who are typically employed, satisfied with their employer, and content in their current role. But, if the right opportunity came along, they might like to learn more. These individuals want to move slower and will ask a lot of questions before making a job change. They are more hesitant to risk leaving a good job for a new challenge and increased risk. This chapter identifies numerous recruitment methods. Some are more useful in identifying active job seekers and others are better used in recruiting passive job seekers. Naturally, some will be directed at both groups.

Legal Considerations

Legal matters also play a significant role in recruitment practices in the United States. This is not surprising, since the candidate and the employer first make contact during the recruitment process. A poorly conceived recruiting process can do much to create problems in the selection process. Therefore, it is essential for organizations to emphasize nondiscriminatory practices at this stage.

The Office of Federal Contract Compliance Programs (OFCCP) has issued guidelines concerning the online recruiting policies of federal contractors and subcontractors. Companies must keep detailed records of each online job search. They must also identify what selection criteria were used and be able to explain why a person with protected status was not hired. EEOC guidelines suggest that companies with more than 100 employees keep staffing records for a minimum of two years. The threshold coverage is 50 employees if dealing with the OFCCP.

A dramatic increase in firms using the Internet for recruiting has added to management's challenge to comply with the OFCCP. Under the rule, there are four criteria to determine whether an individual is an Internet applicant:

- The job seeker has expressed interest through the Internet. Applicants have gone to the corporate career Web site and applied for a particular job that is listed.
- The employer considers the job seeker for employment in a particular open position. If the applicant does not meet specific qualifications spelled out in the job-specification section of the job description, the résumé does not have to be considered.
- The job seeker has indicated that he or she meets the position's basic qualifications. If the position description calls for three years of work experience, and the individual has three years of experience in previous jobs, he or she would believe that meets the basic qualifications.
- The applicant has not indicated he or she is no longer interested in the position.[23]

Employers must keep records of any and all expressions of interest through the Internet, including online résumés and internal databases. Employers are also expected to obtain the gender, race, and ethnicity of each applicant, when possible. This information enables a compilation of demographic data, such as age, race, and gender, based on that applicant pool. This data is used to determine whether a company's hiring practices are discriminatory.

Promotion Policies

Promotion from within (PFW) is the policy of filling vacancies above entry-level positions with current employees.

An organization's promotion policy can have a significant impact on recruitment. A firm can stress a policy of promotion from within its own ranks or one in which positions are generally filled from outside the organization. Depending on specific circumstances, either approach may have merit, but usually a combination of the two approaches proves best.

When an organization emphasizes promotion from within, its workers have an incentive to strive for advancement. When employees see coworkers promoted, they become more aware of their own opportunities. At Costco, most managers have been promoted to their current jobs from within the company. In fact, 68 percent of warehouse managers started out as hourly employees.[24] As another example, employees with Royal Caribbean Cruises have the opportunity to progress over time based on performance from an entry-level position such as assistant cabin steward to an officer position. Motivation provided by PFW often improves employee morale. PFW also communicates to the workers that the firm wants them to succeed. In addition, an internal hire understands the firm's culture.

Another advantage of internal recruitment is that the organization is usually well aware of its employees' capabilities. Internal candidates have knowledge of the firm, its policies, and its people. An employee's present job performance, by itself, may not be a reliable criterion for promotion. Nevertheless, management will know many of the employee's personal and job-related qualities. The employee has a track record, as opposed to being an unknown entity. Also, the company's investment in the individual may yield a higher return.

It is unlikely, however, that a firm can, or would even desire to, adhere rigidly to a practice of promotion from within. A strictly applied PFW policy eventually leads to inbreeding, a lack of cross-fertilization, and a lack of creativity. Although seldom achieved, a good goal would be to fill 80 percent of openings above entry-level positions from within. Frequently, new blood provides new ideas and innovation that must take place for firms to remain competitive. In such cases, even organizations with PFW policies may opt to look outside the organization for new talent. In any event, a promotion policy that first considers insiders is great for employee morale and motivation, which is beneficial to the organization.

TRENDS & INNOVATIONS

Social Media Recruiting

Many organizations are leaving newspapers and general-purpose job boards and turning instead to such avenues as social media recruiting. Used properly, social media recruiting can benefit nearly all phases of recruiting.[25] In fact, many recruiters believe that social media and employee referrals will surpass online job boards as the preferred way to acquire talent.[26] It has often been said that if you are not using social media to get recruits, your competitors likely are. *Social media* is the catchword in recruiting these days. Terry Terhark, CEO of the Findlay, Ohio-based RPO firm the RightThing, said, "It's amazing to me, and I've been recruiting for 20-plus years, how fast it changes."[27] Social media recruiting is based on the principle that people are social animals. They have lots of friends, so send them job postings and they will circulate them to their friends. If you are looking for a job, tell your "friends" and they may be able to help.[28]

Networking is one of the best recruiting tools, and sites such as Twitter, Facebook, LinkedIn, Google+, YouTube, and blogging are available to utilize social media recruiting. However, prior to introducing social media recruiting, it is important that the proper employer branding strategy is in place.[29] Then these sites can be used to drive the brand to attract top talent to the organization.

Contracting an employment agency or executive search firm to find a manager who earns $150,000 annually can cost over $50,000 in fees or more. Posting ads on job search sites such as Monster.com could mean spending thousands of dollars and precious hours studying résumés. In contrast, social media tools are mostly free and offer added value as candidates use their own online networks, blog content, and references, which speeds up the interview process. Bill Peppier, managing partner at Kavaliro Staffing Services in Orlando, Florida, said, "Social media is at the heart of everything we do. We make numerous job placements that we never would have been able to do without Facebook, LinkedIn and Twitter. Pretty soon everyone will be finding jobs that way."[30]

Giant consulting firm Accenture hired 50,000 in 2010 and plans to make as many as 40 percent of new hires in the next few years through social media. John Campagnino, Accenture's head of global recruiting, said, "This is the future of recruiting for our company."[31] Using social media as a strategy in the recruiting process permits a firm to interact with potential hires on Facebook, LinkedIn, and Twitter. Jobs can be posted daily on those sites. Such sites also permit talent groups to be developed by linking professional groups and preserving contact with potential hires.

Today many workers live out a large portion of their lives online. Most of the new talent entering the job market these days is quite comfortable with social media and firms are increasingly being led to use it in their recruitment effort. Restaurant chain Raising Cane's has a jobs section on its Facebook page where it lists current openings and uses extensive photos and video to convey messages about the company culture. Giuseppe Rosati, founder of the restaurant jobs portal www.restogigs.com, said, "When passive job seekers stumble upon your job postings on social media sites, it opens up a whole new group of potential candidates, candidates that would not see the job on a traditional job site because they're not actively looking."[32]

There are some downsides to social media recruiting. If the applicant pool is unfamiliar or uncomfortable with using social media, then employing social media can be ineffective or even risky. Also, decision makers could become aware of an individual's race, ethnicity, or other protected information. Then, candidates might complain that they were rejected for a job based on content posted on their social networking site.[33]

FIGURE 5-1

The Recruitment Process

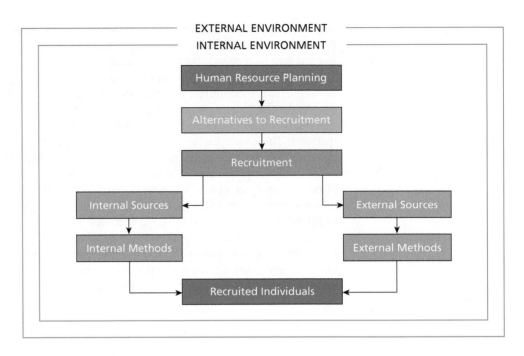

Recruitment Process

OBJECTIVE 5.4

Describe the recruitment process and explain internal recruitment methods.

employee requisition
Document that specifies job title, department, the date the employee is needed for work, and other details.

recruitment sources
Where qualified candidates are located.

recruitment methods
Specific means used to attract potential employees to the firm.

HR Web Wisdom

Social Network Recruiting
https://www.linkedin.com

LinkedIn is an online social network Web site.

When human resource planning indicates a need for employees, the firm may evaluate alternatives to hiring (see Figure 5-1). If these alternatives prove to be inappropriate, the recruitment process starts. Frequently, recruitment begins when a manager initiates an **employee requisition**, a document that specifies job title, department, the date the employee is needed for work, and other details. With this information, managers can refer to the appropriate job description to determine the qualifications the recruited person needs.

The next step in the recruitment process is to determine whether qualified employees are available within the firm (the internal source) or if it is necessary to look to external sources, such as colleges, universities, and other organizations. Because of the high cost of recruitment, organizations need to use the most productive recruitment sources and methods available.

Recruitment sources are where qualified candidates are located, such as colleges or competitors. **Recruitment methods** are the specific means used to attract potential employees to the firm, such as online recruiting.

Identifying productive sources of applicants and using suitable recruitment methods are essential to maximizing recruiting efficiency and effectiveness. When a firm identifies the sources of candidates, it uses appropriate methods for either internal or external recruitment to accomplish recruitment objectives. A candidate responds to the firm's recruitment efforts by submitting professional and personal data on either an application for employment or a résumé, depending on the company's policy.

Companies may discover that some recruitment sources and methods are superior to others for locating and attracting potential talent. Smart recruiters want to post their job where the best prospects are likely to be. For instance, one large, heavy-equipment manufacturer determined that medium-sized, state-supported colleges and universities located in rural areas were good sources of potential managers. Ever wonder why the job ad section of the Sunday paper is not as large as it once was? Recruiters are now placing their recruiting money in areas that are most productive, such as with the use of social media. To maximize recruiting effectiveness, using recruitment sources and methods tailored to specific needs is vitally important (a topic discussed later in this chapter).

Internal Recruitment Methods

Management should be able to identify current employees who are capable of filling positions as they become available. Helpful tools used for internal recruitment include employee databases, job postings and job bidding, and employee referrals.

Human Resource Databases

Human resource databases permit organizations to determine whether current employees possess the qualifications for filling open positions. As a recruitment device, these databases have proven to be extremely valuable to organizations. Databases can be valuable in locating talent internally and supporting the concept of promotion from within.

Job Posting and Job Bidding

job posting
Procedure for informing employees that job openings exist.

job bidding
Procedure that permits employees who believe that they possess the required qualifications to apply for a posted position.

Job posting is a procedure for informing employees that job openings exist. **Job bidding** is a procedure that permits employees who believe that they possess the required qualifications to apply for a posted job.

Hiring managers usually want to give internal candidates priority as a way to improve employees' attitudes and stimulate their interest in the company.[34] The job posting and bidding procedures can help minimize the commonly heard complaint that insiders never hear of a job opening until it is filled. Typically, vacant jobs are posted to internal candidates before external recruiting takes place. A number of forums are available today to advise employees that a vacancy exists. In years past, jobs were literally posted on a bulletin board. Today, companies use the intranet, the Internet, or post the job on the company Web site or company Facebook page. Some companies send out e-mails and voice mail to selected managers and employees advising them that a vacancy exists.

Many organizations, including Whirlpool, BMW Manufacturing Co., Kellogg, Hyatt, and Hewlett-Packard, manage internal candidates with Web-based applications. Employees create profiles that detail their skills and interests for their next ideal position and are notified when such a position exists. FedEx's philosophy is that employees should be doing the kind of work they want to do. Its Web site helps candidates identify their ideal job. Using drop-down lists, it prompts them to enter data about desires, location, type of work, and so forth; it also asks them to describe their skills. When jobs open, managers have instant access to these electronic résumés in which the candidates have specified what they can and want to do.

Today, if a worker does not know about a vacancy, it is usually because he or she did not check the internal posting system regularly. Yet, even with an online system, a job posting and bidding system has some potential negative features. For one thing, an effective system requires the expenditure of time, effort, and money. Organizations need to be sure to treat internal candidates properly so they will not be discouraged or prompted to leave if they do not get the job. When bidders are unsuccessful, someone must explain to them why they were not selected. Management must choose the most qualified applicant or else the system will lack credibility. Still, complaints may occur, even in a well-designed and well-implemented system.

Employee Referrals

employee referral
An employee of the company recommends a friend or associate as a possible member of the company; this continues to be the way that top performers are identified.

Employee referrals involves an employee of the company recommending a friend or associate as a possible member of the company; this continues to be the way that top performers are identified. In many organizations, the use of employee referrals produces the most and best-qualified applicants. Organizations such as Southwest Airlines, Microsoft, Disney, and Ritz typically employ many of their new hires exclusively through employee referrals. It is just human nature that employees do not want to recommend a person unless they believe they are going to fit in and be productive. Thus, it is a powerful recruiting tool. Because of this, many companies have strengthened their employee referral program. These organizations have found that their employees can serve an important role in the recruitment process by actively soliciting applications from among their friends and associates.

Some firms give incentives to their employees for successful referrals. A WorldatWork Bonus Program Practices survey found that 66 percent of companies offer referral bonuses and an additional 18 percent are considering one. Typically, the types of positions that a company would pay referral bonuses include professionals, technical, IT staff, and sales.[35] However, employee referral has also proven valuable for other professions. The trucking firm of CRST Malone offers its drivers a $1,000 bonus for recruiting other drivers.[36]

Typically, those who are referred by a present employee are more productive. Costs can be much lower than using advertising or agencies. Using referrals also reduces turnover among both new and existing employees because applicants come prescreened for culture fit. Small companies especially prefer to find candidates through referrals and networks of people they trust. Groupon, the online discounter, grew from 37 to 7,100 employees in 21 months. It acquires about 40 percent of new hires through employee referrals.[37]

Employee enlistment is a unique form of employee referral in which every employee becomes a company recruiter. This is not the same as merely asking employees to refer friends to the company. The firm supplies employees with simple business cards that do not contain names or positions. Instead, these cards have a message similar to: "We are always looking for great. For additional information, log on to our Web site." Employees then distribute the cards wherever they go, at parties, sports events, family gatherings, picnics, or the park. The purpose is to let people know that the company really does want people to apply. An interesting way of using e-mail in the recruitment process is to ask employees to put a footer in their e-mails reminding people that their company is hiring. It might say something like the following: "Note: We're hiring amazing engineers, BD people, and a star Ops person. Refer a friend and get a fully paid trip to Hawaii for two."[38]

Recruiters can often obtain referrals from new employees when they first join the firm. These new hires may provide leads regarding other candidates that have the skills and competences that the organization needs. Information from such candidates is often easy to obtain because the new hire is excited about joining the company and would like to have their friends and associates join them. Recruiters may simply ask: "Do you know anyone in your field who might like to work here?" A capable recruiter can then develop a list of good candidates with special skills who can be recruited.[39]

A note of caution should be observed with regard to the extensive use of employee referral. The 2006 EEOC Compliance Manual explicitly warns that recruiting only at select colleges or relying on word-of-mouth recruiting, which includes employee referral programs, may generate applicant pools that do not reflect diversity in the labor market.

OBJECTIVE 5.5

Identify external recruitment sources.

External Recruitment Sources

At times, a firm must look beyond its own borders to find employees, particularly when expanding its workforce. External recruitment is needed to (1) fill entry-level jobs; (2) acquire skills not possessed by current employees; and (3) obtain employees with different backgrounds to provide a diversity of ideas. As Figure 5-2 shows, even with internal promotions, firms still have to fill entry-level jobs from the outside. Thus, after the president of a firm retires, a series of internal promotions follows. Ultimately, however, the firm has to recruit externally for the entry-level position of salary analyst. If an outside candidate was selected for the president's position, the chain reaction of promotions from within would not have occurred. If no current employee has the desired qualifications, candidates may be attracted from a number of outside sources.

FIGURE 5-2

Internal Promotion and External Recruitment

High Schools and Vocational Schools

Organizations concerned with recruiting clerical and other entry-level employees often depend on high schools and vocational schools. Many of these institutions have outstanding training programs for specific occupational skills, such as home appliance repair and small engine mechanics. Some companies work with schools to ensure a constant supply of trained individuals with specific job skills. In some areas, companies even loan employees to schools to assist in the training programs.

Community Colleges

Many community colleges are sensitive to the specific employment needs in their local labor markets and graduate highly sought-after students with marketable skills. Typically, community colleges have two-year programs designed for both a terminal education and preparation for a four-year university degree program. Many community colleges also have excellent mid-management programs combined with training for specific trades. Sowela Technical Community College located in Lake Charles, Louisiana, has a well-respected culinary program that is known nationwide. Career centers often provide a place for employers to contact students, thereby facilitating the recruitment process.

Colleges and Universities

Colleges and universities represent a major recruitment source for potential professional, technical, and management employees. Placement directors, faculty, and administrators can be helpful to organizations in their search for recruits. Establishing a relationship with faculty members is important because most professors are well aware of their students' academic performance and abilities. Because on-campus recruitment is mutually beneficial, both employers and universities should take steps to develop and maintain close relationships. It is important that the firm knows the school and the school knows the firm.

Competitors in the Labor Market

When recent experience is required, competitors and other firms in the same industry or geographic area may be the most important source of recruits. Another name for actively recruiting employees from competitors is called *poaching*. It has been estimated that poaching may account for 30 percent of the movement in labor.[40] In fact, the most highly qualified applicants often come directly from competitors in the same labor market, as people typically do not enter the workforce loaded with experience and job skills. Competitors and other firms serve as external sources of recruitment for high-quality talent. Even organizations that have policies of promotion from within occasionally look elsewhere to fill positions.

Smaller firms in particular look for employees trained by larger organizations that have greater developmental resources. For instance, one optical firm believes that its own operation is not large enough to provide extensive training and development programs. Therefore, a person recruited by this firm for a significant management role is likely to have held at least two previous positions with a competitor.

ETHICAL DILEMMA

Unfair Advantage?

You are the vice president of human resources for a high-tech company that is competing for a major government project. You believe that one of your key competitors is ahead of you in project development and you would like to recruit some of its engineers who are knowledgeable about the project. You receive an anonymous e-mail that includes the names and phone numbers of key people involved in your competitor's project. If you use the information and are able to hire some of the competitor's key people, your company has a chance to beat the competitor and you will become a hero. If you do not use the information, your company may lose a great deal of money.

What would you do?
What factor(s) in this ethical dilemma might influence a person to make a less-than-ethical decision?

Former Employees

At one time, when employees quit, their managers and peers tended to view them as being disloyal and ungrateful, and they were "punished" with no-return policies. A common attitude was that if you left your firm, you did not appreciate what the company had done for you. Those days are gone and often "goodbye" may not be forever. In fact according to a recent survey, only 11 percent of HR professionals said that they would not rehire departing workers if they wished to return.[41] Today's young workers are more likely to change jobs and later return to a former employer than their counterparts who entered the workforce 20 or 30 years ago, and smart employers try to get their best ex-employees to come back. The *boomerang* effect might happen because there was a strong bond with previous coworkers or the new job was not what the employee envisioned. Van Alstyne, HR manager for Staffing Plus, based in Haverford, Pennsylvania, said, "If employees depart on good terms, contact should be maintained through proactive networking efforts by the company. It keeps the door open for good employees to return."[42]

The advantage of tracking former employees is that the firm knows their strengths and weaknesses and the ex-employees know the company. Tracking, recruiting, and hiring a former employee can be a tremendous benefit and can encourage others to stay with the firm. It sends the message that things are not always greener on the other side of the fence. The large number of people who will change jobs during their lifetime means businesses would be foolish to lose touch with them.

Unemployed

The unemployed often provide a valuable source of recruits. Qualified applicants join the unemployment rolls every day for various reasons. Companies may downsize their operations, go out of business, or merge with other firms, leaving qualified workers without jobs. Employees are also fired sometimes merely because of personality differences with their bosses. Not infrequently, employees become frustrated with their jobs and quit. Even individuals who have been out of work for extended periods should not be overlooked. In 2012, approximately 14 million Americans were unemployed creating an unemployment rate of around 9 percent. However, if discouraged workers who have given up looking for jobs are counted, the total unemployment rate was about 16 percent.[43]

Military Personnel

Hiring former service members makes sense to a lot of employers because many of these individuals have a proven work history and are flexible, motivated, and drug-free. General Electric found an endless supply of talent in junior military officers. Many were graduates of U.S. military academies who had spent four to five years in the service. They were found to be hardworking, smart, and intense; they had leadership experience and were flexible. They are prompt, used to reporting for work on time, and know the importance of a professional appearance and presence.[44] Walmart, along with many other companies, has discovered the benefits of recruiting military talent. It even hired a retired Army brigadier general, Gary Profit, to expand military recruiting to all levels and divisions of the business.[45]

Service members nationwide looking for jobs can also go to HirePatriots.com. "We help citizens and businesses to thank our current military, veterans, and their spouses by posting their job opportunities on our free military job posting and search Web site," said Mark Baird, president of Patriotic Hearts.[46]

Self-Employed Workers

The self-employed worker may also be a good potential source. These individuals may be true entrepreneurs who are ingenious and creative. For many firms, these qualities are essential for continued competitiveness. Such individuals may constitute a source of applicants for any number of jobs requiring technical, professional, administrative, or entrepreneurial expertise within a firm.

Ex-offenders

Some organizations have found it beneficial to hire ex-offenders.[47] There are approximately 2.3 million criminals behind bars in the United States. Further, 65 million U.S. adults have criminal records, and each year more than 700,000 ex-offenders are released.[48] A recent analysis by the National Employment Law Project shows that more than one in four U.S. adults has an arrest or conviction that would appear in a routine criminal background check.[49] The Bureau of Labor Statistics estimates that as many as 50 percent of ex-offenders are unemployed. Many are non-violent substance abusers who were locked up because of federal and state drug laws. According to Multicultural Foodservice & Hospitality Alliance President Gerry Fernandez, "I'm aware of several chains that have programs to hire ex-offenders, though they do not want publicity. Who do you think works third shift, where they don't come in contact with customers?"[50] In another example, supermarket retail consultant and restaurateur Howard Solganik has launched a program that puts ex-offenders to work helping area farmers increase the supply of local, seasonal produce to consumers. Solganik said, "My experience in the restaurant business exposed me to ex-offenders. I saw that most were hard workers and also were grateful for the jobs they were given."[51]

Many ex-offenders have nothing on their résumé except what they have done while they were in prison. Sweet Beginnings, a wholly owned subsidiary that produces honey and honey-based skin care products, is staffed almost entirely by ex-offenders. Palms Barber, manager and career foundation worker, said, "I had to demonstrate that ex-offenders can be good workers. They can be good for your bottom line." Sweet Beginnings's employees must complete its job-readiness program before they are hired and receive job placement when they are ready to leave.[52]

Mobile Recruiting

OBJECTIVE 5.6

Explain the impact of mobile HR recruiting.

Macy's Inc. executive recruiting director Owen Williams provides an example of the power of mobile recruiting. During his three-block walk to his office, he regularly uses his BlackBerry and the mobile version of LinkedIn to post job listings and connect to potential candidates. Time is money for Owen because he personally fills more than 80 store manager and regional buyer positions a year. "It's amazing what work I can get done in that walk," he says."[53]

The world of recruiting via mobile technology is moving at lightning speed. More and more people are adopting mobile technology, and many organizations are trying to figure out how to use mobile devices in the recruiting process. Recruiters use mobile apps to post jobs, run text message–based recruiting campaigns, create online communities for potential new hires to learn about their companies, monitor social networks for news about industries they hire for, and keep in touch with staff and outside agencies. These tasks previously had to be done from a desktop or laptop computer.[54] The move to mobile recruiting has generated blogs, webinars, seminars, e-newsletters, and online groups. Recruiters who want to keep up with technology and trends can join the LinkedIn group CloudRecruiting.net or read blogs such as RecruiterGuy.net.

Online Recruitment Methods

OBJECTIVE 5.7

Describe online recruitment methods and discuss the possibility of job search scams.

Online recruiting has revolutionized the way companies recruit employees and job seekers search and apply for jobs. In addition, smartphones may be used in many of the methods described below.

Internet Recruiter

internet recruiter
Person whose primary responsibility is to use the Internet in the recruitment process (also called cyber recruiter).

The **Internet recruiter**, also called a cyber recruiter, is a person whose primary responsibility is to use the Internet in the recruitment process.

Most companies currently post jobs on their corporate career Web site. Individuals must be in place to monitor and coordinate these activities. The more companies recruit on the Internet, the greater the need for Internet recruiters. Currently, high-tech firms have the greatest needs.

Virtual Job Fair

virtual job fair
Online recruiting method engaged in by a single employer or group of employers to attract a large number of applicants.

A **virtual job fair** is an online recruiting method engaged in by a single employer or group of employers to attract a large number of applicants. They are designed to be a first step in the recruitment process. Many recruiters have found that traditional job fairs where applicants and recruiters go to a physical location are ineffective. In addition to the time and expense of attending them in person, recruiters often find them wasteful because many people who stop by their booth do not possess the right skills.[55]

At virtual job fairs, recruiters prescreen résumés, contact candidates who are a potential fit, and store e-mail addresses. If applicants pass the initial screening, they typically must complete a questionnaire, take a behavioral test, and do a telephone interview before meeting a recruiter in person.

Virtual fairs usually last about five hours, though recruiters can receive résumés online for as long as a week after the event. In their virtual "booth," recruiters often provide links to their online career site, obtained résumés from candidates, and interact with applicants in a live chat room.

Corporate Career Web Sites

Corporate career Web sites are job sites accessible from a company home page that list the company positions available and provide a way for applicants to apply for specific jobs. They have become a major resource for both job seekers and companies seeking new employees.

A career Web site should be relevant and engaging, informing the reader about the company and the specific position being advertised. It should be used as a selling device that promotes the company to prospective job candidates. Writing effective recruitment ads on the Internet is different from the short, one-inch-column ads in the Sunday newspaper. The Internet provides enough space to fully describe the job, location, and company. It provides an opportunity to convert consumers into great employees. A good Web site should provide a feeling of the kind of corporate culture that exists within the company.

Weblogs (Blogs for Short)

Weblogs, or *blogs,* have changed the ways in which individuals access information. Google or a blog search engine such as Technorati.com can be used. All a person has to do is type in a key phrase like *marketing jobs*. The blogs themselves make it pretty easy to find, with names like HRJobs.com, AttorneyJobs.com, and SalesJobs.com. Some employers and employment agencies have also discovered that blogging is a way to do detailed and stealthy background checks.

General-Purpose Job Boards

Firms use general-purpose job boards by typing in key job criteria, skills, and experience, and indicating their geographic location. Job seekers can search for jobs by category, experience, education, location, or any combination of categories. General-purpose job boards continue to attract large number of applicants, but their use has declined somewhat in recent years. Many believe that the general-purpose big job boards are best for job seekers in professions that experience high turnover like sales but often are less effective for highly qualified applicants or those looking for work in smaller industries. They are also not as effective in finding jobs for senior level positions because most firms prefer referrals or Web sites such as LinkedIn.[56] The two most widely recognized general employment Web sites are, Monster.com and CareerBuilder.com.

MONSTER.COM. Monster Worldwide, Inc. is the parent company of Monster. It is a premier global online employment solution for people seeking jobs and the employers who need people. Information helpful to job seekers such as résumé tips, interview tips, salary information, and networking information is available on the site.[57]

CAREERBUILDER.COM. Owned by Gannett Co, Inc., Tribune Company, The McClatchy Company, and Microsoft Corp., CareerBuilder offers a vast online and print network to help job seekers connect with employers. CareerBuilder.com powers the career sites for more than 9,000 Web sites, including 140 newspapers and broadband portals such as MSN and AOL.[58]

NACElink Network

The **NACElink Network**, the result of an alliance among the National Association of Colleges and Employers, DirectEmployers Association, and Symplicity Corporation, is a national recruiting network and suite of Web-based recruiting and career services automation tools serving the needs of colleges, employers, and job candidates. Currently over 900 colleges use the NACElink system.[59] The system includes three components: job posting, résumé database, and interview scheduling. It is available to employers to post jobs and search for students and new graduates. DirectEmployers Association has also created an employment Web site for returning veterans that uses military codes to help veterans identify jobs in their fields.

.Jobs

.Jobs is a network of employment Web sites where any company can list job openings for free. There are 40,000 sites, with all Web addresses ending in ".jobs." The initiative is being backed by nearly 600 hundred industrial companies such as Google, American Express, IBM, Northrop Grumman, and Lockheed Martin. Finding jobs on the sites is simple. Possible searches might include Nurse.jobs, Attorney.jobs, HR.jobs, and Sales.jobs. For someone looking for a job in the

CHAPTER 5 • RECRUITMENT   **121**

Washington, D.C., there's www.washingtondc.jobs. It works for many professions and is available in every state and any U.S. city with more than 5,000 people.

AllianceQ

AllianceQ
Group of Fortune 500 companies, along with over 3,000 small and medium-sized companies, that have collaborated to create a pool of job candidates.

AllianceQ is a group of Fortune 500 companies, along with over 3,000 small and medium-sized companies, that have collaborated to create a pool of job candidates. AllianceQ provides a way for candidates to be found by top employers.[60] Those passed over by one company are invited to submit their résumés to the AllianceQ database. "It's a no-brainer," says Phil Hendrickson, a recruiting manager at member company Starbucks.[61]

Niche Sites

niche sites
Web sites that cater to highly specialized job markets such as a particular profession, industry, education, location, or any combination of these specialties.

Niche sites are Web sites that cater to highly specialized job markets such as a particular profession, industry, education, location, or any combination of these specialties. They continue to grow in popularity and are giving the top two general-purpose job boards major competition.[62] There seems to be a site for virtually everyone. A few catchy ones include:

- cfo.com (a comprehensive online resource center for senior finance executives)
- accountantsworld.com (an online recruiting service that provides CPA firms with assistance in locating qualified employees)
- dice.com (a leading provider of online recruiting services for technology professionals)
- internshipprograms.com (employers who are exclusively looking for interns)
- joyjobs.com (international employment for teachers)
- techjobbank.com (focuses on the recruiting needs of the technology companies)
- coolworks.com (find seasonal job or career in places such as Yellowstone, Yosemite, or other national parks)
- figurejobs.com (provides executives and experienced professionals with access to some of the most exclusive executive jobs, executive recruiters, and career-management tools available)
- TVjobs.com (jobs in broadcasting)
- layover.com (jobs in trucking)
- college.monster.com (job listings and résumé service that targets college students and alumni)
- JobsInLogistics.com (dedicated to logistics jobs and logistics careers)
- Job.com (maintains sites specialized by geography)

A niche site is also available for professors who desire to change jobs. Formerly, college and university professors went to the campus library and thumbed through the many pages of *The Chronicle of Higher Education* to hunt for a job. Now all they have to do is enter www.chronicle.com, *The Chronicle of Higher Education* Web site. All the jobs listed with the *Chronicle* are available to view for free. Each position announcement has a hot link to a university home page where additional information can be obtained. The universities pay the fees.

Contract Workers' Sites

Earlier, contract workers were mentioned as part of the contingent workforce as an alternative to recruitment. Sites are available to assist these workers. Specialized Web sites let workers advertise their skills, set their price, and pick an employer. Two such sites are listed below:

- Freelance.com is a company that offers to clients the services of talented freelancers.
- Guru.com is an online marketplace for freelance talent.

Hourly Workers' Sites

After years of focusing primarily on professionals and their prospective employers, job sites are now available to attract blue-collar and service workers. Traditionally, there have been major differences between the ways hourly and salaried workers look for jobs. Most hourly workers pursue jobs by filling out applications rather than creating and sending out résumés. So sites allow job seekers to build an application that can be viewed by employers. Recognizing that some hourly workers do not have computer access, they have set up phone-based services to accept applications. Some job boards have bilingual call-center operators who can help job applicants through the process. Many of the large boards such as Monster.com and CareerBuilder.com have moved into this large market.

Job Search Scams

In searching for a job online, one should be alert to the fact that there are those out there who will attempt to steal personal information and set up fraudulent credit-card accounts. Often crooks search for potential victims through posting a high-paying job on popular job search Web sites. Once you apply for a job, naturally in order to conduct a thorough background check, they will need personal information such as your bank-account or credit-card number to check you out. Do not do it! True, firms use bank information, but that happens after you are hired. Countless crooks are out there waiting for a person to make a mistake. Recently, Lloyd's Insurance PLC was subject to a recruitment scam in which people were offered fake jobs with Lloyd's and then asked to send their personal details. Often potential targets receive fake documents that look amazingly real in an attempt to lend credibility to the scam.[63]

The following scenario is not unusual in job scams. A person who posts his or her résumé on the Web one day receives a call from a person who says that he is an HR director with a well-known company. The person says that he is impressed with your résumé wants to meet with you as soon as possible since there appeared to be a perfect match. But before the meeting can take place, a background check needs to be completed. Then a very detailed form is sent with requests for social security number, date of birth, mother's maiden name, even a bank-account number. If you do this, you have been scammed. Often not only are the credit-card accounts maxed out, but new accounts have been opened and also emptied.

Here is another situation that should send out an alert for a possible scam. If a posted job includes an e-mail address with a domain like Gmail, Hotmail, or Yahoo!, caution should be used. Most legitimate companies have a company e-mail address. Susan Joyce, publisher of employment portal Job-Hunt.org, tries to identify fake jobs, first by Googling the hiring firm. "If all you find are other job postings on other job boards, that's a red flag," she says.[64] To verify whether a company is legitimate, corporate phone numbers can be obtained by using sites such as Hoovers.com. Call the company to determine if the position is legitimate.

Your social security number and date of birth are valuable in the hands of the scammer. True, they may be needed to conduct a background a check, but you should hesitate to provide them until after an in-person meeting.

OBJECTIVE 5.8
Identify traditional external recruitment methods.

Traditional External Recruitment Methods

Although online recruiting has greatly impacted how recruiting is accomplished, traditional methods are not dead.

Media Advertising

Advertising communicates the firm's employment needs to the public through media such as newspapers, trade journals, radio, television, and billboards. The firm's previous experience with various media should suggest the most effective approach for specific types of jobs. Although few individuals base their decision to change jobs on advertising, ads create awareness, generate interest, and encourage a prospect to seek more information about the firm and the job opportunities that it provides. A traditional common form of advertising that provides broad coverage at a relatively low cost is the newspaper ad. Firms using the newspaper ad attempt to appeal to the self-interest of prospective employees, emphasizing the job's unique qualities. Recently, the use of newspaper advertising has declined because other recruiting methods are more effective and less expensive. Newspapers continue to lose readership; only two of the top 25 dailies, the *Wall Street Journal* and *USA Today*, gained readers.[65]

Certain media attract audiences that are more homogeneous in terms of employment skills, education, and orientation. Advertisements placed in publications such as the *Wall Street Journal* relate primarily to managerial, professional, and technical positions. The readers of these publications are generally individuals qualified for many of the positions advertised. Focusing on a specific labor market minimizes the likelihood of receiving marginally qualified or even totally unqualified applicants. Like most professional publications, jobs that are advertised in the paper copy of the *Journal* are also available on the publication's Web site. Journals specific to particular trades are also widely used. For example, *Automotive News* might have jobs related to the automobile industry and *American Drycleaner* likely will list jobs in the dry cleaning business.

Qualified prospects who read job ads in newspapers and professional and trade journals may not be so dissatisfied with their present jobs that they will pursue opportunities advertised.

Therefore, in high-demand situations, a firm needs to consider all available media resources such as radio, billboards, and television. These methods are likely more expensive than newspapers or journals, but, in specific situations, they may prove successful. For instance, a regional medical center used billboards effectively to attract registered nurses. One large manufacturing firm had considerable success in advertising for production trainees by means of spot advertisements on the radio. A large electronics firm used television to attract experienced engineers when it opened a new facility and needed more engineers immediately. Thus, in situations where hiring needs are urgent, television and radio may provide good results. Broadcast messages can let people know that an organization is seeking recruits. A primary limitation is the amount of information they can transmit.

Private Employment Agencies

Private employment agencies, often called "headhunters," are best known for recruiting white-collar employees and offer an important service in bringing qualified applicants and open positions together.[66] Firms and job hunters use private employment agencies for virtually every type position. Job seekers should carefully select the employment agency to use because there are both good and bad recruiters. Today, private employment agencies often specialize in filling a particular niche in the job market. Agencies should be selected based on knowledge of the industry and the specific position being sought.

Private employment agencies fees can range up to 35 percent of a person's first year salary. The one-time fees that some agencies charge often turn off candidates, although many private employment agencies also deal with firms that pay the fees. Either way, the headhunter does not get paid until a person is placed. The recent recession has significantly impacted the use of private employment agencies resulting in a general retrenchment of the industry.

Public Employment Agencies

Public employment agencies are operated by each state but receive overall policy direction from the U.S. Employment Service. Public employment agencies have become increasingly involved in matching people with technical, professional, and managerial positions. They typically use computerized job-matching systems to aid in the recruitment process, and they provide their services without charge to either the employer or the prospective employee.

Executive Search Firms

Executive search firms are used by some firms to locate experienced professionals and executives when other sources prove inadequate. The key benefit of executive search firms is the targeting of ideal candidates. In addition, the executive search firm can often find passive candidates, those not actively looking for a job.

An executive search firm's representatives often visit the client's offices and interview the company's management. This enables them to gain a clear understanding of the company's goals and the job qualifications required. After obtaining this information, they contact and interview potential candidates, check references, and refer the best-qualified person to the client for the selection decision. Search firms maintain databases of résumés for this process. Other sources used include networking contacts, files from previous searches, specialized directories, personal calls, previous clients, colleagues, and unsolicited résumés. The search firm's task is to present candidates who are eminently qualified to do the job; it is the company's decision whom to hire.

There are two types of executive search firms: contingency and retained. *Contingency search firms* receive fees only upon successful placement of a candidate in a job opening. The search firm's fee is generally a percentage of the individual's compensation for the first year. The client pays expenses, as well as the fee. A contingency recruiter goes to work when there is an urgent need to fill a position, when an opening exists for a difficult position, or when a hiring executive wants to know about top-notch talent as those people surface, regardless of whether there is an opening.

Retained search firms are considered consultants to their client organizations, serving on an exclusive contractual basis, and typically recruit top business executives. With a retained search firm, the company typically gets a firmer commitment from their search firm, as well as more personalized attention, dedicated time, and customized searches.[67]

Recruiters

Recruiters most commonly focus on technical and vocational schools, community colleges, colleges, and universities. The key contact for recruiters on college and university campuses is often the student placement director. This administrator is in an excellent position to arrange interviews with students possessing the qualifications desired by the firm. Placement services help organizations use their recruiters efficiently. They identify qualified candidates, schedule interviews, and provide suitable rooms for interviews.

The company recruiter plays a vital role in attracting applicants. The interviewee often perceives the recruiter's actions as a reflection of the character of the firm. If the recruiter is dull, the interviewee may think the company is dull; if the recruiter is apathetic, discourteous, or vulgar, the interviewee may well attribute these negative characteristics to the firm. Recruiters must always be aware of the image they present, because it makes a lasting impression. Recruitment success comes down to good personal selling, appealing to the candidate's priorities, and addressing his or her concerns. The recruiter should underscore the job's opportunities and keep the lines of communication open.

A recent trend is the use of videoconferencing with equipment at both corporate headquarters and on college campuses. Recruiters can communicate with college career counselors and interview students through a videoconferencing system without leaving the office.

Job Fairs

job fair
Recruiting method engaged in by a single employer or group of employers to attract a large number of applicants to one location for interviews.

A **job fair** is a recruiting method engaged in by a single employer or group of employers to attract a large number of applicants to one location for interviews.

From an employer's viewpoint, a primary advantage of job fairs is the opportunity to meet a large number of candidates in a short time. Conversely, applicants may have convenient access to a number of employers. As a recruitment method, job fairs offer the potential for a much lower cost per hire than traditional approaches. Job fairs are often organized by universities to assist their students in obtaining jobs. Here, employers from many organizations meet at a single point on the campus. The job fair is available from disciplines from across the university. Students and employers can meet here to ask and answer questions.

At times job fairs are tailored to recruit specific types of individuals. At a Tucson, Arizona, job fair, the event was designed to bring together senior citizens and companies looking to hire them, as well as offer assistance to those seeking to improve their job skills as a first step toward employment. The job fair attracted two dozen companies seeking to fill positions for everything from teachers' aides to bank tellers to tour bus drivers and call-center staff.[68] Job fairs are also held to bring together military service members and companies with openings to fill. Recently the Veterans Career Fair and Expo was held in Washington, D.C. Employers representing companies across the private sector, as well as several government agencies, were on site to discuss career and job opportunities to thousands of veterans from the mid-Atlantic region.[69]

Internships

internship
Special form of recruitment that involves placing a student in a temporary job with no obligation either by the company to hire the student permanently or by the student to accept a permanent position with the firm following graduation.

An **internship** is a special form of recruitment that involves placing a student in a temporary job with no obligation either by the company to hire the student permanently or by the student to accept a permanent position with the firm following graduation.

An internship typically involves a temporary job for the summer months or a part-time job during the school year. It may also take the form of working full-time one semester and going to school full-time the next. Recently nontraditional virtual internships are being used by businesses for students who would be required to commute long distances through the use of Skype, e-mail, and conference calls.[70] Employers are able to *try out* future employees prior to making a job offer. If the trial period proves unsuccessful, there is no obligation on either side. Google has long been known for using the internship as a recruiting method. Even in a slowed economy, Google offered interns competitive pay and on-site perks that include free gourmet food, a gym, fitness classes, massage therapy, bike repair, dry cleaning, a hair stylist, oil changes, and car washes.[71]

During the internship, the student gets to view business practices firsthand. At the same time, the intern contributes to the firm by performing needed tasks. In addition to other benefits, internships provide opportunities for students to bridge the gap from business theory to practice. Through this relationship, a student can determine whether a company would be a desirable employer. Similarly, having a relatively lengthy time to observe the student's job performance, the firm can make a better judgment regarding the person's qualifications.

In today's job market, just having a degree is often not enough to get a job offer; internships are often the deciding factor in getting a good job or not. Students with internship and co-op experience are often able to find jobs easier, and they progress much further and faster in the business world than those without. Paid internships for college students have become even more valuable in recent years for both new graduates and companies. In a NACE's 2011 Student

HR Web Wisdom

Internship Web Site
http://www.internships.com/

The world's largest internship marketplace.

Survey, more than half of the interns from the Class of 2011 were paid, and 61 percent of students with a paid summer internship in the for-profit sector received a full-time job offer after graduation.[72] Steve Canale, manager, global recruiting and staffing services, at General Electric Co., based in Fairfield, Connecticut, said, "If I had my budget slashed and only had $100 to spend, I'd spend it all on my internship program. They become my brand ambassadors".[73]

Social media has now become a prime mover for students seeking internships. Christine Garland found an internship when a Twitter-savvy friend offered to help. "I have a qualified PR student looking for summer internships," he tweeted. He got a response within five minutes from a Chicago-based B2B Web marketing company. The firm interviewed Garland and accepted her as an intern.[74]

Professional Associations

Virtually every professional group publishes a journal and has a Web site that is widely used by its members. Many professional associations in business areas including finance, marketing, accounting, and human resources provide recruitment and placement services for their members. Jobs advertised are placed in the journal in hard copy and also advertised on the professional group's Web site. The Society for Human Resource Management (SHRM), for example, operates a job referral service for members seeking new positions and employers with positions to fill.

Unsolicited Applicants

A company must have a positive image or employer brand in order to attract unsolicited applicants. If an organization has the reputation of being a good place to work, it may be able to attract qualified prospects even without extensive recruitment efforts. Acting on their own initiative, well-qualified workers may seek out a specific company to apply for a job. Unsolicited applicants who apply because they are favorably impressed with the firm's reputation often prove to be valuable employees. In the Internet age, applicants can go to the firm's corporate career Web site and *walk in* by making an application online.

Open Houses

Open houses pair potential hires and recruiters in a warm, casual environment that encourages on-the-spot job offers. Open houses are cheaper and faster than hiring through recruitment agencies, and they are also more popular than job fairs. There are pros and cons to holding a truly *open* house. If the event is open, it may draw a large turnout, but it also may attract a number of unqualified candidates. Some companies prefer to control the types of candidates they host, and so they conduct invitation-only sessions. In this scenario, someone screens résumés in response to ads, then invites only preselected candidates. Open house advertising may be through both conventional media and the Internet, where a firm might feature its open house on its home page.

Event Recruiting

event recruiting
Recruiters going to events being attended by individuals the company is seeking.

Event recruiting involves having recruiters go to events being attended by individuals the company is seeking. Cisco Systems pioneered event recruiting as a recruitment approach. In the case of programmers in the Silicon Valley, the choice spots have been marathons and bike races. Companies that participate in these events become involved in some way that promotes their name and cause. For example, they might sponsor or cosponsor an event, pass out refreshments, and give away prizes. Individuals get to know that the company is recruiting and the types of workers it is seeking. Event recruiting gives a company the opportunity to reflect its image.

Sign-on Bonuses

Employers use sign-on bonuses to attract top talent, particularly in high-demand fields such as health care, sales, marketing, and accounting. Bonuses allow a firm to pay a premium to attract individuals without dramatically upsetting its salary scale. Even as Wall Street continued to lay off workers, some firms were offering sign-on bonuses for top management talent. Overall, in 2011, 54 percent of firms surveyed by Altura Consulting Group offered signing bonuses.[75] Roadrunner Transportation Services was offering up to a $10,000 bonus spread over five quarters to experienced drivers.[76]

Competitive Games

Google has a unique way to get individuals interested in applying for technical positions. Google Code Jam is an international programming competition hosted and administered by Google. The competition began in 2003 as a means to identify top engineering talent for potential employment at Google. The competition consists of a set of algorithmic problems that must be solved in a fixed amount of time. Competitors may use any programming language and development environment to obtain their solutions. The final round for the 2011 Code Jam was in Tokyo. The 30,000 coders came from far and wide to contend in the international Code Jam competition.[77]

Google is not the only company that uses games as a recruiting tool. TopCoder is a Glastonbury, Connecticut, company that creates software coding competitions. Internet advertising firm DoubleClick hired TopCoder to run a software coding competition contest between students from Columbia University and New York University. TopCoder identified about 100 programmers to participate in this software competition, and 10 made it to the final round. DoubleClick Chief Information Officer Mok Choe says the company has already hired a few of the winners. "We can filter out the cream of the crop," says Choe.[78]

OBJECTIVE **5.9**

Describe how recruitment methods and sources are tailored to each other.

Tailoring Recruitment Methods to Sources

Because each organization is unique, so are the needed types and qualifications of workers to fill positions.[79] Thus, to be successful, a firm must tailor its recruitment sources and methods to its specific needs.

Suppose, for example, that a large firm has an immediate need for an experienced information technology manager and no one within the firm has these qualifications. Figure 5-3 shows a matrix that depicts sources and methods of recruitment for such a manager. Managers must first identify the *source* (where prospective employees are located) before choosing the *methods* (how to attract them). It is likely that other firms, possibly competitors, employ such individuals. After considering the recruitment source, the recruiter must then choose the method (or methods) of recruitment that offers the best prospects for attracting qualified candidates. Perhaps it would be appropriate to advertise the job in the classified section of the *Wall Street Journal* and use online recruiting. Alternatively, an executive search firm may serve as a viable option. In addition, the recruiter may attend meetings of professional information technology associations. One or more of these methods will likely yield a pool of qualified applicants.

In another scenario, consider a firm's need for 20 entry-level machine operators, whom the firm is willing to train. High schools and vocational schools would probably be good recruitment sources. Methods of recruitment might include newspaper ads, public employment agencies, recruiters, visiting vocational schools, and employee referrals.

reshoring

Reverse of offshoring and involves bringing work back to the United States.

OBJECTIVE **5.10**

Define *reshoring* and explain why some firms are rejecting outsourcing and returning the lost jobs to the United States.

FIGURE 5-3

Methods and Sources of Recruitment for an Information Technology Manager

External Sources	Online recruiting	Advertising	Employment agencies	Recruiters	Job fairs	Internships	Executive search firms	Professional associations	Walk-in applicants	Open houses	Event recruiting	Sign-on bonuses	High Tech Competition
High/Vocational schools													
Community colleges													
Colleges and universities													
Competitors in the labor market	X	X	X				X	X					
Unemployed													
Self-employed													
Former employees													
Military personnel													
Ex-offenders													

Reshoring

Reshoring is the reverse of off-shoring and involves bringing work back to the United States. Advocates of reshoring believe that manufacturers should calculate the total impact of offshoring because there are often hidden expenses such as higher costs for travel, packaging, shipping, and inventory.[80] Harry Moser, who has emerged as the champion of reshoring in the United States, said, "Reshoring is bringing back work, parts or tools that will finally be used in North America."[81] Reshoring has also become a part of recent labor agreements. For instance, a portion of the 2011 labor agreement between Ford Motor Company and the United Auto Workers involved Ford agreeing to reshore some work presently being done in Mexico, China, and Japan.

There are numerous examples of reshoring by American firms. GE is reshoring its appliance manufacturing with an investment of about $432 million in its facilities in Kentucky, Tennessee, Alabama, and Indiana. Some of the reasons cited included rising costs for currency exchange, transportation, and labor in countries that were once much less expensive.[82] Wham-O, a company that makes inexpensive toys, recently announced it was moving 50 percent of its Frisbee and Hula Hoop production back to the United States from China and Mexico, which will create hundreds of new American jobs.[83] Vaniman Manufacturing, a dental equipment producer that has been offshoring most of its sheet metal fabrication to China since 2002, is now returning to the United States. NCR Corporation, which has been producing its ATMs in China, India, and Hungary, is returning all of its production to a facility in Columbus, Georgia.[84]

There are those who believe that reshoring is destined to happen as wages in countries where the manufacturing has been outsourced increase. According to a study by The Boston Consulting Group, net labor costs in the United States and China are expected to converge by 2015 thereby making it more attractive to return to the United States. Also, the decline of the U.S. dollar has provided a fiscal climate advantageous to manufacturing machine tools in North America.[85]

MyManagementLab

Go to **mymanagementlab.com** to complete the problems marked with this icon ⭐.

Summary

1. **Describe the possibility of contingent workers replacing full-time employees.** *Contingent workers* have a nontraditional relationship with the worksite employer and work as part-timers, temporaries, or independent contractors. The United States Government Accountability Office has estimated that so-called contingent workers make up nearly a third of the workforce. And forecasters believe that amount will rise.

2. **Define recruitment and explain alternatives to recruitment.** *Recruitment* is the process of attracting individuals on a timely basis, in sufficient numbers, and with appropriate qualifications to apply for jobs with an organization.

   Even when HR planning indicates a need for additional employees, a firm may decide against increasing the size of its workforce. Recruitment and selection costs are significant when you consider all the related expenses. Alternatives include contingent workers, outsourcing, off-shoring, onshoring, and overtime.

3. **Explain the external environment of recruitment and describe how promotion policies influence recruitment.**

   External factors that affect recruiting include labor market conditions, legal considerations, and whether an applicant is active or passive.

   An organization's promotion policy can have a significant impact on recruitment. *Promotion from within* is the policy of filling vacancies above entry-level positions with current employees.

4. **Describe the recruitment process and explain internal recruitment methods.** Recruitment frequently begins when a manager initiates an employee requisition. Next, the firm determines whether qualified employees are available from within (the internal source) or must be recruited externally from sources such as colleges, universities, and other firms. Sources and methods are then identified.

   Human resource databases permit organizations to determine whether current employees possess the qualifications for filling open positions. *Job posting* is a method of internal recruitment that is used to communicate the fact that job openings exist. *Job bidding* is a system that permits individuals in an organization to apply for a specific job within the organization. *Employee referrals* involves an employee of the company recommending to management a friend or associate as a possible member of the company and continues to be the way that top performers are identified.

5. *Identify external recruitment sources.* External sources of recruitment include high schools and vocational schools, community colleges, colleges and universities, competitors and other firms, the unemployed, older individuals, military personnel, self-employed workers, and ex-offenders.

6. *Explain the impact of mobile HR recruiting.* The world of recruiting via mobile technology is moving at lightning speed. More and more people are adopting mobile technology, and many organizations are trying to figure out how to start using mobile devices in the recruiting process.

7. *Describe online recruitment methods and discuss the possibility of job search scams.* Some online methods include Internet recruiter, virtual job fairs, corporate career Web sites, blogs, general-purpose job boards, NACElink Network, .jobs, AllianceQ, niche sites, contract workers' sites, and hourly workers' job sites.

In searching for a job online, one should be alert to the fact that there are those out there who will attempt to steal personal information from you and set up fraudulent credit-card accounts.

8. *Identify traditional external recruitment methods.* Traditional external recruitment methods include media advertising, private employment agencies, public employment agencies, recruiters, job fairs, internships, executive search firms, professional associations, unsolicited applicants, open houses, event recruiting, sign-on bonuses, and high-tech competition.

9. *Describe how recruitment methods and sources are tailored to each other.* Recruitment must be tailored to the needs of each firm. In addition, recruitment sources and methods often vary according to the type of position being filled.

10. *Define reshoring and explain why some firms are rejecting outsourcing and returning the lost jobs to the United States.* Reshoring is the reverse of offshoring and involves bringing work back to the United States. Advocates of reshoring believe that manufacturers should calculate the real impact of offshoring because there are often hidden expenses such as higher costs for travel, packaging, shipping, and inventory.

Key Terms

contingent workers   108
recruitment   110
outsourcing   110
offshoring   110
onshoring   110
active job seekers   111
passive job seekers   112
promotion from within (PFW)   112
employee requisition   114

recruitment sources   114
recruitment methods   114
job posting   115
job bidding   115
employee referral   115
Internet recruiter   119
virtual job fair   119
corporate career Web sites   120
NACElink Network   120

.jobs   120
AllianceQ   121
niche sites   121
job fair   124
internship   124
event recruiting   125
reshoring   127

Exercises

1. The HRM in Action at the beginning of the chapter entitled "Will Contingent Workers Replace Full-Time Employees?" creates a situation where the workforce of the future is quite different from that which existed in the past. What might be some pros and cons for replacing full-time employees with temporary workers?

2. You see the following ad in your local newspaper: Telephone sales: Woman, age 25–40, needed for telephone sales. Selected applicant must have high school diploma and good credit rating. Call Mr. Smith at Acme Manufacturing Co., Inc.
Are there possibly hiring standards to avoid in this ad? Discuss.

3. The process of matching sources and methods of recruitment was discussed in this chapter. For the following positions, match sources and methods. Assume that in all cases you must use external recruitment to fill the position. Justify your choices.
a. college professor who just received his or her Ph.D.
b. senior accountant with a CPA
c. entry-level accountant
d. skilled automobile mechanic
e. entry-level machine operator

Questions for Review

1. Define *recruitment*.
2. What are the typical alternatives to recruitment that a firm may use?
3. What are factors external to the organization that can significantly affect the firm's recruitment efforts?
4. What is meant by the policy of *promotion from within*?
5. How has social media emerged as an important force in recruiting?
6. What are the steps involved in the recruitment process?
7. Distinguish between recruitment sources and recruitment methods.
8. What are some internal recruitment methods?
9. Why is employee referral so important in the recruitment process?
10. What external sources of recruitment are available?
11. What might be some advantages of using mobile recruiting?
12. What online recruitment methods are available?
13. What traditional external methods of recruitment are available?
14. Define *reshoring*. Why is it being used as an alternative to offshoring?

INCIDENT 1 A Problem Ad?

Dorothy Bryant was the new recruiting supervisor for International Manufacturing Company in Salt Lake City, Utah. One of Dorothy's first assignments was to recruit two software design engineers for International. Design engineers are hard to recruit because of the difficulty of their training and the high demand for them. After considering various recruitment alternatives, Dorothy placed the following ad in a local newspaper with a circulation in excess of 1,000,000:

Employment Opportunity for Software Design Engineers

2 positions available for engineers desiring career in growth industry.

Prefer recent college graduates with good appearance.

Good credit rating

Apply Today! Send your résumé,

in confidence, to: D. A. Bryant

International Manufacturing Co., P.O. Box 1515

Salt Lake City, UT 84115

More than 300 applications arrived in the first week, and Dorothy was elated. When she reviewed the applicants, however, it appeared that few people possessed the desired qualifications for the job.

Questions

1. Dorothy overlooked some of the proper recruiting practices, which resulted in an excessive number of unqualified people applying. What are they?
2. Are there any hiring standards that should be avoided? Identify them and explain why they should be avoided.
3. What recruitment sources and methods might have been used to have generated a better applicant pool for the two software design engineer positions for International Manufacturing? Defend your recommendations.

INCIDENT 2 I Am Qualified, Why Not Me?

Five years ago when Bobby Bret joined Crystal Productions as a junior accountant, he felt that he was on his way up. He had just graduated with a B+ average from college, where he was well liked by his peers and by the faculty and had been an officer in several student organizations. Bobby had shown a natural ability to get along with people as well as to get things done. He remembered what Roger Friedman, the controller at Crystal, had told him when he was hired: "I think you will do well here, Bobby. You've come highly recommended. You are the kind of guy that can expect to move right on up the ladder."

Bobby felt that he had done a good job at Crystal, and everybody seemed to like him. In addition, his performance appraisals had been excellent. However, after five years he was still a junior accountant. He had applied for two senior accountant positions that had opened, but they were both filled by people hired from outside the firm. When

the accounting supervisor's job came open two years ago, Bobby had not applied. He was surprised when his new boss turned out to be a hotshot graduate of State University whose only experience was three years with a large accounting firm. Bobby had hoped that Ron Greene, a senior accountant he particularly respected, would get the job.

On the fifth anniversary of his employment at Crystal, Bobby decided it was time to do something. He made an appointment with the controller. At that meeting Bobby explained to Mr. Friedman that he had worked hard to obtain a promotion and shared his frustration about having been in the same job for so long. "Well," said Mr. Friedman, "you don't think that you were all that much better qualified than the people that we have hired, do you?" "No," said Bobby, "but I think I could have handled the senior accountant job. Of course, the people you have hired are doing a great job too." The controller responded, "We just look at the qualifications of all the applicants for each job, and considering everything, try to make a reasonable decision."

Questions

1. Do you believe that Bobby has a legitimate complaint? Explain.
2. Explain the benefits of a promotion from within policy. Would such a policy be appropriate for Crystal?

MyManagementLab

Go to **mymanagementlab.com** for Auto-graded writing questions as well as the following Assisted-graded writing questions:

5-1. Why might a firm want to use contingent workers as opposed to full-time employees?

5-2. Why is it important to match sources and methods of recruitment?

5-3. Mymanagementlab Only – comprehensive writing assignment for this chapter.

Notes

1. "The End of the Office," *Growth Strategies* (2010): 3–4.
2. Irwin Speizer, "Contingency Plan," *Workforce Management* 89 (October 2010): 28.
3. Robert J. Grossman, "The Art of Choosing a Staffing Agency," *HR Magazine* 57 (March 2012): 33–35.
4. Robert J. Grossman, "Strategic Temp-tations," *HR Magazine* 57 (March 2012): 24–31.
5. Daniel N. Janich, "Without Proper Planning, Contingent Workers Pose Serious Legal Risks to Employer Benefit Plans," *Employee Benefit Plan Review* 66 (July 2011): 8–11.
6. Irwin Speizer, "An On-Demand Workforce," *Workforce Management* 88 (October 19, 2009: 45–49.
7. "Temporary Workforce Stronger Than Ever," *T+D* 65 (May 2011): 21.
8. Ed Frauenheim, "Companies Focus Their Attention on Flexibility," *Workforce Management* 90 (February 2011): 3–4.
9. Matthew Beecher, "Only Assets Need Apply," *HR Magazine* 56 (November 2011): 84–85.
10. Kevin Ryan, "Gilt Groupe's CEO on Building a Team of A Players," *Harvard Business Review* 90 (January/February 2012): 43–46.
11. Lisa V. Gillespie, "Climbing the Corporate Lattice?" *Employee Benefit News* 26 (January 2012): 17–18.
12. Bene Creswick, "Looking Outside," *Accountancy* 147 (February 2011): 44–45.
13. "Desktop Support Outsourcing Ranks Best in Lowering Costs, While IT Security Outsourcing Leads in Service Improvement," *Computer Economics Report* 24 (January 2011): 15–19.
14. Ann Pace, "Searching for Innovation Overseas," *T+D* 65 (April 2011): 24.
15. Aditya Pande, "How to Make Onshoring Work," *Harvard Business Review* 89 (March 2011): 30.
16. Julie Bos, "Top Trends in Staffing: Is Your Organization Prepared for What Lies Ahead?" *Workforce Management* 90 (February 2011): 18–21.
17. John Helyar and Douglas MacMillan, "In Tech, Poaching Is the Sincerest Form of Flattery," *Bloomberg Businessweek* (March 7, 2011): 17–18.
18. Vickie Elmer, "The Return of Multiple Offers," *Fortune* 164 (July 25, 2011): 31–33.
19. James E. Leemann, "The Jobs Are Out There," *Industrial Safety & Hygiene News* 46 (January 2012): 18–20.
20. Stephen Whitaker and Mary Zenker, "Are Underemployed Graduates Displacing Nongraduates?" *Economic Trends* (July 2011): 21–23.
21. David J. Lynch, "Did That Robot Take My Job?" *Bloomberg Businessweek* (January 19, 2012): 15–16.
22. Anthony P. Carnevale, "Old Jobs, New Jobs: Here's the Difference," *HR Magazine* 57 (January 2012): 25.
23. Office of Federal Contract Compliance Programs.
24. Stephenie Overman, "On the Right Track," *HR Magazine* 56 (April 2011): 73–75.
25. Jacob Stoller, "Recruiting with Social Media Online Tools Open Doors," *CMA Magazine* 86 (January 2012): 40–41.
26. Phaedra Brotherton, "Social Media and Referrals Are Best Sources for Talent," *T+D* 66 (January 2012): 24.
27. Susan G. Hauser, "Tech Turbo Boosters on Hyperdrive," *Workforce Management* 90 (August 2011): 24–26.
28. Raghav Singh, "Social Media: It's about Engagement," *Journal of Corporate Recruiting Leadership* 6 (February 2011): 14–16.
29. Kendra Ramirez, "Recruiting via Social Media," *Smart Business Cincinnati/Northern Kentucky* 7 (August 2011): 6.
30. Rita Pyrillis, "The Bait Debates," *Workforce Management* 90 (February 2011): 18–21.
31. Jessi Hempel, "How LinkedIn Will Fire Up Your Career," *Fortune* 161 (April 1, 2010): 74–82.
32. Dana Tanyeri, "How to Hire Now," *Restaurant Business* 109 (January 2010): 18.
33. Jonathan A. Segal, "Dancing on the Edge of a Volcano," *HR Magazine* 56 (April 2011): 83–86.
34. Victoria Neal, Inga Y. Fong, and John Sweeney, "Strikebreaking, Providing Toilets, Job Postings," *HR Magazine* 55 (December 2010): 24–25.
35. "Study Finds Bonus Pay Geared to Attract, Not Retain, Talent," *Report on Salary Surveys* 9 (March 2009): 1–7.
36. William B. Cassidy, "Flatbed Carrier Doubles Driver Referral Bonus," *JOC Online* (March 19, 2010): 5.
37. Vickie Elmer, "Hiring without a Net: Groupon's Recruiter Speaks," *Fortune* 164 (July 25, 2011): 34.
38. Auren Hoffman, "Seeking Great Candidates Online," *BusinessWeek Online* (December 10, 2009): 1.
39. Yvette Lee, John Sweeney, and Lesa Albright, "Electronic Harassment, Recruiters' Sources, Global Benefits," *HR Magazine* 55 (September 2010): 24–25.

40. Alice Andore, "The Value of Poaching," *HR Magazine* 57 (April 2012): 36–37.

41. "Technology Talent Poaching to Get More Aggressive in 2011," *Channel Insider* (March 3, 2011): 1.

42. Michael A. Tucker, "Don't Say Goodbye," *HR Magazine* 56 (August 2011): 71–73.

43. Dori Meinert, "Ready, Set, Hire!" *HR Magazine* 57 (January 2012): 22–28.

44. Elaine Dumier, "Hiring Veterans," *Massachusetts Family Business* (2011 2nd Quarter): 20–21.

45. Brian O'Keefe, Jon Birger, and Doris Burke, "Battle-Tested," *Fortune* 161 (March 22, 2010): 108–118.

46. Agency Group 09, "America Supports You: Group Helps Troops, Families Find Jobs," FDCH Regulatory Intelligence Database (January 30, 2008): Department of Defense, 703-695-0192.

47. Margaret Waldo, "Second Chances: Employing Convicted Felons," *HR Magazine* 57 (March 2012): 36–41.

48. Dana Wilkie, "EEOC Weighs Need for Hiring Guidelines Revisions," *SHRM Online Staffing Management Discipline* (August 2, 2011).

49. Eric Krell, "Criminal Background," *HR Magazine* 57 (February 2012): 45–54.

50. David Farkas, "Employee Search," *Chain Leader* 13 (June 2008): 44–45.

51. Roseanne Harper, "CSA Offers Second Chance," *Supermarket News* 57 (September 14, 2009): 30.

52. Leigh Buchanan, "Hive of Activity," *Inc.* 33 (April 2011): 87–88.

53. Michelle V. Rafter, "Goin' Mobile In," *Workforce Management* 90 (February 2011): 26–28.

54. "Growing Use of Apps Expanding Operations of HR Professionals," *HR Focus* 87 (November 2010): 4–5.

55. Gary N. Stern, "Virtual Job Fairs Becoming More of a Reality," *Workforce Management* 90 (February 2011): 11.

56. Jena McGregor, "Job Sites: Are They Worth It?" *Fortune* 161 (June 14, 2010): 45–46.

57. http://about-monster.com/content/who-we-are

58. http://www.careerbuilder.com/share/AboutUs/

59. http://www.nacelink.com/nl_about.php

60. http://jobsearch.about.com/od/jobsdatabases/a/allianceq.htm July 13, 2011

61. "This Résumé Pool Is Deepening Fast," *BusinessWeek* (July 13, 2009): 72.

62. Deborah Silver, "Niche Sites Gain Monster-Sized Following," *Workforce Management* 90 (March 2011): 10–11.

63. "Lloyd's Is Victim of Recruitment Fraud," *Reactions* (November 2010): 181.

64. Barbara Kiviat, "Job Search Scams," *Time* 174 (October 26, 2009): 53.

65. Sean Callahan, "Can Newspapers Still Deliver?" *B to B* 94 (January 19, 2009): 1/27.

66. Chris McCarthy, "The Art of Headhunting," *Accountancy* 147 (June 2011): 60.

67. Lin Grensing-Pophal, "Executive Search," *Credit Union Management* 35 (January 2012): 32–35.

68. Philip S. Moore, "Seniors Flood Older Worker Fair," *Inside Tucson Business* 14 (March 3, 2005): 15–17.

69. "Vets Descend on Washington for Career Fair and Expo," Agency Group 09, *FDCH Regulatory Intelligence Database* (January 19, 2012).

70. Alison Damast, "Virtual Internships in Rising Demand," *BusinessWeek.com* (January 19, 2012): 2.

71. "Employers Are Being Creative with Perks & Pay for Internships," *HR Focus* 87 (March 2010): 9.

72. Richard Rothschild, "Basic Chemistry? Paid Internships Tend to Yield Full-Time Jobs," *Workforce Management* 90 (August 2011): 3–4.

73. Rita Pyrillis, "Companies, Again, Are Giving It the Old College Try," *Workforce Management* 90 (February 2011): 16–17.

74. Mallie Jane Kim, "Network via Social Media," *U.S. News & World Report* 147 (December 2010): 53.

75. "Signing Bonuses, Severance Plans Strong, Surveys Show," *Payroll Practitioner's Monthly* 2011 (October 2011): 13–15.

76. Max Kvidera, "Carriers Up the Ante for Owner-Operators," *Overdrive* 51 (August 2011): 20.

77. http://code.google.com/codejam/ July 23, 2011.

78. Spence Ante, "Hiring Techies Is as Tricky as Ever," *BusinessWeek Online* (April 4, 2004).

79. R. Wayne Mondy, Robert M. Noe, and Robert E. Edwards, "Successful Recruitment: Matching Sources and Methods," *Personnel* 64 (September 1987): 42–46.

80. John Sprovieri, "Bringing It All Back Home," *Adhesives & Sealants Industry* 18 (April 2011): 14–18.

81. Josh Cable, "Making the Case for Made in America," *Industry Week* 259 (April 2010): 56.

82. Chris Koepfer, "A Look at Total Cost Can Change the View," *Production Machining* 11 (January 2011): 6.

83. Bill Powell, "The End of Cheap Labor in China," *Time* 177 (June 27, 2011): 1–4.

84. "Off-Shoring Comes Full Circle," *Trends Magazine* (January 2012): 25–28.

85. "Reshoring: It's Going to Happen Anyway," *Modern Machine Shop* 84 (August 2011): 42–50.

6

Selection

HRM in Action

Biometrics for HR?

OBJECTIVE 6.1

Describe the use of biometrics in HR.

*B*iometrics deal with a variety of traits that are not subject to change, including fingerprints, palm prints, facial features, DNA, retinas, irises, odors, rhythm, gait, and voice.[1] It can be used in any situation requiring accurate identification of an individual. For example, iris-pattern and retina-pattern authentication methods are being used in some bank automatic teller machines. Voice wave recognition is being used to grant access to proprietary databanks in research facilities. Facial-recognition technology has been used by law enforcement to pick out individuals in large crowds with considerable accuracy. Palm prints are being used to provide physical access to buildings.[2] Walt Disney World obtains an image of each person entering its gates, and ties that copy to the bar code information on the ticket. Buying and reselling multiday passes, which had been costly for the park in the past, has been eliminated.[3] Ceelox, Inc. uses fingerprint authentication to ensure secure login to cloud applications.[4]

Even behavioral identifiers such as handwriting that measure the pressure, speed, and rhythm of a person's writing and gait analysis technologies that recognize the way a person walks are possibilities for biometrics. A biometric system designed for identification purposes attempts to determine who a particular person is. It gathers biometric information from a person and compares it with the matching information in its database. Some believe that biometric technology is so important that it could rival the social impact of penicillin, the assembly line, and the airplane.[5]

E-passports implant an electronic chip and antenna into the paper document to confirm the carrier's identity. The chip holds the same information printed in the passport such as name, date of birth, and other biographical information. In some cases, it also contains biometric identifiers such

1. Describe the use of biometrics in HR.

2. Explain the significance of employee selection and identify environmental factors that affect the selection process.

3. Describe the selection process and explain the importance of preliminary screening.

4. Describe reviewing applications and résumés.

5. Explain the significance of recruitment and selection with LinkedIn.

6. Describe the use of tests in the selection process.

7. Explain the use of the employment interview in the selection process.

8. Explain pre-employment screening, negligent hiring, and the selection decision.

9. Describe human capital metrics and explain the metrics for evaluating recruitment/selection effectiveness.

10. Explain leadership styles in the global environment.

---

as fingerprints.[6] Hand scanners have replaced the punch cards used for clocking into work. The age-old problem of having a buddy clock in for you is a thing of the past. A person cannot sign in without the correct handprint.

The U.S. Department of Defense Common Access ID Card has been issued to all military and service personnel and contractors on U.S. military sites. This card contains biometric data and digitized photographs as well as laser-etched photographs and holograms to add security. Ultimately a similar system may be used in a national system for identifying people. To do this, every U.S. worker would need to have a birth certificate and other means of identification, then have his or her biometric, such as a fingerprint, captured.

Some believe that such databases would create privacy and security risks.[7] However, databases in the federal government already have significant data on each of us, such as Social Security, IRS, and passports. Lawrence P. Lataif, senior immigration counsel at the Florida law firm of Shutts & Bowen LLP, said, "Can anyone imagine any data on an ID card that is not already in a computer database?"[8] Ultimately HR would likely be responsible for collecting and storing this vast amount of data as part of the employment process.

Significance of Employee Selection

selection
Process of choosing from a group of applicants the individual best suited for a particular position and the organization.

Selection is the process of choosing from a group of applicants the individual best suited for a particular position and the organization. Properly matching people with jobs and the organization is the goal of the selection process. If individuals are overqualified, underqualified, or for any reason do not fit either the job or the organization's culture, they will be ineffective and probably leave the firm, voluntarily or otherwise. There are many ways to improve productivity, but none is more powerful than making the right hiring decision. A firm that selects high-quality employees reaps substantial benefits, which recur every year the employee is on the payroll. On the other hand, poor selection decisions can cause irreparable damage. A bad hire can negatively affect the morale of the entire staff, especially in a position where teamwork is critical.

Many companies would rather go short and work overtime than hire one bad apple. If a firm hires many bad apples, it cannot be successful for long even if it has perfect plans, a sound organizational structure, and finely tuned control systems. Competent people must be available to ensure the attainment of organizational goals. Today, with many firms having access to the same technology, *people* make the real difference.

OBJECTIVE 6.2

Explain the significance of employee selection and identify environmental factors that affect the selection process.

Environmental Factors Affecting the Selection Process

A standardized selection process followed consistently would greatly simplify the selection process. However, circumstances may require making exceptions. The following sections describe environmental factors that affect the selection process.

Other HR Functions

The selection process affects, and is affected by, virtually every other HR function. For example, if the compensation package is inferior to those provided by competitors, hiring the best-qualified applicants will be difficult or impossible to achieve. The same situation applies if the firm's safety and health record is substandard or if the firm has a reputation for providing minimal training. Certainly, if marginal workers are hired, additional training will be needed to get them qualified.

Legal Considerations

Legal matters play a significant role in HR management because of legislation, executive orders, and court decisions. Although the basic purpose of selection is to determine candidates' eligibility for employment, it is also essential for organizations to maintain nondiscriminatory practices. The guiding principles in determining what information to get from an applicant are: why am I asking this question and why do I want to know this information? If the information is job related, usually asking for the information is appropriate.

Speed of Decision Making

The time available to make the selection decision can also have a major effect on the selection process. Conditions also can impact the needed speed of decision making. Suppose, for instance, that the only two quality-control inspectors on a production line just had a fight and both resigned, and the firm cannot operate until the positions are filled. In this situation, speed is crucial, and a few phone calls, two brief interviews, and a prayer may constitute the entire selection procedure. On the other hand, conducting a national search to select a chief executive officer may take months or even a year. In bureaucracies, it is not uncommon for the selection process to take a considerable amount of time.

Organizational Hierarchy

Organizations usually take different approaches to filling positions at varying levels. For instance, consider the differences in hiring a chief executive officer versus filling a clerical position. Extensive background investigations and multiple interviews would most likely apply for the executive position. On the other hand, an applicant for a clerical position would probably take a word-processing test and perhaps have a short employment interview.

Applicant Pool

The number of qualified applicants recruited for a particular job makes up the **applicant pool**. The process can be truly selective only if there are several qualified applicants. Yet, only one or two applicants with the required skills may be available. The selection process then becomes a matter of choosing from whoever is at hand. The expansion and contraction of the labor market also affects the size of the applicant pool. A low unemployment rate often means that the applicant pool is smaller, whereas a high unemployment rate may expand the pool. According to the Bureau of Labor Statistics, the total number of job openings in January 2011 was 2.8 million, with over 13.9 million unemployed workers. That meant there were no jobs available for four out of every five workers in the job market.[9]

The number of people hired for a particular job compared to the number of qualified individuals in the applicant pool is often expressed as a **selection ratio**, or

$$\text{Selection Ratio} = \frac{\text{Number of people hired}}{\text{Number of qualified applicants (applicant pool)}}$$

A selection ratio of 1.00 indicates that there was only one qualified applicant for an open position. The lower the ratio falls below 1.00, the more alternatives the manager has in making a selection decision. For example, a selection ratio of 0.10 indicates that there were 10 qualified applicants for an open position.

Note in the above selection ratio formula that "qualified" applicants are sought and not just a warm body to fill a vacant position. One might think that during a recession it would be easy to find "qualified" applicants for vacant positions. True, in a recession there are often many candidates, but after screening for qualified applicants, the realistic selection pool may be greatly reduced. Often companies are finding it difficult to attract critical-skills employees. The jobs that are going unfilled often require a combination of new skills or entirely new skill sets compared with those that were required before the recession.

Type of Organization

The type of organization employing individuals, such as private, governmental, or not for profit, can also affect the selection process. A private-sector business is heavily profit oriented. Prospective employees who can help achieve profit goals are the preferred candidates. Consideration of the total individual, including job-related personality factors, is involved in the selection of employees for this sector.

Government civil service systems typically identify qualified applicants through competitive examinations. Often a manager may select only from among the top three applicants for a position. A manager in this sector may not have the prerogative of interviewing other applicants.

Individuals considered for positions in not-for-profit organizations (such as the Boy Scouts and Girl Scouts, YMCA, or YWCA) confront still a different situation. The salary level in these organizations may not be competitive with those of private and governmental organizations.[10] Therefore, a person who fills one of these positions must be not only qualified but also dedicated to this type of work.

Probationary Period

Many firms use a probationary or introductory period that permits them to evaluate an employee's ability based on established performance. The purpose of a probationary period is to establish the suitability of a new employee for the position and to resolve any issues there might be in the new employee's performance over the first three months or so. This practice may be either a substitute for certain phases of the selection process or a check on the validity of the process. The rationale is that if an individual can successfully perform the job during the probationary period, the process does not require other selection tools. From a legal viewpoint, the use of a probationary period in the selection process is certainly job related.

Even in unionized firms, the labor–management agreement typically does not protect a new employee until after a certain probationary period. This period is typically from 60 to 90 days. During that time, an employee can be terminated with little or no justification. On the other hand, firing a marginal employee in a union environment may prove to be quite difficult after the probationary period.

organizational fit
Management's perception of the degree to which the prospective employee will fit in with the firm's culture or value system.

Organizational Fit

Organizational fit refers to management's perception of the degree to which the prospective employee will fit in with the firm's culture or value system. There are numerous reasons that a new hire does not work out but none is as important as cultural fit. Knowledge and skill are important but the most lasting component of the employment relationship is cultural match.[11] The commonly heard statement, "the chemistry was just not right" may describe a poor fit. This was supported by Steven Rice, executive vice president of HR Juniper Networks Inc., who said, "If the customer sees you as team-oriented and such and the customer service guy is different, you have a problem. You have to hire against the brand."[12] A poor fit harms organizational effectiveness, hurts morale, and drains creativity. Nina Brody, head of talent for Take Care Health Systems in Conshohocken, Pennsylvania, said, "If we have 10 qualified clinical people in front of us, we want to know who will fit best with our culture, because that's where we tend to experience trouble, not necessarily with someone's ability to do the job technically."[13]

Using *fit* as a criterion may raise legal and diversity questions, and perhaps this explains the low profile of its use.[14] Nevertheless, there is considerable evidence that managers use it in making selection decisions and that it is not a minor consideration. Complicating the situation further is the fact that the same employee may be a poor fit with one firm and a perfect fit with another. Applicants also should consider organizational fit when assessing whether to accept a job offer.

OBJECTIVE **6.3**

Describe the selection process and explain the importance of preliminary screening.

Selection Process

The general purpose of the selection process is to determine if the applicant is qualified, to educate the candidate, and to assess his or her cultural fit. Figure 6-1 illustrates a generalized selection process, but it may vary from organization to organization and also according to the type of job being filled. It typically begins with preliminary screening. Next, applicants complete the firm's application for employment or provide a résumé. Then they progress through a series of selection tests, one or more employment interviews, and pre-employment screening, including background and reference checks. The hiring manager then offers the successful applicant a job, subject to successful completion of a medical examination. Notice that an applicant may be rejected or opt out at any time during the selection process. To a point, the more screening tools used to assess an applicant, the greater the chance of making a good selection decision.

Selection Technology

Two tools that are invaluable to the selection process in the technology boom that is sweeping HR today are applicant-tracking systems (ATSs) and candidate relationship management (CRM). "ATS and CRM are really your backbone," says Jim McCoy, vice president of solutions for ManpowerGroup Solutions, the RPO software division of Milwaukee-based ManpowerGroup.[15]

An *applicant-tracking system (ATS)*, also called a talent management system, is a software application designed to help an enterprise select employees more efficiently. Current ATSs permit human resource and line managers to oversee the entire selection process. They often involve screening résumés and spotting qualified candidates, conducting personality and skills tests, and handling background investigations. They allow companies to compile job applications electronically, to more quickly gather candidates, set up interviews, and get new hires on board. An ATS can be used to post job openings on a corporate Web site or job board and generate interview requests to potential candidates by e-mail. Other features may include individual applicant tracking, requisition tracking, automated résumé ranking, customized input forms, prescreening questions and response tracking, and multilingual capabilities. ATSs are used extensively to help ease the labor-intensive process of sorting résumés from online job boards. In most cases, the goal is not merely to reduce costs but also to speed up the hiring process and find people who fit an organization's success profile. ATSs continue to be enhanced to make recruiters more efficient and extend sourcing into the global market. Developers of ATSs are now focusing efforts on developing quality-of-hire metrics.

Helene Richter, director of talent operations for Liz Claiborne, New York City, said, "People choose an applicant-tracking tool to streamline process. But you have EEO and compliance issues that you need to streamline as well." The applicant-tracking function does both.[16] Hiring information is tracked to comply with Office of Federal Contract Compliance Programs.

FIGURE 6-1

Selection Process

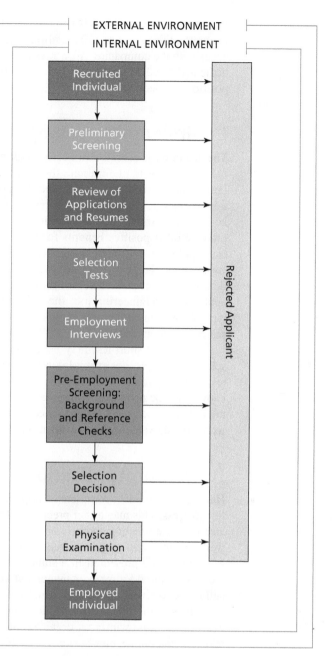

The purpose of *candidate relationship management (CRM)* is to help manage potential and actual applicants in an organized manner. It is useful in managing the relationship between the company and prospective applicants.[17] CRM can be used to send job postings and job descriptions to job boards and other sites. It has the capability to search the Internet, including social media sites, for résumés, and then adds and catalogues them and other information to the database. CRM systems have the ability to link with other ATSs and any Web site. CRM systems permit candidates to get to know more about the company and allow the company to get to know more about the candidate.

CRM systems are used to communicate with those who have applied or appear qualified for jobs with the firm. Once the CRM system identifies an individual who might be appropriate for an open position, the system can e-mail that person asking them to respond. Gerry Crispin, a principal at the consulting firm CareerXroads in Kendall Park, New Jersey, said, "Candidate relationship management systems can provide information that helps a candidate recognize himself as an employee of the company, creating an 'I'd fit there' attitude."[18]

The Internet has created a situation where a large number of résumés can be received. Often, candidates send an application and never get a reply. Whether as a result of arrogance, ignorance, or incompetence, companies sometime fail to inform applicants after they have been rejected. To overcome this situation, organizations use CRM software to help job seekers have good experiences with the companies' Web sites and to bolster efforts to build talent pools. Companies truly dedicated to CRM do not stop after sending an auto reply; they also let them know when the position has been filled.

Preliminary Screening

The selection process often begins with preliminary screening. The basic purpose of preliminary screening is to eliminate those who obviously do not meet the position's requirements. Preliminary screening may take the form of reviewing for obviously unqualified applicants with a brief interview, test, or only a review of the application or résumé for clear mismatches. In addition to eliminating clearly unqualified job applicants quickly, preliminary screening may produce other positive benefits for the firm. It is possible that the position for which the applicant applied is not the only one available. If the person doing the screening knows about other vacancies in the firm, he or she may be able to steer the prospective employee to another position. For instance, the assessor may decide that although an applicant is not a good fit for the applications-engineering job, she is an excellent candidate for an internal R&D position. This type of assessment not only builds goodwill for the firm but also can maximize recruitment and selection effectiveness.

At times a short test may be administered to determine if a person should proceed in the selection process. For example, in the recruitment of sales representatives, a brief sales aptitude test may be given to determine if the applicant has a talent or interest in sales. Then the company knows that the people they interview are already more likely to succeed in the role. By conducting a quick assessment before scheduling interviews, the company is more likely to hire people who will add value to the organization.

Review of Applications

Having the candidate complete an application for employment is another early step in the selection process. This may either precede or follow preliminary screening. The employer then evaluates it to see whether there is an apparent match between the individual and the position. A well-designed and properly used application form can be helpful, since essential information is included and presented in a standardized format. Completion of an application may not be initially required for many management and professional positions. In these cases, a résumé may suffice. A complete application usually is obtained at a later time.

The specific information requested on an application form may vary from firm to firm, and even by job type within an organization. An application typically contains sections for name, address, telephone number, e-mail address, military service, education, and work history. Managers compare the information contained in a completed application to the job description to determine whether a potential match exists between the firm's requirements and the applicant's qualifications. As you might expect, this judgment is often difficult.

Several preprinted statements are usually included on the application form. First, by signing the form, the applicant certifies that information provided on the form is accurate and true. Employers will likely reject candidates who make false claims for major issues. Candidates may be terminated after employment if they made any representation or statement that was not accurate or if they did not disclose matters that might significantly prejudice the employer's hiring decision. Second, when not prohibited by state law, the form should also state that the position is *employment at will* and that either the employer or the employee can terminate employment at any time for any reason. Finally, the form should contain a statement whereby the candidate gives permission to have his or her background and references checked.

An employment application form must reflect not only the firm's informational needs but also legal requirements. Potentially discriminatory questions inquiring about such factors as gender, race, age, convictions, national origin, citizenship, birthplace, dependents, disabilities, religion, color, and marital status should be avoided.

Applicants sometimes deliberately leave out information on the application that may present them in a negative light. To combat this, many employers are requiring applicants to use online applications that force a person to complete a required field before the application is successfully submitted. In fact, corporations have increasingly declined to accept a printed résumé and applicants are directed to company Web sites for employment application and résumé submission.

OBJECTIVE **6.4**

Describe reviewing applications and résumés.

Review of Résumés

A **résumé** is a goal-directed summary of a person's experience, education, and training developed for use in the selection process.

résumé

Goal-directed summary of a person's experience, education, and training developed for use in the selection process.

Professional and managerial applicants often begin the selection process by submitting a résumé. Figure 6-2 illustrates a traditional résumé. Note that the résumé includes the career objective for the specific position the applicant is seeking (a vita does not contain a career objective). Some HR professionals suggest that a professional summary at the beginning of the résumé is more useful to the recruiter. However, young job seekers with little work experience may be best served by using a career objective statement. The remainder of the résumé should be directed toward showing how a person has the skills and competencies necessary to accomplish the position identified in the career objective statement.[19] Using keywords from the job description or employment ad will help an applicant get past the résumé-scanning programs many firms use.[20] Only information necessary to show a relationship to the objective should be included. The all-important concept of relevancy is crucial in selling the applicant to the company. A new

FIGURE 6-2

Example of a Traditional Résumé

Marianne Sanders

Current Address
4289 Tiger Bend Road
Baton Rouge, LA 71220
Phone: 555.555.5151
E-mail: MSanders@internet.com

Objective:	To obtain an entry level position in accounting.
Education:	McNeese State University **Bachelor of Science, Accounting,** **Expected date of graduation, May 2013** **GPA: 3.5/4.0**
Experience:	January 2012 – Present Accounting Internship with McElroy, Quirk, & Burch, APC (Accounting firm) Lake Charles, LA January 2010 – December 2011 McNeese State University Student worker (Financial Aid) Lake Charles, LA • Assist full-time worker with office work • Help students complete financial aid question/forms
Honors:	Beta Gamma Sigma Honor Fraternity Beta Alpha Psi Honor Fraternity Pi Beta Lambda – Business Professionals President Honor Role (Six times)
Personal:	Hard working, goal-oriented, conscientious, positive thinker, work well in teams, excellent people skills
Interests:	Accounting, physical fitness, traveling, tennis
Software Proficiency:	Microsoft Office 2010, Excel, Word, PowerPoint, Windows 7, Social Networking (Facebook, Twitter, LinkedIn)

trend that has evolved over time is that the content of the résumé is more important than fitting an applicant's entire career onto one page. Historically, a one-page résumé was the standard that applicants were told to use.

In developing a résumé, the sender should be careful not to misrepresent the truth. An applicant who is three hours away from graduation has not graduated. Certainly, the résumé should be designed to present the applicant in a positive light but without exaggeration. With regard to job history, dates of employment should be accurate. It goes without saying that résumés should not contain grammar and spelling errors. The résumé should show that the applicant has an understanding of the job and how his or her work history can assist in accomplishing the job.

When sending a résumé via the Internet, applicants should realize that most large companies now use applicant-tracking systems. These systems assume a certain résumé style. Résumés that deviate from the assumed style are ignored or deleted. These systems scan résumés into databases, search the databases on command, and rank the résumés according to the number of resulting "hits" they receive. At times such searches use multiple (10–20) criteria. Some systems flag résumés that appear to misrepresent the truth, present misleading information, or are in other ways suspicious.

The use of applicant-tracking systems coupled with the downsizing of human resource departments has resulted in a situation where many résumés are never seen by human eyes once they enter the system. Therefore, a job applicant should make his or her résumé as computer/scanner friendly as possible so that its life in a database will be extended. Even if you are a perfect match for the job, your résumé may never get to someone who could decipher your potential

OBJECTIVE 6.5

Explain the significance of recruitment and selection with LinkedIn.

TRENDS & INNOVATIONS

Recruitment and Selection with LinkedIn

LinkedIn went public in 2011 when it priced its initial offering at $45 per share, giving it a market value of over $4 billion, and the value has increased significantly since then. Basically, LinkedIn is an online social network for professionals. Unlike Facebook, LinkedIn members tend to go to the site for very specific reasons, such as to connect with those who can help them grow professionally or help their business grow.[21] It may also be valuable in finding a job by letting employers know about a person's skills and background through the LinkedIn profile. In fact, in a recent survey, LinkedIn was the top networking site used by North American companies to find job candidates.[22] LinkedIn is also valuable in researching potential employers or in obtaining recommendations for technology or other purchases.[23]

As of March 2012, LinkedIn has more than 161 million members in the world who have created free online profiles about themselves, and the number is seemingly growing daily. Kevin Donlin, codirector of Guerrilla Job Search International, said, "If you're not on LinkedIn, you do not exist to recruiters."[24] The profile typically contains the member's current occupation and employer, contact information, education, job history, skills, and other details. Members can post updates about their professional activities, such as speaking schedules or conventions attended. Through LinkedIn, a professional portrait can be developed, which is critical for any job seeker, either active or passive. Members can post favorable references from friends or business associates. LinkedIn provides social networking from a professional aspect.[25]

LinkedIn is very useful for companies in their recruitment efforts.[26] In fact, the largest and fastest-growing part of LinkedIn's business is "hiring solutions," which include a variety of services for in-house and external recruiters. These services include online job postings and ways to organize job searches. A major benefit is the ability to quickly identify and contact passive candidates, those who seem to have the necessary background, education, and skills but are not actively seeking work.[27]

Corporate recruiter Elisa Bannon of U.S. Cellular in Chicago used to spend up to $4 million a year to post jobs and screen résumés through Monster and CareerBuilder. Then her budget was cut to $1 million and she had 2,500 openings to fill. She could no longer afford the big boards and turned to LinkedIn. For an annual fee of $60,000, she now has access to the network's millions of members.[28] More and more companies are looking to cut costs and are shifting recruiting money to LinkedIn.[29]

Since companies value passive candidates for more senior positions, LinkedIn has become an even more valuable source for hiring to fill these positions. Filling senior positions once meant paying executive search firms thousands of dollars for each job. But with social networks like LinkedIn, in-house recruiters now have another way to reach such talent.

LinkedIn profiles have become essentially digital-era résumés. They are one of the most dominant ways for an employer to build a human presence in the social network environment.

The site also makes it easy to ask for references by providing an outline for those requests. There is a potential problem, however, with providing references for a coworker. Companies do not want it to appear as if the organization is providing the reference should a negative action be taken against the person. Workers can still write a reference about a coworker, but it should not suggest that it reflects the opinion of the company.[30]

ETHICAL DILEMMA

Employee Selection Criteria?

You are the newly appointed sales manager for a large manufacturing organization that has been struggling of late, even though your region is the firm's most successful one. Your office is located in a very close-knit community where people place a high value on local basketball. In fact, it didn't take you long to realize that to most people, local basketball is even more important than the Super Bowl. While you were watching a game the other night with your biggest customer, who purchases almost 40 percent of your yearly volume, he told you that the star on the team may soon be leaving the community because his father was laid off. He has heard that your region has an opening for

a sales representative, and he asks you to hire the boy's father. You tell him that you will be glad to review the man's résumé, but you think that you have already found an extremely qualified person.

As you are reviewing the résumé of your customer's recommended candidate the next day, the person you are replacing comes by the office to say good-bye. In the conversation he mentions that in this town, people do each other favors, and that is how they build trust. He also tells you that if the boy's father is not hired, the firm may lose most, if not all, of the buyer's business. That is quite a shock because you realize that the customer's candidate lacks some qualifications for the position.

What would you do?
What factor(s) in this ethical dilemma might influence a person to make a less-than-ethical decision?

---

value. To make the process work, a keyword résumé style should be used. **Keywords** refer to those words or phrases that are used to search databases for résumés that match. A **keyword résumé** contains an adequate description of the job seeker's characteristics and industry-specific experience presented in keyword terms in order to accommodate the computer search process. The keywords are often job titles, skills, or areas of expertise related to the position. Keywords tend to be more of the noun or noun-phrase type (Office 2010, Windows 7, UNIX, Biochemist) as opposed to power action verbs often found in traditional résumés (developed, coordinated, empowered, organized). Another way to look at keyword phrases is to think in terms of job duties. The terms employers search for most often are problem solving and decision making, oral and written communication, customer service or retention, performance and productivity improvement, leadership, technology, team building, project management, and bilingual.

Applicants should study the job posting and industry ads to get an overview of the phrases that keep reappearing. Detailing an individual's job duties may require a change in mindset away from traditional résumé writing. Recruiters should be mindful that applicants have gotten smarter in résumé preparation and at times include words that hardly resemble their past accomplishment.

Selection Tests

Recognizing the shortcomings of other selection tools, many firms have added selection tests to their hiring process. These tests rate factors such as aptitude, personality, abilities, and motivation of potential employees, allowing managers to choose candidates according to how they will fit into the open positions and corporate culture. However, tests alone are not enough to make a sufficient evaluation of a candidate because they are not foolproof. Firms need to use them in conjunction with other selection tools.

Advantages and Disadvantages of Selection Tests

Research indicates that customized tests can be a reliable and accurate means to predict on-the-job performance. Organizations use tests to identify attitudes and job-related skills that interviews cannot recognize. Also, the cost of employment testing is small in comparison to ultimate hiring costs. They are a more efficient way to get at information that results in better-qualified people being hired.

Job performance depends on an individual's ability and motivation to do the work. Selection tests may accurately predict an applicant's ability to perform the job, the "can do," but they are less successful in indicating the extent to which the individual will be motivated to perform it, the "will do." The most successful employees have two things in common: they identify with their firm's goals, and they are highly motivated. For one reason or another, some employees with high potential never seem to reach it. The factors related to success on the job are so numerous and complex that selection may always be more of an art than a science.

Employers should be aware that tests might be unintentionally discriminatory. Office of Federal Contract Compliance Programs (OFCCP) former director Charles E. James Sr. said, "Testing is a 'necessary business tool' to help employers select qualified candidates. Hiring the wrong person puts your company at risk. The key is to make the test fit the job you're using it for."[31] When a test excludes a protected class at a significant rate, the test should be avoided unless the employer can show that the test is job related for the position in question and consistent with business necessity. Using selection tests carries with it legal liabilities of two types. One is a lawsuit from rejected applicants who claim a test was not job related or that it unfairly discriminated against a protected group, violating federal employment laws. The second potential legal problem relates to *negligence hiring* lawsuits filed by victims of employee misbehavior or incompetence (a topic discussed later in this chapter).

Test anxiety can also be a problem. Applicants often become quite anxious when confronting yet another hurdle that might eliminate them from consideration. The test administrator's reassuring manner and a well-organized testing operation should serve to reduce this threat. Actually, although a great deal of anxiety is detrimental to test performance, a slight degree is helpful.

The problems of hiring unqualified or less-qualified candidates and rejecting qualified candidates will continue regardless of the procedures followed. Well-developed tests administered by competent professionals help organizations minimize such consequences.

Characteristics of Properly Designed Selection Tests

Properly designed selection tests are standardized, objective, based on sound norms, reliable, and, of utmost importance, valid. The application of these concepts is discussed next.

standardization
Uniformity of the procedures and conditions related to administering tests.

STANDARDIZATION The uniformity of the procedures and conditions related to administering tests is **standardization**. To compare the performance of several applicants taking the same test, it is necessary for all to take the test under conditions that are as identical as possible. For example, the content of instructions provided and the time allowed must be the same, and the physical environment must be similar. If one person takes a test in a room with jackhammers operating just outside and another takes it in a more tranquil environment, differences in test results are likely.

objectivity
Condition that is achieved when everyone scoring a given test obtains the same results.

OBJECTIVITY In testing, **objectivity** occurs when everyone scoring a test obtains the same results. Multiple-choice and true–false tests are objective. The person taking the test either chooses the correct answer or does not.

norm
Frame of reference for comparing an applicant's performance with that of others.

NORMS A frame of reference for comparing an applicant's performance with that of others is a **norm**. Specifically, a norm reflects the distribution of many scores obtained by people similar to the applicant being tested. A score by itself is insignificant. It becomes meaningful only when compared with other applicants' scores.

When a sufficient number of employees are performing the same or similar work, employers can standardize their own tests. Typically, this is not the case, and a national norm for a particular test is used. A prospective employee takes the test, the score obtained is compared to the norm, and the significance of the test score is then determined.

reliability
Extent to which a selection test provides consistent results.

RELIABILITY The extent to which a selection test provides consistent results is **reliability**. Reliability data reveal the degree of confidence placed in a test. If a person scores 130 on a certain intelligence test this week and retakes the test next week and scores 80, the test reliability would likely be low. If a test has low reliability, its validity as a predictor will also be low. If after scoring 130 the first week a person scores another 130 the second week, the test is reliable. However, the existence of reliability alone does not guarantee the test's validity.

validity
Extent to which a test measures what it claims to measure.

VALIDITY The basic requirement for a selection test is that it be valid. **Validity** is the extent to which a test measures what it claims to measure. If a test cannot indicate ability to perform the job, it has no value. And, if used, it will result in poor hiring decisions and a potential legal liability for the employer.

Here is an example that describes the difference between reliability and validity. If a person weighs 200 pounds but the scale shows a wide difference, such as 455, 150, 295, and 240, the scale is not reliable. If the scale consistently reads "100" and you weigh 200 pounds, then it is reliable, but not valid. If it reads "200" each time, then the measurement is both reliable and valid.

Validity, commonly reported as a correlation coefficient, summarizes the relationship between two variables. For example, these variables may be the score on a selection test and some measure of employee performance. A coefficient of 0 shows no relationship, whereas coefficients of either +1.0 or −1.0 indicate a perfect relationship, one positive and the other negative. Naturally, no test will be 100 percent accurate, yet organizations strive for the highest feasible coefficient. If a job performance test has a high positive correlation coefficient, most prospective employees who score high on the test will probably later prove to be high performers.

Title VII requires the test to work without having an adverse impact on minorities, females, and individuals with backgrounds or characteristics protected under the law. If using the test results in an adverse impact on certain members of protected groups, the firm must have a compelling reason why it is used; that is, it must validate the test. Employers are not required to validate their selection tests automatically.

Test Validation Approaches

The *Uniform Guidelines on Employee Selection Procedures* established three approaches to validating selection tests: criterion-related validity, content validity, and construct validity.

CRITERION-RELATED VALIDITY A test validation method that compares the scores on selection tests to some aspect of job performance determined, for example, by performance appraisal is **criterion-related validity**. Performance measures might include quantity and quality of work, turnover, and absenteeism. A close relationship between the score on the test and job performance suggests that the test is valid. The two basic forms of criterion-related validity are concurrent and predictive validity.

Concurrent validity is determined when the firm obtains test scores and the criterion data at essentially the same time. For instance, it administers the test to all currently employed telemarketers and compares the results with company records that contain current information about each employee's job performance. If the test is able to identify productive and less productive workers, one could say that it is valid. A potential problem in using this validation procedure results from changes that may have occurred within the work group. For example, firms may have fired the less productive workers, and promoted the more productive employees out of the group.

Predictive validity involves administering a test and later obtaining the criterion information. For instance, all applicants take the test but the firm uses other selection criteria, not the test results, to make the selection decision. After observing employee performance over time, the company analyzes test results to determine whether they differentiate the successful and less successful employees. Predictive validity is a technically sound procedure. Because of the time and cost involved, however, its use is often not feasible.

CONTENT VALIDITY A test validation method whereby a person performs certain tasks that are actually required by the job or completes a paper-and-pencil test that measures relevant job knowledge is **content validity**. Although statistical concepts are not involved, many practitioners believe that content validity provides a sensible approach to validating a selection test. This form of validation requires thorough job analysis and carefully prepared job descriptions. An example of the use of content validity is giving a word-processing test to an applicant whose primary job would be word processing. Court decisions have supported the concept of content validity.

CONSTRUCT VALIDITY A test validation method that determines whether a test measures certain constructs, or traits, that job analysis finds to be important in performing a job is **construct validity**. For instance, a job may require a high degree of creativity or reasoning ability. Or, a sales representative position may require the applicant to be extroverted and aggressive. Construct validity in and of itself is not a primary method for validating selection tests.

Types of Employment Tests

Individuals differ in characteristics related to job performance. These differences, which are measurable, relate to cognitive abilities, psychomotor abilities, job knowledge, work samples, vocational interests, and personality.

criterion-related validity
Test validation method that compares the scores on selection tests to some aspect of job performance determined, for example, by performance appraisal.

content validity
Test validation method whereby a person performs certain tasks that are actually required by the job or completes a paper-and-pencil test that measures relevant job knowledge.

construct validity
Test validation method that determines whether a test measures certain constructs, or traits, that job analysis finds to be important in performing a job.

cognitive aptitude tests
Tests that determine general reasoning ability, memory, vocabulary, verbal fluency, and numerical ability.

COGNITIVE APTITUDE TESTS Tests that determine general reasoning ability, memory, vocabulary, verbal fluency, and numerical ability are **cognitive aptitude tests**.

Cognitive aptitude tests are a form of IQ tests. They may be helpful in identifying job candidates who have extensive knowledge bases. As the content of jobs becomes broader and more fluid, employees must be able to adapt quickly to job changes and rapid technological advances. It is likely that testing will be necessary to match the broader range of characteristics required for successful performance of these flexible jobs. The NFL uses the Wonderlic Personnel Test, which is designed as a way to measure cognitive ability, the applicant's natural aptitude for learning new information.

psychomotor abilities tests
Tests that measure strength, coordination, and dexterity.

PSYCHOMOTOR ABILITIES TESTS Tests that measure strength, coordination, and dexterity are **psychomotor abilities tests**. Miniaturization in assembly operations has accelerated the development of tests to determine these abilities. Much of this work is so delicate that magnifying lenses are necessary, and the psychomotor abilities required to perform the tasks are critical.

job-knowledge tests
Tests designed to measure a candidate's knowledge of the duties of the job for which he or she is applying.

JOB-KNOWLEDGE TESTS Tests that measure a candidate's knowledge of the duties of the job for which he or she is applying are **job-knowledge tests**. Such tests are commercially available but individual firms may also design them specifically for any job, based on data derived from job analysis.

work-sample tests
Tests that require an applicant to perform a task or set of tasks representative of the job.

WORK-SAMPLE TESTS Tests that require an applicant to perform a task or set of tasks representative of the job are **work-sample tests**. For positions that require heavy use of spreadsheets, having the applicant construct a sample spreadsheet, with data the firm provides, will be useful in assessing a required ability. Such tests, by their nature, are job related. A real test of validity, in the opinion of some experts, should be a performance assessment: take individuals to a job and give them the opportunity to perform it.

vocational interest tests
Tests that indicate the occupation a person is most interested in and the one likely to provide satisfaction.

VOCATIONAL INTEREST TESTS Tests that indicate the occupation a person is most interested in and the one likely to provide satisfaction are **vocational interest tests**. These tests compare the individual's interests with those of successful employees in a specific job. The assumption here is that if a person shows a definite interest in a certain vocation they will be more productive on the job. But, having interest in a job and being able to effectively perform it may not be the same. A person may have an interest in being a brain surgeon but not the aptitude for it. Although interest tests have application in employee selection, their primary use has been in counseling and vocational guidance.

personality tests
Self-reported measures of traits, temperaments, or dispositions.

PERSONALITY TESTS Self-reported measures of temperaments, or dispositions, are **personality tests**. Personality tests, unlike ability tests, are not time constrained and do not measure specific problem-solving skills. These questionnaires tap into softer areas, such as leadership, teamwork, and personal assertiveness. A properly designed personality profile can measure and match the appropriate personality dimensions to the requirements of the job.

In sales jobs, personality tests are usually more reliable than the information provided by interviews and résumés. Salespeople possess certain traits that distinguish them, perhaps explaining why some can survive in the competitive world of sales and why others struggle.[32] More and more companies are using specially designed personality tests such as Myers-Briggs to identify top sales recruits. Research indicates that two important predictors for successful salespeople are extroversion and conscientiousness. The ability to test for these traits can mean a significant increase in selection effectiveness.

Most large companies now use psychometric testing to identify future managers. These individuals are being assessed for their ability to bring about long-term change and their ability to handle day-to-day management tasks. Generally, fire departments and law enforcement agencies use the Minnesota Multiphasic Personality Inventory (MMPI) test, which consists of 567 statements that help to determine a subject's degree of paranoia, depression, mania, or anxiety. In police departments the MMPI is used to detect the inclination toward substance abuse. These types of tests are typically used in the early stage of the selection process.

Integrity tests were the first personality tests used in pre-employment screening. Employers have used them to measure candidates' attitudes toward theft, dishonesty, absenteeism, violence, drug use, alcohol abuse, and other counterproductive behaviors. Retail stores, nuclear plants, law enforcement agencies, and child-care facilities typically use integrity tests. Research has shown that integrity tests have high validity for predicting undesirable behaviors at work.[33] Since the polygraph test (discussed later) has been effectively banned in the private sector as a hiring tool, integrity tests have often been used to detect dishonesty in candidates.

Online Assessment

Organizations are increasingly using the Internet to assess various skills required by applicants. Employment assessments can range from online exams for a specific computer skill to personality tests intended to predict customer service competence.[34] Firms may design and have their own tests available online or use an external source. Companies use online assessment to make it faster and easier to process applications. Companies want assessments that can be given directly on their Web-based career centers with the results channeled to an applicant-tracking system.

Simulation-type assessments that use Web-based interactive media, role-playing, and even video games to make test taking more fun and interesting for job applicants have been used. Church's Chicken and Strategic Restaurants Inc. uses a pre-interview service, called JobApp Network, which screens and ranks applicants. It saves unit managers time and effort, and ultimately improves the quality of new hires. Church's reported that during its initial use with 46 restaurants, turnover decreased by 63 percent.[35]

Virtual Job Tryout is an online simulation tool from the Shaker Consulting Group in Cleveland that tests for cultural and team fit as well as assessment of job-specific skills through "day in the life" interactive simulations. Nina Brody, head of talent for Take Care Health Systems believes "the assessment gives candidates a highly realistic job preview—causing some to self-select out early and others to solidify their commitment."[36]

Assessment Centers

assessment center

Selection technique that requires individuals to perform activities similar to those they might encounter in an actual job.

An **assessment center** is a selection approach that requires individuals to perform activities similar to those they might encounter in an actual job. The assessment center is one of the most powerful tools for assessing managerial talent because it is designed to determine if they will be effective in performing a specific job. Research has established the validity of the assessment center approach to predicting performance. Many of America's top companies have set up assessment centers where they can first interview potential employees and then evaluate them in real work situations. It provides an excellent way to determine an individual's capabilities to perform an entry-level management job.

In an assessment center, candidates perform a number of exercises that simulate the tasks they will carry out in the job they seek. Typical assessment center tests include having applicants complete *in-basket exercises* and perform in *management games, leaderless discussion groups, mock interviews,* and other simulations. The traditional in-basket exercise has received a technological boost by replacing the paper memos with e-mail messages, faxes, tweets, or voice mail. Assessment centers measure candidates' skills in prioritizing, delegating, and decision making. The professional assessors who evaluate the candidates' performances usually observe them away from the workplace over a certain period of time, perhaps a single day. The assessors selected are typically experienced managers who may not only evaluate performances, but also participate in the exercises.

An advantage of the assessment center approach is the increased reliability and validity of the information provided. Research has shown that the in-basket exercise, a typical component of assessment centers, is a good predictor of management performance. Its validity provides an alternative to paper-and-pencil tests.

Unique Forms of Testing

HR Web Wisdom

Genetic Testing
http://ghr.nlm.nih.gov/

A guide to understanding genetic conditions.

genetic tests

Tests given to identify predisposition to inherited diseases, including cancer, heart disease, neurological disorders, and congenital diseases.

GENETIC TESTING Tests performed to identify predisposition to inherited diseases, including cancer, heart disease, neurological disorders, and congenital diseases are **genetic tests**. DNA-testing companies can tell us our potential risk for breast cancer, cystic fibrosis, Alzheimer's disease, and other common chronic conditions. Scientists have assembled the entire set of genetic instructions for building a human body, and world leaders likened this achievement to putting a human being on the moon. This brings both hope and concerns to the forefront in employment testing.

Genetic tests may predict a predisposition to having a disease. However, such tests cannot tell whether a person is certain to get the disease or when he or she would become ill. In addition, everyone has some disposition to genetic disease and a genetic predisposition is not the same as a preexisting condition.

The EEOC has issued guidelines stating that healthy individuals with a genetic pre-disposition to a disease, and thus perceived as disabled, are protected by the Americans with Disabilities Act. The Genetic Information Nondiscrimination Act of 2008 (GINA) is designed to prohibit the improper use of genetic information in health insurance and employment. Recently the EEOC issued a final regulation, which generally bars employers, unions, employment agencies, and joint apprenticeship programs from requesting, requiring, or purchasing an individual's genetic information and making employment decisions based on such data.[37] The cap on combined losses ranges from $50,000 for employers with 15 to 100 employees to $300,000 for employers with more than 500 employees.[38] These are the same caps that were applied with the Civil Rights Act of 1991. Although GINA's provisions expressly protect employees and applicants, the new regulations clarify that GINA protects former employees as well.

GRAPHOANALYSIS (HANDWRITING ANALYSIS) The use of handwriting analysis as a selection factor is **graphoanalysis**. Many in the United States view handwriting analysis in the same context as psychic readings or astrology. In Europe, however, many employers use graphoanalysis to help screen and place job applicants. It is not unusual for European companies to have full-time handwriting analysts on staff. With graphoanalysis, every stroke of handwriting has a meaning that can be understood only within the context of the other strokes present in the handwriting.

Although no definitive study exists on the extent of its use in the United States, according to some handwriting experts, graphoanalysis is becoming more common. A basic reason for the reluctance of U.S. employers to use this approach appears to be a concern over the ability to validate such tests. And, there is little research demonstrating the effectiveness of graphology in employee selection. This and the worry about possible legal action seem to make many American employers wary of the process.

POLYGRAPH TESTS For many years, another means used to verify background information was the polygraph, or lie-detector test. One purpose of the polygraph was to confirm or refute the information contained in a candidate's application. However, the Employee Polygraph Protection Act of 1988 severely limited the use of polygraph tests in the private sector. It made unlawful the use of a polygraph test by any employer engaged in interstate commerce. However, the act does not apply to governmental employers, and there are other limited exceptions. Even here, the technology has been found to be flawed. Effective techniques for beating lie detectors, which only measure stress and anxiety have been developed and are available for use.

The act permits use of polygraph tests in the private sector in screening certain prospective employees for security service firms and pharmaceutical manufacturers, distributors, and dispensers. The act also permits, with certain restrictions, polygraph testing of certain employees reasonably suspected of involvement in a workplace incident, such as theft or embezzlement. Persons who take polygraph tests have a number of specific rights. For example, they have the right to a written notice before testing, the right to refuse or discontinue a test, and the right not to have test results disclosed to unauthorized persons.

Employment Interview

OBJECTIVE 6.7

Explain the use of the employment interview in the selection process.

employment interview
Goal-oriented conversation in which an interviewer and an applicant exchange information.

graphoanalysis
Use of handwriting analysis as a selection factor.

The **employment interview** is a goal-oriented conversation in which the interviewer and applicant exchange information. Traditionally, interviews have not been valid predictors of success on the job. In fact, courts are often suspicious of hiring decisions based primarily on interview results because of their inherently subjective nature. For 500 years, Leonardo da Vinci's *Mona Lisa* has confounded viewers who try to read her expression. Like the *Mona Lisa*, every job applicant presents a mysterious façade. Nevertheless, interviews continue to be the primary method companies use to evaluate applicants. The employment interview is especially important because the applicants who reach this stage are the survivors. They have endured preliminary screening, had their applications reviewed, and scored satisfactorily on selection tests. At this point, the candidates appear to be qualified, at least on paper. Every seasoned manager knows, however, that appearances can be quite misleading. Additional information is needed to indicate whether the individual is willing to work and can adapt to that particular organization (organizational fit).

Interview Planning

Interview planning is essential to effective employment interviews. A primary consideration should be the speed in which the process occurs. Many studies have demonstrated that the top candidates for nearly any job are hired and off the job market within anywhere from one to 10 days.

The physical location of the interview should be both pleasant and private, providing for a minimum of interruptions. The interviewer should possess a pleasant personality, empathy, and the ability to listen and communicate effectively. He or she should become familiar with the applicant's qualifications by reviewing the data collected from other selection tools. As preparation for the interview, the interviewer should develop a job profile based on the job description/specification. After listing job requirements, it is helpful to have an interview checklist that involves comparing an applicant's application and résumé with the job description. Also, questions should be prepared that relate to the qualities needed in a person being sought. In doing so, it is helpful to ask for examples of past job-related applicant behavior.

Content of the Interview

Both the interviewer and the candidate have agendas for the interview.[39] After establishing rapport with the applicant, the interviewer seeks additional job-related information to complement data provided by other selection tools. The interview permits clarification of certain points, the uncovering of additional information, and the elaboration of data needed to make a sound selection decision. The interviewer should provide information about the company, the job, and expectations of the candidate. Other areas typically included in the interview are discussed next.

OCCUPATIONAL EXPERIENCE The interviewer will explore the candidate's knowledge, skills, abilities, and willingness to handle responsibility. Although successful performance in one job does not guarantee success in another, it does provide an indication of the person's ability and willingness to work.

ACADEMIC ACHIEVEMENT In the absence of significant work experience, a person's academic record takes on greater importance. Managers should, however, consider grade point average in the light of other factors. For example, involvement in work, extracurricular activities, or other responsibilities may have affected an applicant's academic performance.

INTERPERSONAL SKILLS An individual may possess important technical skills significant to accomplishing a job. However, if the person cannot work well with others, chances for success are slim. This is especially true in today's world, with the increasing use of teams. The biggest mistake an interviewee can make is thinking that firms hire people only for their technical skills.

PERSONAL QUALITIES Personal qualities normally observed during the interview include physical appearance, speaking ability, vocabulary, poise, adaptability, assertiveness, leadership ability, and cooperative spirit.[40] As with all selection criteria, these attributes should be considered only if they are relevant to job performance.

Candidate's Role and Expectations

Although the interviewer will provide information about the company, it is still important for candidates to do their homework, including studying the job description and checking the Internet (including the firm's Web site) prior to the interview. Employees are also conducting background checks on companies to check out potential employers on such things as financial stability, whether or not the company would be a good place to work, and career opportunities.[41] Most company sites include information tailored to job seekers. They often provide a history of the company and a description of its products and customers. Applicants can often find out the culture of the firm by doing a thorough search of the Internet and the news media.[42] WetFeet .com provides insightful profiles of companies, careers, and industries to guide job seekers toward finding the right career, the right industry, the right company, and the right job for them. A person applying for a management position, especially, should have a thorough understanding of the firm's business priorities, its strengths and weaknesses, and its major competitors. Applicants should consider how they would address some of the issues facing the company. They need to be able to show how their experiences can help in addressing these issues.

Recruiters need to remember that interviewees also have objectives for the interview. One might be to determine what the firm is willing to pay as a starting salary. Job seekers have other goals that may include the following:

HR Web Wisdom

WetFeet.com

Helps equip job seekers with the advice, research, and inspiration needed to plan and achieve a successful career

- To be listened to and understood
- To have ample opportunity to present their qualifications
- To be treated fairly and with respect
- To gather information about the job and the company
- To make an informed decision concerning the desirability of the job

Candidates can learn what interviewing skills they need to improve by undergoing a mock interview or two. Having a colleague or friend interview them and afterwards critically reviewing their own responses can be beneficial. This mock interview allows candidates to analyze the strengths and interests that they would bring to a job. The process would also help them prioritize the points they want to make in the real interview.

General Types of Interviews

Types of interviews are often broadly classified as structured, unstructured, behavioral, and situational. A discussion of the differences follows.

unstructured interview
Interview in which the job applicant is asked probing, open-ended questions.

UNSTRUCTURED INTERVIEW An **unstructured interview** is one in which the interviewer asks probing, open-ended questions. This type of interview is comprehensive, and the interviewer encourages the applicant to do much of the talking. Questions such as "What professional accomplishments are you most proud of and why?" "What is your greatest professional strength, and how have you used it to overcome a challenge in your career?" and "What specifically attracted you to our organization?" might be asked. The unstructured interview is often more time consuming than the structured interview and results in obtaining different information from different candidates. This adds to the potential legal woes of organizations using this approach. Compounding the problem is the likelihood of discussing ill-advised, potentially discriminatory information. Applicants who are being encouraged to pour their heart out may volunteer facts that the interviewer does not need or want to know. Unsuccessful applicants subjected to this interviewing approach may later claim in court that the reason for their failure to get the job was the employer's use of this information.

structured interview
Interview in which the interviewer asks each applicant for a particular job the same series of job-related questions.

STRUCTURED INTERVIEW In the **structured interview**, the interviewer asks each applicant for a particular job the same series of job-related questions. Although interviews have historically been very poor predictors of job success, use of structured interviews increases reliability and accuracy by reducing the subjectivity and inconsistency of unstructured interviews. With the structured interview, questions are developed and asked in the same order of all applicants applying for the vacant position. This makes it easier to compare candidates fairly. There is a better chance that the best candidate will be selected using this technique. Often benchmark answers are determined beforehand.

Certainly, job-knowledge questions would be asked to probe the applicant's job-related knowledge; these questions may relate to basic educational skills or complex scientific or managerial skills. Worker requirements questions might also be asked of each applicant to determine the applicant's willingness to conform to the requirements of the job. For example, the interviewer may ask whether the applicant is willing to perform repetitive work or move to another city. Determining what questions to ask involves a thorough analysis of the position including a detailed analysis of the job description. Questions related to major job requirements in the job description makes the process extremely job related.

behavioral interview
Structured interview in which applicants are asked to relate actual incidents from their past relevant to the target job.

BEHAVIORAL INTERVIEW Traditional interviewing has a reputation of being a poor predictor of job success. Because of the low success rate of traditional interviews, the behavioral interview is often used. The **behavioral interview** is a structured interview in which applicants are asked to relate actual incidents from their past relevant to the target job. Once used exclusively for senior executive positions, behavioral interviewing is now a popular technique for lower-level positions also. The assumption is that past behavior is the best predictor of future behavior.

Behavioral interviewers look for three main things: a description of a challenging situation, what the candidate did about it, and measurable results. In the behavioral interview, the questions are selected for their relevance to job success in a particular job. Questions are formed from the behaviors by asking applicants how they performed in the described situation. For example, when probing to determine how creative an applicant is, the candidate might be requested to "Describe an experience when you were faced with a new problem and how you handled it."[43] Or, if seeking to determine the applicant's enthusiasm, the request might be, "Relate a scenario during which you were responsible for motivating others." Behavioral interviewers ask each candidate the same open-ended questions, then score responses on a scale. Interviewing is based on the principle that what you did previously in your life is a good predictor of what you will do in the future. Interviewees are asked to give an example of a situation when they faced a dilemma, a problem, or a situation.

In behavioral interviews, candidates may unwittingly reveal information about their attitudes, intelligence, and truthfulness. Arrogance, lack of cooperation with team members, and anger can all spill out during such an interview. Although some candidates may think the interview is all about technical skills, it is as much about them as a person as anything.

Questions asked during behavioral interviews are legally safe since they are job related. Equally important, since both questions and answers are related to successful job performance, they are more accurate in predicting whether applicants will be successful in the job they are hired to perform. It answers the one question both the hiring manager and the candidate want to know most: Is this a good fit?

situational interview

Gives interviewers better insight into how candidates would perform in the work environment by creating hypothetical situations candidates would be likely to encounter on the job and asking them how they would handle them.

SITUATIONAL INTERVIEW Whereas the behavioral interview focuses on how an individual handled circumstances in the past, the **situational interview** creates hypothetical situations candidates would likely encounter on the job and ask how they would handle them. For example, the question might be asked: "One of your employees has experienced a significant decline in productivity. How would you handle it?" As another example, "You completely disagree with the way that your boss has told you to handle a project. What would you do?" Basically, a situational interview provides a preview of the how a candidate might handle situations in a simulated work environment.

Methods of Interviewing

Organizations conduct interviews in several ways. The level of the open position and the appropriate labor market determine the most fitting approach. A discussion of these methods follows.

ONE-ON-ONE INTERVIEW In a typical employment interview, the applicant meets one-on-one with an interviewer. As the interview may be a highly emotional occasion for the applicant, meeting alone with the interviewer is often less threatening. This method provides a better opportunity for an effective exchange of information to take place.

group interview

Meeting in which several job applicants interact in the presence of one or more company representatives.

GROUP INTERVIEW In a **group interview**, several applicants interact in the presence of one or more company representatives. This approach, although not mutually exclusive of other interview types, may provide useful insights into the candidates' interpersonal competence as they engage in a group discussion. Another advantage of this technique is that it saves time for busy professionals and executives.

board interview

An interview approach in which several of the firm's representatives interview a candidate at the same time.

BOARD (OR PANEL) INTERVIEW In a **board interview**, several of the firm's representatives interview a candidate at the same time. Companies use the board interview to gain multiple viewpoints, because there are many cross-functional workplace relationships in business these days. Once the interview is complete, the board members pool their evaluation of the candidate. Most Ph.D. recipients are quite familiar with the board interview, as they were required to defend their dissertation as their professors asked questions. At times, some candidates claimed that professors having opposing views were deliberately placed on the board and the candidate had to tiptoe through the session, hoping not to offend anyone.

MULTIPLE INTERVIEWS At times, applicants are interviewed by peers, subordinates, and potential superiors. This approach permits the firm to get a more encompassing view of the candidate. It also gives the candidate a chance to learn more about the company from a variety of perspectives. The result of this type of interview is a stronger, more cohesive team that shares the company's culture and helps ensure organizational fit.

VIDEO INTERVIEW The *video interview* involves an applicant being interviewed with both individuals being in different locations. It saves time and money when having the first face-to-face meeting with a top prospect. When the video interview is used, candidates get a better feel for the firm's culture or employer brand. Skype, the free video service, is fine for one-on-one screens, so long as the candidate has a webcam and is also a Skype user. There are, however, many vendors available for video interviewing. Prices for some are as low as $10 or $20, but may be $100 to $200 depending on the service.[44]

STRESS INTERVIEW What would you do if you were in an interview that was going quite well and all at once the interviewer said, "I think your answer is totally inadequate: it doesn't deal with my concerns at all, can't you do better than that?" You may not realize it, but you have just been exposed to a stress interview. In the **stress interview**, the interviewer intentionally creates anxiety.

stress interview
Form of interview in which the interviewer intentionally creates anxiety.

Most interviewers strive to minimize stress for the candidate. However, in the stress interview, the interviewer deliberately makes the candidate uncomfortable by asking blunt and often discourteous questions. The purpose is to determine the applicant's tolerance for stress that may accompany the job. Knowledge of this factor may be important if the job requires the ability to deal with a high level of stress.

Amazon.com interviewers have been known to ask job candidates to guess how many gas stations there are in the United States or to estimate the cost to wash all of Seattle's windows. Google interviewers have also been known to ask, "You are shrunk to the height of a nickel and your mass is proportionally reduced so as to maintain your original density. You are then thrown into an empty glass blender. The blades will start moving in 60 seconds. What do you do?"[45] The answer is not as important as your logic in approaching an answer.

Stress interviews are not new. The late Admiral Hyman G. Rickover, father of the U.S. Navy's nuclear submarine program, was known to offer interviewees a chair that had one or two legs shorter than the other. The candidates' problems were compounded by the chair's polished seat. The admiral once stated that "they had to maintain their wits about them as they answered questions while sliding off the chair."[46]

realistic job preview (RJP)
Method of conveying both positive and negative job information to an applicant in an unbiased manner.

REALISTIC JOB PREVIEW A **realistic job preview (RJP)** conveys both positive and negative job information to the applicant in an unbiased manner. Many applicants have unrealistic expectations about the prospective job they are seeking. They may have been told the exciting part of the job, but the less glamorous areas are not mentioned. Realistic job previews have become increasingly common in certain fields because of the high turnover rates and the constant cost of replacing those individuals who do not work out.[47] For instance, when conducting an interview in the fast-food restaurant industry, an applicant might be taken behind the counter to see what it is like to work in a hot, greasy environment, smell food cooking all day, and scramble around other bodies in close quarters.[48] An inaccurate perception may occur when interviewers paint false, rosy pictures of the job and the company. This practice leads to mismatches of people and positions. What compounds the problem is when candidates exaggerate their own qualifications. The RJP should typically be done early in the selection process and, definitely, before a job offer is made.

An RJP conveys information about tasks the person would perform and the behavior required to fit into the culture of the organization. This approach helps applicants develop a more accurate perception of the job and the firm. Employers who give detailed RJPs get two results: fewer employees accept the job offer, and applicants who do accept the offer are less likely to leave the firm. Given an RJP, some candidates will take themselves out of the selection process, minimizing the number of unqualified candidates. Another reason to use RJPs is the benefit a firm receives from being an up-front, ethical employer.

Potential Interviewing Problems

Potential interviewing problems that can threaten the success of employment interviews are discussed next.

INAPPROPRIATE QUESTIONS Although no questions are illegal, many are clearly hiring standards to avoid. When they are asked, the responses generated create a legal liability for the employer. The most basic interviewing rule is this: "Ask only job-related questions." The definition of a test in the *Uniform Guidelines* includes "physical, education, and work experience requirements *informal or casual interviews*." Because the interview is a test, if adverse impact is shown, it is subject to the same validity requirements as any other step in the selection process. For unstructured interviews, this constraint presents special difficulties. Historically, the interview has been more vulnerable to charges of discrimination than any other tool used in the selection process.

The Americans with Disabilities Act also provides a warning for interviewers. Interviewers should inquire about the need for reasonable accommodations in only a few situations. For example, the topic is appropriate if the applicant is in a wheelchair or has an obvious disability that will require accommodation. Also, the applicant may voluntarily disclose a disability or even ask for some reasonable accommodation. Otherwise, employers should refrain from broaching the subject. Instead, interviewers should frame questions in terms of whether applicants can perform the essential functions of the jobs for which they are applying.

PERMITTING NON-JOB-RELATED INFORMATION If a candidate begins volunteering personal information that is not job related, the interviewer should steer the conversation back on course. The interviewer might do well to begin the interview by tactfully stating something like, "This selection decision will be based strictly on qualifications. Let's not discuss topics such as religion, social activities, national origin, gender, or family situations. We are definitely interested in you, personally. However, these factors are not job related and will not be considered in our decision." This enables better decisions to be made while decreasing the likelihood of discrimination charges.[49]

To elicit needed information in any type of interview, the interviewer must create a climate that encourages the applicant to speak freely. However, the conversation should not become too casual. Whereas engaging in friendly chitchat with candidates might be pleasant, in our litigious society, it may be the most dangerous thing an interviewer can do. Asking a woman a question about her children that has nothing to do with the job would not be appropriate.

INTERVIEWER BIAS Often a problem that may arise in an interview is interviewer bias where the interviewer makes assumptions about the interviewee that may be incorrect and lets these biases influence the selection decision. Various forms of biases will next be discussed.

Stereotyping bias occurs when the interviewer assumes that the applicant has certain traits because they are members of a certain class. The classic case of stereotyping bias is when an interviewer assumes that a women applicant cannot meet a certain physical requirement such as being able to lift 50 pounds.

A *halo error bias* occurs when the interviewer generalizes one positive first impression feature of the candidate. Such might be the case with discovering that you have something in common with the applicant. The opposite could occur with *horn error bias* where the interviewer's first impression of the candidate creates a negative first impression that exists throughout the interview.

Contrast bias may occur when, for example, an interviewer meets with several poorly qualified applicants and then confronts a mediocre candidate. By comparison, the last applicant may appear to be better qualified than he or she actually is. The opposite can also occur. Suppose that a clearly outstanding candidate is followed by a very good candidate. The second candidate may not be considered even if the first candidate turns down the job offer.

Premature judgment bias suggests that interviewers often make a judgment about candidates in the first few minutes of the interview.[50] Apparently, these interviewers believe that they have the ability to determine immediately whether a candidate will be successful or not. When this occurs, a great deal of potentially valuable information is not considered. Even if an interviewer spent a week with an applicant, the sample of behavior might be too small to judge the candidate's qualifications properly. In addition, the candidate's behavior during an interview is seldom typical or natural, thereby making a quick judgment difficult.

Interview illusion bias is closely related to premature judgment but not the same. Managers may say something to the effect "Give me just five minutes with an applicant and I can tell if they will be successful with our company." Their belief in their interview ability was likely exaggerated. Recruiters are often overconfident about their ability to judge others in general. Interviewers have to be careful about placing excessive weight on interviews and thinking "I just feel good about this applicant" when making the hiring decision.[51]

INTERVIEWER DOMINATION In successful interviews, relevant information must flow both ways. Sometimes, interviewers begin the interview by telling candidates what they are looking for, and then are excited to hear candidates parrot back their own words. Other interviewers are delighted to talk through virtually the entire interview, either to take pride in their organization's accomplishments or to express frustrations over their own difficulties. After dominating the meeting for an hour or so, these interviewers feel good about the candidate. Therefore, interviewers must learn to be good listeners as well as suppliers of information.

LACK OF TRAINING Anyone who has ever conducted an interview realizes that it is much more than carrying on a conversation with another person. The interviewer is attempting to gain insight into how the applicant answers job-related questions. There should be a reason for asking each question. For instance, suppose the applicant is told, "Tell me about yourself." A trained interviewer asks this question to determine whether the applicant's life experiences qualify the applicant for the job, not the fact that he or she had a little dog named Moe as a child.

Interviewers should be trained to have a job-related purpose for asking each question. When the cost of making poor selection decisions is considered, the expense of training employees in interviewing skills can be easily justified.

NONVERBAL COMMUNICATION *Body language* is the nonverbal communication method in which physical actions such as motions, gestures, and facial expressions convey thoughts and emotions. The interviewer is attempting to view the nonverbal signals from the applicant. Applicants are also reading the nonverbal signals of the interviewer. Therefore, interviewers should make a conscious effort to view themselves as applicants do to avoid sending inappropriate or unintended nonverbal signals.

Concluding the Interview

When the interviewer has obtained the necessary information and answered the applicant's questions, he or she should conclude the interview. Management must then determine whether the candidate is suitable for the open position and organization. If the conclusion is positive, the process continues; if there appears to be no match, the candidate is no longer considered. Also, in concluding the interview, the interviewer should tell the applicant that he or she will be notified of the selection decision shortly. Keeping this promise helps maintain a positive relationship with the applicant.

<table>
<tr><td>

OBJECTIVE 6.8

Explain pre-employment screening, negligent hiring, and the selection decision.

</td></tr>
</table>

Pre-employment Screening: Background Investigations

Pre-employment screening has experienced tremendous growth since the terrorist attack of 9/11. It went from a possible step in the selection process to that of a necessary step. Background investigation is more important than ever due to the rise in negligent hiring (to be discussed later in this chapter) lawsuits, recent corporate scandals, and national security concerns. At this stage of the selection process, an applicant has normally completed an application form or submitted a résumé, taken the necessary selection tests, and undergone an employment interview. On the surface the candidate looks qualified. It is now time to determine the accuracy of the information submitted or to determine whether vital information was not submitted.

Background investigations involve obtaining data from various sources, including previous employers, business associates, credit bureaus, government agencies, and academic institutions. Fingerprinting also is becoming a more common part of checks, especially for companies that employ workers in charge of securing a worksite—for example, airports, the financial services industry, hospitals, schools, the gaming industry, and hazardous materials services. Reasons for leaving jobs or gaps in employment may be cleverly disguised to present a work history that does not provide an accurate or complete picture. Letters of recommendation from companies that are no longer in existence and differences between their résumé and completed job application may raise a red flag.

Checking for criminal records is important because many applicants with criminal records tend to lie about it on their applications. A 2010 Society for Human Resource Management (SHRM) survey that found criminal background investigations are conducted to ensure a safe work environment, to reduce legal liability for negligent hiring, and to eliminate or reduce criminal activity in the workplace.[52]

The intensity of background investigations depends on the nature of the open position's tasks and its relationship to customers or clients. To be legally safe, employers should ask applicants to sign a liability waiver permitting a background investigation. The waiver is typically a statement on the application form that releases former employers, business references, and others from liability. It also authorizes checks of court records and the verification of the applicant's educational history and other credentials.

Employment Eligibility Verification (Form I-9)

The employment eligibility verification form I-9 must be filled out by American job applicants, but it allows any number of documents to be used to demonstrate their legal right to work in the United States. Every employee hired since 1986 must have a completed Form I-9 on file.[53] In an audit, federal immigration agents review the Form I-9 that employers are required to keep on file.[54] The law provides for penalties from $100 to $1,000 for each incorrect or missing I-9. Recently, the government required 1,000 companies to turn over employment records for inspection. Organizations including Chipotle Mexican Grill, apple grower Gebbers Farms, and clothing retailer Abercrombie

& Fitch have received substantial fines for I-9 violations.[55] Disneyland in California was accused of having more than 1,000 paperwork violations and received a $395,000 fine.[56]

An additional level of verification involves the use of *E-Verify* to check out new hires, and its use is required for federal contractors and subcontractors with contracts of $100,000 or more. Recently, the U.S. Supreme Court granted states the right to require employers to use the federal E-Verify system to check on the eligibility of employees to work in the United States.[57] E-Verify is a Web-based system that lets employers check Social Security and visa numbers submitted by workers against government databases. The system is not checking for citizenship, but for eligibility to be lawfully employed in the United States. The E-Verify system is not flawless, since a recent report found that six percent passed the E-Verify checks because they had used fraudulent or stolen identities.[58]

Continuous Background Investigation

Background investigations are not just for pre-employment any more. Some employers are screening their employees on an ongoing basis.[59] In certain industries, such as banking and health care, employers are required by regulation to routinely research the criminal records of employees. People and events are ever-changing. For example, financial devastation, marital collapse, or a medical crisis can send a person with the cleanest record over the edge. It has been estimated that every year one or two of every 1,000 existing employees acquire a new criminal record. Since only a small percent of convictions lead to jail time, the employer may never know of a conviction unless there is an ongoing background investigation.

Background Investigation with Social Networking

An increasing number of employers are using social networking to conduct background investigations.[60] Employers use an applicant's Facebook page, LinkedIn profile, and postings made on an industry blog to find out about individuals they are considering hiring. According to one study, more than eight out of 10 employers say that a positive online reputation influences their hiring decisions at least to some extent, and nearly half say a strong online reputation influences their decisions to a great extent.[61] Industries most likely to conduct background investigations on applicants are those that specialize in technology or that use sensitive information.

Employers reported that they have found content on social networking sites that caused them not to hire the candidate. Some examples include posting provocative or inappropriate photographs or information, posting content about alcohol or drug use, and posting negative comments about their previous employer, coworkers, or clients. Other information found on these sites supported their decision to hire the candidate. For example, the profile provided a good feel for the candidate's personality and fit within the organization, the profile supported candidate's professional qualifications, and other people posted good references about the candidate.

As the cost of background checking has dropped and technology has improved, background checking has entered new dating relationships. Prior to accepting an invitation for a date with a new person, that individual can be "checked out" to determine if what was said was fact or fiction. Apps are now available to conduct a background check before entering into any relationship. Through these new apps, one can quickly determine if a person is telling the truth about factors such as age, relatives, addresses, criminal history, bankruptcies, judgments, liens, aliases, and current contact information. The cost for these background checks is under $10.00.

Remembering Hiring Standards to Avoid

Some of the standards used in the background investigation have the potential to violate a hiring standard to avoid. A word of caution is advised in situations where an applicant *acknowledges* that he or she has been convicted of a crime. A major implication of the *Griggs v Duke Power Company* Supreme Court case was that when human resource management practices eliminate substantial numbers of minority or women applicants (prima facie evidence), the burden of proof is on the employer to show that the practice is job related. If a criminal record automatically eliminates a candidate that means that approximately 65 million people who have been convicted of felonies and misdemeanors may struggle to find employment.[62] Some states and cities have done away with asking about criminal convictions on applications, and there is a push to do it also on the national level.[63] Therefore, caution should be taken using criminal conviction as a hiring criterion if it cannot be shown to be job related.

The same rationale can be said for conducting credit checks. If a disproportionate number of members of a protected group are rejected through the use of the credit check, the company would need to validate its use. Certainly, if a company does a credit check on all applicants, it is difficult to say that the credit check is job related. Presently four states have laws on their books limiting credit check uses, and 13 other states are considering credit check proposals.[64]

Congress created somewhat of an obstacle for employers when it amended the federal Fair Credit Reporting Act (FCRA). Employers' obligations are triggered under the act when they use consumer reports that contain information about an individual's personal and credit characteristics, character, general reputation, and lifestyle. To avoid legal problems, employers need to allow sufficient time between notifying an applicant or employee of a less than favorable consumer report and taking adverse action. If an unfavorable credit check surfaces, the potential employee should be given time to dispute and correct the errors.[65] The FCRA covers only reports that are prepared by a consumer reporting agency such as a credit bureau.

The EEOC has recently conducted hearings claiming there are employers that hire only individuals who are presently employed.[66] Paul C. Evans, a partner with law firm Morgan Lewis & Bockius LLP in Philadelphia, said, "I do think the EEOC will look to see whether or not employers are de facto, even without an explicit policy, precluding or eliminating from consideration" those who have been out of work for long periods of time.[67]

Much of the social media content contains information regarding possible hiring standards to avoid. The typical Facebook page will reveal race, sex, age, ethnic background, and more by just looking at the pictures and profile. Religion, especially if it is a strong part of the member's belief system, is often easy to detect. None of these factors should be considered in the selection process. However, information is usually available that is legal to consider. In fact, according to a survey by Microsoft Corporation, seven out of 10 U.S. hiring managers reject candidates based on information they have posted online even though 90 percent of these managers are concerned that the information they find can be inaccurate and unreliable.[68]

Pre-employment Screening: Reference Checks

reference checks
Validations from individuals who know the applicant that provide additional insight into the information furnished by the applicant and verification of its accuracy.

Reference checks are validations from those who know the applicant that provide additional insight into the information furnished by the applicant and allow verification of its accuracy. They are a valuable source of information to supplement the background investigation. Applicants are often required to submit the names of several references who can provide additional information about them. A possible flaw with reference checking is that virtually everyone can name three or four individuals willing to make favorable statements about him or her. Even so, there is anecdotal evidence that personal references do not always provide favorable information. They may not necessarily be committed to shading the truth for the applicant.

A related problem in obtaining information from previous employers is their general reluctance to reveal such data and this trend continues to grow. In a 2010 Society for Human Resource Management poll on background investigations, 98 percent of respondents said their organizations would verify dates of employment for current or former employees, 68 percent said they would not discuss work performance, and 82 percent said they would not discuss character or personality.[69]

There are two schools of thought with regard to supplying information about former employees. One is, "Don't tell them anything." The other is, "Honesty is the best policy." In the more conservative approach, the employer typically provides only basic data such as name, job title, and dates of employment. The honesty approach is based on the reality that facts honestly given or opinions honestly held constitute a solid legal defense. It is helpful to know why the person left that job. If the response differs from that given by the applicant, it is definitely a red flag. Although protective laws regarding reference checking do exist, apparently there is a wait-and-see attitude among some employers. It will likely take litigation and court rulings before employers fully understand, and have confidence in, the statutes.

Traditional reference checking has been heavily labor intense. *Automated reference checking (ARC)* has been a boom in this area. With ARC, references are anonymous and more efficient and a more comprehensive report can be provided. ARC automates one of the last elements of recruiting that used to be heavily manual. Because it is confidential, people are more forthcoming. And because it is online, the process goes faster. Reference checking requires an e-mail link to the job candidate. It is the candidate, not the recruiter, who contacts references to fill out the questionnaire. The system collects the surveys and prepares a report for the recruiter. Referencing is much faster, going from an average of four to an average of 1.2 days. ARC can help reduce the legal risks for the company seeking the reference because the request comes from the candidate, not the organization. The company does not run the risk of a recruiter asking an inappropriate question, because the applicant has preapproved the questions.

Negligent Hiring

negligent hiring

Liability a company incurs when it fails to conduct a reasonable investigation of an applicant's background, and then assigns a potentially dangerous person to a position in which he or she can inflict harm.

Negligent hiring is the liability an employer incurs when it fails to conduct a reasonable investigation of an applicant's background, and then assigns a potentially dangerous person to a position in which he or she can inflict harm. The typical negligent hiring case involves a deliberate inflicting of harm committed by an employee including fraud, assault, or battery. Reasonable investigation varies according to the nature of the job. The risk of harm to third parties, for example, requires a higher standard of care when hiring a taxi driver as opposed to a machinist. The taxi cab driver is alone and has control of his or her customer during the time the customer is in the car. This would not be the case for the machinist. Employers who operate home-service businesses, day-care centers, and home health care operations are particularly at risk, as are those with employees who drive company vehicles, visit customer locations, handle money, or work with children, the elderly, or the impaired.[70] The primary consideration in negligent hiring is whether the risk of harm from a dangerous employee was reasonably foreseeable. Accusers will argue that employers knew, or should have known, about a hire's potential threat to others.[71] In one negligent hiring case a hospital nursing assistant was hired without a background investigation and the medical center did not ask former employers why the worker had left. If it had, the medical center would have discovered that the worker had previously sexually harassed, assaulted, and inappropriately touched female patients. Once hired, the worker was left alone in rooms with vulnerable female patients and sexually abused them.[72]

Selection Decision

At this point, the focus is on the manager who must take the most critical step of all: the actual hiring decision. If a firm is going to invest thousands of dollars to recruit, select, and train an employee, it is important for the manager to hire the most qualified available candidate, according to the firm's criteria. The final choice is made from among those still in the running after selection tests, interviews, background investigations, and reference checks have been evaluated. Usually, the person selected has qualifications that most closely conform to the requirements of the open position and the organization.

The person who normally makes the final selection is the manager who will be responsible for the new employee's performance. In making this decision, the manager will review results of the selection methods used. All will not likely be weighted the same. The question then becomes, "Which data are most predictive of job success?" For each firm or group of jobs, the optimal selection method may be different.

Medical Examination

The Americans with Disabilities Act (ADA) does not prohibit pre-employment medical examinations. However, it does determine the point at which they may be administered during the selection process. The ADA explicitly states that all exams must be directly relevant to the job requirements and that a firm cannot order a medical exam until the applicant is offered employment. Typically, a job offer is contingent on the applicant's passing this examination. The basic purpose of the medical examination is to determine whether an applicant is physically capable of performing the work. The *Uniform Guidelines* state that these examinations can be used to reject applicants only when the results show that job performance would be adversely affected.

Notification of Candidates

Management should notify both successful and unsuccessful candidates of selection decisions as soon as possible. This action is a matter of courtesy and good public relations. Any delay may also result in the firm losing a prime candidate, as top prospects often have other employment options.

Employers may reject applicants at any time during the selection process. Most people can accept losing if they lose fairly. Problems occur when the selection process appears to be less than objective. It is therefore important for firms to develop and use rational selection tools. Time constraints prevent firms from spending much time explaining a decision to an unsuccessful candidate. If the person rejected was an internal candidate, managers may visit or make a personal phone call to the rejected applicant. A rejection letter is a more likely method if the candidate was not an internal candidate. However, a letter with a personal touch may reduce the stigma of rejection and avoid the applicant's having a negative feeling about the company. An impersonal letter is likely to have the opposite effect. The best an organization can do is to make selection decisions objectively. Hopefully, most unsuccessful individuals can, with time, accept the fact that they were not chosen.

Human Capital Metrics

OBJECTIVE **6.9**

Describe human capital metrics and explain the metrics for evaluating recruitment/selection effectiveness.

human capital metrics
Measures of HR performance.

Human capital metrics are measures of HR performance. Even though employees account for as much as 80 percent of the worth of a corporation, the task of measuring and understanding how they contribute to the bottom line is often difficult. Al Adamsen, founder and managing partner of People-Centered Strategies LLC in San Francisco, said, "Historically, HR has grown up in a void of unaccountability and had not been held accountable for delivering metrics that show the value of their programs or investments."[73] This is not the case today and human capital metrics need to be closely tied to whether company strategic goals are being achieved.[74] Management has for years been able to measure the success or failure of a production process. They focused on return on investment, the bottom line, and profit. Currently, HR is under the same scrutiny and management wants to know how HR activities contribute to the organization's bottom line.

There is, however, no one-size-fits-all metric that employers can adopt to achieve greater hiring efficiency. The metrics that best suit each company depends on a variety of factors, including its business goals. The recent recession heightened the need to have metrics regarding the productivity of employees. When employee cost-cutting decisions must be made, it is important that the most productive employees are retained. One survey revealed that companies with best-in-class talent acquisition programs were most successful at measuring the following four performance criteria: time to hire, quality of hire, new-hire retention, and hiring managers' overall satisfaction with the program.[75]

Metrics for Evaluating the Effectiveness of Recruitment/Selection

Possible metrics for evaluating the effectiveness of recruitment/selection are described next. Metrics for evaluating other functions are discussed at the appropriate time.

Quality of Hire

Many recruiters believe that quality of hire is the most important metric to use in the selection process. Some possible measures to determine the quality of hire might be communication effectiveness, ability to motivate others, leadership ability, and cultural fit.[76] Even though the question of how to measure quality of hire and set standards for new-hire performance is difficult to determine, it is an important decision that HR professionals are constantly striving to determine. Realistically, the answer depends on the system and the company involved. For quality of hire to be usable, one needs to have performance assessment for two or three years before the real capabilities of a new hire will be understood.

Time Required to Hire

The shorter the time to hire, the more efficient the HR department is in finding the replacement for the job. The top candidates for nearly any job are hired and off the job market within anywhere from one to 10 days. It then becomes crucial that the time required to hire be as low as possible while still ensuring quality of hire. Otherwise your best prospect will have already signed on to work for a competitor.

New-Hire Retention

It is important to measure new-hire retention because costs go up dramatically if a position has to be filled again in a short period. New-hire retention is calculated by determining the percentage of the new hires that remain with the company at selected intervals, typically one or two years. If this situation is happening excessively, HR should analyze the selection process to determine if there are flaws in the system that cause new hires to terminate prematurely. Perhaps, as was mentioned earlier, a realistic job preview needs to be instituted.

Hiring Manager Overall Satisfaction

The manager is largely responsible for the success of his or her department. It is the quality of the employees in the workgroup that have a major impact on success of the department. A manager's belief that employees being hired through the recruitment and selection system do not perform as well as expected casts doubt on the entire selection process. Some measure manager satisfaction based on the survey of hiring managers, compared to previous period. Other firms provide a rating scale for the manager to evaluate how a new hire is performing after the employee's first 90 or 120 days.

HR Web Wisdom

Business Owner's Toolkit
http://www.toolkit.cch.com

Offers detailed instructions for the small business owner to hire, manage, and retain employees.

Turnover Rate

Turnover rate is the number of times on average that employees have to be replaced during a year. For example, if a company has 200 employees and 200 workers had been hired during the year, a 100 percent turnover rate would be experienced. As one might expect, a 100 percent rate is quite costly to the organization, and ways need to be found to reduce the rate. Employees who are hired and then quit within 120 days are called "False Starts" and are considered to be especially expensive, since the company spends money on their hire but then quickly must spend even more to replace them. Across all industries, the average turnover rate is 15 percent, whereas companies in the service industries typically have the highest turnover rates at 35 percent.[77]

Cost Per Hire

In determining the recruiting cost per hire, the total recruiting expense must first be calculated. Then, the cost per hire may be determined by dividing the recruiting expenses (calculation of advertising, agency fees, employee referrals, relocation, recruiter pay, and benefits costs) by the number of recruits hired. Naturally, the difficulty associated with this measure is in determining the exact costs to include as recruiting expenses. It may be beneficial for a firm to use a benchmark cost per hire to compare to the specific cost for the company.

Selection Rate

The number of applicants hired from a group of candidates expressed as a percentage is the *selection rate*. For example, if 100 qualified candidates are available and 25 are chosen, the selection rate would be 25 percent. Certainly, the selection rate is affected by the condition of the economy. Also, the validity of the selection process (previously discussed) will impact the selection rate.

OBJECTIVE 6.10

Explain leadership styles in the global environment.

Acceptance Rate

Once an offer has been extended, the firm has said that this applicant meets the requirements for the position. The *acceptance rate* is the number of applicants who accepted the job divided by the number who were offered the job. If this rate is unusually low, it would be wise to determine the reason that jobs are being turned down. A low acceptance rate increases recruiting cost.

Yield Rate

It has been suggested that the selection process can be viewed somewhat as a funnel, with the number of applicants available at each stage of the selection process getting smaller. A *yield rate* is the percentage of applicants from a particular source and method that make it to the next stage of the selection process. For example, if 100 applicants submitted their résumés through the firm's corporate career Web site and 25 were asked in for an interview, the yield rate for the corporate career Web site would be 25 percent. Each recruitment method would be analyzed in a similar manner.

Leadership Styles in the Global Environment

Organizational fit was discussed in this chapter as management's perception of the degree to which the prospective employee will fit in with the firm's culture or value system. When determining which leadership style will be more appropriate for a company, a country's culture plays a major role in determining whether an executive will be successful or not. Regardless of how far-flung their markets and operations, multinational leaders typically retain and reflect the cultural mores of their home countries. Since the vast majority of firms are deeply rooted in the culture of their home countries, leaders who adhere to the cultural norms have a better chance of success.[78] D. Quinn Mills, professor emeritus of business administration at Harvard Business School, said, "They are very much shaped by national culture. That's why it's very hard to lead an organization that's of a different national culture."[79] A perfect example of where style and culture clashed was with the ill-fated, co-presidency between Germany's Daimler and Detroit's Chrysler when one president was unwilling to share the authority resulting in the resignation of the other president. Even though there does not appear to be a global market for CEOs, there are a few exceptions. Carlos Ghosn provides one exception. He was born in Brazil to Lebanese parents, educated in France, and speaks four languages fluently. He is chief executive officer of both French automaker Renault and its alliance partner Nissan, the Japanese car company.

Think of global business styles as a continuum with U.S. executives at one end and their Asian counterparts at the other. America and Japan provide an excellent example for studying cross-cultural leadership interaction due to the cultural differences between the countries. American CEOs differ in styles, but most have a common denominator; they have more leeway to make large, strategic decisions themselves.[80] Japanese leaders tend to make decisions by consensus. Some wonder if it is possible for the various styles of executives to ever come together. It is too early to tell. However, there appears to be a shift away from emulating American leaders, especially since the recent financial crisis.

Philip R. Harris and Robert T. Moran, in their book, *Managing Cultural Differences*, summarize feedback from Arab businesspeople regarding how they perceive many Westerners. To them, Westerners act superior, as if they know the answer to everything; are not willing to share credit for joint efforts; are unable or unwilling to respect and adjust to local customs and culture; prefer solutions based on their home cultures rather than meeting local needs; resist working through local administrative and legal channels and procedures; manage in an autocratic and intimidating way; and are too imposing and pushy.[81] In such an environment, an American leader chosen for duty in an Arab country would have difficulties being successful.

MyManagementLab

Go to **mymanagementlab.com** to complete the problems marked with this icon ⭐.

Summary

1. *Describe the use of biometrics in HR. Biometrics* deal with a variety of traits that are not subject to change, including fingerprints, palm prints, facial features, DNA, retinas, irises, odors, rhythm, gait, and voice. It can be used in any situation requiring accurate identification of an individual.

2. *Explain the significance of employee selection and identify environmental factors that affect the selection process. Selection* is the process of choosing from a group of applicants the individual best suited for a particular position. There are many ways to improve productivity, but none is more powerful than making the right hiring decision.

   The environmental factors that affect the selection process include legal considerations, speed of decision making, organizational hierarchy, applicant pool, type of organization, and probationary period.

3. *Describe the selection process and explain the importance of preliminary screening.* The selection process typically begins with preliminary screening, during which obviously unqualified candidates are rejected. Next, applicants complete the firm's application form, and this is followed by the administration of selection tests and a series of employment interviews with reference and background investigations. Once the selection decision has been made, the prospective employee may be given a company medical examination.

4. *Describe reviewing applications and résumés.* Having the applicant complete an application for employment is another early step in the selection process. The employer evaluates this application to see whether there is an apparent match between the individual and the position.

When writing their résumés, applicants should realize that most companies now use automated résumé systems. These systems assume a certain résumé style. Résumés that deviate from the assumed style are ignored or deleted.

5. **Explain the significance of recruitment and selection with LinkedIn.** LinkedIn is an online social network for professionals. The largest and fastest-growing part of LinkedIn's business is "hiring solutions," which include a variety of services for in-house and external recruiters. These services include online job postings and ways to organize job searches.

6. **Describe the use of tests in the selection process.** Recognizing the shortcomings of other selection tools, many firms have added pre-employment tests to their hiring process. Selection tests may accurately predict an applicant's ability to perform the job, the "can do," but they are less successful in indicating the extent to which the individual will be motivated to perform it, the "will do." Employers should also be aware that tests might be unintentionally discriminatory. Test anxiety can also be a problem.

7. **Explain the use of the employment interview in the selection process.** The interview permits clarification of certain points, the uncovering of additional information, and the elaboration of data needed to make a sound selection decision. The interviewer should provide information about the company, the job, and expectations of the candidate.

The general types of interviews are the unstructured interview and the structured interview, including the behavioral interview and the situational interview.

8. **Explain pre-employment screening, negligent hiring, and the selection decision.** Background investigations primarily seek data from various sources, including professional references.

Negligent hiring is the liability an employer incurs when it fails to conduct a reasonable investigation of an applicant's background, and then assigns a potentially dangerous person to a position in which he or she can inflict harm.

The selection decision is when the final choice is made from among those still in the running after reference checks, selection tests, background investigations, and interview information are evaluated.

9. **Describe human capital metrics and explain the metrics for evaluating recruitment/selection effectiveness.** Metrics available to assess HR efficiency are numerous, and a comprehensive set of metrics can be produced to evaluate recruitment and selection. Possible metrics include quality of hire, time required to hire, new-hire retention, hiring manager overall satisfaction, turnover rate, costs per hire, selection rate, acceptance rate, and yield rate.

10. **Explain leadership styles in the global environment.** More often than not, trying to make different styles of leadership work in foreign lands is an exercise in frustration. The vast majority of firms are deeply rooted in their home countries.

Key Terms

selection   134
applicant pool   135
selection ratio   135
organizational fit   136
résumé   139
keywords   141
keyword résumé   141
standardization   142
objectivity   142
norm   142
reliability   142
validity   142

criterion-related validity   143
content validity   143
construct validity   143
cognitive aptitude tests   144
psychomotor abilities tests   144
job-knowledge tests   144
work-sample tests   144
vocational interest tests   144
personality tests   144
assessment center   145
genetic tests   145
graphoanalysis   146

employment interview   146
unstructured interview   148
structured interview   148
behavioral interview   148
situational interview   149
group interview   149
board interview   149
stress interview   150
realistic job preview (RJP)   150
reference checks   154
negligent hiring   155
human capital metrics   156

Exercises

1. What would be the selection ratio if there were 15 applicants to choose from and only one position to fill? Interpret the meaning of this selection ratio.

2. What do you believe would be the most important components of the selection process for the following jobs?
   a. social media recruiter
   b. experienced salesperson
   c. new hire for McDonalds
   d. plant manager for major chemical company

3. A friend of yours with another company about the same size as yours showed you their application form. They asked a lot more questions and you wonder if your company could also ask them. Could the following items be added to our application blank? Why or why not?
   a. Marital Status,
   b. Height and Weight,
   c. Age,
   d. Sex,

e. Do you have children?

f. What is your credit score?

g. Have you ever been convicted?

h. If you are a female, do you plan to have any more children?

i. What handicaps do you have?

4. Calculate the metrics for the following situations:

a. A company hires 100 new workers at first of the year and only 50 of them are remaining at the end of the year. What is the new-hire retention rate for the firm?

b. A company employs 200 workers and 100 of them had to be replaced during the year. What is the turnover rate for the firm?

c. A firm makes an offer of employment to 50 applicants and 20 of them accept the offer. What is the acceptance rate for the firm?

Questions for Review

1. How are biometrics used in business today?

2. What environmental factors could affect the selection process? Discuss each.

⭐ 3. In terms of employee selection, what is the significance of organizational fit?

4. What are the typical steps in the selection process?

5. Distinguish between an applicant-tracking system and candidate relationship management.

6. What is the general purpose of preliminary screening?

7. What is the purpose of the application form?

8. What types of questions should be asked on an application form?

9. Define résumé, keyword, and keyword résumé.

⭐10. What are the advantages and potential problems in the use of selection tests?

11. What are the basic characteristics of a properly designed selection test?

12. What are the test validation approaches? Define each.

13. Identify and describe the various types of employment tests.

14. Describe genetic testing, graphoanalysis, and polygraph tests.

15. Explain the use of online assessment.

16. What is the purpose of an assessment center?

17. What are the general types of interviews? Explain each.

18. What types of questions would make up a behavioral interview?

19. What are the various methods of interviewing? Define each.

20. What are some potential interview problems?

⭐21. Why should an employer be concerned about negligent hiring?

22. Why should the selection decision be made before conducting a medical examination?

23. What are human capital metrics? What are some metrics for evaluating recruitment and selection?

INCIDENT 1 A Matter of Priorities

As production manager for Thompson Manufacturing, Sheila Stephens has the final authority to approve the hiring of any new supervisors who work for her. The human resource manager performs the initial screening of all prospective supervisors and then sends the most likely candidates to Sheila for interviews.

One day recently, Sheila received a call from Pete Peterson, the human resource manager: "Sheila, I've just spoken to a young man who may be just who you're looking for to fill the final line supervisor position. He has some good work experience and appears to have his head screwed on straight. He's here right now and available if you could possibly see him."

Sheila hesitated a moment before answering. "Gee, Pete" she said, "I'm certainly busy today, but I'll try to squeeze him in. Send him on down."

A moment later Allen Guthrie, the applicant, arrived at Sheila's office and she introduced herself. "Come on in, Allen," said Sheila. "I'll be right with you after I make a few phone calls." Fifteen minutes later Sheila finished the calls and began talking with Allen. Sheila was quite impressed. After a few minutes Sheila's door opened and a supervisor yelled, "We have a small problem on line one and need your help." Sheila stood up and said, "Excuse me a minute, Allen." Ten minutes later Sheila returned, and the conversation continued for ten more minutes before a series of phone calls again interrupted the pair.

The same pattern of interruptions continued for the next hour. Finally, Allen looked at his watch and said, "I'm sorry, Mrs. Stephens, but I have to pick up my wife."

"Sure thing, Allen," Sheila said as the phone rang again. "Call me later today."

Questions

1. What should Sheila have done to avoid interviews like this one?

2. Explain why Sheila, not Pete, should make the selection decision.

3. What steps in the selection process were missed, if any? What problems might occur as a result of these omissions?

INCIDENT 2 But I Didn't Mean To!

David Corbello, the office manager of the *Daily Gazette,* a midwestern newspaper, was flabbergasted as he spoke with the HR manager, Amanda Dervis. He had just discovered that he was the target of a lawsuit filed by an applicant who had not been selected. "All I did was make friendly inquiries about her children. She seemed quite receptive about talking about them. She was proud of her family. She even told me about every aspect of the difficult divorce she had just gone through. She seemed to want to talk so I let her. I thought I was merely breaking the ice and setting the tone for an effective dialogue.

I thought nothing of it when she told me that she needed a day-care facility when she went to work. A year later she claims to have been the victim of discrimination because she believes that a man would not have been asked questions about his children. There's nothing to this lawsuit, is there, Amanda?"

Questions

1. How should Amanda respond to David's question?
2. What hiring standards to avoid did David violate?

MyManagementLab

Go to **mymanagementlab.com** for Auto-graded writing questions as well as the following Assisted-graded writing questions:

6-1. What is the significance of employee selection?

6-2. Why is background investigation important to the selection process?

6-3. Mymanagementlab Only – comprehensive writing assignment for this chapter.

Notes

1. Stephanie Sheridan and Alison Williams, "Employee Training Key to Dodging Business Risks and Protecting Consumer Rights When Utilizing New Technology," *Employee Relations Law Journal* 36 (Spring 2011): 81–85.

2. Tracy Barbour, "Biometrics: Making It Easier to Tell if People Are Who They Say They Are," *Alaska Business Monthly* 27 (February 2011): 24–27.

3. Jeffrey Pheterson, "Privacy—Between the Devil and the Deep Blue Cloud, Trends in Biometric Data Collection and Use," *Employee Relations Law Journal* 37 (Summer 2011): 64–67.

4. "Ceelox Provides Biometric Identity Access to Cloud Apps," *Computer Protocols* 25 (May 2011): 4–5.

5. Ronald Hawkins, "Biometrics Redefined," *Security: Solutions for Enterprise Security Leaders* 48 (January 2011): 44.

6. Sarah Fister Gale, "Passport to the Future," *PM Network* 25 (January 2011): 6–7.

7. Roy Maurer, "Opponents of National ID Card Cite Myriad Concerns, Dangers," *HR Magazine* 55 (June 2010): 20.

8. Aliah D. Wright, "Can HR Professionals Adapt as Biometric Data Become Reality?" *HR Magazine* 55 (June 2010): 20.

9. Marissa Garff, "Career Planning: There's an App for That," *T+D* 65 (July 2011): 25.

10. Susan Ladika, "Not for Profit Woo Veteran Executives," *Workforce Management* 90 (February 2011): 8–10.

11. Anita Weyland, "How to Recruit People Who Fit," *Training Journal* (July 2011): 41–45.

12. Bill Roberts, "Values-Driven HR," *HR Magazine* 57 (March 2012): 44–48.

13. Dave Zielinski, "Effective Assessments," *HR Magazine* 56 (January 2011): 61–64.

14. Jonathan A. Segal, "Hiring Days Are Here Again," *HR Magazine* 56 (July 2011): 58–60.

15. Susan G. Hauser, "Tech Turbo Boosters on Hyperdrive," *Workforce Management* 90 (August 2011): 24–26.

16. "Automate Recruiting and Onboarding," *Chain Store Age* 85 (April 2009): 19.

17. Sue Weeks, "Putting CRM at the Heart of Recruiting," *Recruiter* (April 14, 2010): 32–34.

18. Bill Roberts, "Manage Candidates Right from the Start," *HR Magazine* 53 (October 2008): 73–76.

19. Jacquelyn Smith, "The Most Outlandish Résumé Mistakes Ever," *Forbes.com* (September 22, 2011): 31.

20. Elaine Pofeldt, "Does Your Résumé Make You Look Old?" *Money* 40 (March 2011): 38–39.

21. "Top Talent May Be a Click Away," *Business People* 24 (July 2011): 68.

22. Theresa Witham, "Social Media for Recruiting," *Credit Union Management* 35 (February 2012): 30.

23. Tony Bradley, "Five Ways to Use LinkedIn," *PC World* 29 (August 2011): 30.

24. Mallie Jane Kim, "Network via Social Media," *U.S. News & World Report* 147 (December 2010): 53.

25. Kurt Schiller, "Five Trends Shaking Up the Internet," *Information Today* 27 (October 2010): 1–54.

26. "LinkedIn Top Site to Source Potential Hires," *CA Magazine* 145 (January/February 2012): 8.

27. Manu Kaushik, "Social Media Turns Job Portal," *Business Today* 20 (June 1, 2011): 123.

28. Matthew Boyle, "Enough to Make Monster Tremble," *BusinessWeek* (July 6, 2009): 43–45.

29. Jena McGregor, "Job Sites: Are They Worth It?" *Fortune* 161 (June 14, 2010): 45–46.

30. Ed Frauenheim, "LinkedIn," *Workforce Management* 90 (February 2011): 21–22.

31. "Validate Hiring Tests to Withstand EEO Scrutiny: DOL & EEOC Officials," *HR Focus* 85 (May 2008): 8–9.

32. Ilona Jerabek, "Sales Personality," *Sales & Service Excellence* 10 (July 2010): 12.

33. Bill Roberts, "Your Cheating Heart," *HR Magazine* 56 (June 2011): 54–60.

34. Ed Frauenheim, "More Companies Go with Online Tests to Fill in the Blanks," *Workforce Management* 90 (May 2011): 12–13.

35. Dana Tanyeri, "How to Hire Now," *Restaurant Business* 109 (January 2010): 18.

36. Dave Zielinski, "Effective Assessments," *HR Magazine* 56 (January 2011): 61–64.

37. "EEOC Issues Final Rule Interpreting Federal Law on Genetic Information," *HR Focus* 88 (January 2011): 1–5.

38. Susan G. Hauser, "Sincerely Yours, GINA," *Workforce Management* 90 (July 2011): 16–21.

39. Melissa Carslake, "How Not to Conduct a Job Interview," *Recruiter* (March 9, 2011): 21.

40. Kimberly Thompson, "Remember Intangibles When Applying for Work," *Phi Kappa Phi Forum* 90 (Spring 2010): 23.

41. Haley Armand, "Background Checks Aren't Just for Employers," *Thrive Magazine* (January 2012): 24–25.

42. Diane Borhani, "Getting to Know Your Employer," *Wall Street Journal Online* (May 23, 2011).

43. "How to: Hire for Creativity," *Inc.* 32 (October 2010): 53–56.

44. John Zappe, "For Recruiting, Video Is Hot (and Cold)," *Journal of Corporate Recruiting Leadership* 6 (February 2011): 17–21.

45. Michael Kaplan, "Job Interview Brainteasers," *Business 2.0* 8 (September 2007): 35–37.

46. Martha Frase-Blunt, "Games Interviewers Play," *HR Magazine* 46 (January 2001): 107–108.

47. Michael A. Tucker, "Show and Tell," *HR Magazine* 57 (January 2012): 51–53.

48. Stephenie Overman, "Hiring Candidates Who Will Stay," *Staffing Management* 6 (July-September 2011): 1.

49. "Job Interviews: How to Pose Risky Questions the Legal Way," *HR Specialist: New Jersey Employment Law* 5 (April 2010): 6.

50. "Why Should We Pick You?" *Director* 63 (April 2010): 31–33.

51. "The Hidden Risks of Hiring Based on 'Chemistry,'" *HR Specialist* 8 (February 2010): 1–2.

52. Dana Wilkie, "EEOC Weighs Need for Hiring Guidelines Revisions," *SHRM Online Staffing Management Discipline* (August 2, 2011).

53. Jeffrey W. Larroca, "Global Diversity and the American Workforce," *INSIGHT into Diversity* (December 2010): 29.

54. Stephenie Overman, "Avoiding Immigration Audits," *HR Magazine* 56 (January 2011): 57–59.

55. Dave Zielinski, "Automating I-9 Verification," *HR Magazine* 56 (May 2011): 57–60.

56. Craig J. Davidson, "Know the Five Core Disciplines of HR," *Employee Benefit Advisor* 8 (October 2010): 68–72.

57. "High Court Upholds E-Verify Mandate," *Payroll Manager's Letter* 27 (July 7, 2011): 1.

58. Bill Leonard, "Researchers: Stolen Identities Often Slip Through E-Verify," *HR Magazine* 55 (April 2010): 11.

59. "Continuous Screening May Create Issues for Employers," *Workforce Management* 89 (February 1, 2010): 30.

60. Jonathan A. Segal, "Dancing on the Edge of a Volcano," *HR Magazine* 56 (April 2011): 83–86.

61. Sherrie A. Madia, "Why Shifting Efforts to Social Media Is Smart Strategy for 2011," *Journal of Corporate Recruiting Leadership* 5 (December 2010): 12–13.

62. "Vast Majority of Large Employers Screen Applicants for Criminal Records, Survey Says," *HR Focus* 88 (May 2011): 11–12.

63. Heather O'Neill, "Thinking Outside the Box," *Workforce Management* 91 (January 2012): 3.

64. Joanne Deschenaux, "States Seek to Limit Credit Checks for Hiring," *HR Magazine* 56 (April 2011): 20.

65. Juliette Fairley, "Employers Face Challenges in Screening Candidates," *Work force Management* 89 (November 2010): 7–9.

66. Kathryn M. Nash, "Get Ready for a New Federally Protected Class: The Unemployed," *HR Specialist: Minnesota Employment Law* 5 (January 2012): 6.

67. Judy Greenwald, "New Type of Hiring Discrimination Claim in Works," *Business Insurance* 45 (February 28, 2011): 1–20.

68. Andrea Siedsma, "Are Background Checks on Web Posts Too Much Information?" *Workforce Management* 91 (January 2012): 10.

69. Dori Meiert, "Seeing Behind the Mask," *HR Magazine* 56 (February 2011): 30–37.

70. Michael L. Forte, "Sexual Assaults at Work: When Can the Employer Be Held Liable?" *Florida Underwriter* 28 (2011): 10.

71. Bill Roberts, "Backgrounds to the Foreground," *HR Magazine* 55 (December 2010): 46–51.

72. "Stakes Rise for Preventing Sexual Harassment and Age Discrimination," *Security Director's Report* 9 (March 2009): 8.

73. Drew Robb, "Creating Metrics for Senior Management," *HR Magazine* 56 (December 2011): 109–111.

74. "Every Metric Tells a Story if HR Measures and Communicates Effectively," *HR Focus* 89 (April 2012): 6.

75. Theresa Minton-Eversole, "Quality Measurement: Key to Best-in-Class Talent Acquisition," *HR Magazine* 53 (December 2008): 64–66.

76. "Quality of Hires Is Vital," *Recruiter* (June 9, 2010): 6.

77. "Every Metric Tells a Story if HR Measures and Communicates Effectively," *HR Focus* 89 (April 2012): 6.

78. Pankaj Ghemawat, "The Cosmopolitan Corporation," *Harvard Business Review* 89 (May 2011): 92–99.

79. Thomas K. Grose, "When in Rome, Do as Roman CEOs Do," *U.S. News & World Report* 146 (November 2009): 38–41.

80. Vimal Babu, "Divergent Leadership Styles Practiced by Global Managers in India," *Indian Journal of Industrial Relations* 46 (January 2011): 478–490.

81. Gary Wederspahn, "Expatriate Training: Don't Leave Home Without It," *T&D* 56 (February 2002): 67.

Part Four
Human Resource Development

7

Training and Development

HRM in Action ## Executive Onboarding for External Hires

OBJECTIVE 7.1

Describe executive onboarding for external hires, define *training* and *development*, and explain factors influencing T&D.

Up to 40 percent of externally hired executives in the private sector fail within the first 18 months and many others who are recruited from outside the firm leave within five years.[1] Although considerable time, effort, and money are spent recruiting top talent, companies often do a poor job of onboarding new executives. In fact, few companies take the time to familiarize new executives about the workings of the corporate culture beyond the standard, one-size-fits-all orientation session. However, what new executives need to know in order to be effective differs significantly from the focus of most general employee orientation programs. If an executive is coming in from another company, a great deal of attention needs to be paid to explaining how things really work in the new environment.[2] For example, to succeed new executives must understand the unwritten rules, processes, and networks that influence how things get done in the organization. Too often they are just given the key to the executive suite and are expected to sink or swim. That approach will not work if an organization is searching for ways to help these new executives succeed.

When a CEO fails, it often creates a loss of value for the firm. Think of the turmoil that has existed at Hewlett-Packard; former eBay CEO Meg Whitman was hired as its eighth CEO since 1999 and the second one in 2011.[3] Although impossible to calculate precisely, the costs resulting from a failed CEO are usually significant, particularly for an "outsider." When executives are unsuccessful, usually it is because they did not understand how to operate in the new culture. What was a

CHAPTER OBJECTIVE   After completing this chapter, students should be able to:

1 Describe executive onboarding for external hires, define *training* and *development,* and explain factors influencing T&D.

2 Describe the T&D process and explain the various T&D methods.

3 Explain mobile learning and describe training and development delivery systems.

4 Describe management development, mentoring, coaching, and reverse mentoring.

5 Define *orientation* and explain implementing training and development programs.

6 Explain the metrics for evaluating training and development.

7 Define *organization development (OD)* and describe various OD techniques.

8 Distinguish between job security and career security.

9 Describe career planning and explain career paths and career development.

10 Describe career development methods, identify various career paths, and explain global meetings through telepresence.

strength in their old company may be a weakness in their new one. The board needs to take a pro-active stance to ensure that new executives are successfully integrated into the organization.[4]

Billie Blair, president and CEO of Change Strategists, Inc. believes that newly hired executives often "feel they've lassoed the moon."[5] To help these new CEOs achieve success, firms need to use executive onboarding programs. When Bristol-Myers Squibb, the global pharmaceutical manu-facturer, studied the retention rates of its recently hired executives, it discovered they were losing promising new executives by not taking steps to ensure their success. It then focused on provid-ing new executives guidelines, meetings with influential colleagues, role clarification, and a better understanding of the company's culture for the first 100 days of employment.[6] The onboarding pro-cess for a new CEO should provide a guide to the new corporate culture and its people and person-alities. It is not a onetime event that occurs only in the first few days after the CEO comes on board. It is a continuous process that lasts until the new CEO is ready to succeed in the new environment.

The problem of early failure of executives also extends itself to the public sector. According to the Office of Personnel Management, 16 percent of newly hired executives failed to complete the first year successfully through voluntary termination or for poor performance.[7] Although not as severe as within the private sector, the cause of the problem was quite similar; they were not able to effectively operate in the new culture.

training and development (T&D)

Heart of a continuous effort designed to improve employee competency and organizational performance.

training

Activities designed to provide learners with the knowledge and skills needed for their present jobs.

Strategic Training and Development

Training and development (T&D) is the heart of a continuous effort designed to improve employee competency and organizational performance. **Training** provides learners with the knowledge and skills needed for their present jobs. Showing a worker how to operate a lathe or a supervisor how to schedule daily production are examples of training. On the other hand, **development** involves learning that goes beyond today's job and has a more long-term focus. It prepares employees to keep pace with the organization as it changes and grows. T&D activities have the potential to align a firm's employees with its corporate strategies. Some possible strategic benefits of T&D include employee satisfaction, improved morale, higher retention, lower turnover, improved hiring, a better bottom line, and the fact that satisfied employees produce satisfied customers.

OBJECTIVE 7.2

Describe the T&D process and explain the various T&D methods.

development

Learning that goes beyond today's job and has a more long-term focus.

learning organization

Firm that recognizes the critical importance of continuous performance-related T&D and takes appropriate action.

Learning Organization

Improved performance, the bottom-line purpose of T&D, is a strategic goal for organizations. Toward this end, many firms have become or are striving to become learning organizations. A **learning organization** is a firm that recognizes the critical importance of continuous performance-related T&D and takes appropriate action. A learning organization needs to provide a supportive learning environment and it provides specific learning processes and practices. Also, it is vital that management supports and reinforces learning.

A learning management system moves beyond delivering tactical training projects to initiating learning programs aligned with strategic corporate goals. Once undervalued in the corporate world, training programs are now credited with strengthening customer satisfaction, contributing to partnership development, enhancing research and development activities, and finally, reinforcing the bottom line. Being recognized as a company that encourages its employees to continue to grow and learn can be a major asset in recruiting. Learning organizations view learning and development opportunities in all facets of their business and try to constantly look ahead and ensure that all employees are taking full advantage of their learning opportunities.[8] In a learning organization employees are rewarded for learning and are provided enriched jobs, promotions, and compensation. Organizations with a reputation for having a culture of being a learning leader tend to attract more and better-qualified employees.

In the competition to become listed in the "100 Best Companies to Work for in America," learning and growth opportunities were a high priority. On nearly every survey, training and development ranks in the top three benefits that employees want from their employers, and they search for firms that will give them the tools to advance in their profession. It is clear that T&D is not merely a nice thing to provide. It is a strategic resource; one that firms must tap to energize their organizations in the 21st century.

Factors Influencing Training and Development

There are numerous factors that both impact and are impacted by T&D.

Top Management Support

For T&D programs to be successful, top management support is required; without it, a T&D program will not succeed. The most effective way to achieve success is for executives to provide the needed resources to support the T&D effort. The comments by Carol Freeland, principal/owner of ACTS+ in Hot Springs Village, Arizona, best described the importance of support from the CEO when she said, "If the CEO does not believe in the inherent value of training, any training effort on the part of the company will be fruitless and languish."[9]

The recession saw many training budgets suffer as executives looked for ways to reduce costs. By 2011 firms had started to boost the size of their training staffs.[10] However, even as the economy improved, training professionals were having to do more with less. As Karen O'Lonard, principal analyst of Bersin & Associates, said, "Companies aren't rolling out more training, but are trying to get better results from existing programs."[11]

HR Web Wisdom

American Society for Training and Development

http://www.astd.org

The homepage for the American Society for Training and Development is presented.

Shortage of Skilled Workers

Shortage of future skilled workers was first projected in the 1980s but has recently received additional attention. Mark Tomlinson, executive director and general manager of the Society of Manufacturing Engineers, compares the shortage of skilled workers to viewing an iceberg in stormy seas. "We're just approaching it; we haven't hit it yet but we know it's there. People are starting to see it. They just don't know how to deal with it."[12] There will likely be major shortages of future skilled workers; for example, 240,000 jobs for skilled workers go unfilled annually, even in a recession. It took Cianbro Corporation, a heavy construction company in the Northeast, 18 months to hire 80 experienced welders.[13] As another example, the number one problem facing surface finishers today is finding qualified employees.[14]

Unemployment figures are misleading because they do not show employers who are begging for skilled workers. Worldwide many companies are struggling to find skilled workers. Baby boomers—the best-educated and most-skilled workforce in U.S. history—are preparing to retire. Labor experts are concerned that workers in the United States lack the critical skills needed to replace baby boomers. Silicon Valley companies are having difficulty finding software engineers; Union Health Service and the Harvard hospital system find it hard to find nurses and technicians; and manufacturers such as Caterpillar and Westinghouse cannot hire enough welders and machinists to operate their state-of-the-art lathes.[15]

Part of the problem in finding qualified people for manufacturing jobs is that there is a generation of young people for which manufacturing has not been an attractive job prospect because they have seen many jobs outsourced and they question the long-term future in these jobs. In addition, training needs are changing and the old skill requirements of reading, writing, and arithmetic have been expanded. Executives are increasingly demanding additional skills of their new hires such as critical thinking and problem solving, communication, collaboration, and creativity.[16]

Technological Advances

Change is occurring at an amazing speed, with knowledge doubling every year. Perhaps no factor has influenced T&D more than technology. The Internet, computers, smartphones, text messaging, and e-mail have dramatically affected how training is conducted. Informal instructional delivery methods such as blogs, wikis, and social networks are being used. Even Facebook, LinkedIn, and Twitter can assist in training. As emphasized throughout this chapter, technology has played a huge role in changing the way knowledge is delivered to employees, and this change is constantly being extended.

World Complexity

The world is simply getting more complex, and this has had an impact on how an organization operates. No longer does a firm just compete against other firms in the United States. The entire world provides opportunities and threats that must be confronted. Organizations have to think how the workforce will be staffed and trained in this global environment.

ETHICAL DILEMMA

The Tough Side of Technology

You are the human resource director for a large manufacturing firm that is undergoing major changes. Your firm is in the process of building two technologically advanced plants. When these are completed, the company will close four of its five old plants. It is your job to determine who will stay with the old plant and who will be retrained for the newer plants.

One old-plant employee is a 56-year-old production worker who has been with your firm for 10 years. He seems to be a close personal friend of your boss, as they are often seen together socially. However, in your opinion, he is not capable of handling the high-tech work required at the new plants, even with additional training. He is not old enough to receive any retirement benefits and there are other qualified workers with more seniority who want to remain at the old plant.

What would you do?
What factor(s) in this ethical dilemma might influence a person to make a less-than-ethical decision?

Lifetime Learning

Largely due to the work environment workers confront today, learning can never stop; it is a continuous process. The psychological value of lifelong learning cannot be overstated. Employees who participate in ongoing education will feel as if their careers are advancing and they are better able to provide for their families. Things will change faster tomorrow than they did today, and will be even faster the day after that. Employees who are not staying ahead of the curve are going to be left behind and their value to the firm diminishes.

Learning Styles

Although much remains unknown about the learning process, what is known affects the way firms conduct training. It is known that adults retain approximately 20 percent of what they read and hear, 40 percent of what they see, 50 percent of what they say, 60 percent of what they do, and 90 percent of what they see, hear, say, and do.[17] Because of these differences, it is important to use a wide range of T&D methods. Learning style supports the concept that people have a natural preference, based on their dominant sense, in how they choose to learn and process information. It may be visual, hearing, or touching.[18] Some learn best from working in a group whereas others prefer studying on an individual basis. Still others absorb best by seeing how the material provides a practical application, and others want to know the theoretical basis. Some learners can readily absorb information by reading written words whereas others learn best through hearing the words spoken.

In studying the information in this text, the different learning styles will become apparent. There are exercises at the end of each chapter to provide hands-on application of the material. Being able to read the words in the text will appeal to some whereas others will learn best through hearing the instructor's lecture. Each chapter's PowerPoint slides provide a visual representation of the material. The incidents at the end of each chapter require extending your newfound knowledge in a practical manner.

blended training
The use of multiple training methods to deliver T&D.

To cope with the different learning styles, firms use multiple methods, called **blended training** (also referred to as blended learning), to deliver T&D. This involves using a combination of training methods that are strategically combined to best achieve a training program's objectives.[19] John Leutner, head of global learning services for Xerox corporate human resources, said, "The new blended learning is about creating a richer, more meaningful development experience that relates to a person's work and performance."[20]

Another learning principle is that learners progress in an area of learning only as far as they need to in order to achieve their purposes. Professors have long known that telling students which concepts are important motivates them to study the material, especially if the information is prime test material. Research indicates that unless there is relevance, meaning, and emotion attached to the material taught, trainees will not learn.

just-in-time training
Training provided anytime, anywhere in the world when it is needed.

Another learning principle is that the best time to learn is when the learning can be useful. One way this impacts T&D is the need for training on a timely basis. **Just-in-time training (on-demand training)** is training provided anytime, anywhere in the world when it is needed. Computer technology, the Internet, intranets, smartphones, and similar devices have made these approaches economically feasible to a degree never before possible. The ability to deliver knowledge to employees on an as-needed basis, anywhere on the globe, and at a pace consistent with their learning styles greatly enhances the value of T&D.

Other Human Resource Functions

Successful accomplishment of other human resource functions can also have a crucial impact on T&D. For instance, if recruitment-and-selection efforts or its compensation package attract only marginally qualified workers, a firm will need extensive T&D programs. Hiring marginally qualified workers will likely have a significant impact on the firm's safety and health programs. Therefore, additional training will be required.

Training and Development Process

Major adjustments in the external and internal environments necessitate corporate change. The general T&D process that anticipates or responds to change may be seen in Figure 7-1. First, an organization must determine its specific training needs. Then specific objectives need to be

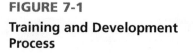

FIGURE 7-1

Training and Development Process

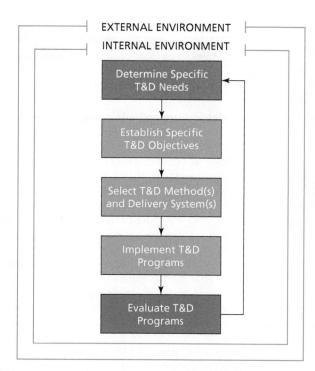

established. The objectives might be quite narrow if limited to the supervisory ability of a manager, or they might be broad enough to include improving the management skills of all first-line supervisors. In exemplary organizations, there is a close link between the firm's strategic mission and the objectives of the T&D program. Review and periodic updating of these objectives is necessary to ensure that they support the changing strategic needs of the organization. After setting the T&D objectives, management can determine the appropriate methods and the delivery system to be used. Naturally, management must continuously evaluate T&D to ensure its value in achieving organizational objectives.

Determine Specific Training and Development Needs

The first step in the T&D process is to determine specific T&D needs. In today's highly competitive business environment, undertaking a program because other firms are doing it is asking for trouble. A systematic approach to addressing bona fide needs must be undertaken and must be done taking into consideration the mission of the organization.

Training and development needs may be determined by conducting analyses on several levels:

- *Organizational analysis:* From an *overall organizational* perspective, the firm's strategic mission, goals, and corporate plans are studied, along with the results of strategic human resource planning.
- *Task analysis:* The next level of analysis focuses on the *tasks* required to achieve the firm's purposes. Job descriptions are important data sources for this analysis level.
- *Person analysis:* Determining *individual training needs* is the final level. The relevant questions are, "Who needs to be trained?" and "What kind of knowledge, skills, and abilities (KSAs) do employees need?" Performance appraisals and interviews or surveys of supervisors and job incumbents are helpful at this level.

Companies now train for specific needs and trainers are asking, "What knowledge do you want your people to have? What skills do they need? What do they need to do differently from what they're doing today?" Trainers want to find out what job knowledge and skills the person needs to have to get the job done.

Mobile Learning

Mobile learning (m-learning) is any learning that takes place via mobile or portable devices such as cell phones, personal digital assistants, tablets, media players, and e-readers. Some benefits of mobile learning are that it is more convenient and can take place at any time, eliminates technological barriers, and improves retention.[21] Even the iPod has been used effectively as a learning device. Learning is also being delivered by devices a person can wear such as glasses or earpieces.[22] Mobile learning can take place anywhere and does not require the learner to be at a fixed location. Therefore, the definition of "the office" takes on new meaning. A worker can be at home, a restaurant, a car, or virtually anywhere and still be "at work." Mobile learning is relevant because it can take place in the setting where the learning is to be put into practice such as a hospital ward or a client's office. It has been estimated that 75 percent of the U.S. workforce will be mobile by 2013.[23] If this is so, training this mobile workforce will mean developing and deploying new mobile learning possibilities. According to new ASTD-i4cp research, 65 percent of employers are either using, considering, or currently developing learning for mobile devices.[24] Indeed, some predict that the "m" will soon disappear in m-learning.

Mobile learning really took off with the improved versions of smartphones, e-readers, and the iPad. Training apps for these devices were then developed. Screen technology has also improved, and employees are often seen watching training films and videos on their iPods or iPhones while on a train or walking to work. Cloud computing can now manage mobile devices. M-learning permits virtually instant feedback and portability because the learner does not need traditional media. Efforts should be made to make sure that m-learning is short and purposeful. Alex Heiphetz, founder and president of AHG, a software solutions company, said, "Contrary to traditional training units, mobile learning is best suited for short, two- to six-minute sessions that provide a single learning point or a summary of previously learned key points."[25]

Cheesecake Factory Inc., which has 160 restaurants nationwide, recently increased its training staff from 10 to 15 employees. The new employees all possessed multimedia expertise, which is the emphasis of the new training approach. Traditional textbooks and classrooms have been eliminated. VideoCafé, a YouTube system, permits employees to upload and share job-related videos, such as customer greetings and food preparation. The company also uses interactive games, including a simulation tool to teach employees how to make the "perfect hamburger."[26]

Mobile learning has proven quite effective for training in the hotel industry. MetaMedia Training International supplied one major hotel chain with more than 900 Sony PlayStation Portable (PSP) devices to deliver mobile training. Using the PSP, employees can receive training while walking around the hotel.[27] The ability to train while on the job has become a reality.

OBJECTIVE 7.3

Explain mobile learning and describe training and development delivery systems.

mobile learning
Any learning that takes place via mobile or portable devices such as cell phones, personal digital assistants, tablets, media players, and e-readers.

Establish Specific Training and Development Objectives

T&D must have clear and concise objectives and be developed to achieve organizational goals. Without them, designing meaningful T&D programs would not be possible. Worthwhile evaluation of a program's effectiveness would also be difficult, at best. Consider these purposes and objectives for a training program involving employment compliance:

Training Area: Employment Compliance

PURPOSE To provide the supervisor with

1. Knowledge and value of consistent human resource practices
2. The intent of Equal Employment Opportunity Commission (EEOC) legal requirements
3. The skills to apply them

OBJECTIVES To be able to

1. Cite the supervisory areas affected by employment laws on discrimination
2. Identify acceptable and unacceptable actions
3. State how to get help on EEOC matters
4. Describe why we have disciplinary action and grievance procedures
5. Describe our disciplinary action and grievance procedures, including who is covered

As you see, the *purpose* is established first. The specific *learning objectives* that follow leave little doubt about what the training should accomplish. With these objectives, managers can determine whether training has been effective. For instance, in the example above, a trainee either can or cannot state how to get help on equal employment opportunity matters.

Training and Development Methods

When a person is working in a garden, some tools are more helpful in performing certain tasks than others. The same logic applies when considering T&D methods, and these methods are changing continuously and improving. Regardless of whether programs are in-house or outsourced, firms use a number of methods for imparting knowledge and skills to the workforce and usually more than one method, called *blended training* (previously mentioned), is used to deliver T&D. As part of the blended training process, mobile learning is enhancing or replacing some traditional training methods. T&D methods are discussed next. Each of these training methods should be evaluated and selected for what it does best.

Instructor-Led

The instructor-led method, where the instructor physically stands in front of students, continues to be effective for many types of training. One advantage of instructor-led training is that the instructor may convey a great deal of information in a relatively short time. The effectiveness of instructor-led programs improves when groups are small enough to permit discussion, and when the instructor is able to capture the imagination of the class and use new technology to provide a better classroom learning experience. Also, the charisma or personality that the instructor brings to class may excite the students to want to learn. The classroom setting allows for real-time discussion that is not easily replicated, even with the most advanced technology.

E-Learning

The tradition of instructors physically lecturing in front of live corporate students has diminished somewhat in recent years. **E-learning** is the T&D method for online instruction using technology-based methods such as the Internet, intranet, and CD-ROM. The benefits of e-learning are numerous and include decreased costs, greater convenience and flexibility, improved retention rates, and a positive environmental impact.[28] It can be self-paced, can often be individualized, and can be done while at work or off-shift. A concept can be viewed as often as needed. Individuals using e-learning can be working on different parts of a program, at varying speeds, and in different languages.

Luxottica is an Italian eyewear and optical company whose chain stores include LensCrafters, Pearle Vision, and Sunglass Hut, with 38,000 employees worldwide. Angi Willis, Luxottica's learning technology project manager said, "We just didn't have the manpower, technology or budget to efficiently and effectively manage and execute our various training programs." Luxottica put training online so employees could have instant access to information they needed to do their jobs, including details on new products and regulations as well as continuing education.[29]

The advantages of using e-learning are numerous; however, the biggest advantage is cost savings. According to Gordon Johnson, vice president of marketing for infrastructure provider Expertus, "Online meetings are one-third the cost of face-to-face meetings, so the question becomes not which is best, but whether face-to-face training is three times better. Usually not."[30]

For Union Pacific, the largest railroad company in North America, both distance and time have been hurdles to learning. About 19,000 of its 48,000 widely disbursed employees work on the railroad's locomotives and freight cars, many on different schedules. So the company uses a blend of traditional learning and e-learning that provides the kind of training far-flung employees require, at a time when they can use it.

Firms that consistently have a high turnover rate have turned to e-learning because classroom learning is not cost-effective. Nike faced a challenge that a number of retailers today are confronting. Nike designed an online training program that the company could offer to employees in its own stores as well as at other retailers that sell Nike products. The program conveys a lot of information quickly, but it is also easy to learn. This is important because the training is directed at 16- to 22-year-olds.[31]

A takeoff on e-learning is the *live virtual classroom*, often referred to as *virtual instructor led*, that uses a Web-based platform to deliver live, instructor-led training to geographically dispersed learners. Organizations can bring together entire teams for just an hour or two per week. They can also bring content specialists into the classroom for only the necessary time required from two minutes to two

e-learning
The T&D method for online instruction using technology-based methods such as the Internet, intranet, and CD-ROM.

hours. *Virtual instructor led* training is ideal for organizations that have many technicians needing frequent training while they continue to do their job in the field.[32] The need to have large blocks of time that takes workers away from their jobs is thus eliminated. Training can now be provided in blocks of time as opposed to several days. For example, a two-day live training session might be provided in five 75-minute modules delivered over time. These provide both cost savings and convenience.[33]

Case Study

case study
T&D method in which trainees are expected to study the information provided in the case and make decisions based on it.

The **case study** is a T&D method in which trainees study the information provided in the case and make decisions based on it.

If an actual company is involved, the student would be expected to research the firm to gain a better appreciation of its financial condition and environment. Research on companies has been significantly enhanced through the availability of library databases such as EBSCOhost. Often, the case study method occurs with an instructor who serves as a facilitator.

Behavior Modeling and Twittering

behavior modeling
T&D method that permits a person to learn by copying or replicating behaviors of others to show managers how to handle various situations.

Behavior modeling is a T&D method that permits a person to learn by copying or replicating behaviors of others. Behavior modeling has been used to train supervisors in such tasks as conducting performance reviews, correcting unacceptable performance, delegating work, improving safety habits, handling discrimination complaints, overcoming resistance to change, orienting new employees, and mediating individuals or groups in conflict.

Social networking has been used as a learning tool involving behavior modeling. "In a corporation, micro-blogging can be a way to augment behavior modeling," says Sarah Millstein, author of the *O'Reilly Radar Report*. This works by having a person who excels at a task send out frequent updates about what he or she is doing. The company might even formalize the process to the extent that it would select exemplary performers to post on a regular basis and determine those employees who should follow their posts.[34]

Role-Playing

role-playing
T&D method in which participants are required to respond to specific problems they may encounter in their jobs by acting out real-world situations.

Role-playing is a T&D method in which participants are required to respond to specific problems they may encounter in their jobs by acting out real-world situations. Rather than hearing an instructor talk about how to handle a problem or by discussing it, they learn by doing. Role-playing is often used to teach such skills as administering disciplinary action, interviewing, grievance handling, conducting performance appraisal reviews, team problem solving, effective communication, and leadership-style analysis. A successful role-playing activity occurs if the activity actually mirrors real-life situations. It has also been used successfully to teach workers how to deal with individuals who are angry, irate, or out of control. Some restaurant chains use role-playing to train servers how to deal with difficult situations such as a couple having an argument at the dinner table. The classic case of using role-playing is when a manager must take disciplinary against a worker for something they did improperly. Managers never know how an employee will react when being reprimanded. When acting out the role of the worker, he or she may randomly choose from a variety of roles such as being stoic, starting to cry, promising never to do it again, or take this job and shove it.

Training Games

Games can be quite useful learning tools to aid in the group dynamic process. Games are a cost-effective means to encourage learner involvement and stimulate interest in the topic thereby enhancing employees' knowledge and performance.[35] According to Elizabeth Treher, founder, president, and CEO of The Learning Key Inc., "Team-based business games result in better knowledge retention, provide focused, memorable learning and a more enjoyable learning atmosphere than traditional methods."[36] A major benefit of games is that learners retain 75 percent of the knowledge they acquire when playing games, according to research by the National Training Laboratories. McDonald's in Japan estimates new employee training time to prepare burgers has been cut in half as a result of a video game created in conjunction with Nintendo.[37] Microsoft Xbox support agents use the Xbox Customer Care Framework (CCF) Assessment simulator training game. The game simulates real-life circumstances caused by generating the stress and anxiety of receiving difficult customer relations calls.[38] Even the U.S. Marine Corps uses a game-based training program called Mission Impact, which places learners in a simulated battalion to improve their environmental performance.

business games
T&D method that permits participants to assume roles such as president, controller, or marketing vice president of two or more similar hypothetical organizations and compete against each other by manipulating selected factors in a particular business situation.

Business games is a T&D method that permits participants to assume roles such as president, controller, or marketing vice president of two or more similar hypothetical organizations and compete against each other by manipulating selected factors in a particular business situation. Participants make decisions affecting such factors as price levels, production volumes, and inventory levels. Typically, a computer program manipulates their decisions, with the results simulating those of an actual business situation. Participants are able to see how their decisions affect other groups and vice versa. The best thing about this type of learning is that if a poor decision costs the company $1 million, no one gets fired, yet the business lesson is learned.

In-Basket Training

in-basket training
T&D method in which the participant is asked to establish priorities for and then handle a number of business papers, e-mail messages, memoranda, reports, and telephone messages that would typically cross a manager's desk.

In-basket training is a T&D method in which the participant is asked to establish priorities for and then handle a number of business papers, e-mails, texts, memoranda, reports, and telephone messages that would typically cross a manager's desk. The messages, presented in no particular order, call for anything from urgent action to routine handling. The participant is required to act on the information contained in these messages. In this method, the trainee assigns a priority to each particular situation before making any decisions. This form of training has been quite beneficial to help predict performance success in management jobs. Assessment centers commonly make use of this method in the selection process.

On-the-Job Training

on-the-job training (OJT)
An informal T&D method that permits an employee to learn job tasks by actually performing them.

On-the-job-training (OJT) is an informal T&D method that permits an employee to learn job tasks by actually performing them. Often OJT will also have a significant impact on personal development. The key to this training is to transfer knowledge from a highly skilled and experienced worker to a new employee, while maintaining the productivity of both workers. OJT is used to pass on critical "how to" information to the trainee. Individuals may also be more highly motivated to learn because it is clear to them that they are acquiring the knowledge needed to perform the job. At times, however, the trainee may feel so much pressure to produce that learning is negatively affected. Firms should be selective about who provides on-the-job training. Regardless of who does the training, that person must have a good work ethic and correctly model the desired behavior.

Apprenticeship Training

apprenticeship training
Training method that combines classroom instruction with on-the-job training.

Apprenticeship training is a training method that combines classroom instruction with on-the-job training. While in training, the employee earns less than the master craftsperson, who is the instructor. The National Association of Manufacturers projects that by 2020 some 10 million skilled workers will be needed and apprenticeships remain one of the most vital sources for securing skilled labor.[39] Such training is common with craft jobs, such as those of plumber, carpenter, machinist, welder, fabricator, laser operator, electrician, and press brake operator. As baby boomers continue to leave the workforce, they must be replaced by competent operators, and apprenticeship programs provide an effective way of accomplishing this. Many organizations are partnering with high schools, vocational schools, and universities as they search for new skilled workers. Organizations often donate look-alike equipment to the schools so students can be trained on the system.

The U.S. Department of Labor has implemented new regulations governing apprenticeships. Historically apprenticeships were defined by the amount of instruction time—typically 10,000 hours over four years. The new regulations offer provisions for competency-based apprenticeships, electronic and distance training, and the issuance of interim credentials. These credentials can be used toward college credits. "It's nice because a person isn't waiting until the end of the program to get some kind of reward," says Steve Mandes, executive director at National Institute for Metalworking Skills (NIMS).[40]

Training and Development Delivery Systems

The section above focused on the various T&D methods available to organizations, and the list is constantly changing. In this section, our attention is devoted to how training may be delivered to participants.

Corporate Universities

A T&D delivery system provided under the umbrella of the organization is referred to as a **corporate university**. The corporate T&D institution's focus is on creating organizational change that involves areas such as company training, employee development, and adult learning. It aims to achieve its goals by conducting activities that foster individual and organizational learning and knowledge. It is proactive and strategic rather than reactive and tactical and can be closely aligned to corporate goals. Even though called universities, they are not so in the straightest sense since degrees in specific subjects are not granted. GE has its Crotonville campus and McDonald's has its Hamburger University. Intel University in Arizona administers programs developed by training groups located worldwide. The university also teaches nontechnical skills such as dealing with conflict and harassment avoidance.

Recent years has seen the decline of corporate universities as companies such as Xerox, Andersen, Ford, Pfizer, Aetna, and Merrill Lynch moved away from them. However, in New York City, North Shore-Long Island Jewish Health System's corporate university serves 42,000 employees across 15 hospitals.[41] Deloitte LLP has recently built a $300 million corporate university in Westlake, Texas. Its 750,000 square feet will house state-of-the-art learning technology, 800 sleeping rooms, and even a ballroom. Marc Rosenberg, a learning consultant, says, "There's only so much you can do with social networking on the Internet, especially in services firms where you rely so much on your colleagues for help."[42] Also, firms are better able to control the quality of training and to ensure that all employees receive the same messages.

Colleges and Universities

For decades, colleges and universities have been the primary delivery system for training professional, technical, and management employees. Many public and private colleges and universities are taking similar approaches to training and education as have the corporate universities. Corporate T&D programs often partner with colleges and universities or other organizations, such as the American Management Association, to deliver both training and development.

Community Colleges

Community colleges are publicly funded higher education establishments that deliver vocational training and associate degree programs. Some employers have discovered that community colleges can provide certain types of training better and more cost effectively than the company can. Rapid technological changes and corporate restructuring have created a new demand by industry for community college training resources.

Online Higher Education

A form of online e-learning that has increased substantially in recent years is the use of online higher education. **Online higher education** is defined as formal educational opportunities including degree and training programs that are delivered, either entirely or partially, via the Internet. One reason for the growth of online higher education is that it allows employees to attend class at lunchtime, during the day, or in the evening. It also saves employees time because it reduces their need to commute to school. It increases the range of learning opportunities for employees and increases employee satisfaction. Another point that needs to be made is that skepticism regarding the quality of online degrees appears to be fading. John Challenger, chief executive of outplacement firm Challenger, Gray & Christmas, agrees. "We did once have a clear line between online and brick-and-mortar degrees, but that's changing," he says. "Hiring managers are catching up."[43]

Enrollment in online universities continues to grow. The University of Phoenix has the largest student body in North America. The university has more than 200 campuses worldwide and confers degrees in over 100 degree programs at the bachelor's, master's, and doctoral levels. Clemson University's Master of Human Resource Development is a fully online course designed for in-career practitioners. The 36-credit program follows a cohort structure, with approximately 40 students in each unit. Class sessions are offered several times a week, to allow for an average of 10 students in each class. Students are assigned a "home group" within the cohort, but can choose another class to attend when work–life demands such as schedule conflicts or travel arise.[44]

In recent years, programs have been introduced that provide students with more and more autonomy and control of their programs of study. There are basically three categories of online higher education programs available: hybrid, synchronous, and asynchronous. *Hybrid programs* permit students to take some classes online and some in a traditional university setting. *Online synchronized study* offers students the choice of studying through an online portal system; however, the student is expected to appear for most classes on a real-time schedule. With this approach, students interact with a real professor and obtain real-time support for the learning material. With *asynchronous learning,* students have a series of assignments that need to be completed in a certain time frame. A system is available that allows students to communicate with the professor and classmates. Marianne Mondy, a legislative auditor for Louisiana, received her MBA through the University of Phoenix. She was given the option of totally completing her MBA online or to do a portion of her work on campus. She chose the online option because of her work schedule. All courses were six weeks in length and each assignment had to be completed in a fixed time frame. Online higher education is not for everyone and the key to success is discipline. Jeff Seaman of Babson Survey Research Group, which studies online education, said, "You need discipline. Otherwise, the 'anytime, anywhere' aspect frees you to put off the work."[45]

Vestibule System

vestibule system
T&D delivery system that takes place away from the production area on equipment that closely resembles equipment actually used on the job.

Vestibule system is a T&D delivery system that takes place away from the production area on equipment that closely resembles equipment actually used on the job. For example, a group of lathes may be located in a training center where the trainees receive instruction in their use. A primary advantage of the vestibule system is that it removes the employee from the pressure of having to produce while learning. The emphasis is focused on learning the skills required by the job.

Video Media

The use of video media such as DVDs continues to be a popular T&D delivery system. These media are especially appealing to small businesses that cannot afford more expensive training methods and are often incorporated in e-learning and instructor-led instruction. In addition, they provide the flexibility desired by any firm. Behavior modeling, previously mentioned, has long been a successful training method that uses video media.

Simulators

simulators
T&D delivery system comprised of devices or programs that replicate actual job demands.

Simulators are a T&D delivery system comprised of devices or programs that replicate actual job demands. The devices range from simple paper mock-ups of mechanical devices to computerized simulations of total environments. Training and development specialists may use simulated sales counters, automobiles, and airplanes. A prime example is the use of simulators to train pilots. Simulated crashes do not cost lives or deplete the firm's fleet of jets. John Deere uses an Excavator Training Simulator to train new operators in a risk-free environment. The simulator provides specific realistic lessons on proper operator techniques, machine controls, and safe operation at a virtual job site.[46] Crane operator trainees use a software simulator based on actual crane functions. Trainees sit in an authentic crane cab, with real control options while the simulation offers a realistic experience.[47]

Informal Training Through Social Networking

Today's employees interact, learn, and work in much different ways and styles than in the not-so-distant past. Increasingly mobile and geographically dispersed workforces are becoming the norm. At the same time, dwindling or stagnant travel budgets are creating a need for different training methods. As a result, some organizations are using social networking and collaborative tools to enable informal learning. In a recent study, 55 percent of respondents also expect an increase in informal learning usage, which includes social media, blogs, wikis, and discussion groups.[48] Informal learning often takes place outside the corporate training departments. It does not necessarily follow a specified curriculum and often begins accidentally. It is experienced directly in the course of everyday life or work. By embracing informal learning, learners may be more motivated to gain knowledge. Thus, informal learning has surfaced as an important part of employee development.

The premise behind the educational success of social networking is the learning approach referred to as *constructivism.* A constructivist learning environment differs from the traditional model. In this setting, the teacher guides the learner toward multiple learning sources, rather than acting as the sole source of knowledge.[49] With more workers around the world using social media, they are getting and trusting information from their peer group more than in the past.[50] Often organizations are using communication meetings called huddles, which are usually called daily for a short period of time such as seven minutes, as informal learning opportunities.[51] Many believe that using shared, social learning solutions will grow.

Management Development

OBJECTIVE **7.4**

Describe management development, mentoring, coaching, and reverse mentoring.

management development

Consists of all learning experiences provided by an organization resulting in upgrading skills and knowledge required in current and future managerial positions.

Management development consists of all learning experiences provided by an organization resulting in upgrading skills and knowledge required in current and future managers. Although leadership is often depicted as an exciting and glamorous endeavor, there is another side; failure can quickly result in losing one's position. The risks are especially high because of today's rapid changes. This situation magnifies the importance of providing development opportunities for a firm's management group. Even in the recent recession, the demand for management development continued to be strong. Although budgets were being slashed, managers and executives were asking for more help. A recent study found that almost 70 percent of companies believe that senior executives need to improve their leadership skills. More than half of companies reported that their top leaders needed to also improve their strategic planning skills. Several other skills that leaders need are encouraging teamwork, motivating people, and creativity.[52] The DDI's *Global Leadership Forecast 2011* found that organizations with the highest-quality leaders were 13 times more likely to outperform their competition in metrics such as financial accomplishment, product quality and services, employee engagement, and customer approval.[53]

A firm's future lies largely in the hands of its managers. This group performs certain functions essential to the organization's survival and prosperity. Managers must make the right choices in most of their decisions; otherwise, the firm will not grow, and may even fail. Therefore, it is imperative that managers keep up with the latest developments in their respective fields and, at the same time, manage an ever-changing workforce operating in a dynamic environment. Also note that as managers reach higher levels in the organization, it is not so much their technical skills that they need, but their interpersonal skills and their business knowledge.

First-line supervisors, middle managers, and executives may all participate in management development programs. These programs are available in-house, by professional organizations, and at colleges and universities. T&D specialists often plan and present in-house programs, at times using line managers. Organizations such as the Society for Human Resource Management and the American Management Association conduct conferences and seminars in a number of specialties. Numerous colleges and universities also provide management development programs. Colleges and universities may possess expertise not available within business organizations. In these cases, academicians and management practitioners can advantageously present T&D programs jointly.

Mentoring and Coaching

Mentoring and coaching have become important means of management development. Because the purposes of mentoring and coaching are similar in concept and the terms are often used interchangeably in the literature, they are discussed together. Coaching and mentoring activities, which may occur either formally or informally, are primarily development approaches emphasizing one-on-one learning.

mentoring

Approach to advising, coaching, and nurturing for creating a practical relationship to enhance individual career, personal, and professional growth and development.

Mentoring is an approach to advising, coaching, and nurturing for creating a practical relationship to enhance individual career, personal, and professional growth and development. The concept of a mentor is believed to have its origins in Greek mythology when Odysseus set out for the Trojan War and placed the running of his palace in the hands of his trusted friend, Mentor.[54] Mentors may be anywhere in the organization or even in another firm. For years, mentoring has repeatedly been shown to be the most important factor influencing careers. In a study done by Gartner Research, having a mentor helps a person get promoted five times more often than his or her peers who do not have mentors. They are also promoted six times more than the competition.[55]

Most *Fortune* 500 companies have a mentoring program. Mentors equip protégés to learn for themselves by sharing experiences, asking demanding questions, challenging decision making, and expanding problem-solving skills. It focuses on skills to develop protégés to perform to their highest potential, leading to career advancement. Mentors have the potential to help mentees discover their strengths and weaknesses, formulate a career path, set goals, manage stress, and balance work and personal obligations. Organizations are using mentoring to prepare a successor and also to transition knowledge and skills within the organization. Technology can be used to match up mentors and mentees. These relationships may be quite fluid and form and dissolve around specific issues, such as helping younger people to build their professional networks. Government-sponsored mentor organizations may be seen in Table 7-1.

E-mentoring, or open mentoring, is being used more and more today as opposed to face-to-face interaction with positive results. Many keep in touch with their mentors via e-mail, Facebook, and Twitter, but they may get together for lunch if they happen to be in the same location.

Most believe that women can truly benefit from a female mentor who has knowledge and experience and can show them "the ropes." For various reasons, mentors tend to seek out their mirror images. Since women and minorities are not equally represented at the firm's top levels, they sometimes are left without a female mentor. Women who are mentored, particularly by other women, are more likely to enhance and expand career skills, advance in their careers, receive higher salaries, and enjoy their work more. Women want and need to have advice provided by

TABLE 7-1

Government-sponsored Mentor Organizations for Small Businesses

Once a small business has been started many important decisions have to be made. This is especially true in the first months for a new small business. A mentor can be an invaluable resource in making these initial decisions because it is someone who has been down the same path. A mentor is experienced, successful and willing to provide advice and guidance—for no real personal gain. Government-sponsored mentor organizations offer a great deal of free resources and services to support small business owners, both online and locally.

SCORE: Provides free and confidential counseling, mentoring and advice to small business owners nationwide via its network of more than 12,400 retired business executives, leaders and volunteers. SCORE is sponsored by SBA and has volunteers share their expertise through in-person and online counseling (http://www.score.org/).

Small Business Development Centers: Provides management assistance to current and prospective small business owners. Centers are located in all 50 states as well as the District of Columbia, Puerto Rico, and the U.S. Territories. SBDC services assisting small businesses with financial, marketing, production, organization, engineering and technical problems and feasibility studies. All services given at SBDCs are free and confidential. Additional low cost training options are available. Assistance from an SBDC is available to anyone interested in beginning a small business for the first time or improving or expanding an existing small business, who cannot afford the services of a private consultant.

Women's Business Centers (WBC): Provides business training, counseling and other resources to help women start and grow successful businesses. The Center represents a national network of nearly 100 educational centers designed to assist women start and grow small businesses. WBCs operate with the mission to "level the playing field" for women entrepreneurs, who still face unique obstacles in the world of business. Through the management and technical assistance provided by the WBCs, entrepreneurs—especially women who are economically or socially disadvantaged—are offered comprehensive training and counseling on a vast array of topics in many languages to help them start and grow their own businesses.

Minority Business Development Centers: The Minority Business Development Agency was created specifically to foster the establishment and growth of minority-owned businesses in America, with more than 40 centers nationwide.

General Services Administration (GSA): The GSA offers a Mentor/Protégé Program that is specifically designed to encourage prime contractors to help small businesses be more successful in government contracting and enhance their ability to perform successfully on government contracts and subcontracts. The program is designed to encourage and motivate GSA prime contractors to assist small businesses and enhance their capability of performing successfully on GSA contracts and subcontracts. The goal is to increase the overall number of small businesses receiving GSA prime contract and subcontract awards, resulting from mentorship and refined business practices. The mentor firms also benefit from their collaboration with small businesses. The mentors receive exposure to new business ideas and technology, a higher profile within the GSA community, as well as the satisfaction of helping mentors to reach their subcontracting goals.

Source: http://www.sba.gov/content/steps-finding-mentor

mentors to effectively use their talents and realize their potential, not only for their personal benefit but to assist their firms.[56]

Coaching is often considered a responsibility of the immediate boss, who provides assistance, much like a mentor, but the primary focus is about performance. Coaching involves helping workers see why they have been selected to perform the task or why they have been selected for the team. The coach has greater experience or expertise than the protégé and is in the position to offer wise advice. It is employee development that is customized to each individual and is therefore immediately applicable and does not require stepping away from work for extended periods of time.

Reverse Mentoring

Reverse mentoring is a process in which older employees learn from younger ones. There are people in organizations who are approaching retirement who do not want to retire and who have tremendous knowledge that should not go to waste. There are young people who know things others do not know and who are anxious to expand their horizons. The existence of these two diverse, but potentially mutually helpful, populations has led to reverse mentoring. At Procter & Gamble, the reverse mentoring program allows senior management to be mentored in areas such as biotechnology. It pairs scientists and top managers in order to explore the potential impact of biotechnology on P&G's customers, suppliers, and overall business. Time Warner has a Digital Reverse Mentoring Program between their executives and technology savvy college students.[57] Phil McKinney, a vice president at Hewlett-Packard, uses reverse mentoring by spending time with his company's college interns to understand what motivates them and how they work.[58]

Orientation (Onboarding)

Orientation is the initial T&D effort to inform new employees about the company, the job, and the work group. It becomes a way to engage new employees and reinforce the fact that they made the proper career choice. It also familiarizes them with the corporate culture and helps them to quickly become productive. A good orientation program is quite important because first impressions are often the most lasting and need to start the minute an applicant accepts an offer of employment. One of the orientation goals at Booz Allen is to make a positive first impression and create excitement before the new hire's first day on the job, using their online new-hire portal.[59]

New employees usually decide whether or not to stay at a company within their first six months of employment, and orientation programs give organizations an opportunity to get the relationship off to a good start. Therefore, new-hire orientation programs are particularly crucial for the rapid transition from new hires to contributing members of the organization. Orientation formats are unique to each firm. However, some basic purposes are listed below.

- *The Employment Situation.* At an early point in time, it is helpful for the new employee to know how his or her job fits into the firm's organizational structure and goals.
- *Company Policies and Rules.* Every job within an organization must be performed within the guidelines and constraints provided by policies and rules. Employees must understand these to ensure a smooth transition into the workplace.
- *Compensation.* Employees have a special interest in obtaining information about the reward system. Management normally provides this information during the recruitment-and-selection process and often reviews it during orientation.
- *Corporate Culture.* The firm's culture reflects, in effect, "How we do things around here." This relates to everything from the way employees dress to the way they talk.
- *Team Membership.* A new employee's ability and willingness to work in teams was likely determined before he or she was hired. In orientation, the program may again emphasize the importance of becoming a valued member of the company team.
- *Employee Development.* An individual's employment security is increasingly becoming dependent on his or her ability to acquire needed knowledge and skills that are constantly changing. Thus, firms should keep employees aware not only of company-sponsored developmental programs, but also of those available externally.
- *Socialization.* To reduce the anxiety that new employees may experience, the firm should take steps to integrate them into the informal organization. Some organizations have found that employees subjected to socialization programs, including the topics of politics and career management, perform better than those who have not undergone such training.

To the above list, add the fact that there are numerous forms and documents a new employee must complete or read and acknowledge.

Supervisors represent the front line of orientation. Roger Chevalier, California-based management consultant and author of *A Manager's Guide to Improving Workplace Performance,* said, "If employees are selected properly, 85 percent of whether or not they will succeed is based on the environment created by a supervisor."[60] Peers also often serve as excellent information agents. There are several reasons for using peers in performing this function. For one thing, they are accessible to newcomers, often more so than the boss. Peers also tend to have a high degree of empathy for new people. In addition, they have the organizational experience and technical expertise to which new employees need access. Some organizations assign a mentor or "buddy" to new hires to work with them until they are settled in.

While orientation can occupy a new employee's first few days on the job, some firms believe that learning is more effective if spread out over time. For example, a company may deliver a program in a system of 20 one-hour sessions over a period of several weeks. Some firms are sensitive to information overload and make information available to employees on an as-needed basis. For example, a new supervisor may eventually have the responsibility for evaluating his or her subordinates. But, knowledge of how to do this may not be needed for six months. A training segment on performance evaluation may be placed on the Internet or a firm's intranet and be available when the need arises. This approach is consistent with *just-in-time training,* mentioned earlier.

Implementing Training and Development Programs

A perfectly conceived training program will fail if management cannot convince the participants of its merits. Participants must believe that the program has value and will help them achieve their personal and professional goals. A long string of successful programs certainly enhances the credibility of T&D.

Implementing T&D programs is often difficult. One reason is that managers are typically action-oriented and feel that they are too busy for T&D. According to one management development executive, "Most busy executives are too involved chopping down the proverbial tree to stop for the purpose of sharpening their axes." Another difficulty in program implementation is that qualified trainers must be available. In addition to possessing communication skills, the trainers must know the company's philosophy, its objectives, its formal and informal organization, and the goals of the training program. Training and development requires more creativity than perhaps any other human resource function.

Implementing training programs presents unique problems. Training implies change, which employees may vigorously resist. It may also be difficult to schedule the training around present work requirements. Unless the employee is new to the firm, he or she undoubtedly has specific full-time duties to perform. Another difficulty in implementing T&D programs is record keeping. It is important to maintain training records, including how well employees perform during training and later on the job. This information helps measure program effectiveness and chart the employees' progress in the company.

OBJECTIVE **7.6**

Explain the metrics for evaluating training and development.

Metrics for Evaluating Training and Development

Managers should strive to develop and use T&D metrics because such information can smooth the way to budget approval and executive buy-in. Most managers agree that training does not cost, it pays, and that training is an investment, not an expense. However, the actual value of the training must be determined if top management will be ready to invest in it. Some possible metrics for evaluating training and development will next be discussed.

Participants' Opinions

Evaluating a T&D program by asking the participants' opinions of it is an approach that provides a response and suggestions for improvements, essentially a level of customer satisfaction. You cannot always rely on such responses, however. The training may have taken place in an exotic location with time for golfing and other fun activities, and the overall experience may bias some reports. Nevertheless, this approach is a good way to obtain feedback and to get it quickly and inexpensively.

Extent of Learning

Some organizations administer tests to determine what the participants in a T&D program have learned. The pretest–posttest control group design is one evaluation procedure that may be used. In this procedure, both groups receive the same test before and after training. The experimental group receives the training but the control group does not. Each group receives randomly assigned trainees. Differences in pretest and posttest results between the groups are attributed to the training provided. A potential problem with this approach is controlling for variables other than training that might affect the outcome.

Behavioral Change

Tests may accurately indicate what trainees learn, but they give little insight into whether the training leads participants to change their behavior. For example, it is one thing for a manager to learn about motivational techniques but quite another matter for this person to apply the new knowledge. A manager may sit in the front row of a training session dealing with empowerment of subordinates, absorb every bit of the message, understand it totally, make a grade of 100 on a test on the material, and then return the next week to the workplace and continue behaving in the same old autocratic way. The best demonstration of value occurs when learning translates into lasting behavioral change. Michael Allen, winner of the Distinguished Contribution to Workplace Learning and Performance Award, said, "We don't care about what people know. We care about what they can do…with what they know. Our challenge, as effective instructional designers, is to get people to make the leap from knowing to doing and that's where we often fail."[61]

Accomplishment of T&D Objectives

Still another approach to evaluating T&D programs involves determining the extent to which T&D objectives were accomplished. Here metrics address the business's bottom line, such as productivity data, rather than numbers of training sessions completed or the satisfaction employees gained from a training session. For instance, if the objective of an accident-prevention program is to reduce the number and severity of accidents by 15 percent, comparing accident rates before and after training provides a useful metric of success. Leslie Joyce, vice president of global talent management at Novelis and former CLO at Home Depot, said, "If there is change in behavior or improvement in performance, most CEOs I've worked with will agree that training has had an impact."[62]

Return on Investment from Training

CEOs want to see training in terms that they can appreciate such as business impact, business alignment, and return on investment (ROI). However, a recent study from the ROI Institute showed that while 96 percent of executives want to see the business effects of learning, only 8 percent receive it.[63] Nevertheless, in today's global competitive environment, training will not be rewarded with continued investment unless training results in improved performance that impacts the bottom line. Today, organizations can only justify investing in training that is clearly essential to business success and that actually delivers results that enable the company to compete effectively.

Benchmarking

Benchmarking is the process of monitoring and measuring a firm's internal processes, such as operations, and then comparing the data with information from companies that excel in those areas. Because training programs for different firms are unique, the training measures are necessarily broad. Common benchmarking questions focus on metrics such as training costs, the ratio of training staff to employees, and whether new or more traditional delivery systems are used. Information derived from these questions probably lacks the detail to permit specific improvements of the training curricula. However, a firm may recognize, for example, that another organization is able to deliver a lot of training for relatively little cost. This information could then trigger the firm to follow up with interviews or site visits to determine whether that phenomenon represents a "best practice."

HR Web Wisdom

Benchmarking
http://www.benchnet.com

The Benchmarking Exchange and Best Practices homepage is provided.

benchmarking
Process of monitoring and measuring a firm's internal processes, such as operations, and then comparing the data with information from companies that excel in those areas.

ISO 9001 Quality Assurance Training Standards

One ISO 9001 quality assurance standard states: "Employees should receive the training and have the knowledge necessary to do their jobs." To comply with the standard, companies must maintain written records of their employee training to show that employees have been properly trained. Think of possible questions that a compliance auditor might ask when auditing a firm. Some might be "How does your firm assess the need for the types and amounts of training and education received by all categories of employees? What percent of employees receives training annually? What is the average number of hours of training and education per employee?" Under ISO 9001, monitoring the quality of training is important.

Workforce Investment Act

HR Web Wisdom

Workforce Investment Act
**http://www.careeronestop
.org/**
Career One Stop Pathways to
Career Success.

The Workforce Investment Act (WIA) replaced the problem-riddled Job Training Partnership Act and consolidated more than 70 federal job-training programs. These federally funded programs allow state and local organizations to offer training and skill enhancement that benefit employers, dislocated workers, and low-income youth. A primary focus of WIA is to meet the needs of business for skilled workers while satisfying the training, education, and employment needs of individuals.

One-stop service centers are at the heart of the system. These centers provide job seekers with a range of services, including career counseling, skill assessments, training, job search assistance, and referrals to programs and services, depending on need. Each year, one-stop centers provide about 15 million workers with information about the characteristics of available jobs, strategies to land the best possible new jobs, and the benefits and costs of enrolling in training programs.

Recently the VOW to Hire Heroes Act was signed into law, which provides additional training to veterans in what the Department of Labor defines as high-demand job sectors. To qualify, veterans must participate in the Transition Assistance Program, which provides employment training and job search skills.

OBJECTIVE 7.7

Define *organization development (OD)* and describe various OD techniques.

**organization development
(OD)**

Planned and systematic attempts to change the organization, typically to a more behavioral environment.

Organization Development: A Strategic HR Tool

Individuals and groups receive the bulk of T&D effort. However, some firms believe that to achieve needed change, they must move the entire organization in a different direction. Efforts to achieve this are the focus of **organization development (OD)**—planned and systematic attempts to change the organization, typically to a more behavioral environment. OD education and training strategies are designed to develop a more open, productive, and compatible workplace despite differences in personalities, culture, or technologies. The OD movement has been strongly advocated by researchers such as Chris Argyris and Warren Bennis.[64] Organization development applies to an entire system, such as a company or a plant, and is a major means of achieving change in the corporate culture. Various factors in the firm's corporate culture affect employees' behavior on the job. To bring about desired changes in these factors and behavior, organizations must be transformed into market-driven, innovative, and adaptive systems if they are to survive and prosper in today's highly competitive global environment. This type of development is increasingly important as both work and the workforce diversify and change.

Numerous OD interventions are available to the practitioner. Interventions covered in the following sections include survey feedback, a technique often combined with other interventions such as quality circles and team building.

Survey Feedback

survey feedback

Organization development method of basing change efforts on the systematic collection and measurement of subordinate's attitudes through anonymous questionnaires.

The organization development method of basing change efforts on the systematic collection and measurement of subordinate's attitudes through anonymous questionnaires is **survey feedback**. It enables management teams to help organizations create working environments that lead to better working relationships, greater productivity, and increased profitability. Survey feedback generally involves the following steps:

1. Members of the organization, including top management, are involved in planning the survey.
2. All members of the organizational unit participate in the survey.
3. The OD consultant usually analyzes the data, tabulates results, suggests approaches to diagnosis, and trains participants in the feedback process.
4. Data feedback usually begins at the top level of the organization and flows downward to groups reporting at successively lower levels.
5. Feedback meetings provide an opportunity to discuss and interpret data, diagnose problem areas, and develop action plans.

Quality Circles

quality circles
Groups of employees who voluntarily meet regularly with their supervisors to discuss problems, investigate causes, recommend solutions, and take corrective action when authorized to do so.

America received the concept of quality circles from Japan several decades ago. This version of employee involvement is still in use today, improving quality, increasing motivation, boosting productivity, and adding to the bottom line. **Quality circles** are groups of employees who voluntarily meet regularly with their supervisors to discuss their problems, investigate causes, recommend solutions, and take corrective action when authorized to do so. The team's recommendations are presented to higher-level management for review, and the approved actions are implemented with employee participation.

Toyota North America Inc. uses quality circles to develop a competitive workforce spirit. Approximately 37 percent of the automaker's assemblers participate in Toyota's global "Quality Circles" competition that pits worker against worker in a friendly competition to develop more efficient manufacturing methods. The ultimate target is 100 percent. Quality circles are one way that Toyota sees as providing an edge over the competition. Toyota holds competitions twice a year to identify the best ideas.[65]

Team Building

team building
Conscious effort to develop effective work groups and cooperative skills throughout the organization.

Team building is a conscious effort to develop effective work groups and cooperative skills throughout the organization. It helps members diagnose group processes and devise solutions to problems. Effective team building can be the most efficient way to boost morale, employee retention, and company profitability. Whether it's a lieutenant leading troops into battle or executives working with their managers, the same principles apply. An important by-product of team building is that it is one of the most effective interventions for improving employee satisfaction and work-related attitudes. Individualism has deep roots in American culture. This trait has been a virtue and will continue to be an asset in our society. However, there are work situations that make it imperative to subordinate individual autonomy in favor of cooperation with a group. It seems apparent that teams are clearly superior in performing many of the tasks required by organizations. The building of effective teams, therefore, has become a business necessity.

Team building uses self-directed teams, each composed of a small group of employees responsible for an entire work process or segment. Team members work together to improve their operation or product, to plan and control their work, and to handle day-to-day problems. They may even become involved in broader, company-wide issues, such as vendor quality, safety, and business planning. There are basically two types of team-building exercises. In the first, there is an attempt to break down barriers to understanding that workers have built. In the second, participants "place their lives" in the hand of others such as falling backwards believing that the team will catch you.[66] Team-building exercises run the spectrum from a paint-ball battle[67] to the raw egg exercise that Southwest Airlines creates. At Southwest Airlines, the firm divides new employees into teams and gives them a raw egg in the shell, a handful of straws, and some masking tape. Their task is, in a limited amount of time, to protect that delicate cargo from an eight-foot drop. The exercise prepares teams of employees for creative problem solving in a fast-paced environment.[68]

In one team-building exercise, participants were instructed to untangle a 60-foot yellow rope. At first participants tried to untangle the rope on an individual basis, which resulted in failure. Ultimately, they began to share their ideas on how to untangle the rope, and within minutes it was untangled.[69] A classic team-building exercise is called "blind man's bluff" where a blindfolded person who is "it" has to chase others with only the verbal assistance of team members to guide him or her.[70]

Pump It Up sells inflatable playgrounds throughout the United States and uses the playgrounds and childlike activities to create team-building exercises. The head office worked with team-building experts to devise a handbook of business-related team-building activities, including "Leading the Crowd Playfully" (to break the ice) and "Tag Team Climbing" (to improve cooperation). However, just bouncing around—in socks, in full view of the boss—may improve team morale.[71]

A classic team-building exercise is called "Team Banquets," where workers with different knowledge, skills, and experience are brought together to accomplish a single goal: create a banquet. The Team Banquet brings together 25 to 30 employees and challenges them to prepare a gourmet banquet within two hours. Only the raw ingredients and equipment are provided.[72] Through team building, management and participants discover that the exercises provide an excellent analogy to the workplace and provide an outstanding means for developing teamwork.

Job Security versus Career Security

OBJECTIVE 7.8
Distinguish between job security and career security.

The job environment is experiencing tremendous changes now and will likely see more in the future. Jobs are being eliminated, changed, and created. Not long ago students went to the library, pulled journals and books from the shelves, copied pertinent pages, and wrote term papers. Today, students can be virtually anywhere with a notebook computer or smartphone and access libraries through the Internet. Grocery stores do not need as many cashiers, because checkout stands are being automated. FedEx and UPS do not need as many workers, because machines will do more sorting. Not as many loaders will be needed because machines determine which packages belong on which trucks. Recently Walmart eliminated the position of greeters from the overnight shift at its 3,800-plus U.S. stores and also redefined the role of daytime greeters.[73]

On the other hand, wireless and mobile devices have created some of the hottest jobs today. Think of the different types of jobs that have been created as a result of the social media explosion. For example, as a result of the development and expansion of the many uses of social media, jobs in cyber security have been formed. Other "hot jobs" include social media manager and technical recruiter. There is also a high demand for doctors and nurse practitioners, pharmacists, therapists, and virtually everybody with an advanced degree in health care. The increased use of cloud computing has created high demand for cloud computer experience.[74]

job security
Implies security in one job, often with one company.

Jobs now identified for extinction were historically thought to be very secure. In the past, most people remained with one company and career for the majority of their adult years. The term **job security** implies security in one job, often with one company. Historically, this type of security depended on an employee doing a good job and keeping out of trouble. But, for most workers today, this assumption is not valid. Today, there is no such thing as job security even if you worked at your job for many years. Today's employees will work for approximately nine companies during their careers, and on average, individuals will change careers (not merely "jobs") three times in their life. In fact, the Department of Labor estimates that individuals will remain with a firm an average of 3.6 years before changing jobs. The old social contract between employers and employees no longer exists. The country has largely become a free-agent nation, in which employees are no more loyal to companies than companies are to employees. The decision to leave or stay is based not only on an employee's career prospects in the present company, but also on how it might prepare him or her to move on elsewhere. Therefore, the way people approached their careers in the past is history.

career security
Requires developing marketable skills and expertise that help ensure employment within a range of careers.

Career security is distinctly different from job security; it requires developing marketable skills and expertise that help ensure employment within a range of careers. Career security results from the ability to perform within a broad range of careers well enough to be marketable in more than one job and to more than one organization. With career security, workers are offered opportunities to improve their skills, and thus their employability in an ever-changing work environment. Employees owe the company their commitment while employed and the company owes its workers the opportunity to learn new skills, but that is as far as the commitment goes. Loyalty in either direction is not expected. Security comes from employability rather than paternal protection.

There is just one way to achieve true career security and that is to be ready to re-create yourself, no matter what your age, your education, or your skill set. The Denali Group, a procurement-services company, predicts that Generation Y workers will have 15 to 25 jobs in their lifetime, requiring frequent changes in professional identities.[75]

OBJECTIVE **7.9**

Describe career planning and explain career paths and career development.

career

General course that a person chooses to pursue throughout his or her working life.

career planning

Ongoing process whereby an individual sets career goals and identifies the means to achieve them.

Career and Career Planning Defined

A **career** is a general course that a person chooses to pursue throughout his or her working life. Historically, a *career* was a sequence of work-related positions an individual occupied during a lifetime, although not always with the same company. However, today there are few relatively static jobs. **Career planning** is an ongoing process whereby *an individual* sets career goals and identifies the means to achieve them. Individuals in today's job market must truly manage their careers. Career planning should not concentrate only on advancement opportunities, since the present work environment has reduced many of these opportunities. At some point, career planning should focus on achieving successes that do not necessarily entail promotions.

Career Planning

"If you don't know where you're going, any road will get you there" is certainly true in career planning. Career planning must now accommodate a number of objectives and enable us to prepare for each on a contingency basis. It will need updating to accommodate changes in our own interests as well as in the work environment. Historically, it was thought that career planning was logical, linear, and indeed, planned. Today, a new job assignment often is thought of as being paid to learn a new task and increase your experience level in case you must leave your job. Because of the many changes that are occurring, career planning is essential for survival for individuals and organizations. Individuals should have a strategy or plan for unexpected career events that begins while they are still employed.

Career Planning: Self-Assessment

Through career planning, a person continuously evaluates his or her abilities and interests, considers alternative career opportunities, establishes career goals, and plans practical developmental activities. A career plan lets you know where you are and where you are going. At times career planning occurs not at the beginning of a person's career but may occur in planning for a second career or even a third career. Being fired from a job is not an uncommon experience in today's work environment, and a thorough self-assessment may be needed to be able to reenter the job market. Workers should attempt to identify and overcome shortcomings. Thus, starting over can be a natural phase of building a career. In any event, career planning must begin with self-understanding or self-assessment. Then, the person is in a position to establish realistic goals and determine what to do to achieve these goals. This action also lets the person know whether his or her goals are realistic.

self-assessment

Process of learning about oneself.

   Self-assessment is the process of learning about oneself. Anything that could affect one's performance in a future job should be considered. It is one of the first things that a person should do in planning a career. A self-assessment can help a person target career choices and goals. Conducting a realistic self-assessment may help a person avoid mistakes that could affect his or her entire career progression. A person should take time to analyze his or her past successes and failures. A thorough self-assessment will go a long way toward helping match an individual's specific qualities and goals with the right job or profession. Remember, you cannot get what you want until you know what you want. The self-assessment is not something that is done once and forgotten. It is something that spans a career and into retirement. The self-assessment may show that you do not want to retire at 65. Some enjoy working well past what traditionally has been thought of as the retirement age. As a 95-year-old former mentor said, "work is what keeps me alive and going. Everyone I know who retired died young, and certainly much younger than me."[76]

   Some useful tools include a strength/weakness balance sheet and a likes and dislikes survey. However, any reasonable approach that assists self-understanding is helpful.

strength/weakness balance sheet

A self-evaluation procedure, developed originally by Benjamin Franklin, that assists people in becoming aware of their strengths and weaknesses.

STRENGTH/WEAKNESS BALANCE SHEET A self-evaluation procedure, developed originally by Benjamin Franklin, that assists people in becoming aware of their strengths and weaknesses is the **strength/weakness balance sheet**. Employees who understand their strengths can use them to maximum advantage. By recognizing their weaknesses, they are in a better position to overcome them. This statement sums up that attitude: "If you have a weakness, understand it and make it work for you as a strength; if you have a strength, do not abuse it to the point at which it becomes a weakness."

To use a strength/weakness balance sheet, the individual lists strengths and weaknesses as he or she perceives them. This is quite important, because believing, for example, that a weakness exists even when it does not can equate to a real weakness. Thus, if you believe that you make a poor first impression when meeting someone, you will probably make a poor impression. The perception of a weakness often becomes a self-fulfilling prophecy.

The mechanics for preparing the balance sheet are quite simple. To begin, draw a line down the middle of a sheet of paper. Label the left side *Strengths* and the right side *Weaknesses*. Record all perceived strengths and weaknesses. You may find it difficult to write about yourself. Remember, however, that no one else need see the results. The primary consideration is complete honesty.

Table 7-2 shows an example of a strength/weakness balance sheet. Obviously, Wayne (the person who wrote the sheet) did a lot of soul-searching in making these evaluations. Typically, a person's weaknesses will outnumber strengths after the first few attempts. However, as the individual repeats the process, some items that first appeared to be weaknesses may eventually be seen as strengths and should then be moved from one column to the other. A person should devote sufficient time to the project to obtain a fairly clear understanding of his or her strengths and weaknesses. Typically, the process should take a minimum of one week. The balance sheet will not provide all the answers regarding a person's strengths and weaknesses, but many people have gained a better understanding of themselves by completing it. Analyzing oneself should not

TABLE 7-2

Strength/Weakness Balance Sheet

Strengths	Weaknesses
Work well with people.	Get very close to few people.
Like to be given a task and get it done in my own way.	Do not like constant supervision.
Good manager of people.	Am extremely high-strung.
Hard worker.	Often say things without realizing consequences.
Lead by example.	Cannot stand to look busy when there is no work to be done.
People respect me as being fair and impartial.	Cannot stand to be inactive. Must be on the go constantly.
Tremendous amount of energy.	Cannot stand to sit at a desk all the time.
Function well in an active environment.	Basically a rebel at heart but have portrayed myself as just the opposite. My conservatism has gotten me jobs that I emotionally did not want.
Relatively open-minded.	
Feel comfortable in dealing with high-level businesspersons.	Am sometimes nervous in an unfamiliar environment.
Like to play politics. (This may be a weakness.)	Make very few true friends.
Get the job done when it is defined.	Not a conformist but appear to be.
Excellent at organizing other people's time.	Interest level hits peaks and valleys.
Can get the most out of people who are working for me.	Many people look on me as being unstable. Perhaps I am. Believe not.
Have an outgoing personality—not shy.	Divorced.
Take care of those who take care of me. (This could be a weakness).	Not a tremendous planner for short range. Long-range planning is better.
Have a great amount of empathy.	Impatient—want to have things happen fast.
Work extremely well through other people.	Do not like details.
	Do not work well in an environment where I am the only party involved.

Source: Wayne Sanders

be just a one-time event. People change, and every few years the process should again be undertaken. You can determine means to react to your findings and, perhaps, overcome a weakness after you have conducted the self-assessment.

LIKES AND DISLIKES SURVEY A **likes and dislikes survey** assists individuals in recognizing restrictions they place on themselves. Connecticut-based career counselor Julie Jansen said, "It's important in identifying what you want to do, what your skills are, and what you don't—and do—like about your current occupation."[77] You are looking for qualities you want in a job and attributes of a job you do not want. For instance, some people are not willing to live in certain parts of the country, and such feelings should be noted as a constraint. Some positions require a person to spend considerable amount of time traveling. Thus, an estimate of the amount of time a person is willing to travel would also be helpful. Recognition of such self-imposed restrictions may reduce future career problems.

The size of the firm might also be important. Some like a major organization whose products or services are well known; others prefer a smaller organization, believing that the opportunities for advancement may be greater or that the environment is better suited to their tastes. All factors that could affect an individual's work performance should be listed in the likes and dislikes survey. An example of this type of survey is shown in Table 7-3.

A self-assessment such as this helps a person understand his or her basic motives and sets the stage for pursuing a career or seeking further technical competence. People who know themselves can more easily make the decisions necessary for successful career planning. Many people get sidetracked because they choose careers based on haphazard plans or the wishes of others, rather than on what they believe to be best for them.

Getting to know yourself is not a singular event. As individuals progress through life, priorities change. Individuals may think they know themselves quite well at one stage of life and later begin to see themselves quite differently. Therefore, the self-assessment should be viewed as a continuous process. Career-minded individuals must heed the Red Queen's admonition to Alice: "It takes all the running you can do, to keep in the same place."[78] This admonition is very true in today's work environment.

Using the Web for Self-Assessment Assistance

The Internet has valuable information to assist in developing a self-assessment. Some sites are free and others charge a modest fee. Some Web sites that might be valuable as you conduct your self-assessment include:

- *CareerMaze:* An assessment of vocational interests and weaknesses, interests, and capabilities for every job seeker at every level is provided. There is a charge of $19.95 for the Career Maze report.[79]
- *Career-intelligence:* A by-women, for-women career resource with a philosophy of Stretch, Grow, and Achieve. Its mission is to help women achieve personal and professional satisfaction by providing the information, support, and tools needed to succeed in today's competitive economy.[80]
- *Holland's Theory of Career Choice:* The Career Key is based on the theory that people like to be around others who have similar personalities. In choosing a career, it means that people choose jobs where they can be around other people who are like them. The test takes about 15 minutes to complete and costs $9.95.[81]

TABLE 7.3

Likes and Dislikes Survey

Likes	Dislikes
Enjoy traveling	Do not want to work for a large firm
Would like to live in the Southeast U.S.	Would not want to work in a large city
Enjoy being my own boss	Would not like to work behind a desk all day
Would like to live in a medium-sized city	Would not like to wear suits all the time
Enjoy watching football and baseball	
Enjoy playing racquetball	

Using the Web for Career-Planning Assistance

The Web can often be an excellent tool for assisting you in planning your career. Listed below is some advice on how the Web can assist you.

- There is a large amount of free information available on the Web that should prove helpful. Virtually all of the major job boards provide tips for securing the position you desire.
- The Web can be used to develop and maintain a professional network. It is much easier and more convenient to keep in touch with other professionals through such means as e-mail, texting, LinkedIn, Twitter, and Facebook. This is important, since the number one way people find a job is through some kind of networking or referral. Individuals whom you have met at conferences, business meetings, or on LinkedIn or Facebook may provide useful assistance in a job search. A network should be maintained with these individuals even though you are satisfied with your present job.
- The Web should be used to investigate specific companies before seeking employment or going for an interview. For instance, with WetFeet.com, a job seeker can research companies, careers, and industries.

OBJECTIVE 7.10

Describe career development methods, identify various career paths, and explain global meetings through telepresence.

career path

A flexible line of movement through which a person may travel during his or her work life.

career development

Formal approach used by the organization to ensure that people with the proper qualifications and experiences are available when needed.

Career Paths and Career Development

A **career path** is a flexible line of movement through which a person may travel during his or her work life. Following an established career path, the employee can undertake career development with the firm's assistance. From a worker's perspective, following a career path may involve weaving from company to company and from position to position as he or she obtains greater knowledge and experience.

Career development is a formal approach used by the organization to ensure that people with the proper qualifications and experiences are available when needed. Beverly Kaye, coauthor of *Love 'Em or Lose 'Em: Getting Good People to Stay,* studied the top 20 reasons employees remain with their company and discovered that career development opportunities was number one on the list. It was even more important than receiving greater pay.[82] With career development, the organization identifies paths and activities for individual employees as they develop.

Career planning rests with the employee. However, career development must closely parallel individual career planning if a firm is to retain its best and brightest workers. Employees must see that the firm's career development effort is directed toward furthering their specific career objectives. Companies must therefore help their employees obtain their career objectives and, most notably, career security. They must provide them with opportunities to learn and do different things. Performing the same or a similar task over and over provides little development. Through effective career development, a pool of men and women can be developed who can thrive in any number of organizational structures in the future.

Properly designed and implemented career development programs can aid in recruiting and hiring and ensure that the best employees are in the pipeline for future leadership positions. Formal career development is important to maintain a motivated and committed workforce. In fact, Gen Y workers tend to favor personalized career guidance as opposed to big salaries and retirement packages. Further, high-potential employees are more likely to remain with organizations that are willing to invest in their development.

Career development should begin with a person's job placement and initial orientation. Management then observes the employee's job performance and compares it to job standards. At this stage, strengths and weaknesses will be noted, enabling management to assist the employee in making a tentative career decision. Naturally, this decision can be altered later as the process continues. This tentative career decision is based on a number of factors, including personal needs, abilities, and aspirations, and the organization's needs. Management can then schedule development programs that relate to the employee's specific needs.

Career development programs are expected to achieve one or more of the following objectives:

- *Effective development of available talent.* Individuals are more likely to be committed to career development that is part of a specific career plan. This way, they can better understand the purpose of development. Career development consistently ranks high on employees' *want lists,* and they can often be a less expensive option than pay raises and bonuses.
- *Self-appraisal opportunities for employees considering new or nontraditional career paths.* Some excellent workers do not view traditional upward mobility as a career option, since firms today have fewer promotion options available. Other workers see themselves in dead-end jobs and seek relief. Rather than lose these workers, a firm can offer career planning to help them identify new and different career paths.
- *Development of career paths that cut across divisions and geographic locations.* The development should not be limited to a narrow spectrum of one part of a company.
- *A demonstration of a tangible commitment to developing a diverse work environment.* Individuals who recognize a company as desiring a diverse environment often have greater recruiting and retention opportunities.
- *Satisfaction of employees' specific development needs.* Individuals who see their personal development needs being met tend to be more satisfied with their jobs and the organization. They tend to remain with the organization.
- *Improvement of performance.* The job itself is the most important influence on career development. Each job can provide different challenges and experiences.
- *Increased employee loyalty and motivation, leading to decreased turnover.* Individuals who believe that the firm is interested in their career planning are more likely to remain with the organization.
- *A method of determining training and development needs.* If a person desires a certain career path and does not currently have the proper qualifications, this identifies a training and development need.

Career Development Methods

There are numerous methods for career development. Some currently used methods, most of which are used in various combinations, are discussed next.

Manager/Employee Self-Service

Manager and employee self-service have proven to be useful in career development. Many companies are providing managers with the online ability to assist employees in planning their career paths and developing required competencies. Through employee self-service, employees are provided with the ability to update performance goals online and to enroll in training courses.

Discussions with Knowledgeable Individuals

In a formal discussion, the superior and subordinate employees may jointly agree on what career development activities are best. The resources made available to achieve these objectives may also include developmental programs. In some organizations, human resource professionals are the focal point for providing assistance on the topic. In other instances, psychologists and guidance counselors provide this service. In an academic setting, colleges and universities often provide career planning and development information to students. Students often go to their professors for career advice.

Company Material

Some firms provide material specifically developed to assist in career development. Such material is tailored to the firm's special needs. In addition, job descriptions provide valuable insight for individuals to personally determine whether a match exists between their strengths and weaknesses and specific positions.

Performance Appraisal System

The firm's performance appraisal system can also be a valuable tool in career development. Discussing an employee's strengths and weaknesses with his or her supervisor can uncover developmental needs. If overcoming a particular weakness seems difficult or even impossible, an alternative career path may be the solution.

Workshops

Some organizations conduct workshops lasting two or three days for the purpose of helping workers develop careers within the company. Employees define and match their specific career objectives with the needs of the company. At other times, the company may send workers to workshops available in the community or workers may initiate the visit themselves. Consider just two of the developmental activities available for HR professionals:

- *Society for Human Resource Management Seminar Series.* Many HR seminars are available to SHRM members.
- *American Management Association, Human Resource Seminars.* There are numerous human resource seminars offered through the AMA.

Possible career paths will next be discussed.

Career Paths

Career paths have historically focused on upward mobility within a particular occupation, a choice not nearly as available as in the past. The days of the cradle to the grave job have largely disappeared. Other career paths include the network, lateral skill, dual-career paths, adding value to your career, demotion, and being your own boss as a free agent. Most careers are no longer a straight ascent up the corporate ladder. By selecting an alternative career path, a person may transfer current skills into a new career, one that was only dreamed about in the past. Typically, these career paths are used in combination and may be more popular at various stages of a person's career.

Traditional Career Path

Although the traditional career path is not as viable a career path option as it previously was, understanding it furthers one's comprehension of the other career path alternatives. The **traditional career path** is one in which an employee progresses vertically upward in the organization from one specific job to the next. The assumption is that each preceding job is essential preparation for the next-higher-level job. Therefore, an employee must move, step-by-step, from one job to the next to gain needed experience and preparation. One of the biggest advantages of the traditional career path is that it was straightforward and very predictable.[83] The path was clearly laid out, and the employee knew the specific sequence of jobs through which he or she must progress.

Today, the old model of a career in which an employee worked his or her way up the ladder in a single company is becoming somewhat rare. The up-or-out approach, in which employees have to keep getting promoted quickly or get lost, is becoming outmoded. The certainties of yesterday's business methods and growth have disappeared in most industries. However, the one certainty that still remains is that there will always be top-level managers and individuals who strive to achieve these positions. The manner in which these positions are obtained may be different.

Network Career Path

The **network career path** contains both a vertical sequence of jobs and a series of horizontal opportunities. The network career path recognizes the interchangeability of experience at certain levels and the need to broaden experience at one level before promotion to a higher level. Often, this approach provides more realistic opportunities for employee development in an organization than does the traditional career path. For instance, a person may work as an inventory manager for a few years and then move to a lateral position of shift manager before being considered for a promotion. The vertical and horizontal options lessen the probability of blockage in one job. Royal Caribbean crew members are often given several different work assignments prior to a promotion. One major disadvantage of this type of career path is that it is more difficult to explain to employees the specific route their careers may take for a given line of work.

Lateral Skill Path

The **lateral skill path** allows for lateral moves within the firm, taken to permit an employee to become revitalized and find new challenges. Neither pay nor promotion may be involved, but by learning a different job, an employee can increase his or her value to the organization and

---

traditional career path
Employee progresses vertically upward in the organization from one specific job to the next.

network career path
Method of career progression that contains both a vertical sequence of jobs and a series of horizontal opportunities.

lateral skill path
Career path that allows for lateral moves within the firm, taken to permit an employee to become revitalized and find new challenges.

also become rejuvenated and reenergized. Firms that want to encourage lateral movement may choose to use a skill-based pay system that rewards individuals for the type and number of skills they possess. Another approach is job enrichment. This approach rewards (without promotion) an employee by increasing the challenge of the job, giving the job more meaning, and giving the employee a greater sense of accomplishment.

Dual-Career Path

dual-career path
Career path that recognizes that technical specialists can and should be allowed to contribute their expertise to a company without having to become managers.

The dual-career path was originally developed to deal with the problem of technically trained employees who had no desire to move into management through the normal upward mobility procedure. The **dual-career path** recognizes that technical specialists can and should be allowed to contribute their expertise to a company without having to become managers. A dual-career approach is often established to encourage and motivate professionals in fields such as engineering, sales, marketing, finance, and human resources. Individuals in these fields can increase their specialized knowledge, make contributions to their firms, and be rewarded without entering management. Whether on the management or technical path, compensation would be comparable at each level. The dual system has been a trademark in higher education, where individuals can move through the ranks of instructor, assistant professor, associate professor, and professor without having to go into administration.

Adding Value to Your Career

Adding value to your career may appear to be totally self-serving, but nevertheless, it is a logical and realistic career path. In the rapidly changing world today, professional obsolescence can creep up on a person. What makes a person valuable in today's work environment is the knowledge and experience he or she brings to a job. An individual's knowledge must be ever expanding, and continual personal development is a necessity. The better an employee's qualifications, the greater the opportunities he or she has with the present firm and in the job market. A person must discover what companies need, then develop the skills necessary to meet these needs as defined by the marketplace. Individuals should always be doing something that contributes significant, positive change to the organization. If any vestige of job security exists, this is it. Basically, the primary tie that binds a worker to the company, and vice versa, is mutual success resulting in performance that adds value to the organization.

Demotion

demotion
Process of moving a worker to a lower level of duties and responsibilities, which typically involves a reduction in pay.

Demotion is the process of moving a worker to a lower level of duties and responsibilities, which typically involves a reduction in pay. Demotions have long been associated with failure, but limited promotional opportunities in the future and the fast pace of technological change may make demotion a legitimate career option. If the stigma of demotion can be removed, more employees, especially older workers, might choose to make such a move. Some people get into a position only to find their skills were better suited to their old job. Sometimes they decide they do not want to have as much responsibility because of things going on in their personal lives. Working long hours for limited promotional opportunity loses its appeal to some after a while, especially if the worker can financially afford the demotion. In certain instances, this approach might open up a clogged promotional path and at the same time permit a senior employee to escape unwanted stress without being viewed as a failure.

Free Agents (Being Your Own Boss)

free agents
People who take charge of all or part of their careers by being their own bosses or by working for others in ways that fit their particular needs or wants.

Free agents are people who take charge of all or part of their careers by being their own bosses or by working for others in ways that fit their particular needs or wants. Many became free agents because of company downsizing and have no desire or would have difficulty reentering the corporate world.[84] Some free agents work full-time; others work part-time. Others work full-time and run a small business in the hope of converting it into their primary work. Free agents come in many shapes and sizes, but what distinguishes them is a commitment to controlling part or all of their careers. They have a variety of talents and are used to dealing with a wide range of audiences and changing their approach on the spot in response to new information or reactions. They also tend to love challenges and spontaneity.[85]

Global Meetings through Telepresence

Business traveling is based on the belief that there is no substitute for reading the body language of the person in front of you. Rich Redelfs, a partner at the venture firm Foundation Capital said, "You want to look somebody in the eye and say, do I trust this person enough to write them a multimillion-dollar check? We feel we can do that with telepresence."[86]

Videoconferencing has been around for decades and has been greatly improved with the development of telepresence. It has been estimated that by 2015, companies will spend $5 billion on videoconferencing and telepresence.[87] Telepresence systems provide the illusion of sitting across a conference table from the individuals you are "meeting" and "looking them in the eye."[88] Until recently, the status of business travelers was measured by frequent-flier miles, their admission to VIP lounges, and names of famous people they met at conferences. For years, Irv Rothman, CEO of Hewlett-Packard's Financial Services division, flew at least once a quarter with his top three lieutenants from his New Jersey base to HP's Silicon Valley headquarters. After a six-and-a-half hour flight, he would meet with their boss, and then do it all over again. With telepresence, the flight time is eliminated.[89]

Telepresence systems are made by companies such as Polycom and Cisco Systems. Polycom immersive rooms range from $200,000 to $600,000 and require a service plan, while Cisco's telepresence suite starts at over $300,000.[90] Here is a description of how a telepresence videoconferencing system works. A telepresence facility generally has half a conference room with table and chairs. The other half of the table contains extra-large monitors displaying video feeds, creating the impression that participants are in the same room. In one unique application, participants in Scotland and England held a joint Christmas party.[91]

Starwood Hotels recently made its telepresence suite at the Sheraton on the Park in Sydney, Australia, available for public use. Rates run $500 per hour and since it is a hotel setting, the service is available 24 hours a day. Telepresence is especially important in Australia where long-distance travel is unavoidable. Telepresence addressed the continuing need to cut costs and increase productivity.[92] The future looks bright for telepresence and teleconferencing. Predictions are that future teleconferencing suites will be equipped with computer programs that can translate languages instantaneously, furthering conversations among associates who do not speak the same language.[93]

MyManagementLab

Go to **mymanagementlab.com** to complete the problems marked with this icon ⭐.

Summary

1. **Describe executive onboarding for external hires, define training and development, and explain factors influencing T&D.** Although considerable time, effort, and money are spent recruiting top talent, companies often do a poor job of onboarding. If an executive is coming in from another company, a great deal of attention needs to be paid to explaining how things work in the new environment. To succeed, new executives must understand the unwritten rules, processes, and networks that influence how things get done in the organization.

   Training is designed to permit learners to acquire knowledge and skills needed for their present jobs. *Development* involves learning that goes beyond today's job.

   There are numerous factors that both impact and are impacted by T&D including top management support, shortage of skilled workers, technological advances, world complexity, lifetime learning, learning styles, and other human resource functions.

2. **Describe the T&D process and explain the various T&D methods.** First, an organization must determine its specific training needs. Then specific objectives need to be established. After setting the T&D objectives, management can determine the appropriate methods and the delivery system to be used. Management must continuously evaluate T&D to ensure its value in achieving organizational objectives.

   Training and development methods include instructor-led training, e-learning, case study, behavior modeling, role-playing, training games, in-basket training, on-the-job training, and apprenticeship training.

3. **Explain mobile learning and describe training and development delivery systems.** *Mobile learning* is any learning that takes place via mobile or portable devices such as cell phones, personal digital assistants, tablets, media players, and e-readers. It can take place anywhere and does not require the learner to be at a fixed location.

   Delivery systems include corporate universities, colleges and universities, community colleges, online higher education, vestibule system, video media, and simulators.

4. **Describe management development, mentoring, coaching, and reverse mentoring.** *Management development*

consists of all learning experiences provided by an organization for the purpose of providing and upgrading skills and knowledge required in current and future managers.

Mentoring is an approach to advising, coaching, and nurturing for creating a practical relationship to enhance individual career, personal, and professional growth and development. *Coaching*, often considered a responsibility of the immediate boss, provides assistance much like a mentor.

Reverse mentoring is a process in which older employees learn from younger ones.

5. *Define* orientation *and explain implementing training and development programs.* *Orientation* is the guided adjustment of new employees to the company, the job, and the work group.

Implementing T&D programs is often difficult. One reason is that managers are typically action-oriented and feel that they are too busy for T&D. Training and development requires more creativity than perhaps any other human resource function.

6. *Explain the metrics for evaluating training and development.* Some possible metrics for evaluating training and development include participants' opinion, extent of learning, behavioral change, accomplishment of T&D objectives, return on investment from training, and benchmarking.

7. *Define* organization development (OD) *and describe various OD techniques.* *Organization development* is planned and systematic attempts to change the organization, typically to a more behavioral environment. OD techniques include survey feedback, a technique often combined with other interventions such as quality circles and team building.

8. *Distinguish between job security and career security.* *Job security* implies security in one job, often with one company. *Career security* requires developing marketable skills and expertise that help ensure employment within a range of careers.

9. *Describe career planning and explain career paths and career development.* *Career planning* is an ongoing process whereby an individual sets career goals and identifies the means to achieve them.

A *career path* is a flexible line of movement through which a person may travel during his or her work life.

Career development is a formal approach used by the organization to ensure that people with the proper qualifications and experiences are available when needed.

10. *Describe career development methods, identify various career paths, and explain global meetings through telepresence.* Career development methods include manager/employee self-service, discussions with knowledgeable individuals, company material, performance appraisal system, and workshops.

Career paths include traditional career path, network career path, lateral skill path, dual-career path, adding value to your career, demotion, and free agents.

Telepresence systems provide the illusion of sitting across a conference table from the individuals you are "meeting" and "looking them in the eye."

Key Terms

training and development (T&D)   166
training   166
development   166
learning organization   166
blended training   168
just-in-time training (on-demand
    training)   168
mobile learning (m-learning)   170
e-learning   171
case study   172
behavior modeling   172
role-playing   172
business games   173
in-basket training   173
on-the-job training (OJT)   173

apprenticeship training   173
corporate university   174
online higher education   174
vestibule system   175
simulators   175
management development   176
mentoring   176
coaching   178
reverse mentoring   178
orientation   178
benchmarking   180
organization development (OD)   181
survey feedback   181
quality circles   182
team building   182

job security   183
career security   183
career   184
career planning   184
self-assessment   184
strength/weakness balance sheet   184
likes and dislikes survey   186
career path   187
career development   187
traditional career path   189
network career path   189
lateral skill path   189
dual-career path   190
demotion   190
free agents   190

Exercises

1. What do you believe would be the best method(s) of training for the following jobs? Discuss.
    a. entry-level machine operator
    b. new assistant manager for a McDonald's restaurant
    c. salesperson for a new automobile dealership

2. What do you believe would be the best delivery system(s) for the above-listed jobs?

3. The Trends & Innovation in this chapter entitled "Mobile Learning" creates a situation in which the workplace of the future is quite different from that which existed in the past. What might be some pros and cons for using mobile learning in organizations?

Questions for Review

1. Define *training* and *development*.
2. What is a learning organization?
3. What are the steps in the T&D process?
4. What has caused the rapid growth in mobile learning?
5. What are the various training and development methods? Briefly describe each.
6. What are the various training and development delivery systems? Briefly describe each.
7. How is social networking used in informal training?
8. Define *management development*. Why is it important?
9. Distinguish between mentoring and coaching. What is reverse mentoring?
10. Define *orientation*, and explain the purposes of orientation.
11. What are some metrics for evaluating training and development?
12. What is the Workforce Investment Act?
13. Define each of the following:
    (a) organization development
    (b) survey feedback
    (c) quality circles
    (d) team building
14. Distinguish between job security and career security.
15. Define *career*. Why is it important for individuals to conduct career planning?
16. What is the process of developing a strength/weakness balance sheet?
17. How might the Web be used for self-assessment assistance? For career-planning assistance?
18. Why is it important for a firm to conduct career development?
19. What are some career development methods?
20. What are the various career paths that individuals may use?
21. What has caused the surge in the use of telepresence?

INCIDENT 1   Training at Keller-Globe

Lou McGowen was worried as she approached the training director's office. She supervises six punch press operators at Keller-Globe, a maker of sheet metal parts for the industrial refrigeration industry. She had just learned that her punch presses would soon be replaced with a continuous-feed system that would double the speed of operations. She was thinking about how the workers might feel about the new system when the training director, Bill Taylor, opened the door and said, "Come on in, Lou. I've been looking forward to seeing you."

After a few pleasantries, Lou told Bill of her concerns. "The operators really know their jobs now. But this continuous-feed system is a whole new ball game. I'm concerned, too, about how the workers will feel about it. The new presses are going to run faster. They may think that their job is going to be harder."

Bill replied, "After talking with the plant engineer and the production manager, I made a tentative training schedule that might make you feel a little better. I think we first have to let the workers know why this change is necessary. You know that both of our competitors changed to this new system last year. After that, we will teach your people to operate the new presses."

"Who's going to do the teaching?" Lou asked. "I haven't even seen the new system."

"Well, Lou," said Bill, "the manufacturer has arranged for you to visit a plant with a similar system. They'll also ship one of the punch presses in early so you and your workers can learn to operate it."

"Will the factory give us any other training help?" Lou asked.

"Yes, I have asked them to send a trainer down as soon as the first press is set up. He will conduct some classroom sessions and then work with your people on the new machine."

After further discussion about details, Lou thanked Bill and headed back to the production department. She was confident that the new presses would be a real benefit to her section and that her workers could easily learn the skills required.

Questions

1. Evaluate Keller-Globe's approach to training.
2. How might the use of social media assist Lou in training her employees?

INCIDENT 2   There's No Future Here!

"Could you come to my office for a minute, Bob?" asked Terry Geech, the plant manager.

"Sure, be right there," said Bob Glemson. Bob was the plant's quality control director. He had been with the company for four years. After completing his degree in mechanical engineering, he worked as a production supervisor and then as a maintenance supervisor prior to moving to his present job. Bob thought he knew what the call was about.

"Your letter of resignation catches me by surprise," began Terry. "I know that Wilson Products will be getting a good person, but we sure need you here, too."

"I thought about it a lot," said Bob, "but there just doesn't seem to be a future for me here."

"Why do you say that?" asked Terry.

"Well," replied Bob, "the next position above mine is yours. Since you're only 39, I don't think it's likely that you'll be leaving soon."

"The fact is that I *am* leaving soon," said Terry. "That's why it's even more of a shock to learn that you're resigning. I think I'll be moving to the corporate office in June of next year. Besides, the company has several plants that are larger than this one, and we need good people in those plants from time to time, both in quality control and in general management."

"Well, I heard about an opening in the Cincinnati plant last year," said Bob, "but by the time I checked, the job had already been filled. We never know about opportunities in the other plants until we read about the incumbent in the company paper."

"All this is beside the point now. What would it take to get you to change your mind?" asked Terry.

"I don't think I will change my mind now," replied Bob, "because I've given Wilson Products my word that I'm going to join them."

Questions

1. Evaluate the career planning and development program at this company.
2. What actions might have prevented Bob's resignation?

MyManagementLab

Go to **mymanagementlab.com** for Auto-graded writing questions as well as the following Assisted-graded writing questions:

7-1. Why is executive onboarding for external hires so difficult?

7-2. What are some factors that influence T&D?

7-3. Mymanagementlab Only – comprehensive writing assignment for this chapter.

Notes

1. Marilyn S. Nyman, "The Executive On-Boarding Challenge," *Industry Week* 259 (September 2010): 40–42.
2. "Four Keys to Effective Onboarding," *Healthcare Executive* 26 (November/December 2011): 44.
3. "'HP Matters' Says Incoming CEO Meg Whitman," *Channel Insider* (September 23, 2011): 1–2.
4. Randall S. Cheloha and Jacob Kumaresan, "On-Boarding a New Outside CEO," *Corporate Board* 32 (March/April 2011): 1–6.
5. Gail Dutton, "Training the Revolving-Door CEO," *Training* 47 (November/December 2010): 42–43.
6. Rita L. Fritz, "The First 100 Days: How to Accelerate the Learning Curve for Executives," *Healthcare Executive* 22 (November/December 2007): 8–14.
7. Stephanie Castellano, "OPM Establishes New Model for Executive Onboarding," *T+D* 66 (February 2012): 20.
8. Rich Cordivari, "From Training Company to Learning Organization," *T+D* 64 (January 2010): 60–63.
9. Emily Johnson, "Maximize Your Training Investment," *Collector* 77 (February 2012): 42–43.
10. Garry Kranz, "Training Wheels Back in Motion," *Workforce Management* 91 (January 2012): 4.
11. Gary Kranz, "More to Learn," *Workforce Management* 90 (January 2011): 27–30.
12. Dennis Seeds, "Scouting for Talent: What the Shortage in Skilled Manufacturing Workers Means to a Hungry Industry," *Smart Business Indianapolis* 8 (July 2011): 9–13.
13. Joanne L. Stewart, "Train for the Future," *T+D* 65 (July 2011): 54–57.
14. Matthew Kirchner, "The Number One Problem Facing Surface Finishers Today," *Products Finishing* 76 (January 2012): 45.
15. Drake Bennett, "Do the Unemployed Get a Second Act?" *Bloomberg Businessweek* (September 9, 2011): 64–70.
16. "The 21st Century Requires More Skilled Workers," *MWorld* 10 (Summer 2011): 17–19.
17. Fred E. Fanning, "Engaging Learners: Techniques to Make Training Stick," *Professional Safety* 56 (August 2011): 42–48.
18. "Using Your Clients' Learning Style to Close Sales," *Kitchen & Bath Design News* 30 (February 2012): 20.
19. Armin Hopp, "Soft Steps Towards Digital Learning," *Training Journal* (January 2012): 51–54.
20. Lance Dublin, "Finding the Right Learning Mix," *Chief Learning Officer* 10 (August 2011): 36–39.
21. Naomi Norman, "Mobile Learning Made Easy," *Learning Circuits* (January 2012): 3.
22. Bob Little, "Moving to a New Kind of Learning," *Training Journal* (July 2011): 24–27.
23. Eric Savitz and Bernardo Albergaria, "Telepresence for Everyone," *Forbes.com* (August 22, 2011): 33.
24. David Wentworth and Michael Green, "Mobile Learning: Anyplace, Anytime," *T+D* 65 (July 2011): 25.
25. Marissa Garff, "Implementing M-Learning: Make the Dream a Reality," *T+D* 66 (January 2012): 16.
26. Gary Kranz, "More to Learn," *Workforce Management* 90 (January 2011): 27–30.
27. Doug Stone, "Entering the Mobile Zone," *T+D* 64 (December 2010): 27–29.
28. "A Closer Look at E-learning: Expert Advice on Why Technology-based Training Works," *Industrial Safety & Hygiene News* 46 (January 2012): 56.
29. Greg Wright, "Retailers Buy Into E-Learning," *HR Magazine* 55 (December 2010): 87–90.
30. Gail Dutton, "Tech Check," *Training* 46 (January 2009): 24–26.
31. Michael A. Tucker, "E-Learning Evolves," *HR Magazine* 50 (October 2005): 74–78.
32. Margery Weinstein, "Is Technology Fulfilling Its Promise?" *Training* 48 (September/October 2011): 32–34.
33. Martyn Lewis, "Moving Into the Live Virtual Classroom," *T+D* 65 (July 2011): 76–77.

34. Pat Galagan, "Twitter as a Learning Tool, Really," *T+D* 63 (March 2009): 28–31.
35. Dave Zielinski, "Gaming for Engagement," *HR Magazine* 57 (January 2012): 16.
36. "Companies Are Using Team-Based Business Games to Increase Productivity, Expert Says," *CPA Practice Management Forum* 6 (2010): 22.
37. "Training Budgets Bounce Back: Where to Spend," *HR Specialist* 9 (March 2011): 1–5.
38. Brandon Hall, "Learning at Play," *Chief Learning Officer* 10 (May 2011): 18.
39. James Warren, "Develop a Strategy for Recruiting Future Employees," *Quality* 48 (October 2009): 40–43.
40. Peter B. Alpern, "Need Skilled Workers? Try Growing Your Own," *American Machinist* 153 (May 2009): 40–43.
41. Kathryn Tyler, "A New U," *HR Magazine* 57 (April 1, 2012): 27–34.
42. Pat Galagan, "Back to Bricks and Mortar," *T+D* 65 (March 2011): 30–31.
43. Laura Cohn, "Grad Degrees from a Distance," *Kiplinger's Personal Finance* 64 (August 2010): 49.
44. Ann Pace, "Higher Education: Paves the Way for New Career Opportunities," *T+D* 65 (September 2011): 74–77.
45. Elaine Pofeldt, "Make a Digital Degree Pay Off," *Money* 40 (June 2011): 32.
46. Jeff Griffin, "Simulator Provides Effective—And Fun—Training," *Underground Construction* 64 (August 2009): 16–18.
47. Euan Youdale, "Open View," *International Cranes & Specialized Transport* 19 (May 2011): 23–24.
48. Ladan Nikravan, "Back to Class," *Chief Learning Officer* 11 (January 2012): 18–21.
49. Daniel W. Bixby, "To Be Continued: Using Social Media for Training Conversations," *T+D* 64 (July 2010): 30–33.
50. Dave Zielinski, "Group Learning," *HR Magazine* 57 (May 2012): 49–52.
51. "Four Ways to Facilitate Informal Learning," *T+D* 66 (February 2012): 18.
52. Aparna Nancherla, "C-Level Boot Camp," *T+D* 64 (January 2010): 24.
53. Jazmine Boatman and Rich Wellins, "It's Time for a Leadership: [R]Evolution," *T+D* 65 (April 2011): 52–58.
54. Kristy Allen, "Mentoring Builds a Stronger Profession," *Charter* 81 (February 2010): 54.
55. Amy Alexander, "Mentoring Give-and-Take," *Investor's Business Daily* (January 24, 2012): 3.
56. Michael Laff, "The Guiding Hand: Mentoring Women," *T+D* 63 (September 2009): 32–35.
57. Christian Hamaker, "An Example in Their Youth," *Rural Telecom* 28 (September/October 2009): 9.
58. Richard R. Reilly and Karen Sobel Lojeski, "Leading the Dispersed Workforce," *Mechanical Engineering* 131 (November 2009): 30–34.
59. David Milliken, "Poised for Discovery," *T+D* 65 (August 2011): 70–71.
60. Angelia Chapin, "How to Get Your New Hires from Zero to 100 in Weeks," *Canadian Business* 83 (November 23, 2010): 72.
61. Paula Ketter, "Creative Instructional Design Equals Successful Learning Transfer," *T+D* 65 (July 2011): 10.
62. Pat Galagan, "Measure for Measure," *T+D* 65 (May 2011): 28–30.
63. Edward Trolley, "Lies About Learning," *Chief Learning Officer* 10 (June 2011): 82.
64. R. Wayne Mondy and Shane R. Premeaux, *Management: Concepts, Practices, and Skills,* 7th ed. (Englewood Cliffs, NJ, Prentice Hall, 1995): 497.
65. Byron Pope, "Toyota Says Quality Circles Still Paying Dividends," *Ward's Auto World* 44 (June 2008): 20.
66. Mike Donlin, "Take One for the Team," *Corporate Meetings & Incentives* 28 (August 2009): 26.
67. "Team Building Treachery," *Accountancy* 143 (March 2009): 20.
68. Kathryn Tyler, "Take New Employee Orientation off the Back Burner," *HR Magazine* 43 (May 1998): 49.
69. René Street, "We Move Forward as a Team," *Women in Business* 61 (December 2009/January 2010): 6.
70. Swati Karve, "Facilitation Skills: Using Training Games," *T+D* 65 (July 2011): 30–31.
71. Belinda Luscombe, "Getting Jumpy at Work," *Time International (South Pacific Edition)* 173 (May 25, 2009): 30.
72. Howard Prager, "Cooking Up Effective Team Building," *Training & Development* 53 (December 1999): 14–15.
73. Diane Brady and David Welch, "The Obsolete Jobs Club," *Bloomberg Businessweek* (February 6, 2012): 22–24.
74. "Cloud-Savvy IT Professionals See Abundant Opportunity," *Channel Insider* (January 9, 2012): 1.
75. Douglas Warshaw, Joan Caplin, and Tara Moore, "Pulling Off the Ultimate Career Makeover," *Fortune International (Europe)* 164 July 4, 2011): 40–49.
76. Rebecca Weingarten, "Thinking of Retiring? Not So Fast," *BusinessWeek Online* (March 26, 2009): 20.
77. John Mullins, "Career Planning the Second Time Around," *Occupational Outlook Quarterly* 53 (Summer 2009): 12–15.
78. Lewis Carroll, *Through the Looking Glass* (New York: Norton, 1971): 127.
79. http://www.careermaze.com/home.asp?licensee=CareerMaze
80. http://www.career-intelligence.com/about/about_career-intelligence.asp
81. http://www.careerkey.org/asp/your_personality/take_test.html
82. Ann Field, "Do Your Stars See a Reason to Stay?" *Harvard Management Update* 13 (June 2008): 3–5.
83. Beverly Kaye and C. Patrick Smith, "Career Development: Shifting from Nicety to Necessity," *T+D* 66 (January 2012): 52–55.
84. Julie Bos, "Top Trends in Staffing: Is Your Organization Prepared for What Lies Ahead?" *Workforce Management* 90 (February 2011): 33–38.
85. Thomas Lawrence, "Integrating Contingent Workers," *Baseline* 114 (January/February 2012): 3.
86. Drake Bennett, "I'll Have My Robots Talk to Your Robots," *Bloomberg Businessweek* (February 21, 2011): 52–61.
87. Lauren Brousell, "Things You Need to Know," *CIO* 24 (May 1, 2011): 26.
88. Scot Case, "Look Them in the Eye," *Government Procurement* 17 (August/September 2009): 26–28.
89. Michelle Conlin, "The Waning Days of the Road Warrior," *BusinessWeek* (June 2, 2008): 65–66.
90. "Will High-del 'Telepresence' Conferences Nix Need for Business Travel?" *Public Relations Strategist* 17 (Spring 2011): 7.
91. "The Twin-location Christmas Party with a Live Telepresence Link," *Conference & Incentive Travel* (June 2011): 29.
92. "Telepresence and Video Conferencing: The Business Case," *CIO* (August 9, 2010): 2.
93. Geoff Colvin, "Brave New Work: The Office of Tomorrow," *Fortune* 165 (January 16, 2012): 49–55.

8

Performance Management and Appraisal

HRM in Action Employee Engagement for a Committed Workforce

OBJECTIVE 8.1

Describe employee engagement, define *performance management*, and describe the importance of performance management.

employee engagement
Level of commitment workers make to their employer, seen in their willingness to stay at the firm and to go beyond the call of duty.

Employee engagement refers to the level of commitment workers make to their employer, seen in their willingness to stay at the firm and to go beyond the call of duty. The concept of engagement serves as a reminder that people ultimately drive an organization's success. Engagement is found in employees' minds, hearts, and hands. It evolves into the positive culture that exists within the organization.[1] Engaged workers want to come to work every day and do what is needed to get the job done right. "Engaged people feel good about coming to work every day," says Fred Lorestani, vice president of North American Implant Operations for Stryker.[2] They are like marathon runners who are in it for the long haul.[3]

The recent recession significantly impacted employee engagement as layoffs, pay cuts, and freezes caused employee engagement to decline. Some employers became complacent when fewer workers appeared to be getting the same job done as effectively and productively as they were before the recession. In such a climate, workers feel pressured to surpass normal production levels not because they want to but because they had to just to keep their jobs. However, if they are not truly engaged and all they are getting is a paycheck, they can get that elsewhere when the recession ends.[4] Watson Wyatt's Employee Engagement Index reported that in companies where layoffs occurred, the number of highly disengaged workers reached as high as 24 percent.[5] So if you have 10 employees, two or three of them are coming to work every day actively disengaged and working against the goals of the firm.[6] That is a frightening thought.

David Lacey, vice president of human resource business development at VIST Insurance, said, "Without an engaged workforce, a company is merely going through the motions instead of being a top performer."[7] Towers Perrin-ISR reports that companies with highly engaged workforces have an average of 19 percent higher net income and a slightly higher operating margin. This information provides a clear link between engagement and profitability.[8]

CHAPTER OBJECTIVES   After completing this chapter, students should be able to:

1. Describe employee engagement, define *performance management*, and describe the importance of performance management.

2. Define *performance appraisal* and identify the uses of performance appraisal.

3. Discuss the performance appraisal environmental factors, describe the performance appraisal process, and discuss whether or not a case can be made for getting rid of performance appraisals.

4. Identify the various performance criteria (standards) that can be established.

5. Identify who may be responsible for performance appraisal and explain the performance period.

6. Identify the various performance appraisal methods.

7. List the problems that have been associated with performance appraisal.

8. Explain the characteristics of an effective appraisal system.

9. Describe the legal implications of performance appraisal.

10. Explain how the appraisal interview should be conducted and discuss how performance appraisal is affected by a country's culture.

Colleen O'Neill, a senior partner at Mercer and the firm's talent leader in the United States and Canada, said, "Employee engagement reflects the total work experience, and a big part of it is how you are treated, what kind of work you do, and how you feel about your co-workers, bosses, and the general work environment."[9] An important relationship at work is between employees and their immediate supervisors. Supervisors can improve employee engagement by assigning workers to jobs that best use their skills and abilities, encouraging innovation, and trusting and respecting them.[10] Respected employees are more likely to be engaged employees.[11] In some companies managers are being evaluated based on their ability to maintain high levels of employee engagement. WD-40's President and Chief Executive Officer Garry Ridge said, "Holding managers accountable for employee engagement starts with identifying the business' strategic goals, then linking engagement to strategy."[12]

While virtually all companies say they value employee engagement, the most successful ones consistently monitor it. With some firms, engagement can be measured in terms of productivity and performance.[13] For instance, Best Buy can quantify the value of a one percent increase in engagement among employees at a particular store. At Best Buy the value is more than $100,000 in the store's annual operating income.[14] At highly successful Costco Wholesale Corporation, the issue of trust is addressed by the company's open door policy that permits employees to directly communicate with Costco's top executives. John Matthews, the company's senior vice president of human resources and risk management, said "Our employees are candid, and they tell us when we screw up."[15]

JetBlue monitors employee engagement monthly by asking employees annually on their hiring date if they would recommend the company.[16] Perhaps this is a major reason JetBlue received high customer satisfaction ratings in a 2011 *Consumer Reports*.[17]

performance management (PM)
Goal-oriented process directed toward ensuring that organizational processes are in place to maximize the productivity of employees, teams, and ultimately, the organization.

HR Web Wisdom

Performance Management
http://www.opm.gov/perform/ overview.asp

Office of Personnel Management Web site on performance management.

OBJECTIVE 8.2

Define *performance appraisal* and identify the uses of performance appraisal.

performance appraisal (PA)
Formal system of review and evaluation of individual or team task performance.

Performance Management

Performance management (PM) is a goal-oriented process directed toward ensuring that organizational processes are in place to maximize the productivity of employees, teams, and ultimately, the organization. It is a major player in accomplishing organizational strategy in that it involves measuring and improving the value of the workforce. PM includes incentive goals and the corresponding incentive values so that the relationship can be clearly understood and communicated. There is a close relationship between incentives and performance.

PM systems are one of the major focuses in business today. Although every HR function contributes to performance management, training, performance appraisal, and compensation appraisal play a more significant role. While performance appraisal occurs at a specific time, performance management is a dynamic, continuous process. Every individual in the organization is a part of the PM system. Every component of the system is integrated to ensure continuous organizational effectiveness. With PM, every worker's efforts should focus on achieving strategic goals. A well-developed job description is needed to determine whether performance expectations have been achieved. If workers' skills need improvement, additional training should be provided. In PM systems, training has a direct tie-in to achieving organizational effectiveness, as does pay and performance. A good PM system ensures that people make good, effective use of their time.

Performance management may be the single largest contributor to organizational effectiveness in recent years. An effective performance management system should be the responsibility of everyone in the organization starting with the CEO and moving throughout the entire organization because companies that disregard performance management do not prosper.[18]

Performance Appraisal

Performance appraisal (PA) is a formal system of review and evaluation of individual or team task performance. A critical point in the definition is the word *formal*, because in actuality, managers should be reviewing an individual's performance on a continuing basis.

PA is especially critical to the success of performance management. Although performance appraisal is but one component of performance management, it is a vital one, in that it directly reflects the organization's strategic plan. Although evaluation of team performance is critical when teams exist in an organization, the focus of PA in most firms remains on the individual employee. Regardless of the emphasis, an effective appraisal system evaluates accomplishments and initiates plans for development, goals, and objectives.

Performance appraisal is often a negative and dreaded activity.[19] It is a task that often seems to elude mastery. If this is so, why not just eliminate it? Actually, some managers might do just that *if* they did not need to provide feedback, encourage performance improvement, make valid decisions, justify terminations, identify training and development needs, and defend personnel decisions. Performance appraisal serves many purposes, and improved results and efficiency are increasingly critical in today's globally competitive marketplace. Therefore, abandoning the only program with *performance* in its name and *employees* as its focus would seem to be an ill-advised overreaction. On top of these considerations, managers must be concerned about legal ramifications. Developing an effective performance appraisal system has been and will continue to be a high priority for management.

Uses of Performance Appraisal

For many organizations, the primary goal of an appraisal system is to improve individual and organizational performance. There may be other goals, however. A potential problem with PA, and a possible cause of much dissatisfaction, is expecting too much from one appraisal plan. For example, a plan that is effective for developing employees may not be the best for determining pay increases. Yet, a properly designed system can help achieve organizational objectives and enhance employee performance. In fact, PA data are potentially valuable for virtually every human resource functional area.

Human Resource Planning

In assessing a firm's human resources, data must be available to identify those who have the potential to be promoted or for any area of internal employee relations. Through performance appraisal it may be discovered that there is an insufficient number of workers who are prepared to enter management. Plans can then be made for greater emphasis on management development. Succession planning is a key concern for all firms. A well-designed appraisal system provides a profile of the organization's human resource strengths and weaknesses to support this effort.

Recruitment and Selection

Performance evaluation ratings may be helpful in predicting the performance of job applicants. For example, it may be determined that a firm's successful employees (identified through performance evaluations) exhibit certain behaviors when performing key tasks. These data may then provide benchmarks for evaluating applicant responses obtained through the selection process. Also, in validating selection tests, employee ratings may be used as the variable against which test scores are compared. In this instance, determination of the selection test's validity would depend on the accuracy of appraisal results.

Training and Development

Performance appraisal should point out an employee's specific needs for training and development. For instance, if Pat Compton's job requires skill in technical writing and her evaluation reveals a deficiency in this factor, she may need additional training to overcome this shortcoming. If a firm finds that a number of first-line supervisors are having difficulty in administering disciplinary action, training sessions addressing this problem may be appropriate. By identifying deficiencies that adversely affect performance, T&D programs can be developed that permit individuals to build on their strengths and minimize their deficiencies. An appraisal system does not guarantee properly trained and developed employees. However, determining T&D needs is more precise when appraisal data are available.

Career Planning and Development

Career planning is an ongoing process whereby *an individual* sets career goals and identifies the means to achieve them. On the other hand, *career development* is a formal approach used by the organization to ensure that people with the proper qualifications and experiences are available when needed. Performance appraisal data is essential in assessing an employee's strengths and weaknesses and in determining the person's potential. Managers may use such information to counsel subordinates and assist them in developing and implementing their career plans.

Compensation Programs

Performance appraisal results provide a basis for rational decisions regarding pay adjustments. Most managers believe that you should reward outstanding job performance tangibly with pay increases. They believe that *the behaviors you reward are the behaviors you get*. Rewarding behaviors necessary for accomplishing organizational objectives is at the heart of a performance management system. To encourage good performance, a firm should design and implement a reliable performance appraisal system and then reward the most productive workers and teams accordingly. Creators of total rewards systems want to ensure that individual performance supports organizational objectives.

Internal Employee Relations

Performance appraisal data are also used for decisions in several areas of internal employee relations, including promotion, demotion, termination, layoff, and transfer. For example, an employee's performance in one job may be useful in determining his or her ability to perform another job on the same level, as is required in the consideration of transfers. Certainly, performance appraisal data is vital when promotions are considered or layoffs must be made. However, when the performance level is unacceptable, demotion or even termination may be appropriate.

Assessment of Employee Potential

Some organizations attempt to assess an employee's potential as they appraise his or her job performance. Although past behaviors may be a good predictor of future behaviors in some jobs, an employee's past performance may not accurately indicate future performance in other jobs. The best salesperson in the company may not have what it takes to become a successful district sales manager, where the tasks are distinctly different. Similarly, the best systems analyst may, if promoted, be a disaster as an information technology manager. Overemphasizing technical skills and ignoring other equally important skills is a common error in promoting employees into management jobs. Recognition of this problem has led some firms to separate the appraisal of performance, which focuses on past behavior, from the assessment of potential, which is future oriented.

OBJECTIVE **8.3**

Discuss the performance appraisal environmental factors, describe the performance appraisal process, and discuss whether or not a case can be made for getting rid of performance appraisals.

Performance Appraisal Environmental Factors

External and internal environmental factors can influence the appraisal process. For example, legislation requires that appraisal systems be nondiscriminatory. In the case of *Mistretta v Sandia Corporation* (a subsidiary of Western Electric Company, Inc.), a federal district court judge ruled against the company, stating, "There is sufficient circumstantial evidence to indicate that age bias and age based policies appear throughout the performance rating process to the detriment of the protected age group." The *Albemarle Paper v Moody* case also supported validation requirements for performance appraisals, as well as for selection tests. Organizations should avoid using any appraisal method that results in a disproportionately negative impact on a protected group.

The labor union is another external factor that might affect a firm's appraisal process. Unions have traditionally stressed seniority as the basis for promotions and pay increases. They may vigorously oppose the use of a management-designed performance appraisal system used for these purposes.

Factors within the internal environment can also affect the performance appraisal process. For instance, a firm's corporate culture can assist or hinder the process. Today's dynamic organizations, which increasingly use teams to perform jobs, recognize overall team results as well as individual contributions. A nontrusting culture does not provide the environment needed to encourage high performance by either individuals or teams. In such an atmosphere, the credibility of an appraisal system will suffer regardless of its merits.

Performance Appraisal Process

As shown in Figure 8-1, the starting point for the PA process is identifying specific performance goals. An appraisal system probably cannot effectively serve every desired purpose, so management should select the specific goals it believes to be most important and realistically achievable. For example, some firms may want to stress employee development, whereas other organizations may want to focus on pay adjustments. Too many PA systems fail because management expects too much from one method and does not determine specifically what it wants the system to accomplish.

FIGURE 8-1

Performance Appraisal Process

Can a Case Be Made for Getting Rid of Traditional Performance Appraisal?

Most managers do not like administering performance appraisal and employees do not like receiving them. One management guru, Edward Lawler, believes that performance appraisal systems neither motivate individuals nor effectively guide their development. Instead, he maintains, they create conflict between supervisors and subordinates and lead to poor behaviors.[20] Historically, the performance appraisal process involved managers telling workers what they wanted them to do, determining the degree to which the task was completed, and rewarding or punishing them based on how well the job was done. Today firms stress employee empowerment and engagement. They also want employees to work in teams to accomplish their duties. Teams, not managers, are often making the decisions, which runs counter to the traditional appraisal system.[21] There are those who believe that a firm cannot have an empowered and engaged workforce and still use a traditional performance appraisal system.

Perhaps one of the failures of the performance appraisal process lies in lack of ownership by line managers and employees. For line managers, performance appraisal is often one of the most dreaded chores of the job. For supervisors and workers alike, the yearly review is usually not viewed as a positive event.[22] It is often seen as a required practice having little real value and not a means of improving performance. Dan Walker, HR consultant and former chief talent officer at Apple Inc., does not believe in performance appraisal. He said, "What

if I told my kids that I was going to give them a once-a-year discussion on their behavior? Sometimes we do stupid things." Apple left it up to managers to assess performance anyway they saw fit, or not at all.[23]

At times, it appears that performance appraisal systems are developed for the wrong reasons. Often they are conducted out of habit and used only if it becomes necessary to fire an employee. Frequently the legal department encourages management to use the appraisal system to document poor performance. But, since managers find it difficult to provide constructive criticism, they often succumb and give poor performers unearned high scores.[24] Employees are happy and the manager does not have to be seen as the carrier of negative information. No problem exists unless the manager decides to fire a poor performer. Those same high performance evaluations could end up in court as evidence of discrimination.[25]

There may be a better way to conduct performance appraisal. Companies have developed performance management software to help employers automate and streamline performance reviews. Rypple's software is a goal-setting application that helps human resource managers give employees feedback about how they are performing. The software is used by such firms as Facebook, Gilt Group, Mozilla, and Rackspace.[26] Rypple's performance systems had the younger workers in mind when it developed its performance management system, which resembles a Facebook page. Jennifer Ricci, vice president of employee experience at Kobo, a Rypple Flow user, said, "With Rypple people can immediately recognize people in other departments and recognize collaboration on goals."[27] A person can quickly give feedback to anyone in his or her company with the Rypple system.

The next step in this ongoing cycle continues with establishing performance criteria (standards) and communicating these performance expectations to those concerned. Then the work is performed and the supervisor appraises the performance. At the end of the appraisal period, the appraiser reviews work performance and evaluates it against established performance standards. This review helps determine how well employees have met these standards, determines reasons for deficiencies, and develops a plan to correct the problems. At this meeting, goals are set for the next evaluation period, and the cycle repeats.

OBJECTIVE 8.4

Identify the various performance criteria (standards) that can be established.

Establish Performance Criteria (Standards)

There is an old adage that says "What gets watched gets done." Therefore, management must carefully select performance criteria as it pertains to achieving corporate goals.[28] The most common appraisal criteria are traits, behaviors, competencies, goal achievement, and improvement potential.

Traits, Behaviors, and Competencies

Traits, behaviors, and competencies are often used as performance appraisal standards. *Traits* are usually thought of as being biologically created. A personality trait is more ingrained with an individual as with a person being introverted or extroverted. Certain employee traits such as appearance and cognitive aptitude may be the basis for some evaluations.

Behaviors are typically viewed as resulting from life experiences. A behavior may have been learned from parents, from significant friends, or from a certain work environment. A behavior can be changed but traits are usually more established. Often a young person who joins the military will have many behavioral changes take place prior to returning to civilian life. An appropriate behavior to evaluate for a manager might be leadership style. For individuals working in teams, developing others, teamwork and cooperation, or customer service orientation might be appropriate. Desired behaviors may be appropriate as evaluation criteria because if they are recognized and rewarded, employees tend to repeat them. If certain behaviors result in desired outcomes, there is merit in using them in the evaluation process.

Competencies include a broad range of knowledge, skills, traits, and behaviors that are needed to perform a job successfully. They may be technical in nature, relate to interpersonal skills, or are business oriented. For example, analytical thinking and achievement orientation might be essential in professional jobs. In leadership jobs, relevant competencies might include developing talent, delegating authority, and people management skills. The competencies selected for evaluation purposes should be those that are closely associated with job success.

Many of these commonly used traits, behaviors, and competencies are subjective and may be either unrelated to job performance or difficult to define. In such cases, inaccurate evaluations may occur and create legal problems for the organization as well. This was the case in *Wade v Mississippi Cooperative Extension Service* where the circuit court ruled:

> *In a performance appraisal system, general characteristics such as leadership, public acceptance, attitude toward people, appearance and grooming, personal conduct, outlook on life, ethical habits, resourcefulness, capacity for growth, mental alertness, and loyalty to organization are susceptible to partiality and to the personal taste, whim, or fancy of the evaluator as well as patently subjective in form and obviously susceptible to completely subjective treatment by those conducting the appraisals.*

At the same time, certain traits, behaviors, and competencies may relate to job performance and, if this connection is established, using them may be appropriate.

Goal Achievement

If organizations consider *ends* more important than *means*, goal achievement outcomes become an appropriate factor to evaluate. The outcomes established should be within the control of the individual or team and should be those results that lead to the firm's success. At upper levels, the goals might deal with financial aspects of the firm such as profit or cash flow, and market considerations such as market share or position in the market. At lower organizational levels, the outcomes might be meeting the customer's quality requirements and delivering according to the promised schedule.

To assist the process, the manager needs to provide specific examples of how the employee can further his or her development and achieve specific goals. Both parties should reach an agreement as to the employee's goals for the next evaluation period and the assistance and resources the manager needs to provide. This aspect of employee appraisal should be the most positive element in the entire process and help the employee focus on behavior that will produce positive results for all concerned.

Improvement Potential

When organizations evaluate their employees' performance, many of the criteria used focus on the past. From a performance management viewpoint, the problem is that you cannot change the past. Unless a firm takes further steps, the evaluation data become merely historical documents. Therefore, firms should emphasize the future, including the behaviors and outcomes needed to develop the employee, and, in the process, achieve the firm's goals. This involves an assessment of the employee's potential. Including *potential* in the evaluation process helps to ensure more effective career planning and development.

You should remember that the evaluation criteria presented here are not mutually exclusive. In fact, many appraisal systems are hybrids of these approaches.

OBJECTIVE 8.5

Identify who may be responsible for performance appraisal and explain the performance period.

Responsibility for Appraisal

Often the human resource department is responsible for coordinating the design and implementation of performance appraisal programs. However, it is essential that line managers play a key role from beginning to end. These individuals usually conduct the appraisals, and they must directly participate in developing the program if it is to succeed. In a recent survey of 1,143 U.S. employees, 53 percent get feedback about their performance from their managers. But many would like to get an expanded view of their performance and receive input from others such as from peers, project leaders, and even clients.[29] Several possibilities exist with regard to the person(s) who will actually rate the employee.

Immediate Supervisor

An employee's immediate supervisor has traditionally been the most logical choice for evaluating performance, and this continues to be the case. The supervisor is usually in an excellent position to observe the employee's job performance, and the supervisor has the responsibility for managing a particular unit. When someone else has the task of evaluating subordinates, the supervisor's authority may be undermined. Also, subordinate training and development is an important element in every manager's job and, as previously mentioned, appraisal programs and employee development are usually closely related.

On the negative side, the immediate supervisor may emphasize certain aspects of employee performance and neglect others. Also, managers have been known to manipulate evaluations to justify pay increases and promotions and vice versa.

In most instances, the immediate supervisor will probably continue to be involved in evaluating performance. Organizations will seek alternatives, however, because of technological advances and a desire to broaden the perspective of the appraisal.

Subordinates

Historically, our culture has viewed evaluation by subordinates negatively. However, this thinking has changed somewhat. Some firms conclude that evaluation of managers by subordinates is both feasible and needed. They reason that subordinates are in an excellent position to view their superiors' managerial effectiveness. Advocates believe that this approach leads supervisors to become especially conscious of the work group's needs and to do a better job of managing. In the higher education environment, it is a common practice for instructors to be evaluated by students. Critics are concerned that managers (and instructors) will be caught up in a popularity contest or that employees will be fearful of reprisal. If this approach has a chance for success, one thing is clear: the evaluators must be guaranteed anonymity. Ensuring this might be particularly difficult in a small department and especially if demographic data on the appraisal form could identify raters.

Peers and Team Members

A major strength of using peers to appraise performance is that they work closely with the evaluated employee and probably have an undistorted perspective on typical performance, especially in team assignments. Problems with peer evaluations include the reluctance of some people who work closely together, especially on teams, to criticize each other. On the other hand, if an employee has been at odds with another worker, he or she might really "unload on the enemy," resulting in an unfair evaluation. Another problem concerns peers who interact infrequently and lack the information needed to make an accurate assessment.

Organizations are increasingly using teams, including those that are self-directed. Team members know each other's performance better than anyone and can, therefore, evaluate performance more accurately. Also, peer pressure is a powerful motivator for team members. In addition, members who recognize that peers within the team will be evaluating their work show increased commitment and productivity. When employees work in teams, and their appraisal system focuses entirely on individual results, it is not surprising that they show little interest in their teams. But, this problem can be corrected. If teamwork is essential, make it a criterion for evaluating employees; rewarding collaboration will encourage teamwork.

Self-Appraisal

If employees understand their objectives and the criteria used for evaluation, they are in a good position to appraise their own performance. Many people know what they do well on the job and what they need to improve. If they have the opportunity, they will criticize their own performance objectively and take action to improve it. Many times employees are tougher on themselves than the supervisor will be. Also, because employee development is self-development, employees who appraise their own performance may become more highly motivated. Self-appraisal provides employees with a means of keeping the supervisor informed about everything they have done during the appraisal period.[30]

Even if a self-appraisal is not a part of the system, the employee should at least provide the manager a list of his or her most important accomplishments and contributions over the appraisal period. This will prevent the manager from being blindsided when the employee complains, perhaps justifiably, "You didn't even mention the Bandy contract I landed last December!"

As a complement to other approaches, self-appraisal has great appeal to managers who are primarily concerned with employee participation and development. For compensation purposes, however, its value is considerably less. Some individuals are masters at attributing good performance to their own efforts and poor performance to someone else's.

Customer Appraisal

Customer behavior determines a firm's degree of success. Therefore, some organizations believe it is important to obtain performance input from this critical source. Organizations use this approach because it demonstrates a commitment to the customer, holds employees accountable, and fosters change. Customer-related goals for executives generally are of a broad, strategic nature, whereas targets for lower-level employees tend to be more specific. For example, an objective might be to improve the rating for accurate delivery or reduce the number of dissatisfied customers by half. It is important to have employees participate in setting their goals and to include only factors that are within the employees' control.

Performance Appraisal for Telecommuters

Telecommuting is a work arrangement whereby employees are able to remain otherwise away from the office and perform their work using computers and other electronic devices that connect them with their offices. When conducting performance appraisal for telecommuters, there are some general guidelines to follow to ensure that employees who are not in the office are not treated differently. Certainly there should be a well-defined understanding of job roles and performance measures. Telecommuters should have objective measurements that apply to all employees. Employers must take care not to vary the performance standards and metrics for virtual workers who have job duties that are similar to those of office-based counterparts.[31]

Appraisal Period

Formal performance evaluations are usually prepared at specific intervals. Although there is nothing magical about the period for formal appraisal reviews, in most organizations they occur either annually or semiannually. Even more significant, however, is the continuous interaction (primarily informal), including coaching and other developmental activities, that continues throughout the appraisal period. Managers should be conditioned to understand that managing performance is a continuous process that is built into their job every day.

In the current business climate, firms may want to consider monitoring performance more often. Changes occur so fast that employees need to look at objectives and their own roles throughout the year to see whether changes are in order. Southwest Airlines has asked its managers to have monthly check-ins with staff rather than semiannual ones.[32] Employees with Royal Caribbean Cruises are evaluated approximately three weeks prior to the completion of their contract, which is typically six months.

Some organizations use the employee's date of hire to determine the rating period. At times a subordinate's first appraisal may occur at the end of a probationary period, anywhere from 30 to 90 days after his or her start date. However, in the interest of consistency, it may be advisable to perform evaluations on a calendar basis rather than on anniversaries. If firms do not conduct all appraisals at the same time, it may be impossible to make needed comparisons between employees.

OBJECTIVE **8.6**

Identify the various performance appraisal methods.

Choosing a Performance Appraisal Method

Managers may choose from among a number of appraisal methods. The type of performance appraisal system chosen depends on its purpose. If the major emphasis is on selecting people for promotion or merit pay increases, a traditional method, such as rating scales, may be appropriate.

Collaborative methods, such as the 360-degree feedback method, include input from the employees themselves and may prove to be more suitable for training and development.

The various methods are next presented as if they are separate and distinct when in actuality each may be used in conjunction with another method. For instance, the 360-degree feedback method may incorporate portions of the ranking scale and even the essay method.

360-Degree Feedback Evaluation Method

The **360-degree feedback evaluation method** is a popular performance appraisal method that involves evaluation input from multiple levels within the firm as well as external sources.

The 360-degree method is unlike traditional performance reviews, which provide employees with feedback only from supervisors. The 360-degree feedback provides an all-inclusive view of each employee.[33] In this method, people all around the rated employee may provide ratings, including senior managers, the employee himself or herself, supervisors, subordinates, peers, team members, and internal or external customers. As many as 90 percent of *Fortune* 500 companies use some form of 360-degree feedback for either employee evaluation or development. Many companies use results from 360-degree programs not only for conventional applications but also for succession planning, training, and professional development.[34]

Unlike traditional approaches, 360-degree feedback focuses on skills needed across organizational boundaries. Also, by shifting the responsibility for evaluation to more than one person, many of the common appraisal errors can be reduced or eliminated. Software is available to permit managers to give the ratings quickly and conveniently. The 360-degree feedback method may provide a more objective measure of a person's performance. Including the perspective of multiple sources results in a more comprehensive and fair view of the employee's performance by minimizing biases resulting from limited views of performance.[35]

Having multiple raters also makes the process more legally defensible. However, it is important for all parties to know the evaluation criteria, the methods for gathering and summarizing the feedback, and the use to which the feedback will be put. An appraisal system involving numerous evaluators will naturally take more time and, therefore, be more costly. Nevertheless, the way firms are being organized and managed may require innovative alternatives to traditional top-down appraisals.

In a recent survey of training participants, 84 percent said their 360-degree experience was useful.[36] However, some managers believe that the 360-degree feedback method has problems. GE's former CEO Jack Welch maintains that the 360-degree system in his firm had been "gamed" and that people were saying nice things about one another, resulting in all good ratings.[37] Another critical view with an opposite twist is that input from peers, who may be competitors for raises and promotions, might intentionally distort the data and sabotage the colleague. Yet, since so many firms use 360-degree feedback evaluation, it seems that many firms have found ways to avoid the pitfalls.

The biggest risk with 360-degree feedback is confidentiality. Many firms outsource the process to make participants feel comfortable that the information they share and receive is completely anonymous. Information is very sensitive and, in the wrong hands, could impact careers.

Rating Scales Method

The **rating scales method** is a performance appraisal method that rates employees according to defined factors.

Using this approach, evaluators record their judgments about performance on a scale. The scale includes several categories; normally five to seven in number, defined by adjectives such as *outstanding, meets expectations*, or *needs improvement*. Although systems often provide an overall rating, the method generally allows for the use of more than one performance criterion. One reason for the popularity of the rating scales method is its simplicity, which permits quick evaluations of many employees. When you quantify the ratings, the method facilitates comparison of employees' performances.

The factors chosen for evaluation are typically of two types: job-related and personal characteristics. Note that in Figure 8-2, job-related factors include quality and quantity of work, whereas personal factors include such behaviors as interpersonal skills and traits, such as *adaptability*. The rater (evaluator) completes the form by indicating the degree of each factor that is most descriptive of the employee and his or her performance. In this illustration, evaluators total

FIGURE 8-2

Rating Scales Method of Performance Appraisal

Performance Factors	Needs Improvement (1) (Unacceptable)	Below Expectations (2) (Marginal)	Meets Expectations (3) (Normal)	Exceeds Expectations (4)	Clearly Outstanding (5)
Judgment					
Initiative					
Creativeness					
Problem Solving					
Interpersonal Skills					
Job Knowledge					
Leadership Ability					
Adaptability					
Attitude					
Quality of Work					
Quantity of work					

Total Points_____

Comments:

Performance goals for next appraisal period:

- _____
- _____
- _____

Self-development activities for this employee

- _____
- _____
- _____

_____   _____   _____
Employee's Signature   Date   Rating Supervisor's Signature

and then average the points. The final score (total points) for the employee is the total of each section's points. Then, each employee's total can be compared to all employees in the unit to determine how he or she relates.

Some firms provide space for the rater to comment on the evaluation given for each factor. This practice may be especially encouraged, or even required, when the rater gives an extreme rating, either the highest or lowest. For instance, if an employee is rated *needs improvement* on any of the evaluation factors, the rater provides written justification for this low evaluation. The purpose of this requirement is to focus on correcting deficiencies and to discourage arbitrary and hastily made judgments.

The more precise the definition of factors and degrees, the more accurately the rater can evaluate worker performance. For instance, to receive a *clearly outstanding* rating for a factor such as *quality of work*, a person must consistently go beyond the prescribed work requirements. When the various performance levels are described merely as *clearly outstanding* or *needs improvement* without further elaboration, what has the employee really learned? These generalities do not provide the guidance needed for improving performance. It is important that each rater interpret the factors and degrees in the same way. Raters acquire this ability through performance appraisal training. Many rating scale forms also provide for consideration of future behavior. Notice that the form shown in Figure 8-2 has space for performance goals and self-development activities for the next appraisal period.

Critical Incident Method

The **critical incident method** is a performance appraisal method that requires keeping written records of highly favorable and unfavorable employee work actions.

When such an action, a "critical incident," affects the department's effectiveness significantly, either positively or negatively, the manager writes it down. At the end of the appraisal period, the rater uses these records along with other data to evaluate employee performance. With this method, the appraisal is more likely to cover the entire evaluation period and not focus on the past few weeks or months.

Essay Method

The **essay method** is a performance appraisal method in which the rater writes a brief narrative describing the employee's performance.

This method tends to focus on extreme behavior in the employee's work rather than on routine day-to-day performance. Ratings of this type depend heavily on the evaluator's writing ability. Supervisors with excellent writing skills, if so inclined, can make a marginal worker sound like a top performer. Comparing essay evaluations might be difficult because no common criteria exist. However, some managers believe that the essay method is not only the most simple but also an acceptable approach to employee evaluation.

Work Standards Method

The **work standards method** is a performance appraisal method that compares each employee's performance to a predetermined standard or expected level of output.

Standards reflect the normal output of an average worker operating at a normal pace. Firms may apply work standards to virtually all types of jobs, but production jobs generally receive the most attention. An obvious advantage of using work standards as appraisal criteria is objectivity. However, for employees to perceive that the standards are objective, they should understand clearly how the standards were set. Management must also explain the rationale for any changes to the standards.

Ranking Method

The **ranking method** is a performance appraisal method in which the rater ranks all employees from a group in order of overall performance.

For example, the best employee in the group is ranked highest, and the poorest is ranked lowest. You follow this procedure until you rank all employees. A difficulty occurs when all individuals have performed at comparable levels (as perceived by the evaluator).

Paired comparison is a variation of the ranking method in which the performance of each employee is compared with that of every other employee in the group. A single criterion, such as overall performance, is often the basis for this comparison. The employee who receives the greatest number of favorable comparisons receives the highest ranking.

Some professionals in the field argue for using a comparative approach, such as ranking, whenever management must make human resource decisions. They believe that employees are promoted or receive the highest pay increases not because they achieve their objectives, but rather because they achieve them better than others in their work group.

Forced Distribution Method

The **forced distribution method** of performance appraisal requires the rater to assign individuals in a work group to a limited number of categories, similar to a normal frequency distribution. The purpose of forced distribution is to keep managers from being excessively lenient and having a disproportionate number of employees in the "superior" category.[38]

Forced distribution systems have been around for decades and firms such as General Electric, Cisco Systems, EDS, Hewlett-Packard, Microsoft, Pepsi, Caterpillar, Sun Microsystems, Goodyear, Ford Motor, and Capital One use them today.[39] Proponents of forced distribution believe they facilitate budgeting and guard against weak managers who are too timid to get rid of poor performers. They think that forced rankings require managers to be honest with workers about how they are doing.

The forced distribution systems tend to be based on three levels. In GE's system, the best performers are placed in the top 20 percent, the next group in the middle 70 percent, and the poorest performing group winds up in the bottom 10 percent. The underperformers are, after being given a time to improve their performance, generally let go.

Although used by some prestigious firms, the forced distribution system appears to be unpopular with many managers.[40] Some believe it fosters cutthroat competition, paranoia, and general ill will, and destroys employee loyalty.[41] Many believe that a "rank-and-yank" system such as forced distribution is not compatible when a company encourages teamwork. Critics of forced distribution contend that they compel managers to penalize a good, although not a great, employee who is part of a superstar team. Another reason employees are opposed to forced ranking is that they suspect that the rankings are a way for companies to rationalize firings more easily.

Behaviorally Anchored Rating Scale Method

The **behaviorally anchored rating scale (BARS) method** is a performance appraisal method that combines elements of the traditional rating scales and critical incident methods; various performance levels are shown along a scale with each described in terms of an employee's specific job behavior.

Table 8-1 illustrates a portion of a BARS system that was developed to evaluate college recruiters. Suppose the factor chosen for evaluation is *Ability to Present Positive Company Image*. On the *very positive* end of this factor would be "Makes excellent impression on college recruits. Carefully explains positive aspects of the company. Listens to applicant and answers questions in a very positive manner." On the *very negative* end of this factor would be "Even with repeated instructions continues to make a poor impression. This interviewer could be expected to turn off college applicant from wanting to join the firm." As may be noted, there are several levels in between the very negative and the very positive. The rater is able to determine more objectively how frequently the employee performs in each defined level.

A BARS system differs from rating scales because, instead of using terms such as *high*, *medium*, and *low* at each scale point, it uses behavioral anchors related to the criterion being measured. This modification clarifies the meaning of each point on the scale and reduces rater bias and error by anchoring the rating with specific behavioral examples based on job analysis

HR Web Wisdom

Appraisal News
http://www.performance-appraisal.com/home.htm

Performance appraisal news and general PA information is provided.

TABLE 8-1

BARS for Factor: Ability to Present Positive Company Image

Clearly Outstanding Performance:	Makes excellent impression on college recruits. Carefully explains positive aspects of the company. Listens to applicant and answers questions in a very positive manner.
Excellent Performance:	Makes good impression on college recruits. Answers all questions and explains positive aspects of the company. Answers questions in a positive manner.
Good Performance:	Makes a reasonable impression on college recruits. Listens to applicant and answers questions in knowledgeable manner.
Average Performance:	Makes a fair impression on college recruits. Listens to applicant and answers most questions in a knowledgeable manner.
Slightly Below Average Performance:	Attempts to make a good impression on college recruits. Listens to applicants but at times could be expected to have to go to other sources to get answers to questions.
Poor Performance:	At times makes poor impression on college recruits. Sometimes provides incorrect information to applicant or goes down blind avenues before realizing mistake.
Very Poor Performance:	Even with repeated instructions continues to make a poor impression. This interviewer could be expected to turn off college applicant from wanting to join the firm.

information. Instead of providing a space for entering a rating figure for a category such as *Above Expectations*, the BARS method provides examples of such behavior. This approach facilitates discussion of the rating because it addresses specific behaviors, thus overcoming weaknesses in other evaluation methods. Regardless of apparent advantages of the BARS method, reports on its effectiveness are mixed. A specific deficiency is that the behaviors used are activity oriented rather than results oriented. Also, the method may not be economically feasible since each job category requires its own BARS. Yet, among the various appraisal techniques, the BARS method is perhaps the most highly defensible in court because it is based on actual observable job behaviors.

Results-Based System

results-based system
Performance appraisal method in which the manager and subordinate jointly agree on objectives for the next appraisal period; in the past a form of *management by objectives.*

The manager and subordinate jointly agree on objectives for the next appraisal period in a **results-based system**, in the past a form of *management by objectives* (MBO). Although all aspects of an MBO system did not work effectively, there were sections that remain as part of an effective appraisal system.

The crucial phase of the MBO process requires that challenging but attainable objectives and standards be established through interaction between superiors and subordinates. Individuals jointly established objectives with their superiors, who then give them some latitude in how to achieve the objectives. Action plans require clear delineation of what specifically is to be accomplished and when it is to be completed. For example, if a sales manager has a performance objective of increasing sales in his or her area by 38 percent next year, the action plan might include the employment of three experienced salespersons, six calls a week by the sales manager on major customers, and assignment of appropriate sales quotas to all the salespeople.

With MBO, performance is evaluated on the basis of progress toward objective attainment. Having specific performance objectives provides management with a basis for comparison. When objectives are agreed on by the manager and the subordinate, self-evaluation and controls become possible. In fact, with MBO, performance appraisal can be a joint effort, based on mutual agreement.

With MBO, it is left up to the managers to take corrective action when results are not as planned. Such action may take the form of changes in personnel, changes in the organization, or even changes in the objectives. Other forms of corrective action may include providing additional training and development of individual managers or employees to enable them to better achieve the desired results. Corrective action should not necessarily have negative connotations. Under MBO, objectives can be renegotiated downward without penalty or fear of job loss. Various segments of the MBO process can easily be integrated into an effective *results-based system.*

OBJECTIVE 8.7

List the problems that have been associated with performance appraisal.

Problems in Performance Appraisal

As indicated in the previous "Trends & Innovations," performance appraisal is constantly under a barrage of criticism. The rating scales method seems to be the most vulnerable target. Yet, in all fairness, many of the problems commonly mentioned are not inherent in this method but, rather, reflect improper implementation. The following section highlights some of the more common problem areas.

Appraiser Discomfort

Conducting performance appraisals is often a frustrating task for managers. If a performance appraisal system has a faulty design, or improper administration, employees will dread receiving appraisals and the managers will despise giving them. In fact, some managers have always loathed the time, paperwork, difficult choices, and discomfort that often accompanies the appraisal process. Going through the procedure cuts into a manager's high-priority workload and the experience can be especially unpleasant when the employee in question has not performed well.

Lack of Objectivity

A potential weakness of traditional performance appraisal methods is that they lack objectivity. In the rating scales method, for example, commonly used factors such as traits, behaviors, and competencies are often difficult to measure. In addition, these factors may have little to do with an employee's job performance. Although subjectivity will always exist in appraisal methods, employee appraisal based primarily on personal characteristics may place the evaluator and the company in untenable positions with the employee and equal employment opportunity guidelines. The firm may be hard-pressed to show that some of these factors are job related.

Halo/Horn Error

A **halo error** occurs when a manager generalizes one positive performance feature or incident to all aspects of employee performance, resulting in an excessively high rating.[42]

For example, Rodney Pirkle, accounting supervisor, placed a high value on neatness, a factor used in the company's performance appraisal system. As Rodney was evaluating the performance of his senior accounting clerk, Jack Hicks, he noted that Jack was a very neat individual and gave him a high ranking on this factor. Also, consciously or unconsciously, Rodney permitted the high ranking on neatness to carry over to other factors, giving Jack undeserved high ratings on all factors. Of course, if Jack had not been neat, the opposite could have occurred. This phenomenon is known as the **horn error**, an evaluation error that occurs when a manager generalizes one negative performance feature or incident to all aspects of employee performance, resulting in a lower rating.

Leniency/Strictness

Giving undeserved high ratings to an employee is referred to as **leniency**. This behavior is often motivated by a desire to avoid controversy over the appraisal. However, leniency provides a false sense of confidence to the employee and diminishes exceptional performance by other workers. It is most prevalent when highly subjective (and difficult to defend) performance criteria are used, and the rater is required to discuss evaluation results with employees. When managers know they are evaluating employees for administrative purposes, such as pay increases, they are likely to be more lenient than when evaluating performance to achieve employee development. Leniency, however, may result in failure to recognize correctable deficiencies. The practice may also deplete the merit budget and reduce the rewards available for superior employees. Rather than confronting employees whose performance is not acceptable, a managers may avoid the situation by giving "false positive" performance evaluations. An organization may find itself in a difficult situation when after firing a problem employee, the recent excellent performance evaluation shows up as part of a lawsuit.[43] Rating an employee as outstanding and then firing him or her because of poor performance will make a supervisor look foolish if taken to court.

Being unduly critical of an employee's work performance is referred to as **strictness**. Although leniency is usually more prevalent than strictness, some managers, on their own initiative, apply an evaluation more rigorously than the company standard. This behavior may be due to a lack of understanding of various evaluation factors. The worst situation is when a firm has both lenient and strict managers and does nothing to level the inequities. Here, the weak performers get relatively high pay increases and promotions from a lenient boss, whereas the strict manager shortchanges the stronger employees. This can have a demoralizing effect on the morale and motivation of the top-performing people.

Central Tendency

Central tendency error is an evaluation appraisal error that occurs when employees are incorrectly rated near the average or middle of a scale. This practice may be encouraged by some rating scale systems that require the evaluator to justify in writing extremely high or extremely low ratings. With such a system, the rater may avoid possible controversy or criticism by giving only average ratings. However, since these ratings tend to cluster in the *fully satisfactory* range, employees do not often complain. Nevertheless, this error does exist and it influences the accuracy of evaluations. Typically, when pay raises are given, they will be based on an employee's rated performance. When a manager gives an underachiever or overachiever an average rating, it undermines the compensation system.[44]

Recent Behavior Bias

Anyone who has observed the behavior of young children several weeks before Christmas can readily identify with the problem of recent behavior bias. Suddenly, the wildest kids in the neighborhood develop angelic personalities in anticipation of the rewards they hope to receive from

Old Saint Nick. Individuals in the workforce are not children, but they are human. Virtually every employee knows precisely when a performance review is scheduled. Although his or her actions may not be conscious, an employee's behavior often improves and productivity tends to rise several days or weeks before the scheduled evaluation. It is only natural for a rater to remember recent behavior more clearly than actions from the more distant past. Therefore, managers need to track a worker's performance over the entire time covered by the performance review.[45]

Personal Bias (Stereotyping)

This pitfall occurs when managers allow individual differences to affect the ratings they give. If there are factors to avoid such as gender, race, or age, not only is this problem detrimental to employee morale, but it is obviously illegal and can result in costly lawsuits. The effects of cultural bias, or stereotyping, can definitely influence appraisals.[46] Managers establish mental pictures of what are considered ideal typical workers, and employees who do not match this picture may be unfairly judged. While all people have biases of some type that can affect the appraisal process, a successful evaluator will manage these biases.[47]

Prejudice in appraisal can be based on other factors as well. For example, mild-mannered employees may be appraised more harshly because they do not seriously object to the results. This type of behavior is in sharp contrast to the more outspoken employee, who often confirms the adage: *the squeaky wheel gets the grease.*

Manipulating the Evaluation

In some instances, managers control virtually every aspect of the appraisal process and are therefore in a position to manipulate the system. For example, a supervisor may want to give a pay raise to a certain employee or the supervisor may just "favor" one worker more than another. To justify this action, the supervisor may give the employee an undeserved high performance evaluation and perhaps a less favored, but productive, employee a lower rating.[48] Or, the supervisor may want to get rid of an employee and so may give the individual an undeserved low rating. In either instance, the system is distorted and the goals of performance appraisal cannot be achieved. In addition, in the latter example, if the employee is a member of a protected group, the firm may wind up in court. If the organization cannot adequately support the evaluation, it may suffer significant financial loss.

Employee Anxiety

The evaluation process may also create anxiety for the appraised employee.[49] This may take the form of discontent, apathy, and turnover. In a worst-case scenario, a lawsuit is filed based on real or perceived unfairness. Opportunities for promotion, better work assignments, and increased compensation may hinge on the results. This could cause not only apprehension, but also outright resistance. One opinion is that if you surveyed typical employees, they would tell you performance appraisal is management's way of highlighting all the bad things they did all year.

OBJECTIVE **8.8**

Explain the characteristics of an effective appraisal system.

Characteristics of an Effective Appraisal System

The basic purpose of a performance appraisal system is to improve the performance of individuals, teams, and the entire organization. The system may also serve to assist in making administrative decisions concerning pay increases, promotions, transfers, or terminations. In addition, the appraisal system must be legally defensible. Although a perfect system does not exist, every system should possess certain characteristics. The following factors assist in accomplishing these purposes.

Job-Related Criteria

Job-relatedness is perhaps the most basic criterion needed in employee performance appraisals. The evaluation instrument should tie in closely to the accomplishment of organizational goals.[50] The *Uniform Guidelines on Employee Selection Procedures* and court decisions are quite clear on this point. More specifically, evaluation criteria should be determined through job analysis. Subjective factors, such as initiative, enthusiasm, loyalty, and cooperation may be important; however, unless clearly shown to be job related, they should not be used.

Abdication of Responsibility

You are the new vice president for human resources of a company that has not been performing well, and everyone, including yourself, has a mandate to deliver results. The pressure has never been greater. Shareholders are angry after 31 months of a tough market that has left their stock underwater. Many shareholders desperately need stock performance to pay for their retirement. Working for you is a 52-year-old manager with two kids in college. In previous evaluations, spineless executives told him he was doing fine, when he clearly was not, and his performance is still far below par.

If you are to show others in the company that you are willing to make tough decisions, you feel you must fire this individual. The question is who's going to suffer: the firm and ultimately shareholders whose retirements are in jeopardy, or a nice guy who's been lied to for 20 years.

What would you do?
What factor(s) in this ethical dilemma might influence a person to make a less-than-ethical decision?

Performance Expectations

Subordinates must understand in advance what is expected of them. How can employees function effectively if they do not know what they are being measured against? On the other hand, if employees clearly understand the expectations, they can evaluate their own performance and make timely adjustments as they perform their jobs, without having to wait for the formal evaluation review. The establishment of highly objective work standards is relatively simple in many areas, such as manufacturing, assembly, and sales. For numerous other types of jobs, however, this task is more difficult. Still, evaluation must take place based on clearly understood performance expectations.

Standardization

Firms should use the same evaluation instrument for all employees in the same job category who work for the same supervisor. Supervisors should also conduct appraisals covering similar periods for these employees. Regularly scheduled feedback sessions and appraisal interviews for all employees are essential. Most large companies require groups of supervisors to come together to standardize employee performance reviews. They hash out the rationale behind each employee's performance rating and adjust them to ensure that they reflect similar standards and expectations.[51]

Formal documentation of appraisal data serves several purposes, including protection against possible legal action. Employees should sign their evaluations. If the employee refuses to sign, the manager should document this behavior. Records should also include a description of employee responsibilities, expected performance results, and the role these data play in making appraisal decisions. Although performance appraisal is important for small firms, they are not expected to maintain performance appraisal systems that are as formal as those used by large organizations. Courts have reasoned that objective criteria are not as important in firms with only a few employees because in smaller firms top managers are more intimately acquainted with their employees' work.

Trained Appraisers

A common deficiency in appraisal systems is that the evaluators seldom receive training on how to conduct effective evaluations. Unless everyone evaluating performance receives training in the art of giving and receiving feedback, the process can lead to uncertainty and conflict. The training should be an ongoing process in order to ensure accuracy and consistency. It should cover how to rate employees and how to conduct appraisal interviews. Instructions should be rather detailed and the importance of making objective and unbiased ratings should be emphasized.

Continuous Open Communication

Most employees have a strong need to know how well they are performing. A good appraisal system provides highly desired feedback on a continuing basis. There should be few surprises in the performance review. However, in one survey, only 45 percent of individuals felt their managers consistently communicated their performance concerns throughout the year.[52] Managers should handle daily performance problems as they occur and not allow them to pile up for six months or a year and then address them during the performance appraisal interview. When something new surfaces during the appraisal interview, the manager probably did not do a good enough job communicating with the employee throughout the appraisal period. Even though the interview presents an excellent opportunity for both parties to exchange ideas, it should never serve as a substitute for the day-to-day communication and coaching required by performance management.

Conduct Performance Reviews

In addition to the need for continuous communication between managers and their employees, a special time should be set for a formal discussion of an employee's performance. Since improved performance is a common goal of appraisal systems, withholding appraisal results is absurd. Employees are severely handicapped in their developmental efforts if denied access to this information. A performance review allows them to detect any errors or omissions in the appraisal, or an employee may disagree with the evaluation and want to challenge it.

Constant employee performance documentation is vitally important for accurate performance appraisals. Although the task can be tedious and boring for managers, maintaining a continuous record of observed and reported incidents is essential in building a useful appraisal. The appraisal interview will be discussed in a later section.

Due Process

Ensuring due process is vital. If the company does not have a formal grievance procedure, it should develop one to provide employees an opportunity to appeal appraisal results that they consider inaccurate or unfair. They must have a procedure for pursuing their grievances and having them addressed objectively.

OBJECTIVE 8.9
Describe the legal implications of performance appraisal.

Legal Implications

Employee lawsuits may result from negative evaluations. Employees often win these cases, thanks in part to the firm's own performance appraisal procedures. A review of court cases makes it clear that legally defensible performance appraisal systems should be in place. Perfect systems are not expected, and the law does not preclude supervisory discretion in the process. However, the courts normally require an absence of adverse impact on members of protected classes or validation of the process. It also expects a system that keeps one manager from directing or controlling a subordinate's career. There should also be a system whereby the appraisal is reviewed and approved by someone or some group in the organization. Another requirement is that the evaluator must have personal knowledge of the employee's job performance. In addition, the system uses predetermined norms that limit the manager's discretion.

Mistakes in appraising performance and decisions based on invalid results can have serious repercussions. For example, discriminatory merit pay increases have resulted in costly legal action. In settling cases, courts have held employers liable for back pay, court costs, and other costs related to training and promoting certain employees in protected classes. Further, giving higher-than-earned evaluations and then firing an employee may set the stage for a suit, especially if the individual is a member of a protected group. The seemingly inconsistency may give the employee a basis for claiming discrimination.[53]

An employer may also be vulnerable to a *negligent retention* claim if an employee who continually receives unsatisfactory ratings in safety practices, for example, is kept on the payroll and he or she causes injury to a third party. In these instances, firms might reduce their liability if they provide substandard performers with training designed to overcome the deficiencies.

It is unlikely that any appraisal system will be immune to legal challenge. However, systems that possess the characteristics discussed above are more legally defensible. At the same time, they can provide a more effective means for achieving performance management goals.

Appraisal Interview

The appraisal interview is the Achilles' heel of the entire evaluation process. In fact, appraisal review sessions often create hostility and can do more harm than good to the employee–manager relationship. To minimize the possibility of hard feelings, the face-to-face meeting and the written review must have performance improvement, not criticism, as their goal. The reviewing manager must use all the tact he or she can muster in discussing areas needing improvement. Managers should help employees understand that they are not the only ones under the gun. Rating managers should emphasize their own responsibility for the employee's development and commitment for support.

The appraisal interview definitely has the potential for confrontation and undermining the goal of motivating employees. The situation improves considerably when several sources provide input, including perhaps the employee's own self-appraisal. Regardless of the system used, employees will not trust a system they do not understand.

Scheduling the Interview

Supervisors usually conduct a formal appraisal interview at the end of an employee's appraisal period. It should be made clear to the employee as to what the meeting is about.[54] Employees typically know when their interview should take place, and their anxiety tends to increase if their supervisor delays the meeting. Interviews with top performers are often pleasant experiences for all concerned. However, supervisors may be reluctant to meet face-to-face with poor performers. They tend to postpone these anxiety-provoking interviews.

Interview Structure

A successful appraisal interview should be structured in a way that allows both the supervisor and the subordinate to view it as a problem-solving rather than a fault-finding session. The manager has several purposes when planning an appraisal interview. Certainly the employee's performance should be discussed, focusing on specific accomplishments.[55] Also, the employee should be assisted in setting goals and personal-development plans for the next appraisal period. The manager should suggest means for achieving established goals, including support from the manager and firm. For instance, a worker may receive an average rating on a factor such as *quality of production*. In the interview, both parties should agree to the specific improvement needed during the next appraisal period and specific actions that each should take.[56]

During performance reviews, managers might ask employees whether their current duties and roles are effective in achieving their goals. In addition to reviewing job-related performance, they might also discuss subjective topics, such as career ambitions. For example, in working on a project, perhaps an employee discovered an unrealized aptitude. This awareness could result in a new goal or serve as a springboard to an expanded role in the organization.

The amount of time devoted to an appraisal interview varies considerably with company policy and the position of the evaluated employee. Although costs are a consideration, there is merit in conducting separate interviews for discussing (1) employee performance and development and (2) pay. Many managers have learned that as soon as the topic of pay emerges in an interview, it tends to dominate the conversation, with performance improvement taking a back seat. For this reason, if pay increases or bonuses are involved in the appraisal, it might be advisable to defer those discussions for one to several weeks after the appraisal interview.

Use of Praise and Criticism

Some managers believe that they should focus only on negative items. However, focusing only on weaknesses has the potential to damage relationships with subordinates.[57] No one wants a lengthy interview where they are constantly bombarded with criticism. A person might reason that "If I am this bad, I had better find another job."

As suggested earlier, conducting an appraisal interview requires tact and patience on the part of the evaluator. Praise is appropriate when warranted, but it can have limited value if not clearly deserved. If an employee must eventually be terminated because of poor performance, a manager's false praise could bring into question the "real" reason for being fired.

Criticism, even if warranted, is especially difficult to give. The employee may not perceive it as being constructive. It is important that discussions of these sensitive issues focus on the deficiency, not the person. Effective managers minimize threats to the employee's self-esteem whenever possible. When giving criticism, managers should emphasize the positive aspects of performance; criticize actions, not the person; and ask the employee how he or she would change things to improve the situation. Also, the manager should avoid supplying all the answers and try to turn the interview into a win–win situation so that all concerned gain.

Employees' Role

From the employees' side, two weeks or so before the review, they should go through their diaries or files and make a note of all projects worked on, regardless of whether or not they were successful.[58] The best recourse for employees in preparing for an appraisal review is to prepare a list of creative ways they have solved problems with limited resources. They will look especially good if they can show how their work contributes to the value of the company. This information should be on the appraising manager's desk well before the review. Reminding managers of information they may have missed should help in developing a more objective and accurate appraisal.

Concluding the Interview

Ideally, employees will leave the interview with positive feelings about management, the company, the job, and themselves. If the meeting results in a deflated ego, the prospects for improved performance will be bleak. Although you cannot change past behavior, future performance is another matter. The interview should end with specific and mutually agreed-upon plans for the employee's development. Managers should assure employees who require additional training that it will be forthcoming and that they will have the full support of their supervisor. When management does its part in employee development, it is up to the individual to perform in an acceptable manner.

A GLOBAL PERSPECTIVE

Performance Appraisal versus a Country's Culture

Performance appraisal is an area of human resource management that has special problems when translated into different countries' cultural environments. The use of performance appraisal in the United States is relatively new compared to many older countries. Here, formal performance appraisal came into systematic use toward the beginning of the 20th century. However, performance appraisal in China has evolved over many centuries. As early as the third century A.D., Sin Yu, Chinese philosopher, criticized a biased rater employed by the Wei dynasty saying, "The Imperial Rater of Nine Grades seldom rates men according to their merits but always according to his likes and dislikes."[59]

Chinese managers often have a different idea about what performance is than do Western managers, as Chinese companies tend to focus appraisals on different criteria. Chinese managers appear to define performance in terms of personal characteristics, such as loyalty and obedience, rather than outcome measurement. Chinese performance appraisals place great emphasis on moral characteristics. On the other hand, Western performance appraisal seeks to help achieve organizational objectives, and this is best obtained by concentrating on individual outcomes and behaviors that are related to the attainment of those objectives.[60]

Culture also plays a significant role in the success and failure of performance appraisal systems in the Middle East. In the Middle East there is a view called *wasta*, which significantly affects how business is conducted. Wasta refers to using mutual favors instead of merit to get things done. Because wasta implies reciprocity, it remains entrenched in society, and it has a major effect on human resources, especially performance appraisal. Wasta affects many aspects of HR such as selection and promotions since friendship and family connections is the criteria used instead of merit.[61]

Summary

1. *Describe employee engagement, define* **performance management,** *and describe the importance of performance management.* *Employee engagement* refers to the level of commitment workers make to their employer, seen in their willingness to stay at the firm and to go beyond the call of duty.

   Performance management is a goal-oriented process that is directed toward ensuring that organizational processes are in place to maximize productivity of employees, teams, and ultimately, the organization.

   Performance management systems are one of the major focuses in business today. With PM, the effort of each and every worker should be directed toward achieving strategic goals.

2. *Define* **performance appraisal** *and identify the uses of performance appraisal.* *Performance appraisal* is a system of review and evaluation of individual or team task performance.

   Performance appraisal data are potentially valuable for use in numerous human resource functional areas, including human resource planning, recruitment and selection, training and development, career planning and development, compensation programs, internal employee relations, and assessment of employee potential.

3. *Discuss the performance appraisal environmental factors, describe the performance appraisal process, and discuss whether or not a case can be made for getting rid of performance appraisals.* Legislation requires that appraisal systems be nondiscriminatory. Unions have traditionally stressed seniority as the basis for promotions and pay increases. A firm's corporate culture can assist or hinder the process.

   The identification of specific goals is the starting point for the PA process and the beginning of a continuous cycle. Then job expectations are established with the help of job analysis. The next step involves examining the actual work performed. Performance is then appraised. The final step involves discussing the appraisal with the employee.

   Edward Lawler noted the considerable documentation showing that performance appraisal systems neither motivate individuals nor effectively guide their development.

4. *Identify the various performance criteria (standards) that can be established.* The most common appraisal criteria are traits, behaviors, competencies, goal achievement, and improvement potential.

5. *Identify who may be responsible for performance appraisal and explain the performance period.* People who are usually responsible for performance appraisal include immediate supervisors, subordinates, peers and team members, self-appraisal, and customer appraisal.

   Formal performance evaluations are usually prepared at specific intervals. Although there is nothing magical about the period for formal appraisal reviews, in most organizations they occur either annually or semiannually.

6. *Identify the various performance appraisal methods.* Performance appraisal methods include 360-degree feedback evaluation, rating scales, critical incidents, essay, work standards, ranking, forced distribution, behaviorally anchored rating scales, and results-based approaches.

7. *List the problems that have been associated with performance appraisal.* The problems associated with performance appraisals include appraiser discomfort, lack of objectivity, halo/horn error, leniency/strictness, central tendency, recent behavior bias, personal bias (stereotyping), manipulating the evaluation, and employee anxiety.

8. *Explain the characteristics of an effective appraisal system.* Characteristics include job-related criteria, performance expectations, standardization, trained appraisers, continuous open communication, conduct performance reviews, and due process.

9. *Describe the legal implications of performance appraisal.* A review of court cases makes it clear that legally defensible performance appraisal systems should be in place. Perfect systems are not expected, and the law does not preclude supervisory discretion in the process. However, systems that possess certain characteristics are more legally defensible.

10. *Explain how the appraisal interview should be conducted and discuss how performance appraisal is affected by a country's culture.* A successful appraisal interview should be structured in a way that allows both the supervisor and the subordinate to view it as a problem-solving rather than a fault-finding session.

    Performance appraisal is an area of human resource management that has special problems when translated into different countries' cultural environments. The use of performance appraisal in the United States is relatively new compared to many older countries. Here, formal performance appraisal came into systematic use toward the beginning of the 20th century. However, performance appraisal in other countries has evolved over many centuries and is strongly affected by a country's culture.

Key Terms

employee engagement   196
performance management (PM)   198
performance appraisal (PA)   198
360-degree feedback evaluation
    method   205
rating scales method   205
critical incident method   207

essay method   207
work standards method   207
ranking method   207
forced distribution method   207
behaviorally anchored rating scale
    (BARS) method   208

results-based system   209
halo error   210
horn error   210
leniency   210
strictness   210
central tendency error   210

Exercises

1. The Trends & Innovations in the chapter entitled "Can a Case Be Made for Getting Rid of Traditional Performance Appraisal?" provides an argument to eliminate the use of performance appraisal. Do you accept or reject the suggestion that performance appraisals should not be used? Be prepared to defend your decision.
2. Visit an HR manager in your local area. What performance appraisal method does this firm use? Ask how well the performance appraisal method is accepted in the organization.

3. Your performance appraisal uses a rating form with the following characteristics: leadership, public acceptance, attitude toward people, appearance and grooming, personal conduct, outlook on life, ethical habits, resourcefulness, capacity for growth, mental alertness, and loyalty to organization. Could any of these characteristics pose a problem with regard to a legal challenge? Why? Discuss.

Questions for Review

1. Define *performance management* and *performance appraisal*.
2. What are the uses of performance appraisal?
3. What environmental factors affect performance appraisal?
⭐ 4. What are some reasons that people give for getting rid of performance appraisal?
5. What are the steps in the performance appraisal process?
6. What aspects of a person's performance might an organization evaluate?
7. Many different people can conduct performance appraisals. What are the various alternatives?
8. What appraisal intervals are often used in appraisal reviews?
9. Briefly describe each of the following methods of performance appraisal:
    (a) 360-degree feedback evaluation
    (b) rating scales
    (c) critical incidents

(d) essay
(e) work standards
(f) ranking
(g) forced distribution
(h) behaviorally anchored rating scales
(i) results-based systems
10. What are the various problems associated with performance appraisal? Briefly describe each.
⭐11. What are the legal implications of performance appraisal?
⭐12. Explain why the following statement is often true: "The *Achilles' heel* of the entire evaluation process is the appraisal interview itself."
⭐13. How might different countries' cultures view performance appraisal?

INCIDENT 1   These Things Are a Pain

"There, at last it's finished," thought Rajiv Chaudhry, as he laid aside the last of 12 performance appraisal forms. It had been a busy week for Rajiv, who supervises a road maintenance crew for the Georgia Department of Highways.

In passing through Rajiv's district a few days earlier, the governor had complained to the area superintendent that repairs were needed

on several of the highways. Because of this, the superintendent assigned Rajiv's crew an unusually heavy workload. In addition, Rajiv received a call from the human resource office that week reminding him that the performance appraisals were late. Rajiv explained his predicament, but the HR specialist insisted that the forms be completed right away.

Looking over the appraisals again, Rajiv thought about several of the workers. The performance appraisal form had places for marking *quantity of work*, *quality of work*, and *cooperativeness*. For each characteristic, the worker could be graded *outstanding*, *good*, *average*, *below average*, or *unsatisfactory*. As Rajiv's crew had completed all of the extra work assigned for that week, he marked every worker *outstanding* in *quantity of work*. He marked Joe Blum *average* in *cooperativeness* because Joe had questioned one of his decisions that week. Rajiv had decided to patch a pothole in one of the roads, and Joe thought the small section of road surface ought to be broken out and replaced. Rajiv didn't include this in the remarks section of the form, though. As a matter of fact, he wrote no remarks on any of the forms.

Rajiv felt a twinge of guilt as he thought about Roger Short. He knew that Roger had been goofing off, and the other workers had been carrying him for quite some time. He also knew that Roger would be upset if he found that he had been marked lower than the other workers. Consequently, he marked Roger the same to avoid a confrontation. "Anyway," Rajiv thought, "these things are a pain, and I really shouldn't have to bother with them."

As Rajiv folded up the performance appraisals and put them in the envelope for mailing, he smiled. He was glad he would not have to think about performance appraisals for another six months.

Questions

1. What weaknesses do you see in Rajiv's performance appraisals?
2. Should HR have the ability to "insist that the forms be completed right away"? Discuss.
3. Many managers would agree with Rajiv in saying that "these things are a pain, and I really shouldn't have to bother with them." What are the disadvantages in doing away with performance appraisal?

INCIDENT 2   Performance Appraisal?

As the production supervisor for Sweeny Electronics, Nakeisha Joseph was generally well regarded by most of her subordinates. Nakeisha was an easygoing individual who tried to help her employees in any way she could. If a worker needed a small loan until payday, she would dig into her pocket with no questions asked. Should an employee need some time off to attend to a personal problem, Nakeisha would not dock the individual's pay; rather, she would take up the slack herself until the worker returned.

Everything had been going smoothly, at least until the last performance appraisal period. One of Nakeisha's workers, Bill Overstreet, had been experiencing a large number of personal problems for the past year. Bill's wife had been sick much of the time, and her medical expenses were high. Bill's son had a speech impediment, and the doctors had recommended a special clinic. Bill, who had already borrowed the limit the bank would loan, had become upset and despondent over his circumstances.

When it was time for Bill's annual performance appraisal, Nakeisha decided she was going to do as much as possible to help him. Although Bill could not be considered more than an average worker, Nakeisha rated him outstanding in virtually every category. Because the firm's compensation system was heavily tied to performance appraisal, Bill would be eligible for a merit increase of 10 percent in addition to a regular cost-of-living raise.

Nakeisha explained to Bill why she was giving him such high ratings, and Bill acknowledged that his performance had really been no better than average. Bill was very grateful and expressed this to Nakeisha. As Bill left the office, he was excitedly looking forward to telling his work buddies about what a wonderful boss he had. Seeing Bill smile as he left gave Nakeisha a warm feeling.

Questions

1. From Sweeny Electronics' standpoint, what difficulties might Nakeisha's performance appraisal practices create?
2. What can Nakeisha do now to diminish the negative impact of her evaluation of Bill?
3. Might a forced distribution performance appraisal system overcome the problem that Nakeisha has created? Discuss.

MyManagementLab

Go to **mymanagementlab.com** for Auto-graded writing questions as well as the following Assisted-graded writing questions:

8-1. Why is employee engagement so important to a firm?

8-2. What are the characteristics of an effective appraisal system?

8-3. Mymanagementlab Only – comprehensive writing assignment for this chapter.

Notes

1. Ronald J. Alsop, "Cultural Awareness," *Workforce Management* 90 (July 2011): 42.
2. Jennifer Robison, "Boosting Engagement at Stryker," *Gallup Management Journal Online* (January 5, 2012): 1.
3. Gretchen Spreitzer and Christined Porath, "Creating Sustainable Performance," *Harvard Business Review* 90 (January/February 2012): 92–99.
4. Robert R. Hasting, "Expert: Too Many Employees Have 'Checked Out,'" *HR News* (August 11, 2011): 1.
5. Tom Roth, "How-to Lead Employee Engagement," *Training* 47 (July/August 2010): 12.
6. Michelle Sterling, "Want to Enhance Employee Engagement? Ask Three Critical Questions," *MWorld* 10 (Spring 2011): 25–27.
7. Vasishtha Preeti, "Why You Need an Employee-Retention Program," *Advisor Today* 104 (August 2009): 60.
8. Mark Shearon, "The Cost of Employee Disengagement Can't Wait," *MWorld* 10 (Spring 2011): 44–47.
9. Phaedra Brotherton, "Employee Loyalty Slipping Worldwide; Respect, Work-Life Balance Are Top Engagers," *T+D* 66 (February 2012): 24.
10. "Employee Engagement Correlates to Career Advancement and Training," *T+D* 65 (February 2011): 21.
11. Jack Wiley, "Give Employees What They Want? Absolutely!" *Supervision* 73 (February 2012): 14–17.
12. Michael A. Tucker, "Make Managers Responsible," *HR Magazine* 57 (March 2012): 75–78.
13. Sue Elsworth, "Achieving a New Level of Employee Engagement," *Human Resources Magazine* 16 (June/July 2011): 6–7.
14. Ross McCammon, "Approval Ratings," *Entrepreneur* 40 (February 2012): 16–18.
15. Garry Kranz, "Losing Life Blood," *Workforce Management* 90 (July 2011): 25–28.
16. Thomas H. Davenport, Jeanne Harris, and Jeremy Shapiro, "Competing on Talent Analytics," *Harvard Business Review* 88 (October 2010): 52–58.
17. "Best & Worst Airlines," *Consumer Reports* 76 (June 2011): 19.
18. Ann Pace, "The Performance Management Dilemma," *T+D* 65 (July 2011): 22.
19. "Resolve Conflict: Conduct Performance Reviews Without Rancor," *Managing People at Work* (January 2012): 8.
20. Edward E. Lawler III, "Performance Management: The Next Generation," *Compensation & Benefits Review* 26 (May/June 1994): 16.
21. Barry Johnson and Mandy Geal, "Is Performance Appraisal Valid?" *Training Journal* (October 2010): 49–53.
22. Jeffrey Russell and Linda Russell, "Talk Me Through It: The Next Level of Performance Management," *T+D* 64 (April 2010): 42–48.
23. Rita Pyrillis, "The Reviews Are In," *Workforce Management* 90 (May 2011): 20–25.
24. Brad Bjelke, "Performance Review Nightmares," *Smart Business Orange County* 6 (September 2011): 18.
25. Jathan Janove, "Reviews—Good for Anything?" *HR Magazine* 56 (June 2011): 121–126.
26. "Salesforce.com Acquires HR Software Maker," *Channel Insider* (December 16, 2011): 1.
27. Timio Geron, "Rypple Flow Is Social HR Management on a Big Screen," *Forbes.com* (August 24, 2011).
28. Hugh J. Watson and Jim Hill, "What Gets Watched Gets Done: How Metrics Can Motivate," *Business Intelligence Journal* 14 (2009): 4–7.
29. "U.S. Employees Desire More Sources of Feedback for Performance Reviews," *T+D* 66 (February 2012): 18.
30. Joan Lloyd, "Performance Reviews Never Easy," *Receivables Report for America's Health Care Financial Managers* 24 (March 2009): 8–10.
31. Bill Leonard, "Managing Virtual Teams," *HR Magazine* 56 (June 2011): 38–42.
32. Jena McGregor, "The Midyear Review's Sudden Impact," *BusinessWeek* (July 6, 2009): 50–52.
33. Kyle Couch, "Talent Management," *Leadership Excellence* 29 (February 2012): 18.
34. G. N. Salunke, "Colleagues, Managers, Customers and Competitors Keys to Development: 360 Degree Approach to Development," *Advances in Management* 3 (August 2010): 32–35.
35. Jean Fagan, "What Can It Do for Medical Group Practices?" *Physician Executive* 37 (May/June 2011): 85–87.
36. "Full-Circle Assessments," *Training* 47 (November/December 2010): 7.
37. John F. Welch Jr., *Jack: Straight from the Gut* (New York: Warner Business Books, 2001): 157–158.
38. D.G., "Driving the Truth Into Performance Management," *Conference Board Review* 45 (September/October 2008): 42.
39. Stephen Garcia, "Forced Rankings of Employees Bad for Business," *Machine Design* 79 (September 13, 2007): 4–5.
40. Anita Flynn, "Performance Reviews—A Test of Leadership," *Supervision* 72 (January 2011): 14–15.
41. Liz Ryan, "Ten Management Practices to Throw Overboard in 2012," *BusinessWeek.com* (January 23, 2012): 1.
42. "Writing and Giving Job Reviews: 8 Do's and Don'ts," *HR Specialist* 8 (February 2010): 6.
43. "10 HR Mistakes Your Employee's Lawyer Will Try to Exploit," *HR Specialist: Texas Employment Law* 7 (January 2012): 4.
44. Tom Krattenmaker, "Appraising Employee Performance in a Downsized Organization," *Harvard Management Update* 14 (May 2009): 3–5.
45. Leigh Sujanto, "Performance Anxiety," *Charter* 82 (April 2011): 24–26.
46. Jeffrey Pfeffer, "Low Grades for Performance Reviews," *BusinessWeek* (August 8, 2009): 68.
47. Eric Krell, "An Impartial Review," *HR Magazine* 56 (October 2011): 97–99.
48. Adrienne Fox, "Curing What Ails Performance Reviews," *HR Magazine* 54 (January 2009): 52–56.
49. Sarah Raj, "How to Impress at Appraisals," *Enterprise Innovation* 6 (December 2010/January 2011): 40–41.
50. Nishchae Suri, "Career Journal: Making Performance Appraisals More Effective," *Wall Street Journal Online* (April 29, 2011).
51. Rebecca R. Hastings, "Most Large Companies Calibrate Performance, Poll Finds," *HR Magazine* 57 (February 2012): 87.
52. Alexandra Bradley, "Taking the Formality Out of Performance Reviews," *T+D* 64 (June 2010): 18.

53. Jonathan A. Segal, "The Dirty Dozen Performance Appraisal Errors," *BusinessWeek.com* (January 17, 2011): 2.

54. "Addressing Performance Problems: 7 Steps to Success," *HR Specialist* 7 (October 2009): 6.

55. "Cite Specifics," *Communication Briefings* 29 (April 2010): 6.

56. "Performance Prep," *Communication Briefings* 29 (March 2010): 9.

57. Rick Wartzman, "Yes, You Can Make Performance Reviews Worthwhile," *BusinessWeek.com* (April 11, 2011): 4.

58. Charlene Kesee, "Toot Your Horn…Loudly," *OfficePro* 70 (March/April 2010): 14–17.

59. Harouna Saibou, "Performance Appraisal in the Public Sector in Niger," *International Journal of Business & Management* 6 (June 2011): 263–266.

60. Paul S. Hempel, "Differences between Chinese and Western Managerial Views of Performance," *Personnel Review* 30 (2001): 203–226.

61. Antonio Giangreco, Andrea Carugati, Massimo Pilati, and Antonio Sebastiano, "Performance Appraisal Systems in the Middle East: Moving Beyond Western Logics," *European Management Review* 7 (2010): 155–168.

Part Five
Compensation

9 Direct Financial Compensation

HRM in Action

Executive Pay as a Lightning Rod for Criticism

OBJECTIVE 9.1

Discuss executive pay as a lightning rod for criticism, define *compensation*, and describe the various forms of compensation.

For some time now, executive pay for the nation's highest-paid chief executives, including salary, bonuses, perks, and stock options, has been a lightning rod for criticism and debate.[1] In fact, every day there seems to be another story related to excessive executive pay. The AFL-CIO has even set up an Executive PayWatch Web site. According to the site, CEOs of the top 299 companies in the Standard & Poor's 500 Index received, on average, $11.4 million in total compensation in 2011. That is 343 times the average worker's median pay of $33,190.[2] Other studies have estimated the pay difference as even higher. No matter what figure is chosen, it is evident that the pay gap between the most affluent executives and the average worker has become enormous. It is difficult for workers who make $12 to $18 an hour to appreciate why these executives merit such large salaries. This obvious disparity has caused considerable discussion regarding the proper ratio of CEO compensation to that of the average worker.[3] Peter Drucker, the famous management author, once said, "I have often advised managers that a 20-to-1 salary ratio between senior executives and rank-and-file white-collar workers is the limit beyond which they cannot go if they don't want resentment and falling morale to hit their companies."[4]

The outrage over excesses has focused heavily on Wall Street. Extreme examples have occurred all too often. Merrill Lynch paid former CEO E. Stanley O'Neal $87 million in the five years through 2006, much in incentive pay, for posting record profits by becoming a top mortgage securities player. O'Neal's leadership ultimately led to $40 billion in write-downs and Merrill's sale to Bank of America. He was permitted to step down keeping his pay and collecting an additional $136 million.[5] Occidental Petroleum chief Ray Irani received a five-year total compensation of $127,447,000. In 2006, thanks to a rise in oil prices and the company's payment scheme, Irani took home a total of $460 million. In 2010 he took home nearly $59 million in salary, perks, bonuses, and other stock awards.[6] Some CEOs, like Michael Jefferies of Abercrombie & Fitch, took home more pay, despite the fact that their businesses did so badly that their stocks fell and they laid off many employees.[7] The question of what is excessive compensation has emerged as the number one concern of shareholders.

There continues to be attempts to hold down executive salaries. However, sometimes it appears as though as soon as one compensation loophole is filled, another one emerges. IRS rules, for instance, state that performance-based compensation does not count toward the $1 million maximum deduction that companies can take on compensation paid to top executives. Thus, there was an explosion in bonuses and deferred compensation. Once that loophole was defused, another one was found. IRS restrictions are relaxed once an executive has left the firm, so there was an increase in generous postretirement perks.[8] Many believe the Dodd–Frank Act will have a significant impact on excessive executive compensation.[9] Its effect on say on pay, golden parachutes, and clawback policies will be discussed in the Trends & Innovation later in the chapter. However, a recent survey found average CEO total compensation increased 39 percent in 2010, while average total shareholder return equaled only 25 percent, and average net income increased 30 percent.[10] And some CEOs still receive compensation packages that most would perceive as excessive. Larry Ellison, CEO of Oracle, has accepted more than $60 million in stock options every year since 2008. Apple's new CEO Tim Cook got a package worth $378 million for his first year.[11]

The compensation of CEO Paul Stebbins of World Fuel Services provides an excellent example of tying compensation to performance results. Under his executive pay plan almost all compensation is tied to the financial performance of the company. Restricted stock is tied to annual net income growth. Stock appreciation rights (similar to stock options) are linked to three-year earnings-per-share growth. He also has $23 million, two-thirds of his net worth, tied up in World Fuel stock.[12] Now if World Fuel Services does well in the long run, both Stebbins and World Fuel benefit.

compensation

Total of all rewards provided to employees in return for their services.

direct financial compensation

Pay that a person receives in the form of wages, salary, commissions, and bonuses.

indirect financial compensation (benefits)

All financial rewards that are not included in direct financial compensation.

nonfinancial compensation

Satisfaction that a person receives from the job itself or from the psychological and/or physical environment in which the person works.

| OBJECTIVE **9.2**

Define *financial equity* and explain the concepts of equity in direct financial compensation.

equity theory

Motivation theory that people assess their performance and attitudes by comparing both their contribution to work and the benefits they derive from it to the contributions and benefits of comparison others whom they select—and who in reality may or may not be like them.

financial equity

Perception of fair pay treatment for employees.

Compensation: An Overview

Compensation administration is one of management's most difficult and challenging human resource functions because it contains many elements and has a far-reaching impact on an organization's strategic goals. **Compensation** is the total of all rewards provided employees in return for their services. The overall purpose of compensation is to attract, retain, and motivate employees. The components of a total compensation program are shown in Figure 9-1.

Direct financial compensation consists of the pay that a person receives in the form of wages, salaries, commissions, and bonuses. **Indirect financial compensation (benefits)** consists of all financial rewards that are not included in direct financial compensation. This form of compensation includes a wide variety of rewards normally received indirectly by the employee such as paid vacation and medical care. **Nonfinancial compensation** consists of the satisfaction that a person receives from the job itself or from the psychological and/or physical environment in which the person works.

Equity in Financial Compensation

Equity theory is the motivation theory that people assess their performance and attitudes by comparing both their contribution to work and the benefits they derive from it to the contributions and benefits of *comparison others* whom they select—and who in reality may or may not be like them. Equity theory states that a person is motivated in proportion to the *perceived* fairness of the rewards received for a certain amount of effort as compared with what others receive. Someone might say, "I'm going to stop working so hard. I work harder than Susan and she gets all the raises." This individual has compared his effort and the rewards he received to the effort exerted and the rewards received by Susan.[13] In fact, no actual inequity may exist, but the perception of inequity influences subsequent actions. According to equity theory, individuals are motivated to reduce any perceived inequity.[14] They strive to make the ratios of outcomes to inputs equal. When inequity exists, the person making the comparison strives to make the ratios equal by changing either the outcomes or the inputs.

Understanding equity theory is very important as it pertains to compensation. Organizations must attract, motivate, and retain competent employees. Because a firm's financial compensation system plays a huge role in achieving these goals, organizations ought to strive for equity. **Financial equity** means a perception of fair pay treatment for employees. As will be seen, firms and individuals view fairness from several perspectives. Ideally, compensation will be even-handed to all parties concerned and employees will perceive it as such. However, this is a very elusive goal.

FIGURE 9-1

Components of a Total Compensation Program

Compensation

Financial		Nonfinancial	
Direct	**Indirect (Benefits)**	**The Job**	**Job Environment**
Wages	***Legally Required Benefits***	Meaningful	Sound Policies
Salary	Social Security	Appreciated	Capable Managers
Commissions	Unemployment Compensation	Satisfying	Competent Employees
Bonuses	Workers' Compensation	Learning	Congenial Coworkers
	Family & Medical Leave	Enjoyable	Appropriate Status Symbols
		Challenging	Working Conditions
	Discretionary Benefits		**Workplace Flexibility**
	Payment for Time Not Worked		Flextime
	Health Care		Compressed Workweek
	Life Insurance		Job Sharing
	Retirement Plans		Telecommuting
	Employee Stock Option Plans		Part-Time Work
	Employee Services		
	Premium Pay		
	Voluntary Benefits		

external equity
Equity that exists when a firm's employees receive pay comparable to workers who perform similar jobs in other firms.

internal equity
Equity that exists when employees receive pay according to the relative value of their jobs within the same organization.

employee equity
Equity that exists when individuals performing similar jobs for the same firm receive pay according to factors unique to the employee, such as performance level or seniority.

team equity
Equity that is achieved when teams are rewarded based on their group's productivity.

External equity exists when a firm's employees receive pay comparable to workers who perform similar jobs in other firms. A problem that exists is that often employees perceive that workers in other companies earn more. However, a recent survey by HR Solutions International Inc. found that although employees frequently think that peers at other firms earn more, in reality they typically are paid about the same.[15] Compensation surveys help organizations determine the extent to which external equity is present. **Internal equity** exists when employees receive pay according to the relative value of their jobs within the same organization.[16] It was with regard to internal equity that Peter Drucker was referring to at the beginning of the chapter.

Job evaluation (discussed later in the chapter) is a primary means for determining internal equity. Most workers are concerned with both internal and external pay equity. From an employee relations perspective, internal pay equity may be more important because employees have more information about pay matters within their own organizations, and they use this information to form perceptions of equity. On the other hand, an organization must be competitive in the labor market, which is external equity. In a competitive environment, and especially for high-demand employees, it becomes clear that the market is of primary importance (external equity).

Employee equity exists when individuals performing similar jobs for the same firm receive pay according to factors unique to the employee, such as performance level or seniority. Suppose that two accountants in the same firm are performing similar jobs, and one is clearly the better performer. If both workers receive equal pay increases, employee equity does not exist, and the more productive employee is likely to be unhappy. **Team equity** is achieved when teams are rewarded based on their group's productivity. However, achieving equity may be a problem when it comes to team incentives. If all team members contributed equally, there would not likely be a problem. But, that is usually not the case, as more productive team members may cover for less productive ones.

Inequity in any category can result in morale problems. If employees feel that their compensation is unfair, they may leave the firm. Even greater damage may result for the firm if the employees choose not to leave but stay and restrict their efforts. In either event, the organization's overall performance is damaged.

OBJECTIVE 9.3
Identify the determinants of direct financial compensation.

Determinants of Direct Financial Compensation

Compensation theory has never been able to provide a completely satisfactory answer to what an individual's service for performing a job is worth. Although no scientific approach is available, organizations typically use a number of relevant factors to determine individual pay. These determinants appear in Figure 9-2. Historically, the *organization*, the *labor market*, the *job*, and the *employee* all have influenced job pricing and the ultimate determination of an individual's financial compensation. These factors continue to play an important role.

FIGURE 9-2

Primary Determinants of Direct Financial Compensation

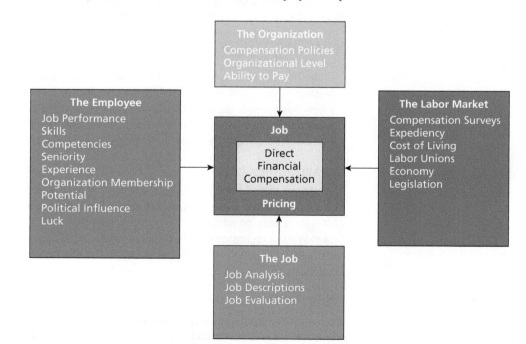

OBJECTIVE **9.4**

Describe the organization as a determinant of direct financial compensation.

Organization as a Determinant of Direct Financial Compensation

Managers tend to view financial compensation as both an expense and an asset. It is an expense in the sense that it reflects the cost of labor. However, financial compensation is clearly an asset when it is instrumental in recruiting and hiring good people and in encouraging them to put forth their best efforts and remain in their jobs. A firm that pays well attracts many applicants, enabling management to pick and choose the skills and traits it values. It holds on to these quality hires by equitably sharing the fruits of its financial success, not only among the management team but also with the rank and file. Compensation programs have top management's attention because they have the potential to influence employee work attitudes and behavior that lead to improved organizational performance and achieving the firm's strategic plan.

Compensation Policies

compensation policy
Policy that provides general guidelines for making compensation decisions.

A **compensation policy** provides general guidelines for making compensation decisions. Some employees may perceive their firm's compensation policies as being fair and unbiased and others may have different opinions. The result of these perceptions may have an effect on employees' perceptions of fairness and result in lower productivity or they may choose to leave the firm. An organization often, formally or informally, establishes compensation policies that determine whether it will be a pay leader, be a pay follower, or strive for an average position in the labor market.

pay leaders
Organizations that pay higher wages and salaries than competing firms.

PAY LEADERS **Pay leaders** are organizations that pay higher wages and salaries than competing firms. Using this strategy, they feel that they will be able to attract high-quality, productive employees and thus achieve lower per-unit labor costs. Higher-paying firms usually attract more highly qualified applicants than lower-paying companies in the same labor market.

market (going) rate
Average pay that most employers provide for a similar job in a particular area or industry.

MARKET RATE The **market (going) rate** is the average pay that most employers provide for a similar job in a particular area or industry. Many organizations have a policy that calls for paying the market rate. In such firms, management believes that it can still employ qualified people and remain competitive.

pay followers
Companies that choose to pay below the going rate because of a poor financial condition or a belief that they do not require highly capable employees.

PAY FOLLOWERS Companies that choose to pay below the market rate because of poor financial conditions or a belief that they do not require highly capable employees are **pay followers**. When organizations follow this policy, difficulties often occur. Consider the case of Trig Ekeland.

> *Trig managed a large, but financially strapped farming operation in South Dakota. Although no formal policies were established, Trig had a practice of paying the lowest wage possible. One of his farmhands, Charlie Roberts, was paid minimum wage. During a period of three weeks, Charlie wrecked a tractor, severely damaged a combine, and tore out the transmission in a new pickup truck. Charlie's actions prompted Trig to remark, "Charlie is the most expensive darned employee I've ever had."*

As Trig discovered, paying the lowest wage possible did not save money; actually, the practice was quite expensive. In addition to hiring unproductive workers, organizations that are pay followers may have a high turnover rate, as their most qualified employees leave to join higher-paying organizations. Equally important, in situations in which incompetent or disgruntled employees make contact with customers, they may not provide the kind of customer service management desires.

Organizational Level

The organizational level in which compensation decisions are made can also have an impact on pay. Upper management often makes these decisions to ensure consistency. However, in some cases, there may be advantages to making pay decisions at lower levels, where better information may exist regarding employee performance. Extreme pressure to retain top performers may override the desire to maintain consistency in the pay structure. Organizations increasingly make exceptions for just this reason.

Ability to Pay

An organization's assessment of its ability to pay is also an important factor in determining pay levels. Financially successful firms tend to provide higher-than-average compensation. However, an organization's financial strength establishes only the upper limit of what it will pay. To arrive at a specific pay level, management must consider other factors.

OBJECTIVE 9.5

Describe the labor market as a determinant of direct financial compensation and explain how the job is a determinant of direct financial compensation.

labor market

Potential employees located within the geographic area from which employees are recruited.

Labor Market as a Determinant of Direct Financial Compensation

Potential employees located within the geographic area from which employees are recruited constitute the **labor market**. Labor markets for some jobs extend far beyond the location of a firm's operations. An aerospace firm in St. Louis, for example, may be concerned about the labor market for engineers in Fort Worth or Orlando, where competitive firms are located. Managerial and professional employees are often recruited from a wide geographic area. As global economics increasingly sets the cost of labor, the global labor market grows in importance as a determinant of financial compensation for individuals.

Pay for the same jobs in different labor markets may vary considerably. Administrative assistant jobs, for example, may carry an average salary of over $50,000 or more per year in a large, urban community but only $25,000 or less in a smaller town. Compensation managers must be aware of these differences in order to compete successfully for employees. The market rate is an important guide in determining pay. Many employees view it as the standard for judging the fairness of their firm's compensation practices.

Compensation Surveys

compensation survey

A means of obtaining data regarding what other firms are paying for specific jobs or job classes within a given labor market.

A **compensation survey** is a means of obtaining data regarding what other firms are paying for specific jobs or job classes within a given labor market. Virtually all compensation professionals use compensation surveys either directly or indirectly. Surveys may be purchased, outsourced to a consulting firm, or conducted by the organization itself. Organizations use surveys for two basic reasons: to identify their relative position with respect to the chosen competition in the labor market, and to provide input in developing a budget and compensation structure. Of all the wage criteria, market rates remain the most important standard for determining pay. In a competitive environment, the marketplace determines economic worth, and this is the critical factor. During the recent recession, pay raises were nonexistent in many organizations. As the country has moved out of the recession, firms were racing to conduct compensation surveys to determine what the competition was doing with regard to salary increases.[17]

Expediency

Although standard compensation surveys are generally useful, managers in highly technical and specialized areas occasionally need to use nontraditional means to determine what constitutes competitive compensation for scarce talent and niche positions. They need real-time information and must rely on recruiters and hiring managers on the front lines to let them know what is happening in the job market. Quick compensation decisions often have to be made to secure high-demand employees as these individuals are typically not on the market for long.

Cost of Living

Although not a problem in recent years, the logic for using cost of living as a pay determinant is both simple and sound: when prices rise over time and pay does not, *real pay* is actually lowered. A pay increase must be roughly equivalent to the increased cost of living if a person is to maintain his or her previous level of real wages. For instance, if someone earns $42,000 during a year in which the average rate of inflation is 4 percent, a $140-per-month pay increase will be necessary merely to maintain the purchasing ability of that employee.

People living on fixed incomes (primarily the elderly and the poor) are hit hard by inflation, but they are not alone, as most employees also suffer financially. In recognition of this problem some firms index pay increases to the inflation rate. In fact, in a questionable practice, some organizations sacrifice *merit pay* (discussed later in the chapter) to provide across-the-board increases designed to offset the results of inflation.

Inflation is not the only factor affecting cost of living; location also comes into play. The cost of working in New York City is certainly higher than Ames, Iowa. You can calculate comparative salaries in one city to another by going to www.homefair.com.

HR Web Wisdom

Calculate Salary Differences from City to City

http://www.homefair.com

Web site to determine numerous costs of a move to another city.

Official measures of inflation such as the *Consumer Price Index* (CPI) are market oriented, measuring only the decrease in our money's power to purchase products currently available for sale. An alternative way to view cost of living includes nonmarket elements of our existence, such as the rising costs from crime, lawsuits, pollution, and family breakdown.

Labor Unions

The National Labor Relations Act (Wagner Act) declared legislative support, on a broad scale, for the right of employees to organize and engage in collective bargaining. Unions normally prefer to determine compensation through the process of collective bargaining. An excerpt from the Wagner Act prescribes the areas of mandatory collective bargaining between management and unions as "wages, hours, and other terms and conditions of employment." These broad bargaining areas obviously have great potential to impact compensation decisions. When a union uses comparable pay as a standard in making compensation demands, the employer needs accurate labor market data. When a union emphasizes cost of living, it may try to pressure management into including a cost-of-living allowance. A **cost-of-living allowance (COLA)** is an escalator clause in the labor agreement that automatically increases wages as the U.S. Bureau of Labor Statistics' cost-of-living index rises. Recently, cost-of-living allowances in union contracts have been disappearing.

cost-of-living allowance (COLA)
Escalator clause in a labor agreement that automatically increases wages as the U.S. Bureau of Labor Statistics' cost-of-living index rises.

Economy

The economy definitely affects financial compensation decisions. For example, a depressed economy generally increases the labor supply, and this serves to lower the market rate. A booming economy, on the other hand, results in greater competition for workers and the price of labor is driven upward. In addition, the cost of living typically rises as the economy expands.

Legislation

Federal and state laws can also affect the amount of compensation a person receives. The Equal Pay Act prohibits an employer from paying an employee of one gender less money than an employee of the opposite gender, if both employees do work that is substantially the same. Equal employment legislation, including the Civil Rights Act, the Age Discrimination in Employment Act, and the Americans with Disabilities Act, prohibits discrimination against specified groups in employment matters, including compensation. The same is true for federal government contractors or subcontractors covered by Executive Order 11246 and the Rehabilitation Act. States and municipal governments also have laws that affect compensation practices. Our focus in the next section, however, is on the federal legislation that provides broad coverage and specifically deals with compensation issues.

DAVIS–BACON ACT OF 1931 The Davis–Bacon Act of 1931 was the first national law to deal with minimum wages. It mandates a *prevailing wage* for all federally financed or assisted construction projects exceeding $2,000. The Secretary of Labor sets the prevailing wage at the union wage, regardless of what the average wage is in the affected locality. The act is currently being debated in Congress as many believe it has outlived its usefulness.[18]

WALSH–HEALY ACT OF 1936 The Walsh–Healy Act of 1936 requires companies with federal contracts for the manufacture or furnishing of goods exceeding $10,000 to pay prevailing wages as determined by the Secretary of Labor. This legislation also requires one-and-a-half times the regular pay rate for hours over eight per day or 40 per week.

FAIR LABOR STANDARDS ACT OF 1938, AS AMENDED (FLSA) The most significant law affecting compensation is the Fair Labor Standards Act of 1938. The purpose of the FLSA is to establish minimum labor standards on a national basis and to eliminate low wages and long working hours. The FLSA attempts to eliminate low wages by setting a minimum wage, and to make long hours expensive by requiring a higher overtime pay rate for excessive hours. It also requires record keeping and provides standards for child labor. The Wage and Hour Division of the U.S. Department of Labor (DOL) administers this act. The amount of the minimum wage has changed several times since it was first introduced in 1938 and continues to do so; it rose from $6.55 to $7.25 per hour in 2009. Tipped workers, on the other hand, may receive a minimum wage of $5.12.[19] However, if hourly wage plus tips do not add up to the minimum wage, the company must make up the difference. It is here that minimum-wage violations often occur.[20]

The act also requires overtime payment at the rate of one-and-one-half times the employee's regular rate after 40 hours of work in a 168-hour period. Aggressive action is being taken against companies that fail to pay the overtime requirement.[21] Although the act covers most organizations and employees, certain classes of employees are specifically exempt from overtime provisions. **Exempt employees** are categorized as executive, administrative, professional, or outside salespersons.

An *executive employee* is essentially a manager (such as a production manager) with broad authority over subordinates. An *administrative employee,* although not a manager, occupies an important staff position in an organization and might have a title such as account executive or market researcher. A *professional employee* performs work requiring advanced knowledge in a field of learning, normally acquired through a prolonged course of specialized instruction.[22] This type of employee might have a title such as company physician, legal counsel, or senior statistician. *Outside salespeople* sell tangible or intangible items away from the employer's place of business.

The escalation in the use of smartphones and related devices by organizations has the potential to violate the FLSA. What happens if a company issues a nonexempt employee a smartphone and tells him or her to be on call 24 hours/7 days a week? The *Gomez v Lincare* case was decided by the California Court of Appeals in 2009 and permitted a group of employees to recover overtime wages for the time they spent responding to pages. However, no case has yet been decided by the Supreme Court.[23]

DODD–FRANK WALL STREET REFORM AND CONSUMER PROTECTION ACT The Dodd–Frank Act was signed into law in 2010 and has provisions relating to executive compensation and corporate governance that impact the executives, directors, and shareholders of publicly traded companies. Specific provisions of the act will be covered later under topics on "Say on Pay," "Golden Parachutes," and the "Clawback Provision" in this chapter's Trends & Innovation.

Job as a Determinant of Direct Financial Compensation

The individual employee and market forces are most prominent as wage criteria. However, the job itself continues to be a factor, especially in firms that have internal pay equity as an important consideration. These organizations pay for the value they attach to certain duties, responsibilities, and other job-related factors such as working conditions. Management techniques used for determining a job's relative worth include job analysis, job descriptions, and job evaluation.

Before an organization can determine the relative difficulty or value of its jobs, it must first define their content. Normally, it first does job analysis. The primary by-product of job analysis is the job description. Job descriptions serve many different purposes, including data for evaluating jobs. They are essential to all *job evaluation* methods that depend heavily on their accuracy and clarity for success.

Job Evaluation

Job evaluation is a process that determines the relative value of one job in relation to another. Basically, it determines the value of the job to the company. The primary purpose of job evaluation is to eliminate internal pay inequities that exist because of illogical pay structures. For example, pay inequity probably exists if the mailroom supervisor earns more than the chief accountant. For obvious reasons, organizations prefer internal pay equity. However, when a job's pay rate is ultimately determined to conflict with the market rate, the latter is almost sure to take precedence. Job evaluation measures job worth in an administrative rather than an economic sense. The latter can be determined only by the marketplace and made known through compensation surveys.[24] Nevertheless, some firms continue to use job evaluation for the following purposes:

- To identify the organization's job structure.
- To eliminate pay inequities and bring order to the relationships among jobs.
- To develop a hierarchy of job value for creating a pay structure.

The human resource department may be responsible for administering job evaluation programs. However, committees made up of individuals familiar with the specific jobs to be evaluated often perform the actual evaluations. A typical committee might include the human resource executive and representatives from other functional areas such as finance, production, information technology, and marketing. The composition of the committee usually depends on the type and level of the jobs being evaluated. In all instances, it is important for the committee to keep personalities out of the evaluation process and to remember that it is evaluating the *job,* not the person(s) performing the job. Some people have difficultly making this distinction. This is understandable, since some job evaluation systems are very similar to some performance appraisal methods. In addition, the duties of a job may, on an informal basis, expand, contract, or change depending on the person holding the job.

Small and medium-sized organizations often lack job evaluation expertise and may elect to use an outside consultant. When employing a consultant, management should require that the consultant not only develop the job evaluation system, but also train company employees to administer it properly.

The four traditional job evaluation methods are the *ranking, classification, factor comparison,* and *point.* There are innumerable versions of these methods, and a firm may choose one and modify it to fit its particular purposes. Another option is to purchase a proprietary method such as the Hay Plan. The ranking and classification methods are nonquantitative, whereas the factor comparison and point methods are quantitative approaches.

Ranking Method

The ranking method is the simplest of the four job evaluation methods. In the **job evaluation ranking method**, the raters examine the description of each job being evaluated and arrange the jobs in order according to their value to the company. The procedure is essentially the same as the ranking method for evaluating employee performance. The only difference is that you evaluate jobs, not people.

Classification Method

The **classification method** involves defining a number of classes or grades to describe a group of jobs. In evaluating jobs by this method, the raters compare the job description with the class description. Class descriptions reflect the differences between groups of jobs at various difficulty levels. The class description that most closely agrees with the job description determines the classification for that job. For example, in evaluating the job of receptionist, the description might include these duties:

1. Greet and announce visitors.
2. Answer phone and route calls.
3. Receive and route mail.

Assuming that the remainder of the job description includes similar routine work, this job would probably be placed in the lowest job class.

Each class is described in such a way that it captures sufficient work detail, yet is general enough to cause little difficulty in slotting a job description into its appropriate class.

Factor Comparison Method

The factor comparison method is somewhat more involved than the two previously discussed qualitative methods. The **factor comparison method** of job evaluation assumes that there are five universal factors consisting of mental requirements, skills, physical requirements, responsibilities, and working conditions; the evaluator makes decisions on these factors independently.

The five universal job factors are:

- Mental requirements, which reflect mental traits such as intelligence, reasoning, and imagination.
- Skills, which pertain to facility in muscular coordination and training in the interpretation of sensory impressions.
- Physical requirements, which involve sitting, standing, walking, lifting, and so on.
- Responsibilities, which cover areas such as raw materials, money, records, and supervision.
- Working conditions, which reflect the environmental influences of noise, illumination, ventilation, hazards, and hours.

job evaluation ranking method
Job evaluation method in which the raters examine the description of each job being evaluated and arrange the jobs in order according to their value to the company.

classification method
Job evaluation method in which classes or grades are defined to describe a group of jobs.

factor comparison method
Job evaluation method that assumes there are five universal factors consisting of mental requirements, skills, physical requirements, responsibilities, and working conditions; the evaluator makes decisions on these factors independently.

point method

Job evaluation method in which the raters assign numerical values to specific job factors, such as knowledge required, and the sum of these values provides a quantitative assessment of a job's relative worth.

HR Web Wisdom

The Hay Group Guide Chart-Profile Method
http://www.haygroup.com

Homepage of the Hay Plan, the most widely used job measurement system in the world, is provided.

Hay Group Guide Chart-Profile Method (Hay Plan)

Refined version of the point method used by approximately 8,000 public and private-sector organizations worldwide to evaluate clerical, trade, technical, professional, managerial, and/or executive-level jobs.

OBJECTIVE 9.7

Describe job pricing and identify factors related to the employee that are essential in determining direct financial compensation.

job pricing

Placing a dollar value on a job's worth.

pay grade

Grouping of similar jobs to simplify pricing jobs.

wage curve

Fitting of plotted points to create a smooth progression between pay grades (also known as the pay curve).

pay range

Minimum and maximum pay rate with enough variance between the two to allow for a significant pay difference.

In this method, the evaluation committee creates a monetary scale, containing each of the five universal factors, and ranks jobs according to their value for each factor. Unlike most other job evaluation methods, which produce relative job worth only, the factor comparison method determines the absolute value as well.

Point Method

In the **point method**, raters assign numerical values to specific job factors, such as knowledge required, and the sum of these values provides a quantitative assessment of a job's relative worth. Historically, some variation of the point plan has been the most popular option.

Point plans require time and effort to design. Historically, a redeeming feature of the method has been that, once developed, the plan was useful over a long time. In today's environment, the shelf life may be considerably less. In any event, as new jobs are created and old jobs substantially changed, job analysis must be conducted and job descriptions rewritten on an ongoing basis. The job evaluation committee then evaluates the jobs. Only when job factors change, or for some reason the weights assigned become inappropriate, does the plan become obsolete.

Hay Group Guide Chart-Profile Method (Hay Plan)

The **Hay Group Guide Chart-Profile Method (Hay Plan)** is a widely used refined version of the point method used by public and private-sector organizations worldwide to evaluate clerical, trade, technical, professional, managerial, and/or executive-level jobs.[25] It uses the compensable factors of know-how, problem solving, accountability, and additional compensable elements. Point values are assigned to these factors to determine the final point profile for any job.

Job pricing, and the details involved, is the topic of the next section.

Job Pricing

The process of job evaluation results in a job hierarchy. It might reveal, for example, that the job of senior accountant is more valuable than the job of machinist, which, in turn, is more valuable than the job of receptionist. At this point, you know the *relative* value of these jobs to the company, but not their *absolute* value. **Job pricing** results in placing a dollar value on a job's worth. It takes place after evaluation of a job and the relative value of each job in the organization has been determined. Firms often use pay grades and pay ranges in the job-pricing process.

Pay Grades

A **pay grade** is the grouping of similar jobs to simplify pricing jobs. For example, it is much more convenient for organizations to price 15 pay grades than 200 separate jobs. The simplicity of this approach is similar to a college or university's practice of grouping grades of 90–100 into an *A* category, grades of 80–89 into a *B*, and so on. In following this approach, you also avoid a false suggestion of preciseness. Although job evaluation plans may be systematic, none are scientific.

Plotting jobs on a scatter diagram is often useful to managers in determining the appropriate number of pay grades for a company. Looking at Figure 9-3, notice that each dot on the scatter diagram represents one job. The location of the dot reflects the job's relationship to pay and evaluated points, which reflect its worth. When this procedure is used, a certain point spread determines the width of the pay grade (100 points in this illustration). Although each dot represents one job, it may involve dozens of individuals who have *positions* in that one job. The large dot at the lower left represents the job of receptionist, evaluated at 75 points. The receptionist's hourly rate of $12.90 represents either the average wage currently paid for the job or its market rate. This decision depends on how management wants to price its jobs.

A **wage curve** (or *pay curve*) is the fitting of plotted points to create a smooth progression between pay grades. The line drawn minimizes the distance between all dots and the line; a line of best fit may be straight or curved. However, when the point system is used, a straight line is often the result, as in Figure 9-3. You can draw this wage line either freehand or use a statistical method.

Pay Ranges

After pay grades have been determined, the next decision is whether all individuals performing the same job will receive equal pay or whether pay ranges should be used. A **pay range** includes a minimum and maximum pay rate with enough variance between the two to allow for

Summary Evaluated Points	Pay Grade	Minimum	Pay Range Midpoint	Maximum
0–99	1	$12.00	$13.30	$14.60
100–199	2	13.30	14.60	15.90
200–299	3	14.60	15.90	17.20
300–399	4	15.90	17.20	18.50
400–500	5	17.20	18.50	19.80

a significant pay difference. Pay ranges are generally preferred over single pay rates because they allow a firm to compensate employees according to performance and length of service. Pay then serves as a positive incentive. When pay ranges are used, a firm must develop a method to advance individuals through the range. Companies typically use different range spreads for jobs that are more valuable to the company.

POINTS ALONG THE RANGE Referring again to Figure 9-3, note that anyone can readily determine the minimum, midpoint, and maximum pay rates per hour for each of the five pay grades. For example, for pay grade 5, the minimum rate is $17.20, the midpoint is $18.50, and the maximum is $19.80. The minimum rate may be the *hiring in* rate that a person receives when joining the firm, although in practice, new employees often receive pay that starts above this level. The maximum pay rate represents the maximum that an employee can receive for that job regardless of how well he or she performs the job.

PROBLEM OF TOPPING OUT A person at the top of a pay grade will have to be promoted to a job in a higher pay grade in order to receive a pay increase unless (1) an across-the-board adjustment is made or (2) the job is reevaluated and placed in a higher pay grade. This situation has caused numerous managers some anguish as they attempt to explain the pay system to an employee who is doing a tremendous job but is at the top of a pay grade. Consider this situation:

> *Everyone in the department realized that Beth Smithers was the best administrative assistant in the company. At times, she appeared to do the job of three people. Bob Marshall, Beth's supervisor, was especially impressed. Recently, he had a discussion with the human resource manager to see what he could do to get a raise for Beth. After Bob described the situation, the human resource manager's only reply was, "Sorry, Bob. Beth is already at the top of her pay grade. There is nothing you can do except have her job upgraded or promote her to another position."*

Situations like Beth's present managers with a perplexing problem. Many would be inclined to make an exception to the system and give Beth a salary increase. However, this action would violate a traditional principle, which holds that every job in the organization has a maximum value, regardless of how well an employee performs the job. The rationale is that making exceptions to the compensation plan would result in widespread pay inequities. Having stated this, today many organizations are challenging traditional concepts as they strive to retain top-performing employees. For example, if Beth Smithers worked for Microsoft or Southwest Airlines, she might get a raise.

RATE RANGES AT HIGHER LEVELS The rate ranges established should be large enough to provide an incentive to do a better job. At higher levels, pay differentials may need to be greater to be meaningful. There may be logic in having the rate range become increasingly wide at each consecutive level. Consider, for example, what a $200-per-month salary increase would mean to a file clerk earning $2,000 per month (a 10 percent increase) and to a senior cost accountant earning $5,000 per month (a 4 percent increase). Assuming an inflation rate of 4 percent, the accountant's *real pay* would remain unchanged.

Broadbanding

Broadbanding is a technique that collapses many pay grades (salary grades) into a few wide bands to improve organizational effectiveness.

Employees today perform more diverse tasks than they previously did. Broadbanding creates the basis for a simpler compensation system that de-emphasizes structure and control and places greater importance on judgment and flexible decision making. Bands may also promote lateral development of employees and direct attention away from vertical promotional opportunities. The decreased emphasis on job levels should encourage employees to make cross-functional moves to jobs that are on the same or an even lower level because their pay rate would remain unchanged. Broadbanding allows for more flexibility within ranges, allows more movement of employees within the ranges, and can reduce the need for promotions.[26]

The use of broadbanding has declined in recent years. Although broadbanding is successful in some organizations, the practice is not without pitfalls. Since each band consists of a broad range of jobs, the market value of these jobs may also vary considerably. Unless carefully monitored, employees in jobs at the lower end of the band could progress to the top of the range and become overpaid.[27]

Single-Rate System

Pay ranges are not appropriate for some workplace conditions, such as assembly-line operations. When all jobs within a unit are routine, with little opportunity for employees to vary their productivity, a single-rate (or fixed-rate) system may be more appropriate. When single rates are used, everyone in the same job receives the same base pay. This rate may correspond to the midpoint of a range determined by a compensation survey.

Adjusting Pay Rates

When pay ranges have been determined and jobs assigned to pay grades, it may become obvious that some jobs are overpaid and others underpaid. Underpaid jobs are normally brought up to the minimum of the pay range as soon as possible. Referring again to Figure 9-3, you can see that a job evaluated at about 225 points and having a rate of $14.00 per hour is represented by a circled dot immediately below pay grade 3. The job was determined to be difficult enough to fall in pay grade 3 (200–299 points). However, employees working in the job are being paid 60 cents per hour less than the minimum for the pay grade ($14.60 per hour). If one or more female employees should be in this circled job, the employer might soon learn more than desired about the Equal Pay Act and the Fair Pay Act. Good management practice would be to correct this inequity as rapidly as possible by placing the job in the proper pay grade and increasing the pay of those in that job.

Overpaid jobs present a different problem. Figure 9-3 illustrates an overpaid job for pay grade 4 (note the circled dot above pay grade 4). Employees in this job earn $19.00 per hour, or 50 cents more than the maximum for the pay grade. An ideal solution to the problem of an overpaid job is to promote the employee to a job in a higher pay grade. This is a great idea if the employee is qualified for a higher-rated job and a job opening is available. Another possibility would be to bring the job rate and employee pay into line through a pay cut. Although this decision may appear logical, it is generally not a good management practice, as this action would punish employees for a situation they did not create. Somewhere in between these two possible solutions is a third: to freeze the rate until across-the-board pay increases bring the job into line.

Pricing jobs is not an easy task. It requires effort that never ends. It is one of those tasks that managers may dislike but must do anyway.

Employee as a Determinant of Direct Financial Compensation

In addition to the organization, the labor market, and the job, factors related to the employee are also essential in determining an individual's compensation. These factors include job performance, skills/competencies, seniority, experience, organization membership, potential, political influence, luck, and salary compression.

Job Performance—Performance-Based Pay

Performance-based pay is governed by how well one performs the job. To maximize company objectives of the firm, it is important to link employee compensation to performance. This basic rule applies to all within the organization ranging from the company president to hourly employee. Basically, what you reward is what you get. It recognizes that some workers are just better than other workers in performing the same job. In recent years there has been a definite move in the United States toward pay for performance.

The objective of performance-based pay is to improve productivity by rewarding those who best assist in achieving this goal. It is based on the assumption that given the proper incentives, most employees will work harder and smarter. In a recent survey, companies that reported the best results from their pay-for-performance programs used multiple rewards to recognize and reward performance including base pay increases (91 percent), short-term incentives (71 percent), spot bonuses (49 percent), equity awards (33 percent), other long-term incentives (18 percent), and profit sharing (7 percent).[28] An effective performance appraisal program is a prerequisite for any pay system tied to performance. Using this approach, workers would need to first have a clear understanding of what goals the organization wanted them to achieve. Then, based on the result of performance appraisal, rewards would be forthcoming.

When Sprint's CEO Dan Hesse took over the wireless provider, he wanted employees to clearly understand what he thought was important and what they should focus on to achieve maximum rewards. He wanted compensation to be based on improving the customer experience, strengthening the brand, and generating cash to increase profits. The amount paid for performance extended from 5 percent for entry-level employees to 50 percent and higher at the vice president level.[29] As another example, if it is important to improve safety in the workplace, this must be communicated to employees and included in their performance review. If worker behavior leads to fewer accidents, workers should be rewarded.[30] Rewards might be as simple as a pat on the back or additional money in their paychecks. Appraisal data provide input for such approaches as merit pay, bonuses, and piecework. Each of these approaches to compensation management will be discussed in the following sections.

Merit Pay

merit pay
Pay increase added to employees' base pay based on their level of performance.

Merit pay is a pay increase added to employees' base pay based on their level of performance. In practice, however, it historically has been merely a cost-of-living increase in disguise.[31] However, as John Rubino, president of Rubino Consulting Services, an international human resources consulting firm, said, "Companies with base-salary programs and automatic annual pay increases offer little to motivate employees."[32] Past studies by compensation professionals have determined that merit pay is *marginally successful* in influencing pay satisfaction and performance. From the employer's viewpoint, a distinct disadvantage to the typical merit pay increase is that it increases the employee's base pay. Therefore, employees receive the added amount each year they are on the payroll regardless of later performance levels.

The recent recession may have created a compensation revolution with regard to merit pay. Pay increases where everyone is treated essentially the same with only small differences between the best performer and mediocre ones are a thing of the past for some firms. Craig E. Schneier, the HR boss at biotechnology giant Biogen Idec, does not believe that all employees and positions are equal. At Biogen, one vice president might get double what another VP in the next office will get.[33] Certainly this philosophy bodes well for many Generation Y employees as they want to be rewarded based on their individual performance and do not believe the time a person devotes to the job should be a primary consideration.[34]

It has become increasingly difficult to justify merit pay increases based on a previous employment period but added perpetually to base pay. There are many long-term employees who are poor performers who have high salaries because of past automatic cost-of-living increases. Although numerous companies continue with traditional merit pay plans, some companies are starting to quietly freeze or cut pay for some so as to be able to reward others. According to Myrna Hellerman, senior vice president at Sibson Consulting, "much can be learned from best-practices companies where base pay increases must be earned, based on demonstrated individual achievement. Pay raises are not an entitlement; the entitlement era is over."[35]

Bonuses

bonus
One-time annual financial award, based on productivity that is not added to base pay.

Companies are increasingly placing a higher percentage of their compensation budget in **bonuses**, a one-time annual financial award, based on productivity that is not added to base pay.

More and more companies embrace the concept of *pay for performance*. Recently when the economy was slowing down and employers were holding down across-the-board pay raises, companies still put a large percent of salary budgets toward bonuses.[36] A recent survey found that 70 percent of employers offer bonuses as a reward to employees.[37] The use of bonuses helps managers control their cash outlay in a tough business environment while laying the foundation to share success with top producers.[38] Managers commonly contend that the use of bonuses is a win–win situation because it boosts production and efficiency and gives employees some control over their earning power. A positive side effect of using bonuses to reward high performance is that it may encourage coworkers to increase their productivity so that they can also receive the bonuses.

spot bonus
Relatively small monetary gifts provided to employees for outstanding work or effort during a reasonably short period of time.

Many organizations today are providing *spot bonuses* for critical areas and talents. **Spot bonuses** are relatively small monetary gifts provided to employees for outstanding work or effort during a reasonably short period of time. If an employee's performance has been exceptional, the employer may reward the worker with a one-time bonus of as low as $50 and $100 or $500. For certain professional jobs it is not unheard of for a highly productive worker to receive $5,000 shortly after a noteworthy achievement.

Piecework

piecework
Incentive pay plan in which employees are paid for each unit they produce.

Piecework is an incentive pay plan in which employees are paid for each unit they produce. For example, if a worker is paid $8 a unit and produces 10 units a day, the worker earns $80. Sometimes a guaranteed base is included in a piece-rate plan, meaning that a worker would receive this base amount no matter what the output. Historically, piecework is especially prevalent in the production/operations area. Requirements for the plan include developing output standards for the job and being able to measure the output of a single employee. Piecework pay plans have declined in use somewhat because the plan requires constant monitoring. For instance, if on day one the worker produced 8 units and on day two the worker produced 12 units, each day must be counted separately. Also professionals such as industrial engineers are needed to maintain the system. Obviously, a piecework plan would not be feasible for many jobs.

Skills—Skill-Based Pay

skill-based pay
System that compensates employees for their job-related skills and knowledge, not for their job titles.

Although quite similar in nature, skill- and competency-based pay will be discussed separately. **Skill-based pay** is a system that compensates employees for their job-related *skills* and *knowledge,* rather than how well he or she performs on the present job. Essentially, job descriptions, job evaluation plans, and job-based salary surveys are replaced by skill profiles, skill evaluation plans, and *skill-based* salary surveys. The system assumes that employees who know more are more valuable to the firm and, therefore, they deserve a reward for their efforts in acquiring new skills. When employees obtain additional job-relevant skills, both individuals and the departments they serve benefit. For example, a department may have six different types of machines, each requiring different skills to operate. Under a skill-based pay system, the worker would increase his or her pay as additional machines are learned.

Although skill-based pay appears to have advantages for both employer and employee, there are some challenges for management. The firm must provide adequate training opportunities or else the system can become a demotivator. Also, since it takes an average of only three years for a worker to reach a maximum level in a skill-based pay system, what will keep employees motivated? As a result, the use of skill-based pay among organizations has declined.[39]

Competencies—Competency-Based Pay

competency-based pay
Compensation plan that rewards employees for the capabilities they attain.

Competency-based pay is a compensation plan that rewards employees for the capabilities they attain. It is a type of skill-based pay plan for professional and managerial employees. Today, there are many alternatives to choose from—core, organizational, behavioral, and technical competencies. The disappearance of the traditional job provides the primary rationale for this change. Today, employees often have variable and unstable work assignments, with roles that cannot be assigned a valid pay rate through traditional job evaluation plans. Often, considerable time must be spent determining the specific competencies needed for the different jobs. Blocks of competencies are then priced and management must invest considerable time in developing, implementing, and continuing such a system.

Seniority

seniority
Length of time an employee has been associated with the company, division, department, or job.

Seniority is the length of time an employee has been associated with the company, division, department, or job. Although management generally prefers performance as the primary basis for compensation changes, unions tend to favor seniority. They believe the use of seniority provides an objective and fair basis for pay increases. Many union leaders consider performance evaluation systems to be too subjective, permitting management to reward favorite employees arbitrarily.

Experience

Regardless of the nature of the task, experience has the potential for enhancing a person's ability to perform. However, this possibility materializes only if the experience acquired is positive. Knowledge of the basics is usually a prerequisite for effective use of a person's experience. This is true for a person starting to play golf, learn a foreign language, or manage people in organizations. People who express pride in their many years of managerial experience may be justified in their sentiments, but only if their experience has been beneficial. Today, it is possible that *experience* is becoming somewhat irrelevant. In fact, technology may have rendered experience useless unless the person with the experience has kept up with the technology available. Managing in the dot-com world is certainly different from the old economy. Still, employees receive compensation for their experience and the practice is justified if the experience is positive and relevant to the work.

Organization Membership

Employees receive some compensation components without regard to the particular job they perform or their level of productivity. They receive them because they are members of the organization. For example, an average performer occupying a job in pay grade 1 may receive the same number of vacation days, the same amount of group life insurance, and the same reimbursement for educational expenses as a superior employee working in a job classified in pay grade 10. In fact, the worker in pay grade 1 may get more vacation time if he or she has been with the firm longer. The purpose of rewards based on organizational membership is to maintain a high degree of stability in the workforce and to recognize loyalty.

Potential

Potential is useless if it is never realized. However, organizations do pay some individuals based on their potential. To attract talented young people to the firm, for example, the overall compensation program must appeal to those with no experience or any immediate ability to perform difficult tasks. Many young employees are paid well, perhaps not because of their ability to make an immediate contribution, but because they have the *potential* to add future value to the firm as a professional, first-line supervisor, manager of compensation, vice president of marketing, or possibly even chief executive officer.

Political Influence

Firms should obviously try not to permit political influence to be a factor in determining financial compensation. However, to deny its existence would be unrealistic. There is an unfortunate element of truth in the statement, "It's not *what* you know, it's *who* you know." To varying degrees in business, government, and not-for-profit organizations, a person's *pull* or political influence may sway pay and promotion decisions. It may be natural for a manager to favor a friend or relative in granting a pay increase or promotion. Nevertheless, if the person receiving the reward is not deserving of it, the work group will soon know about it. The result will probably be devastating to employee morale.

Luck

You have undoubtedly heard the expression, "It helps to be in the right place at the right time." There is more than a little truth in this statement as it relates to compensation. Opportunities are continually presenting themselves in firms. Realistically, there is no way for managers to foresee many of the changes that occur. For instance, who could have known that the purchasing agent, Joe Flynn, a seemingly healthy middle-aged man, would suddenly die of a heart attack? Although the company may have been grooming several managers for Joe's position, none were capable of immediately assuming the increased responsibility. The most experienced person, Tommy Loy, had been with the company only six months. Tommy had been an assistant buyer for a competitor for four years. Because of his experience, Tommy received the promotion and the increased financial compensation. Tommy Loy was lucky; he was in the right place at the right time.

When asked to explain their most important reasons for success and effectiveness as managers, two chief executives responded candidly. One said, "Success is being at the right place at the right time and being recognized as having the ability to make timely decisions. It also depends on having good rapport with people, a good operating background, and the knowledge of how to develop people." The other replied, "My present position was attained by being in the right place at the right time with a history of getting the job done." Both executives recognize the significance of luck combined with the ability to perform. Their experiences lend support to the idea that luck works primarily for the efficient.

Salary Compression

Salary compression occurs when less experienced employees are paid as much as or more than employees who have been with the organization a long time due to a gradual increase in starting salaries and limited salary adjustment for long-term employees. Salary compression continues to be a major challenge for compensation managers even in a recession when pay cuts and freezes were the focus of the daily news. As workers discover inequities in their pay, resentment and lower productivity may follow with the employees ultimately leaving the company when the economy improves. Further, from a risk management perspective, companies need to make sure that salary compression is not causing problems with such laws as the Equal Pay Act. Unfortunately, no easy solution is available and it is projected that the gap between current and new employees is getting wider, and will continue to do so.

Salary compression typically occurs when there is only a minimum pay differential with various skills and responsibility levels. Salary compression can cause people in jobs of less responsibility to make more than workers in jobs that have more responsibility. For example, salary compression occurs when a worker earns as much or more than their supervisor. Reasons for this imbalance may be caused by the employee being paid overtime or a premium for the job while the supervisor cannot earn these benefits.

The solution to salary compression is simple; unfortunately the solution usually requires money, which is limited for most organizations. A company can build in compression funding to any annual budget increases. Still yet another way to remedy salary compression is to focus a primary portion of raises to your best employees and not waste compensation on across-the-board adjustments.

OBJECTIVE 9.8

Describe team-based pay, company-wide pay plans, professional employee compensation, sales representative compensation, and contingent worker compensation.

Team-Based Pay

Team-based pay is determined by how well the team performs in the accomplishment of the job. Since team performance consists of individual efforts, individual employees should be recognized and rewarded for their contributions. However, if a team is to function effectively, firms should also provide a reward based on the overall team performance as well. Changing a firm's compensation structure from an individual-based system to one that involves team-based pay can have powerful results. By so doing, a firm can improve efficiency, productivity, and profitability.

Team incentives have both advantages and disadvantages. On the positive side, firms find it easier to develop performance standards for groups than for individuals. For one thing, there are fewer standards to determine. Also, the output of a team is more likely to reflect a complete product or service. Another advantage is that employees may be more inclined to assist others and work collaboratively if the organization bases rewards on the team's output. When teams perform highly, it is the interaction among team members, not the members themselves, that creates the high performance. If a team member is asked who was responsible for the high performance of the team, he or she would likely say "We were" and mean it. A potential disadvantage for team incentives relates to exemplary performers. If individuals in this category perceive that they contribute more than other employees in the group, they may become disgruntled and leave. Christopher Avery, a Texas-based speaker and consultant who specializes in issues concerning individual and shared responsibility in the workplace and the author of *Teamwork Is an Individual Skill: Getting Your Work Done When Sharing Responsibility,* said, "If management wants to reward a high-performing team member, give that person a raise."[40]

Company-Wide Pay Plans

In baseball, as with other team sports, you do not judge the team based on its ace pitcher or great outfielder. The criterion for success is overall team performance, its win–loss record. In business, company-wide plans offer a possible alternative to the incentive plans previously discussed. Organizations normally base company-wide plans on the firm's productivity, cost savings, or profitability. Company-wide plans include profit sharing and gainsharing.

Profit Sharing

profit sharing
Compensation plans that result in the distribution of a predetermined percentage of the firm's profits to employees.

Profit sharing is a compensation plan that results in the distribution of a predetermined percentage of the firm's profits to employees. Many firms use this type of plan to integrate the employees' interests with those of the company. Profit-sharing plans can aid in recruiting, motivating, and retaining employees, which usually enhances productivity.

There are several variations of profit-sharing plans, but three basic kinds of plans used today are current profit sharing, deferred profit sharing, and combination plans.

- *Current plans* provide payment to employees in cash or stock as soon as profits have been determined.
- *Deferred plans* involve placing company contributions in an irrevocable trust, credited to individual employees' accounts. The funds are normally invested in securities and become available to the employee (or his or her survivors) at retirement, termination, or death.
- *Combination plans* permit employees to receive payment of part of their share of profits on a current basis, while deferring payment of part of their share.

Normally, most full-time employees are included in a company's profit-sharing plan after a specified waiting period. *Vesting* determines the amount of profit an employee owns in his or her account. Firms often determine this sum on a graduated basis. For example, an employee may become 25 percent vested after being in the plan for two years; 50 percent vested after three years; 75 percent vested after four years; and 100 percent vested after five years. This gradual approach to vesting encourages employees to remain with the firm, thereby reducing turnover.

The results of profit sharing include increased efficiency and lower costs. However, variations in profits may present a special problem. When employees have become accustomed to receiving added compensation from profit sharing, and then there is no profit to share, they may become disgruntled.

A basic problem with a profit-sharing plan stems from the recipients' seldom knowing precisely how they helped generate the profits, beyond just doing their jobs. And, if employees continue to receive a payment, they will come to expect it and depend on it. If they do not know what they have done to deserve it, they may view it as an entitlement program and the intended ownership attitude may not materialize.

Gainsharing

gainsharing
Plans designed to bind employees to the firm's productivity and provide an incentive payment based on improved company performance.

Gainsharing plans are designed to bind employees to the firm's productivity and provide an incentive payment based on improved company performance. Gainsharing programs, such as the

ETHICAL DILEMMA

But, He's a Friend

You have worked for your company for over 30 years and you have been the CEO much of this time. The company has grown to be one of the most successful firms in the world and your reputation is viewed as impeccable. The company was basically nothing when you arrived.

You have a very close friend who joined the firm shortly after you did. You went to the same university and were friends in the same fraternity. As you built the company, your friend prospered with you. In fact, many believe that if something happened to you, he would be offered your position. As your chief financial officer, you have given your friend tremendous power. But, you believe that he has earned it because he has developed the most productive and well-respected unit in the company. In fact, many of the rising stars in the country want to work for him. Seemingly, he can do no wrong.

But, a shocking tale is related to you one morning by a young CPA, and a friend of the family who works in the department overseen by your friend. He tells you of a plot he believes your friend has devised that can significantly improve the financial picture for the firm in the short run. The plan involves delaying reporting of certain expenses that could result in a significant stock price increase and a bonanza for your friend if he chooses to exercise his stock options. You are aware that he has recently gone through a bitter divorce that has had a devastating effect on his financial well-being. You think, "He is not a bad guy, just in a bad situation."

Your young friend is obviously fearful of the repercussions of reporting what he has discovered. If what he said is true and your friend exercises his stock options, it could result in the SEC getting involved and a public relations disaster for you. Because everyone is aware of your friendship, both reputations could be severely damaged. There would also likely be financial penalties for the firm. You believe the young man will keep quiet about what he believes is occurring if you ask him to, but you are left with a dilemma. He is your closest friend and you both have survived many business encounters in the past.

What would you do?
What factor(s) in this ethical dilemma might influence a person to make a less-than-ethical decision?

Scanlon, Multicost Scanlon, Rucker, and Improshare plans, are the most popular company-wide plans that have been adopted by American corporations. The goal of gainsharing is to focus on improving cost-efficiency, reducing costs, improving throughput, and improving profitability. Gainsharing helps align an organization's people strategy with its business strategy. Gainsharing plans (also known as *productivity incentives, team incentives,* and *performance sharing incentives*) generally refer to incentive plans that involve many or all employees in a common effort to achieve a firm's performance objectives.

Joseph Scanlon, after whom the Scanlon plan was named, developed the first gainsharing plan during the Great Depression, and it continues to be a successful approach to group incentive. The **Scanlon plan** provides a financial reward to employees for savings in labor costs resulting from their suggestions. Employee-management committees evaluate these suggestions. Participants in these plans calculate savings as a ratio of payroll costs to the sales value of what that payroll produces. If the company is able to reduce payroll costs through increased operating efficiency, it shares the savings with its employees. Scanlon plans are not only financial incentive systems, but also systems for participative management. The Scanlon plan embodies management–labor cooperation, collaborative problem solving, teamwork, trust, gainsharing, open-book management, and servant leadership.

Scanlon plan
Gainsharing plan that provides a financial reward to employees for savings in labor costs resulting from their suggestions.

HR Web Wisdom

Scanlon Leadership Network
http://www.scanlon.org/

A promoter of the Scanlon principles to advance their applications among organizations.

Professional Employee Compensation

As defined by the Fair Labor Standards Act, a *professional employee* performs work requiring advanced knowledge in a field of learning, normally acquired through a prolonged course of specialized instruction. Examples of exempt professionals often employed in industry include scientists and engineers. Their pay, initially, is for the knowledge they bring to the organization. Gradually, however, some of this knowledge becomes obsolete, and their salaries reflect this. At times, this encourages professionals to want to enter management to make more money. A problem with this move is that they may not be suited for management.

The unstable nature of professional jobs and their salaries result in a heavy emphasis on market data for job pricing. This has resulted in the use of *maturity curves* that reflect the relationship

TRENDS & INNOVATIONS

Say on Pay, Golden Parachutes, and Clawback Policies

Three provisions in the Dodd–Frank Act relate to say on pay, golden parachute contracts, and clawback policies.[41] The provision for **say on pay** gives shareholders in all but the smallest companies an advisory vote on executive pay. This is something that governance advocates have long wanted. Those who support the concept of say on pay believe that the vote will cause greater accountability on executive pay decisions.[42] The Dodd–Frank Act requires 5,000 companies to hold nonbinding shareholder say-on-pay votes at least every three years. Companies must also hold shareholder votes on the frequency of say on pay with the option of one, two, or three years, or to abstain. Frequency votes are required to be held every six years.[43] Thus far, shareholder votes appear to be highly favorable in support of company pay plans. However, a recent study found that boards that give chief executive officers higher pay opportunities are more likely to receive lower levels of support in shareholder say-on-pay votes than those with lower CEO pay.[44] Also, shareholders appear to want their say on pay on an annual basis as opposed to every two or three years.[45] Institutional Shareholder Services (ISS), which recommends mutual funds and other large shareholders on how to vote in corporate elections, has recommended "no" votes on executive pay in about 13 percent of the proposals it has reviewed this proxy season.[46] All of the companies with a failed say-on-pay vote in 2011 had a negative recommendation from the proxy advisory firm ISS.[47] One major company to receive a negative vote on say on pay was Hewlett-Packard. The negative vote may have been influenced by the resignation of CEO Mark Hurd after an investigation into sexual harassment allegations; he still received nearly $13 million in severance.[48]

A **golden parachute contract** is a perquisite that protects executives in the event that another company acquires their firm or if the executive is forced to leave the firm for other reasons. To hire and retain talented individuals, some corporations negotiate employment agreements that include golden parachutes.[49] At times golden parachute contracts have been abused. As an extreme example, CEO Robert Nardelli left Home Depot with a golden parachute worth $210 million even though Home Depot's stock performed poorly.[50]

The Dodd–Frank Act has disclosure requirements for golden parachute arrangements between the companies and their executive officers. It requires a shareholder advisory vote on certain parachute arrangements where shareholder approval of the business combination itself is sought. Legally, a "no" vote has little effect because the vote is advisory, and the vote cannot bind a company or its board to overrule any company or board decision or change or add to the company's or board's duties. But from a shareholder relations viewpoint, the answer is more problematic. A "no" vote may indicate future shareholder involvement.[51] Largely as a result of the Dodd–Frank Act, although golden parachutes continue to exist, many companies have scaled back the change-in-control severance payments to ward off shareholders' concerns and line up with evolving best practices.[52]

A **clawback policy** allows the company to recover compensation if a later review indicates that payments were not calculated accurately or performance goals were not met. The Dodd–Frank Act requires companies to develop *clawback policies* to recover compensation later deemed excessive.[53] The clawback is a procedure included in an executive's employment contract that allows the company to recover payments made through performance-based incentives under certain circumstances.[54] It requires executives to return incentive pay if the results on which it was granted are later adjusted downward for any reason. The CEO of Atlanta-based homebuilder Beazer Homes paid back $6.5 million in bonus pay and stock profits to settle an SEC complaint. According to the complaint, CEO Ian McCarthy failed to reimburse the company for cash bonuses, incentive and equity-based compensation, and profits from Beazer stock sales that he received in the year after the company filed fraudulent financial statements.[55]

OBJECTIVE 9.9

Explain say on pay, golden parachutes, and clawback policies.

between professional compensation and years of experience. These curves are used primarily to establish rates of pay for scientists and engineers involved in technical work at the professional level. Such maturity curves reveal a rapid increase in pay for roughly five to seven years, and then a more gradual rise as technical obsolescence erodes the value of these jobs.[56]

Sales Representative Compensation

Designing compensation programs for sales employees involves unique considerations. Bob Cartwright, SPHR, president and CEO of Texas-based Intelligent Compensation LLC, advises companies on sales strategies saying, "Understanding what the business needs are, where the gaps exist and what needs to be driven to get business from point A to point B—that's the key."[57] Proper ratio of base pay, commissions, and bonuses must be established. For this reason, this task may belong to the sales staff rather than to human resources. Nevertheless, many general compensation practices apply to sales jobs. For example, job content, relative job worth, and job market value are all relevant factors.

The *straight salary* approach is one extreme in sales compensation. In this method, salespersons receive a fixed salary regardless of their sales levels. Organizations use straight salary primarily to emphasize continued product service after the sale. For instance, sales representatives who deal largely with the federal government on a continuous basis often receive this form of compensation.

At the other extreme is *straight commission,* in which the person's pay is totally determined as a percentage of sales. If the salesperson makes no sales, the individual receives no pay. On the other hand, highly productive sales representatives can earn a great deal of money under this plan.

Between these extremes are the endless varieties of *part-salary, part-commission* combinations. The possibilities increase when a firm adds various types of *bonuses* to the basic compensation package. The emphasis given to either commission or salary depends on several factors, including the organization's philosophy toward service, the nature of the product, and the amount of time required to close a sale.

Contingent Worker Compensation

Contingent workers are employed through an employment agency or on an on-call basis and often earn less than traditional employees. Flexibility and lower costs for the employer are key reasons for the growth in the use of contingent workers. An inherent compensation problem relates to internal equity. You may have two employees working side by side, one a contingent worker and the other a regular employee, performing the same or near identical tasks, and one makes more money than the other. In most cases, contingents earn less pay and are far less likely to receive health or retirement benefits than their permanent counterparts.

OBJECTIVE 9.10

Explain the various elements of executive compensation and discuss executive compensation in the global environment.

Executive Compensation

Although there has been considerable discussion regarding what some say are excessive salaries by executives, one should remember that the skills possessed by company executives largely determine whether a firm will prosper, survive, or fail. A company's executive compensation program is a critical factor in attracting and retaining the best available talent. Thus, compensation programs need to be developed that motivate these executives to strive to achieve long-term success for the firm.

Executive pay has risen markedly over the past two decades, significantly outdoing shareholder earnings in most years. Some say that the reason for this exceptional rise is because corporate boards were not doing their jobs. Others believe that the salary upsurge was a necessary fact of life if the firm was to hire the best CEO possible in a highly competitive market.[58] Corporate board of directors are now taking a more active role since the financial services meltdown when the question was often asked "Where were the boards?"[59] Companies are under the proverbial gun to devise compensation plans that reward performance rather than greed. In fact the Dodd–Frank Act requires open disclosure of the relationship between the actual pay of executives and the financial performance of the company.

The act also focuses on ensuring that pay for performance is used throughout the company.[60] It is one thing for a chief executive to receive lavish compensation when the company is doing well, but it is something else to pay them millions when the company is failing. It is very important to shareholders to bring compensation in line with performance and directors today appear to be listening carefully, and responding, to the concerns expressed by shareholders, regulators, and other stakeholders.[61] Boards of directors and compensation professionals look for "red flags" that could signal corporate risk, such as direct loans to executives, payments of executive taxes, uncapped incentive and discretionary bonus payments, excessive relocation benefits and sign-on bonuses, excessive severance when termination is voluntary, and so on.[62] Some combinations of base salary, bonuses and performance-based pay, stock options, and perquisites make up the total compensation package of most executive pay plans.

Base Salary

Although it may not represent the largest portion of the executive's compensation package, base salary is obviously important. It is a factor in determining the executive's standard of living. Salary also provides the basis for other forms of compensation; for example, it may determine the amount of bonuses and certain benefits. The U.S. tax law does not allow companies to deduct more than $1 million of an executive's salary unless it is performance based and meets specified criteria.[63]

say on pay

Provision that gives shareholders in all but the smallest companies an advisory vote on executive pay.

golden parachute contract

Perquisite that protects executives in the event that another company acquires their firm or the executive is forced to leave the firm for other reasons.

clawback policy

Allows the company to recover compensation if subsequent review indicates that payments were not calculated accurately or performance goals were not met.

Bonuses and Performance-Based Pay

As shareholders become increasingly disenchanted with the high levels of executive compensation for less-than-stellar accomplishments, performance-based pay is gaining in popularity. While the Dodd–Frank Act has influenced executive pay, it appears that the greater influence has been the initiative to link pay to performance.[64] If pay for performance is appropriate for lower-level employees, should top executives be exempt from the same practice? The true superstars can still have huge earnings if their targets are met.

Payment of bonuses reflects a managerial belief in their incentive value. Cash bonuses, paid periodically based on performance goals, often provide real incentives. In the past, bonuses could be quite large and often were not tied to "real" performance goals. Hopefully, million-dollar pay packages not tied to performance are a thing of the past.

The Dodd–Frank Act requires the Securities and Exchange Commission and other agencies to regulate incentive pay at financial institutions. The SEC requires that institutions with $1 billion or more in assets (about 380 firms) be required to discourage "inappropriate risk" and disclose bonus details. Firms with $50 billion in assets (about 30 firms) would have to defer at least half of the top executives' bonuses for three years. These mechanisms are designed to discourage short-term thinking.

Stock Option Plans

stock option plan
Incentive plan in which executives can buy a specified amount of stock in their company in the future at or below the current market price.

Stock option plans give the executive the option to buy a specified amount of stock in the future at or below the current market price. The stock option is a long-term incentive designed to integrate the interests of management with those of the organization. To ensure this integration, some boards of directors require their top executives to hold some of the firm's stock. Stock options have lost some of their appeal because of accounting rule changes that require companies to value and book an appropriate expense for options as they are granted. Nevertheless, there are several bona fide reasons for including stock ownership in executive compensation plans. In addition to potentially aligning employees' interests with those of shareholders, retaining top executives is also a factor.

Perquisites (Perks)

perquisites (perks)
Special benefits provided by a firm to a small group of key executives and designed to give the executives something extra.

Perquisites (perks) are any special benefits provided by a firm to a small group of key executives and designed to give the executives "something extra." Possible executive's perks include a company-provided car, limousine service, and the use of company plane and yacht. The Securities and Exchange Commission has lowered the threshold for disclosure of executive perks from $50,000 to $10,000. Once-hidden information regarding perks must now be disclosed. Compensation committees are now focusing more on core incentives such as salaries, bonuses, and long-term incentives, and cutting perks and severance pay. Perks such as having a corporate jet or yacht are things that upset the public and legislators. David E. Gordon of Frederic W. Cook & Co., a compensation consultancy, said, "These kinds of perks just aren't worth it. They are a small fraction of overall compensation but have the ability to get 50 percent of the attention."[65]

A decrease in executive perquisites is a key prediction of the Dodd–Frank Act. Over one-third of Fortune 100 companies reported they had eliminated various executive perks listed as "other" perquisites.[66]

Severance Packages

What most people may not understand is that massive severance payments are not set up by a board of directors after a CEO has quit or been fired. These payments were negotiated prior to being hired. Not only should CEO pay be considered but CEO pay contracts should also be examined. But hopefully the environment is changing.

The Securities and Exchange Commission has adopted far-reaching executive compensation disclosure rules that apply to publicly traded companies. The new rules require companies to list all the agreements for each executive, to disclose the payment triggers, and, most importantly, to give an estimated dollar value of potential payments and benefits and the specific factors used to determine them. For the first time, investors will see the estimated total dollar value of the exit packages. No longer will these agreements become exposed only at the time of a merger and acquisition deal or when the board removes a CEO.

Executive Compensation in the Global Environment

The pay gap between the most affluent executives and the average worker in the United States remains wide. Earlier it was reported that the ratio between CEO and the average worker was 343 to 1. By contrast, the ratio is 50 in Venezuela, 22 in Britain, 20 in Canada, and 11 in Japan.[67] Whereas people in the United States derive great status from high pay, nations in large parts of Europe and Asia shun conspicuous wealth.

Governance of executive pay varies from country to country but there is a definite increase in shareholder influence on executive pay issues from Europe to North America to Asia Pacific and beyond. This trend will likely continue. Shareholders in Europe have been the leaders of the push. Executives at French firms face binding shareholder votes on certain aspects of their pay packages, including share options and retirement packages. Another proposal in France requires that severance payments be conditional on performance—a practice essentially unheard of in the past. European governments are trying to exert more direct influence over executive pay as well. Legislators in the Netherlands want to limit non-performance-based compensation by imposing an additional tax on salary and severance payments.[68] Starting in 2003, public companies in the United Kingdom were required to give shareholders an advisory up-or-down vote on executive pay packages. Although the say-on-pay vote is nonbinding, advocates believe that it has increased the discussion between companies and large investors, which resulted in an improved alignment between pay and performance. As an example, share option plans, which were criticized for rewarding short-term share price volatility over long-term value creation, have been largely replaced with performance-contingent stock.[69]

Investors in the Netherlands, Sweden, and Norway can cast a binding vote on executive pay. Some firms in Spain and Switzerland have voluntarily introduced advisory votes. Across Europe, companies are making efforts to improve executive pay disclosure.[70] It is quite likely these trends will continue in the wake of the recent recession. The United States has been slow to react to compensation governance, but there is evidence that this may be changing. Remember from the Trends & Innovations, as part of the Dodd–Frank Wall Street Reform and Consumer Protection Act, shareholders get a nonbinding vote on executive pay and generous packages set up for executives who part ways with the company.

MyManagementLab

Go to **mymanagementlab.com** to complete the problems marked with this icon ⭐.

Summary

1. **Discuss executive pay as a lightning rod for criticism, define compensation, *and describe the various forms of compensation.*** Executive pay has been a lightning rod for criticism and debate. The pay gap between the most affluent executives and the average worker has become enormous. It is difficult for workers who make $12 to $18 an hour to appreciate why these executives are making such outrageous salaries.

   Compensation is the total of all rewards provided employees in return for their services. *Direct financial compensation* consists of the pay that a person receives in the form of wages, salaries, commissions, and bonuses. *Indirect financial compensation (benefits)* consists of all financial rewards that are not included in direct financial compensation. *Nonfinancial compensation* consists of the satisfaction that a person receives from the job itself or from the psychological and/or physical environment in which the person works.

2. **Define financial equity *and explain the concepts of equity in direct financial compensation.*** *Financial equity* is workers' perceptions that they are being treated fairly.

   Forms of compensation equity include external equity, internal equity, employee equity, and team equity. *External equity* exists when a firm's employees receive pay comparable to workers who perform similar jobs in other firms. *Internal equity* exists when a firm's employees receive pay according to the relative value of their jobs within the same organization. *Employee equity* exists when individuals performing similar jobs for the same firm receive pay according to factors unique to the employee, such as performance level or seniority. *Team equity* is achieved when teams are rewarded based on their group's productivity.

3. **Identify the determinants of direct financial compensation.** The organization, the labor market, the job, and the employee all have an impact on job pricing and the ultimate determination of an individual's financial compensation.

4. **Describe the organization as a determinant of direct financial compensation.** Compensation policies, organizational level, and ability to pay are organizational factors to be considered.

5. *Describe the labor market as a determinant of direct financial compensation and explain how the job is a determinant of direct financial compensation.* Factors that should be considered include compensation surveys, expediency, cost-of-living increases, labor unions, the economy, and certain federal and state legislation.

  Management techniques used for determining a job's relative worth include job analysis, job descriptions, and job evaluation.

6. *Define* job evaluation *and describe the four traditional job evaluation methods.* Job evaluation is a process that determines the relative value of one job in relation to another. In the job evaluation ranking method, the raters examine the description of each job being evaluated and arrange the jobs in order according to their value to the company. The classification method involves defining a number of classes or grades to describe a group of jobs. In the factor comparison method, raters need not keep the entire job in mind as they evaluate; instead, they make decisions on separate aspects or factors of the job. In the point method, raters assign numerical values to specific job factors, such as knowledge required, and the sum of these values provides a quantitative assessment of a job's relative worth.

7. *Describe job pricing and identify factors related to the employee that are essential in determining direct financial compensation.* Placing a dollar value on the worth of a job is *job pricing*.

  The factors include pay for performance, seniority, experience, membership in the organization, potential, political influence, luck, and salary compression.

8. *Describe team-based pay, company-wide pay plans, professional employee compensation, sales representative compensation, and contingent worker compensation.* If a team is to function effectively, firms should provide a reward based on the overall team performance.

  Company-wide plans include profit sharing and gain-sharing. Organizations normally base company-wide plans on the firm's productivity, cost savings, or profitability.

Compensation for professionals is for the knowledge they bring to the organization. The unstable nature of professional jobs and their salaries result in a heavy emphasis on market data for job pricing.

Designing compensation programs for sales employees involves unique considerations.

Contingent workers are employed through an employment agency or on an on-call basis and often earn less than traditional employees. Flexibility and lower costs for the employer are key reasons for the growth in the use of contingent workers.

9. *Explain say on pay, golden parachutes, and clawback policies.* The Dodd–Frank Act requires 5,000 companies to hold nonbinding shareholder say-on-pay votes. Under the law, *say-on-pay* votes are required at least every three years.

  A *golden parachute contract* is a perquisite that protects executives in the event that another company acquires their firm or if the executive is forced to leave the firm for other reasons.

  A *clawback policy* allows the company to recover compensation if subsequent review indicates that payments were not calculated accurately or performance goals were not met.

10. *Explain the various elements of executive compensation and discuss executive compensation in the global environment.* In determining executive compensation, firms typically prefer to relate salary growth for the highest-level managers to overall corporate performance. Executive compensation often has five basic elements: (1) base salary, (2) bonuses and performance-based pay, (3) stock option plans, (4) perquisites, and (5) severance packages.

  The pay gap between the most affluent executives and the average worker in the United States remains wide. Earlier it was reported that the ratio between CEO and the average worker was 343 to 1. By contrast, the ratio is 50 in Venezuela, 22 in Britain, 20 in Canada, and 11 in Japan. Whereas people in the United States derive great status from high pay, nations in large parts of Europe and Asia shun conspicuous wealth.

Key Terms

Exercises

1. What form of incentive compensation might be used for the following jobs to increase productivity?
   a. machine operator
   b. automobile salesperson
   c. group of five people cooperating to get the job done
⭐ 2. The HRM in Action at the beginning of the chapter entitled "Executive Pay as a Lightning Rod for Criticism" suggested that some executives today are paid excessive salaries. What might be some pros and cons for paying large salaries to top executives?

3. What form of equity is involved if you hear one of your employees say the following?
   a. That guy at XYZ Company does the same type work I do but gets $10,000 more a year.
   b. That person in maintenance makes more than I do as the maintenance manager.
   c. I joined the firm the same time he did and now he is making $10,000 more than me for doing the same job.

Questions for Review

1. Define each of the following terms:
   (a) compensation
   (b) direct financial compensation
   (c) indirect financial compensation
   (d) nonfinancial compensation
2. What are the differences among external equity, internal equity, employee equity, and team equity?
3. What are the determinants of direct financial compensation?
4. What factors should be considered when the labor market is a determinant of direct financial compensation?
⭐ 5. How has government legislation affected compensation?
6. What is the difference between an exempt and a nonexempt employee?
7. Define *job evaluation*. Give the primary purpose of job evaluation.
8. Distinguish between the following job evaluation methods:
   (a) ranking
   (b) classification
   (c) factor comparison
   (d) point method
   (e) Hay Group Guide Chart-Profile Method
9. Define *job pricing*. What is the purpose of job pricing?

10. Define *pay grades*. State the basic procedure for determining pay grades.
11. Define *pay ranges*. What is the purpose of establishing pay ranges?
12. Define *broadbanding*. What is the purpose of using broadbanding?
13. Distinguish between merit pay, bonus, spot bonuses, and piecework.
14. Identify factors related to the employee as a determinant of direct financial compensation.
15. What are some company-wide pay plans? Briefly discuss each.
16. How is the compensation for professionals determined?
17. How is the compensation for sales representatives determined?
18. Describe each of the following:
   (a) say on pay
   (b) golden parachute contract
⭐ (c) clawback policies
19. What are the various types of executive compensation?
20. How does executive pay in the United States compare to executive compensation in the global environment?

INCIDENT 1 A Motivated Worker

Bob Rosen could hardly wait to get back to work Monday morning. He was excited about his chance of getting a large bonus. Bob is a machine operator with Ram Manufacturing Company, a Wichita, Kansas, producer of electric motors. He operates an armature-winding machine. The machine winds copper wire onto metal cores to make the rotating elements for electric motors.

Ram pays machine operators on a graduated piece-rate basis. Operators are paid a certain amount for each part made, plus a bonus. A worker who produces 10 percent above standard for a certain month receives a 10 percent additional bonus. For 20 percent above standard, the bonus is 20 percent. Bob realized that he had a good chance of earning a 20 percent bonus that month. That would be $1,787.

Bob had a special use for the extra money. His wife's birthday was just three weeks away. He was hoping to get her a car. He had already saved $4,000, but the down payment on the car was $5,500. The bonus would enable him to buy the car.

Bob arrived at work at seven o'clock that morning, although his shift did not begin until eight. He went to his workstation and checked the supply of blank cores and copper wire. Finding that only one spool of wire was on hand, he asked the forklift truck driver to bring another. Then, he asked the operator who was working the graveyard shift, "Sam, do you mind if I grease the machine while you work?"

"No," Sam said, "that won't bother me a bit."

After greasing the machine, Bob stood and watched Sam work. He thought of ways to simplify the motions involved in loading, winding, and unloading the armatures. As Bob took over the machine after the eight o'clock whistle, he thought, "I hope I can pull this off. I know the car will make Kathy happy. She won't be stuck at home while I'm at work."

Questions

1. Explain the advantages of a piecework pay system such as that at Ram.
2. What might be problems associated with the piecework pay system?

INCIDENT 2 The Controversial Job

David Rhine, compensation manager for Farrington Lingerie Company, was generally relaxed and good-natured. Although he was a no-nonsense, competent executive, David was one of the most popular managers in the company. This Friday morning, however, David was not his usual self. As chairperson of the company's job evaluation committee, he had called a late-morning meeting at which several jobs were to be considered for reevaluation. The jobs had already been rated and assigned to pay grade 3. But the office manager, Ben Butler, was upset that one was not rated higher. To press the issue, Ben had taken his case to two executives who were also members of the job evaluation committee. The two executives (production manager Bill Nelson and general marketing manager Betty Anderson) then requested that the job ratings be reviewed. Bill and Betty supported Ben's side of the dispute, and David was not looking forward to the confrontation that was almost certain to occur.

The controversial job was that of receptionist. Only one receptionist position existed in the company, and Marianne Sanders held it. Marianne had been with the firm 12 years, longer than any of the committee members. She was extremely efficient, and virtually all the executives in the company, including the president, had noticed and commented on her outstanding work. Bill Nelson and Betty Anderson were particularly pleased with Marianne because of the cordial manner in which she greeted and accommodated Farrington's customers and vendors, who frequently visited the plant. They felt that Marianne projected a positive image of the company.

When the meeting began, David said, "Good morning. I know that you're busy, so let's get the show on the road. We have several jobs to evaluate this morning and I suggest we begin . . ." Before he could finish his sentence, Bill interrupted, "I suggest we start with Marianne." Betty nodded in agreement. When David regained his composure, he quietly but firmly asserted, "Bill, we are not here today to evaluate Marianne. Her supervisor does that at performance appraisal time. We're meeting to evaluate jobs based on job content. In order to do this fairly, with regard to other jobs in the company, we must leave personalities out of our evaluation." David then proceeded to pass out copies of the receptionist job description to Bill and Betty, who were obviously very irritated.

Questions

1. Do you feel that David was justified in insisting that the job, not the person, be evaluated? Discuss.
2. Do you believe that there is a maximum rate of pay for every job in an organization, regardless of how well the job is being performed? Justify your position.
3. Assume that Marianne is earning the maximum of the range for her pay grade. In what ways could she obtain a salary increase?

MyManagementLab

Go to **mymanagementlab.com** for Auto-graded writing questions as well as the following Assisted-graded writing questions:

9-1. Why do many believe that executive compensation is the lightning rod for criticism?

9-2. Why might a firm want to be a pay leader as opposed to paying market rate?

9-3. Mymanagementlab Only – comprehensive writing assignment for this chapter.

Notes

1. A. G. Lafley, "Executive Pay: Time for CEOs to Take a Stand," *Harvard Business Review* 88 (May 2010): 40.
2. "CEOs' Pay Search," *HR Magazine* 56 (July 2011): 20.
3. Matt Turner, "Executive Compensation Programs Can Help or Hurt CEO Succession," *NACD Directorship* 36 (June/July 2010): 47–48.
4. Peter Drucker, "Beyond Capitalism," *Across the Board* 42 (November/December 2005): 14.
5. Neil Weinberg, "Pity the Bankers," *Forbes* 187 (April 25, 2011): 78–79.
6. Geoff Colvin, "As Executive Compensation Becomes Topics (Again), the Real Outrage Is How CEOs Are Paid, Not How Much," *Fortune* 161 (May 3, 2010): 86.
7. Robert J. Grossman, "Executive Pay: Perception and Reality," *HR Magazine* 54 (April 2009): 26–32.
8. Karen Dillon, "The Coming Battle over Executive Pay," *Harvard Business Review* 87 (September 2009): 96–103.
9. "Executive Compensation Impact of the Dodd-Frank Act: Considerations for the Remainder of 2011 and for 2012," *Employee Benefit Plan Review* 65 (August 2011): 22–25.
10. "Pay for Performance Is Working," *Corporate Board* 32 (May/June 2011): 27.
11. Robert Lowenstein, "Is Any CEO Worth $189,000 Per Hour?" *Bloomberg Businessweek* (February 20, 2012): 8–9.
12. Emily Lambert, "The Right Way to Pay," *Forbes* 183 (May 11, 2009): 78–80.
13. R. Wayne Mondy and Shane R. Premeaux, *Management: Concept, Practices, and Skills* (Englewood Cliffs, NJ: Prentice Hall, 7th Edition, 1995): 323–325.

14. Reginald L. Bell, "Addressing Employees' Feelings of Inequity: Capitalizing on Equity Theory in Modern Management," *Supervision* 72 (May 2011): 3–6.

15. Todd Hennenman, "Pay 'Philosophy' Could Prompt Workers to Stay," *Workforce Management* 90 (March 2011): 18.

16. Philippa Youngman, "Show Me the Money," *Human Resources Magazine* 16 (April/May 2011): 18–19.

17. "Salary Data Sources Critical to Compensation Planning," *Report on Salary Surveys* 12 (January 2012): 11–13.

18. Don Marsh, "OSH, Davis-Bacon Acts Bring Taxpayer Divergent Returns," *Concrete Products* 114 (May 2011): 4.

19. "Rule Clarifies Tip Credit; Comp Time, Fluctuating Workweek Left Intact," *HR Focus* (May 2011): 8–9.

20. Fay Hansen, "Study Finds Widespread Wage Theft," *Workforce Management* 88 (November 16, 2009): 29.

21. Judy Greenwald, "Top Wage-hour Class Action Settlements Soared in 2009," *Business Insurance* 44 (January 25, 2010): 4–19.

22. Roger S. Achille, "FLSA Requires Education for Professional Exemption," *HR Magazine* 55 (February 2010): 70.

23. Cassandra Dillenberger, "Is Overtime Pay Required for PDA, Cell Phone, or Blackberry Use?" *Contractor's Business Management Report* 2-10 (November 2010): 1–7.

24. Nancy Hatch Woodward, "Matching Jobs with Pay," 57 *HR Magazine* (May 2012): 55–58.

25. http://www.haygroup.com/ww/about/index.aspx?ID=68

26. "Strategic Use of Pay Ranges Can Maximize a Tight Budget," *Report on Salary Surveys* (May 2010): 8–9.

27. Frank L. Giancola, "A Framework for Understanding New Concepts in Compensation Management," *Benefits & Compensation Digest* 46 (September 2009): 1–16.

28. "Study Says Pay for Performance Linked to Positive Results," *Report on Salary Surveys* 11 (March 2011): 10–11.

29. Eric Krell, "All for Incentives, Incentives for All," *HR Magazine* 56 (January 2011): 34–38.

30. Kathryn Tyler, "Design an Effective Rewards Program," *HR Magazine* 56 (October 2011): 94.

31. "Pay for Performance," *Controller's Report 2010* (January 2010): 6–8.

32. "Use Variable Pay to Promote Success in the Workplace," *HR Focus* 87 (July 2010): 5–6.

33. Michelle Conlin, "The Case for Unequal Perks," *BusinessWeek* (March 23, 2009): 54–55.

34. Justin G. Roy, "Ten Tips for Retaining the Next Generation," *Offshore* 72 (January 2012): 10–11.

35. "Compensation & Incentives, The Entitlement Era Is Over," *HR Magazine* 57 (Special Supplement, SHRM 2012 HR Trend Book): 60.

36. "Raises Cut in '09, But Bonus Budgets Inch Up," *Treasury & Risk* (September 2009): 8.

37. "Compdata Survey Finds 70 Percent of Employers Offer Bonuses as Rewards," *Report on Salary Surveys* 12 (January 2012): 15.

38. Angie Herbers, "Bonus Babies," *Investment Advisor* 30 (February 2010): 47–48.

39. Frank L. Giancola, "Skill-Based Pay: Fad or Classic?" *Compensation & Benefits Review* 43 (July 2011): 220–226.

40. Matt Bloch, "Rewarding the Team," *HR Magazine* 52 (February 2007): 91–93.

41. "Executive Compensation Impact of the Dodd-Frank Act: Considerations for the Remainder of 2011 and for 2012," *Employee Benefit Plan Review* 65 (August 2011): 22–25.

42. David Lynn, "Implementing Say-On-Pay in 2011," *Corporate Board* 32 (July/August 2011): 17–20.

43. Melissa Klein Anguilar, "Say-on-Pay Rules Include Delay for Small Companies," *Compliance Week* 8 (March 2011): 14–52.

44. Dori Meinert, "High CEO Pay Leads to Lower Shareholder Support," 57 *HR Magazine* (May 2012): 18.

45. Melissa Klein Aguilar, "Lack of Investor Support for Less-Frequent Say-on-Pay Votes," *Compliance Week* 8 (April 2011): 9–10.

46. "Company Dinged for Failure to Disclose CEO Perks," *Compliance Week* 8 (March 2011): 8–10.

47. John K. Wilson and Joshua A. Agen, "Say on Pay Best Practices for 2012," *Corporate Board* 33 (March/April 2012): 6–10.

48. Arielle Bikard, "Say-on-Pay Losses Catch HP, Others Off Guard," *Compliance Week* 8 (June 2011): 44–45.

49. William G. Ruffner, "The Golden Parachute Paradox," *Pennsylvania CPA Journal* 82 (Summer 2011): 1.

50. Jeremy Smerd, "The 'Big' News Stories That Weren't," *Workforce Management* 86 (December 10, 2007): 30.

51. "Compliance Clarified: Safely Landing Golden Parachutes," *Compliance Reporter* (February 28, 2011): 2.

52. Sarah Hiester, "Golden Parachutes: Still with Us, But for How Long?" *Corporate Governance Advisor* 20 (January/February 2012): 1–8.

53. "Firms Gear Up for Dodd-Frank Pay Rules," *Compliance Reporter* (February 21, 2011): 32.

54. Jesse Fried and Nitzan Shilon, "The Dodd-Frank Clawback and the Problem of Excess Pay," *Corporate Board* 32 (January/February 2012): 15–21.

55. Melissa Klein Aguilar, "Beazer CEO Returns $6.5M to Settle SEC Clawback Suit," *Compliance Week* 8 (April 2011): 7–8.

56. Richard I. Henderson, *Compensation Management in a Knowledge-Based World* (Upper Saddle River, NJ: Prentice Hall, 2006): 181.

57. Scott Ladd, "May the Sales Force Be with You," *HR Magazine* 55 (September 2010): 105–107.

58. Charles M. Elson and Craig K. Ferrere, "What Is a CEO Worth? Don't Look to Peers," *Directors & Boards* 35 (2011 3rd Quarter): 40–45.

59. Richard M. Steinberg, "On the Hot Seat with Today's Challenges," *Financial Executive* 25 (October 2009): 28–31.

60. Myrna Hellerman, "Wanted: 'Pay for Performance' CEOs," *Corporate Board* 32 (September/October 2011): 17–20.

61. "Boards Tighten Their Focus on Pay, Risk and Succession Planning," *Corporate Board* 32 (January/February 2012): 26–27.

62. "Red Flags," *Trustee* 64 (April 2011): 7.

63. Michael J. Collins, "Eleven Executive Compensation Problems (and Some Possible Solutions)," *Benefits Law Journal* 24 (Fall 2011): 7–19.

64. "Executive Pay Recovers Heartily in 2010, Three Surveys Find," *Report on Salary Surveys* 11 (June 2011): 1–5.

65. Jessica Silver-Greenberg, Tara Kalwarski, and Alexis Leondis, "CEO Pay Drops...But Cash Is King," *BusinessWeek* (April 5, 2010): 50–56.

66. "Executive Perks Declining," *HR Magazine* 55 (December 2010): 62.

67. Doris Burke, "The Growing Wealth Gap," *Fortune* 164 (November 7, 2011): 28.

68. "Lack of Global Pay Rules Creates Challenges," *Compliance Reporter* (January 29, 2010): 17.

69. Diane Doubleday and Jennifer Wagner, "New Era for Boards and Executive 'Pay For Performance,'" *Corporate Board* 30 (September/October 2009): 5–12.

70. Aubrey E. Bou and Ira T. Kay, "When Should Shareholders Say 'Yes' on Pay?" *Rotman International Journal of Pension Management* 4 (Spring 2011): 12–17.

10

Indirect Financial Compensation (Benefits) and Nonfinancial Compensation

HRM in Action

Unique Employee Benefits

OBJECTIVE 10.1

Describe some unique employee benefits, define *indirect financial compensation* (benefits), and explain what is included in a total reward package.

As the recession moved on, more and more companies were providing unique benefits to keep employees involved, even as traditional employee benefit costs continued to rise. Companies were trying out what some might call unique benefits as they attempted to brand their organization as a good place to work. They used employee benefits to clearly separate them from their competitors. Employers are looking at what types of unique benefits they can bring to their organization to show employees they are interested in providing additional improvements at work. Listed below are some unique benefits that employees currently enjoy.

- Akraya Inc., a staffing services firm based in Sunnyvale, California, provides a cleaning service for employees' homes twice a month. This benefit is especially important to employees who have to clean their homes on the weekend after working all week at the office.[1]
- At Zynga, a gaming company headquartered in San Francisco, the wellness center includes a sports court and exercise equipment, as well as yoga, tai chi, and acupuncture rooms. The roughly 100 dogs that come to work every day with their owners enjoy pet insurance, free dog food , and Zynga-issued dog tags.[2]
- At Kimpton, the privately owned operator of 55 hotels across the United States, animal owners can take advantage of discounted pet insurance, and employees are free to bring their dogs to work every day.[3]
- The Liberty Hotel in Boston holds a Yappier Hour (a takeoff on Happy Hour) every week in the summer where guests and employees can bring their pets for "Puptails" and socializing. It also offers group pet insurance as part of the employee benefits program.[4]

1 Describe some unique employee benefits, define *indirect financial compensation* (benefits), and explain what is included in a total reward package.

2 Describe legally required benefits.

3 Define *discretionary benefits* and explain the various types of discretionary benefits.

4 Explain the different kinds of health care legislation and describe the relationship between smoke-free workplaces and the Patient Protection and Affordable Care Act.

5 Explain premium pay.

6 Explain voluntary benefits.

7 Describe customized benefit plans.

8 Describe the importance of communicating information about the benefits package.

9 Describe the job itself and the job environment as components of nonfinancial compensation.

10 Describe workplace flexibility (work–life balance) factors and global customized benefits.

- Colgate-Palmolive offers emergency home child care, with complete coverage for the first 10 days and then 50 percent for days 11 through 30. The company also has backup child care at some locations, and parents get time off on the morning of the first day of school. Its mortgage assistance program helps employees refinance existing loans or obtain a discounted mortgage to buy a new home. U.S. employees can buy additional vacation days at the beginning of each year—or sell unused days.[5]

- At the New Belgium Brewing Company in Fort Collins, Colorado, employees get a cruiser bicycle after their first year and after five years they receive a free trip to Belgium to visit breweries. After 10 years, workers are given a four-week sabbatical and a tree is planted in their name. The company has a stock ownership plan in which employees have 42 percent ownership in the company. A free beer after work is a valued benefit for some.[6]

Other possible unique benefits might be paying for child care for a parent who is on company travel, pet care when an employee travels, or paid travel for an employee's spouse. Some small to midsize organizations in the United States allow parents to bring their babies to work as a benefit, although most firms accept babies only until they can crawl.[7] If any of the mentioned items are important to the workforce, it may be worthwhile to incorporate them into the benefit package.

Indirect Financial Compensation (Benefits)

Most organizations recognize that they have a responsibility to their employees to provide certain benefits such as insurance and other programs for their health, safety, security, and general welfare (see Figure 10-1). **Indirect financial compensation (benefits)** consists of all financial rewards not included in direct financial compensation. They typically account for about 30 percent of a firm's financial compensation costs. According to a recent SHRM survey, benefits are the second most important driver of job satisfaction, coming in just behind job security.[8] Benefits generally cost the firm money, but employees usually receive them indirectly. For example, an organization may spend thousands of dollars a year contributing to health insurance premiums for each employee. The employee does not receive the money but does obtain the health insurance coverage benefit.

As a rule, employees receive benefits because of their membership in the organization. Benefits are typically unrelated to employee productivity; therefore, although they may be valuable in recruiting and retaining employees, they do not generally serve as motivation for improved performance. Legislation mandates some benefits, and employers provide other discretionary and voluntary benefits. *Discretionary benefits* are benefit payments made as a result of unilateral management decisions in nonunion firms and from labor–management negotiations in unionized firms. *Voluntary benefits*, on the other hand, are usually 100 percent paid by the employee but the employer typically pays the administrative cost. Voluntary benefits have two distinct advantages: (1) they are generally nontaxable to the employee and (2) the cost may be much less for large groups of employees than for individuals. Often a hybrid situation exists in which employers pay a portion of the benefit and the employee pays for additional services.

HR Web Wisdom

Total Rewards
http://www.worldatwork.org/waw/aboutus/html/aboutus-whatis.html

Total rewards include everything the employee perceives to be of value resulting from the employment relationship.

A Total Rewards Package

Historically, compensation practitioners focused primarily on direct financial compensation and indirect financial compensation (benefits). However, this approach has expanded into the concept of total rewards, and the emphasis is now more encompassing as reflected in the name change of the compensation's professional organization. The American Compensation Association is now WorldatWork, the Professional Association for Compensation, Benefits, and *Total Rewards*. Total rewards is about all the ways in which people are rewarded when they come to work—pay, benefits, and the other nonfinancial rewards (psychological and/or physical environment factors). Managers today should consider a broad rewarding work environment and not just focus on pay

FIGURE 10-1

Indirect Financial Compensation (Benefits) in a Total Compensation Program

EXTERNAL ENVIRONMENT
INTERNAL ENVIRONMENT
Compensation

Financial   Nonfinancial

<u>Direct</u>   <u>Indirect (Benefits)</u>   <u>The Job</u>   <u>Job Environment</u>

Legally Required Benefits
Social Security
Unemployment Compensation
Workers' Compensation

Discretionary Benefits
Payment for Time Not Worked
Health Care
Life Insurance
Retirement Plans
Disability Protection
Employee Stock Option Plans
Employee Services
Premium Pay

Voluntary Benefits

and benefits plans. The definition of compensation goes beyond money and benefits and looks at learning and development, including career development, and the work environment.[9] One survey of more than 250,000 large U.S. companies revealed that a comprehensive benefit plan including opportunities for career advancement and work–life flexibility are the top factors in workers' happiness, even more important than salary.[10]

Everything included in the total reward package is directed toward maximum attainment of corporate goals. Everything the company provides is included, from base pay and benefits to the organization's culture and environment. With total rewards, the idea of a three-legged stool provides an example of how the three forms of compensation are tied together. If one leg of the stool breaks or is weaker than the others, the total compensation package will be less effective. Such would be the case with a person attempting to sit on a stool on which one leg was shorter than the others.

Some companies are using a total reward statement to show employees the total value of everything they enjoy as a member of the organization. All items that add value to an employee should be included. If it cost $3,000 for training provided an employee, this also should be included. However, there may be a problem in determining the actual value of an item to a specific employee. For instance, it may be easy to compute the training cost for an employee as $3,000 but what value does the employee actually place on the training? It could be zero or it could be much more than $3,000.

OBJECTIVE 10.2
Describe legally required benefits.

Legally Required Benefits

Employers provide most benefits, but the law requires others. These legally required benefits currently account for about 10 percent of total compensation costs. They include Social Security, unemployment insurance, and workers' compensation.

Social Security

The Social Security Act of 1935 created a system of retirement benefits. It also established the Social Security Administration. Subsequent amendments to the act added other forms of protection, such as disability insurance, survivors' benefits, and Medicare.

Disability insurance protects employees against loss of earnings resulting from total incapacity. *Survivors' benefits* are provided to certain members of an employee's family when the employee dies. These benefits are paid to the widow or widower and unmarried children. Unmarried children may be eligible for survivors' benefits until they are 18 years old. In some cases, students retain eligibility until they are 19. *Medicare* provides hospital and medical insurance protection for individuals 65 years of age and older and for those who have become disabled.

Although employees must pay a portion of the cost of Social Security coverage, the employer makes a contribution and considers this cost to be a benefit. The present employer tax rate is 6.2 percent for the Social Security portion and 1.45 percent for Medicare. The Social Security rate is applied to a maximum taxable wage of $106,800. The rate for Medicare applies to all earnings.

ETHICAL DILEMMA

A Poor Bid

You are vice president of human resources for a large construction company, and your company is bidding on an estimated $2.5 million public housing project. A local electrical subcontractor submitted a bid that you realize is 20 percent too low because labor costs have been incorrectly calculated. It is obvious to you that benefits amounting to over 30 percent of labor costs have not been included. In fact, the bid was some $30,000 below those of the other four subcontractors. But, accepting it will improve your chance of winning the contract for the big housing project.

What would you do?
What factor(s) in this ethical dilemma might influence a person to make a less-than-ethical decision?

Approximately 95 percent of the workers in this country pay into and may draw Social Security benefits. The Social Security program currently is running a surplus, but the retirement of the 77-million-member baby-boom generation has begun. Unless Congress makes changes by 2041, the program will have used up its surplus and will no longer be able to pay full benefits.

The retirement age today is 66. It will increase gradually until in 2027, it reaches age 67. These changes will not affect Medicare, with full eligibility under this program holding at age 65.

Unemployment Compensation

Unemployment compensation provides workers whose jobs have been terminated through no fault of their own monetary payments for up to 26 weeks or until they find a new job. The basic program is state-run with oversight from the U.S. Department of Labor. States pay the benefits; the federal government pays the states for administrative costs. Employers pay the Federal Unemployment Tax at a rate of 6.2 percent on the first $7,000 each employee earns. If they pay it on time, the percent is offset by 5.8 percent so the actual rate is .8 percent. The permanent Extended Benefits Program provides an additional 13 or 20 weeks of compensation to workers who exhaust basic benefits in states where unemployment has worsened.

The intent of unemployment payments is to provide an unemployed worker time to find a new job equivalent to the one lost without suffering financial distress. Without this benefit, workers might have to take jobs for which they are overqualified or end up on welfare. Unemployment compensation also serves to sustain consumer spending during periods of economic adjustment. In the United States, unemployment insurance is based on both federal and state statutes and, although the federal government provides guidelines, the programs are administered by the states and therefore benefits vary by state. A payroll tax paid solely by employers funds the unemployment compensation program. Unemployment rates range from 3.4 percent in North Dakota to 13.0 percent in Nevada. The construction industry and hospitality businesses have been hit the hardest.[11]

Workers' Compensation

Workers' compensation provides a degree of financial protection for employees who incur expenses resulting from job-related accidents or illnesses. As with unemployment compensation, the various states administer individual programs, which are subject to federal regulations. Employers pay the entire cost of workers' compensation insurance, and their past experience with job-related accidents and illnesses largely determines their premium expense. These circumstances should provide further encouragement to employers to be proactive with health and safety programs.

Discretionary Benefits

Although the law requires some benefits, organizations provide numerous other benefits that assist in accomplishing the objectives of both the company and the employee. **Discretionary benefits** are benefit payments made as a result of unilateral management decisions in nonunion firms and from labor–management negotiations in unionized firms. An employee's desire for a specific benefit may change, requiring organizations to continuously check the pulse of its workforce to determine the most sought after benefits.

Major categories of discretionary benefits include payment for time not worked, health care, life insurance, retirement plans, employee stock option plans, and employee services. Employers continuously reevaluate their benefits program, adding some and reducing some as the need arises. Bank-at-work programs are now being used as a discretionary benefit because they provide something new to the benefits offerings without increasing costs.[12]

Payment for Time Not Worked

In providing payment for time not worked, employers recognize that employees need time away from the job for many purposes. Discussed in the following sections are paid vacations, sick pay and paid time off, sabbaticals, and other forms of payment for time not worked.

Paid Vacations

Vacation time serves important compensation goals. For instance, paid vacations help workers to be more creative and productive, reduce stress, brings families and friends closer to families, and improves job performance.[13] They may also encourage employees to remain with the firm. Paid vacation time typically increases with seniority. For example, employees with one year of service might receive two weeks; ten years' service, three weeks; and fifteen years' service, four weeks.

In a climate of increased outsourcing and job insecurity, it is not surprising that many Americans do not take full advantage of their vacation benefits. In a Right Management survey, over two-thirds of employees said they were not using all their annual leave in 2011, which was down from less than half in 2010.[14] Some employees believe their employers do not want them to take vacations or are afraid to ask for time off. As compared with other countries, the average 13 days Americans take annually is small. According to the World Tourism Organization, Italians take 42 days, French take 37 days, and Brazilians take 34 days. Canadians double the number of vacation days per year that are taken in the United States.[15] In one survey, 63 percent of Americans work more than 40 hours a week and lose more than $21 billion in unused vacation each year.[16]

Vacation time may vary with organizational rank. For instance, an executive, regardless of time with the firm, may be given a month of vacation. With an annual salary of $1,440,000, this manager would receive a benefit worth approximately $120,000 each year while not working. A junior accountant earning $39,000 a year might receive two weeks of vacation time worth about $1,500.

Sick Pay and Paid Time Off

Each year many firms allocate to each employee a certain number of days of sick pay they may use when ill. Employees who are too sick to report to work continue to receive their pay up to the maximum number of days accumulated. As with vacation pay, the number of sick pay days often depends on seniority.

Some managers are very critical of sick pay programs. At times individuals have abused the system by calling in sick when all they really wanted was an additional day of paid vacation. One approach in dealing with the problem of unscheduled absences is *paid time off*. In lieu of sick leave, vacation time, and a personal day or two, a growing number of companies are providing **paid time off** (PTO), a certain number of days off provided each year that employees can use for any purpose. With a PTO plan, all categories of time off such as sick leave, vacation, and personal days are grouped together. Possible benefits from PTOs include simpler administration, fewer carryover issues, high employee satisfaction, fewer creative excuses for time off, earlier advance notice of time-off needs, fewer last-minute absences, and fewer conflicts about time-off usage.

Some companies are experimenting with different forms of PTO plans. A few companies are using what is referred to as a *results-only work environment* (ROWE). This plan allows employees to work wherever and whenever they wish as long as they complete projects on time. It often provides the "perfect blend" to the younger generation or those who are young at heart where both work life and personal life can be enjoyed.[17] The attitude of many workers today is that if I can get it done, and get it done well, why does it matter where or when I work?[18] Employers Resource Council, a human resource services company based in Mayfield Village, Ohio, gives employees all the time off that they want. There is no schedule and no limit for earned vacation and leave time. The firm's 30 employees just have to get their work done on time.[19]

Sabbaticals

Sabbaticals are temporary leaves of absence from an organization, usually at reduced pay. Although sabbaticals have been used for years in the academic community, they are now entering the private sector. In fact, over 20 percent of companies on Fortune magazine's list of the Top 100 Best Companies to Work For provide sabbaticals.[20] Often sabbaticals help to reduce turnover and keep workers from burning out, hopefully returning revitalized and more committed to their work. At Intel Corporation, which has 44,209 employees in the United States, workers who complete seven years with the company are eligible to take an eight-week sabbatical with full pay.[21] Stonyfield Farm instituted a two-month paid sabbatical for anyone who has worked at least five years with the firm. The program has been one of the most popular benefits with almost 200 employees taking advantage of it.[22]

Sabbaticals are not without challenges. Overachievers may experience difficulty in letting go of their work and worry about their job if they are gone for extended periods. Then there is the problem of scheduling who will take up the slack while the person on sabbatical is gone. But, most organizations using sabbaticals have discovered that the benefits outweigh the challenges.

paid time off (PTO)
Means of dealing with the problem of unscheduled absences by providing a certain number of days each year that employees can use for any purpose.

sabbaticals
Temporary leaves of absence from an organization, usually at reduced pay.

Other Types of Payment for Time Not Worked

Although paid vacations, sick pay, paid time off, and sabbaticals constitute the largest portion of payment for time not worked, there are numerous other types that companies use. It is common for organizations to pay workers for their time in performing civic duties. For example, companies often give employees time off to work with the United Way. At times an executive may be on loan to work virtually full time on such an endeavor.

Some companies routinely permit employees to take off during work hours to handle personal affairs without taking vacation time. When a worker is called for jury duty, some organizations continue to pay their salary; others pay the difference between jury pay and their salary. When the National Guard or military reserve are called to duty, as has been the case in Afghanistan and Iraq, some companies pay their employees a portion of their salary while on active duty. Further, during an election, many companies permit employees voting time. Still other firms permit bereavement time for the death of a close relative. Finally, there is the payment for time not worked while at the company such as rest periods, coffee breaks, lunch periods, cleanup time, and travel time. The Fair Labor Standards Act does not require employers to give workers a rest break, and only 10 states require it to be given. In these states, usually the break mandated is 10 minutes for every four hours worked.

Health Care

Health care represents the most expensive item in indirect financial compensation. In fact, according to research from the Kaiser Family Foundation, the United States spends more per capita on health care than any other country and threatens to go even higher.[23] The Office of Management and Budget estimates that the United States spends approximately $700 billion per year in health care costs due to inefficiency and waste. An additional $360 billion per year is spent in the administration of the system.[24] Some companies have reduced or eliminated salary increases or bonuses, or both, in order to provide increasingly expensive medical benefits for employees.

A number of factors have combined to create the high cost of health care:

- An aging population
- A growing demand for medical care
- Increasingly expensive medical technology
- Inefficient administrative processes

There appears to be a light at the end of the tunnel. Employers are using programs to better manage costs, such as managed-care health organizations and consumer-driven plans, to help reduce and control health care costs. Also, the health care bill passed in 2010 (discussed later) will likely have a significant impact on health care.

Managed-Care Health Organizations

Historically, managed-care systems have been the general response to increased medical costs. These networks are comprised of doctors and hospitals that agree to accept negotiated prices for treating patients. Employees receive financial incentives to use the facilities within the network. The following are various forms of managed-care health organizations:

- **Health maintenance organizations (HMOs)** cover all services for a fixed fee but exercise control over which doctors and health facilities a member may use.
- **Preferred provider organizations (PPOs)** are managed-care health organizations in which incentives are provided to members to use services within the system; out-of-network providers may be used at greater cost.
- **Point-of-service (POS)** requires a primary care physician and referrals to see specialists, as with HMOs, but permits out-of-network health care access.
- **Exclusive provider organizations (EPOs)** offer a smaller PPO provider network and usually provide little, if any, benefits when an out-of-network provider is used.

Managed-care health organizations are losing their luster for some in favor of consumer-driven health care plans.

---

health maintenance organization (HMO)
Managed-care health organization that covers all services for a fixed fee but exercises control over which doctors and health facilities a member may use.

preferred provider organization (PPO)
Managed-care health organization in which incentives are provided to members to use services within the system; out-of-network providers may be used at greater cost.

point-of-service (POS)
Managed-care health organization that requires a primary care physician and referrals to see specialists, as with HMOs, but permits out-of-network health care access.

exclusive provider organization (EPO)
Managed-care health organization that offers a smaller preferred provider network and usually provides few, if any, benefits when an out-of-network provider is used.

Consumer-Driven Health Care Plans

Companies are increasingly placing the responsibility for health care on employees.[25] With health insurance costs still rising faster than the cost of living, consumer-driven health care plans are being used more because they have proven to lower costs. **Consumer-driven health care plans** give each employee a set amount of money annually to purchase health care coverage that involves high-deductible insurance coverage combined with a tax-advantaged account such as a health savings account (HSA), health reimbursement account (HRA), and flexible spending account (FSA). Membership in these plans was about 21 million in 2011, or approximately 12 percent of the private insurance market, according to a report by the Employee Benefit Research Institute.[26] They are a good way for employers to provide the same caliber of benefits to their employees while also reducing premiums and involving employees in the cost of coverage. Patients who pay for health care services using pretax funds are not subject to the same lengthy, burdensome payments cycle. General Electric requires its salaried U.S. employees and retirees under the age of 65 to choose a consumer-driven health plan, which includes deductibles that run as high as $4,000 a year.[27] Consumer-driven plans are more popular with large employers with 1,000 or more workers, and about one-third of these sponsor such plans. According to America's Health Insurance Plans, the average premiums for consumer-driven plans are approximately 15 to 20 percent lower than average premiums in the overall market.[28] A recent McKinsey & Company study found that with these plans, patients are twice as likely to ask about costs and three times as likely to choose less-expensive treatment options. Thirty percent are more likely to get an annual check-up. Chronic patients are 20 percent more likely to carefully follow physicians' orders.[29]

consumer-driven health care plan

Gives each employee a set amount of money annually with which to purchase health care coverage that involves high-deductible insurance coverage combined with a tax-advantaged account such as a health savings account, health reimbursement accounts, and flexible spending account.

HEALTH SAVINGS ACCOUNT A **health savings account (HSA)** is a tax-free health spending and savings account available to individuals and families who have qualified high-deductible health insurance policies as determined by IRS regulations. HSAs are an important tool in the search to change consumers' health care spending behaviors and better manage health costs. It gives individuals a stake in managing their own health care dollars. Individuals deposit up to $6,250 a year in a pretax account that can be used for deductibles for doctor visits, prescriptions and other expenses, as well as saving for future and long-term medical expenses. HSA-eligible health plans typically have lower premiums than other plans because of their higher deductibles. Another advantage is that even if a worker takes another job, the HSA stays with that individual.[30] The health care reform law contains two direct changes to health savings accounts. It eliminates the ability to use the HSA for over-the-counter drugs and increases the early withdrawal penalty from 10 percent to 20 percent.

health savings account (HSA)

Tax-free health spending and savings accounts available to individuals and families who have qualified high-deductible health insurance policies as determined by IRS regulation.

HEALTH REIMBURSEMENT ACCOUNTS **Health reimbursement accounts (HRAs)** allow an employer to set aside funds to reimburse medical expenses paid by participating employees. HRAs allow both employees and employers to save on the cost of health care. All employer contributions are 100 percent tax deductible to the employer and tax free to the employee. Although HRA plans are flexible, the primary requirement for an HRA is that the plan must be funded solely by the employer. There is no limit on the employer's contributions, which are excluded from an employee's income, and a credit balance in the employee's account can be rolled over from year to year like a savings account.

health reimbursement accounts (HRAs)

Allows an employer to set aside funds to reimburse medical expenses paid by participating employees.

FLEXIBLE SPENDING ACCOUNT A **flexible spending account (FSA)** is a health benefit plan established by employers that allows employees to deposit a certain portion of their salary (before paying income taxes) into an account to be used for eligible expenses. The employee consents to this reduced salary allowing the employer to contribute to an FSA, and account holders are generally issued a Visa or MasterCard Flexible Spending Account card. This keeps an employee from having to personally pay whenever expenses arise. There is also no requirement to submit receipts for reimbursement; instead, the purchase is deducted from the account balance. Payroll contributions made to an FSA are exempt from federal income tax, Social Security taxes and, in most cases, state income tax. As a result, employees who use an FSA can essentially shield a portion of their income from taxes to pay for approved medical and dependent care expenses. Examples of permissible reimbursement expenses include asthma prescriptions, braces for a teenager, or monthly daycare. A major disadvantage of an FSA is that generally employees forfeit any amounts left unspent in the accounts at year-end. Under the Patient Protection and Affordable Care Act of 2010 there is a limit of $2,500 on a FSA. Also employees will no longer be able to use FSA funds to pay for over-the-counter medications.

flexible spending account (FSA)

Benefit plan established by employers that allows employees to deposit a certain portion of their salary into an account (before paying income taxes) to be used for eligible expenses.

On-Site Health Care (Work-Site Clinics)

On-site health care is another way of curbing health care costs and also providing an employee benefit. Employers have increasingly gotten into the business of providing direct health care to their workers through on-site clinics because it permits employers to better manage and at times reduce the growth of health care costs. On-site health care assists in treating minor illnesses and injuries, vaccinations, physical therapy, and providing follow-up care. Employers can reduce the number of visits employees make to more costly facilities, such as physicians' offices and hospital emergency rooms. This approach reduces time required for doctors' visits and recovery, and encourages employees to adopt healthier lifestyles. In some organizations employees who use on-site health care can receive the same quality of care that is expected during a visit to a primary care physician or even an urgent care center or emergency room.[31]

Walgreens has aggressively moved into the growing market for work-site medical clinics as part of its effort to rebrand itself as a health and wellness company. Walgreens bought Take Care Health Systems and two of the largest work-site clinic companies in the country, CHD Meridian Healthcare and Whole Health Management. Walgreens is now the largest provider of work-site medical care, with more than 375 Take Care Clinics.[32] After analyzing its health claims and wellness data, Intel opened an on-site clinic at its Jones Farm campus in Hillsboro, Oregon. The clinic serves about 5,700 employees and provides primary care, urgent care, allergy and flu shots, travel medicine, vaccinations, and physical therapy.[33]

Major Medical Benefits

Some plans provide for major medical benefits to cover extraordinary expenses that result from long-term or serious health problems. The use of *deductibles* is a common feature of medical benefits. For example, the employee may have to pay the first $500 of medical bills before the insurance takes over payment.

Dental and Vision Care

Dental and vision care are popular benefits in the health care area. Employers typically pay the entire costs for both types of plans except for a deductible, which may amount to $50 or more per year. Dental plans may cover, for example, 70 to 100 percent of the cost of preventive procedures and 50 to 80 percent of restorative procedures. Most health care plans offer dental coverage. Some plans also include orthodontic care.

Americans spend more than $50 billion a year on vision problems and more and more companies are providing vision care as a benefit. Vision care plans may cover all or part of the cost of eye examinations and eyewear.

OBJECTIVE **10.4**

Explain the different kinds of health care legislation and describe the relationship between smoke-free workplaces and the Patient Protection and Affordable Care Act.

Health Care Legislation

Seven pieces of federal legislation related to health care are discussed in the next sections.

Employee Retirement Income Security Act

The Employee Retirement Income Security Act (ERISA) of 1974 strengthens existing and future retirement programs. Mismanagement of retirement funds was the primary spur for this legislation. Some employees were entering retirement only to find that the retirement income they had counted on was not available. The act's intent was to ensure that when employees retire, they receive deserved pensions. The purpose of the act is described here:

> It is hereby declared to be the policy of this Act to protect ... the interests of participants in employee benefit plans and their beneficiaries ... by establishing standards of conduct, responsibility and obligations for fiduciaries of employee benefit plans, and by providing for appropriate remedies, sanctions, and ready access to the federal courts.

Note that the word *protect* is used here because the act does not force employers to create employee retirement plans. It does set standards in the areas of participation, vesting of benefits, and funding for existing and new plans.

Consolidated Omnibus Budget Reconciliation Act

With the high cost of medical care, an individual without health care insurance is vulnerable. The Consolidated Omnibus Budget Reconciliation Act (COBRA) of 1985 was enacted to give employees the opportunity to temporarily continue their coverage, which they would otherwise lose because of termination, layoff, or other changes in employment status. The act applies to employers with 20 or more employees. Under COBRA, individuals may keep their coverage, as well as coverage for their spouses and dependents, for up to 18 months after their employment ceases. Certain qualifying events can extend this coverage for up to 36 months. The individual, however, must pay for this health insurance, and it is expensive.

Older Workers Benefit Protection Act

The Older Workers Benefit Protection Act (OWBPA) of 1990, an amendment to the Age Discrimination in Employment Act, prohibits discrimination in the administration of benefits on the basis of age, but also permits early retirement incentive plans as long as they are voluntary. Employers must offer benefits to older workers that are equal to or greater than the benefits given to younger workers, with one exception. The act does not require employers to provide equal or greater benefits to older workers when the cost to do so is greater than for younger workers. The act establishes wrongful termination waiver requirements as a means of protecting older employees by ensuring that workers are fully informed before signing a waiver.

Health Insurance Portability and Accountability Act

The Health Insurance Portability and Accountability Act (HIPAA) of 1996 provides protection for Americans who move from one job to another, who are self-employed, or who have preexisting medical conditions. The prime objective of this legislation is to make health insurance portable and continuous for employees, and to eliminate the ability of insurance companies to reject coverage for individuals because of a preexisting condition. As an element of HIPAA, there is now a regulation designed to protect the privacy of personal health information.

Family and Medical Leave Act

The Family and Medical Leave Act (FMLA) of 1993 applies to private employers with 50 or more employees and to all governmental employers. The FMLA provides employees up to 12 weeks a year of unpaid leave in specified situations. The overall intent of the act is to help employees balance work demands without hindering their ability to attend to personal and family needs. FMLA rights apply only to employees who have worked for the employer for at least 12 months and who have at least 1,250 hours of service during the 12 months immediately preceding the start of the leave. The FMLA guarantees that health insurance coverage is maintained during the leave and also that the employee has the right to return to the same or an equivalent position after a leave.

Pension Protection Act

The Pension Protection Act made a large number of reforms to U.S. pension plan laws and regulations. This law made several pension provisions in the Economic Growth and Tax Relief Reconciliation Act of 2001 permanent, including increased IRA contribution limits and increased salary deferral contribution limits to a 401(k). It also attempts to strengthen pension systems and reduce reliance on the federal pension system and the Pension Benefit Guaranty Corporation (PBGC). The act seeks to ensure that employers make greater contributions to their pension funds, ensuring pension fund solvency and avoiding a potential multibillion-dollar taxpayer bailout of the PBGC.

Companies with underfunded pensions pay additional premiums along with the elimination of loopholes that allowed underfunded pensions to miss pension payments. The act also requires that pension plans provide more accurate assessments of their obligations and contains provisions designed to strengthen the funding rules for defined benefit pension plans. One of the long-term requirements of the act is for pensions to be fully funded in by 2013.

Patient Protection and Affordable Care Act

The Patient Protection and Affordable Care Act of 2010, often called the "Health Care Reform Bill," created considerable political debate because it effectively reshaped major portions of the health care industry in the United States.[34] The act is based on the idea that when more people have health insurance—young, healthy people in addition to older, sicker people—risk will be spread out and costs will come down. Following are some of the major features of the bill:

1. All individuals will be required to have health insurance coverage by 2014. Those who choose not to have insurance would pay a penalty. The act will also require employers to offer employees affordable health insurance or pay a penalty. Coverage is considered excessive if an employee premium contribution is above 9.5 percent of family income. To handle this situation, some companies are considering offering wage-based premiums where lower-wage earners pay less than those who are higher paid.[35]
2. Children can stay on their parents' policy until they are 26.
3. Insurance companies cannot cancel a policy if the insured gets sick.
4. A person cannot be denied insurance simply because of a preexisting condition.
5. There is no maximum limit on insurance coverage.
6. There is no waiting time with regard to coverage for preexisting conditions.

The law does not require an individual to drop the health coverage he or she had on the date of enactment. Existing employer plans are "grandfathered" under the new law and can continue to renew current employees and enroll new employees. One of the impacted areas from the act pertains to creating a smoke-free workplace, discussed in the following Trends & Innovations.

TRENDS & INNOVATIONS

Smoke-free Workplaces and the Patient Protection and Affordable Care Act

It may appear odd to have a topic regarding smoke-free workplaces in the chapter on benefits, but the Patient Protection and Affordable Care Act justifies the placement. The cost gap for health care between smokers and non-smokers likely will widen beginning in 2018 when, under a provision of the act, companies with health plans that spend much more than average will have to pay an additional federal tax. It is well documented that smokers increase health care costs. Therefore, employers have two choices: cut benefits or cut the trend of rising medical costs to avoid the levy. Many firms are taking the second choice. The following section highlights the cost of smoking to organizations.

Ann Skye, wellness manager at Quintiles Transnational Corporation, said, "Smoking is the number one culprit in poor health, and its negative effects are indisputable. We feel it would be irresponsible for any employee wellness program not to aggressively address tobacco use."[36] Smoking is the biggest factor in controllable health care costs. According to the Centers for Disease Control and Prevention, cigarette smoking is the leading cause of preventable death in this country, accounting for roughly 443,000 deaths, or one out of every five deaths. Numerous studies have concluded that workplace smoking is not only hazardous to employees' health, but also detrimental to the firm's financial health. Statistics show that cigarette smoking costs $92 billion in productivity losses in the workplace annually.[37] Employees who smoke consume more health care resources, experience greater absenteeism, and tend to be less productive while at work.

Employers have grown increasingly intolerant of smokers and many workplaces are smoke-free, although about 21 percent of adult Americans continue to smoke.[38] Even though some smokers remain adamant that passive cigarette smoke is not harmful, the Surgeon General has concluded that there is no safe level of secondhand smoke exposure. The evidence that secondhand tobacco smoke causes serious harm becomes more concrete every day and may be an underrecognized cause of heart attack deaths. Having smoke-free workplace policies helps to fulfill an employer's legal obligation to provide a safe workplace under the Occupational Safety and Health Act's general duty clause, which requires organizations to furnish a workplace free from recognized hazards that are causing or are likely to cause death or serious physical harm. The policy also reduces the risk of litigation, potentially reduces workers' compensation premiums, and protects employees from harm.

According to the American Lung Association, 50,000 people die from exposure to secondhand smoke each year.[39] A study released by the University of Minnesota Cancer Center revealed that nonsmoking employees had up to 25 times more nicotine in their bodies on days when they worked in restaurants and bars than on days they were not at work.[40]

Recently companies are also using penalties against workers for unhealthy behaviors. The most common penalty is higher premium benefits and increased deductibles. At PepsiCo, smokers pay an annual $600 insurance surcharge, and Gannett Publishing charges an additional $60 a month. Some business owners have taken a personal stand against smoking in general, not just smoking in the workplace. Alaska Airlines, Union Pacific, and Turner Broadcasting have refused to hire smokers for more than 20 years.[41] Four employees from Weyco, a firm that manages benefit plans for workers on behalf of other companies, were fired after refusing to take a nicotine test to determine whether they had smoked. President Howard Weyers said, "Some call this a violation of privacy, pointing to the principle that what you do in your own home is your own business. But they forget the part about so long as it doesn't harm anyone else."[42] There potentially may be a problem with such a policy because 30 states and the District of Columbia have "lifestyle" statutes that limit an employer's ability to make adverse employment decisions based on what employees or applicants do while off duty. Some of those statutes may prevent an employer from terminating an employee or refusing to hire an applicant who smokes.[43]

Life Insurance

Group life insurance is a benefit provided to protect the employee's family in the event of his or her death. Although the cost of group life insurance is relatively low, some plans call for the employee to pay part of the premium. Coverage may be a flat amount (for instance, $50,000) or based on the employee's annual earnings. For example, workers earning $40,000 per year may have $80,000, twice their annual earnings, worth of group life coverage.

Retirement Plans

Retirement is currently a hot topic because of the aging baby-boomer generation. Employers are in the middle of this challenge since they are one of our society's primary providers of retirement income. Various types of employer retirement plans will be discussed next.

Defined Benefit Plans

defined benefit plan
Retirement plan that provides the participant with a fixed benefit upon retirement.

HR Web Wisdom

Types of Retirement Plans
**http://www.dol.gov/dol/topic/
retirement/typesofplans.htm**

Retirement information from the U.S. Department of Labor.

Retirement plans are generally either *defined benefit* or *defined contribution*. A **defined benefit plan** is a formal retirement plan that provides the participant with a fixed benefit upon retirement. Although defined benefit formulas vary, they are typically based on the participant's final years' average salary and years of service. Plans that are considered generous provide pensions equivalent to 50 to 80 percent of an employee's final earnings. Use of defined benefit plans has declined in recent years. However, many workers lost considerable money in their 401(k)s during the recent recession, causing them to have more faith in defined benefit plans.

In today's job markets younger workers are more interested in defined benefits plans but are often unable to obtain them. In a Towers Watson study, nearly two-thirds of workers under 40 said defined benefit plans are a key factor in their decision to stay with their companies compared with only a quarter of those with defined contribution plans. As firms begin to hire again, retirement benefits are becoming a factor for employees. David Speier, senior retirement consultant in Towers Watson's Arlington, Virginia, office, said, "I think younger individuals are looking at their parents and seeing the struggles they are going through—having to delay retirement—and are reacting."[44]

Defined Contribution Plans

defined contribution plan
Retirement plan that requires specific contributions by an employer to a retirement or savings fund established for the employee.

A **defined contribution plan** is a retirement plan that requires specific contributions by an employer to a retirement or savings fund established for the employee. One of the most significant changes in the composition of individual retirement savings over the past 10 years has been the shift from defined *benefits* to defined *contribution* pension plans such as 401(k). Only as far back as 1996, most companies with retirement plans had defined benefit plans. However, today a majority of Fortune 100 companies offer employees only a defined contribution plan. Employees know in advance how much employers will contribute to a defined benefit plan; the amount of retirement income from a defined contribution plan will depend on the investment success of the pension fund.

401(k) plan
Defined contribution plan in which employees may defer income up to a maximum amount allowed.

A **401(k) plan** is a defined contribution plan in which employees may defer income up to a maximum amount allowed. Some employers match employee contributions 50 cents for each dollar deferred. Although employers typically pay the expenses for their defined benefit pension plans, there is a wide variety of payment arrangements for 401(k) plans. Some plan sponsors pay for everything, including investment fees and costs. Others pay for virtually nothing, with the result that nearly all fees are paid out of the plan's assets. In the middle are those plans in which the sponsor and participants share the expenses.

The recent recession was not kind to 401(k) accounts. As a result, some firms reduced or eliminated their matches to accounts. As the economy improved, employers began reinstating their matching contributions, usually at the same level, but sometimes higher or lower than the original match.[45]

Cash Balance Plans

cash balance plan
Retirement plan with elements of both defined benefit and defined contribution plans.

For some organizations, a hybrid fund may be the desired approach to retirement plans. A **cash balance plan** is a plan with elements of both defined benefit and defined contribution plans. During the recent recession, many 401(k) accounts took a beating. As a result, many employers felt having employees assume 100 percent of the risks was too much. A middle ground was found using a cash balance plan in connection with a defined contribution plan. When used as a stand-alone plan, a cash balance plan provides all of the benefits that would otherwise be available under a standard defined benefit plan. It has the additional benefit of allowing for different targeted benefit amounts for different participants in the plan. Cash balance plans help employers who are looking for ways to maximize retirement contributions for their workers beyond a 401(k) plan, such as professionals seeking to contribute more than $49,000 to their retirement plan. It resembles a defined contribution plan because it uses an account balance to communicate the benefit amount. However, it is closer to being a defined benefit plan because the employer normally bears the responsibility for and the risks of managing the assets.[46]

Coca-Cola has a cash balance plan for all employees. Kevin Wagner, a senior retirement consultant in the Atlanta office of Watson Wyatt Worldwide, which worked with Coca-Cola in designing the cash balance plan, said, "It is refreshing to see a company understand the value of its defined benefit plan, which, at least in Coca-Cola's situation, brings great value to both the company and its employees."[47] Other companies that have converted to cash balance plans include FedEx, MeadWestvaco, SunTrust Banks, and Dow Chemical.

Disability Protection

Workers' compensation protects employees from job-related accidents and illnesses. Some firms, however, provide additional protection that is more comprehensive. When the short-term plan runs out, a firm's long-term plan may become active; such a plan may provide 50 to 70 percent of an employee's pretax pay. Long-term disability provides a monthly benefit to employees who due to illness or injury are unable to work for an extended period.

Employee Stock Option Plans

employee stock option plan (ESOP)

Plan in which a firm contributes stock shares to a trust, which then allocates the stock to participating employee accounts according to employee earnings.

An **employee stock option plan (ESOP)** is a plan in which a firm contributes stock shares to a trust, which then allocates the stock to participating employee accounts according to employee earnings. ESOP advocates have promoted employee ownership plans as a means to align the interests of workers and their companies to stimulate productivity. This practice, long reserved for executives, now often includes employees working at lower levels in the firm. The difficulty some see in the plan is that you have to wait until retirement to receive the benefits, and that is a long time for Gen Y employees to see into the future. Robert J. Larison, president of Atlantic Coast Bank in Waycross, Georgia, said, "We lose people to non-ESOP banks all the time. They go across the street for $5,000 a year more in salary when they might have been awarded a $15,000 or $20,000 vesting in their ESOP that year."[48]

Although the potential benefits of ESOPs are attractive, some employees want the ability to sell their shares prior to retirement, which ESOPs do not allow. Many people do not want to take the chance that the stock is going to be less valuable when they retire. Periods of wild rides in the stock market also dampen worker enthusiasm for ESOPs. Although the potential advantages of ESOPs are impressive, the other side of the coin is the danger of having all your eggs in one basket. The Enron experience makes this point only too well.

Employee Services

Organizations offer a variety of benefits that can be termed "employee services." These benefits encompass a number of areas, including child care, educational assistance, food services/subsidized cafeterias, scholarships for dependents, relocation benefits, and domestic partner benefits.

Child Care

A benefit offered by some firms is subsidized child care. According to the National Conference of State Legislatures, an estimated 80 percent of employees miss work due to unexpected child-care coverage issues. It is estimated that every $1 invested in backup child care yields $3 to $4 in returned productivity and benefit. At the Abbott Laboratories headquarters campus 30 miles north of Chicago, the company has built a $10 million state-of-the-art child-care center for more than 400 preschool children of Abbott workers. For parents who prefer a different arrangement, if their babysitter is sick, Abbott provides emergency backup service. Company child-care arrangements tend to reduce absenteeism, protect employee productivity, enhance retention and recruiting, promote the advancement of women, and make the firm an employer of choice.

Educational Assistance

Educational assistance plans can go a long way in improving employee retention. In a recent survey of HR professionals, 58 percent said their organizations offered educational assistance for undergraduate education, and 54 percent offered graduate assistance.[49] Some companies reimburse employees after they have completed a course with a grade of "C" or above, whereas others provide for advance payment of these expenses. Other employers provide half the reimbursement up front and the rest upon satisfactory completion of the course. United Technologies Corporation pays for an employee's entire tuition and books up front. It also offers paid time off—as much as three hours a week, depending on the course load—to study. IBM has a unique form of tuition reimbursement; employees could contribute up to $1,000 a year to an interest-bearing education account supplemented by company-paid matches. The funds do not have to be used for education related to the employees' present job. Mutual of Omaha provides 100 percent repayment up to $150 per credit hour at the employee's school of choice, with an annual maximum of $3,600 for employees working 30 or more hours per week. Employees can select any course pertinent to their job or that would be helpful in helping them advance professionally and become accomplished employees.[50] Internal Revenue Service regulations allow for educational assistance benefits to be nontaxable up to $5,250 per year, although the average educational reimbursement by employers is $1,600 per year.

Food Services/Subsidized Cafeterias

There is generally no such thing as a free lunch. However, firms that supply food services or subsidized cafeterias provide an exception to this rule. What they hope to gain in return is increased productivity, less wasted time, enhanced employee morale, and, in some instances, a healthier workforce. Most firms that offer free or subsidized lunches feel that they get a high payback in terms of employee relations. Northwestern Mutual is one such company. Free lunches are available in its cafeterias, where the menus list calories instead of prices. Keeping the lunch hour to a minimum is an obvious advantage, but employees also appreciate the opportunity to meet and mix with people they work with. Making one entree a heart-healthy choice and listing the calories, fat, cholesterol, and sodium content in food is also appealing to a large number of employees.

Scholarships for Dependents

Often companies provide scholarships for dependents of employees. Scholarship programs can help boost employee recruitment and retention. Franciscan Health Systems, a nonprofit health care provider in Tacoma, Washington, targets its awards primarily to employees' children who are interested in entering the health care field, although it also awards scholarships for study in other areas.

Relocation

relocation benefits
Company-paid shipments of household goods and temporary living expenses, covering all or a portion of the real estate costs associated with buying a new home and selling the previously occupied home.

Relocation benefits are company-paid shipments of household goods and temporary living expenses, covering all or a portion of the real estate costs associated with buying a new home and selling the previously occupied home. Relocation packages vary but most companies will pay for household moving and packing expenses and temporary living expenses for up to six months until the home sells. Companies may also pay for weekly or bimonthly trips back home over the weekends. It has been estimated that approximately $25 billion is spent annually on corporate relocation.[51]

Although relocating can be a hassle, it can also produce many benefits. Employees typically feel an investment has been made by their employer if they are asked to relocate and the firm pays all relocation expenses. Some companies have programs that help trailing spouses or partners secure employment. Some firms also provide outplacement help to spouses.

Often employees who once viewed a transfer as a step up are now taking a closer look at not only the economic impact of the move, but also what it does to quality of life. Recently, the primary reasons for declining a relocation were housing and mortgage concerns, followed by family issues/ties and spouses' or partners' jobs. John A. Challenger, CEO of the outplacement firm Challenger, Gray & Christmas Inc., said, "Continued weakness in the housing market is undoubtedly a leading factor behind the decline in relocation."[52] Losing money on the sale of their house is certainly not an enticement to relocate.

Domestic Partner Benefits

A challenge facing managers and human resource professionals is deciding whether to offer domestic partner benefits. Unmarried domestic partners are more often being included as qualified for coverage under employee benefit plans with larger companies. Among Fortune 500 companies, about 57 percent offer same-sex partner benefits.[53] A number of companies are reimbursing gay and lesbian employees for the additional taxes they incur for their same-sex domestic partnership health care benefits. For example, New York–based Ernst & Young recently announced it would reimburse eligible employees for the tax, which averaged $1,100 per employee annually.[54]

There are also a growing number of counties, states, and municipalities that offer domestic partner benefits and provide a basis for comparison of policies, legal hurdles, coverage, and costs. Thirteen U.S. states, such as California, Connecticut, New Jersey, New York, and Vermont, have joined this trend, as have 139 cities/counties.[55] Recently, Blue Cross & Blue Shield of Rhode Island began covering domestic partners. Domestic partners must be of the same sex, have resided together for a year or more prior to application, and be financially interdependent. In addition, supporting documentation including a Declaration of Domestic Partnership is required; but once the domestic partner is added, dependent children are also eligible for coverage.[56]

OBJECTIVE 10.5

Explain premium pay.

premium pay
Compensation paid to employees for working long periods of time or working under dangerous or undesirable conditions.

hazard pay
Additional pay provided to employees who work under extremely dangerous conditions.

shift differential
Additional money paid to employees for the inconvenience of working less-desirable hours.

Premium Pay

Premium pay is compensation paid to employees for working long periods of time or working under dangerous or undesirable conditions. Payment for overtime is legally required for nonexempt employees who work more than 40 hours in a given week. However, some firms voluntarily pay overtime for hours worked beyond eight in a given day and pay double time, or even more, for work on Sundays and holidays.

Additional pay provided to employees who work under extremely dangerous conditions is called **hazard pay**. A window washer for skyscrapers in New York City might receive extra compensation because of the precarious working conditions. Military pilots collect extra money in the form of *flight pay* and *combat pay* because of the risks involved in the job. When the U.S. State Department was having difficulty enticing members of the Foreign Service to be assigned to the U.S. Embassy in Baghdad, Iraq, it offered a form of hazard pay. It enticed workers to take jobs in unstable regions with a 70 percent boost in base salary, premium pay for overtime, and 10 weeks off.

Some employees receive **shift differential** pay for the inconvenience of working less-desirable hours. This type of pay may be provided as additional compensation per hour and is used extensively in the health care and technical occupations. For example, employees who work the second shift (swing shift), from 4:00 P.M. until midnight, might receive $2.00 per hour above the base rate for that job. The third shift (graveyard shift) often warrants an even greater differential; for example, an extra $3.00 per hour may be paid for the same job. Shift differentials are sometimes based on a percentage of the employee's base rate.

OBJECTIVE 10.6

Explain voluntary benefits.

voluntary benefits
Benefits that are 100 percent paid by the employee but the employer typically pays the administrative cost.

Voluntary Benefits

Many firms are moving away from discretionary benefits where the cost is shouldered totally or partially by the company to voluntary benefits. **Voluntary benefits** are 100 percent paid by the employee but the employer typically pays the administrative cost. Employees gain because their premiums typically reflect group discounts and thus are lower than the employees could obtain on their own. Elana D'Arciprete, southeast vice president at Colonial Life, said, "Voluntary benefits set employers apart by allowing them to offer a more expansive benefits package at any or little direct cost to them."[57] Some of the discretionary benefits in this chapter have been converted either partially or fully to voluntary benefits. The most common voluntary products provided include term life insurance, vision insurance, long-term care insurance, long-term disability insurance, accident insurance, and dental insurance. Other voluntary benefits include automobile insurance, homeowners'/renters' insurance, debt counseling and financial planning, identity theft coverage, college savings plans, and pet insurance. Of recent many firms are offering discount programs. A recent survey of HR managers found that 58 percent of their employers had employee discount programs. Possible discounts provide a range of options including Sprint or AT&T cell phones and discounted tickets, such as for amusement parks.[58]

OBJECTIVE **10.7**

Describe customized benefit plans.

customized benefit plan

Benefit plan that permits employees to make yearly selections to largely determine their benefit package by choosing between taxable cash and numerous benefits.

Customized Benefit Plans

Customized benefit plans permit employees to make yearly selections to largely determine their benefit package by choosing between taxable cash and numerous benefits.

Not long ago firms offered a uniform package that generally reflected a typical employee based on tradition, budgets, and management choices. Today, the workforce has become considerably more heterogeneous, and this prototype is no longer representative. Different interests must be served in this new workforce today.[59] With four generations of workers now in the workplace, customization and flexibility become very important in developing a benefits package that meets the needs of everyone. Workers have considerable latitude in determining how much they will take in the form of salary, life insurance, pension contributions, and other benefits. Customized cafeteria plans permit flexibility in allowing each employee to determine the compensation components that best satisfy their needs.

Obviously, organizations cannot permit employees to select all their benefits. For one thing, firms must provide the benefits required by law. In addition, it is probably wise to require that each employee have core benefits, especially in areas such as retirement and medical insurance. However, the freedom to select highly desired benefits would seem to maximize the value of an individual's compensation. Employees' involvement in designing their own benefit plans would also effectively communicate to them the cost of their benefits. In keeping the program current, management depends on an upward flow of information from employees to determine when benefit changes are needed.

The downside to customized benefit plans is that they are costly. Development and administrative costs for these plans exceed those for traditional plans. Even though customized benefit plans add to the organization's administrative burden, some firms apparently find that the advantages outweigh shortcomings.

OBJECTIVE **10.8**

Describe the importance of communicating information about the benefits package.

Communicating Information about the Benefits Package

Employee benefits can help a firm recruit and retain a top-quality workforce. Organizations spend millions of dollars each year for benefits. Yet, many do not do a good job of communicating the value of this investment to the employees. Often organizations do not have to improve benefits to keep their best employees; rather, workers need to fully understand the benefits that are provided them.

ERISA (previously discussed) provides still another reason for communicating information about a firm's benefits program. This act requires organizations with a pension or profit-sharing plan to provide employees with specific data at specified times. The act further mandates that the information be presented in a manner that is easy to understand. Also, under the Patient Protection and Affordable Care Act, employers must provide a benefits summary and coverage explanation to all applicants and enrollees at the time of initial enrollment and at the annual enrollment, in addition to the summary plan description required by ERISA.

Nonfinancial Compensation

nonfinancial compensation

Consists of the satisfaction that a person receives from the job itself or from the psychological and/or physical environment in which the person works.

Historically, compensation departments have not dealt with nonfinancial factors. However, the new compensation model suggests that this is changing. **Nonfinancial compensation** consists of the satisfaction that a person receives from the job itself or from the psychological and/or physical environment in which the person works. The components of nonfinancial compensation consist of the job itself and the job environment (see Figure 10.2).

FIGURE 10-2
Nonfinancial Compensation
in a Total Compensation
Program

Compensation		
Direct **Financial**	**Nonfinancial**	
	The Job	**Job Environment**
	Meaningful	Sound Policies
	Appreciated	Capable Managers
	Satisfying	Competent Employees
	Learning	Congenial Co-Workers
	Enjoyable	Appropriate Status Symbols
	Challenging	Working Conditions
		Workplace Flexibility
		Flextime
		Compressed Workweek
		Job Sharing
		Telecommuting
		Part-Time Work

OBJECTIVE **10.9**

Describe the job itself and the job
environment as components of
nonfinancial compensation.

Job Itself as a Nonfinancial Compensation Factor

The job itself can be a very powerful motivational factor in the compensation equation. Some jobs can be so stimulating that the employee is anxious to get to work each day. At the evening meal, details of what happened on the job may be shared with family or friends. Given the prospect of getting a generous raise by leaving this job, this worker may quickly say "No" to the opportunity. Unwillingness to change jobs for additional financial compensation suggests that the job itself is indeed an important reward. Such jobs are meaningful and challenging, workers believe that they are appreciated, the work is enjoyable and satisfying, and learning opportunities are available. Individuals who are engaged in their work find great satisfaction in their job and feel that they are contributing to the success of the organization tend to remain and be productive with the organization.

Job Environment as a Nonfinancial Compensation Factor

Sadly, often when jobs are designed, little time is devoted to addressing employees' motivational needs. The focus is on how to get the work done more efficiently.[60] In such an environment, a job may be so boring or distasteful that an individual dreads going to work. A report from the Conference Board based on a survey of 5,000 workers found that only 45 percent were satisfied with their jobs—down from 61.1 percent in 1987.[61] This condition is sad considering the time a person devotes to his or her job. When work is a drag, life may not be very pleasant and, if a boring job creates excessive and prolonged stress, the person involved may eventually become emotionally or physically ill. Examples of how the job environment has the potential to be nonfinancial compensation factors are discussed below.

Sound Policies

A *policy* is a predetermined guide established to provide direction in decision making. Human resource policies and practices reflecting management's concern for its employees can serve as positive rewards. Consider how the following policies would contribute to the satisfaction of a worker:

- To provide realistic and practical incentives as a means of encouraging the highest standard of individual performance and to ensure increased quality and quantity of performance.
- To create and maintain good working conditions, to provide the best possible equipment and facilities, and plants and offices that are clean, orderly, and safe.
- To employ people without regard to race, sex, color, national origin, or age.

- To encourage employees to improve their skills by participating in available educational or training programs.
- To provide every possible opportunity for advancement so that each individual may reach his or her highest potential.

If a firm's policies show consideration rather than disrespect, fear, doubt, or lack of confidence, the result can be rewarding to both the employees and the organization. Policies that are arbitrary and too restrictive alienate people.

Capable Managers

Anyone who has worked under a manager who does not possess the skills needed to successfully lead the unit understands the importance of having a capable individual in charge. Many workers quit their jobs because of the way the unit is being managed. Just being around an incompetent boss every day may provide the motivation to call in sick when you are not ill. There may be the autocratic manager who only wants it done his or her way. Then, there is the manager who can seemingly never make a decision. There are endless examples of supervisors who are incapable of performing their jobs, thus making the job environment of their employees less than desirable.

Competent Employees

Working with individuals who are capable and knowledgeable can often create a synergistic environment. *Synergism* is the cooperative action of two or more persons working together to accomplish more than they could working separately. Synergy implies the possibility of accomplishing tasks that could not even be done by people working separately. Solving problems together is often exhilarating when a coworker is competent. Successful organizations emphasize continuous development and ensure employment of competent managers and nonmanagers. Competitive environments and the requirement for teamwork will not permit otherwise.

Congenial Coworkers

Although a few individuals in this world may be quite self-sufficient and prefer to be left alone, they will likely be unsuccessful in the team-oriented organizations that exist today. The American culture has historically embraced individualism, yet most people possess, in varying degrees, a desire for acceptance by their work group. It is very important that management develop and maintain congenial work groups. A work group's need for creativity may require individuals with diverse backgrounds. However, to be effective, they must share common values and goals.

Appropriate Status Symbols

Status symbols are organizational rewards that take many forms such as office size and location, desk size and quality, how close one's private parking space is to the office, floor covering, and job title. Status symbols vary from company to company and sometimes are understood only by persons within the company. Some firms make liberal use of these types of rewards; others tend to minimize them. This latter approach reflects a concern about the adverse effect they may have on creating and maintaining a team spirit among members at various levels in the firm. This is true within many workplaces, where the corner office and private washroom have given way to more democratic arrangements.

Working Conditions

The definition of *working conditions* has broadened considerably over the years. Today, an air-conditioned and reasonably safe and healthy workplace is considered necessary.

Workplace flexibility arrangements can often have a positive or negative relationship about how an individual views his or her job. These factors will be discussed in the following sections.

OBJECTIVE 10.10

Describe workplace flexibility (work–life balance) factors and global customized benefits.

Workplace Flexibility (Work–Life Balance)

Effective work–life balance programs focus on solving any personal issues that can detract from an employee's work. For employers, creating a balanced work–life environment can be a key strategic factor in attracting and retaining the most talented employees. As Tina Tchen, executive director of the White House Council on Women and Girls, said, "Flexible work policies are an economic imperative for American families and companies."[62] Workplace flexibility is high on employees' lists of company benefits desired and continues to grow. It has moved from being a great benefit that a company can offer to a business necessity. By providing such an environment, employees are better able to fit family, community, and social commitments into their schedule. The homogeneous workforce that the United States once had is quite different now. Consider the following statistics and envision how the workplace profile has changed: 27 percent of single parents are men, 40 percent of the workforce is unmarried, one in five workers is 50 or older, and four million households are multigenerational. Also, nearly 25 percent of Americans are caring for elders.[63]

For men and women seeking to balance their work and personal lives, time is nearly as important as money and may even be more important for some.[64] According to a Baylor University study, new mothers who return to work are more likely to stay on the job if they have greater control over their work schedules.[65] More employees are requesting workplace flexible benefits to achieve a better work and life balance. Marcee Harris Schwartz, the New York–based director of BDO USA's Flex program, said, "We do not think of flexibility as a set of options, or an employee benefit, or even a program. We really see it as a business strategy—a strategy that can help employees manage their own working life."[66] Some companies offer many of the factors typically associated with workplace flexibility. State Street Corporation, a multinational financial services provider with more than 29,000 employees in 26 countries, provides five options that give employees flexibility on when, how, and where they work.[67] These include flextime, compressed schedule, reduced hours, telecommuting, and job sharing.

Flextime

Flextime is the practice of permitting employees to choose their own working hours, within certain limitations. Even when the economy was depressed, flexible work hours remained high on the priority list of what companies could offer in lieu of a salary increase, although guaranteed job security ranked number one. For many old-economy managers who think they must see their employees every minute to make sure they are working, this may be difficult. Another benefit of flextime is that it can bring better health to employees by reducing employee stress levels.

In a flextime system, employees typically work the same number of hours per day as they would on a standard schedule. However, they work these hours within what is called a bandwidth, which is the maximum length of the workday (see Figure 10.3). Core time is that part of the day when all employees must be present. *Flexible time* is the period within which employees may vary their schedules. A typical schedule permits employees to begin work between 6:00 A.M. and 9:00 A.M. and to complete their workday between 3:00 P.M. and 6:00 P.M. Marianne Mondy, a legislative auditor for the State of Louisiana goes to work at 6:30 and is off at 3:00, a schedule she very much enjoys. This permits her to miss much of Baton Rouge's horrible traffic congestion.

Because flexible hours are highly valued in today's society, providing a flexible work schedule gives employers an edge in recruiting new employees and retaining highly qualified ones.[68] Also, flextime allows employees to expand their opportunities. For example, it may be easier for them to continue their education than if they were on a traditional work schedule. The public also seems to reap benefits from flextime. Transportation services, recreational facilities, medical clinics, and other services can be better used by reducing competition for service at conventional peak times. Yet, flextime is not suitable for all types of organizations. For example, its use may be severely limited in assembly-line operations and companies using multiple shifts.

Compressed Workweek

The **compressed workweek** is an arrangement of work hours that permits employees to fulfill their work obligation in fewer days than the typical five-day, eight-hour-a-day, workweek. A common compressed workweek is four 10-hour days. Another form of the compressed work-week is four nine-hour days and a half day on Friday. Some hospitals permit their registered nurses to work three 12-hour days during a workweek. Still other firms are allowing employees to work longer but fewer days in the summer in exchange for a day off each week. There are endless different combinations of compressed workweeks.

Working under this arrangement, employees have reported greater job satisfaction. In addition, the compressed workweek offers the potential for better use of leisure time for family life, personal business, and recreation. Employers in some instances have cited advantages such as increased productivity and reduced turnover and absenteeism. Other firms, however, have encountered difficulty in scheduling workers' hours and at times employees become fatigued from working longer hours. In some cases, these problems have resulted in lower product quality and reduced customer service.

Job Sharing

job sharing

Two part-time people split the duties of one job in some agreed-on manner and are paid according to their contributions.

In **job sharing**, two part-time people split the duties of one job in some agreed-on manner and are paid according to their contributions. It is an attractive option to people who want to work fewer than 40 hours per week.

Some have equated the benefits job sharing provides to that of running a marathon. Given equal athletic ability, two athletes running half a marathon back to back will invariably run faster than one runner going the entire distance alone. Although the arrangements vary, the outcome is the same: Job sharing provides the flexibility to enjoy life. It provides an option to retain workers, particularly women who often opt out of the workforce to raise families. Often job sharers work as hard in, say, three days, as those working full time and are pleased to have the opportunity to combine work and motherhood or other interests.

There appears to be a growing trend as more companies offer job sharing. Two Ford Motor Company engineers used job sharing as a means of advancing their careers and still have time with their newborns. Julie Levine and Julie Rocco were joint program manager for the 2011 Explorer Crossover and each earned 80 percent of their full-time salaries and benefits. Rocco and Levine supervise 10 people. Rocco worked Monday, Wednesday, and Thursday, and Levine worked Tuesday, Wednesday, and Friday. Both worked about 40 hours a week each, which is considered part-time in the automobile industry.[69]

Job sharing also provides a means of encouraging older workers to remain on the job past retirement age. Sharing jobs has potential benefits that include the broader range of skills the partners bring to the job. For job sharing to work, however, the partners must be compatible, have good communication skills, and have a bond of trust with their manager. Job sharing also can pose challenges, including the need for additional oversight—such as conducting administrative tasks and performance reviews for two employees rather than one. However, if the option is the loss of two valued employees, the additional effort is certainly worth it.

Two-in-a-Box

Some companies are giving two executives the same responsibilities and the same title and letting them decide how the work is to be divided (Two-in-a-Box). Unlike job sharing, it is a full-time job for both executives. It certainly has some risk, as in the case of the 1998 DaimlerChrysler Corporation disaster of an attempt at Two-in-a-Box when one executive was unwilling to share authority, resulting in the resignation of the other executive. Problems certainly can occur as the egos of two executives meet, but it has proven successful in certain instances. A major advantage of this approach is that it can ease transition, permitting a newer manager to learn from a more experienced manager. It is also useful as managers confront the requirement of global traveling. One manager could be at the home office taking care of regular business while the other is traveling. For two-and-a-half years, two executives shared a job as heads of Cisco's routing group. The two had complementary skills and each gained experience from the other. Cisco typically combines a technically oriented manager with a business-oriented one.[70] The Two-in-a-Box approach requires work and constant communication, but for the right two executives, the benefits derived are worth it.

There are other examples of Two-in-a-Box. Aon Consulting is chaired by co-CEOs Kathryn Hayley and Baljit Dail.[71] In 2010, German business software provider SAP AG appointed Bill McDermott and Jim Hagemann Snabe as co-CEOs.[72] Other companies that utilize co-CEOs include BlackBerry maker Research in Motion and restaurant chain P.F. Chang's China Bistro.

Telecommuting

Telecommuting is a work arrangement whereby employees, called "teleworkers" or "telecommuters," are able to remain at home (or otherwise away from the office) and perform their work using computers and other electronic devices that connect them with their offices.

Telecommuting has become more popular in recent years, and it is estimated that by 2020 up to 30 percent of the workforce will be telecommuting brought on by traffic congestion and frustration with commuting and high gas prices. According to a WorldatWork survey of 563 North American companies, 37 percent provided full-time positions away from the office.[73] For self-motivated workers, telecommuting can increase worker productivity and improve job satisfaction and loyalty. Modern communications and information technologies permit people to work just about anywhere. Today, physical location is largely immaterial when it comes to working. Telecommuting is significantly changing not just the way people work but also where they do it. One study indicates that employees who telecommute for the majority of the time are more satisfied with their jobs than those working primarily in an office.[74] Workers like telecommuting because there are fewer interruptions, less company politics, and less face-to-face communication. These benefits improve their work–life balance.

Telecommuters generally are information workers. They accomplish jobs that require, for example, analysis, research, writing, budgeting, data entry, or computer programming. Teleworkers also include illustrators, loan executives, architects, attorneys, and publishers. Employees can accomplish both training and job duties without losing either efficiency or quality by using the Internet. Thanks largely to telecommuting, when the New York City transit union went on strike, knowledge workers were able to work from home, which greatly lessened the effect of the strike.

Another advantage of telecommuting is that it eliminates the need for office space. The expense of employees is not just their salaries and benefits, but also the overhead associated with their office space. Deloitte LLP offers most of its 45,000 employees nationwide the option to telecommute as many as five days a week and have been doing this for 15 years. As leases come up for renewal, the firm is able to reduce office space and energy costs by 30 percent. The facilities are then reconfigured to accommodate mobile workers who do not need permanent offices.[75]

Also, commuting distances are not a factor for teleworkers. The average time it takes to get to work continues to increase, which often contributes to tardiness and lost work hours. With telecommuting, firms may hire the best available employees located virtually anywhere in the world for many jobs. The ability to employ disabled workers and workers with small children further broadens the labor market. Finally, telecommuting is being used as an alternative for executives who are unwilling to relocate. If the company is willing to permit the executive to not work out of headquarters, telecommuting may be the answer.

Part-Time Work

Historically, part-time employees have been viewed as basically second-class citizens. These were the workers who reluctantly accepted a low-paying job until a full-time career break occurred. Today, increasing highly educated professionals are choosing part-time opportunities in their fields to address both job and personal needs. Alison Doyle, an About.com job search and employment expert, said, "Professional moms would be thrilled to lower their hours to spend more time with their children, and they don't mind giving up benefits to achieve that work/life balance."[76]

At Deloitte, each employee's performance is discussed during twice-a-year evaluations focused not just on career targets but also on larger life goals. Employees can request to do more or less travel or client service. The employee can also request to move laterally into a new role that may or may not come with a pay cut. About 10 percent of employees choose to "dial up" or "dial down" at any given time. The program is in response to Millennials demanding a better work–life balance and boomers looking to ease into retirement.[77]

Just described were the positive aspects of part-time. The recent recession caused many workers to take part-time jobs because they could not find full-time ones. In March 2010, the underemployed rate was 20.3 percent.

A GLOBAL PERSPECTIVE

Global Customized Benefits

The trend in the United States is to customize benefit plans and not offer a uniform package that generally reflected a typical employee. That approach also applies to the global environment and often provides a major challenge for organizations. Global companies must recognize that a standardized benefits program for all employees may be impractical and unsuccessful in achieving key benefits objectives. Employers must understand the culture of each country because the culture will have a major impact on the benefits workers desire.[78]

There are three basic groups of global benefits: government-provided, government-mandated, and voluntarily provided by the company. Government-provided benefits are administered and provided directly by the government. Typically they consist of health care and retirement benefits, but may include life insurance, disability insurance, or unemployment insurance. Government-mandated benefits are those provided by employers because the law requires them to do so. Voluntary benefits are provided at the discretion of the employer.[79]

The first thing that a firm must do when considering a benefit package in the global environment is to establish a global corporate benefits strategy and determine what the company identity should be. For example, Helsinki-based Tieto Corporation, an information technology services company with 17,000 employees, wants to present an image that it provides the best benefits in the marketplace. On the other hand, the benefit approach for Nalco Company, a Naperville, Illinois–based water treatment company with more than 11,500 employees operating in 130 countries, just wants to be at the 50th percentile among companies for benefits.[80] These two philosophies will likely have a significant impact on the benefit package offered.

A company operating in India will likely offer an assortment of child incentives, home incentives, and health plans that include grandparents. They also expect a "dearness allowance" that helps to offset inflation as part of the compensation plan.[81] For India's Informa employees, private health insurance, flexible benefits, and dependent coverage are top commodities. But in the United Kingdom, the wellness programs such as gym memberships and health screenings are highly valued benefits.[82]

U.S. multinationals have discovered that U.S. insurance plan designs were not universally acceptable in other countries. This is caused by labor and tax regulations, which strongly influence employee expectations. For instance, U.S. group life insurance plans deliver lump-sum death benefits, but such benefits are not tax-favored in the Netherlands, where employees expect survivorship annuities to spouses and children in the event of death in service. U.S. firms also place a high priority on health care benefits, whereas many European countries have government-sponsored health care arrangements that differ in design in each country. Additionally, in some countries, employer-paid private medical plans are considered taxable income to the employee.[83]

Going global has its challenges with regards to total rewards. An employer not only has to ensure that its strategy fits with the benefits available in each country as well as its culture, but also has to consider issues of communication including language, media, and currency. Elliott Webster, flexible benefits director at consultants PIFC, says, "Different cultures can also be a challenge. For example, in the UK life insurance is seen as a benefit provided by a company but in Norway it is seen as a right."[84]

The United States ranks ninth in terms of the percentage of companies offering flexible work arrangements to their employees according to a survey released by Grant Thornton International. The top two countries in the survey were Finland (92 percent) and Sweden (86 percent), with Australia and Thailand (85 percent) tied at third. The three worst countries, in terms of companies offering flexible work arrangements, were Japan, Greece, and Armenia.[85]

MyManagementLab

Go to **mymanagementlab.com** to complete the problems marked with this icon ⭐.

Summary

1. **Describe some unique employee benefits, define indirect financial compensation *(benefits)*, and explain what is included in a total reward package.** Some companies are experimenting with what some might call unique benefits as they attempt to brand their organization as a good place to work. They want to stand out from the pack.

Indirect financial compensation (benefits) includes all financial rewards that generally are not paid directly to the employee.

The concept of total rewards is now more encompassing as reflected in the name change of the American Compensation Association to WorldatWork, the Professional Association for Compensation, Benefits, and *Total Rewards*.

2. *Describe legally required benefits.* Legally required benefits currently account for about 10 percent of total compensation costs. They include Social Security, unemployment insurance, and workers' compensation.

3. *Define discretionary benefits and explain the various types of discretionary benefits. Discretionary benefits* are benefit payments made as a result of unilateral management decisions in nonunion firms and from labor–management negotiations in unionized firms.

   Categories of discretionary benefits include payment for time not worked, health care, life insurance, retirement plans, disability protection, employee stock option plans (ESOPs), and employee services.

4. *Explain the different kinds of health care legislation and describe the relationship between smoke-free workplaces and the Patient Protection and Affordable Care Act.* The Employee Retirement Income Security Act, the Consolidated Omnibus Budget Reconciliation Act, the Older Workers Benefit Protection Act, the Health Insurance Portability and Accountability Act, the Family and Medical Leave Act, the Pension Protection Act, and the Patient Protection and Affordable Care Act are major care health care legislations.

   The cost gap for health care between smokers and nonsmokers likely will widen beginning in 2018 when, under a provision of Patient Protection and Affordable Care Act, companies with health plans that spend much more than average will have to pay an additional federal tax.

5. *Explain premium pay. Premium pay* is compensation paid to employees for working long periods of time or working under dangerous or undesirable conditions.

6. *Explain voluntary benefits.* Many organizations are moving to *voluntary benefits,* which are essentially 100 percent paid by the employee. However, the employer typically pays the administrative cost. Employees gain because their premiums typically reflect group discounting and thus are lower than the employees could obtain on their own.

7. *Describe customized benefit plans. Customized benefit plans* permit employees to make yearly selections to largely determine their benefit package by choosing between taxable cash and numerous benefits.

8. *Describe the importance of communicating information about the benefits package.* Organizations spend millions of dollars each year for benefits. Yet, many do not do a good job of communicating the value of this investment to the employees. Often organizations do not have to improve benefits to keep their best employees; rather, workers need to fully understand the benefits that are provided them.

9. *Describe the job itself and the job environment as components of nonfinancial compensation.* The components of nonfinancial compensation consist of the job itself and the job environment.

   The job itself can be a very powerful factor in the compensation equation. Some jobs can be so stimulating that the incumbent is anxious to get to work each day. On the other hand, a job may be so boring or distasteful that an individual dreads going to work.

   The job environment also can have a significant impact on compensation. Sadly, often when jobs are designed, little time is devoted to addressing employees' motivational needs. The focus is on how to get the work done more efficiently. Nonfinancial compensation factors include sound policies, capable managers, competent employees, congenial coworkers, appropriate status symbols, and working conditions.

10. *Describe workplace flexibility (work–life balance) factors and global customized benefits.* Workplace flexibility factors include flextime, the compressed workweek, job sharing, Two-in-a-Box, telecommuting, and part-time work.

    When dealing with benefits on the global stage, employers must recognize that a standardized benefits program for all employees across the globe may be impractical and unsuccessful in achieving key benefits objectives.

Key Terms

indirect financial compensation (benefits)   250
unemployment compensation   252
workers' compensation   252
discretionary benefits   252
paid time off (PTO)   253
sabbaticals   253
health maintenance organization (HMO)   254
preferred provider organization (PPO)   254
point-of-service (POS)   254

exclusive provider organization (EPO)   254
consumer-driven health care plan   255
health savings account (HSA)   255
health reimbursement accounts (HRAs)   255
flexible spending account (FSA) 255
defined benefit plan   259
defined contribution plan   259
401(k) plan   259
cash balance plan   259
employee stock option plan (ESOP)   260

relocation benefits   261
premium pay   262
hazard pay   262
shift differential   262
voluntary benefits   262
customized benefit plan   263
nonfinancial compensation   263
flextime   266
compressed workweek   266
job sharing   267
telecommuting   268

Exercises

1. Think of a job you have worked in the past or a job that your parents held. What discretionary and voluntary benefits were provided? In order of importance to you or your parents, rank the value of each benefit. How valuable was the total benefit package?

⭐ 2. The Trends & Innovations in this chapter entitled "Smoke-free Workplaces and the Patient Protection and Affordable Care Act" provides an argument to eliminate nicotine use in the workplace. Do you accept or reject the suggestion that nicotine use is bad for the workplace? Be prepared to defend your decision in class.

3. Customized benefit plans permit employees to make yearly selections to largely determine their benefit package by choosing between taxable cash and numerous benefits. What do you believe would be the most valuable benefits for the following employees?
   a. single person who recently graduated from college
   b. forty-year-old married man with two children in college
   c. single mother with two young children

Questions for Review

1. What are some examples of unique benefits that companies provide?
2. Define *indirect financial compensation (benefits)*. Distinguish between discretionary and voluntary benefits.
3. In compensation terminology, what does *total rewards* mean?
4. What are the mandated or legally required benefits? Briefly describe each.
5. What are the basic categories of discretionary benefits? Describe each.
6. What items are included in the discretionary benefit of payment for time not worked?
7. Define each of the following:
   (a) health maintenance organization (HMO)
   (b) preferred provider organization (PPO)
   (c) point-of-service (POS)
   (d) exclusive provider organization (EPO)
   (e) consumer-driven health care plans
   (f) health savings account (HSA)
   (g) health reimbursement accounts (HRAs)
   (h) flexible spending account (FSA)
8. What is the purpose of on-site health care (work-site clinics)?
9. There are numerous forms of retirement plans. Describe each of the following:
   (a) defined benefit plan
   (b) defined contribution plan
   (c) 401(k) plan
   (d) cash balance plan
10. What is an employee stock option plan (ESOP)?
11. What are topics included within employee services?
12. Distinguish among premium pay, hazard pay, and shift differential pay.
⭐13. What is the purpose of a customized benefit plan?
14. Define each of the following benefit laws:
    (a) Employee Retirement Income Security Act
    (b) Consolidated Omnibus Budget Reconciliation Act
    (c) Health Insurance Portability and Accountability Act
    (d) Family and Medical Leave Act
    (e) Older Workers Benefit Protection Act
    (f) Pension Protection Act
    (g) Patient Protection and Affordable Care Act
15. What is the relationship between smoke-free workplaces and the Patient Protection and Affordable Care Act?
16. What are the components of nonfinancial compensation?
17. What are some nonfinancial compensation factors?
18. Define each the following workplace flexibility factors:
    (a) flextime
    (b) compressed workweek
    (c) job sharing
    (d) telecommuting
19. What is the purpose of the staffing practice called Two-in-a-Box?
⭐20. Why is it important to customize benefits in the global environment?

INCIDENT 1   Flextime

Kathy Collier is a supervisor of a government office in Washington, D.C. Morale in her office has been quite low recently. The workers have gone back to an 8:00 A.M. to 4:30 P.M. work schedule after having been on flextime for nearly two years.

When the directive came down allowing Kathy to place her office on flextime, she spelled out the rules carefully to her people.

Each person was to work during the core period from 10:00 A.M. to 2:30 P.M.; however, they could work the rest of the eight-hour day at any time between 6:00 A.M. and 6:00 P.M. Kathy felt her workers were honest and well motivated, so she did not bother to set up any system of control.

Everything went along well for a long time. Morale improved, and all the work seemed to get done. In November, however, an auditor from the General Accounting Office investigated and found that Kathy's workers were averaging seven hours a day. Two employees had been working only during the core period for more than two months. When Kathy's department manager reviewed the auditor's report, Kathy was told to return the office to regular working hours. Kathy was upset and disappointed with her people. She had trusted them and felt they had let her down.

Questions

1. What are the advantages and disadvantages of flextime?
2. What could Kathy have done to keep the above situation from occurring?
3. Are there other workplace flexibility arrangements that Kathy might use improve morale?

INCIDENT 2 A Benefits Package Designed for Whom?

Wayne McGraw greeted Robert Peters, his next interviewee, warmly. Robert had an excellent academic record and appeared to be just the kind of person Wayne's company, Beco Electric, was seeking. Wayne is the university recruiter for Beco and had already interviewed six graduating seniors at Centenary College.

Based on the application form, Robert appeared to be the most promising candidate to be interviewed that day. He was 22 years old and had a 3.6 grade point average with a 4.0 in his major field, industrial management. Robert was not only the vice president of the Student Government Association, but also activities chairman for Kappa Alpha Psi, a social fraternity. The reference letters in Robert's file reveal that he was both very active socially and a rather intense and serious student. One of the letters from Robert's employer during the previous summer expressed satisfaction with Robert's work habits.

Wayne knew that discussion of benefits could be an important part of the recruiting interview. But he did not know which aspects of Beco's benefits program would appeal most to Robert. The company has an excellent profit-sharing plan, although 80 percent of profit distributions are deferred and included in each employee's retirement account. Health benefits are also good. It also has long-term care insurance. The company's medical and dental plan pays a significant portion of costs. A company lunchroom provides meals at about 70 percent of outside prices, although few managers take advantage of this. Employees get one week of paid vacation after the first year and two weeks after two years with the company. Two weeks are provided each year for sick leave. In addition, there are 12 paid holidays each year. Finally, the company encourages advanced education, paying for tuition and books in full, and, under certain circumstances, allowing time off to attend classes during the day. It also provides scholarships for dependents.

Questions

1. What aspects of Beco's benefits program are likely to appeal to Robert? Explain.
2. In today's work environment, what additional benefits might be more attractive to Robert? Explain.
3. What aspects of Beco's benefits program would likely be the least appealing to Robert? Discuss.

MyManagementLab

Go to **mymanagementlab.com** for Auto-graded writing questions as well as the following Assisted-graded writing questions:

10-1. Why have some firms gone to voluntary benefits as opposed to discretionary benefits?

10-2. Why is it important to communicate information about the benefits package?

10-3. Mymanagementlab Only – comprehensive writing assignment for this chapter.

Notes

1. Ronald J. Alsop, "Perks Do Exist in a Vacuum," *Workforce Management* 90 (September 2011): 42.
2. Miguel Helft, "Check Out Zynga's New Offices," *Fortune* 164 (November 7, 2011): 59–60.
3. Christopher Tkaczyk, "Five-Star Culture," *Fortune* 164 (July 25, 2011): 23.
4. David Weldon, "In This Economy, 'People Pleasers' Can Be Workers' Best Friends," *Workforce Management* 90 (September 2011): 12–13.
5. Christopher Tkacyk, "Colgate-Palmolive," *Fortune* 161 (May 5, 2010): 39.
6. Spencer Bailey, "Benefits On Tap," *Bloomberg Businessweek* (March 21, 2011): 96–97.
7. "Don't Cry! Babies at Work Easier than You Think," *HR Specialist: Compensation & Benefits* 5 (March 2010): 1–2.
8. "Report Finds Job Satisfaction Tied to Security and Benefits," *Credit Union Times* 21 (September 22, 2010): 19.
9. Adrienne Fox, "Make a 'Deal,'" *HR Magazine* 57 (January 2012): 36–42.
10. "Benefits, Advancement Key to Worker Happiness, Report Says," *HR News* (August 12, 2011): 1.
11. Robert J. Grossman, "Hidden Costs of Layoffs," *HR Magazine* 57 (February 2012): 24–29.
12. Joanne Sammer, "Bank on Savings," *HR Magazine* 57 (January 2012): 47–49.
13. "Get Out of Town," *Benefits Magazine* 49 (February 2012): 74.

14. "Fewer Employees Are Using All Their Annual Leave," *Managing Benefits Plans* 14 (February 2012): 16.

15. "Getaway," *New Republic* 237 (August 6, 2007): 3–4.

16. Catherine A. Allen, "Burned Out?" *Personal Excellence* 16 (July 2011): 4.

17. Jason Blumer, "The Perfect Blend: A Firm's Path to Ensuring Work-Life Balance," *CPA Practice Advisor* 22 (February 2012): 21.

18. Justin G. Roy and Sullivan Kreiss, "Ten Tips for Retaining the Next Generation," *Offshore* 72 (January 2012): 10–11.

19. Joseph Coombs, "Flexibility Still Meeting Resistance," *HR Magazine* 56 (July 2011): 72.

20. Kathryn Tyler, "Sabbaticals Pay Off," *HR Magazine* 56 (December 2011): 38–42.

21. "Employers Embracing Programs as Morale Booster, Business Strategy," *HR Focus* 88 (September 2011): 1–4.

22. Meg Cadoux Hirshberg, "The Family Sabbatical," *Inc.* 34 (February 2012): 36–38.

23. Matt Bolch, "Realities Drive Change in Health Care Delivery," *Financial Executive* 28 (January/February 2012): 36–39.

24. Paul Keckley, "My Take on the Current State of Health Care," *Managed Care Outlook* 25 (January 1, 2012): 1–9.

25. Steve Miller, "Employers Change Tactics to Control Health Plan Costs," *HR Magazine* 57 (January 2012): 11.

26. "Consumer-Driven Health Plan Enrollment Still Growing, EBRI Report Finds," *HR Focus* 89 (March 2012): 11.

27. Jena McGregor and Esme Deprez, "Health Care: GE Gets Radical," *BusinessWeek* (November 30, 2009): 30.

28. Michael Johnsen, "HSAs, FSAs Make Consumers More Cost-Aware," *Drug Store News* 33 (March 14, 2011): 16.

29. John Reynolds, "Putting the Consumer Truly in the Driver Seat with Consumer Directed Health Care," *Employee Benefit Plan Review* 65 (April 2011): 14–15.

30. Rhea Brittany Luebke, "Create a Retirement Savings Strategy Using a Health Savings Account," *Journal of Financial Service Professionals* 66 (January 2012): 27–29.

31. Lori Thayer Oliphant and Cheryl Camin Murray, "Fit for an On-Site Clinic," *HR Magazine* 57 (January 2012): 61.

32. Jeremy Smerd, "Work-Site Clinics Gaining Favor as Retail Locations Lag," *Workforce Management* 89 (April 2010): 8–10.

33. Lydell C. Bridgeford, "Employers Adjust Workplace-Clinic Models to Achieve Goals," *Employee Benefit News* 25 (April 2011): 1–49.

34. Lori Chordas, "New Year, New Rules," *Best's Review* 112 (January 2012): 52–53.

35. Nancy Hatch Woodward, "Earn Less, Pay Less," *HR Magazine* 57 (March 2012): 67–70.

36. "Even in Difficult Times, Employees See the Value of Smoking Cessation Programs," *Managed Care Outlook* 22 (June 1, 2009): 10–12.

37. "Put Out That Cigarette! Intensive Worksite Programs Help Smokers Quit," *Managed Care Outlook* 24 (July 1, 2011): 1–9.

38. Lydell C. Bridgeford, "Smoke Gets in Your Eyes," *Employee Benefit News* 22 (January 2008): 33–34.

39. Katherine Harmon, "Carcinogens Detected from 'Thirdhand Smoke,'" *Scientific American* 302 (April 2010): 29.

40. Paul McIntyre, "A Smoking Ban Isn't About Your Bottom Line, It's About Protecting Your Workers' Health," *Nation's Restaurant News* 39 (December 5, 2005): 24–34.

41. Joanne Deschenaux, "Is a 'Smoker-Free' Workplace Right for You?" *HR Magazine* 56 (July 2011): 42–45.

42. Monica Dobie, "Quit Smoking or Lose Your Job," *World Tobacco* (May 2005): 20–21.

43. Susan K. Lessack, "Where There's Smoke … Can You Fire (or Refuse to Hire)?" *HR Specialist: Employment Law* 40 (May 2011): 7.

44. Patty Kujawa, "Young Workers Craving Defined Benefit Plans," *Workforce Management* 90 (March 2011): 16.

45. Vishal Apte and Brendan McFarland, "A Look at Defined Contribution Match Reinstatements," *Pension Benefits* 21 (January 2012): 7–10.

46. Lisa Murton Beets, "Cash Balance Pension Plans," *Smart Business Columbus* 20 (January 2012): 42.

47. Jerry Geisel, "Coca-Cola Makes Move to Cash Balance Plan," *Business Insurance* 43 (February 23, 2009): 3.

48. John Koegel, "Is There an ESOP in Your Future?" *Community Banker* 17 (January 2008): 22–23.

49. Jennifer Schramm, "Undereducated," *HR Magazine* 56 (September 2011): 136.

50. Michael E. Echols, "Pay for Learning—It Pays," *Chief Learning Officer* 11 (February 2012): 44–48.

51. Theresa Minton-Eversole, "Easing the Travails of Trailing Spouses," *HR Magazine* 56 (November 2011): 43–46.

52. Sonia Alleyne, "Relocation Is Down," *Black Enterprise* 41 (April 2011): 46.

53. Janet Aschkenasy, "Work Equality Advances," *Treasury & Risk* (May 2011): 19.

54. Rebecca Vesely "Some Companies Offer Tax Relief for Domestic Partners," *Workforce Management* 91 (February 2012): 15.

55. Evelio E. Astray-Caneda III, "Offering Same-Sex Domestic Partner Benefits to Government Employees: Reasons, Examples, and Methods," *Benefits Magazine* 49 (January 2012): 46.

56. "Regional Briefs," *Managed Care Outlook* 24 (June 15, 2011): 4–5.

57. Kathleen Koster, "Want to Be More Liked? Offer Voluntary Benefits, Survey Concludes," *Employee Benefit News* 25 (February 2011): 42.

58. David Tobenkin, "Here's the Deal," *HR Magazine* 57 (March 2012): 61–65.

59. Todd Henneman, "Workers Pick Their Perfect Perquisites," *Workforce Management* 91 (January 2012): 9.

60. Frank L. Giancola, "Examining the Job Itself as a Source of Employee Motivation," *Compensation & Benefits Review* 43 (January 1, 2011): 23–29.

61. "Employee Satisfaction: Key to Recovery Success?" *HR Focus* 87 (April 2010): 1–15.

62. "Work/Life Policies Enhance Business," *HR Magazine* 57 (January 2012): 69.

63. "Work-Family Conflicts Affect Employees at All Income Levels," *HR Focus* 87 (April 2010): 9.

64. Henry G. Jackson, "Flexible Workplaces: A Business Imperative," *HR Magazine* 56 (October 2011): 10.

65. "Working Moms Need Flexibility," *OfficePro* 71 (August/September 2011): 5.

66. "Employers Embracing Programs as Morale Booster, Business Strategy," *HR Focus* 88 (September 2011): 1–4.

67. Alison Quirk, "The Business Case for Flex," *HR Magazine* (April 2012): 44—45.

68. Justin G. Roy, "Ten Tips for Retaining the Next Generation," *Power Engineering* 116 (January 2012): 11–12.

69. Jamie LaReau, "Ford's 2 Julies Share Devotion—and Job," *Automotive News* 85 (October 25, 2010): 4–26.

70. Scott Thurm, "Power-Sharing Prepares Managers," *Wall Street Journal* (December 5, 2005): B4.

71. Ed Frauenheim, "Co-CEOs: Two at the Top," *Workforce Management* 88 (May 18, 2009): 40–42.

72. "SAP AG Reports Departure of CEO and Appointment of Co-CEOs," *Telecomworldwire (M2)* (February 8, 2010).

73. Michelle V. Rafter, "Out of Site," *Workforce Management* 90 (June 2011): 22–28.

74. "The Virtual Office Gains Momentum," *Trends Magazine* (January 2011): 16–19.

75. Dori Meinert, "Make Telecommuting Pay Off," *HR Magazine* 56 (June 2011): 32–37.

76. Adrienne Fox, "Part-Timers," *HR Magazine* 55 (August 2010): 28–33.

77. Laura Fitzpatrick, "We're Getting Off the Ladder," *Time* 173 (May 25, 2009): 45.

78. Rosaline Chow Koo, "The Global Added Value of Flexible Benefits," *Benefits Quarterly* 27 (2011 Fourth Quarter): 17–20.

79. Yvette Lee, John Sweeney, and Lesa Albright, "Electronic Harassment, Recruiters' Sources, Global Benefits," *HR Magazine* 55 (September 2010): 24–25.

80. David Tobenkin, "Learn the Landscape," *HR Magazine* 56 (May 2011): 51–54.

81. Rudy Bethea, Jr., "Global Benefits Management: Maintaining a Competitive Edge in Multiple Countries," *Employee Benefit Plan Review* 64 (November 2009): 22–23.

82. Lori Chordas, "Multiple Choice," *Best's Review* 109 (March 2009): 65–67.

83. Paul Shimer, "Looking for Land," *Employee Benefit News* 23 (June 2009): 30–32.

84. Jenny Keefe, "Total Rethink," *Employee Benefits* (November 2008): 56–59.

85. Evan Taylor, "United States Ranks Ninth Globally in Flexible Work Schedules," *HR Focus* 88 (August 2011): 9–10.

Part Six
Safety and Health

Chapter 11
A Safe and Healthy
Work Environment

A Safe and Healthy Work Environment

HRM in Action

Resilience Training

OBJECTIVE 11.1

Describe resilience training and explain the nature and role of safety and health and the function of the Occupational Safety and Health Administration.

resilience
Ability to bounce back and adapt in a positive manner to difficult situations.

Resilience is the ability to bounce back and adapt in a positive manner to difficult situations.[1] Most of us have experienced failure or a major disappointment at some time in our life. It might be from being fired, an unsuccessful romance, or failure on a major exam. Certainly disappointments are a nearly inevitable part of living. As Michael Jordan once said, "Twenty six times I've been trusted to take the game-winning shot—and missed. I've failed over and over and over again in my life. And that is why I succeed."[2] Today, the need for employee resilience is based largely on difficult economic times where employees are being asked to do more with less.

Resilience is not something a person in born with; rather it is something one can learn and develop.[3] Many believe that resilience training should be used instead of stress management programs in today's work environment. Resilience training is not intended to help workers reduce stress, rather it is meant to strengthen them after experiencing stress.[4] Resilience training deals with the individual's emotional reactions to situations. Many firms use resilience training to prevent stress as opposed to dealing with the symptoms of stress.[5] They are investing in measures to build a more overall resilient workforce. Each employee is taught how use a mental "toolkit" when confronting a stressful situation.[6] Resilience training actually teaches people how to learn from a stressful situation. For example, how should you deal with an angry customer in the restaurant business? Resilience trainer George S. Everly says the "discipline is winning over decision-makers in industries where employees experience daily stress, such as health care, finance, law enforcement, firefighting, emergency medical services and the military."[7] Aid workers who have to go into places after disasters are now provided resilience training before a disaster. The extreme natural disasters in recent years, such as with Hurricane Katrina and the earthquake in Japan, have increased interest in helping employees cope and making them more resilient.[8]

The first step in resilience training is to set goals; essentially what do you want from resilience training? Is the goal to help workers grow stronger under stress or to be able to work longer hours without burning out? There are several resilience training programs available and each program differs somewhat. Martin E. P. Seligman is presently testing his resilience training program with the U.S. Army where trauma is more common and more severe than in any corporate setting. The $145 million program includes a psychological fitness test, self-improvement courses, and post-test and master resilience training for drill sergeants. Many believe this model would have practical application in business.[9]

Developing a resilience culture where employees have a sense of control over their work is important as a means of dealing with stress. People who have experienced the program feel they can control their environment. They are able to face unfamiliar situations with less anxiety and be more confident when taking risks.[10]

Nature and Role of Safety and Health

In our discussion, **safety** involves protecting employees from injuries caused by work-related accidents. Included within the umbrella definition of safety are factors related to musculoskeletal disorders, stress injuries, and workplace and domestic violence. **Health** refers to employees' freedom from physical or emotional illness. Problems in these areas can seriously affect a worker's productivity and quality of work life. They can dramatically lower a firm's effectiveness and employee morale. In fact, job-related injuries and illnesses are more common than most people realize.

Occupational Safety and Health Administration

The Occupational Safety and Health Act of 1970 created the Occupational Safety and Health Administration (OSHA). The purpose of OSHA is to ensure worker safety and health in the United States by working with employers and employees to create better working environments. The act requires employers to provide employees a safe and healthy place to work and this responsibility extends to providing *safe employees.* The courts have reasoned that a dangerous worker is comparable to a defective machine.

Employers have a responsibility under the **general duty clause** of the Occupational Safety and Health Act to furnish a workplace free from recognized hazards that are causing or are likely to cause death or serious physical harm. To prove a violation of the general duty clause, OSHA has to demonstrate (1) that a condition or activity in the workplace presented a hazard, (2) that the employer or its industry recognized this hazard, (3) that the hazard was likely to cause death or serious physical harm, and (4) that a feasible and effective means existed to eliminate or materially reduce the hazard. In 2008 an employee was trampled to death by shoppers at a Walmart store during the annual "Black" Friday. OSHA cited the store for this fatality even though there is no specific OSHA regulation for crowd control plans. OSHA held that it was Walmart's "general duty" to have developed such a plan.[11]

In 1913, the U.S. Bureau of Labor Statistics documented about 23,000 industrial deaths in a workforce of 38 million, a rate of about 61 deaths per 100,000 workers.[12] The number of fatal work injuries in the United States in 2010 was 4,547, which was the lowest total since the fatality census was first conducted in 1992.[13] Since its beginning in 1970, OSHA has helped to cut workplace fatalities by more than 60 percent and occupational injury and illness by 40 percent. At the same time, U.S. employment has more than doubled from 56 million workers at 3.5 million work sites to 147 million workers at 7.2 million sites. The agency has helped standardize reasonable worker protections. Rules defining confined spaces, machine guards, or hard hat zones have allowed many plant managers and site supervisors to think more about productivity, not accidents. The most frequently mentioned hazard that OSHA addresses has to do with missing or inadequate fall protection.[14]

The mission of OSHA is to promote and ensure workplace safety and health and to reduce workplace fatalities, injuries, and illnesses. OSHA is committed to ensuring—so far as possible—that every working man and woman in the nation has a safe and healthful working environment. It believes that providing workers with a safe workplace is central to their ability to enjoy health, security, and the opportunity to achieve the American dream. Addressing safety and health issues in the workplace also saves the employer money and adds value to the business. To handle this workload, OSHA has approximately 2,000 inspectors.

Even though OSHA would like a successful partnership relationship to exist, at times penalties must be given. Financial penalties serve as reminders to companies of the benefits of maintaining safe and healthy working conditions. A serious hazard citation has a maximum penalty of $7,000. A serious violation occurs when there is substantial probability that death or serious physical harm could result from a hazard about which the employer knew or should have known.[15] A willful citation might have a maximum amount of $70,000 per violation. Calculated instance by instance, if 10 employees were exposed to one hazard the employer intentionally did not eliminate, the penalty amount would immediately jump to $700,000.

OSHA has implemented the Severe Violator Enforcement Program that increases inspections at work sites where "recalcitrant employers" have repeatedly violated safety regulations and endangered workers. It also requires a mandatory follow-up inspection to make sure required changes were made. BP Products North America Inc. received the largest fine in OSHA's history for its failure to correct hazards faced by employees at its Texas City refinery. However, this record will likely be broken as a result of the death and destruction caused by the oil well explosion and the resulting damage to the Gulf Coast in 2010.

OBJECTIVE 11.2

Explain the relationship between OSHA and whistleblowers, describe the economic impact of safety, and explain the focus of safety programs.

HR Web Wisdom

OSHA

http://www.osha.gov

Occupational Safety and Health Administration Web site.

OSHA and Whistleblowers

A little known fact is that OSHA is charged with more than just enforcing health and safety matters. Within the Department of Labor, OSHA enforces the whistleblower protection provisions of 21 statutes, covering not just workplace safety but also the environment, consumer products, the financial system, and other areas. For instance, the Sarbanes–Oxley Act has a provision that makes it illegal to fire or otherwise discriminate against a corporate officer for trying to report possible accounting irregularities to higher corporate officials or enforcement agencies. The U.S. Department of Labor administers this portion of the Sarbanes–Oxley Act, not the U.S. Securities & Exchange Commission. The whistleblower provision of the Dodd–Frank Act prohibits employers from retaliating against employees who raise various protected concerns or provide protected information to the employer or to the government. OSHA Assistant Secretary Dr. David Michaels said, "Whistleblowers play a vital role in ensuring the integrity of our financial system, as well as the safety of our food, air, water, workplaces and transportation systems. The ability of workers to speak out and exercise their legal rights without fear of retaliation is crucial to many of the legal protections and safeguards that all Americans value."[16]

Recently OSHA ruled that Bank of America Corporation (BofA) violated the whistleblower protection provisions of the Sarbanes–Oxley Act by improperly firing an employee. It ordered BofA to reinstate the employee and pay her approximately $930,000 in back wages, interest, compensatory damages, and attorney fees. The employee-led internal investigations revealed widespread and persistent wire, mail, and bank fraud. The employee alleged that those who attempted to report fraud to the firm's employee relations department suffered persistent retaliation. In her case, she was fired.[17]

In 2012, OSHA ordered AirTran Airways, a subsidiary of Dallas, Texas–based Southwest Airlines Company, to reinstate a former pilot who was fired after reporting numerous mechanical concerns. The agency also has ordered that the pilot be paid more than $1 million in back wages plus interest and compensatory damages. An investigation by OSHA's Whistleblower Protection Program found reasonable cause to believe that the termination was an act of retaliation in violation of the whistleblower provision of the Wendell H. Ford Aviation Investment and Reform Act for the 21st Century. OSHA recently ordered a Florida trucking company to reinstate a driver fired for refusing to drive two unsafe trucks. The department ruled that Zurla Trucking, a 42-driver company, violated the Surface Transportation Assistance Act. It was required to pay back wages, plus interest, and compensatory damages and $125,000 in punitive damages. Zurla also had to remove adverse references related to the firing from the employee's records. However, most of the attention regarding health and safety relates to OSHA.

OSHA prohibits any person from discharging or in any manner retaliating against any employee because the employee has exercised rights under the OSHA. Rights provided by the act include employee participation in safety and health activities such as complaining to OSHA and seeking an OSHA inspection, participating in an OSHA inspection, participating or testifying in any proceeding related to an OSHA inspection, and reporting a work-related injury, illness, or fatality. Under OSHA, retaliation is generally defined as any action that would dissuade a reasonable employee from engaging in protected activity. Depending on the circumstances of the case, "adverse" action can include:

- Firing or laying off
- Blacklisting
- Demoting
- Denying overtime or promotion
- Disciplining
- Denial of benefits
- Failure to hire or rehire
- Intimidation

- Making threats
- Reassignment affecting prospects for promotion
- Reducing pay or hours[18]

In another ruling, OSHA ordered Union Pacific Railroad Company to immediately reinstate an employee in Idaho who was terminated after reporting a work-related injury. OSHA also ordered the company to pay the employee more than $300,000 in back wages, compensatory damages, attorney's fees, and punitive damages. The employee had filed a whistleblower complaint with OSHA alleging suspension without pay and then termination 23 days after notifying the company of an on-the-job injury.

OSHA and the Small Business[19]

For a small business owner, a safe workplace is not only critical to employee health and the business's success, it is the law. Under the provisions of OSHA, employers must provide a workplace free from recognized hazards that are causing, or are likely to cause, death or serious physical harm to employees regardless of the size of a business. OSHA provides a Web-based step-by-step occupational health and safety guide that can help determine the government requirements that apply to small businesses. The guide is intended to help small business employers meet the legal requirements imposed by OSHA and achieve an in-compliance status before an OSHA inspection. It covers the basics of an occupational safety and health plan for small business owners, tips on how to self-assess the workplace, employee training strategies, and more.

It also has an on-site consultation service that provides small businesses with free advice from trained state government staff. The service is completely separate from any enforcement programs that the OSHA operates, and is entirely confidential. Sessions identify and uncover potential workplace hazards and are intended to help small business owners improve their workplace safety and health systems. Small businesses that participate can qualify for a one-year exemption from routine OSHA inspections.[19]

Safety: The Economic Impact

Job-related deaths and injuries of all types extract a high toll not only in human misery, but also in economic loss. According to a Liberty Mutual Workplace Safety Index, workplace illnesses and injuries cost U.S. firms $53 billion in workers' compensation costs, an average of more than $1 billion per week.[20] The top leading cause of workplace injuries and their associated costs are overexertion (e.g., lifting, carrying, pushing, pulling, etc.). The significant financial costs are often passed along to the consumer in the form of higher prices. Thus, job-related deaths and injuries affect everyone, directly or indirectly. Safety risks can be significant for employers. In addition to workers' compensation costs, OSHA can levy major fines. Indirect costs related to turnover and lost productivity add to the expense.

Companies have come a long way in recognizing the importance and cost benefits of safety. Workplaces are safer, thanks to efforts of employers, insurance companies, unions, and state and federal agencies. Safety professionals strive for lower workers' compensation costs, as do insurance companies, who work to keep both their clients' and their own costs down. However, death and injuries continue to occur.

Focus of Safety Programs

Every employer needs to have a comprehensive safety program in place regardless of the degree of danger involved. Safety programs may accomplish their purposes in two primary ways: one focusing on *unsafe employee actions* and the other on *unsafe working conditions*.

Unsafe Employee Actions

Training and orientation of new employees emphasizing safety is especially important. The early months of employment are often critical because it has been proven that work injuries decrease with length of service. The first approach in a safety program is to create a psychological environment and employee attitudes that promote safety. A *corporate culture* needs to exist where employees are involved and engaged and have the opportunity to provide input on changes to their workplace. Studies show a positive link between employee engagement and involvement and safety performance.[21] Accident rates decline when workers consciously or subconsciously think about safety. This attitude must permeate the firm's operations, and a strong company policy emphasizing safety and health is crucial. Although there is danger that everyone's responsibility will become no one's responsibility, a truly safe environment takes the effort of everyone from top management to the lowest-level employee. Although every individual in a firm should be encouraged to come up with solutions to potential safety problems, the firm's managers must take the lead. Management's unique role is clear, since OSHA places primary responsibility for employee safety on the employer.

Unsafe Working Conditions

The second approach to safety program design is to develop and maintain a safe physical working environment. Here, altering the environment becomes the focus for preventing accidents. Even if Joe, a machine operator, has been awake all night with a sick child and can barely keep his eyes open, the safety devices on his machine will help protect him. Management should create a physical environment in which accidents cannot occur. It is in this area that OSHA has had its greatest influence.

Developing Safety Programs

Workplace accident prevention requires safety program planning. Plans may be relatively simple, as for a small retail store, or more complex and highly sophisticated, as for a large automobile assembly plant. Regardless of the organization's size, the support of top management is essential if safety programs are to be effective.

Table 11-1 shows some of the reasons for top management's support of a safety program. This information suggests that the lost productivity of a single injured worker is not the only factor to consider. Every phase of human resource management is involved. The firm may have difficulty recruiting if it gains a reputation for being an unsafe place to work. Employee relations erode if workers believe that management does not care enough about them to provide a safe workplace. Firms will see an increase in compensation costs when they must pay a premium to attract and retain qualified applicants. Maintaining a stable workforce may become very difficult if employees perceive their workplace as hazardous. To overcome the above-mentioned problems, safety training must be a continuous process to ensure a safe workplace.

job hazard analysis (JHA)
Multistep process designed to study and analyze a task or job and then break down that task into steps that provide a means of eliminating associated hazards.

JOB HAZARD ANALYSIS **Job hazard analysis (JHA)** is a multistep process designed to study and analyze a task and then break down that task into steps that provide a means of eliminating associated hazards. JHA can have a major impact on safety performance. It results in a detailed written procedure for safely completing many tasks within a plant. A successful JHA program features several key components: management support, supervisor and employee training, written program, and management oversight. It is an effective and useful tool to isolate and address safety issues and risks.

ETHICAL DILEMMA

Illegal Dumping

You have just become aware that the company that disposes of your plant waste is not following Environmental Protection Agency guidelines. The firm is dumping toxic waste at night in a closed landfill six miles from the plant. To make matters worse, your brother-in-law operates the waste disposal company. You have already warned him once, and you have just learned that he is still illegally dumping waste. You confront him, telling him that you are going to use the hotline to report him if he illegally dumps waste one more time, but he threatens to implicate you if you blow the whistle.

What would you do?
What factor(s) in this ethical dilemma might influence a person to make a less-than-ethical decision?

TABLE 11-1

Reasons for Management's Support of a Safety Program

- **Personal loss.** The physical pain and mental anguish associated with injuries are always unpleasant and may even be traumatic for an injured worker. Of still greater concern is the possibility of permanent disability or even death.

- **Financial loss to injured employees.** Most employees are covered by company insurance plans or personal accident insurance. However, an injury may result in financial losses not covered by insurance.

- **Lost productivity.** When an employee is injured, there will be a loss of productivity for the firm. In addition to obvious losses, there are often hidden costs. For example, a substitute worker may need additional training to replace the injured employee. Even when another worker is available to move into the injured employee's position, efficiency may suffer.

- **Higher insurance premiums.** Workers' compensation insurance premiums are based on the employer's history of insurance claims. The potential for savings related to employee safety provides a degree of incentive to establish formal programs.

- **Possibility of fines or imprisonment.** Since the enactment of the Occupational Safety and Health Act, a willful and repeated violation of its provisions may result in serious penalties for the employer.

- **Social responsibility.** Many executives feel responsible for the safety and health of their employees. A number of firms had excellent safety programs years before OSHA existed. They understand that a safe work environment is not only in the best interests of the firm; providing one is the right thing to do.

OSHA has issued a comprehensive booklet to assist in job hazard analysis. The booklet explains what job hazard analysis is and offers guidelines to help firms conduct their own step-by-step analysis.[22]

SUPERFUND AMENDMENTS REAUTHORIZATION ACT, TITLE III (SARA) SARA requires businesses to communicate more openly about the hazards associated with the materials they use and produce and the wastes they generate. Although SARA has been around since 1986, some firms still do not have a satisfactory program in place. The hazard communication standard often leads the list of OSHA violations, since the top category for OSHA citations is for no written hazard communication program. Dealing with this standard appears to be relatively simple and inexpensive, except when organizations ignore its provisions.

EMPLOYEE INVOLVEMENT One way to strengthen a safety program is to include employee input, which provides workers with a sense of involvement. To prevent accidents, each worker must make a personal commitment to safe work practices. A team concept, in which employees watch out for each other as a moral obligation, is a worthy goal. Supervisors can show support for the safety program by conscientiously enforcing safety rules and by closely conforming to the rules themselves. Participation in such teams helps form positive attitudes, and employees develop a sense of ownership of the program. Involved employees may become concerned not only with safety issues but also with ways to improve productivity.

SAFETY ENGINEER In many companies, one staff member coordinates the overall safety program. Titles such as *safety engineer* and *safety director* are common. One of the safety engineer's primary tasks is to provide safety training for company employees. This involves educating line managers about the merits of safety, and recognizing and eliminating unsafe situations. Although the safety engineer operates essentially in an advisory capacity, a well-informed and assertive person in this capacity may exercise considerable influence in the organization. Some major corporations also have *risk management departments* that anticipate losses associated with safety factors and prepare legal defenses in the event of lawsuits.

Accident Investigation

Accidents can happen even in the most safety-conscious firms. Whether or not an accident results in an injury, an organization should carefully evaluate each occurrence to determine its cause and to ensure that it does not recur. The safety engineer and the line supervisor usually jointly investigate accidents. One of the responsibilities of any supervisor is to prevent accidents. To do so, the supervisor must learn, through active participation in the safety program, why accidents occur, how they occur, where they occur, and who is involved. Supervisors gain a great deal of knowledge about accident prevention by helping to prepare accident reports. OSHA Form 300 is a log of work-related injuries and illnesses (see Figure 11-1). The Log is used in the evaluation of safety programs, discussed next. Most employers electronically transmit records of occupational injuries and illnesses directly to OSHA.

Evaluation of Safety Programs

Perhaps the best indicator of a successful safety program is a reduction in the injury frequency rate, OSHA's formula is provided below:

> **Injury Frequency Rate** = (Number of Recordable Injuries x 200,000) divided by the number of hours worked.) The 200,000 is the equivalent of 100 full-time employees working 40 hours per week, 50 weeks a year.

Other OSHA metrics currently in use include total cases, nonfatal cases without lost workdays, total lost workday cases, cases with days away from work, and measure of fatalities. In addition to program-evaluation criteria, an effective reporting system helps to ensure that accidents are reported and receive attention. This is important because almost half of workplaces inspected by OSHA are for underreported numbers of employee injuries or illnesses.[23] With the start of a new safety program, the number of accidents may decline significantly because some supervisors may fail to report certain accidents to make the statistics for their units look better. Proper evaluation of a safety program depends on the accurate reporting and recording of data.

Organizations must use the conclusions derived from an evaluation for them to be of any value in improving the safety program. Gathering data and permitting this information to collect dust on the safety director's desk will not solve problems or prevent accidents. Accident investigators must transmit evaluation results upward to top management and downward to line managers in order to generate improvements.

OBJECTIVE 11.3

Describe the consequences of musculoskeletal disorders and explain the purpose of ergonomics.

musculoskeletal disorders (MSDs)

Conditions that affect the body's muscles, joints, tendons, ligaments, and nerves.

carpal tunnel syndrome (CTS)

Caused by pressure on the median nerve that occurs as a result of a narrowing of the passageway that houses the nerve.

HR Web Wisdom

Musculoskeletal Disorders

http://www.answers.com/ topic/musculoskeletal-disorders

Site offers information on musculoskeletal disorders.

Musculoskeletal Disorders

Musculoskeletal disorders (MSDs) are conditions that affect the body's muscles, joints, tendons, ligaments, and nerves. Work-related MSDs, including tendonitis, carpal tunnel syndrome (CTS), and back pain, cost U.S. companies $61.2 billion annually just to cover lost productivity.[24] Over half a million cases of musculoskeletal disorders are reported annually in the United States.[25] They are the leading cause of nonfatal workplace injuries nationwide, accounting for 28 percent of all such incidences requiring days away from work.[26] Kevin Schmidt, senior vice president at Work Well, an occupational health services company, said, "Employers can reduce and prevent MSDs in their workplaces by hiring workers who are qualified for the jobs at hand, conditioning employees to do the job and modifying the work area if needed."[27]

A major musculoskeletal disorder is **carpal tunnel syndrome (CTS)** caused by pressure on the median nerve that occurs as a result of a narrowing of the passageway that houses the nerve. People who have CTS may experience pain, numbness, or tingling in the hands or wrist, a weak grip, the tendency to drop objects, sensitivity to cold, and in later stages, muscle deterioration, especially in the thumb.

CTS tends to develop in people who use their hands and wrists repeatedly in the same way. Illustrators, carpenters, assembly-line workers, and people whose jobs involve work on personal computers are the ones most commonly affected. Workers in an office environment often experience CTS. If employees keyboard 40 words per minutes, they press 12,000 keys per eight-hour day with approximately eight ounces of force needed to press each key. Using these estimates, employees working full time will exert approximately 16 tons of force each day.[28]

CTS is preventable, or at least its severity can be reduced. Managers can provide ergonomic furniture, especially chairs, and ensure that computer monitors are positioned at eye level and keyboards at elbow level. Employees can also cooperate by reporting early symptoms of CTS. Also, it helps to often rest the hand and wrist in a neutral position trying not to perform the exact activities that caused the syndrome. Often taking nonsteroidal anti-inflammatory drugs will help. Certainly, any physical therapy aimed at exercising the hand muscle-tendon units should be

OSHA's Form 300

Log of Work-Related Injuries and Illnesses

Year:

U.S. Department of Labor
Occupational Safety and Health Administration

Form approved OMB no. 1218-0176

Attention: This form contains information relating to employee health and must be used in a manner that protects the confidentiality of employees to the extent possible while the information is being used for occupational safety and health purposes.

You must record information about every work-related injury or illness that involves loss of consciousness, restricted work activity or job transfer, days away from work, or medical treatment beyond first aid. You must also record significant work-related injuries and illnesses that are diagnosed by a physician or licensed health care professional. You must also record work-related injuries and illnesses that meet any of the specific recording criteria listed in 29 CFR 1904.8 through 1904.12. Feel free to use two lines for a single case if you need to. You must complete an injury and illness incident report (OSHA Form 301) or equivalent form for each injury or illness recorded on this form. If you're not sure whether a case is recordable, call your local OSHA office for help.

Establishment name

City _____ **State** _____

Identify the person

Describe the case

Classify the case

(A) Case No.	(B) Employee's Name	(C) Job Title (e.g., Welder)	(D) Date of injury or onset of illness (mo./day)	(E) Where the event occurred (e.g. Loading dock north end)	(F) Describe injury or illness, parts of body affected, and object/substance that directly injured or made person ill (e.g. Second degree burns on right forearm from acetylene torch)	Death (G)	Days away from work (H)	Job transfer or restriction (I)	Other record-able cases (J)	On job transfer or restriction (days) (K)	Away from work (days) (L)	Injury (M)(1)	Skin Disorder (2)	Respiratory Condition (3)	Poisoning (4)	All other illnesses (5)

Classify the case — Using these categories, check ONLY the most serious result for each case:

Enter the number of days the injured or ill worker was:

Check the "injury" column or choose one type of illness:

Page totals | 0 | 0 | 0 | 0 | 0 | 0 | 0 | 0 | 0 | 0 | 0

	Injury (1)	Skin Disorder (2)	Respiratory Condition (3)	Poisoning (4)	All other illnesses (5)

Be sure to transfer these totals to the Summary page (Form 300A) before you post it.

Page _____ **1** of **1**

Public reporting burden for this collection of information is estimated to average 14 minutes per response, including time to review the instruction, search and gather the data needed, and complete and review the collection of information. Persons are not required to respond to the collection of information unless it displays a currently valid OMB control number. If you have any comments about these estimates or any aspects of this data collection, contact: US Department of Labor, OSHA Office of Statistics, Room N-3644, 200 Constitution Ave, NW, Washington, DC 20210. Do not send the completed forms to this office.

FIGURE 11-1

OSHA's Form 300, Log of Work-Related Injuries and Illnesses

stopped until after symptoms have disappeared. Other suggested actions include keeping wrists straight, taking exercise breaks, alternating tasks, shifting positions periodically, adjusting chair height, working with feet flat on the floor, and being conscious of posture. Many of these actions suggest the need for ergonomics.

Ergonomics

A specific approach to dealing with health problems such as musculoskeletal disorders and enhancing performance is ergonomics. **Ergonomics** is the process of designing the workplace to support the capabilities of people and job or task demands. Through ergonomics, the goal is to fit the machine and work environment to the person, rather than require the person to make the adjustment. Ergonomics includes all attempts to structure work conditions so that they maximize energy conservation, promote good posture, and allow workers to function without pain or impairment. Failure to address ergonomics issues results in fatigue, poor performance, and musculoskeletal disorders. In fact, ergonomic disorders are the fastest-growing category of work-related illness.

ergonomics
Process of designing the workplace to support the capabilities of people and job or task demands.

There is a clear economic payoff in using ergonomics. Blue Grass Energy, a Kentucky distribution cooperative, implemented a proactive and mandatory stretching program for its field crews, purchased battery-operated tools, and tested back-saving technology and has minimized lost labor hours due to injuries in the field. All the line workers are required to stretch their muscles before each strenuous work day, resulting in a dramatic decline in pulled hamstrings and other muscles and back injuries.[29] Other companies have discovered that improving the work environment boosts morale, lowers injury rates, and yields a positive return on investment. A sound ergonomic approach to avoiding workplace injuries is prevention.

The workforce of the future is expected to be increasingly mobile. With mobile devices employees can work virtually anywhere. Ergonomics engineers are concerned that this group is setting itself up for musculoskeletal problems, which can range from discomfort to the development of tendonitis. Margo Fraser, executive director of the Association of Canadian Ergonomists, said, "Workers who find they are pulling laptops out in coffee shops and fast-food restaurants must also remember they are not just sitting in non-ergonomic chairs, but ones that are "anti-ergonomic," purposefully designed to keep people from sitting in them for hours at a time."[30]

Another threat to the safety and security of people on the job is workplace violence, discussed next.

OBJECTIVE **11.4**
Explain the effects of workplace and domestic violence on businesses and describe workplace bullying.

Workplace Violence

All too often, human resource professionals are receiving wake-up calls about the potential for workplace violence. Recently, an employee killed two fellow workers at a Kraft Foods Inc. plant in Philadelphia, and in another instance, a truck driver shot and killed eight coworkers, then himself, at a beer distributor in Connecticut. OSHA defines **workplace violence** as physical assault, threatening behavior, verbal abuse, hostility, or harassment directed toward employees at work or on duty. The fact that OSHA has included verbal abuse in the definition of workplace violence has HR professionals concerned that the general duty clause could even be cited for obscene language.[31]

workplace violence
Physical assault, threatening behavior, verbal abuse, hostility, or harassment directed toward employees at work or on duty.

According to a National Institute for Occupational Safety and Health publication, on average, 1.7 million workers are injured each year, and more than 800 die as a result of workplace violence.[32] Sadly, homicide is the second leading cause of death on the job, second only to motor vehicle crashes. Regardless of who commits the crime, there is the horror of random workplace violence.

Homicide, as terrible as it is, accounts for only a small percentage of the overall incidence of workplace violence. There is no way to estimate the physical and psychological damage to other employees, who are only onlookers to the violent behavior. The issue facing most large employers is not *if* they will ever deal with an act of workplace violence, but *when*.

Vulnerable Employees

Employees at gas stations and liquor stores, taxi drivers, police officers, and convenience store managers working night shifts face the greatest danger from workplace violence. However, no workplace is immune from violence. Hospital managers overwhelmingly say that the biggest threat emergency room workers face is patient violence. Most hospitals now have security guards stationed in their emergency rooms, particularly at times such as Saturday nights, when violence seems to escalate.

There are numerous reasons for violent acts committed by employees or former employees. Among the most common are personality conflicts, marital or family problems, drug or alcohol abuse, and firings or layoffs.

Legal Consequences of Workplace Violence

In addition to the horror of workplace violence, there is also the ever-present threat of legal action. Civil lawsuits claiming *negligent hiring* or *negligent retention* are a constant threat. *Negligent hiring* is the liability an employer incurs when it fails to conduct a reasonable investigation of an applicant's background, and then assigns a potentially dangerous person to a position in which he or she can inflict harm. **Negligent retention** is the liability an employer may incur when a company keeps persons on the payroll whose records indicate a strong potential for wrongdoing and fails to take steps to defuse a possibly violent situation. If an employer ignores warning signs leading up to a violent incident, it could be held legally liable. As previously mentioned, under OSHA's *general duty clause,* employers are required to furnish, to each employee, a place of employment that is free from recognizable hazards that are causing, or likely to cause, death or serious harm to the employee.

negligent retention
Liability an employer may incur when a company keeps persons on the payroll whose records indicate a strong potential for wrongdoing and fails to take steps to defuse a possibly violent situation.

Individual and Organizational Characteristics to Monitor

Some firms that have experience with workplace violence are trying an alternative approach. Instead of trying to screen out violent people, they are attempting to detect employees who commit minor aggressive acts and exhibit certain behaviors. These individuals often go on to engage in more serious behaviors. Once identified, these people are required to meet with trained staff members for counseling as long as needed. This approach may require more commitment on the part of the firm, but the alternative cost of violence may make this expenditure reasonable in the long run.

Although there are no sure signs an employee will commit an act of violence, certain behaviors can signal a problem, such as erratic behavior, increased irritability or hostility, reduced quality of work, poor organizational and time management skills, absenteeism, and a look of physical exhaustion. There are usually signs preceding workplace violence. Workers who shoot and kill their coworkers are likely to be employees who recently experienced a negative change in employment status, including those who have been fired, whose contracts have not been renewed, or who have been suspended because of a dispute with management. In one instance, a Domino's Pizza employee was discharged and later arrested after setting fires at two stores, causing more than $1 million in damages. The worker entered the buildings using keys he had not been required to turn in.[33] All terminations should require employees to return all company property issued such as keys, access cards and ID badges, and uniforms. Workers who are fired for a violent conflict should be escorted off company property. If possible, a heightened security alert should be made at the perimeter for several hours afterwards in the event the employee returns to "get even."

Preventive Actions

The best protection employers can offer is to establish a zero tolerance policy for workplace violence by and against employees.[34] However, there is no way an employer can completely avoid risk when it comes to violence. Incidences of some unbalanced person coming in and shooting people happen randomly, and organizations can do little to anticipate or prevent them. However, there are things that can be done to reduce the risk. There are basically two parts to violence prevention. First, there must be a process in place to help with early detection of worker anger. Second, supervisors and HR staff need to be trained in how to skillfully handle difficult employment issues.

A firm can take certain actions to minimize violent acts and to avoid lawsuits. It should have policies that ban weapons on company property, including parking lots, and under suspicious circumstances, require employees to submit to searches for weapons or examinations to determine their mental fitness for work. A firm should also have a policy stating that it will not tolerate any incidents of violence or even threats of violence; and it should encourage employees to report all suspicious or violent activity to management. In addition, many firms are equipping receptionists and those responsible for checking workers into the facility with panic buttons to enable them to alert security officers instantly.

Can the selection process predict applicants who will be prone to violence? The answer is "No." On the other hand, the profiles of individuals *not* prone to violence tend to have certain things in common. The most important characteristic and one with the highest correlation is that an applicant has no history of substance abuse. Other positive factors include being outwardly focused and having outside interests and friendships rather than being mainly self-involved. Finally, applicants with a good work history often are a strong predictor of a person not inclined to violence.

To confirm these characteristics, the firm must conduct a thorough background investigation prior to hiring. Gordon Basichis, cofounder of Corra Group, an international corporate security firm, said, "At first glance, a person's background check for misdemeanors may not look so bad, but it can get worse because sexual and violent crimes, especially domestic ones, can get plea-bargained down or dropped by family members."[35]

Domestic Violence

Spillover from domestic violence is a threat to employees and their coworkers because one of the easiest places to the find the victim is at his or her workplace.[36] One study suggested that one in 10 employees is currently being abused, which often carries itself over to the workplace.[37] Another study examined 500 assaults that occurred in the workplace as a result of domestic violence and just over half of the incidents ended in at least one homicide.[38] For example, Robert Reza slipped into the Emcore manufacturing plant in Albuquerque, New Mexico, and shot six employees—killing two—before taking his own life because he was angry with his girlfriend, a plant employee.[39] Domestic violence can have an impact on a firm's bottom line, costing about $5.8 billion each year in absenteeism, lower productivity, and turnover.[40] Therefore, business organizations have a huge stake in the problem of domestic violence.

Judith A. Lampley, general counsel of the Equal Employment Advisory Council, said, "The biggest mistake an employer can make is to ignore the issue."[41] The *general duty clause* of the Occupational Safety and Health Act requires a firm to furnish a workplace free from recognized hazards that are causing or are likely to cause death or serious physical harm. This includes protecting not only an intended victim of domestic violence, but also coworkers, who can become victims when angry partners bring weapons to a workplace. An employer could potentiality face claims by the victim, coworkers, third parties, and even the person who caused the domestic violence.

Laws Related to Domestic Violence

Laws passed since the early 1980s recognize the seriousness of domestic violence. In 1984, the Family Violence Prevention and Services Act was passed to help prevent domestic violence and provide shelter and related assistance for victims. The Violence Against Women Act was passed in 1994, creating new federal criminal laws and establishing additional grant programs within the Department of Health and Human Services and the Department of Justice (DOJ). The Violence Against Women and DOJ Reauthorization Act of 2005 required a study to be prepared to determine the prevalence of domestic violence, dating violence, sexual assault, and stalking among men, women, youth, and children. At least 29 states plus the District of Columbia have laws that allow people who leave jobs because of domestic violence to become eligible for unemployment benefits. Also, some states such as Florida, California, Colorado, Hawaii, Illinois, Kansas, and Maine give domestic violence victims the right to take time off. Florida law permits employees to take up to three days leave from work in any 12-month period for a variety of activities connected with domestic violence issues.

OBJECTIVE 11.5

Define *stress*, explain the consequences of stress including identifying stressful jobs, and explain burnout.

stress

Body's nonspecific reaction to any demand made on it.

Nature of Stress

Stress is the body's nonspecific reaction to any demand made on it. It affects people in different ways and therefore is highly individualized. Certain events may be quite stressful to one person but not to another. Moreover, the effect of stress is not always negative. For example, mild stress

Workplace Bullying

The definition of workplace violence has been expanded to include bullying because it has become more common, is costly, and is a possible predictor of physical violence. **Workplace bullying** includes acts of continual hostile conduct that deliberately hurt another person emotionally, verbally, or physically. It is often seen as a means of gaining power over another person through repeated aggressive behavior. Bullying may cause severe psychological pain for victims and for coworkers who witness the attacks.[42] According to a study by the National Institute for Occupational Safety and Health, bullying tends to occur when there is a lack of trust of management, a poor organizational climate, higher absenteeism and turnover rates, reduced productivity, and higher litigation costs.[43] In recent years, employers have noted increased workplace rudeness, which may lead to increased bullying.[44] According to one study, 35 percent of employees report being bullied at work. Currently, 11 states have proposed legislation regarding bullying in the workplace.[45]

There are basically two types of bullying—physical and psychological. Physical bullying involves intimidation and/or threatening actions.[46] Screaming, pushing, shoving, or invading a person's personal space provide examples of physical bullying. Psychological bullying involves activities such as jokingly ridiculing a person in a harmful manner, or even staring at somebody in a hostile way. Most companies include bullying behaviors within their workplace violence policy. Usually employees will accept a firm's expectations if they are clearly stated.

Experts use the term *status-blind harassment* to separate workplace bullying from workers protected under federal and state statutes. Adeola Adele, EPLI product leader for Marsh's FINPRO group, says, "Workplace violence starts with bullying." She tells of a case where an individual shot his coworkers. The worker had been bullied at work, and no one would listen.[47]

Some researchers make the case that a definition of bullying should include social hostility, which includes gossiping or social rejection. According to one survey, this is the most common type of bullying committed by women, who are responsible for more than 40 percent of workplace bullying.[48]

It is quite important for a company to develop a culture that does not accept bullying. Firms should strive to make civility part of the culture.[49] Workplace bullying does not occur in a culture where leaders send the message that each employee is valued, respected, and appreciated. Creating a culture of civility may require careful planning and may require a change in thinking and behaviors for corporate leaders.

---

workplace bullying
Acts of continual hostile conduct that deliberately hurt another person emotionally, verbally, or physically.

actually improves productivity, and it can be helpful in developing creative ideas. For many students, a small bit of stress prior to an exam actually improves performance. However, excessive stress may have the opposite effect.

Many believe their stress has increased over the past five years. Several factors account for this rise, including increased workloads, terrorism, corporate scandals, and economic conditions. The recent recession increased stress levels even among employees who still had jobs.[50] Although much of the world has reduced the number of hours worked each year per person over the past decade, Americans have done just the opposite. Each year, more than 275,000,000 working days are lost in the United States because of absenteeism resulting from stress.[51] If people work longer hours, they often do not have time to refresh, resulting in a deterioration of their personal lives.

Potential Consequences of Stress

Although everyone lives under a certain amount of stress, if it is severe enough and persists long enough, it can be harmful. In fact, stress can be as disruptive to an individual as any accident. It can result in poor attendance, excessive use of alcohol or other drugs, poor job performance, or even overall poor health. There is increasing evidence indicating that severe, prolonged stress is related to the six leading causes of death including heart disease, cancer, lung ailments, accidents, cirrhosis of the liver, and suicide.[52] This is in addition to the everyday headaches, back spasms, overeating, and other annoying ailments the body has developed in response to stress. Stress tops the list of changeable health risks that contribute to health care costs, ahead of other top risks such as current and past tobacco use, obesity, lack of exercise, high blood-glucose levels, depression, and high blood pressure.

Stressful Jobs

Many workers could identify with Jet Blue flight attendant Steven Slater when he imploded on the job and exited down the plane's emergency slide.[53] After a rude passenger's bag hit his

TABLE 11-2

Stressful Jobs

The 12 Jobs with the Most Stress

1. Laborer	**7.** Manager/administrator
2. Secretary	**8.** Waitress/waiter
3. Inspector	**9.** Machine operator
4. Clinical lab technician	**10.** Farm owner
5. Office manager	**11.** Miner
6. Supervisor	**12.** Painter

Other High-Stress Jobs (in Alphabetical Order)

Bank teller	Nurse's aide
Clergy member	Plumber
Computer programmer	Police officer
Dental assistant	Practical nurse
Electrician	Public relations worker
Firefighter	Railroad switchperson
Guard	Registered nurse
Hairdresser	Sales manager
Health aide	Sales representative
Health technician	Social worker
Machinist	Structural-mental worker
Meat cutter	Teacher's aide
Mechanic	Telephone operator
Musician	Warehouse worker

Source: From a ranking of 130 occupations by the federal government's National Institute for Occupational Safety and Health.

head, he used the plane's intercom to curse the customer, thanked the other passengers, grabbed two beers, activated the emergency chute, left the plane, and went home. There are probably many workers who would like to take similar actions in their workplaces. John Challenger, chief executive officer of Challenger, Gray & Christmas, a Chicago-based outplacement firm, said, "Slater tapped into a vein of anger that a lot of people have toward their employers. They are mad about all the layoffs they've gone through at work. They are mad about having their benefits cut."[54] Stress and workload strains are very real challenges now. Estimates are that one in three people in the United States is living with extreme stress, with a large percentage of all doctor visits being related to stress.

The National Institute for Occupational Safety and Health has studied stress as it relates to work and found that some jobs are generally perceived as being more stressful than other jobs. The 12 most stressful jobs are listed in Table 11-2. The common factor among these jobs is lack of employee control over work.[55] Workers in such jobs may feel that they are trapped, treated more like machines than people. Workers who have more control over their jobs, such as college professors and master craftpersons, hold some of the less stressful jobs.

The fact that certain jobs are identified as more stressful than others has important managerial implications. Managers are responsible for recognizing significantly deviant behavior and referring employees to health professionals for diagnosis and treatment. Telling signs of stress may include a reduction in the quantity and quality of work, frequent short periods of absence, increased alcohol consumption, poor time keeping, or becoming tearful or withdrawn. Under excessive stress, a person's dominant trait may become even more obvious. For example, if the individual is a private person, he or she withdraws from colleagues; if the person is upbeat, he or she becomes hyperactive. Ideally, stress should be dealt with before this occurs. To do so, managers must be aware of potential sources of stress. These sources exist both within and outside the organization. Regardless of its origin, stress possesses devastating potential.

Burnout

Burnout, although rarely fatal, is an incapacitating condition in which individuals lose a sense of the basic purpose and fulfillment of their work. It is a special form of stress where individuals become exhausted either physically or mentally or both. Seemingly the body or the mind can no longer handle the overwhelmingly high demands placed on it. Burnout differs from stress in that it causes people who have previously been highly committed to their work to become disillusioned and lose interest and motivation. Individuals who experience burnout often experience emotional exhaustion and lose interest in work.[56] Burnout is often associated with a midlife or midcareer crisis, but it can happen at different times to different people. When this occurs, they may lose their motivation to perform. Burnout is the most common factor leading to the decision to *check out* temporarily.

When burnout occurs, individuals seem to lose their enthusiasm for their job. Burnout is frequently associated with people whose jobs require them to work closely with others under stressful and tension-filled conditions. However, any employee may experience burnout, and no one is exempt. The dangerous part of burnout is that it is contagious. A highly cynical and pessimistic burnout victim can quickly transform an entire group into burnouts. Virtual teams that exist over the long term (more than a year) often run a strong risk of declining performance due to team burnout.

Burnout's price tag is high: it results in reduced productivity, higher turnover, and generally lousy performance. According to the American Institute of Stress, employee burnout costs the U.S. economy about $300 million annually. People often become physically and psychologically weakened from trying to deal with it. Although some employees try to hide their problems, shifts in their behavior may indicate dissatisfaction. They may start procrastinating or go to the opposite extreme of taking on too many assignments. They may lose things and become increasingly disorganized. Good-natured individuals may turn irritable. They may become cynical, disagreeable, pompous, or even paranoid. Their motivation toward a project may not be the same as it used to be, and they may dread doing work that they used to enjoy. It is very important that the problem be dealt with quickly. Some means of dealing with burnout include keeping expectations realistic, reducing workload, finding means to relax at work, and developing and maintaining interests outside work.

Wellness Programs

Wellness programs are becoming more widespread as more employers become conscious of the impact employee health has on performance. Employers that start wellness programs not only help lower health-related costs, but also find that employees are more engaged and productive at work. A recent analysis of data from the Johnson and Johnson Family of Companies revealed that its work-site wellness program created a return on investment of $1.88 to $3.92 in decreased health care costs for every dollar spent on the program.[57] A survey by the American Institute for Preventive Medicine found a $3 cost savings for every $1 invested in corporate wellness efforts.[58] Further program growth is being prompted by the shift toward wellness and prevention in the design of employer-sponsored health care benefits and by federal health care reform legislation. Barry Hall, global wellness research leader at Buck Consultants LLC's Boston office, said, "Wellness is currently the biggest area of growth in benefits, and it's primarily fueled by employer demand."[59] The Patient Protection and Affordable Care Act provides employers with additional incentives to help workers stay healthy. The cap on premium discounts will increase from 20 percent to 30 percent in 2014. Employers can use these discounts to entice employees to participate and meet certain goals in company wellness programs. Under certain situations, employers can move the incentive up to 50 percent. Small businesses with fewer than 100 employees are now eligible for grants to implement new wellness programs.

The traditional view that health is dependent on medical care and is the absence of disease is changing. Today, it is clear that optimal well-being is often achieved through environmental safety, organizational changes, and healthier lifestyles. Laura Karkula, vice president of Wellness Products at OptumHealth, said, "The research shows that companies that deploy health and wellness programs and take the approach of building an overall culture of health have a stronger commitment to those values."[60] Health and wellness programs have also been shown to encourage employees to remain at their companies longer. Important factors in making these programs successful include active strong leadership, especially from the CEO.[61]

There is growing evidence that in addition to containing direct medical costs, effective health programs boost productivity, reduce absenteeism, lower turnover and recruiting costs, and improve morale. Infectious diseases, over which a person has little control, are not the problem they once were. From 1900 to 1970, the death rate from major infectious diseases dropped dramatically. However, the death rate from major chronic diseases, such as heart disease, cancer, and stroke, has significantly increased. Today, heart disease and stroke are the top two killers worldwide. Chronic obstructive pulmonary disease and lung cancer are also growing threats to life. Healthy lifestyle measures such as not smoking, eating healthy foods, and exercising more may help prevent these diseases.

Chronic lifestyle diseases are much more prevalent today than ever before. The good news is that people have a great deal of control over many of them. These are diseases related to smoking, excessive stress, lack of exercise, obesity, and alcohol and drug abuse. Increased recognition of this has prompted employers to become actively involved with their employees' health and to establish wellness programs. Focusing on health care is inherently reactive; focusing on health is proactive and, potentially, a game changer.

There has been a shift toward an approach to improving health that includes involving workers in identifying problems and developing solutions. Wellness programs often expand their focus to include other health issues, such as diet, stress, substance abuse, employee assistance programs, and smoking cessation.

In developing a wellness program, firms should first conduct a health-risk assessment by surveying their employees to determine which workers could benefit from lifestyle change. Then, a wellness program to address appropriate employee health needs can be implemented. Sometimes getting everyone on board to take a health-risk assessment is difficult and incentives such as gift cards and use of big-screen televisions and travel opportunities are used as grand prizes. At Integris Health, employees who completed a health-risk assessment received preferred pricing on benefits, but those who completed the assessment and brought it to a physician during a preventive care visit collected extra incentive.[62] Penalties such as increased insurance premiums are also being used to increase employee participation in wellness programs.[63] Beth Umland, director of research for health and benefits at Mercer LLC in New York City, said, "Premium discounts are becoming a real mainstay incentive and the amount of premium discounts is growing."[64]

Once companies have identified high-risk employees and the health issues they face, they can determine what programs are needed and offer incentives for participation in activities such as smoking cessation classes or joining Weight Watchers. At Lincoln Plating, everyone gets quarterly health-risk appraisals that include blood-pressure screening and body weight, body fat, and flexibility measurements. Each employee reviews the quarterly results with the wellness manager or occupational nurse and sets individual wellness objectives.

The growth in wellness programs has created new leaders with titles such as wellness manager, health and wellness manager, well-being director, wellness coordinator, wellness specialist, and wellness champion. Most of these employees report to a company's top HR or employee benefits executive who is responsible for defining the wellness mission and working to improve health and well-being.[65]

Social Networking and Wellness

Employers increasingly are adopting social networking to strengthen the success of their wellness programs. In his research, Dr. Nicholas Christakis of the Harvard Medical School found that good health is pervasive. When someone loses weight or quits smoking, their friends and family are more likely to also do so. He said, "The implication of this research is that interventions can leverage this phenomenon to purposefully spread healthy behaviors."[66] Social networking brings employees together and works to increase peer support. Social networking also generates participation rates higher than any traditional form of wellness initiative. Using social network tools such as Twitter and Facebook, employees can tell others how well they are doing with regard to quitting smoking or losing weight. Jamie Curtis, vice president of business development with Spectrum Health Systems, said, "If employees are given access to a social platform as part of a Wellness program, they feel more empowered to participate."[67] Once workers quit smoking or lose weight they are certain to tell others, creating a sort of competition. Can you imagine the impact before and after pictures of a person who has lost weight would have on other friends? Such might be the same case with a Tweet that says, "I lost another 10 pounds."

Limeade Inc. of Washington offers social media–based wellness programs that permit employees to engage in healthy activities. The system permits workers to track their progress and share tips with colleagues. Limeade CEO Henry Albrecht said, "Our programs are social because the science of behavioral change shows that people make changes when they have support of friends and peers."[68]

OBJECTIVE **11.7**

Describe the importance of physical fitness programs.

Physical Fitness Programs

The most commonly offered in-house corporate wellness programs involve efforts to promote exercise and fitness. To understand the interest in such programs, consider the results of physical inactiv-
ity: obesity, hypertension, heart disease, diabetes, anxiety, depression, and certain types of cancer.

From management's viewpoint, physical fitness programs make a lot of sense. Loss of productivity resulting from coronary disease alone costs U.S. businesses billions of dollars annually.
Company-sponsored fitness programs often reduce absenteeism, accidents, and sick pay. There
is increasing evidence that if employees stick to company fitness programs, they will experience
better health, and the firm will have lower health costs.

Kenneth Cooper, who coined the term *aerobics* (which literally means *with oxygen*), has
advice for those with or without access to fitness centers. To begin, he feels that moderate exercise is important. He recommends 30 minutes of exercise four to five days a week. People do
not need to train for a marathon to be healthy; they just need to stop being couch potatoes.[69]
His studies also show that cardiovascular training is not enough. He promoted eating a heart-
healthy diet and using vitamin supplements such as antioxidants. He felt that eliminating tobacco
products and habit-forming drugs, controlling alcohol, keeping stress levels down, and getting
periodic health exams helps everyone's fitness.[70]

OBJECTIVE **11.8**

Explain substance abuse, describe
substance-abuse-free workplaces,
and describe how to implement a
drug-testing program.

HR Web Wisdom

*National Council on
Alcoholism & Drug
Dependence*

http://www.ncadd.org/

Fights the stigma and the disease
of alcoholism and drug addictions.

substance abuse
Use of illegal substances or the
misuse of controlled substances such
as alcohol and drugs.

Substance Abuse

Failure to test for drugs can sometimes have a disastrous effect on companies large and small.
For instance, Cake for You is a small specialty bakery. Its service includes making and delivering wedding cakes to receptions. In hiring a delivery driver, Cake for You owners always carefully determined that job candidates had a valid driver's license. The owners were quite pleased
with their new employee, Mike. He was prompt, neatly attired, and seemed to have a pleasant
demeanor. Unfortunately, while making a delivery one morning, Mike was involved in, and in
fact caused, a four-vehicle accident that resulted in one fatality. The investigation revealed that
Mike was high on marijuana. Had the owners of the firm included drug testing as part of their
screening process, they might not be facing a huge lawsuit. In certain industries, such as transportation, for example, drug use on the job is especially hazardous and potentially devastating
to the firm. Think of the damage that could be caused by a 40-ton truck careening out of control.
Under ideal conditions, a fully loaded truck in daylight on a dry road cannot stop in less than 300
feet, or the length of a football field.

Substance abuse involves the use of illegal substances or the misuse of controlled substances such as alcohol and drugs. About 14 million people who are employed either full time or
part time abuse alcohol and/or drugs.[71] These workers use more sick days and are late more often.
They remain in jobs for shorter lengths of time, and their health care costs are twice that of other
employees.[72] According to the Substance Abuse and Mental Health Services Administration,
drug-using employees are 3.6 times as likely to be involved in workplace accidents and five
times as likely to file workers' compensation claims.[73] Further, research indicates that between
10 and 20 percent of the nation's workers who die on the job test positive for alcohol or drugs.[74]
Even so, few issues generate more controversy today than substance-abuse testing. Yet, alcohol
and drug abuse are definitely workplace issues.

Alcohol Abuse

alcoholism
Medical disease characterized
by uncontrolled and compulsive
drinking that interferes with normal
living patterns.

Although our society often attaches a stigma to alcoholism, in 1956, the American Medical
Association described it as a treatable disease. **Alcoholism** is a medical disease characterized by
uncontrolled and compulsive drinking that interferes with normal living patterns. The National
Council on Alcoholism & Drug Dependence reports that 40 percent of workplace fatalities and
47 percent of workplace injuries are related to alcohol consumption. Stress plays an important
role in a person becoming an alcoholic. It is a significant problem that affects people at every
level of society, and it can both result from and cause excessive stress. When under stress, people
with a particular genetic arrangement are inclined to act impulsively, increasing their danger of
problem drinking.[75] As a person starts to drink excessively, the drinking itself produces greater
stress. A vicious cycle is created as this increased stress is dealt with by more drinking. Early
signs of alcohol abuse are especially difficult to identify. Often the symptoms are nothing more

than an increasing number of days absent from work. Alcohol abusers are also much more likely to be using other substances.[76]

Drug Abuse

Drug users are increasingly gravitating to the workplace, which is also an ideal place to sell drugs. Drug use in the workplace costs employers approximately $81 billion each year in lost productivity, according to the U.S. Department of Labor. The National Institute of Drug Abuse cites that employees at risk for illegal on-the-job substance use have been shown to have three times more sick days, three times the tardiness rate, three times more accidents, and are five times more likely to file workers' compensation claims than individuals not engaging in illegal substance use.[77] Since most of *Fortune* 500 companies conduct pre-employment drug screening, a large number of employed drug users work for smaller businesses, many of which do not use drug testing. In fact, 71 percent of companies with 2,500 or more employees require pre-employment drug tests, whereas less than 40 percent of businesses with fewer than 100 employees even had a pre-employment drug-testing policy.[78]

It has also been estimated that over 120 million prescriptions for controlled substance painkillers are dispensed annually. These substances include powerful painkillers that also carry an extremely high risk of addiction.[79] Prescription drugs can be as addictive, impairing, and destructive as common street drugs.

Substance-Abuse-Free Workplace

The Drug-Free Workplace Act of 1988 requires some federal contractors and all federal grantees to agree that they will provide drug-free workplaces as a condition of receiving a contract or grant from a federal agency (details of the act may be seen in Table 11-3). The U.S. Department of Transportation (DOT) requires drug and alcohol testing for drivers of commercial vehicles, as well as employees that perform "safety-sensitive duties." Unless public safety and security are at risk, employers decide if drug testing is performed.

Firms have tackled the drug-abuse problem head-on by establishing a drug-free workplace program. But, some cautions should be taken. Some philosophies and practices that can undermine the effectiveness of drug-free workplace programs may be seen in Table 11-4.

The steps for establishing a substance-abuse-free workplace may be seen in Figure 11-2. Note that the first step is to establish a drug- and alcohol-free policy. The U.S. Department of Labor offers a Drug-Free Workplace Advisor that provides guidance on how to develop a drug- and alcohol-free workplace. At Texas Instruments, the policy is simple and straightforward: "There will be no use of any illegal drug."

TABLE 11-3

Drug-Free Workplace Act of 1988

The Drug-Free Workplace Act of 1988 requires some Federal Contractors and all Federal grantees to agree that they will provide drug-free workplaces as a condition of receiving a contract or grant from a Federal agency.

Organizations, with contracts from any U.S. Federal agency, must comply with the provisions of the Act if the contract is in the amount of $100,000 or more. Organizations must do the following:

(A) publish a statement notifying employees that the unlawful manufacture, distribution, dispensation, possession, or use of a controlled substance is prohibited in the person's workplace. The statement should also notify employees of any punitive actions that will be taken.

(B) establish a drug-free awareness program to inform employees about
   (i)   the dangers of drug abuse in the workplace;
   (ii) the policy of maintaining a drug-free workplace;
   (iii) any available drug counseling, rehabilitation, and employee assistance programs; and
   (iv) the penalties that many be imposed upon employees for drug abuse violations.

(C) make it a requirement that each employee be given a copy of the workplace substance abuse policy.

If a contractor is found not to have a drug-free workplace, each contract awarded by any federal agency shall be subject to suspension of payments under the contract or termination of the contract, or both. The contractor may also be ineligible for award of any contract by any federal agency, and for participation in any future procurement by any federal agency, for a period not to exceed 5 years.

TABLE 11-4

Philosophies and Practices That Can Undermine the Effectiveness of Drug-free Workplace Programs

- Focusing only on illicit drug use and failing to include alcohol—the number one drug of abuse in our society
- Accepting drug use and alcohol abuse as part of modern life and a cost of doing business
- Overreliance on drug testing
- Focusing on termination of users rather than rehabilitation
- Reluctance of supervisors to confront employees on the basis of poor performance
- Reinforcing an individual's denial regarding the impact of his/her alcohol and drug use
- Restricting benefits and/or access to treatment of alcoholism and addiction
- Allowing insurers to restrict access to treatment programs

Source: http://www.dol.gov/elaws/asp/drugfree/drugs/screen5.asp?selection_list=, January 3, 2006.

The second step is to provide education and training for supervisors and workers. At a minimum, supervisor training should include a review of the drug-free workplace policy, the supervisor's specific responsibilities in implementing the policy, and ways to recognize and deal with employees who have job performance problems that could be related to alcohol and drug use. Managers must learn to recognize impaired or intoxicated employees and those who may be addicted. Possible signs that suggest an employee may be a substance abuser includes excessive absenteeism, radical mood swings, and a decline in personal appearance. However, the existence of these indicators alone is not adequate to determine the presence or absence of any condition. The supervisor should never try to diagnose, make accusations, or treat such problems. The indicators provide the supervisor a basis for making a referral to a person who can help the employee, such as an Employee Assistance Program.

Employees should also be educated as to the purpose and ramifications of the drug- and alcohol-free environment. The purpose of this training is to familiarize employees with the drug-free workplace program and provide general education awareness about the dangers of alcohol and drug abuse. Employees should be informed about the requirements of the organization's drug-free workplace policy, the prevalence of alcohol and drug abuse and their impact on the workplace, how to recognize the connection between poor performance and alcohol and/or drug abuse, the progression of the disease of alcohol and drug addiction, and what types of assistance may be available. The program should send a clear message that use of alcohol and drugs in the workplace is prohibited. Employees are encouraged to voluntarily seek help with alcohol and drug problems. It should be noted that individuals who are in recovery from a problem with alcohol or with legal or illegal drugs are protected from discrimination under the Americans with Disabilities Act.[80]

There are hundreds of substances that people abuse. These include marijuana, cocaine, amphetamines, heroin and other opiates, ecstasy, LSD, PCP, inhalants, alcohol, and steroids. The two most commonly abused drugs are marijuana and cocaine. Some signs of marijuana use include red eyes, dry mouth, slowed reaction time, increased hunger, paranoia, short-term memory loss, and a distorted sense of time. The most common signs of cocaine use are dilated pupils, increased energy, and excited speech. Some cocaine users may also experience frequent nose bleeds.[81]

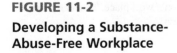

FIGURE 11-2

Developing a Substance-Abuse-Free Workplace

Implementing a Drug-Testing Program

The third step in establishing a substance-abuse-free workplace is to implement a drug-testing program. Proponents of drug-testing programs contend that they are necessary to ensure workplace safety, security, and productivity. A drug-free workplace program should balance the rights of employees and the rights of employers, balance the need to know and rights to privacy, balance detection and rehabilitation, and balance the respect for employees and the safety of all. The difficulty is not in formulating the policy, but rather in implementing it. Also, remember that the Americans with Disabilities Act protects an employee in a substance-abuse rehabilitation program.

Urine, blood, oral fluids, or hair samples are possible drug-testing methods, with most employers relying on urine testing. However, the majority regards blood tests as the forensic benchmark against which to compare others. The problem with this approach is that it is invasive and requires trained personnel for administration and analysis. The use of hair samples is unique in that drug traces will remain in the hair and will not likely diminish over time. Human hair samples are easy to collect, store, and transport, and they are difficult to change. Although urine and blood testing can detect only current drug use, advocates of hair sample analysis claim it can detect drug use from 3 days to 90 days after drug consumption. This would prohibit an applicant from compromising the test by short-term abstinence. A new method is able to detect drugs and other substances from the sweat in fingerprints, permitting mobile drug testing with immediate results.[82]

When the oral fluid method is used, the collection pad is saturated and the individual places the swab in a collection vial, snaps off the handle, seals the container, and hands it over for analysis. Oral fluid testing is especially well-suited to cases of reasonable suspicion and post-accident testing. Oral fluid is a great deterrent because it can be done immediately in the workplace and it does not give an individual an opportunity to adulterate or substitute a urine specimen.[83] From a prospective employee's viewpoint, oral fluid and hair testing may be less embarrassing than a urine test. For example, it is humiliating for a candidate to hear, "We're really happy to have you on board. But, will you take this cup and fill it?"

The final step in obtaining a substance-abuse-free workplace is the creation of an employee assistance program.

OBJECTIVE 11.9

Describe employee assistance programs and health care in the global environment.

employee assistance program (EAP)

Comprehensive approach that many organizations have taken to deal with burnout, alcohol and drug abuse, and other emotional disturbances.

Employee Assistance Programs

The Drug-Free Workplace Act also requires federal employees and employees of firms under government contract to have access to employee assistance program services. An **employee assistance program (EAP)** is a comprehensive approach that many organizations have taken to deal with numerous problem areas such as burnout, alcohol and drug abuse, and other emotional disturbances.

As you would imagine, EAPs grew rapidly in number following that act. Returns on investment in EAPs will vary but one estimate is that a mature, well-run program will return a minimum of three dollars for every dollar spent on it. Advantages claimed for EAPs include lower absenteeism, decreases in workers' compensation claims, and fewer accidents.

Whether managed in-house or outsourced, EAPs have traditionally focused first on mental health, including substance-abuse counseling. Today, companies are aware that the advantages of an EAP extend well beyond assistance for alcohol or drug-related problems. Many have expanded to include financial and legal advice, referrals for day care and elder care, and a host of other services, including assistance with marital or family difficulties, job performance problems, stress, and grief. The recent recession caused some EAPs to move beyond mental health to serve recession-induced employee issues such as financial and legal challenges. EAPs are also being used to provide assistance with managing critical events in the workplace such as mass shooting in domestic violence cases. In an EAP, most or all of the costs (up to a predetermined amount) are borne by the employer. The EAP concept includes a response to personal psychological problems that interfere with both an employee's well-being and overall productivity. The purpose of employee assistance programs is to provide emotionally troubled employees with the same consideration and assistance given employees with physical illnesses. Just having an EAP sends a message that the employer cares, and this can provide considerable encouragement for employees.

A primary concern with an EAP is getting employees to use the program. Some employees perceive that there is a stigma attached to *needing help*. Supervisors must receive training designed to provide specialized interpersonal skills for recognizing troubled employees and encouraging them to use the firm's employee assistance program. Addicted employees are often experts at denial and deception, and they can fool even experienced counselors.

Health Care in the Global Environment

U.S.-based global operations are often safer and healthier than host-country operations, but frequently not as safe as similar operations in the United States. Safety and health laws and regulations often vary greatly from country to country. Such laws can range from virtually nonexistent to as stringent as those in the United States. For example, Abu Dhabi has compulsory coverage for expatriates and requires a full refund for maternity costs and coverage for chronic conditions.[84] In Switzerland, the rules vary between districts. Some require the expatriate to buy medical insurance from an organization in that district. The Dutch require any person who resides in the Netherlands to hold a health insurance policy that meets certain requirements, including preexisting and chronic conditions.[85] Australia requires that all non-Australian citizens coming from countries without reciprocal health care agreements must provide a new proof of insurance. This affects all countries except for Finland, Ireland, Italy, Malta, the Netherlands, Belgium, New Zealand, Norway, Sweden, and the UK.[86]

Health care facilities across the globe vary greatly in their state of modernization. The vast majority of health care in developing world countries do not have acceptable systems for drinking water, sewage treatment, or reliable power.[87] If expats are assigned to these more remote or less-developed areas, companies should be aware that in many medical facilities needles are often reused, equipment is not properly used, and there is a lack of basic medical supplies.

Health care coverage in the United States, Australia, United Kingdom, and Western Europe is generally well established. But, a growing number of expats are being sent to emerging markets, including Central and Eastern Europe, the Far East, and Africa. Expats going to these countries expect to be supported with health care benefits such as private medical insurance, life insurance, and evacuation and repatriation coverage in the event of a medical emergency. Medical evacuation can be an essential benefit for overseas workers, particularly if they are in a location that may not offer the same level of medical treatment they would receive in their home country. For example, staff working in Southeast Asia may have to be transported to Singapore or Hong Kong for adequate treatment.[88] Firms that are sending people to work in places where standards of local health care and medical treatment are uncertain need to provide sufficient insurance coverage.

MyManagementLab

Go to **mymanagementlab.com** to complete the problems marked with this icon ⭐.

Summary

1. *Describe resilience training and explain the nature and role of safety and health and the function of the Occupational Safety and Health Administration.* *Resilience* is the ability to bounce back and adapt in a positive manner to difficult situations. The increasing demand for resilience training is based to a large extent on the difficult economic climate being experienced and the increased job pressure as employees are being asked to do more with less.

   Safety involves protecting employees from injuries due to work-related accidents. *Health* refers to the employees' freedom from physical or emotional illness.

   The role of the Occupational Safety and Health Administration is to ensure a safe and healthful workplace for every American worker.

2. *Explain the relationship between OSHA and whistle-blowers, describe the economic impact of safety, and explain the focus of safety programs.* Within the Department of Labor, OSHA enforces the whistleblower protection provisions of 21 statutes, covering not just workplace safety but also the environment, consumer products, the financial system, and other areas.

   Job-related deaths and injuries of all types extract a high toll not only in human misery, but also in economic loss. The significant financial costs are often passed along to the consumer in the form of higher prices. Thus, job-related deaths and injuries affect everyone, directly or indirectly. Safety risks can be significant for employers. In addition to workers' compensation costs, OSHA can levy major fines.

   Safety programs may be designed to accomplish their purposes in two primary ways. The first approach is to create a psychological environment and attitudes that promote safety. The second approach to safety program design is to develop and maintain a safe physical working environment.

3. *Describe the consequences of musculoskeletal disorders and explain the purpose of ergonomics. Musculoskeletal disorders (MSDs)* are conditions that affect the body's muscles, joints, tendons, ligaments, and nerves. Work-related MSDs, including tendonitis, carpal tunnel syndrome (CTS), and back pain, cost American businesses $61.2 billion annually just to cover the lost productivity costs associated with these ailments. A major musculoskeletal disorder is *carpal tunnel syndrome (CTS)* caused by pressure on the median nerve that occurs as a result of a narrowing of the passageway that houses the nerve.

   Ergonomics is the study of human interaction with tasks, equipment, tools, and the physical environment.

Through ergonomics, the goal is to fit the machine and work environment to the person, rather than require the person to make the adjustment.

4. *Explain the effects of workplace and domestic violence on businesses and describe workplace bullying.* OSHA defines *workplace violence* as physical assault, threatening behavior, verbal abuse, hostility, or harassment directed toward employees at work or on duty. Workplace violence affects more than two million workers each year.

Spillover from domestic violence is a threat to both women and their companies. Domestic violence has become an epidemic in this country.

Workplace bullying includes acts of continual hostile conduct that deliberately hurt another person emotionally, verbally, or physically. Companies have expanded the definition of workplace violence to include bullying because they recognize that it is common, costly, and a possible forerunner to acts of physical violence.

5. *Define* **stress***, explain the consequences of stress including identifying stressful jobs, and explain burnout.* *Stress* is the body's nonspecific reaction to any demand made on it. Stress may be coped with through numerous means.

Although everyone lives under a certain amount of stress, if it is severe enough and persists long enough, it can be harmful. In fact, stress can be as disruptive to an individual as any accident. It can result in poor attendance, excessive use of alcohol or other drugs, poor job performance, or even overall poor health.

The National Institute for Occupational Safety and Health has studied stress as it relates to work and found that some jobs are generally perceived as being more stressful than other jobs. The common factor among these jobs is lack of employee control over work.

Burnout, although rarely fatal, is an incapacitating condition in which individuals lose a sense of the basic purpose and fulfillment of their work.

6. *Describe the purposes of wellness programs and explain social networking and wellness.* Wellness programs are becoming more widespread as more employers become conscious of the impact employee health has on performance. Today, the prevailing opinion is that optimal health can generally be achieved through environmental safety, organizational changes, and changed lifestyles.

Employers increasingly are adopting social networking to strengthen the success of their wellness programs. If used effectively and thoughtfully, these strategies have the potential to create high participation rates, long-term engagement, sustainable behavior change, and significant health outcomes for employee populations.

7. *Describe the importance of physical fitness programs.* Many U.S. business firms have exercise programs designed to help keep their workers physically fit. These programs often reduce absenteeism, accidents, and sick pay.

8. *Explain substance abuse, describe substance-abuse-free workplaces, and describe how to implement a drug-testing program.* *Substance abuse* involves the use of illegal substances or the misuse of controlled substances such as alcohol and drugs. The Drug-Free Workplace Act of 1988 requires some federal contractors and all federal grantees to agree that they will provide drug-free workplaces as a condition of receiving a contract or grant from a federal agency.

The first step for establishing a substance-abuse-free workplace is to establish a drug- and alcohol-free policy. The second step is to provide education and training for supervisors and workers. The third step in establishing a substance-abuse-free workplace is to implement a drug-testing program. The final step in obtaining a substance-abuse-free workplace is the creation of an employee assistance program.

9. *Describe employee assistance programs and health care in the global environment.* An *employee assistance program* is a comprehensive approach that many organizations develop to deal with marital or family problems; job performance problems; stress, emotional, or mental health issues; financial troubles; alcohol and drug abuse; and grief.

U.S.-based global operations are often safer and healthier than host-country operations, but frequently not as safe as similar operations in the United States. Safety and health laws and regulations often vary greatly from country to country. Such laws can range from virtually nonexistent to as stringent as those in the United States.

Key Terms

resilience 276	carpal tunnel syndrome (CTS) 283	burnout 290
safety 278	ergonomics 285	substance abuse 292
health 278	workplace violence 285	alcoholism 292
general duty clause 278	negligent retention 286	employee assistance program (EAP) 295
job hazard analysis (JHA) 281	stress 287	
musculoskeletal disorders (MSDs) 283	workplace bullying 288	

Exercises

1. Calculate the OSHA injury frequency rate, using the following data:
   Total Working Hours: 1,500,000; three injured
2. How stressful do you consider the following jobs? Explain your answer.

a. college professor
b. stockbroker on New York Stock Exchange
c. student (yourself)
d. executive administrative assistant for a global corporation

Questions for Review

1. Define *resilience*. What is the purpose of resilience training?
2. Define *safety* and *health*.
3. What is the purpose of the Occupational Safety and Health Act?
⭐ 4. What relationship does OSHA have with small businesses?
5. What are the primary ways in which safety programs are designed? Discuss.
6. What is the purpose of job hazard analysis?
7. What is the purpose of the Superfund Amendments Reauthorization Act, Title III (SARA)?
8. Why are companies concerned with musculoskeletal disorders? What is carpal tunnel syndrome?
9. Define *ergonomics*. What is the purpose of ergonomics?
⭐10. What effect does workplace and domestic violence have on an organization?
11. What laws were passed because of domestic violence?
12. Define *workplace bullying*. What are the basic forms of workplace bullying?
13. Define *stress*. Why should a firm attempt to identify stressful jobs?
⭐14. Why are firms adopting social networking to strengthen the success of their wellness programs?
15. Why might physical fitness programs be established in organizations?
16. What is the purpose of substance-abuse-free workplaces in organizations?
17. What are the steps for establishing a substance-abuse-free workplace?
18. What is an employee assistance program?

INCIDENT 1   What a Change!

"Just leave me alone and let me do my job," said Manuel Gomez. Dumbfounded, Bill Brown, Manuel's supervisor, decided to count to 10 and did not respond to Manuel's comment. As he walked back to his office, Bill thought about how Manuel had changed over the past few months. He had been a hard worker and extremely cooperative when he started working for Bill two years earlier. The company had sent Manuel to two training schools and had received glowing reports about his performance in each of them.

Until about a year ago, Manuel had a perfect attendance record and was an ideal employee. At about that time, however, he began to have personal problems, which resulted in a divorce six months later. Manuel had several times requested a day off to take care of personal business. Bill attempted to help in every way he could without getting directly involved in Manuel's personal affairs. But Bill was aware of the strain Manuel must have experienced as his marriage broke up, and he and his wife engaged in the inevitable disputes over child custody, alimony payments, and property.

During the same time period, top management initiated a push for improving productivity. Bill found it necessary to put additional pressure on all his workers, including Manuel. He tried to be considerate, but he had to become much more performance-oriented, insisting on increased output from every worker. As time went on, Manuel began to show up late for work, and actually missed two days without calling Bill in advance. Bill attributed Manuel's behavior to extreme stress. Because Manuel had been such a good worker for so long, Bill excused the tardiness and absences, only gently suggesting that Manuel should try to do better.

Sitting at his desk, Bill thought about what might have caused Manuel's outburst a few minutes earlier. Bill had suggested to Manuel that he shut down the machine he was operating and clean up the surrounding area. This was a normal part of Manuel's job and something he had been careful to do in the past. Bill felt the disorder around Manuel's machine might account for the increasing number of defects in the parts he was making. "This is a tough one. I think I'll talk to the boss about it," thought Bill.

Questions

1. What do you think is likely to be Manuel's problem? Discuss.
2. Might a substance-free workplace be appropriate for Bill Brown's company? If so, what would be the steps in establishing such a workplace?
3. How might use of an employee assistance program help in this situation?

INCIDENT 2   A Commitment to Safety?

Wanda Zackery was extremely excited a year ago when she joined Landon Electronics as its first safety engineer. She had graduated from Florida State University with a degree in electrical engineering and had a strong desire to enter business. Wanda had selected her job at Landon Electronics over several other offers. She believed that it would provide her with a broad range of experiences that she could not receive in a strictly engineering job. Also, when the company president, Martha Lincoln, interviewed her, she promised her that the firm's resources would be at her disposal to correct any safety-related problems.

Her first few months at Landon were hectic but exciting. She immediately identified numerous safety problems. One of the most dangerous involved a failure to install safety guards on all exposed equipment. Wanda carefully prepared her proposal, including expected costs, to make needed minimum changes. She estimated that it would take approximately $50,000 to complete the necessary conversions. Wanda then presented the entire package to Ms. Lincoln. She explained the need for the changes to her, and Ms. Lincoln cordially received her presentation. She said that she would like to think it over and get back to her.

But that was six months ago! Every time Wanda attempted to get some action on her proposal, Ms. Lincoln was friendly but still wanted some more time to consider it. In the meantime, Wanda had become increasingly anxious. Recently, a worker had barely avoided a serious injury. Some workers had also become concerned. She heard through the grapevine that someone had telephoned the regional office of OSHA.

Her suspicions were confirmed the very next week when an OSHA inspector appeared at the plant. No previous visits had ever been made to the company. Although Ms. Lincoln was not overjoyed, she permitted the inspector access to the company. Later she might have wished that she had not been so cooperative. Before the inspector left, he wrote violations for each piece of equipment that did not have the necessary safety guards. The fines could total $70,000 if the problems were not corrected right away. The inspector cautioned that repeat violations could cost $700,000 and possible imprisonment.

As the inspector was leaving, Wanda received a phone call. "Wanda, this is Ms. Lincoln. Get up to my office right now. We need to get your project under way."

Questions

1. Discuss Ms. Lincoln's level of commitment to occupational safety.
2. Is there a necessary trade-off between Landon's need for low expenses and the workers' need for safe working conditions? Explain.
3. Safety programs may accomplish their purposes in two primary ways: one focusing on *unsafe employee actions* and the other on *unsafe working conditions*. Which areas of Wanda's proposal was she directing her efforts? Discuss.

MyManagementLab

Go to **mymanagementlab.com** for Auto-graded writing questions as well as the following Assisted-graded writing questions:

11-1. What are the purposes of wellness programs?

11-2. Why should a firm be concerned with employee burnout?

11-3. Mymanagementlab Only – comprehensive writing assignment for this chapter.

Notes

1. Rhett Morris, "Resilience—Reducing Professional Risk and Personal Crisis," *Keeping Good Companies* 63 (July 2011): 372–375.
2. Stephen Balzac, "Who Betrays One Master," *Journal of Corporate Recruiting Leadership* 6 (July 2011): 8–10.
3. Marti MacGibbon, "Resilience: Bend and Bounce—So You Won't Break," *Communication Briefings* 31 (January 2012): 3.
4. Kathleen Koster, "From Lead Balloon to Air Balloon," *Employee Benefit News* 26 (January 2012): 10–11.
5. "The Big Question: What Are Employers Doing About Stress in the Workplace?" *Employee Benefits* (November 2011): 17.
6. "Resilience Training Revives Productivity," *Communication Briefings* 31 (November 2011): 2.
7. William Atkinson, "Turning Stress into Strength," *HR Magazine* 56 (January 2011): 49–52.
8. Susan Ladika, "A Resilient Bunch," *Workforce Management* 90 (November 2011): 26.
9. Martin E. P. Seligman, "Building Resilience," *Harvard Business Review* 89 (April 2011): 100–106.
10. Jan Ferri-Reed, "Release Stress and Build Resilience," *Chief Learning Officer* 10 (July 2011): 42–47.
11. Dan Markiewicz, "A Growing Obligation to Prevent Harm," *Industrial Safety & Hygiene News* 45 (July 2011): 22.
12. Samuel Greengard, "Playing it Safe: The Roaring '20s & Now," *Workforce Management* 91 (January 2012): 1.
13. http://stats.bls.gov/iif/oshwc/cfoi/cfoi_revised09.pdf July 10, 2011.
14. Michael T. Heenan, "What Is OSHA Citing?" *Pit & Quarry* 104 (January 2012): 38–43.
15. "Recycling Company Cited for Baling Machine Death," *Industrial Safety & Hygiene News* 46 (January 2012): 16.
16. "OSHA to Improve Whistleblower Protections," *Material Handling & Logistics* 66 (August 2011): 8.
17. "OSHA Says BofA Broke Whistleblower Law," *Pratt's Bank Law & Regulatory Report* 17 (2011): 14–15.
18. http://www.whistleblowers.gov/index.html
19. http://www.osha.gov/dcsp/compliance_assistance/quickstarts/index.html
20. http://www.osha.gov/dsg/topics/safetyhealth/ December 23, 2011.
21. Megan S. Raines, "Engaging Employees," *Professional Safety* 56 (April 2011): 36–43.
22. http://www.osha.gov/Publications/osha3071.pdf
23. Dave Zielinski, "What's Safe? Employers Underreport Injuries and Illnesses," *HR Magazine* 57 (February 2012): 12.
24. Swati Deshkar, "Ergonomics Investment," *Professional Safety* 55 (October 2010): 48–50.
25. "Assessing Your Company's Manual Material Handling," *Safety Compliance Letter* (July 1, 2011): 7–11.
26. "OSH Act Clause Used Sparingly to Cite Employers for Violations," *HR Focus* 88 (February 2011): 14–15.
27. Beth Mirza, "Identify, Treat and Prevent Employees' Aches and Pains," *HR Magazine* 56 (September 2011): 22.
28. Cynthia Roth, "The Importance of Ergonomics for the Safety Professional," *EHS Today* 4 (February 2011): 45–47.
29. Dathan Lane, "Ergonomics Protection," *Transmission & Distribution World* 63 (April 2011): 64F–64I.
30. Lawrence Cummer, "Office? I Don't Need an Office," *Backbone* (April 2011): 20–21.
31. Arthur G. Sapper, "Sticks and Stones," *HR Magazine* 56 (September 2011): 115–118.
32. Cassandra Dillenberger, "Avoiding Workplace Violence Incidents," *Contractor's Business Management Report* 2010 (February 2010): 1/13.

33. "Making Difficult Terminations as Safe as Possible," *Security Director's Report* 11 (March 2011): 1–15.

34. Kathryn Tyler, "Safer Separations," *HR Magazine* 56 (December 2011): 43.

35. Juliette Fairley, "Strategies that Avoid Workplace Violence, a Rising Threat," *Business Insurance* 44 (November 11, 2010): 31.

36. "Preventing Serious Domestic Violence Spillover Events," *Security Director's Report* 10 (January 2010): 1–13.

37. Dori Meinert, "Out of the Shadows," *HR Magazine* 56 (October 2011): 50–55.

38. "What to Do When Domestic Violence Comes to Work," *HR Focus* 87 (January 2010): 10–11.

39. Kathryn Hawkins, "Domestic Violence & the Workplace," *OfficePro* 70 (October 2010): 16–19.

40. Lydell C. Bridgeford, "Piercing the Veil of Silence: Domestic Violence and the Workplace," *Employee Benefit News* 20 (August 2006): 21.

41. "Employer Policies on Domestic Violence Paramount, Experts Assert," *HR Focus* 88 (February 2011): 3–5.

42. Jacqueline Munson and Christopher Thompson, "Addressing Bullying at Work," *Profiles in Diversity Journal* 14 (January/February 2012): 78.

43. "Bullying Proves the Point—You Should Be a Team Player," *Security Director's Report* 12 (January 2012): 1–15.

44. Kristy Armand, "Standing Up to the Office Bully," *Thrive Magazine* (January 2012): 28–29.

45. Kelly Tilden, "Battle Workplace Bullying," *Credit Union Magazine* 77 (August 2011): 46.

46. Susanne Sclafane, "Do You Work with a Jerk?" *National Underwriter / Property & Casualty Risk & Benefits Management* 115 (March 28, 2011): 14–15.

47. Susanne Sclafane, "What Employers Need to Know about Workplace Bullying," *National Underwriter / Property & Casualty Risk & Benefits Management* 115 (April 11, 2011): 22.

48. "The Next Step in Curbing Workplace Bullying?" *Security Director's Report* 10 (October 2010): 2–4.

49. Donna M. Owens, "Incivility Rising," *HR Magazine* 57 (February 2012): 33.

50. Rita Pyrillis, "EAPS: First Responders in a 'Work-More Economy,'" *Workforce Management* 91 (January 2012): 16.

51. Stephanie Schomer, "Under Pressure," *Fast Company* (April 2010): 112.

52. Cris W. Cannon, "The Reality of Stress and the Need for Management," *Managed Care Outlook* 23 (August 15, 2010): 1–8.

53. "Flight Attendant Incident Puts the Spotlight on Workplace Stress," *EHS Today* 3 (September 2010): 18.

54. Devin Leonard, "Mad as Hell," *Bloomberg Businessweek* (August 16, 2010): 5–6.

55. Katherine Hobson, "Beware: Your Job May Be Killing You," *U.S. News & World Report* 147 (February 2010): 50.

56. Steven Berglas, "Can You Prevent Burnout?" *Forbes* 187 (March 14, 2011): 66.

57. "Bottom Line Benefits of Building a Healthier Workforce," *HR Focus* 89 (April 2012): 17–20.

58. Alex Palmer, "Wellness Incentives Work," *Incentive* 185 (October 2011): 10.

59. Susan J. Wells, "Navigating the Expanding Wellness Industry," *HR Magazine* 56 (March 2011): 45–50.

60. "Employees Value Wellness Programs, But Opportunities Exist for Employers to Do Even More," *Managed Care Outlook* 24 (March 1, 2011): 1–9.

61. Sandra Price, "Ante Up for Wellness," *HR Magazine* 57 (February 2012): 40–42.

62. "With Incentives, Wellness Program Makes Employees Accountable," *Managing Benefits Plans* 11 (July 2011): 16.

63. "More Employers Using Wellness Incentives, Experts Say," *Managing Benefits Plans* 14 (February 2012): 11–13.

64. Susan J. Wells, "Wellness Rewards," *HR Magazine* 57 (February 2012): 67–69.

65. Susan J. Wells, "New Calling: Wellness Officer," *HR Magazine* 56 (February 2011): 43–49.

66. "Using Social Networks to Bolster Your Wellness Programs," *Managing Benefits Plans* 11 (June 2011): 6–8.

67. Jamie Curts, "Social Well-being," *Smart Business Indianapolis* 8 (September 2011): 18.

68. Lisa Beyer, "Companies Are Turning to Technology to Help to Keep Workers Well," *Workforce Management* 90 (October 2011): 6.

69. Pamela Kufahl, "Success Requires the Facts," *Fitness Business Pro* 24 (September 2008): 6.

70. Jodi Schneider, "More Fit in Less Time," *U.S. News & World Report* 132 (May 13, 2002): 50–51.

71. Linda B. Dwoskin, Melissa Bergman Squire, and Jennifer F. Burdick, "Substance Abuse in the Workplace: ADA and FMLA Issues to Consider, Part I," *Employee Benefit Plan Review* 66 (January 2012): 27–32.

72. Robert J. Grossman, "What to Do about Substance Abuse," *HR Magazine* 55 (November 2010): 32–38.

73. "Are Your Workers Accidents Just Waiting to Happen?" *Safety Compliance Letter* (February 2012): 7–11.

74. T. L. Stanley, "Workplace Substance Abuse: A Grave Problem," *Supervision* 70 (June 2009): 18–21.

75. "Genes Linked to Alcoholism," *Investor's Business Daily* (April 15, 2011): 1.

76. "Facts about Recovery," *Psychology Today* (2012 Best in Treatment): 16–17.

77. Paul Meskanick, "Critical Success Factors for Recruitment Process Outsourcing (RPO)," *Offshore* 69 (June 2009): 8–11.

78. Bill Leonard, "Poll: Majority Favors Drug Testing Applicants," *HR Magazine* 56 (November 2011): 87.

79. "Employers Reluctant to Play Role in Preventing Abuse of Painkillers," *HR Focus* 88 (April 2011): 1–4.

80. Jonathan Segal, "Elephant in the Living Room," *HR Magazine* 57 (March 2012): 95–98.

81. "Creating Drug-free Workplace: How to Draft a Policy, Conduct Legal Tests," *HR Specialist: Employment Law* 40 (May 2010): 4.

82. "Fingerprint Drug Testing Seen," *Investor's Business Daily* (November 11, 2011): 2.

83. Catherine McGuire, "What's New in Oral Drug Testing," *Safety Compliance Letter* (January 2012): 7–11.

84. "International Healthcare: Taking Care in New Regions," *Marketing Week* 32 (January 15, 2009): S9.

85. Sam Barrett, "Keep Global Perks at a Healthy Level," *Employee Benefits* (Special Section February 2008): 13–14.

86. Mark Coleman, "The Emperor's New Clothes or Global Healthcare Savvy?" *Employee Benefits* (Special Section January 2010): 2.

87. Robin Guenther and Walt Vernon, "Global Lessons in Healthcare," *Healthcare Design* 10 (October 2010): 10–14.

88. Tynan Barton, "Care in Crisis," *Employee Benefits* (April 2011): 36.

Part Seven
Employee and Labor Relations

12

Labor Unions and Collective Bargaining

HRM in Action

Project Labor Agreements (PLA)

OBJECTIVE 12.1

Describe project labor agreements and explain why employees join unions.

project labor agreement
Prehire collective bargaining agreement between construction firm owners and one or more labor organizations establishing the terms and conditions of employment for a specific construction project.

President Obama signed EO 13502 into law in 2009, which encourages the use of project labor agreements (PLAs) on federal construction contracts of $25 million or more. A **project labor agreement** is a prehire collective bargaining agreement between construction firm owners and one or more labor organizations establishing the terms and conditions of employment for a specific construction project.[1] These agreements require collective bargaining wages and benefits for project employees. PLAs typically mandate that the contractor hire its workers through union halls and require union and nonunion workers alike to pay dues for the length of the project. Prime and subcontractors must follow union rules. PLAs do not prevent nonunion contractors from bidding on construction projects, but they authorize the unions to negotiate the wages and work rules under which a contractor (whether it uses union labor or not) must operate. In exchange, the unions agree to no strike or work disruptions, coordinated work hours, and a reduction of featherbedding. Generally, nonunion contractors oppose PLAs.[2]

Democrats and Republicans have disagreed over the use of PLAs dating back to 1992, when President George H.W. Bush prohibited agencies from requiring construction contractors to use them. President Bill Clinton overturned Bush's order, recommending PLAs on contracts worth more than $5 million. Eight years later, President George W. Bush added a stipulation that agencies stay neutral on the use of labor agreements. In 2009, President Obama issued EO 13502 stating, "Project labor agreements provide 'structure and stability to large-scale construction projects.'"

1 Describe project labor agreements and explain why employees join unions.

2 Describe organized labor's strategies for a stronger movement and explain the basic structure of a union.

3 Discuss laws affecting collective bargaining, including revisiting the NLRB and pay secrecy, and identify the steps that lead to establishing the collective bargaining relationship.

4 Describe the collective bargaining process and explain collective bargaining issues.

5 Describe preparation for negotiations, negotiating the agreement, the two-tier wage system, and breakdowns in negotiations.

6 Describe what is involved in reaching, ratifying, and administering the labor–management agreement.

7 Describe the grievance procedure in a union environment.

8 Explain recent labor–management legal trends and describe collective bargaining in the public sector.

9 Explain union decertification.

10 Describe the state of unions today and discuss labor unrest in China.

Government spokespersons say EO 13502 simply encourages the use of PLAs and does not require them. "It gives each contracting agency the discretion to decide for itself when, on a project-by-project basis, a PLA may provide economy and efficiency," says Dan Gordon, administrator of the Office of Federal Procurement Policy at the Office of Management and Budget.[3] Critics of project labor agreements say the agreements limit competition, increase costs, discriminate against nonunion companies, and are unfair to taxpayers and local municipalities struggling to find money for public works projects.

Subcommittee Chairman Jim Jordan, R-Ohio, contends that Obama's order can be interpreted as a policy mandate. He said that PLAs "tip the scale of an open bid process in favor of organized labor and shut out nonunion shops, many of which are minority and women owned."[4] Only 13 percent of construction workers belong to a labor union. Associated Builders & Contractors President Kirk Pickerel said, "Less than 2 percent of the construction workforce in Florida are affiliated with a labor organization, yet the federal government was willing to increase costs for taxpayers and discriminate against 98 percent of the industry just to reward special interests."[5]

The construction industry has seen an increased use of PLAs on both federal and local government projects.[6] The AFL-CIO Building and Construction Trades Department reported that nearly 100 PLA construction contracts, valued in excess of $80 billion, were awarded in nine months in 2010.[7]

Why Employees Join Unions

Individuals join unions for many different reasons, which tend to change over time, and may involve job, personal, social, or political considerations. It would be impossible to discuss them all, but the following are some of the major reasons.

Dissatisfaction with Management

Every job holds the potential for real dissatisfaction. Each individual has a boiling point that can cause him or her to consider a union as a solution to actual or perceived problems. Union organizers look for arbitrary or unfair management decisions and then emphasize the advantages of union membership as a means of solving these problems. Some of the other common reasons for employee dissatisfaction are described in the following.

COMPENSATION Employees want their compensation to be fair and equitable. Wages are important because they provide both the necessities and pleasures of life. If employees are dissatisfied with their wages, they may look to a union for assistance in improving their standard of living. An important psychological aspect of compensation involves the amount of pay an individual receives in relation to that of other workers performing similar work (employee equity). If an employee perceives that management has shown favoritism by paying someone else more to perform the same or a lower-level job, the employee will likely become dissatisfied. Union members know precisely the basis of their pay and how it compares with that of others. In the past, union members have accepted pay inequities if seniority was the criterion used.

JOB SECURITY Historically, young employees have been less concerned with job security than older workers. Young employees seem to think, "If I lose this job, I can always get another." But if they witness management consistently terminating older workers to make room for younger, more aggressive employees, they may begin to think differently about job security. If the firm does not provide its employees with a sense of job security, workers may turn to a union.

ATTITUDE OF MANAGEMENT People like to feel that they are important. They do not like to be considered a commodity that can be bought and sold. Employees do not like to be subjected to arbitrary actions by management. In some firms, management is insensitive to the needs of its employees. In such situations, employees may perceive that they have little or no influence in job-related matters. Workers who feel that they are not really part of the organization are prime targets for unionization. About 100 hourly workers at North Tonawanda's Smurfit-Stone Container Corporation's corrugated box plant voted to join the United Steelworkers union, claiming the company's disciplinary and promotional policies reflected favoritism.[8] Organizations that treat people with dignity and respect are typically difficult to organize.

Management's attitude may be reflected in even small actions. Employees may begin to feel they are being treated more as machines than as people. Supervisors may fail to give reasons for unusual assignments and may expect employees to dedicate their lives to the firm without providing adequate rewards. The prevailing philosophy may be: "If you don't like it here, leave." A management philosophy that does not consider the needs of employees as individuals makes the firm ripe for unionization. Management must keep in mind that unions will never gain a foothold if management is not abusive of its power. Companies that are pro-employees are not likely to be unionized.

Social Outlet

By nature, many people have strong social needs. They generally enjoy being around others who have similar interests and desires. Some employees join a union for no other reason than to take advantage of union-sponsored recreational and social activities that members and their families find fulfilling. Some unions offer day-care centers and other services that appeal to working men and women, which increases their sense of solidarity with other union members. People who develop close personal relationships, whether in a unionized or union-free organization, will likely stand together in difficult times.

Opportunity for Leadership

Some individuals aspire to leadership roles, but it is not always easy to progress into management. However, employees with leadership ambitions can often satisfy those aspirations through union membership. As with the firm, the union also has a hierarchy of leadership that begins with the union steward, and individual members have the opportunity to work their way up through its various levels.

Forced Unionization

In the 27 states without right-to-work laws, it is legal for an employer to agree with the union that a new employee must join the union after a certain period of time (generally 30 days) or be terminated. This is referred to as a "union-shop agreement." **Right-to-work laws** prohibit management and unions from entering into agreements requiring union membership as a condition of employment. These laws are state statutes or constitutional provisions that ban the practice of requiring union membership or financial support as a condition of employment. They establish the legal right of employees to decide for themselves whether or not to join or financially support a union.[9] Twenty-three states, located primarily in the South and West, have adopted such laws, which are a continuing source of irritation between labor and management. In 2012, Indiana became the most recent right-to-work state.[10]

Peer Pressure

Some individuals will join a union because they are urged to do so by other members of the work group. Friends and associates may constantly remind an employee that he or she is not a member of the union. In extreme cases, union members have threatened nonmembers with physical violence and sometimes have carried out these threats.

OBJECTIVE **12.2**

Describe organized labor's strategies for a stronger movement and explain the basic structure of a union.

Organized Labor's Strategies for a Stronger Movement

Even though the labor movement has suffered setbacks over the past few decades, it is likely that union membership would have been even lower if the following strategies had not been used.

Strategically Located Union Members

The importance of the jobs held by union members significantly affects union power. For instance, an entire plant may have to be shut down if unionized machinists performing critical jobs decide to strike. Thus, a few strategically located union members may exert a disproportionate amount of power. The type of firm that is unionized can also determine a union's power. Unionization of truckers or dockworkers can affect the entire country and, subsequently, enhance the union's power base. This is precisely what the longshoremen did in the West Coast strike of 2002, which affected commerce from San Francisco to Maine. Through control of key industries, a union's power may extend to firms that are not unionized.

Pulling the Union Through

One union tactic that has worked effectively at times is to put pressure on the end user of a company's product in order to have a successful organizing attempt. The United Automobile, Aerospace and Agricultural Implement Workers of America (UAW) authorized a strike against four Johnson Controls Inc. (JCI) factories that made interior parts for some of the country's best-selling vehicles. The quick two-day strike cost workers little lost income, but it hurt General Motors Corporation and DaimlerChrysler Group by shutting down production of their popular Chevy Trail Blazer and Jeep Liberty sport-utility vehicles. Worried about lost sales in a profitable segment and desiring to preserve good relations with the UAW, GM and DaimlerChrysler played an active behind-the-scenes role by pressuring JCI to settle the dispute. The result was a major UAW victory. Not only did raises increase up to $6 an hour, but the strikers won a promise from JCI not to interfere with UAW efforts to organize some 8,000 workers at the 26 other JCI factories that supply the Big Three.[11]

Political Involvement

The political arm of the AFL-CIO is the **Committee on Political Education (COPE)**. Founded in 1955, its purpose is to support politicians who are friendly to the cause of organized labor. The union recommends and assists candidates who will best serve its interests. In presidential and congressional elections, union support may have a significant impact. Union members also encourage their friends and families to support those candidates. Joshua Freeman, professor of labor history at the City University of New York Graduate Center, said, "Unions have gotten weaker, but that weakness is not reflected in the political arena. They are very effective in mobilizing their members and families. It's now fairly common to have one out of four votes in an election coming from a union household."[12] The union's political influence increases as the size of the voting membership grows. With friends in government, the union is in a stronger position to maneuver against management. Political involvement means more than endorsing candidates at all levels of politics, and then attempting to deliver the union membership's vote. Unions give money to candidates who pledge to help pass pro-labor legislation. Of the top 20 biggest political donors at the federal level over the past 20 years, 10 are unions while only four are corporations. The three biggest public unions donated $171.5 million for the 2010 elections.[13]

A 2010 Supreme Court decision ruled that corporations and labor unions can finance political advertising directly linked to political campaigns. The Court ruled that limits are an unconstitutional violation of the First Amendment.[14] Previously, companies, unions, and other groups were prevented from directly paying for political ads during election campaigns.

Union Salting

union salting

Process of training union organizers to apply for jobs at a company and, once hired, working to unionize employees.

Union salting is the process of training union organizers to apply for jobs at a company and, once hired, working to unionize employees.[15] Although traditionally used by blue-collar labor unions within the construction and building industries, it is a strategy labor unions are also using in other sectors, such as the hotel and restaurant industries. The U.S. Supreme Court has ruled that employers cannot discriminate against "union salts" (*NLRB v Town & Electric Inc.*). Therefore, a company cannot terminate these employees solely because they also work for a union. However, if productivity suffers, the worker can be terminated.

Flooding the Community

flooding the community

Process of the union inundating communities with organizers to target a particular business.

Flooding the community is the process of the union inundating communities with organizers to target a particular business in an organizing attempt. With their flooding campaigns, unions typically choose companies in which nonunionized employees have asked for help in organizing. Generally, organizers have been recruited and trained by the national union. They are typically young, ambitious, college-educated people with a passion for the American labor movement. Organizers meet with employees in small groups and even visit them at home. They know every nuance of a company's operations and target weak managers' departments as a way to appeal to dissatisfied employees who may be willing to organize.

Public Awareness Campaigns

public awareness campaigns

Labor maneuvers that do not coincide with a strike or organizing campaign to pressure an employer for better wages, benefits, and the like.

Public awareness campaigns involve labor maneuvers that do not coincide with a strike or an organizing campaign to pressure an employer for better wages, benefits, and the like. Increasingly, these campaigns are used as an alternative to strikes because more employers are willing to replace their striking employees.[16] Employers have less recourse against labor campaigns that involve joining political and community groups that support union goals or picketing homes of a company's board of directors. They are also defenseless in dealing with the union's initiating proxy challenges to actions negative to labor, writing letters to the editors of the local newspapers, and filing charges with administrative agencies such as the Occupational Safety and Health Administration and the National Labor Relations Board. These types of public awareness campaigns, which are not tied directly to labor gains, are often effective methods of developing union leverage. Also, fighting such campaigns is time consuming and costly for companies.

Building Organizing Funds

To encourage workers to come together, the AFL-CIO often asks its affiliates to increase organizing funds. The federation may also increase funding to its Organizing Institute, which trains organizers, and even launches advertising campaigns to create wider public support for unions. National unions also create organizing funds.

Unions Partnering with High Schools

Some high schools are pairing up with labor unions to prepare students for a career. Ten students from Saydel High School's construction shop class have entered a pilot program that allows them direct entry into the United Association Plumbers and Steamfitters Local Union 33 once they graduate. As Local 33, apprentices receive training in plumbing, heating, air conditioning, medical gas, high purity piping, and water treatment. Greg Foshe, business manager of Local 33, said, "The goal of this program is to bring people into the union at a younger age. When students go from high school directly into their trade, they are going from learning situation to learning situation, creating a fast track educational experience."[17]

Organizing Younger Workers

A major strategy now being pursued by union organizers is to recruit younger workers, and it may be coming at the right time since the lowest union membership rate is occurring among this group. In fact, according to the Bureau of Labor Statistics, the lowest union membership rate occurred among those ages 16 to 24 (4.4 percent). In the past, younger organizers were often considered second-class citizens. Consider what Rachael Hunt, a young union organizer, said: "Too many times, more experienced trade unionists have spoken to me as if I were a blank slate: ready to mold and be shaped to meet older organizers' viewpoints and goals. This same top-down, stale, bureaucratic organizational model that is crippling unions is also its biggest barrier to recruiting young people."[18] Richard Trumka, AFL-CIO president, said the following regarding including the ideas of younger workers: "I'm not suggesting that the labor movement ought to abandon all its traditions. But what I am saying is that nostalgia for the past is no strategy for the future. Tradition should always have a vote; we just can't let it have a veto."[19]

Organizing Through the Card Check

card check

Organizing approach by labor in which employees sign a nonsecret card of support if they want unionization, and if 50 percent of the workforce plus one worker sign a card, the union is formed.

The **card check** is an organizing approach by labor in which employees sign a nonsecret card of support if they want unionization, and if 50 percent of the workforce plus one worker sign a card, the union is formed. This organizing method is based on management not objecting to the use of card check. It permits workers to decide in a nonsecret election their union status. Essentially, organizations decide to remain neutral and peacefully permit their employees to decide whether they want to unionize and not interfere as the union passes out authorization cards.

In 2008, the Teamsters launched its nationwide card-check campaign, a procedure in which workers sign cards to join a union instead of going through a secret voting process. A majority of workers in a bargaining unit must sign cards, which are then certified, before the company recognizes the union. Bargaining units from across the country signed authorization cards and were recognized as a union.[20] The largest was the drivers and dockworkers employed by UPS Freight, which added more than 9,900 members.[21]

ETHICAL DILEMMA

A Strategic Move

You are the plant manager for a medium-sized manufacturing company that has been experiencing growing employee tensions, and there has been a lot of talk among workers about forming a union. You have even seen what appear to be authorization cards being passed out around the plant. Sandy Marshall, one of the workers in your plant, has been seen talking to many of the workers, obviously about forming a union. Sandy is very influential with the workers throughout the plant and appears to be a natural leader. You believe that if Sandy continues to promote the union, she will have a major impact among the workers in organizing the union. You have a supervisory position that has just come open. It pays a lot more than what Sandy currently makes. You think, "If I make her a supervisor, she won't be able to use her influence to help get the union started." However, there is another worker in your department who is more qualified and has been with the firm several years longer than Sandy, although he is less influential with other workers throughout the plant.

What would you do?
What factor(s) in this ethical dilemma might influence a person to make a less-than-ethical decision?

Union Structure

The labor movement has developed a multilevel organizational structure. This complex of organizations ranges from local unions to the two principal federations—the AFL-CIO and the Change to Win Coalition.

Local Union

local union
Basic element in the structure of the U.S. labor movement.

The basic element in the structure of the American labor movement is the **local union** (or, the *local*). To the individual union member, the local is the most important level in the structure of organized labor. Through the local, individuals deal with the employer on a day-to-day basis. A local union may fill a social role in the lives of its members, sponsoring dances, festivals, and other functions. It may be the focal point of the political organization and activity of its members.

craft union
Bargaining unit, such as the Carpenters and Joiners Union, which is typically composed of members of a particular trade or skill in a specific locality.

There are two basic kinds of local unions: craft and industrial. A **craft union**, such as the Carpenters and Joiners Union, is typically composed of members of a particular trade or skill in a specific locality. Members usually acquire their job skills through an apprenticeship-training program. An **industrial union** generally consists of all the workers in a particular plant or group of plants. The type of work they do and the level of skill they possess are not a condition for membership in the union. An example of an industrial union is the United Auto Workers.

industrial union
Bargaining unit that generally consists of all the workers in a particular plant or group of plants.

The local union's functions are many and varied. Administering the collective bargaining agreement and representing workers in handling grievances are two very important activities. Other functions include keeping the membership informed about labor issues, promoting increased membership, maintaining effective contact with the national union, and, when appropriate, negotiating with management at the local level.

National Union

national union
Organization composed of local unions, which it charters.

The most powerful level in the union structure is the national union. As stated previously, most locals are affiliated with national unions. A **national union** is composed of local unions, which it charters. As such, it is the parent organization to local unions. The local union, not the individual worker, holds membership in the national union. Each local union provides financial support to the national union based on its membership size. The Service Employees International Union (SEIU) is the largest and fastest-growing national union in North America, with 2.1 million members in the United States, Canada, and Puerto Rico. The SEIU has more than 1.1 million members in the health care field, including nurses, LPNs, doctors, lab technicians, nursing home workers, and home care workers.[22] The International Brotherhood of Teamsters has about 1.4 million members.[23]

The national union is governed by a national constitution and a national convention of local unions, which usually meets every two to five years. Elected officers, aided by an administrative staff, conduct the day-to-day operations of the national union. The national union is active in organizing workers within its jurisdiction, engaging in collective bargaining at the national level, and assisting its locals in their negotiations. In addition, the national union may provide numerous educational and research services for its locals, dispense strike funds, publish the union newspaper, provide legal counsel, and actively lobby at national and state levels.

American Federation of Labor and Congress of Industrial Organizations

American Federation of Labor and Congress of Industrial Organizations (AFL-CIO)
Central trade union federation in the United States.

The **American Federation of Labor and Congress of Industrial Organizations (AFL-CIO)** is the central trade union federation in the United States. It is a loosely knit organization of national unions that has little formal power or control. The member national unions remain completely autonomous and decide their own policies and programs.

The AFL-CIO is a voluntary federation of 57 national and international labor unions representing 12.2 million members, including 3.2 million members in Working America, its community affiliate.[24] It represents the interests of labor and its member national unions at the highest level. The federation does not engage in collective bargaining; however, it provides the means by which member unions can cooperate to pursue common objectives and attempt to resolve internal problems faced by organized labor. The federation is financed by its member national unions and is governed by a national convention, which meets every two years.

The structure of the AFL-CIO is complex. National unions can affiliate with one or more of the trade and industrial departments. These departments seek to promote the interests of specific groups of workers who are in different unions but have common interests. The federation's

Change to Win Coalition

Union federation consisting of seven unions that broke from the AFL-CIO and formally launched a rival labor federation representing about 6 million workers in 2005.

OBJECTIVE 12.3

Discuss laws affecting collective bargaining, including revisiting the NLRB and pay secrecy, and identify the steps that lead to establishing the collective bargaining relationship.

major activities focus on improving the image of organized labor and lobbying on behalf of labor interests. Also, politically educating constituencies is crucial, as is resolving disputes between national unions and policing internal affairs of member unions.

Change to Win Coalition

The **Change to Win Coalition** is a union federation consisting of unions that broke from the AFL-CIO and formally launched a rival labor federation representing six million workers from seven labor unions.

The coalition, led by the Service Employees International Union, focuses its energies on new membership growth and not as much on lobbying. Also included in the new coalition are the International Brotherhood of Teamsters, Unite Here, the United Food and Commercial Workers International Union, United Brotherhood of Carpenters and Joiners of America, the United Farm Workers of America, and the Laborers' International Union of North America. The coalition wanted to direct its efforts at workers in industries in which employers could not easily outsource jobs. The primary targets for organizing included industries in cleaning, health care, hotels and restaurants, retailing, and transportation.

The mission of the Change to Win Coalition is "to unite the 50 million American workers who work in industries that cannot be outsourced or shipped overseas into strong unions that can win them a place in the American middle class—where their jobs provide good wages, decent working conditions and a voice on the job."[25]

Laws Affecting Collective Bargaining

The National Labor Relations Act (Wagner Act) of 1935 is one of the most significant labor–management relations statutes ever enacted. The act declared legislative support, on a broad scale, for the right of employees to organize and engage in collective bargaining. The spirit of the Wagner Act is stated in Section 7, which defines the substantive rights of employees:

Employees shall have the right to self-organization, to form, join, or assist labor organizations, to bargain collectively through representatives of their own choosing, and to engage in other concerted activities, for the purpose of collective bargaining or other mutual aid or protection.

The National Labor Relations Act created the National Labor Relations Board (NLRB). At the time, the board helped the labor movement, which at times resulted in heated and sometimes violent management resistance.[26] The NLRB was given two principal functions: (1) to establish procedures for holding bargaining unit elections and to monitor the election procedures, and (2) to investigate complaints and prevent unlawful acts involving unfair labor practices. Much of the NLRB's work is delegated to 33 regional offices throughout the country. Appointments to the NLRB are made by the president and confirmed by the Senate. They decide on detailed rules governing union and management behavior and how elections should be conducted.

The rights defined in Section 7 were protected against employer interference by Section 8, which detailed and prohibited five management practices deemed to be unfair to labor:

1. Interfering with or restraining or coercing employees in the exercise of their right to self-organization.
2. Dominating or interfering in the affairs of a union.
3. Discriminating in regard to hire or tenure or any condition of employment for the purpose of encouraging or discouraging union membership.
4. Discriminating against or discharging an employee who has filed charges or given testimony under the act.
5. Refusing to bargain with chosen representatives of employees.

Following passage of the Wagner Act, union membership increased from approximately three million to 15 million between 1935 and 1947.

In 1947, with public pressure mounting, Congress overrode President Truman's veto and passed the Labor–Management Relations Act (Taft–Hartley Act). The Taft–Hartley Act extensively revised the National Labor Relations Act. A new period began in the evolution of public policy regarding labor. The pendulum had begun to swing toward a more balanced position between labor and management.

Some of the important changes introduced by the Taft–Hartley Act included the following:

1. Modifying Section 7 to include the right of employees to refrain from union activity as well as engage in it.
2. Prohibiting the closed shop and narrowing the freedom of the parties to authorize the union shop.
3. Broadening the employer's right of free speech.
4. Providing that employers need not recognize or bargain with unions formed by supervisors.
5. Giving employees the right to initiate decertification petitions.
6. Providing for government intervention in national emergency strikes.

Another significant change extended the concept of unfair labor practices to unions. Labor organizations were to refrain from the following:

1. Restraining or coercing employees in the exercise of their guaranteed collective bargaining rights.
2. Causing an employer to discriminate in any way against an employee in order to encourage or discourage union membership.
3. Refusing to bargain in good faith with an employer regarding wages, hours, and other terms and conditions of employment.
4. Engaging in certain types of strikes and boycotts.
5. Requiring employees covered by union-shop contracts to pay initiation fees or dues in an amount which the board finds excessive or discriminatory under all circumstances.
6. *Featherbedding,* or requiring that an employer pay for services not performed.

One of the most controversial elements of the Taft–Hartley Act is its Section 14b, which permits states to enact right-to-work legislation.

Revisiting the National Labor Relations Board

The NLRB has recently been thrust into the forefront stemming from a pattern of controversial decisions that may significantly influence labor–management activities. Since the 2008 presidential election, the NLRB has been reconstituted and has resumed a full caseload. Some believe that the board is promoting the interests and political agenda of labor unions.[27] In 2010, President Obama installed two new members, Craig Becker and Mark Pearce, to the five-member board. Using recess appointments, President Obama appointed three new members to the NLRB in 2012 resulting in a full compliment of members.

John N. Raudabaugh, who served on the National Labor Relations Board from 1990 to 1993, said, "Unions surely are going to change, but I don't see unions disappearing. The question is what will the next generation of unions look like, and what rules will govern employer interactions with them."[28] However, many business groups believe that the board has tilted toward labor, changing the rules that govern employer–labor relations. For example, recently the NLRB voted to change the union election rules, which speeded up the process of securing union representation in workplaces nationwide. The new rule reduces the time between the filing of an election petition and actual voting. Estimations are that most elections will most likely occur within half the current median period of 38 days.[29] This makes it easier for unions to win elections and more difficult for employers to tell their side of the story.

In 2012 the NLRB ruled that a Florida-based home builder committed an unfair labor practice under federal labor law by maintaining a mandatory arbitration agreement that waived the rights of employees to participate in class or collective actions. If this ruling holds up, it may effectively eliminate alternative dispute resolution, a procedure whereby the employee and the company agree ahead of time that any problems will be addressed by an agreed-upon means.[30]

Other examples of decisions made by the board may reveal a trend. The NLRB nullified results of a controversial union vote at Berkeley Bowl, an independent specialty grocer. Workers voted down representation of United Food and Commercial Workers Local 5, but the union later alleged the retailer had violated labor law by intimidating workers. According to a settlement, the retailer must post documents indicating it would not punish or intimidate workers for discussing union representation but is not required to admit to violating labor laws.[31]

A Connecticut ambulance company fired a worker who complained about her supervisor on Facebook. She used offensive language to express her feelings about her boss, and several coworkers joined in. The company fired the woman, citing its policy prohibiting employees from depicting the company "in any way" on social media sites. The NLRB ruled that to be an unfair labor practice. It was the first case in which the NLRB argued that workers' criticisms on social networking sites are "protected concerted activity."[32]

In 2009, the NLRB alleged Boeing illegally punished the local machinists' union when it decided to locate a new plant to build its new 787 Dreamliner jet liner in South Carolina. The NLRB determined Boeing's decision violated federal labor law because it amounted to retaliation for strikes. Boeing initially offered to build the 787 plant near Puget Sound on the condition that the union agrees not to strike for at least 10 years. After talks broke down, Boeing accepted $170 million in grants and tens of millions more in tax breaks to construct the plant in South Carolina, a right-to-work state. The NLRB wanted Boeing to move the work back to Washington.[33] In defining the move as illegal retaliation, the labor board mentioned company executives' public statements about their desire to avoid strikes. That demonstrated the executives' intention to punish the workers, who had staged strikes at Boeing factories four times since 1989.[34] Recently, the NLRB decided to drop its case against Boeing after the union struck a lucrative deal with Boeing covering its workers in Washington.[35]

Pay Secrecy

The NLRB and the courts have declared many times that employers violate the National Labor Relations Act if they issue verbal or written statements that discourage or prohibit nonsupervisory employees from discussing their pay with each other or the media. Pay confidentiality clauses in employment contracts are also illegal. The NLRB also protects pay dialogues among coworkers, which also apply to conversations about benefits and working conditions.

A recent survey found that half of all employees believe that discussing pay is discouraged or formally prohibited by their employers. Among private-sector workers, 61 percent say they believe they are discouraged or prohibited from discussing wages and salaries.[36] Some organizations tend to keep their pay rates secret for various reasons. If a firm's compensation plan is illogical, secrecy may indeed be appropriate because only a well-designed system can stand careful scrutiny. An open system would almost certainly require managers to explain the rationale for pay decisions to subordinates. Secrecy, however, can have some negative side effects including a distortion of the actual rewards people receive. Secrecy also spawns a low-trust environment in which people have trouble understanding the relationship between pay and performance. In such an environment, an otherwise sound program loses its effectiveness. The NLRB is expected take an even more aggressive stance on pay secrecy in the future.

Steps that Lead to Forming a Bargaining Unit

Before a union can negotiate a contract, it must first be formed or certified. The primary law governing the relationship of companies and unions is the National Labor Relations Act, as amended. Collective bargaining is one of the key parts of the act. Section 8(d) of the act defines **collective bargaining** as:

> *The performance of the mutual obligation of the employer and the representative of the employees to meet at reasonable times and confer in good faith with respect to wages, hours, and other terms and conditions of employment, or the negotiation of an agreement, or any question arising thereunder, and the execution of a written contract incorporating any agreement reached if requested by either party, but such obligation does not compel either party to agree to a proposal or require the making of a concession.*

The act further provides that the designated representative of the employees shall be the exclusive representative for all the employees in the unit for purposes of collective bargaining. A **bargaining unit** consists of a group of employees, not necessarily union members, recognized by an employer or certified by an administrative agency as appropriate for representation by a labor organization for purposes of collective bargaining.

---

collective bargaining
Performance of the mutual obligation of the employer and the representative of the employees to meet at reasonable times and confer in good faith with respect to wages, hours, and other terms and conditions of employment, or the negotiation of an agreement, or any question arising thereunder, and the execution of a written contract incorporating any agreement reached if requested by either party; such obligation does not compel either party to agree to a proposal or require the making of a concession.

bargaining unit
Group of employees, not necessarily union members, recognized by an employer or certified by an administrative agency as appropriate for representation by a labor organization for purposes of collective bargaining.

FIGURE 12-1

Steps That Lead to Forming a Bargaining Unit

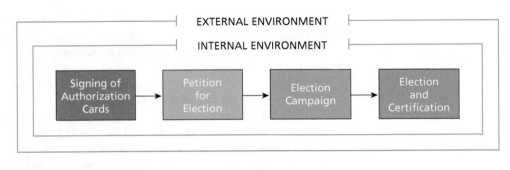

A unit may cover the employees in one plant of an employer, or it may cover employees in two or more plants of the same employer. Although the act requires the representative to be selected by the employees, it does not require any particular procedure to be used so long as the choice clearly reflects the desire of the majority of the employees in the bargaining unit. The employee representative is normally chosen in a secret-ballot election conducted by the NLRB. When workers desire to become the bargaining representative for a group of employees, several steps leading to certification have to be taken (see Figure 12-1).

Prior to observing authorization cards passed out, there are usually signs of an upcoming union organizing attempt. Some indications might be an increase in the number or intensity of employee complaints on wages, hours, working conditions, or management practices; unusual or more frequent employee challenges to management authority; and an increase in the number of formal complaints to government agencies such as Occupational Health and Safety Administration, U.S. Department of Labor, and state or federal equal employment agencies.

Signing of Authorization Cards

A prerequisite to becoming a recognized bargaining unit is to determine whether there is sufficient interest on the part of employees to justify the unit. Evidence of this interest is expressed when at least 30 percent of the employees in a work group sign an authorization card (see Table 12-1). The **authorization card** is a document indicating that an employee wants to be represented by a labor organization in collective bargaining. Most union organizers will not proceed unless at least 50 percent of the workers in the group sign cards.

Petition for Election

After the authorization cards have been signed, a petition for an election may be made to the appropriate regional office of the NLRB. When the petition is filed, the NLRB will conduct an investigation. The purpose of the investigation is to determine, among other things, the following:

1. Whether the board has jurisdiction to conduct an election.
2. Whether there is a sufficient showing of employee interest to justify an election.

authorization card

Document indicating that an employee wants to be represented by a labor organization in collective bargaining.

TABLE 12-1

Example of an Authorization Card

YES, I WANT THE UNION

I, the undersigned, and employee of

(Name of Company)

Hereby authorize the (<u>Name of the Union</u>) to act as my collective bargaining agent with the company for wages, hours, and other terms and conditions of employment.

NAME _____ DATE _____

ADDRESS _____

CITY _____ STATE _____ ZIP _____

JOB TITLE _____

SIGN HERE _____

NOTE: THIS AUTHORIZATION IS TO BE SIGNED AND DATED IN EMPLOYEE'S OWN HANDWRITING. YOUR RIGHT TO SIGN THIS CARD IS PROTECTED BY LAW.

3. Whether a question of representation exists (for example, the employee representative has demanded recognition, which has been denied by the employer).
4. Whether the election will include appropriate employees in the bargaining unit (for instance, the board is prohibited from including plant guards in the same unit with the other employees).
5. Whether the representative named in the petition is qualified (for example, a supervisor or any other management representative may not be an employee representative).
6. Whether there are any barriers to an election in the form of existing contracts or prior elections held within the past 12 months.[37]

If these conditions have been met, the NLRB will ordinarily direct that an election be held within 30 days. Election details are left largely to the agency's regional director.

Election Campaign

When an election has been ordered, both union and management usually promote their causes actively. Unions will continue to encourage workers to join the union, and management may begin a campaign to tell workers the benefits of remaining union-free. The supervisor's role during the campaign is crucial. Supervisors need to conduct themselves in a manner that avoids violating the law and committing unfair labor practices. Specifically, they should be aware of what can and cannot be done during the pre-election campaign period. Throughout the campaign, supervisors should keep upper management informed about employee attitudes.

Theoretically, both union and management are permitted to tell their stories without interference from the other side. At times, the campaign becomes quite intense. Election results will be declared invalid if the campaign was marked by conduct that the NLRB considers to have interfered with the employees' freedom of choice. Examples of such conduct include the following:

- An employer or a union threatens loss of jobs or benefits to influence employees' votes or union activities.
- An employer or a union misstates important facts in the election campaign when the other party does not have a chance to reply.
- Either an employer or a union incites racial or religious prejudice by inflammatory campaign appeals.
- An employer fires employees to discourage or encourage their union activities or a union causes an employer to take such an action.
- An employer or a union makes campaign speeches to assembled groups of employees on company time within 24 hours of an election.

Election and Certification

The NLRB monitors the secret-ballot election on the date set. Its representatives are responsible for making sure that only eligible employees vote, and for counting the votes. Following a valid election, the board will issue a certification of the results to the participants. If a union has been chosen by a majority of the employees voting in the bargaining unit, it will receive a certificate showing that it is now the official bargaining representative of the employees in the unit. However, the right to represent employees does not mean they have the right to dictate terms to management that would adversely affect the organization. The bargaining process does not require either party to make concessions; it only compels them to bargain in good faith in collective bargaining.

Collective Bargaining

Once the NLRB certifies the union, labor and management can engage in collective bargaining. Most union–management agreements in the United States are for a three-year period. Thus, on average, one-third of collective bargaining agreements occur each year. The bargaining structure can affect the conduct of collective bargaining. The four major structures are one company dealing with a single union, several companies dealing with a single union, several unions dealing with a single company, and several companies dealing with several unions. Most contract bargaining is carried out under the first type of structure. The process can become quite complicated when several companies and unions are involved in the same negotiations. However, even when there is only one industry involved and one group of workers with similar skills, collective bargaining can be very difficult.

OBJECTIVE **12.4**

Describe the collective bargaining process and explain collective bargaining issues.

Collective Bargaining Process

The collective bargaining process is fundamental to union and management relations in the United States. Regardless of the current state of labor–management relations, the general aspects of the collective bargaining process are the same and are illustrated in Figure 12-2. Depending on the type of relationship encountered, the collective bargaining process may be relatively simple, or it may be a long, tense struggle for both parties. Regardless of the complexity of the bargaining issues, the ability to reach agreement is the key to any successful negotiation.

As you can see, both external and internal environmental factors can influence the process. The first step in the collective bargaining process is preparing for negotiations. This step is often extensive and ongoing for both union and management. After the issues to be negotiated have been determined, the two sides confer to reach a mutually acceptable contract. Although breakdowns in negotiations can occur, both labor and management have at their disposal tools and arguments that can be used to convince the other side to accept their views. Eventually, however, management and the union usually reach an agreement that defines the rules for the duration of the contract. The next step is for the union membership to ratify the agreement. There is a feedback loop from "Administration of the Agreement" to "Preparing for Negotiation." Collective bargaining is a continuous and dynamic process, and preparing for the next round of negotiations often begins the moment a contract is ratified.

FIGURE 12-2

Collective Bargaining Process

Bargaining Issues

Because of the complex issues facing labor and management today, negotiating teams must carefully prepare for the bargaining sessions. Prior to meeting at the bargaining table, the negotiators should thoroughly know the culture, climate, history, present economic state, and wage and benefits structure of both the organization and similar organizations. Because the length of a typical labor agreement is three years, negotiators should develop a contract that is successful both now and in the future. This consideration should prevail for both management and labor, although it rarely does. During the term of an agreement, the two sides usually discover contract provisions that need to be added, deleted, or modified. These items become proposals to be addressed in the next round of negotiations.

Bargaining issues can be divided into three categories: mandatory, permissive, and prohibited. **Mandatory bargaining issues** fall within the definition of wages, hours, and other terms and conditions of employment. These issues generally have an immediate and direct effect on workers' jobs. A refusal to bargain in these areas is grounds for an unfair labor practice charge. At times, collective bargaining toward new wage, rules, and benefits agreements may drag on for a long time. **Permissive bargaining issues** may be raised, but neither side may insist that they be bargained over. For example, management may want to bargain over health benefits for retired workers, but the union may choose not to bargain over the issue. Another permissive bargaining issue might be the union wanting management to provide child-care arrangements.

Prohibited bargaining issues, such as the issue of the closed shop, an arrangement whereby union membership is a prerequisite, are statutorily outlawed. The Taft–Hartley Act made the closed shop illegal. However, the act was modified 12 years later by the Landrum–Griffin Act to permit a closed shop in the construction industry. This is the only exception allowed.

Despite much dissimilarity, certain topics are included in virtually all labor agreements. Each topic discussed in the following may be an issue in negotiations.

mandatory bargaining issues
Bargaining issues that fall within the definition of wages, hours, and other terms and conditions of employment.

permissive bargaining issues
Issues that may be raised, but neither side may insist that they be bargained over.

prohibited bargaining issues
Issues that are statutorily outlawed from collective bargaining.

Recognition

This section usually appears at the beginning of the labor agreement. Its purpose is to identify the union that is recognized as the bargaining representative and to describe the bargaining unit—that is, the employees for whom the union speaks. A typical recognition section might read as follows:

The XYZ Company recognizes the ABC Union as the sole and exclusive representative of the bargaining unit employees for the purpose of collective bargaining with regard to wages, hours, and other conditions of employment.

Management Rights

A section that is often but not always written into the labor agreement spells out the rights of management. If no such section is included, management may reason that it retains control of all topics not described as bargainable in the contract. The precise content of the management rights section will vary by industry, company, and union. When included, management rights generally involve three areas:

1. Freedom to select the business objectives of the company.
2. Freedom to determine the uses to which the material assets of the enterprise will be devoted.
3. Power to take disciplinary action for cause.

Basically management has the right to determine what work is to be done and where, when, and how it is to be done, to determine the number of employees who will do the work, to supervise and instruct employees in doing the work, to correct employees whose work performance or personal conduct fails to meet reasonable standards, and to hire, dismiss, and promote workers based on performance.

Union Security

Union security is typically one of the first items negotiated in a collective bargaining agreement. The objective of union security provisions is to ensure that the union continues to exist and perform its functions. A strong union security provision makes it easier for the union to enroll and retain members. Some basic forms of union security clauses are next described.

closed shop
Arrangement making union membership a prerequisite for employment.

union shop
Requirement that all employees become members of the union after a specified period of employment (the legal minimum is 30 days) or after a union-shop provision has been negotiated.

maintenance of membership
Employees who are members of the union at the time the labor agreement is signed or who later voluntarily join must continue their memberships until the termination of the agreement as a condition of employment.

agency shop
Labor agreement provision requiring, as a condition of employment, that each nonunion member of a bargaining unit pay the union the equivalent of membership dues as a service charge in return for the union acting as the bargaining agent.

open shop
Employment on equal terms to union members and nonmembers alike.

checkoff of dues
Agreement by which a company agrees to withhold union dues from members' paychecks and to forward the money directly to the union.

CLOSED SHOP A **closed shop** is an arrangement whereby union membership is a prerequisite for employment.

UNION SHOP A **union shop** arrangement requires that all employees become members of the union after a specified period of employment (the legal minimum is 30 days) or after a union-shop provision has been negotiated. Employees must remain members of the union as a condition of employment for the duration of the contract. The union shop is generally legal in the United States, except in states that have right-to-work laws.

MAINTENANCE OF MEMBERSHIP With **maintenance of membership**, employees who are members of the union at the time the labor agreement is signed or who later voluntarily join must continue their memberships until the termination of the agreement as a condition of employment. This form of recognition is also prohibited in most states that have right-to-work laws.

AGENCY SHOP An **agency shop** provision does not require employees to join the union; however, the labor agreement requires that, as a condition of employment, each nonunion member of the bargaining unit pay the union the equivalent of membership dues as a kind of tax, or service charge, in return for the union acting as the bargaining agent. The National Labor Relations Act requires the union to bargain for all members of the bargaining unit, including nonunion employees. The agency shop is outlawed in most states that have right-to-work laws.

OPEN SHOP An open shop describes the absence of union security, rather than its presence. The **open shop**, strictly defined, is employment on equal terms to union members and nonmembers alike. Under this arrangement, no employee is required to join or contribute to the union financially.

CHECKOFF OF DUES Another type of security that unions attempt to achieve is the checkoff of dues. A checkoff agreement may be used in addition to any of the previously mentioned shop agreements. Under the **checkoff of dues** provision, the company agrees to withhold union dues from members' paychecks and to forward the money directly to the union. Because of provisions in the Taft–Hartley Act, each union member must voluntarily sign a statement authorizing this deduction. Dues checkoff is important to the union because it eliminates much of the expense, time, and hassle of collecting dues from each member every pay period or once a month.

Compensation

This section typically constitutes a large portion of most labor agreements. Virtually any item that can affect compensation may be included in labor agreements. Some of the items frequently covered include the following.

WAGE RATE SCHEDULE The base rates to be paid each year of the contract for each job are included in this section. At times, unions are able to obtain a cost-of-living allowance (COLA), or escalator clause, in the contract to protect the purchasing power of employees' earnings.

OVERTIME AND PREMIUM PAY Another section of the agreement may cover hours of work, overtime pay, hazard pay, and premium pay, such as shift differentials.

JURY PAY For some firms, jury pay amounts to the employee's entire salary when he or she is serving jury duty. Others pay the difference between the amount employees receive from the court and the compensation that would have been earned. The procedure covering jury pay is typically stated in the contract.

LAYOFF OR SEVERANCE PAY The amount that employees in various jobs and/or seniority levels will be paid if they are laid off or terminated is a frequently included item.

HOLIDAYS The holidays recognized and the amount of pay that a worker will receive if he or she has to work on a holiday is specified here. In addition, the pay procedure for times when a holiday falls on a worker's normal day off is provided.

VACATION This section spells out the amount of vacation that a person may take based on seniority. Any restrictions as to when the vacation may be taken are also stated.

Grievance Procedure

Virtually all labor agreements include some form of grievance procedure. A **grievance** can be broadly defined as an employee's dissatisfaction or feeling of personal injustice relating to his or her employment. A **grievance procedure** (discussed later in this chapter) is a formal, systematic process that permits employees to express complaints without jeopardizing their jobs.

Employee Security

This section of the labor agreement establishes the procedures that cover job security for individual employees. Seniority is a key topic related to employee security. **Seniority** is the length of time an employee has been associated with the company, division, department, or job. Seniority may be determined company-wide, by division, by department, or by job. Agreement on seniority is important because the person with the most seniority, as defined in the labor agreement, is typically the last to be laid off and the first to be recalled. The seniority system also provides a basis for promotion decisions. When qualifications are met, employees with the greatest seniority will likely be considered first for promotion to higher-level jobs.

Job-Related Factors

Many of the rules governing employee actions on the job are also included. Some of the more important factors are company work rules, work standards, and rules related to safety. This section varies, depending on the nature of the industry and the product manufactured.

Preparation for Negotiations

The union must continuously gather information regarding membership needs to isolate areas of dissatisfaction. The union steward is normally in the best position to collect such data.[38] Because they are usually elected by their peers, stewards should be well informed regarding union members' attitudes. The union steward constantly funnels information up through the union's chain of command, where the data are compiled and analyzed. Union leadership attempts to uncover any areas of dissatisfaction because the general union membership must approve any agreement before it becomes final. Because they are elected, union leaders will lose their positions if the demands they make of management do not represent the desires of the general membership.

Management also spends long hours preparing for negotiations. All aspects of the current contracts are considered, including flaws that should be corrected. When preparing for negotiations, management should listen carefully to first-line managers. These individuals administer the labor agreement on a day-to-day basis and must live with errors made in negotiating the contract. An alert line manager is also able to inform upper management of the demands unions may plan to make during negotiations.

Management also attempts periodically to obtain information regarding employee attitudes. Surveys are often administered to workers to determine their feelings toward their jobs and job environment. Union and management representatives like to know as much as possible about employee attitudes when they sit down at the bargaining table.

Another part of preparation for negotiations involves identifying various positions that both union and management will take as the negotiations progress. Each usually takes an initially extreme position, representing the optimum conditions union or management would prefer. The two sides will likely determine absolute limits to their offers or demands before a breakdown in negotiations occurs. They also usually prepare fallback positions based on combinations of issues. Preparations should be detailed, because clear minds often do not prevail during the heat of negotiations.

A major consideration in preparing for negotiations is the selection of the bargaining teams. The makeup of the management team usually depends on the type of organization and its size. Normally, labor relations specialists, with the advice and assistance of operating managers, conduct bargaining. Sometimes, top executives are directly involved, particularly in smaller firms. Larger companies use staff specialists (a human resource manager or industrial relations executive), managers of principal operating divisions, and, in some cases, an outside consultant, such as a labor attorney.

The responsibility for conducting negotiations for the union is usually entrusted to union officers. At the local level, rank-and-file members who are elected specifically for this purpose will normally supplement the bargaining committee. In addition, the national union will often send a representative to act in an advisory capacity or even to participate directly in the bargaining sessions. The real task of the union negotiating team is to develop and obtain solutions to the problems raised by the union's membership.

Negotiating the Agreement

There is no way to ensure speedy and mutually acceptable results from negotiations. At best, the parties can attempt to create an atmosphere that will lend itself to steady progress and productive results. For example, the two negotiating teams usually meet at an agreed-on neutral site, such as a hotel. When a favorable relationship can be established early, eleventh-hour (or last-minute) bargaining can often be avoided. It is equally important for union and management negotiators to strive to develop and maintain clear and open lines of communication. Collective bargaining is a problem-solving activity; consequently, good communication is essential to its success. Negotiations should be conducted in the privacy of the conference room, not in the news media. Often in the media, the unions belittle management and naturally management strikes back. The media love it because it sells. The results are harmful, often to both sides. If the negotiators feel that publicity is necessary, joint releases to the media may avoid unnecessary conflict.

The negotiating phase of collective bargaining begins with each side presenting its initial demands. Because a collective bargaining settlement can be expensive for a firm, the cost of various proposals should be estimated as accurately as possible. Some changes can be quite expensive, and others cost little or nothing, but the cost of the various proposals being considered must always be carefully deliberated. The term *negotiating* suggests a certain amount of give-and-take, the purpose of which is to lower the other side's expectations. For example, the union might bargain to upgrade its members' economic and working conditions and the company might negotiate to maintain or enhance profitability.

One of the most costly components of any collective bargaining agreement is a wage increase provision. An example of the negotiation of a wage increase is shown in Figure 12-3. In this example labor initially demands a 40-cent-per-hour increase. Management counters with an offer of only 10 cents per hour. Both labor and management, as expected, reject each other's demand. Plan B calls for labor to lower its demand to a 30-cents-per-hour increase. Management counters with an offer of 20 cents. The positions in plan B are feasible to both sides, as both groups are in the bargaining zone. Wages within the bargaining zone are those that management and labor can both accept, in this case, an increase of between 20 cents and 30 cents per hour. The exact amount will be determined by the power of the bargaining unit and the skills of the negotiators.

The realities of negotiations are not for the weak of heart and at times are similar to a high-stakes poker game. A certain amount of bluffing and raising the ante takes place in many negotiations. The ultimate bluff for the union is when a negotiator says, "If our demands are not met, we are prepared to strike." Management's version of this bluff would be to threaten a lockout. Each

FIGURE 12-3

Example of Negotiating a Wage Increase

TRENDS & INNOVATIONS

The Two-Tier Wage System Returns

Years ago, I was a coauthor of an article entitled, "The Two-Tier Wage System: A Major Breakthrough in the Reindustrialization of America?" for *Personnel Administrator,* now entitled *HR Magazine*. In the article the **two-tier wage system** was defined as "a wage structure where newly hired workers are paid less than current employees for performing the same or similar jobs."[39] In the article we said that the trend in labor–management wage negotiations was this so-called two-tier wage system. At the time of the writing of the article, two-tier contracts had already been negotiated in the airline, copper, trucking, auto, and aerospace industries. Shortly afterward, our projections proved to be incorrect and the two-tier wage system died.

But over two decades later it came back to life. In 2007 the UAW and General Motors negotiated a contract that included provisions for a two-tier wage system. The negotiated wage scale for any new *non-core employees* was $14 per hour, which was half of what a typical worker would earn. Twenty percent of GM's employees were in this category. This category of workers did, however, receive traditional health care benefits and had the possibility to ultimately convert to a traditional job.[40] With the settlement between the UAW and General Motors, Chrysler and Ford were not far behind.[41]

The two-tier system was also a major negotiating point in the 2011 labor agreement between General Motors and the UAW. The agreement allowed GM to hire thousands of new "tier two" employees, who will get about half the pay of longer-serving blue-collar workers for the same work. By 2015, projections are that 36,000 workers will be hired by the Big Three automakers and virtually everyone will be hired at tier-two, entry-level wages and benefits.[42]

The two-tier system has not received universal support and many argue that it is not a long-term wage solution.[43] Some argue that the two-tier contracts will increase employee turnover, lower employee morale, and reduce productivity. Chrysler Group CEO Sergio Marchionne even said, "The automaker's two-tier wage structure with the UAW is not viable over the long run."[44] He hinted that the next round of labor agreements will not include the two-tier system.

two-tier wage system
A wage structure where newly hired workers are paid less than current employees for performing the same or similar jobs.

of these tactics will be discussed later as a means of overcoming breakdowns in negotiations. The party with the greater leverage can expect to extract the most concessions.

Even though one party in the negotiating process may appear to possess the greater power, negotiators often take care to keep the other side from losing face. They recognize that the balance of power may switch rapidly. By the time the next round of negotiations occurs, the pendulum may be swinging back in favor of the other side. Even when management appears to have the upper hand, it may make minor concessions that will allow the labor leader to claim gains for the union. Management may demand that workers pay for grease rags that are lost (assuming that the loss of these rags has become excessive). To obtain labor's agreement to this demand, management may agree to provide new uniforms for the workers if the cost of these uniforms would be less than the cost of lost rags. Thus, labor leaders, although forced to concede to management's demand, could show the workers that they have obtained a concession from management. Each side usually does not expect to obtain all the demands presented in its first proposal. Labor can lose a demand and continue to bring it up in the future. Demands for benefits that the union does not expect to receive when they are first made are known as **beachhead demands**.

beachhead demands
Demands that the union does not expect management to meet when they are first made.

Breakdowns in Negotiations

At times negotiations break down, even though both labor and management may sincerely want to arrive at an equitable contract settlement. Several means of removing roadblocks may be used to get negotiations moving again.

Third-Party Intervention

Often an outside person can intervene to provide assistance when an agreement cannot be reached and the two sides reach an impasse. The reasons behind each party's position may be quite rational, or the breakdown may be related to emotional disputes that tend to become distorted during the heat of negotiations. Regardless of the cause, something must be done to continue the negotiations. The two basic types of third-party intervention are mediation and arbitration.

mediation

Neutral third party enters the negotiations and attempts to facilitate a resolution to a labor dispute when a bargaining impasse has occurred.

MEDIATION In **mediation**, a neutral third party enters the negotiations and attempts to facilitate a resolution to a labor dispute when a bargaining impasse has occurred. A mediator basically acts like a facilitator. The objective of mediation is to persuade the parties to resume negotiations and reach a settlement. A mediator has no power to force a settlement but can help in the search for solutions, make recommendations, and work to open blocked channels of communication. Successful mediation depends to a substantial degree on the tact, diplomacy, patience, and perseverance of the mediator. The mediator's fresh insights are used to get discussions going again. Mediation is voluntary at every step of the process. The mediator serves as an informal coach, helping to ensure that the discussions are fair and effective.

The principal organization involved in mediation efforts, other than some state and local agencies, is the Federal Mediation and Conciliation Service (FMCS). The Taft–Hartley Act established the FMCS as an independent agency. Either one or both parties involved in negotiations can seek the assistance of the FMCS, or the agency can offer its help if it feels that the situation warrants it. Federal law requires that the party wishing to change a contract must give notice of this intention to the other party 60 days prior to the expiration of a contract. If no agreement has been reached 30 days prior to the expiration date, the FMCS must be notified.

arbitration

Process in which a dispute is submitted to an impartial third party for a binding decision; an arbitrator basically acts as a judge and jury.

rights arbitration

Arbitration involving disputes over the interpretation and application of the various provisions of an existing contract.

interest arbitration

Arbitration that involves disputes over the terms of proposed collective bargaining agreements.

ARBITRATION In **arbitration**, a dispute is submitted to an impartial third party for a binding decision; an arbitrator basically acts as a judge and jury. There are two principal types of union management disputes: rights disputes and interest disputes. Disputes over the interpretation and application of the various provisions of an existing contract are submitted to **rights arbitration**, which will be discussed shortly under the heading of "Grievance Procedure in a Union Environment." This type of arbitration is common in the United States.

The other type of arbitration, **interest arbitration**, involves disputes over the terms of proposed collective bargaining agreements. In the private sector, the use of interest arbitration as an alternative for impasse resolution has not been a common practice. Unions and employers rarely agree to submit the basic terms of a contract (such as wages, hours, and working conditions) to a neutral party for disposition. They prefer to rely on collective bargaining and the threat of economic pressure (such as strikes and lockouts) to decide these issues.

For either rights or interest arbitration, the disputants are free to select any person as their arbitrator, so long as they agree on the selection. Most commonly, however, the two sides make a request for an arbitrator to either the American Arbitration Association (AAA) or the FMCS. The AAA is a nonprofit organization with offices in many cities. Both the AAA and the FMCS maintain lists of arbitrators. When considering potential arbitrators, both management and labor will study the arbitrator's previous decisions in an attempt to detect any biases. Obviously, neither party wants to select an arbitrator who might tend to favor the other's position.

HR Web Wisdom

American Arbitration Association
http://www.adr.org/

Provides services to individuals and organizations who wish to resolve conflicts out of court.

After the arbitrator has been selected and has agreed to serve, a time and place for a hearing will be determined. The issue to be resolved will be presented to the arbitrator in a document that summarizes the question(s) to be decided. It will also point out any contract restrictions that prohibit the arbitrator from making an award that would change the terms of the contract.

At the hearing, each side presents its case. Arbitration is an adversarial proceeding, so a case may be lost because of poor preparation and presentation. The arbitrator may conduct the hearing much like a courtroom proceeding. Witnesses, cross-examination, transcripts, and legal counsel may all be used. The parties may also submit or be asked by the arbitrator to submit formal written statements. After the hearing, the arbitrator studies the material submitted and testimony given and is expected to reach a decision within 30 to 60 days. The decision is usually accompanied by a written opinion giving reasons for the decision.

The courts will generally enforce an arbitrator's decision unless (1) the arbitrator's decision is shown to be unreasonable or capricious in that it did not address the issues; (2) the arbitrator exceeded his or her authority; or (3) the award or decision violated a federal or state law. In one arbitration case that ultimately went to the Supreme Court, the arbitrator's decision appeared to run counter to public policy of prohibiting workers who had tested positive for drugs from operating heavy machinery or being permitted to return to work. However, the Supreme Court wrote, "We recognize that reasonable people can differ as to whether reinstatement or discharge is the more appropriate remedy here. But both employer and union have agreed to entrust this remedial decision to an arbitrator."[45]

Union Strategies for Overcoming Negotiation Breakdowns

There are times when a union believes that it must exert extreme pressure to get management to agree to its bargaining demands. Strikes and boycotts are the primary means that the union may use to overcome breakdowns in negotiations.

strike
Action by union members who refuse to work in order to exert pressure on management in negotiations.

STRIKES When union members refuse to work in order to exert pressure on management in negotiations, their action is referred to as a **strike**. A strike halts production, resulting in lost customers and revenue, which the union hopes will force management to submit to its terms. In recent times, strikes have rarely been part of contract negotiation processes. There were 11 strikes involving 1,000 or more workers in 2010, idling approximately 45,000 workers.[46] This is in comparison to the over 200 strikes each year in the 1970s.[47]

The timing of a strike is important in determining its effectiveness. An excellent time is when business is thriving and the demand for the firm's goods or services is expanding. However, the union might be hard-pressed to obtain major concessions from a strike if the firm's sales are down and it has built up a large inventory. In this instance, the company would not be severely damaged.

Contrary to many opinions, unions prefer to use the strike only as a last resort. During a strike, workers have little income. The strike fund may only pay for items such as food, utilities, and motor fuel. In recent years, many union members have been even more reluctant to strike because of the fear of being replaced. When a union goes on an economic strike and the company hires replacements, the company does not have to lay off these individuals at the end of the strike. For example, Edw. C. Levy Co., headquartered in Detroit, Michigan, hired permanent replacements for the 130 members of the International Union of Operating Engineers Local 150 who struck the contractor's operations at Mittal Steel Company's Burns Harbor plant.[48]

A union's treasury is often depleted by payment of strike benefits to its members. In addition, members suffer because they are not receiving their normal pay. Striking workers during one General Motors strike got paid about $150 a week strike pay instead of the roughly $1,000 a week that they normally took home. Although strike pay helps, union members certainly cannot maintain a normal standard of living with these minimal amounts.

Sometimes during negotiations (usually at the beginning), the union may want to strengthen its negotiating position by taking a strike vote. Members often give overwhelming approval to a strike. This vote does not necessarily mean that there will be a strike, only that the union leaders now have the authority to call one if negotiations reach an impasse. A favorable strike vote can add a sense of urgency to efforts to reach an agreement.

Successful passage of a strike vote has additional implications for union members. Virtually every national union's constitution contains a clause requiring the members to support and participate in a strike if one is called. If a union member fails to comply with this requirement, he or she can be fined as high as 100 percent of wages for as long as union pickets remain outside the company. However, the Supreme Court has ruled that an employee on economic strike may resign from the union and avoid being punished by the union. In today's economy, union members are using more subtle measures, such as sick-outs and work slowdowns, to successfully avoid the impact of a strike while still bringing pressure on the company to meet union demands.

boycott
Agreement by union members to refuse to use or buy the firm's products.

BOYCOTTS The boycott is another of labor's weapons to get management to agree to its demands. A **boycott** involves an agreement by union members to refuse to use or buy the firm's products.

A boycott exerts economic pressure on management, and the effect often lasts much longer than that of a strike. Once shoppers change buying habits, their behavior will likely continue long after the boycott has ended. At times, significant pressures can be exerted on a business when union members, their families, and their friends refuse to purchase the firm's products. This approach is especially effective when the products are sold at retail outlets and are easily identifiable by brand name. For instance, the classic boycott against Adolph Coors Company was effective because the name of the product, Coors beer, was directly associated with the company. Ultimately, the AFL-CIO signed an agreement with Coors that ended a labor boycott of the company.[49]

secondary boycott
Union attempt to encourage third parties (such as suppliers and customers) to stop doing business with a firm; declared illegal by the Taft–Hartley Act.

The practice of a union attempting to encourage third parties (such as suppliers and customers) to stop doing business with the company is known as a **secondary boycott**. The Taft–Hartley Act declared this type of boycott to be illegal.

Management Strategies for Overcoming Negotiation Breakdowns

There are times when management believes that it must exert extreme pressure to get the union to back away from a demand. The lockout and operating the firm by placing management and nonunion workers in the striking workers' jobs are the primary means management may use to overcome breakdowns in negotiations.

LOCKOUT Management may use the lockout to encourage unions to come back to the bargaining table. In a **lockout**, management keeps employees out of the workplace and runs the operation with management personnel and/or replacements. In 2011, Cooper Tire & Rubber Company's Findlay tire plant locked out the union workers and began hiring temporary workers to fill any voids.[50] The lockout continued for 13 weeks into 2012 and was costly to both the company and the union. The National Football League and the National Basketball Association used a lockout in an attempt to get players to return to negotiations. Unable to work, the employees do not get paid; the fear of a lockout may bring labor back to the bargaining table. A lockout is particularly effective when management is dealing with a weak union, when the union treasury is depleted, or when the business has excessive inventories. The lockout is also used to inform the union that management is serious regarding certain bargaining issues.

lockout
Management keeps employees out of the workplace and runs the operation with management personnel and/or replacements.

CONTINUE OPERATIONS WITHOUT STRIKING WORKERS A course of action that a company can take if the union goes on strike is to operate the firm by placing management and nonunion workers in the striking workers' jobs. The type of industry involved has considerable effect on the impact of this maneuver. If the firm is not labor-intensive and if maintenance demands are not high, such as at a petroleum refinery or a chemical plant, this practice may be quite effective. When appropriate, management may attempt to show how using nonunion employees can actually increase production. At times, management personnel will actually live in the plant and have food and other necessities delivered to them. This was the situation that occurred when the 900 members of Local 470 of the International Association of Machinists struck the PPG Plant in Lake Charles, Louisiana. Management continued to run the plant with management and contract labor personnel. The union members struck because of an increase in insurance payments and a new hiring-in rate for entry-level workers. Prior to the strike, the local had taken a strike vote, and an overwhelming number of workers had voted in favor of the strike. Later on in negotiations, the union permitted members to vote on whether to accept or reject management's proposal. It was rejected by a majority of the workers. Then management sent registered letters to all union members suggesting that they were not willing to maintain the current work situation, and the company was considering hiring replacement workers. Another vote was taken and the contract was accepted. Prior to the final vote, approximately 100 workers had resigned from the union and crossed the picket line.

OBJECTIVE 12.6
Describe what is involved in reaching, ratifying, and administering the labor–management agreement.

Reaching the Labor–Management Agreement

The document that emerges from the collective bargaining process is known as a "labor–management agreement" or "contract." It regulates the relationship between employer and employees for a specified period of time. It is still an essential but difficult task because each agreement is unique, and there is no standard or universal model.

Ratifying the Labor–Management Agreement

Most collective bargaining leads to an agreement without a breakdown in negotiations or disruptive actions. Typically, agreement is reached before the current contract expires. After the negotiators have reached a tentative agreement on all contract terms, they prepare a written agreement covering those terms, complete with the effective and termination dates. The approval process for management is often easier than for labor. The president or CEO has usually been briefed regularly on the progress of negotiations. Any difficulty that might have stood in the way of obtaining approval has probably already been resolved with top management by the negotiators.

However, the approval process is more complex for the union. Until a majority of members voting in a ratification election approve it, the proposed agreement is not final. At times, union members reject the proposal and a new round of negotiations must begin. Many of these rejections might not occur if union negotiators were better informed about members' desires.

Administration of the Labor–Management Agreement

Negotiating, as it relates to the total collective bargaining process, may be likened to the tip of an iceberg. It is the visible phase, the part that makes the news. The larger and perhaps more important part of collective bargaining is administration of the agreement, which the public seldom sees. The agreement establishes the union–management relationship for the duration of the contract. Usually, neither party can change the contract's language until the expiration date, except by mutual consent. However, the main problem encountered in contract administration is uniform interpretation and application of the contract's terms. Administering the contract is a day-to-day activity. Ideally, the aim of both management and the union is to make the agreement work to the benefit of all concerned. At times, this is not an easy task.

Management is primarily responsible for explaining and implementing the agreement. This process should begin with meetings or training sessions not only to point out significant features but also to provide a clause-by-clause analysis of the contract. First-line supervisors, in particular, need to know their responsibilities and what to do when disagreements arise. In addition, supervisors and middle managers should be encouraged to notify top management of any contract modifications or new provisions required for the next round of negotiations.

The human resource manager or industrial relations manager plays a key role in the day-to-day administration of the contract. He or she gives advice on matters of discipline, works to resolve grievances, and helps first-line supervisors establish good working relationships within the terms of the agreement. When a firm becomes unionized, the human resource manager's function tends to change rather significantly, and may even be divided into separate human resource and industrial relations departments. In such situations, the vice president of human resources may perform all human resource management tasks with the exception of dealing with union-related matters. All nonunion employees would go to the human resource professional for assistance needed. The vice president of industrial relations would likely deal with all union-related matters.

Grievance Procedure in a Union Environment

OBJECTIVE **12.7**

Describe the grievance procedure in a union environment.

As previously defined, a *grievance procedure* is a formal, systematic process that permits employees to express complaints without jeopardizing their jobs. A grievance procedure under a collective bargaining agreement is normally well defined. It is usually restricted to violations of the terms and conditions of the agreement. There are other conditions that may give rise to a grievance, including the following:

- A violation of law
- A violation of the intent of the parties as stipulated during contract negotiations
- A violation of company rules
- A change in working conditions or past company practices
- A violation of health and/or safety standards

Grievance procedures have many common features. However, variations may reflect differences in organizational or decision-making structures or the size of a plant or company. Some general principles based on widespread practice can serve as useful guidelines for effective grievance administration:

- Grievances should be adjusted promptly.
- Procedures and forms used for airing grievances must be easy to use and well understood by employees and their supervisors.
- Direct and timely avenues of appeal from rulings of line supervision must exist.

The multistep grievance procedure is the most common type. In the first step, the employee usually presents the grievance orally and informally to the immediate supervisor in the presence of the union steward. This step offers the greatest potential for improved labor relations, and a large majority of grievances are settled here. The procedure ends if the grievance is resolved at this initial step. If the grievance remains unresolved, the next step involves a meeting between the plant manager or human resource manager and higher union officials, such as the grievance committee or the business agent or manager. Prior to this meeting, the grievance is written out, dated, and signed by the employee and the union steward. The written grievance states the events, as the employee perceives them, cites the contract provision that allegedly has been violated, and indicates the settlement desired. If the grievance is not settled at this meeting, it moves to the third step, which typically involves the firm's top labor representative (such as the vice president of industrial relations) and high-level union officials. At times, depending on the severity of the grievance, the president may represent the firm. Arbitration is the final step in most grievance procedures. In arbitration, the parties submit their dispute to an impartial third party for binding resolution. Most agreements restrict the arbitrator's decision to application and interpretation of the agreement and the final decision is binding on both parties. If the union decides in favor of arbitration, it notifies management. At this point, the union and the company select an arbitrator.[51]

When arbitration is used to settle a grievance, a variety of factors may be considered to evaluate the fairness of the management actions that caused the grievance. Some factors include:

- Nature of the offense
- Due process and procedural correctness
- Double jeopardy
- Past record of grievant
- Length of service with the company
- Knowledge of rules
- Warnings
- Lax enforcement of rule
- Discriminatory treatment

The large number of interacting variables in each case makes the arbitration process difficult. The arbitrator must possess exceptional patience and judgment in rendering a fair and impartial decision.

Labor relations problems can escalate when a supervisor is not equipped to handle grievances at the first step. Since the union steward, the aggrieved party, and the supervisor usually handle the first step informally, the supervisor must be fully prepared. The supervisor should obtain as many facts as possible before the meeting, because the union steward is likely to have also done his or her homework.

The supervisor needs to recognize that the grievance may not reflect the real problem. For instance, the employee might be angry with the company for modifying its pay policies, even though the union agreed to the change. To voice discontent, the worker might file a grievance for an unrelated minor violation of the contract.

Any disciplinary action administered may ultimately be taken to arbitration, when such a remedy is specified in the labor agreement. Employers have learned that they must prepare records that will constitute proof of disciplinary action and the reasons for it. Although the formats of written warnings may vary, all should include the following information:

1. Statement of facts concerning the offense
2. Identification of the rule that was violated
3. Statement of what resulted or could have resulted because of the violation
4. Identification of any previous similar violations by the same individual

FIGURE 12-4

Example of a Written Warning

Date: August 1, 2013

To: Wayne Sanders

From: Judy Bandy

Subject: Written Warning

We are quite concerned because today you were thirty minutes late to work and offered no justification for this. According to our records, a similar offense occurred on July 25, 2013. At that time, you were informed that failure to report to work on time is unacceptable. I am, therefore, notifying you in writing that you must report to work on time. It will be necessary to terminate your employment if this happens again.

Please sign this form to indicate that you have read and understand this warning. Signing is not an indication of agreement.

_____
Name

_____
Date

5. Statement of possible future consequences should the violation occur again
6. Signature and date

An example of a written warning is shown in Figure 12-4. In this instance, the worker has already received an oral reprimand. The individual is also warned that continued tardiness could lead to termination. It is important to document oral reprimands because they may be the first step in disciplinary action leading ultimately to arbitration.

OBJECTIVE **12.8**

Explain recent labor–management legal trends and describe collective bargaining in the public sector.

Recent Labor–Management Legal Trends

President Obama has signed four executive orders that impact federal government contractors. These orders require the following: (1) all federal contractors must post notices informing employees of their rights to form and join unions (EO 13496)[52]; (2) all federal contractors may not seek reimbursement for funds spent on influencing employees regarding unionization (EO 13494); (3) all federal contractors succeeding to a service contract must provide job opportunities to employees of the previous service contractor (EO 13495); and recommending that federal agencies taking bids for government construction projects in excess of $25 million to accept only those from contractors who agree in advance to a project labor agreement that requires a union workforce (EO 13502).[53] See the HRM in Action at the beginning of the chapter which discussed project labor agreements.

EO 13494 impacts all federal contractors and mandates that costs associated with so-called persuader activities designed to influence employees to join or not join a union are *not reimbursable* by the federal government under the government's contract with the employer. Examples of "unallowable" costs include (a) preparing and distributing materials; (b) hiring or consulting legal counsel or consultants; (c) holding meetings with employees; and (d) planning or conducting activities by managers, supervisors, or union representatives during work hours. Federal contractors are not prohibited from engaging in promotion activities, but they may not seek reimbursement for these expenses.[54]

Collective Bargaining in the Public Sector

Executive Order 10988 established the basic framework for collective bargaining in federal government agencies. Title VII of the Civil Service Reform Act of 1978 regulates most of the labor–management relations in the federal service. It establishes the Federal Labor Relations Authority (FLRA), which is modeled after the National Labor Relations Board. The intent of the FLRA is to bring the public-sector model in line with that of the private sector. Requirements and mechanisms for recognition and elections, dealing with impasses, and handling grievances are covered in the act. Collective bargaining for federal unions has traditionally been quite different from private-sector bargaining because wages were off the table. President Franklin D. Roosevelt recognized that the bargaining relationship that exists in the private sector cannot also exist in the public sector saying, it "cannot be transplanted into the public service ... The employer is the whole people."[55] Title V of the U.S. Code, the law that dictates rules for federal employees, did not allow bargaining over wage issues, except for the U.S. Postal Service.

There is no uniform pattern to state and local bargaining rights. More than two-thirds of the states have enacted legislation granting public-sector collective bargaining rights to some groups such as teachers, police, and firefighters. However, the diversity of state labor laws makes it difficult to generalize about the legal aspects of collective bargaining at the state and local levels.

In the public sector, most governmental jurisdictions prohibit their employees from striking. This was vigorously pointed out in the 1981 strike by air traffic controllers where President Ronald Reagan used replacement workers to end the first declared national strike against the federal government. The Professional Air Traffic Controllers Organization (PATCO) sacrificed a substantial pay increase, a generous benefit package, and its very existence in its attempt to legitimize strikes in the public sector.[56] As a result, interest arbitration is used to a greater extent than in the private sector, although there is no uniform application of this method. A procedure used in the public sector is **final-offer arbitration**, which has two basic forms: package selection and issue-by-issue selection. In package selection, the arbitrator must select one party's entire offer on all issues in dispute. In issue-by-issue selection, the arbitrator examines each issue separately and chooses the final offer of one side or the other on each issue. Final-offer arbitration is often used to determine the salary of a professional baseball player. Both players and management present a dollar figure to an arbitrator. The arbitrator chooses one figure or the other.

final-offer arbitration
An arbitration procedure used in the public sector whereby the arbitrator must select one party's offer either as a package or issue-by-issue selection.

Union Decertification

OBJECTIVE **12.9**
Explain union decertification.

decertification
Reverse of the process that employees must follow to be recognized as an official bargaining unit.

Until 1947, once a union was certified, it was certified forever. However, the Taft–Hartley Act made it possible for employees to decertify a union. **Decertification** is the reverse of the process that employees must follow to be recognized as an official bargaining unit. It results in a union losing its right to act as the exclusive bargaining representative of a group of employees. As union membership has declined, the need for decertification elections has also diminished.

The rules established by the NLRB spell out the conditions for filing a decertification petition; it is essentially the reverse of obtaining union recognition. At least 30 percent of the bargaining unit members must petition for an election. As might be expected, this task by itself may be difficult because union supporters are likely to strongly oppose the move. Few employees know about decertification and fewer still know how to start the process. Also, although the petitioners' names are supposed to remain confidential, many union members are fearful that their signatures on the petition will be discovered. The timing of the NLRB's receipt of the decertification petition is also critical. The petition must be submitted between 60 and 90 days prior to the expiration of the current contract. When all these conditions have been met, the NLRB regional director will schedule a decertification election by secret ballot.

The NLRB carefully monitors the events leading up to the election. Current employees must initiate the request for the election. This is what happened regarding professional football when the National Football League Players Association (NFLPA) decertified in March 2011. If the NLRB determines that management initiated the action, it will not certify the election. After a petition has been accepted, however, management can support the decertification election attempt. If a majority of the votes cast is against the union, the employees will be free from the union. Strong union supporters are all likely to vote. Thus, if a substantial number of employees are indifferent to the union and choose not to vote, decertification may not occur.

OBJECTIVE **12.10**

Describe the state of unions today and discuss labor unrest in China.

Unions Today

The latest figures from the Labor Department's Bureau of Labor Statistics showed that the percentage of wage and salary workers who were members of a union was 11.8 percent, essentially unchanged from 11.9 percent in 2010. The number of wage and salary workers belonging to unions, at 14.8 million, also showed little movement over the year. In 1983, the first year for which comparable union data are available, the union membership rate was 20.1 percent and there were 17.7 million union workers.

In 2011, 7.6 million public-sector employees belonged to a union, compared with 7.2 million union workers in the private sector. Public-sector workers had a union membership rate of 37.0 percent, more than five times higher than that of the private-sector workers rate of 6.9 percent (Figure 12.5). Private-sector industries with high unionization rates included transportation and utilities (21.1 percent) and construction (14.0 percent), whereas low unionization rates occurred in agriculture and related industries (1.4 percent) and in financial activities (1.6 percent).[57]

The recent labor agreement between the UAW and General Motors offers early-retirement buy-outs to thousands of costly skilled workers the firm no longer needs. It gives each of GM's 48,500 production-line workers a $5,000 lump sum now and about $4,000 more spread over four years, plus a slightly higher share of profits. But GM has not had to concede any increase in basic pay. The next contract talks, in 2015, will in effect start with pay reset at the levels of the early 2000s.[58]

Remember my earlier discussion of "Recent Labor–Management Legal Trends" stated that significant changes affecting unions had been made by the new administration. The new NLRB had been reestablished with members who are pro labor. Also, four EOs that favored labor have been signed. Because of these and other pending measures, there are those who believe that labor will experience a membership surge.

FIGURE 12-5

Percentage of the Private Workforce That Is Unionized

Source: U.S. Department of Labor.

A GLOBAL PERSPECTIVE

Labor Unrest in China

The All-China Federation of Trade Unions (ACFTU) is China's only government-recognized union. The recent recession caused the ACFTU to hold up its unionization drives, but it appears that it has resumed its efforts to unionize foreign-invested enterprises. The ACFTU is putting pressure on foreign-invested enterprises to establish unions and sign collective contracts with their employees. Under the People's Republic of China (PRC) Trade Union Law, the employer, not employees, contributes union dues if the company is not unionized. The pressure to unionize through the collection of union dues is likely to continue with the support of ACFTU.[59]

Perhaps because of the renewed push to promote collective bargaining agreements, strikes and protests at factories have become more commonplace. *Outlook Weekly,* an official government publication, reported that labor disputes in Guangdong in the first quarter of 2009 had risen by nearly 42 percent over 2008; and in the Zhejiang province, the annualized increase was almost 160 percent.[60]

A succession of strikes occurred at several factories in Guangdong and China's coastal regions. The strike that received the most attention happened at Honda Motor Company factories in several Guangdong cities. Workers demanded higher wages and better working conditions. Honda gave in providing a 24 percent pay increase, prompting work stoppages at several other facilities.[61]

Humiliation caused by a series of suicides at Foxconn, a subsidiary of Taiwan's Hon Hai Precision Industry Company, forced the company to give a 30 percent pay increase. The suicides were apparently in response to poor working conditions at the firm.[62] The new generation of Chinese factory workers, born during the 1980s and 1990s, are more sensitive to social issues and workplace rights than their parents. Previous generations might have taken any job available, even for low salaries. But these young workers are seeking jobs that not only pay well but also provide a better life for their families, provide career development, and treat employees with respect.

By 2009, 85 percent of the Fortune 500 companies operating in China had been unionized, including Walmart, a firm that has gained a reputation as being anti-union. Chinese union membership grew from 87 million members in 1999 to 212 million members in 2008.[63] The ACFTU reported that by the end of 2009 more than 1.2 million collective contracts were signed involving more than 2 million enterprises and nearly 162 million workers nationwide.

Two years after the strikes and suicides that rocked manufacturers in China, labor problems are again occurring and appear to be happening daily. For example, in late 2011, approximately 7,000 workers at a Taiwanese-owned New Balance supplier in Dongguan protested plans to relocate production to Jiangxi province and cut bonuses. Willie Fung, chairman of Hong Kong bra-maker Top Form International, said, "As the environment goes from bad to worse, a lot of factories want to find a way out. They want to downsize, shut down, or move somewhere else, and this sparks labor disputes." China's leaders are generally not in favor of these strikes because they fear that they will cause social unrest.[64]

MyManagementLab

Go to **mymanagementlab.com** to complete the problems marked with this icon ⭐.

Summary

1. *Describe project labor agreements and explain why employees join unions.* A *project labor agreement* is a prehire collective bargaining agreement between construction firm owners and one or more labor organizations establishing the terms and conditions of employment for a specific construction project.

    Employees join unions because of dissatisfaction with management, the need for a social outlet, the need for avenues of leadership, forced unionization, and social pressure from peers.

2. *Describe organized labor's strategies for a stronger movement and explain the basic structure of a union.* Organized labor's new strategies for a stronger movement include strategically located union members, pulling the union through, political involvement, union salting,

flooding the community, public awareness campaigns, building organizing funds, partnering with high schools, and organizing through the card check.

    The basic element in the structure of the American labor movement is the local union. The national union is the most powerful level, and the American Federation of Labor and Congress of Industrial Organizations (AFL-CIO) is the central trade union federation in the United States.

3. *Discuss laws affecting collective bargaining, including revisiting the NLRB and pay secrecy, and identify the steps that lead to establishing the collective bargaining relationship.* The National Labor Relations Act (Wagner Act) of 1935 is one of the most significant labor–management relations statutes ever enacted. The act declared legislative support, on a broad scale,

for the right of employees to organize and engage in collective bargaining. The Taft–Hartley Act extensively revised the National Labor Relations Act. A new period began in the evolution of public policy regarding labor.

The NLRB has recently been thrust into the forefront stemming from a pattern of controversial decisions that have significantly influenced labor–management activities. Many believe that the board is promoting the interests and political agenda of labor unions.

The NLRB and the courts have declared many times that employers violate the National Labor Relations Act if they issue verbal or written statements that discourage or prohibit nonsupervisory employees from discussing their pay with each other or the media.

The steps involved include signing authorization cards, petitioning for election, campaigning, winning the election, and being certified.

4. *Describe the collective bargaining process and explain collective bargaining issues.* The negotiating phase of collective bargaining begins with each side presenting its initial demands. The term *negotiating* suggests a certain amount of give-and-take. The party with the greater leverage can expect to extract the most concessions. Breakdowns in negotiations can be overcome through third-party intervention (mediation and arbitration), union tactics (strikes and boycotts), and management recourse (lockouts and continued operation without striking workers).

Bargaining issues can be divided into three categories: mandatory, permissive, and prohibited. Certain topics are included in virtually all labor agreements. These are recognition, management rights, union security, compensation, grievance procedure, employee security, and job-related factors.

5. *Describe preparation for negotiations, negotiating the agreement, the two-tier wage system, and breakdowns in negotiations.* The union must continuously gather information regarding membership needs to isolate areas of dissatisfaction. Management also spends long hours preparing for negotiations.

The negotiating phase of collective bargaining begins with each side presenting its initial demands. The term *negotiating* suggests a certain amount of give-and-take. The party with the greater leverage can expect to extract the most concessions.

The *two-tier wage system* is a wage structure where newly hired workers are paid less than current employees for performing the same or similar jobs.

Breakdowns in negotiations can be overcome through third-party intervention (mediation and arbitration), union tactics (strikes and boycotts), and management recourse (lockouts and continued operation without striking workers).

6. *Describe what is involved in reaching, ratifying, and administering the labor–management agreement.* The document that emerges from the collective bargaining process is known as a "labor–management agreement" or "contract."

The approval process for management is often easier than for labor. The president or CEO has usually been briefed regularly on the progress of negotiations. However, the approval process is more complex for the union. Until a majority of members voting in a ratification election approve it, the proposed agreement is not final.

The larger and perhaps more important part of collective bargaining is administration of the agreement, which the public seldom sees. The agreement establishes the union–management relationship for the duration of the contract.

7. *Describe the grievance procedure in a union environment.* A grievance procedure under a collective bargaining agreement is normally well defined. It is usually restricted to violations of the terms and conditions of the agreement.

8. *Explain recent labor–management legal trends and describe collective bargaining in the public sector.* President Obama has signed four executive orders that will greatly impact federal government contractors.

Since the 2008 presidential election, the NLRB has been reconstituted and has resumed a full caseload. Many believe that the board is promoting the interests and political agenda of labor unions.

Collective bargaining for workers in the public sector has traditionally been quite different from private-sector bargaining because wages have been off the table.

9. *Explain union decertification.* Decertification is essentially the reverse of the process that employees must follow to be recognized as an official bargaining unit.

10. *Describe the state of unions today and discuss labor unrest in China.* In 2011, 7.6 million public-sector employees belonged to a union, compared with 7.2 million union workers in the private sector. Public-sector workers had a union membership rate of 37.0 percent, more than five times higher than that of the private-sector workers rate of 6.9 percent. Private-sector industries with high unionization rates included transportation and utilities (21.1 percent) and construction (14.0 percent), whereas low unionization rates occurred in agriculture and related industries (1.4 percent) and in financial activities (1.6 percent).

The All-China Federation of Trade Unions (ACFTU) is China's only government-recognized union. The recent recession caused the ACFTU to hold up its unionization drives, but it appears that it has resumed its efforts to unionize foreign-invested enterprises. The ACFTU is putting pressure on foreign-invested enterprises to establish unions and sign collective contracts with their employees. Under the People's Republic of China (PRC) Trade Union Law, the employer, not employees, contributes union dues if the company is not unionized. The pressure to unionize through the collection of union dues is likely to continue with the support of ACFTU.

Key Terms

Exercises

1. How easy do you believe the following firms would be for unionization (assuming that they are not already unionized)? Explain your rationale.
   a. McDonald's
   b. Chevrolet dealership
   c. Toyota USA
   d. Delta pilots

2. This is a role-playing exercise involving a union member (you) and a new hire in a right-to-work state. Your job is to convince the new hire that joining the union is in his or her best interest.

3. This is a role-playing exercise involving a long-term employee (you) and a new hire in a right-to-work state. Your job is to convince the new hire that not joining the union is in his or her best interest.

Questions for Review

1. What are organized labor's strategies for a stronger movement?
2. Define the following terms:
   (a) local union
   (b) craft union
   (c) industrial union
   (d) national union
3. What is the difference between the National Labor Relations Act and the Labor–Management Relations Act?
4. Why has the NLRB recently been thrust into the forefront with regard to labor relations?
5. Why is pay secrecy discussed in conjunction with the NLRB?
6. What steps must a union take in establishing the collective bargaining relationship? Briefly describe each step.
7. What are the steps involved in the collective bargaining process?
8. Distinguish among mandatory, permissive, and prohibited bargaining issues.
9. What are topics included in virtually all labor agreements?
10. Define each of the following:
    (a) closed shop

   (b) union shop
   (c) agency shop
   (d) maintenance of membership
   (e) checkoff of dues
   (f) two-tier wage system
11. What are the primary means by which breakdowns in negotiations may be overcome? Briefly describe each.
12. What is involved for both management and labor in ratifying the agreement?
13. What is involved in the administration of a labor agreement?
14. What is typically involved in the grievance procedure in a unionized organization?
15. What are some recent labor–management legal trends?
16. How is the collective bargaining process different in the public sector?
17. Define *decertification*. What are the steps in decertification?
18. What is the status of unions today?

INCIDENT 1 Break Down the Barrier

Yesterday, Angelica Angulo was offered a job as a waitress with GEM Hotel Corporation, located in Las Vegas, Nevada. She had recently graduated from high school in Milford, a small town in New Mexico. Since Angelica had no college aspirations upon graduation, she had moved to Las Vegas to look for a job.

Angelica's immediate supervisor spent only a short time with her before turning her over to Laurie Rader, an experienced waitress, for training. After they had talked for a short time, Laurie asked, "Have you given any thought to joining our union? You'll like all of our members."

Angelica had not considered this. Moreover, she had never associated with union members, and her parents had never been members either. At Milford High, her teachers had never really talked about unions. The fact that this union operated as an open shop meant nothing to her. Angelica replied, "I don't know. Maybe. Maybe not."

The day progressed much the same way, with several people asking Angelica the same question. They were all friendly, but there seemed to be a barrier that separated Angelica from the other workers. One worker looked Angelica right in the eyes and said, "You're going to join, aren't you?" Angelica still did not know, but she was beginning to lean in that direction.

After the end of her shift, Angelica went to the washroom. Just as she entered, Stephanie Clements, the union steward, also walked in. After they exchanged greetings, Stephanie said, "I hear that you're not sure about joining our union. You, and everyone else, reap the benefits of the work we've done in the past. It doesn't seem fair for you to be rewarded for what others have done. Tell you what, why don't you join us down at the union hall tonight? We'll discuss it more then."

Angelica nodded yes and finished cleaning up. "That might be fun," she thought.

Questions

1. Why does Angelica have the option of joining or not joining the union? Hint: Nevada is a right-to-work state.
2. What are the pros and cons regarding Angelica joining the union?
3. How are the other workers likely to react toward Angelica if she chooses not to join? Discuss.

INCIDENT 2 You Are Out of What?

Marcus Ned eagerly drove his new company pickup onto the construction site. His employer, Kelso Construction Company, had just assigned him to supervise a crew of 16 equipment operators, oilers, and mechanics. This was the first unionized crew Marcus had supervised, and he was unaware of the labor agreement in effect that carefully defined and limited the role of supervisors. As he approached his work area, he noticed one of the cherry pickers (a type of mobile crane with an extendable boom) standing idle with the operator beside it. Marcus pulled up beside the operator and asked, "What's going on here?"

"Out of gas," the operator said.

"Well, go and get some," Marcus said.

The operator reached to get his thermos jug out of the toolbox on the side of the crane and said, "The oiler's on break right now. He'll be back in a few minutes."

Marcus remembered that he had a five-gallon can of gasoline in the back of his pickup. So he quickly got the gasoline, climbed on the cherry picker, and started to pour it into the gas tank. As he did so, he heard the other machines shutting down in unison. He looked around and saw all the other operators climbing down from their equipment and standing to watch him pour the gasoline. A moment later, he saw the union steward approaching.

Questions

1. Why did all the operators shut down their machines?
2. If you were Marcus, what would you do now?

MyManagementLab

Go to **mymanagementlab.com** for Auto-graded writing questions as well as the following Assisted-graded writing questions:

12-1. What is the purpose of a project labor agreement?

12-2. What are the primary reasons employees join labor unions?

12-3. Mymanagementlab Only – comprehensive writing assignment for this chapter.

Notes

1. Federal Register / Vol. 74, No. 27 /Wednesday, February 11, 2009 / Presidential Documents, Executive Order 13502 of February 6, 2009, Use of Project Labor Agreements for Federal Construction Projects.

2. David G. Tuerck, "Why Project Labor Agreements Are Not in the Public Interest," *CATO Journal* 30 (Winter 2010): 45–65.

3. Deena C. Malley, "Constructing Change," *Central Penn Business Journal* 27 (March 25, 2011): 23–25.

4. Robert Brodsky, "Labor Fight Renewed," *Government Executive* 43 (May 2011): 16–17.

5. "Army Corps Projects Defy Unions' Upbeat Labor Agreement Tally," *Concrete Products* 113 (October 2010): 8.

6. "Fiduciary Duties," *Benefits Magazine* 48 (August 2011): 32–38.

7. "Army Corps Projects Defy Unions' Upbeat Labor Agreement Tally," *Concrete Products* 113 (October 2010): 8.

8. "SSCC Workers Ok Deal to Unionize," *Official Board Markets* 86 (April 17, 2010): 16.

9. Victoria Neal, Inga Y. Fong, and John Sweeney, "Strikebreaking, Providing Toilets, Job Postings," *HR Magazine* 55 (December 2010): 24–25.

10. Mark Mix, "A Right to Work in Indiana," *Investor's Business Daily* (February 3, 2012): A15.

11. Joann Muller, "Has the UAW Found a Better Road?" *BusinessWeek* 3791 (July 15, 2002): 108.

12. Jessica Marquez, "As Elections Near, Unions Look to Sway Senate Races," *Workforce Management* 87 (April 21, 2008): 6.

13. Mark McKinnoon, "Do We Still Need Unions? No," *Newsweek* 157 (March 7, 2011): 19.

14. Michael Learmonth and Ira Teinowitz, "Court Ruling to Deliver $300M Boost to Media," *Advertising Age* 81 (January 25, 2010): 1.

15. Daryll J. Neuser and Daniel D. Barker, "What Every Employer Should Know About the Law of Union Organizing," *Employee Relations Law Journal* 35 (Spring 2010): 3–45.

16. Arthur B. Shostak, "PATCO's 1981 Strike," *Labor Studies Journal* 34 (June 2009): 149–158.

17. "Unions Takes Proactive Approach to Training," *Plant Engineering* 63 (October 2009): 8.

18. Rachel Haut, Natalie Kelly, and Max Mishler, "Youth Activism in the Labor Movement," *New Labor Forum* 18 (Winter 2009): 98–107.

19. Richard. L. Trumka, "Selling Unions to Young Workers," *Vital Speeches of the Day* 75 (October 2009): 475–478.

20. "UPS Freight Workers Become Teamsters," *Toledo Business Journal* 24 (April 2008): 24–28.

21. "Teamsters Ratify UPS Freight Contract," *Florida Shipper* 33 (April 21, 2008): 13.

22. http://www.seiu.org/our-union/

23. http://www.teamster.org/content/fast-facts

24. http://www.afl-cio.org/aboutus/

25. http://www.changetowin.org/about

26. Stephanie Armour and Holly Rosenkrantz, "A Backlash Looms for the Federal Labor Board," *Bloomberg Businessweek* (February 14, 2011): 26–27.

27. Bill Leonard, "Some See Labor Board Favoring Unions," *HR Magazine* 56 (April 2011): 14.

28. "With Membership Bottoming Out, What Does the Future Hold?" *HR Focus* 88 (April 2011): 13–15.

29. Douglas Gilbert, "Expedited Union Elections," *HR Magazine* 57 (April 2012): 77–78.

30. "NLRB Finds Arbitration Provision Unlawful, Calling Class Action Ban NLRA Interference," *HR Focus* 89 (February 2012): 8.

31. "NLRB Nullifies Vote at Independent," *Supermarket News* 59 (January 10, 2011): 6.

32. "NLRB's Solomon Issues Update, Covers Employer Dos and Don'ts," *HR Focus* 89 (March 2012): 7–8.

33. "Don't Bully Boeing, Barack," *Economist* 398 (May 21, 2011): 15–16.

34. "A Labor Complaint That Just Won't Fly," *Bloomberg Businessweek* (June 20, 2011): 10.

35. "Boeing Bullied," *Economist* 401 (December 17, 2011): 115.

36. "Having Their Say on Pay," *Workforce Management* 90 (January 2011): 22–23.

37. *A Guide to Basic Law and Procedures under the National Labor Relations Act* (Washington, D.C.: U.S. Government Printing Office, October 1978): 11–13.

38. T. L. Stanley, "Union Stewards and Labor Relations," *Supervision* 71 (February 2010): 3–6.

39. Shane R. Premeaux, R. Wayne Mondy, and Art L. Bethke, "The Two-Tier Wage System: A Major Breakthrough in the Reindustrialization of America?" *Personnel Administrator* 31 (November 1986): 92–100.

40. Thomas C. Graham, "The GM/UAW Contract: Winners, Losers, Lost Chances," *American Metal Market* 116 (December 2007): 98.

41. David Barkholz and Amy Wilson, "Ford: Benefits of Two-Tier Wages Won't Come Until 2009," *Automotive News* 82 (February 11, 2008): 15.

42. Adam Bruns, "Steep Hill to Climb," *Site Selection* 56 (May/June 2011): 411–415.

43. "2-Tier Time Limit," *Automotive News* 86 (November 7, 2011): 12.

44. Bradford Wernle and David Phillips, "2-Tier Wage Structure Isn't Viable," *Automotive News* 86 (October 31, 2011): 10.

45. "Arbitrator's Decision Upheld," *Business Insurance* 34 (December 4, 2000): 2.

46. http://www.bls.gov/news.release/wkstp.t02.htm

47. Elizabeth A. Ashack, "Profiles of Significant Collective Bargaining Disputes of 2009," *Compensation & Working Conditions* (March 2010): 1.

48. Andrea Holecek, "Levy Co. Replaces Striking Steel Workers, Fires Others," *The Times* (March 29, 2006).

49. Heather Draper, "Coors Facing New Boycott: Workers at Brewer's Supplier Locked Out after Pact Expired," *Rocky Mountain News* (September 24, 2002): 6B.

50. William Schertz, "New Year, Same Old Struggle at Cooper Plant," *Rubber & Plastics News* 41 (January 9, 2012): 1.

51. Charles A. Borell, "How Unions Can Improve Their Success Rate in Labor Arbitration," *Dispute Resolution Journal* 61 (February 2006): 28–38.

52. "Fed Contractors Will Have to Post 'Right to Unionize' Notice," *HR Specialist: Texas Employment Law* 5 (March 2010): 1–5.

53. http://www.archives.gov/federal-register/executive-orders/2009-obama.html May 5, 2010.

54. "New Executive Orders on Labor Relations Will Impact All Federal Contractors," *Venulex Legal Summaries* (2009 Q1, Special section): 1–2.

55. Nina Easton, "Labor Unions: Flailing in D.C. and Making Enemies on Main Street," *Fortune* 163 (March 21, 2011): 68.

56. Michael R. Carrell and Christina Heavrin, *Labor Relations and Collective Bargaining: Cases, Practices, and Law* (Prentice Hall: Upper Saddle River, N.J.: 2010): 241.

57. http://www.bls.gov/news.release/union2.nr0.htm

58. "A Sadder, Wiser Union," *Economist* 400 (September 24, 2011): 75–76.

59. Lesli K. Ligorner and Todd Shengqiang Liao, "Unionization and Collective Bargaining: New Tools for Social Harmony," *China Business Review* 37 (November/December 2010): 28–31.

60. "Strike Breakers," *Economist* 395 (June 5, 2010): 48.

61. Luming Chen and Samuel Estreicher, "A New Labor Era: Higher Costs and Greater Pressures," *China Business Review* 38 (April-June 2011):26–29.

62. "The Next China," *Economist* 396 (July 31, 2010): 48–50.

63. Mingwei Liu, "Union Organizing in China: Still a Monolithic Labor Movement," *Industrial & Labor Relations Review* 64 (October 2010): 30–52.

64. Dexter Roberts and Bruce Einhorn, "Using Propaganda to Stop China's Strikes," *Bloomberg Businessweek* (December 19, 2011): 15–16.

13

Internal Employee Relations

HRM in Action

Worker Retention: Keeping Your Top Performers

OBJECTIVE 13.1

Describe the importance of worker retention and define *internal employee relations.*

Smart organizations know that voluntary turnover of their most talented workers can put an already challenged organization into an even more shaky position. The recent recession caused a reduction in the global workforce, and workers who had jobs chose to stay even if they really wanted to leave.[1] This take-it-or-leave-it retention strategy left many companies with a false sense of security, believing that their workers would not leave. These companies may be in for a shock as the economy recovers. Lisa B. Peters, chief human resources officer of BNY Mellon, said, "The immediate cost of losing talented employees is significant and can be quantified relatively accurately. The long-term costs are more difficult to calculate, and they can have serious consequences."[2] This could be a problem because a recent MetLife study revealed that one in three employees hopes to be working for another company in the next 12 months.[3] Dr. Ron Leopold, vice president and national medical director for MetLife Inc., said, "Observers eventually expect to see a 'résumé tsunami.' They are not feeling the love."[4]

The key to successful retention is to focus on top performers and determine their risk of leaving. Likely these workers are already being recruited and they probably know their value in the job market. There will always be opportunities elsewhere for a firm's best employees.[5]

Some organizations are using high retention bonuses to retain talented people, and an amazing array of perks and benefits are being offered. But, providing money or benefits may not be enough to keep them.[6] It is not just money and benefits that high potential workers look for; those are easy to obtain by simply moving to another company. Roland Smith, lead researcher at the Center for Creative Leadership in Colorado Springs, Colorado, said, "What they're looking for instead are the things that truly differentiate employers. These include opportunities to more directly influence and direct their careers and more-challenging assignments with real risks and rewards."[7]

A culture must be created where the best employees feel valued, respected, and supported. Al Maag, chief communications officer at Avnet, said, "We must make our employee experience a good one, ranging from giving them challenging assignments to providing the right tools, fair pay and training investments for their careers."[8]

Throughout this book, many topics have been discussed that, by themselves, may not appear to be a retention strategy. But, virtually every topic can be viewed in some manner as being a part of a total retention strategy. Let us see how some topics highlighted in the text might affect retention.

- A corporate culture or employer brand in which workers believe "it's fun to work at this company."
- Organizations that have a reputation for being ethically and socially responsible.
- Organizations that encourage workplace diversity.
- Organizations that let employees become aware of new job opportunities.
- Organizations that emphasize promotion from within.
- Employers that seek employees who "fit" into the organizational culture.
- Organizations that encourage employees to continue to grow and learn.
- Organizations that assess and reward employees based on their performance.
- Organizations that pay a fair wage based on employee productivity.
- Employers that create a balanced work–life environment.
- Organizations that provide employees with a safe and healthy work environment.
- Organizations that create a work environment where employees believe they do not need a union to represent them.
- Organizations with an internal employee administration program that is fair to all involved.

Managers play a pivotal role in an individual's retention decision. Throughout your text, the topic of metrics has been addressed. The most important metric in HR today is the retention rate of a firm's most qualified employees, the individuals who are capable of taking an organization to new heights.

Internal Employee Relations Defined

internal employee relations
Those human resource management activities associated with the movement of employees within the organization.

The status of most workers is not permanently fixed in an organization. Employees constantly move upward, laterally, downward, and out of the organization. To ensure that workers with the proper skills and experience are available at all levels, constant and concerted efforts are required to maintain good internal employee relations. **Internal employee relations** comprise the human resource management activities associated with the movement of employees within the organization. Such topics include discipline and disciplinary action, termination, demotion, downsizing, transfers, promotions, and retirement.

Employment at will is first discussed as a factor affecting internal employee relations.

OBJECTIVE 13.2
Explain the concept of employment at will.

Employment at Will

employment at will
Unwritten contract created when an employee agrees to work for an employer but no agreement exists as to how long the parties expect the employment to last.

Employment at will is an unwritten contract created when an employee agrees to work for an employer but no agreement exists as to how long the parties expect the employment to last. Essentially at-will employees can quit any time they want and a company can terminate an at-will employee for no reason. Certainly there are numerous hiring standards to avoid such as race, religion, sex, national origin, age, and disabilities. Notwithstanding various employment standards to avoid that are based on laws, court decisions, and executive orders, approximately two of every three U.S. workers depend almost entirely on the continued goodwill of their employer. Individuals falling into this category are known as "at-will employees." Not included are individuals with a contract for a specified period of time such as with collective bargaining agreements. Teachers usually have an annual contract and are not at-will employees. The Sarbanes–Oxley Act contains broad employee whistleblower protection. Thus, employees who report an illegal act, such as whistleblowers, are not subject to employment at will. However, much of the U.S. legal system presumes that the jobs of such employees may be terminated at the will of the employer and that these employees have a similar right to leave their jobs at any time. Historically, because of a century-old common-law precedent in the United States, employment of indefinite duration could, in general, be terminated at the whim of either party.

The courts have made certain exceptions to the employment-at-will doctrine. One of these is permitting employees to bring claims based on statements made in employment handbooks. Employers can do certain things to help protect themselves against litigation for wrongful discharge based on a breach of implied employment contract. Statements in documents such as employment applications and policy manuals that suggest job security or permanent employment should be avoided if employers want to minimize charges of wrongful discharge. Telling a person during a job interview that he or she can expect to hold the job as long as they want could be considered a contractual agreement and grounds for a lawsuit. Normally, a person should not be employed without a signed acknowledgment of the at-will disclaimer. In addition, the policy manual should have it noticeably stated in bold, larger-than-normal print, so it is very clear to the employee that this is an at-will relationship. Other guidelines that may assist organizations in avoiding wrongful termination suits include clearly defining the worker's duties, providing good feedback on a regular basis, and conducting realistic performance appraisals on a regular basis.

There are those who contend that even though an employer has a legal right to terminate an employee at will there are ethical boundaries to be considered. Some of these include terminate only as a last resort, after all other options have been exhausted; give as much notice as possible; provide as much severance pay and other help as one can; never terminate an employee for anything other than a legitimate business reason; never lie to an employee about the reason for his or her termination; always tell the truth; and treat the employee with as much dignity and respect as possible. However, there is no law that says these ethical considerations have to be followed. Discipline and disciplinary action are next discussed.

discipline
State of employee self-control and orderly conduct that indicates the extent of genuine teamwork within an organization.

disciplinary action
Invoking a penalty against an employee who fails to meet established standards.

OBJECTIVE 13.3
Explain discipline and disciplinary action.

Discipline and Disciplinary Action

Discipline is the state of employee self-control and orderly conduct that indicates the extent of genuine teamwork within an organization. A necessary but often trying aspect of internal employee relations is the application of **disciplinary action**, invoking a penalty against an employee who fails to meet established standards. Even though disciplinary action may be tense, unpleasant, and fraught with conflict, at times it must be done. Don Crosby, vice president of international and corporate HR at McDonald's, said, "It's the hardest thing a manager has to do. It's also rocky terrain for many executives, who simply do not know when or how to hold the stick, swinging it haphazardly and inconsistently, striking too hard, too soft, or not at all."[9]

Effective disciplinary action addresses the employee's wrongful behavior, not the employee as a person. Incorrectly administered disciplinary action is destructive to both the employee and the organization. Thus, disciplinary action should not be applied haphazardly. Disciplinary action is not usually management's initial response to a problem. Normally, there are more positive ways of convincing employees to adhere to company policies that are necessary to accomplish organizational goals. However, managers at times must administer disciplinary action when company rules are violated.

OBJECTIVE 13.4

Describe the disciplinary action process, discuss the various approaches to disciplinary action, and describe the problems in the administration of disciplinary action.

Disciplinary Action Process

The disciplinary action process is dynamic and ongoing. Because one person's actions can affect others in a work group, the proper application of disciplinary action fosters acceptable behavior by other group members. Conversely, unjustified or improperly administered disciplinary action can have a detrimental effect on other group members.

The disciplinary action process is shown in Figure 13-1. The external environment affects every area of human resource management, including disciplinary actions. Changes in the external environment, such as technological innovations, may render a rule inappropriate and may necessitate creating new rules. Laws and government regulations that affect company policies and rules are also constantly changing. For instance, the Occupational Safety and Health Act caused many firms to establish safety rules.

FIGURE 13-1

Disciplinary Action Process

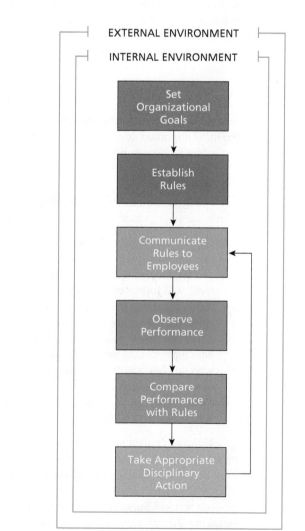

Changes in the internal environment of the firm can also alter the disciplinary action process. Through organization development, the firm may change its employer brand. As a result of this shift, first-line supervisors may begin to handle disciplinary action more positively. Organization policies can also have an impact on the disciplinary action process. Think how a new smoke-free workplace policy might impact the workplace and the possible need for disciplinary action.

The disciplinary action process deals largely with infractions of rules. Notice in Figure 13-1 that rules are established to better facilitate the accomplishment of organizational goals. Rules are specific guides to behavior on the job. The dos and don'ts associated with accomplishing tasks may be highly inflexible. For example, a company may forbid the use of tobacco products anywhere on company property.

After management has established rules, it must communicate these rules to employees. All employees must know the standards in order to be disciplined persons. Individuals cannot obey rules they do not know exist.[10] The manager then observes the performance of workers and compares performance with rules. As long as employee behavior does not vary from acceptable practices, there is no need for disciplinary action, but when an employee's behavior violates a rule, corrective action may need to be taken. Taking disciplinary action against someone often creates an uncomfortable psychological climate. However, managers can still sleep well at night after taking disciplinary action if the rules have been clearly articulated to everyone.

The purpose of disciplinary action is to alter behavior that can have a negative impact on achievement of organizational objectives, not to chastise the violator. The word *discipline* comes from the word *disciple,* and when translated from Latin, it means, *to teach.* Thus, the intent of disciplinary action should be to ensure that the recipient sees disciplinary action as a learning process rather than as something that inflicts pain.

Note that the process shown in Figure 13-1 includes feedback from the point of taking appropriate disciplinary action to communicating rules to employees. When disciplinary action is taken, all employees should realize that certain behaviors are unacceptable and should not be repeated.[11] However, if appropriate disciplinary action is not taken, employees may view the behavior as acceptable and repeat it.

Approaches to Disciplinary Action

Several approaches to the administration of disciplinary action have been developed. Three of the most important concepts are the hot stove rule, progressive disciplinary action, and disciplinary action without punishment.

Hot Stove Rule

According to the hot stove rule, disciplinary action should have the following consequences, which are analogous to touching a hot stove:

1. *Burns immediately.* If disciplinary action is to be taken, it must occur immediately so that the individual will understand the reason for it.
2. *Provides warning.* It is also extremely important to provide advance warning that punishment will follow unacceptable behavior. As individuals move closer to a hot stove, its heat warns them that they will be burned if they touch it; therefore, they have the opportunity to avoid the burn if they so choose.
3. *Gives consistent punishment.* Disciplinary action should also be consistent in that everyone who performs the same act will be punished accordingly. As with a hot stove, each person who touches it with the same degree of pressure and for the same period of time is burned to the same extent.
4. *Burns impersonally.* Disciplinary action should be impersonal. The hot stove burns anyone who touches it, without favoritism.

If the circumstances surrounding all disciplinary action were the same, there would be no problem with this approach. However, situations are often quite different, and many variables may be present in each disciplinary action case. For instance, does the organization penalize a loyal 20-year employee the same way as an individual who has been with the firm for less than six weeks? Supervisors often find that they cannot be completely consistent and impersonal in taking disciplinary action and they need a certain degree of flexibility. Because situations

FIGURE 13-2

Progressive Disciplinary Action Approach

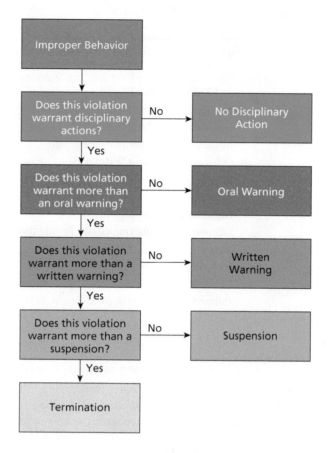

do vary, progressive disciplinary action may be more realistic and more beneficial to both the employee and the organization.

Progressive Disciplinary Action

Progressive disciplinary action is intended to ensure that the minimum penalty appropriate to the offense is imposed. The progressive disciplinary model was developed in response to the National Labor Relations Act. The goal of progressive disciplinary action is to formally communicate problem issues to employees in a direct and timely manner so that they can improve their performance. Its use involves answering a series of questions about the severity of the offense.[12] The manager must ask these questions, in sequence, to determine the proper disciplinary action, as illustrated in Figure 13-2. After the manager has determined that disciplinary action is appropriate, the proper question is, "Does this violation warrant more than an oral warning?" If the improper behavior is minor and has not previously occurred, perhaps only an oral warning will be sufficient. Also, an individual may receive several oral warnings before a *yes* answer applies. The manager follows the same procedure for each level of offense in the progressive disciplinary process. The manager does not consider termination until each lower-level question is answered *yes*. However, major violations, such as assaulting a supervisor or another worker, may justify moving through each level of question to the immediate termination of the employee. It is important for the worker to know what can result if improvement does not result.[13]

To assist managers in recognizing the proper level of disciplinary action, some firms have formalized the procedure. One approach to establish progressive disciplinary action guidelines in a factory environment is shown in Table 13-1. In this example, a worker who is absent without authorization will receive an oral warning the first time it happens and a written warning the second time; the third time, the employee will be terminated. Fighting on the job is an offense that normally results in immediate termination. Specific guidelines for various offenses should be developed to meet the needs of the organization. For example, the wearing of rings or jewelry for aircraft mechanics is strictly prohibited. There would likely be no such rule in an office environment. Basically, the rule should fit the need of the situation.

progressive disciplinary action

Approach to disciplinary action designed to ensure that the minimum penalty appropriate to the offense is imposed.

HR Web Wisdom

Progressive Disciplinary Action

http://humanresources.about .com/od/discipline/

Numerous articles related to disciplinary action and progressive disciplinary action.

TABLE 13-1

Suggested Guidelines for Disciplinary Action

Offenses Requiring First, an Oral Warning; Second, a Written Warning; and Third, Termination
Negligence in the performance of duties
Unauthorized absence from job
Inefficiency in the performance of job
Offenses Requiring a Written Warning and Then Termination
Sleeping on the job
Failure to report to work one or two days in a row without notice
Negligent use of property
Offenses Requiring Immediate Termination
Theft
Fighting on the job
Falsifying time card
Failure to report to work three days in a row without notice

Disciplinary Action without Punishment

disciplinary action without punishment
Process in which a worker is given time off with pay to think about whether he or she wants to follow the rules and continue working for the company.

The process of giving a worker time off with pay to think about whether he or she wants to follow the rules and continue working for the company is called **disciplinary action without punishment**. The approach throws out formal punitive disciplinary action policies for situations such as chronic tardiness or a bad attitude in favor of affirming procedures that make employees want to take personal responsibility for their actions and be models for accomplishment of the corporate mission. When an employee violates a rule, the manager issues an oral reminder. Repetition brings a written reminder, and the third violation results in the worker having to take one, two, or three days off (with pay) to think about the situation. During the first two steps, the manager tries to encourage the employee to solve the problem. If the third step is taken, upon the worker's return, the worker and the supervisor meet to agree that the employee will not violate rules again or the employee will leave the firm. When disciplinary action without punishment is used, it is especially important that all rules are explicitly stated in writing. At the time of orientation, new workers should be told that repeated violations of different rules will be viewed in the same way as several violations of the same rule. This approach keeps workers from taking undue advantage of the process. Walmart has a form of disciplinary action without punishment they call "Decision-Making Day." It provides a paid day off for the employee to decide either to improve or leave the company. It is Walmart's most severe discipline before termination.[14]

Problems in the Administration of Disciplinary Action

As might be expected, administering disciplinary action is not a pleasant task, but it is a job that managers sometimes have to do. Although the manager is in the best position to take disciplinary action, many would rather avoid it even when it is in the company's best interest. Such reluctance often stems from breakdowns in other areas of human resource management. For instance, if a manager has consistently rated an employee high on annual performance appraisals, the supervisor's rationale for taking disciplinary action against a worker for poor performance would be weak. In a possible termination situation, it could be that the employee's productivity has actually dropped substantially. It might also be that the employee's productivity has always been low, yet the supervisor had trouble justifying to upper-level management that the person should be terminated. Rather than run the risk of a decision being overturned, the supervisor retains the ineffective worker.

Occasionally, there may be suits involving members of protected groups who claim that the disciplinary action was taken against them because they are members of a protected group. One

ETHICAL DILEMMA

To Fire or Not to Fire

You are a first-line supervisor for Kwik Corporation, a medium-sized manufacturer of automotive parts. Workers in your company and also your department are quite close, and you view them as family. The work in your department can be quite dangerous. It is especially important that all workers wear their safety glasses, because in the past there have been some serious injuries. The company has a rule that states that any employee who does not follow the stated policy will receive a written reprimand on the first offense and will be terminated on the second violation. You have had to terminate several workers in the past because of similar violations. The other day, Allen Smith, one of your best and most influential employees, violated the safety glasses rule and you gave him a reprimand. You hated to do that because he is by far your best worker and he often helps you if you have a problem with the other workers. He has also been with the company for a long time. You would really be lost without him. You walk up to Allen's workstation and observe him not wearing his safety glasses again. He knows that he has been caught and quickly puts his glasses on and says in a pleading voice, "Please don't fire me. I promise it will never happen again. I have just had a lot on my mind lately."

What would you do?
What factor(s) might in this ethical dilemma might influence a person to make a less-than-ethical decision?

---

of the best ways for a company to protect itself against suits claiming discrimination or harassment is to ensure that it has proper, written policies barring unfair treatment of its staff and a system for ensuring that the policies are followed. Disciplinary actions should be fully documented, and managers should be trained in how to avoid bias claims.[15] Also, although discrimination laws prohibit employers from making employment decisions based on an employee's membership in a protected class, basing decisions solely on performance helps prevent violation of these laws.

A supervisor may be perfectly justified in administering disciplinary action, but there is usually a proper time and place for doing so. For example, taking disciplinary action against a worker in the presence of others may embarrass the individual and actually defeat the purpose of the action. Even when they are wrong, employees resent disciplinary action administered in public. By disciplining employees in private, supervisors prevent them from losing face with their peers.

In addition, many supervisors may be too lenient early in the disciplinary action process and too strict later. This lack of consistency does not give the worker a clear understanding of the penalty associated with the inappropriate action. A supervisor will often endure an unacceptable situation for an extended period of time. Then, when a decision is finally made to take action, he or she is apt to overreact and come down excessively hard. However, consistency does not necessarily mean that the same penalty must be applied to two different workers for the same offense. For instance, managers would be consistent if they always considered the worker's past record and length of service.

| OBJECTIVE **13.5**

Describe terminations, explain termination of employees at various levels, and explain demotion as an alternative to termination.

termination

Most severe penalty that an organization can impose on an employee.

Termination

Termination is the most severe penalty that an organization can impose on an employee; therefore, it should be the most carefully considered form of disciplinary action. The experience of being terminated is traumatic for employees regardless of their position in the organization. They can experience feelings of failure, fear, disappointment, and anger. It is also a difficult time for the person making the termination decision. Knowing that termination may affect not only the employee but also an entire family increases the trauma. Not knowing how the terminated employee will react also may create considerable anxiety for the manager who must do the firing. An individual who is terminated may respond with a wide range of emotions ranging from workplace violence to being totally unemotional in the matter.

Emotional Intelligence Needed in Disciplinary Action

Emotional intelligence (EQ) is the ability to recognize and manage emotions. It is the skill to adapt to the people around us, to consider their emotions, and to recognize our own feelings and those of others, for motivating ourselves and for managing emotions in ourselves and in relationships with others. There are two distinct types of intelligence, intellectual and emotional. One might equate intellectual intelligence with "book smart," measured in terms of IQ, whereas emotional intelligence is usually known as "people smart" and has been measured in terms of EQ.[16] While IQ is genetically determined, EQ can be nurtured.[17] Emotional intelligence may be the reason some very intelligent people fail while some individuals of average intelligence are highly successful.[18]

EQ consists of five aspects including self-awareness, self-relation, motivation, empathy, and social skills.[19] Individuals with high EQ are able to "maneuver their way through potentially volatile situations and walk away without feeling burned."[20] These are qualities managers definitely need should disciplinary action be necessary.

Coca-Cola found that EQ had a major impact on productivity. Division leaders who developed EQ competencies exceeded their performance targets by 15 percent. However, those who did not expand their EQ missed their targets by 15 percent, a 30 percent difference. Likewise, Hallmark Communities discovered that sales representatives who developed EQ skills were 25 percent more productive than representatives with lower EQs.[21]

There are tests to determine a person's emotional intelligence. One of the most used, the Reuven Bar-On's EQ-I, has been endorsed by the American Psychological Association.[22] Some of the areas assessed include "self-regard, interpersonal skills, stress management and handling change to enable employees to play to their strengths and highlight areas to develop."[23] It is also possible to carry out team testing to show the emotional intelligence of a team. Buckman Laboratories International, Inc. uses Thomas International's Personal Profile Analysis (PPA) during the hiring process. The test indicates the likelihood of fit within Buckman's corporate culture.[24]

OBJECTIVE 13.6

Explain the need for emotional intelligence in conducting disciplinary action.

emotional intelligence
Ability to recognize and manage emotions.

HR Web Wisdom

Emotional Intelligence Profile
**http://www.myskillsprofile
.com/tests/eiq16**

Take a test to determine your emotional intelligence.

Most of the time, when the decision is made to terminate a worker, the employee should not really be surprised since he or she should have been given explicit warnings and counseling prior to being fired. The worker should have been advised of specific steps needed to take to keep the job. Support should have been provided to show what needed to be done. The worker also should have been given a reasonable period of time to comply with the supervisor's expectations.

Experts suggest that firings should be on Mondays because it lets the dismissed workers start looking for a job right away.[25] Further, firing a worker at the end of the day leaves little chance for discussion among the remaining staff that may interrupt the workplace. Managers should try to plan the termination and make it based on emotions. Certain steps should be followed in the termination process. In the first place, the worker's manager normally should personally do the firing. Second, the firing process should be kept short, using nonaccusatory language. Third, the manager should not go into the reason for the dismissal and should not answer any questions regarding the decision.[26] In some states, when an employee is involuntarily terminated, the employer must pay all earned and unpaid wages within 24 hours after the employee demands it. To avoid any potential dispute over when a demand was made, most employers simply have the final paycheck available at the termination meeting. Also, select a location where there will be no interruptions. If the employee becomes argumentative, managers may need to get up and leave once the worker has been fired. For that reason, a manager's office is normally not used.[27] Finally, most managers believe that it is best to have a witness since the person being fired may interpret your statements in the worst possible light.[28]

Termination of Employees at Various Levels

Regardless of the similarities in the termination of employees at various levels, distinct differences exist with regard to nonmanagerial/nonprofessional employees, executives, and middle and lower-level managers and professionals.

Termination of Nonmanagerial/Nonprofessional Employees

Individuals in this category are neither managers nor professionally trained individuals, such as engineers or accountants. They generally include employees such as steelworkers, truck drivers, salesclerks, and wait staff. If the firm is unionized, the termination procedure is typically well defined in the labor–management agreement. For example, drinking on the job might be identified as a reason for immediate termination. Absences, on the other hand, may require three written warnings by the supervisor before termination action can be taken.

When the firm is union-free, these workers can generally be terminated more easily since the worker is most likely an at-will employee. In most union-free organizations, violations justifying termination are often included in the firm's employee handbook. At times, especially in smaller organizations, the termination process is informal with the first-line supervisor telling workers what actions warrant termination. Regardless of the size of the organization, management should inform employees of the actions that warrant termination.

Termination of Middle- and Lower-Level Managers and Professionals

Typically, the most vulnerable and perhaps the most neglected groups of employees with regard to termination have been middle- and lower-level managers and professionals. Employees in these jobs may lack the political clout that a terminated executive has. Although certainly not recommended, termination may have been based on something as simple as the attitude or feelings of an immediate superior on a given day.

Termination of Executives

Unlike workers at lower-level positions, CEOs do not have to worry about their positions being eliminated. Their main concern is pleasing the board of directors, because hiring and firing the CEO is a board's main responsibility. Often the reason for terminating a CEO is because the board of directors lost confidence in the executive. Tenure has become increasingly shaky for new CEOs, as the turnover in the *Fortune* 1000 companies is high. According to John Challenger, CEO of the outplacement firm Challenger, Gray & Christmas, Inc., "If you're an executive, you may have noticed the revolving door."[29] This may be a problem because many, such as Jack Welch, a former CEO at General Electric, believe that it takes five years for a chief executive to develop a proper understanding of the company. GE has had just four chief executives since 1970.[30]

Executives usually have no formal appeal procedure. The reasons for termination may not be as clear as those for lower-level employees. Some of the reasons include the following:

1. *Economic downturns.* At times, business conditions may force a reduction in the number of executives.
2. *Reorganization/downsizing.* To improve efficiency or as a result of merging with another company, a firm may reorganize or downsize, resulting in the elimination of some executive positions.
3. *Philosophical differences.* A difference in philosophy of conducting business may develop between an executive and the board. To maintain consistency in management philosophy, the executive may be replaced.
4. *Decline in productivity.* The executive may have been capable of performing satisfactorily in the past but, for various reasons, can no longer perform the job as required.

This list does not include factors related to illegal activities such as sexual harassment or insider trading. Under those circumstances, the firm has no moral obligation to the terminated executive.

An organization may derive positive benefits from terminating executives, but such actions also present a potentially hazardous situation for the company. Terminating a senior executive is an expensive proposition, often in ways more costly than just the separation package. The impact on the organization should be measured in relationships, productivity, strategic integrity, and investor confidence, as well as dollars. Many corporations are concerned about developing a negative public image that reflects insensitivity to the needs of their employees. They fear that such a reputation would impede their efforts to recruit high-quality managers. Also, terminated executives have, at times, made public statements detrimental to the reputation of their former employers.

Demotion as an Alternative to Termination

Demotion is the process of moving a worker to a lower level of duties and responsibilities, which typically involves a reduction in pay. Demotion may be a legitimate career option that had nothing to do with disciplinary action. However, in this section, demotion is addressed as a disciplinary action option. Emotions may run high when an individual is demoted. The demoted person may suffer loss of respect from peers and feel betrayed, embarrassed, angry, and disappointed. The employee's productivity may also decrease further. For these reasons, demotion should be used very cautiously. If demotion is chosen over termination, efforts must be made to preserve the self-esteem of the individual. The person may be asked how he or she would like to handle the demotion announcement. A positive image of the worker's value to the company should be projected.

The handling of demotions in a unionized organization is usually spelled out clearly in the labor–management agreement. Should a decision be made to demote a worker for unsatisfactory performance, the union should be notified of this intent and given the specific reasons for the demotion. Often the demotion will be challenged and carried through the formal grievance procedure. Documentation is necessary for the demotion to be upheld. Even with the problems associated with demotion for cause, it is often easier to demote than to terminate an employee. In addition, demotion is often less devastating to the employee. For the organization, however, the opposite may be true if the demotion creates lingering ill will and an embittered employee.

Downsizing, discussed next, is not the same as termination but the results for workers involved is the same; they no longer have a job.

Downsizing

Downsizing, also known as *restructuring* or *rightsizing,* is essentially the reverse of a company growing; it suggests a one-time change in the organization and the number of people employed. Typically, both the organizational structure and the number of people in the organization shrink for the purpose of improving organizational performance. The retail and investment side of banking is expecting large downsizing. Wall Street is projected to lose 50,000 jobs in 2012, not returning to pre-financial-crisis employment levels until 2023. Globally, more than 220,000 financial service jobs are expected to disappear.[31] And, some believe that these layoffs may only be the tip of the iceberg for the industry.[32]

One big lesson from research on downsizing is that when organizations resist or delay layoffs as long as possible, they tend to bounce back faster when the upturn hits.[33] This is especially true in organizations with skilled workers. This happens, in part, because these organizations save on recruiting and training costs when the demand for their people returns, and by keeping their experienced workforce around, they can move more effectively than their competitors that are scrambling to hire and train new employees with the right skills.[34]

Companies that have downsized should not forget about the workers that remain. Communication channels should be open to let those remaining workers know what and why the downsizing occurred. Often those who remain suffer *survivor's guilt* or *survivor syndrome,* and open communication can do much to get by the feeling. Often it is a good idea to have a venting session where workers are allowed to express their concerns. Questions should be answered clearly and candidly.[35]

Planning is crucial as a company prepares for downsizing. Often there may be age and other discrimination claims if downsizing results in a disproportionately adverse impact on members of a protected class. At times, older workers with higher salaries than their younger counterparts become targets for cost-cutting measures and age discrimination claims occur. It is important to analyze the breakdown of downsized workers to ensure that all protected groups of workers are not disproportionately affected. It is equally imperative that an employer use objective, job-related criteria to decide which positions will be affected. Also, the downsizing organization should be prepared to deal with government requirements such as COBRA and ERISA.

Workers should understand when they are hired how the system will work in the event of layoffs. When the firm is unionized, the layoff procedures are usually stated clearly in the labor–management agreement. Seniority usually is the basis for layoffs, with the least senior employees laid off first. The agreement may also have a clearly spelled-out *bumping procedure*. When senior-level positions are eliminated, the people occupying them have the right to bump workers from lower-level positions, assuming that they have the proper qualifications for the lower-level job. When bumping occurs, the composition of the workforce is altered.

Union-free firms should also establish layoff procedures prior to facing layoff decisions. In union-free firms, productivity and the needs of the organization are typically key considerations. When productivity is the primary factor, management must be careful to ensure that productivity, not favoritism, is the actual basis for the layoff decision. Therefore, it is important to define accurately productivity considerations well in advance of any layoffs.

Negative Aspects of Downsizing

When downsizing is chosen, companies typically describe the positive results, such as improving the bottom line. Many believe that the guaranteed results of employee downsizing on organizational market returns, profitability, and other financial outcomes are at best evasive.[36] There also is a negative side to downsizing. Following are some examples:

- During layoffs, employers and employees must realize that there is a natural grieving period and a desire to go back to the way things used to be. Friendships may be lost, and there is day-to-day uncertainty about the future. It is difficult to think about contributing to the bottom line when you do not know if tomorrow will be your day to be cut.[37]
- Layers are pulled out of a firm, making advancement in the organization more difficult. Thus, more and more individuals find themselves plateaued.
- Workers begin seeking better opportunities because they believe they may be the next in line to be laid off. Often the best workers find other jobs and there is an increase in voluntary departures.[38]
- Employee loyalty is often significantly reduced. For workers who remain after downsizing, the loyalty level is often low.
- Institutional memory or corporate culture is lost.
- Workers who remain after downsizing are also faced with the realization of having to do addition work (some call it "ghost work"). Jim Link, staffing agency Randstad's managing director for human resources, said, "The piling-on of responsibilities is at an all-time high."[39]
- When demand for the products or services returns, the company often realizes that it has cut too deeply. It then begins looking for ways to get the job done.

Worker Adjustment and Retraining Notification Act

The Worker Adjustment and Retraining Notification Act (WARN) requires covered employers to give 60 days advance notice before a plant closing or mass layoff that will affect at least 100 full-time employees.[40] As an example of how the process works: Century Aluminum of West Virginia ceased operations on February 20, 2009. It had issued a federal WARN notice in December 2008 to its 679 employees.[41] Therefore, no penalty was imposed on the company.

There are severe monetary sanctions for failing to comply with the requirements of WARN. The penalties for WARN notice violations include liability to each affected worker for back pay and benefits for up to 60 days.[42] Approximately 1,650 former employees of Mortgage Lenders Network will divide a $2.7 million under a settlement. The company failed to provide the required 60-day warning notice to employees that it would close.[43] However, if an unforeseeable business circumstance causes a business to close earlier than 60 days, WARN does not apply. Such was the case with Hale-Halsell Company. Six days after the retailer United Supermarket, Hale-Halsell's biggest customer, severed ties with the company, the wholesaler announced 200 layoffs.[44]

Outplacement

outplacement
A procedure whereby laid-off employees are given assistance in finding employment elsewhere.

In **outplacement**, laid-off employees are given assistance in finding employment elsewhere.

The use of outplacement began at the executive level, but it has also been used at other organizational levels. Through outplacement, the firm tries to soften the impact of displacement.

Barbara Barra, executive vice president of operations for the consulting firm Lee Hecht Harrison, said, "There is a strong correlation between how a company treats departing employees and its ability to attract and retain top talent now and in the future, particularly when the economy rebounds."[45] Some of the services provided by outplacement include a discussion of pension options, Social Security benefits, expenses for interviews, and wage/salary negotiations. Usually career guidance is provided as well as instructions on how to conduct a self-appraisal directed toward recognizing skills, knowledge, experience, and other qualities recruiters may required in a new job. Tutoring in how to search for a job is usually available, and there is often help available in how to interview in the new employment environment.

When organizational change takes place, there will be a psychological impact on both the individuals who were dismissed and those who remain. Companies use outplacement to take care of employees by moving them successfully out of the company. This proactive response will also likely have a positive influence on those who remain with the company after downsizing. More employers are offering outplacement help to preserve their employer brand and reputation.

Severance Pay

severance pay
Compensation designed to assist laid-off employees as they search for new employment.

Severance pay is compensation designed to assist laid-off employees as they search for new employment.

Although no federal law requires U.S. companies to pay severance, a recent study found that although over half of organizations gave severance pay to all departing employees, 17.7 percent made payments to selected groups only.[46] Even so, U.S. employees earn the least amount of severance pay worldwide, regardless of their job level or tenure.[47] When offered, typically one to two weeks of severance pay for every year of service is provided, up to some predetermined maximum. The employee's organizational level generally affects the amount of severance pay provided. For example, nonmanagers may get eight or nine weeks of pay even if their length of service is greater than eight or nine years. Middle managers may receive severance pay amounts based on the number of years worked.

There are many compelling reasons to pay severance to employees who are involuntarily terminated. Many managers think that treating ousted workers well sends an important message to those who remain behind. There may be a feeling that "we all could be in that situation someday." But a major reason a firm offers severance today is that something in return is provided. The departing worker must waive all rights to sue the company, but the waiver has to be voluntary.[48] In a recent survey, nearly three-quarters of some 400 human resource professionals answered *yes* when asked if they required workers who were laid off to sign a form releasing their organization from liability for employment actions.[49] From the employee's viewpoint, severance is paid so that they will not sue the organization.[50] "It's not love; it's not a gift—it's a business transaction," notes Alan Sklover, author of *Fired, Downsized, or Laid Off.*[51]

Not all internal employee relations situations are as severe as termination and layoffs, and an ombudsperson or alternative dispute resolution may be used to resolve these disputes.

Ombudsperson

ombudsperson
Complaint officer who has access to top management and who hears employee complaints, investigates, and recommends appropriate action.

An **ombudsperson** is a complaint officer who has access to top management and who hears employee complaints, investigates, and recommends appropriate action. Employers use ombudspersons in their organizations to help defuse problems before they become lawsuits or scandals. The more internal mechanisms a corporation has to deal with internal problems, the less likely these problems are to wind up in court. Ombudspersons are impartial, neutral counselors who can give employees confidential advice about problems ranging from abusive managers to allegations of illegal corporate activity. Ombudspersons are used so that all workers may seek informal, confidential assistance to work through problems without losing control over how their concerns will be addressed. The ombudsperson is typically independent of line management and reports near or at the top of the organization.

Melissa Cameron is the ombudsperson for Bayer Corporation North American operations. The firm's 16,600 employees can contact her confidentially to blow the whistle on bad behavior or discuss other workplace issues. She said, "If you find even one or two cases a year that are substantiated, you have more than paid for my salary in terms of addressing a situation on the front end rather than going through litigation."[52]

Alternative Dispute Resolution

alternative dispute resolution (ADR)

Procedure whereby the employee and the company agree ahead of time that any problems will be addressed by an agreed-upon means.

HR Web Wisdom

Alternative Dispute Resolution

http://www.opm.gov/er/ adrguide/toc.asp

Office of Personnel Management, Alternative Dispute Resolution: A Resource Guide.

As the number of employment-related lawsuits increases, companies have looked for ways to protect themselves against the costs and uncertainties of the judicial system. **Alternative dispute resolution (ADR)** is a procedure whereby the employee and the company agree ahead of time that any problems will be addressed by an agreed-upon means.

ADR is based on the use of a jury waiver, which is a contractual provision in which an employee waives the right to a trial by jury in a legal proceeding brought against an employer.[53] Types of ADR include arbitration, mediation, negotiated rulemaking, neutral fact-finding, and minitrials. With the exception of binding arbitration, the goal of ADR is to provide a forum for the parties to work toward a voluntary, consensual agreement, as opposed to having a judge or other authority decide the case. Mediation is the preferred method for most people. ADR cases run the gamut from racial, gender, and age discrimination to unfair firings. The idea behind ADR is to resolve conflicts between employer and employee through means less costly and contentious than litigation. A successful program can save a company thousands of dollars in legal costs and hundreds of hours in managers' time. Just as important, perhaps, it can protect a company from the demoralizing tension and bitterness that employee grievances can spread through a workforce. Compared to litigation, ADR processes are less adversarial, faster and more efficient, relatively lower in cost, and private.

When parties agree to mediate, they are able to reach a settlement in 96 percent of the cases. A Presidential Executive Order requires federal agencies to (1) promote greater use of mediation, arbitration, early neutral evaluation, agency ombudspersons, and other alternative dispute resolution techniques; and (2) promote greater use of negotiated rulemaking.

The Supreme Court rendered an opinion in *Circuit City v Adams* that greatly enhanced an employer's ability to enforce compulsory ADR agreements. The Court held that the ADR was valid and enforceable and made clear that ADR applied to the vast majority of employees and was available to employers seeking to enforce compulsory arbitration agreements.[54] However, in 2012, the NLRB held that a Florida-based home builder committed an unfair labor practice under federal labor law by maintaining a mandatory arbitration agreement that waived the rights of employees to participate in class or collective actions. Only time will tell how this decision will affect ADR.

OBJECTIVE 13.8

Describe transfers, promotions, resignations, and retirements as factors involved in internal employee relations.

transfer

Lateral movement of a worker within an organization.

Transfers

The lateral movement of a worker within an organization is called a **transfer**. A transfer may be initiated by the firm or by an employee. The process does not and should not imply that a person is being either promoted or demoted. Transfers serve several purposes. First, firms often find it necessary to reorganize. Offices and departments are created and abolished in response to the company's needs. In filling positions created by reorganization, the company may have to move employees without promoting them. A similar situation may exist when an office or department is closed. Rather than terminate valued employees, management may transfer them to other areas within the organization. These transfers may entail moving an employee to another desk in the same office or to a location halfway around the world.

A second reason for transfers is to make positions available in the primary promotion channels. At times, very productive but unpromotable workers may clog promotion channels. Other qualified workers in the organization may find their opportunities for promotion blocked. When this happens, a firm's most capable future managers may seek employment elsewhere. To keep promotion channels open, the firm may decide to transfer employees who are unpromotable but productive at their organizational level.

Another reason for transfers is to satisfy employees' personal desires. The reasons for wanting a transfer are numerous. An individual may need to accompany a transferred spouse to a new location or work closer to home to care for aging parents, or the worker may dislike the long commute to and from work. Factors such as these may be of sufficient importance that employees may resign if a requested transfer is not approved. Rather than risk losing a valued employee, the firm may agree to the transfer.

Transfers may also be an effective means of dealing with personality clashes. Some people just cannot get along with one another. Because each of the individuals may be a valued employee, a transfer may be an appropriate solution to the problem. But managers must be cautious regarding the "grass is always greener on the other side of the fence" syndrome. When some workers encounter a temporary setback, they immediately ask for a transfer before they even attempt to work through the problem.

Finally, because of a limited number of management levels, it is becoming necessary for managers to have a wide variety of experiences before achieving a promotion. Individuals who desire upward mobility often explore possible lateral moves so that they can learn new skills.

Promotions

promotion
Movement of a person to a higher-level position in an organization.

A **promotion** is the movement of a person to a higher-level position in the organization.

The term *promotion* is one of the most emotionally charged words in the field of human resource management. An individual who receives a promotion normally receives additional financial rewards and the ego boost associated with achievement and accomplishment. Most employees feel good about being promoted. But for every individual who gains a promotion, there are probably others who were not selected. If these individuals wanted the promotion badly enough or their favorite candidate was overlooked, they may slack off or even resign. If the consensus of employees directly involved is that the wrong person was promoted, considerable resentment may result.

There are numerous laws, court cases, and executive orders that apply when individuals are hired. These same hiring standards apply to promotion decisions. Promotion decisions should not discriminate against employees because of age, race, religion, national origin, color, sex, pregnancy, or disability.[55]

Resignations

Even when an organization is totally committed to making its environment a good place to work, workers will still resign. Some employees cannot see promotional opportunities, or at least not enough, and will therefore move on. A certain amount of turnover is healthy for an organization and is often necessary to afford employees the opportunity to fulfill career objectives. When turnover becomes excessive, however, the firm must do something to slow it. The most qualified employees are often the ones who resign because they are more mobile. On the other hand, marginally qualified workers never seem to leave. If excessive numbers of a firm's highly qualified and competent workers are leaving, a way must be found to reverse the trend.

Analyzing Voluntary Resignations

exit interview
Means of revealing the real reasons employees leave their jobs; it is conducted before an employee departs the company and provides information on how to correct the causes of discontent and reduce turnover.

When a firm wants to determine why individuals leave, it can use the exit interview and/or the postexit questionnaire. An **exit interview** is a means of revealing the real reasons employees leave their jobs; it is conducted before an employee departs the company and provides information on how to correct the causes of discontent and reduce turnover. Determining why employees leave a company can provide an opportunity for the firm to make changes to reduce turnover rates and reduce the associated costs.[56] Also, a good exit interview should assess whether employees felt they had received a good realistic job preview.[57]

Often the reason an employee leaves the job is misleading. Leigh Branham, author of *The 7 Hidden Reasons Employees Leave: How to Recognize the Subtle Signs and Act Before It's Too Late,* believes that employees will cite pay as the reason they quit their jobs, 60 to 80 percent of the time. His research suggests that only 12 to 15 percent of employees leave for this reason.[58] Perhaps departing employees are reluctant to burn bridges by revealing the real reason for leaving because they may need a reference from their supervisor in the future and fear reprisal.

However, only after determining the *real* reason for leaving can a firm develop a strategy to overcome the problem.

At times women who are on the fast track are not candid about why they quit. A consulting firm was hired to discover why top-performing women were quitting in high numbers, saying in their exit interviews that they wanted to spend more time with their kids. But the employers later learned that these women had returned to work with another firm, some starting their own firms and working longer hours. In anonymous interviews, the women who had quit explained the problem. Most said they'd left their jobs because they could not see a future for themselves there. The wanting-to-spend-more-time-with-kids story was just cover—so they could maintain good relations with their former bosses.[59]

Often a third party, such as a person in the HR department or an outsource party, will conduct the exit interview. A third party may be used because employees may not be willing to air their problems with their former bosses. Outsourcing the exit interviews may be beneficial because employers believe that the person who is leaving will be more honest when he or she is not speaking to a company employee. Over time, properly conducted exit interviews can provide considerable insight into why employees leave.[60] Patterns are often identified that uncover weaknesses in the firm's management system. Knowledge of the problem permits corrective action to be taken. Also, exit interviews help to identify training and development needs and identify areas in which changes need to be made. They may also be used to identify hidden biases of managers who are hurting the productivity of the unit.[61]

Another means of determining the real reason employees are leaving the organization is by administering a **postexit questionnaire**, which is sent to former employees several weeks after they leave the organization. Usually, they have already started work at their new company. Ample blank space is provided so that a former employee can express his or her feelings about and perceptions of the job and the organization. Since the individual is no longer with the firm he or she may respond more freely to the questions. However, there are several major weaknesses in the use of the postexit questionnaire. Participation rates are often low because former workers may not care enough to respond and they may be difficult to reach after they have departed.[62] Also, the interviewer is not present to interpret and probe for more information.

To reduce the need to conduct exit interviews and administer postexit questionnaires, some organizations are using a *stay interview,* where management actually meets with employees to assess their attitude regarding their job and the company. According to Beth N. Carvin, chief executive officer for Nobscot Corporation, an HR technology provider, "Stay interviews help a manager uncover what makes the job 'sticky' for each individual. For some employees, it might be purely about money and benefits. For others, it's about the culture and camaraderie."[63]

postexit questionnaire
Questionnaire sent to former employees several weeks after they leave the organization to determine the real reason they left.

Attitude Surveys: A Means of Retaining Quality Employees

Exit and postexit interviews can provide valuable information to improve human resource management practices. The problem, however, is that these approaches are reactions to events that were detrimental to the organization.

An alternative, proactive approach is administering attitude surveys. **Attitude surveys** seek input from employees to determine their feelings about topics such as the work they perform, their supervisor, their work environment, flexibility in the workplace, opportunities for advancement, training and development opportunities, and the firm's compensation system. They can provide valuable information to management, but they should not be a substitute for day-to-day discussion between managers and workers.[64] Since some employees will want their responses to be confidential, every effort should be made to guarantee their anonymity. To achieve this, it may be necessary to have the survey administered by a third party. Regardless of how the process is handled, attitude surveys have the potential to improve management practices. For this reason, they are widely used throughout industry today. Joseph Cabral, senior vice president and chief human resources officer for the North Shore-LIJ Health System in Long Island, N.Y., says "North Shore has been surveying its 38,000 employees annually for the past three years, but it recently went to a quarterly survey to provide more real-time and actionable results and to allow comparisons across worksites and departments."[65]

attitude survey
Survey that seeks input from employees to determine their feelings about topics such as the work they perform, their supervisor, their work environment, flexibility in the workplace, opportunities for advancement, training and development opportunities, and the firm's compensation system.

Employees should be advised of the purpose of the survey. The mere act of giving a survey communicates to employees that management is concerned about their problems, wants to know what they are, and wants to solve them, if possible. Analyzing survey results of various subgroups and comparing them with the firm's total population may indicate areas that should be investigated and problems that need to be solved. For instance, the survey results of the production night shift might be compared with the production day shift. Should problems show up, management must be willing to make the suggested changes. If the survey does not result in some improvements, the process may be a deterrent to employees and future surveys may not yield helpful data. Basically, if you are not going to do anything as a result of the survey, do not bother to administer it.

Advance Notice of Resignation

Most firms would like to have at least a two-week notice of resignation from departing workers. However, a month's notice may be desired from professional and managerial employees who are leaving. When the firm desires notice, the policy should be clearly communicated to all employees. If they want departing employees to give advance notice, companies have certain obligations. For instance, suppose that a worker who gives notice is terminated immediately. Word of this action will spread rapidly to other employees. Later, should they decide to resign, they will likely not give any advance notice.

Firms are now actively recruiting former employees. If the firm views a departing worker as eligible to return in the future, it should avoid treating that person like a second-class citizen. However, in some cases, permitting a worker to remain on the job once a resignation has been submitted may create some problems. If bad feelings exist between the employee and the supervisor or the company, the departing worker may be a disruptive force. On a selective basis, the firm may wish to pay some employees for the notice time and ask them to leave immediately.

Offboarding

offboarding
Facilitates employee departure from the company by assisting in the completion of exit tasks, including exit interviews, forms completion, the return of company property, and ensuring that employees receive the appropriate extended benefits.

Offboarding facilitates employee departure from the company by assisting in the completion of exit tasks, including exit interviews, forms completion, the return of company property, and ensuring that employees receive the appropriate extended benefits.[66] Topics such as the worker's 401(k) and COBRA need to be addressed. Teresa Grote, practice director of composite solutions for Ascendum, an information technology company, said, "I think that in our highly litigious society today, making sure that you go through proper offboarding is probably equally, if not more, important than proper onboarding."[67]

Retirements

Many long-term employees leave an organization by retiring. However, the majority of today's employees are not planning for a traditional retirement, in which they have an immediate and abrupt end to their working career at a specific age, such as 65. Some want to work past the normal retirement age because they are healthy and want to keep active; others have to work because their retirement account has dwindled and they cannot afford to retire.[68] Many want to *phase-in* retirement by working fewer hours as they near 65, or after. This is good for companies because, *flash retirement*, the departure of large numbers of retirement-eligible employees in a short period is lessened.[69] **Phased retirement** is any arrangement that allows people to move from full-time work to retirement in steps. One study found that retirees who transition from full-time work into a temporary or part-time job experience fewer major diseases and are able to function better day-to-day than people who stop working altogether.[70] Retirement is treated as a phased process rather than a sudden event marked by hearing a sentimental speech and receiving a gold watch.[71] About half of all American workers phase into retirement in some way.[72] In addition, 20 percent of employers say that phased retirement is critical to their company's HR strategy today; that number nearly triples, to 61 percent, when employers look ahead 5 years. Allen Steinberg, a principal at Hewitt Associates, said, "Employers will be losing key talent at a time when attracting and retaining skilled workers will be more important."[73] However, a recent study found

phased retirement
Any arrangement that allows people to move from full-time work to retirement in steps.

A GLOBAL PERSPECTIVE

Administering Disciplinary Action in the Global Environment

Previously, the discussion of disciplinary action was examined as it related to managers in the United States. Moving into the international arena often presents different situations. For instance, the punishment for a company employee who stole $10,000 in the United States would likely lead to termination. However, a Japanese judge ruled that the $10,000 was too small an amount to justify termination and the worker was reinstated.[74]

The concept of employment at will is generally accepted in the United States. Remember that employment at will is an unwritten contract created when an employee agrees to work for an employer but no agreement exists as to how long the parties expect the employment to last. When it comes to discharging a worker who is not performing, it is much harder to do in Europe than in North America and other parts of the world. In fact, Europe may have the most employee-friendly laws. Even though they face global competition, unions in several European countries have resisted changing their laws and removing government protections. In many Western European countries, laws on labor unions and employment make it difficult to lay off employees.[75] Laws make it hard to fire workers, so companies are reluctant to hire.[76] It is also difficult to discipline a worker for poor performance in China. Laws tend to come down on the side of the employees when addressing disciplinary action.

In India, as soon as a company hires more than 100 employees, it is legally impossible to terminate anyone without permission of the government and then it must be because of criminal wrongdoing. Such laws have long discouraged foreign investors, held back manufacturing, and prevented the nation from experiencing industrial growth similar to China's. Presently legislators are fighting to push a law through Parliament to let a company expand its workforce without surrendering the power to lay off workers to bureaucrats. The bill faces intense opposition from unions.[77]

Because of the differences in how governments view disciplinary action in the global environment, it is very difficult for a global company to establish a standardized policy on disciplinary action. The company will want to create a precise picture of employment and working conditions in order to establish appropriate practices in each country. Some of the factors that should be considered include hiring and termination rules and regulations covering severance practices.[78]

OBJECTIVE 13.9

Explain problems with conducting disciplinary action in the global environment.

that major corporations do not have phased retirement programs for older workers who can continue adding value.[79]

The Pension Protection Act of 2006 permits limited phased retirement by allowing in-service pension plan withdrawals to begin at age 62 rather than 65.[80] A benefit of phased retirement is that it permits a company to reduce labor costs without hurting morale. It also lets an organization hold on to its experienced workers so they can share their knowledge with a less experienced workforce. Employees at Lee Memorial can work as few as 16 hours a week and still be eligible for benefits. Mercy Health's phased retirement plan allows workers aged 50 and older to reduce the number of hours worked while keeping their benefits.[81] CVS Caremark has set up a "snowbird" employment program to retain valuable employees. The program allows pharmacists to transfer south to places such as Florida for the winter, following the business's customers. Other benefits CVS Caremark provides the more mature workforce include part-time work, training, and flexible scheduling. The workforce of 50 and older has grown from 7 percent in the early 1990s to more than 18 percent today.[82]

Sometimes employees will be offered early retirement before reaching the organization's normal length-of-service requirement. Historically, early retirement has been viewed as an attractive solution when workforce reductions had to be made. Early retirement plans, which gained popularity in the 1980s, appealed to older workers facing layoffs. Early retirement is still being used, but companies often reserve the right to reject a highly productive worker's request.

MyManagementLab

Go to **mymanagementlab.com** to complete the problems marked with this icon ⭐.

Summary

1. *Describe the importance of worker retention and define internal employee relations.* The key to successful retention is to focus on top performers and determine their risk of leaving. It is more than likely that these workers are already being recruited and they probably know their value in the job market.

   Internal employee relations comprise the human resource management activities associated with the movement of employees within the organization.

2. *Explain the concept of employment at will. Employment at will* is an unwritten contract created when an employee agrees to work for an employer but no agreement exists as to how long the parties expect the employment to last.

3. *Explain discipline and disciplinary action. Discipline* is the state of employee self-control and orderly conduct present within an organization.

   Disciplinary action occurs when a penalty is invoked against an employee who fails to meet established standards.

4. *Describe the disciplinary action process, discuss the various approaches to disciplinary action, and describe the problems in the administration of disciplinary action.* After management has established rules, it must communicate these rules to employees. The manager then observes the performance of workers and compares performance with rules. As long as employee behavior does not vary from acceptable practices, there is no need for disciplinary action, but when an employee's behavior violates a rule, corrective action may be necessary.

   Three of the most important concepts are the hot stove rule, progressive disciplinary action, and disciplinary action without punishment.

   As might be expected, administering disciplinary action is not a pleasant task, but it is a job that managers sometimes have to do.

5. *Explain the need for emotional intelligence in conducting disciplinary action. Emotional intelligence* is the capacity for recognizing our own feelings and those of others, for motivating ourselves, and for managing emotions well in ourselves and in our relationships. It is definitely needed should disciplinary action be necessary.

6. *Describe terminations, explain termination of employees at various levels, and explain demotion as an alternative to termination.* Termination is the most severe penalty that an organization can impose on an employee; therefore, it should be the most carefully considered form of disciplinary action. Regardless of the similarities in the termination of employees at various levels, distinct differences exist with regard to nonmanagerial/nonprofessional employees, executives, and middle and lower-level managers and professionals.

   Demotion is the process of moving a worker to a lower level of duties and responsibilities, which typically involves a reduction in pay. If demotion is chosen over termination, efforts must be made to preserve the self-esteem of the individual.

7. *Describe downsizing and explain the use of ombudspersons and alternative dispute resolution. Downsizing,* also known as *restructuring* or *rightsizing,* is essentially the reverse of a company growing; it suggests a one-time change in the organization and the number of people employed.

   An *ombudsperson* is a complaint officer with access to top management who hears employee complaints, investigates, and recommends appropriate action.

   Alternative dispute resolution is a procedure whereby the employee and the company agree ahead of time that any problems will be addressed by an agreed-upon means.

8. *Describe transfers, promotions, resignations, and retirements as factors involved in internal employee relations.* The lateral movement of a worker within an organization is called a *transfer.*

   A *promotion* is the movement of a person to a higher-level position in the organization. Even when an organization is totally committed to making its environment a good place to work, workers will still resign.

   Many long-term employees leave an organization by retiring. The majority of today's employees are not planning for a traditional retirement, in which they have an immediate and abrupt end to their working career at a specific age, such as 65. Some want to work past the normal retirement age because they are healthy and want to keep active; others have to work because their retirement account has dwindled and they cannot afford to retire.

9. *Explain problems with conducting disciplinary action in the global environment.* Because of the differences in how governments view disciplinary action in the global environment, it is very difficult for a global company to establish a standardized policy on disciplinary action.

Key Terms

internal employee relations   336
employment at will   336
discipline   336
disciplinary action   336
progressive disciplinary action   339
disciplinary action without
   punishment   340
termination   341

emotional intelligence (EQ)   342
demotion   344
downsizing   344
outplacement   345
severance pay   346
ombudsperson   346
alternative dispute resolution
   (ADR)   347

transfer   347
promotion   348
exit interview   348
postexit questionnaire   349
attitude survey   349
offboarding   350
phased retirement   350

Exercises

1. Which of the following jobs would likely be covered by employment at will? Explain why or why not.
   a. college professor
   b. software engineer
   c. company president
   d. unionized machine operator

2. Evaluate the following violations of standards. Using progressive disciplinary action, how might a person be fired for each violation?
   a. late for work
   b. unclean work area
   c. insubordination

Questions for Review

1. Define *internal employee relations*.
2. What is meant by the term *employment at will*?
3. What is the difference between discipline and disciplinary action?
4. What are the steps to follow in the disciplinary action process?
5. Describe the following approaches to disciplinary action:
   (a) hot stove rule
   (b) progressive disciplinary action
   (c) disciplinary action without punishment
6. What are the problems associated with the administration of disciplinary action?
7. Why is emotional intelligence needed in conducting disciplinary action?
8. How does termination often differ with regard to non-managerial/nonprofessional employees, executives, and middle and lower-level managers and professionals?
9. Define *demotion*. Why should it be used very cautiously?
10. Define *downsizing*. What are some problems associated with downsizing?
11. What is the purpose of the Worker Adjustment and Retraining Notification Act?
12. Define *outplacement* and *severance pay*.
13. Define *ombudsperson* and *alternative dispute resolution (ADR)*. Why might a firm want to use an ombudsperson or alternative dispute resolution?
14. Distinguish between transfers and promotions.
15. Briefly describe the techniques available to determine the real reasons that an individual decides to leave the organization.
16. Define *offboarding*. Why is it important?
17. Define *phased retirement*. Why do so many employees desire to have a phased retirement?

INCIDENT 1 Should He Be Fired?

Toni Berdit is the Washington, D.C., area supervisor for Quik-Stop, a chain of convenience stores. She has full responsibility for managing the seven Quik-Stop stores in Washington. Each store operates with only one person on duty at a time. Although several of the stores stay open all night, every night, the Center Street store is open all night Monday through Thursday but only from 6:00 A.M. to 10:00 P.M., Friday through Sunday. Because the store is open fewer hours during the weekend, money from sales is kept in the store safe until Monday. Therefore, the time it takes to complete a money count on Monday is greater than normal. The company has a policy that when the safe is being emptied, the manager has to be with the employee on duty, and the employee has to place each $1,000 in a brown bag, mark the bag, and leave the bag on the floor next to the safe until the manager verifies the amount in each bag.

Bill Catron worked the Monday morning shift at the Center Street store and was trying to save his manager time by counting the money prior to his arrival. The store got very busy, and, while bagging a customer's groceries, Bill mistook one of the moneybags for a bag containing three sandwiches and put the moneybag in with the groceries. Twenty minutes later, Toni arrived, and they both began to search for the money. While they were searching, a customer came back with the bag of money. Quik-Stop has a general policy that anyone

violating the money-counting procedure could be fired immediately. However, the ultimate decision was left up to the supervisor and his or her immediate boss.

Bill was very upset. "I really need this job," Bill exclaimed. "With the new baby and all the medical expenses we've had, I sure can't stand to be out of a job."

"You knew about the policy, Bill," said Toni.

"Yes, I did, Toni," said Bill, "and I really don't have any excuse. If you don't fire me, though, I promise you that I'll be the best store manager you've got."

While Bill waited on a customer, Toni called her boss at the home office. With the boss's approval, Toni decided not to fire Bill.

Questions

1. Do you agree with Toni's decision? Discuss.
2. What signal might the decision not to fire Bill give to other store managers?
3. Quik-Stop had a general policy that anyone violating the money-counting procedure could be fired immediately. What would Toni be forced to do if the company had a rule regarding money-counting procedures?

INCIDENT 2 To Heck with Them!

Isabelle Anderson is the North Carolina plant manager for Hall Manufacturing Company, a company that produces a line of relatively inexpensive painted wood furniture. Six months ago Isabelle became concerned about the turnover rate among workers in the painting department. Manufacturing plant turnover rates in that part of the South generally averaged about 30 percent, which was the case at Hall. The painting department, however, had experienced a turnover of nearly 200 percent in each of the last two years. Because of the limited number of skilled workers in the area, Hall had introduced an extensive training program for new painters, and Isabelle knew that the high turnover rate was very costly.

Isabelle conducted exit interviews with many of the departing painters. Many of them said that they were leaving for more money, others mentioned better benefits, and some cited some kind of personal reasons for quitting. But there was nothing to help Isabelle pinpoint the problem. Isabelle had checked and found that Hall's wages and benefits were competitive with, if not better than, those of other manufacturers in the area. She then called in Nelson Able, the painting supervisor, to discuss the problem. Nelson's response was, "To heck with them! They will do it my way or they can hit the road. You know how this younger generation is. They work to get enough money to live on for a few weeks and then quit. I don't worry about it. Our old-timers can take up the slack." After listening to Nelson for a moment, Isabelle thought that she might know what caused the turnover problem.

Questions

1. Interpret a turnover rate of 200 percent. What does it mean?
2. Do you believe that the exit interviews were accurate? Explain your answer.
3. What do you believe was the cause of the turnover problem?

MyManagementLab

Go to **mymanagementlab.com** for Auto-graded writing questions as well as the following Assisted-graded writing questions:

13-1. Why is worker retention of top performers even more important when the economy has slowed?

13-2. What might be some problems associated with conducting disciplinary action in the global environment?

13-3. Mymanagementlab Only – comprehensive writing assignment for this chapter.

Notes

1. "In Rebounding Job Market, Keeping Key Employees Is Growing Challenge," *HR Focus* 89 (April 2012): 1–4.
2. Jan Ferri-Reed, "To Develop Is to Retain," *Chief Learning Officer* 10 (August 2011): 28–35.
3. "Trend #5: Benefits and the Coming Employee Retention Crisis," *Trends Magazine* (October 2011): 30–32.
4. Robert Ceniceros, "'Flight Risks' Need an Anchor," *Business Insurance* 45 (August 8, 2011): 8.
5. "Exit of Corporate Captains Is Reminder to Focus on Engaging Talent Pool," *HR Focus* 89 (February 2012): 16.
6. Jason Boltax, "Love 'Em or Lose 'Em: Retaining Talented Employees," *CPA Practice Management Forum* 7 (2011): 19–22.
7. Robert J. Grossman, "The Care and Feeding of High-Potential Employees," *HR Magazine* 56 (August 2011): 34–39.
8. Alice Hill, "Protect Your 'Gold' Employees," *Baseline* (September/October 2011): 8.
9. Vadim Liberman, "The Perfect Punishment," *Conference Board Review* 46 (January/February 2009): 32–39.
10. Bob Whipple, "8 Be-Attitudes," *Leadership Excellence* 29 (February 2012): 15.
11. Michael S. Lavenant, "The Art of Employee Discipline: How to Retain Control & Increase Production," *Nonprofit World* 28 (July/August 2010): 22–23.
12. T.L. Stanley, "Disciplinary Action and Fairness," *Supervision* 72 (August 2011): 3–6.
13. "What It Means to You," *Legal Alert for Supervisors* 5 (September 1, 2009): 2.
14. David B. Ritter and Mari Kaluza, "Lesson from Walmart: How to Cut Risk when a Co-worker Harasses," *HR Specialist: Illinois Employment Law* 5 (May 2011): 6.
15. "Document All Disciplinary Actions, Including Why and When You Decided to Act," *HR Specialist: New Jersey Employment Law* 6 (May 2011): 3.
16. Daniel C. Finley, "Develop Emotional Intelligence," *Advisor Today* 104 (November 2009): 58–59.
17. Barbara J. A. Eiser, "Emotional Intelligence: Why You Need It for Success," *Pennsylvania CPA Journal* 82 (Spring 2011): 1–3.
18. Richard S. Colfax, John J. Rivera, and Karri T. Perez, "Applying Emotional Intelligence (EQ-1) in the Workplace: Vital to Global Business Success," *Journal of International Business Research* 9 (January 2010): 89–98.
19. Denise Federer, "The Power of Emotional Intelligence," *On Wall Street* 21 (February 2011): 47–48.
20. Martha McCarty, "Emotional IQ," *OfficePro* 70 (March/April 2010): 22–25.
21. Joanne Reid, "The Resilient Leader: Why EQ Matters," *Ivey Business Journal* 72 (May/June 2008): 1–7.

22. Harvey Deutschendorf, "EQ Boost," *T+D* 63 (October 2009): 92–93.

23. Jonathan Perks, "How to Develop Emotional Intelligence," *People Management* 14 (May 1, 2008): 42.

24. Margery Weinstein, "Emotional Evaluation," *Training* 46 (September 2009): 16.

25. "Which Day of the Week Is Best to Fire, Hire and Give Reviews?" *HR Specialist: New York Employment Law* 7 (July 2009): 6.

26. "Don't Pile on Reasons for Firing; You're Spoiling for Retaliation Fight in Court," *HR Specialist: Texas Employment Law* 5 (April 2010): 2.

27. "10 Steps to Stress-free, Lawsuit-free Termination Meetings," *HR Specialist: New York Employment Law* 7 (July 2009): 6.

28. "Three Keys to Keep Terminations from Turning into Lawsuits," *Legal Alert for Supervisors* 5 (March 15, 2010): 3.

29. Liz Wolgemuth, Kimberly Palmer, Katy Marquardt, Matthew Bandy, Rick Newman, and Marty Nemko, "Career Guide 2008," *U.S. News & World Report* 144 (March 24, 2008): 45–61.

30. Kevin Kelly, "The CEO Revolving Door," *BusinessWeek.com* (December 13, 2010): 7.

31. Max Abelson and Ambereen Chaudhury, "After Massive Job Cuts, Wall Street's a Different Place," *Bloomberg Businessweek* (December 5, 2011): 55–57.

32. Jeff Horwitz, "B of A Payroll Cuts the Tip Of the Iceberg for Industry," *American Banker* 176 (August 22, 2011): 1–11.

33. Geoff Colvin, "How Are Most Admired Companies Different? They Invest in People and Keep Them Employed, Even in a Downturn," *Fortune* 161 (March 22, 2010): 82.

34. Robert Sutton, "Layoffs and Creativity: Are You Expelling the Innovators?" *Communication World* 26 (January/February 2009): 48.

35. "Forced to Lay Off People? Don't Forget Those Who Remain," *Legal Alert for Supervisors* 4 (May 4, 2009): 3.

36. Shirley M. Mayton, "Survivor Coping," *OD Practitioner* 43 (Winter 2011): 42–47.

37. Susan Storm Smith, "In a Time of Layoffs, Keep Human Resources Humane," *BusinessWeek Online* (March 19, 2009): 11.

38. Pat Galagan, "The Biggest Losers: The Perils of Extreme Downsizing," *T+D* 64 (November 2010): 27–29.

39. Vickie Elmer, "The Invisible Promotion," *Fortune* 163 (February 7, 2011): 31–32.

40. "Plant Closings: You Must Give 60 Days' Notice," *HR Specialist: California Employment Law* 5 (March 2011): 1–2.

41. "Century Closes W.Va. Smelter," *Metal Producing & Processing* 47 (March/April 2009): 4.

42. "Know Your Layoff Rules of Procedures," *HR Focus* 86 (February 2009): 2.

43. "Employees Get B&C Lender Settlement," *National Mortgage News* 33 (May 18, 2009): 15.

44. Lauren Williamson, "Grocer Gave Fair WARN-ing," *InsideCounsel* 20 (April 2009): 77.

45. "Severance, Outplacement Receive More Attention," *HR Focus* 86 (June 2009): 12.

46. "Compensation Strategies," *Report on Salary Surveys* 11 (February 2011): 8–9.

47. "Survey Finds Severance Pay Declines for U.S. Employees," *Report on Salary Surveys* 9 (January 2009): 4.

48. Anne E. Moran, "Waivers and Severance Arrangements: EEOC Announcement Offers Reminders for Employers," *Employee Relations Law Journal* 35 (2010): 72–80.

49. Rita Zeidner, "Most Employers Require Waivers for Severance Pay," *HR Magazine* 54 (January 2009): 27.

50. "How Employers Are Handling Severance," *Managing Benefits Plans* 10 (February 2010): 12–15.

51. "8 Keys to Negotiating Severance," *Executive Leadership* 24 (June 2009): 8.

52. "5 Questions: Melissa Cameron, Ombudsman, North American Operations, Bayer Corp," *Workforce Management* 88 (October 19, 2009): 8.

53. James J. Rooney, "Jury Waivers: Your New Alternative to Arbitration Agreements?" *HR Specialist: New York Employment Law* 7 (January 2012): 6.

54. "Arbitration Agreements: The Way to Stop Employee Lawsuits Forever," *Supervision* 69 (February 2008): 14–15.

55. "Choosing Employees for Promotion: A 6-step Legal Process," *HR Specialist: New York Employment Law* 4 (August 2009): 4.

56. Patricia M. Buhler, "The Exit Interview: A Goldmine of Information," *Supervision* 72 (August 2011): 11–13.

57. Sue Sommercille and Amy-Kate Snowise, "Get the Most Out of Your Exit Interviewing," *Human Resources Magazine* 16 (June/July 2011): 28–29.

58. Kenya McCullum, "The Retention Intention," *OfficePro* 69 (2009 Special Edition): 8–11.

59. Sharon Meers and Joanna Strober, "When Women Don't Tell the Truth," *Conference Board Review* 46 (Summer 2009): 9–10.

60. Wanda R. Embrey, R. Wayne Mondy, and Robert M. Noe, "Exit Interview: A Tool for Personnel Development," *Personnel Administrator* 24 (May 1979): 46.

61. "Use Exit Interviews to Spot Boss's Hidden Bias," *HR Specialist* 9 (May 2011): 3.

62. Terence E. Shea, "Getting the Last Word," *HR Magazine* 55 (January 2010): 24–25.

63. Kathryn Tyler, "Who Will Stay and Who Will Go?" *HR Magazine* 56 (December 2011): 101–103.

64. Wendy Phaneuf, "Gaining Insight: What Employee Opinion Surveys Can Tell You," *Security: Solutions for Enterprise Security Leaders* 48 (July 2011): 23.

65. Lin Grensing-Pophal, "To Ask or Not to Ask," *HR Magazine* 54 (February 2009): 53–55.

66. John Lamb, "Offboarding: Completing the Cycle Efficiently," *Employee Benefit Advisor* 9 (June 2011): 60–61.

67. Elizabeth Galentine, "Parting Ways Pleasantly," *Employee Benefit News* 23 (June 2009): 42–43.

68. Neal E. Cutler, "Working in Retirement: The Longevity Perplexities Continue," *Journal of Financial Service Professionals* 65 (July 2011): 19–22.

69. Eric Krell, "Ways to Phase Retirement," *HR Magazine* 55 (October 2010): 89–96.

70. "Working After Retirement May Lead to Better Health," *EHS Today* 2 (November 2009): 18.

71. "The Silver Tsunami," *Economist* 394 (February 6, 2010): 74.

72. Anna Rappaport, "Phased Retirement—An Important Part of the Evolving Retirement Scene," *Benefits Quarterly* 25 (2009 Second Quarter): 38–50.

73. Miller Stephen, "Phased Retirement Keeps Boomers in the Workforce," *HR Magazine* (December 2008): 61–62.

74. V. L., "When You Don't Get to Make the Rules," *Conference Board Review* 46 (January/February 2009): 37.

75. Robert J. Samuelson, "The (New) Sick Man of Europe," *Newsweek* 140 (November 18, 2002): 59.

76. Neal E. Boudette, "Searching for Solutions, Germany May Tackle Taboo—Economic Woes Lead Some to Say Beloved Job Law Is Ripe for Rethinking," *Wall Street Journal* (February 28, 2003): A7.

77. Mehul Srivastava, "In India, 101 Employees Pose Big Problems," *Bloomberg Businessweek* (January 17, 2011): 13–14.

78. Neil B. Krupp, "Global Compensation Planning—Establishing and Maintaining a Competitive Edge in the International Marketplace," *Compensation & Benefits Management* 18 (Spring 2002): 54–56.

79. "Firms Don't Focus on Aging Staffers," *Investor's Business Daily* (January 9, 2012): 1.

80. Tomeka M. Hill, "Why Doesn't Every Employer Have a Phased Retirement Program?" *Benefits Quarterly* 26 (2010 Fourth Quarter): 29–39.

81. "Key Steps to Recruiting & Retaining Older Workers," *H&HN: Hospitals & Health Networks* 82 (January 2008): 55–56.

82. Tamara Lytle, "Benefits for Older Workers," *HR Magazine* 57 (March 2012): 52–58.

Part Eight
Operating in a Global Environment

Chapter 14
Global Human Resource
Management

14 Global Human Resource Management

HRM in Action

Global Bribery, the Conviction List Grows

OBJECTIVE 14.1

Describe the impact of global bribery in the international arena.

The United States is rigorously enforcing the Foreign Corrupt Practices Act (FCPA), which prohibits U.S. firms from bribing foreign officials. However, countries other than the United States face far fewer constraints when dealing with bribery. Although the 35 signatories of the Organization of Economic Cooperation and Development's 1997 convention made it a crime to bribe foreign officials, there has been little enforcement of laws by national governments, other than by the United States. Not having the ability to use bribery as a tool of doing business has been costly for American companies.

The 9/11 attacks caused authorities to take a much closer look at financial data as they searched for terrorists' funds, and found bribery corruption in the process.[1] Under the FCPA, it is illegal to pay or attempt to pay bribes to foreign officials in connection with getting business, keeping business, or gaining an improper advantage over competitors. These provisions apply to any U.S. citizen, national, or resident wherever they are, as well as to any U.S.-based or U.S.-listed company. Criminal penalties for individuals include fines of up to $250,000 per violation and imprisonment up to five years, or both. Business entities may be required to pay criminal fines up to $2 million per violation.[2]

The list of convictions under the FCPA continues to grow. In 2011, Johnson & Johnson (J&J) agreed to pay a total of $70 million in a settlement, including $21.4 in criminal penalties and $48.6 million in fines. J&J admitted that its British subsidiary DePuy Inc. had paid bribes to government officials in Greece, Romania, and Poland since 1998. The SEC accused an IBM Korean subsidiary of bribing Korean and Chinese officials from 1998 to 2003. Although IBM did not admit any wrongdoing, it agreed to pay $10 million in fines and penalties.[3] Lucent paid a multimillion-dollar fine for "training" trips it had arranged for executives from state-owned

1. Describe the impact of global bribery in the international arena.
2. Describe the evolution of global business and global strategic human resource management.
3. Explain global staffing.
4. Explain some global issues confronting women.
5. Describe global human resource development.
6. Explain global compensation.

7. Describe global safety and health.
8. Explain global employee and labor relations.
9. Describe legal and political factors affecting global human resource management.
10. Describe possible advantages and disadvantages related to globalization for small and medium-sized businesses.

foreign telecommunications firms to Las Vegas and Orlando, rather than to factories. DynCorp International, a military contractor, fired one of its top lawyers after an internal investigation into potential FCPA violations suggested payments totaling about $300,000 were made to speed up the visa and license process.[4] Avon Products Inc. fired four employees in connection with its ongoing bribery probe in China and additional countries. The investigation focused on expenses, including travel, entertainment, gifts, and payments, to foreign governments, their employees, or other agents connected with its business dealings.[5] Conducting business globally exposes the United States and other companies to an environment that permits bribery, which is against the law in the United States. To ward against problems, some companies have started deploying internal audit teams to help their compliance and legal departments uncover potential FCPA breaches and improve processes and controls.[6]

Some have wondered if ethics can have any middle ground and if there is a middle ground where the answer of "maybe" would be appropriate. The specific culture of a country may answer that question. Western societies are based on the philosophies of Aristotle and Plato and are essentially black and white with no middle ground. On the other hand, Asians believe that ethics depend on the situation. Therefore, Asians may violate their company's code of ethics or even the Foreign Corrupt Practices Act without realizing anything is wrong.[7]

OBJECTIVE **14.2**

Describe the evolution of global business and global strategic human resource management.

Evolution of Global Business

The environment confronted by businesses today is so vastly different from doing business in one or two countries of only a few decades ago. The world is becoming more of a multinational community in which the interdependencies between countries and between organizations are increasing dramatically. It is now one large marketplace consisting of 6.6 billion people speaking 6,700 languages, with thousands of governments all having different regulations and tax requirements. There are more than 900,000 organizations; the top 500 companies generate over $21 trillion.[8] In fact, only five percent of the total amount of consumers worldwide resides in the United States.[9]

With globalization, everybody in the organization, and especially in the HR department, has had to change focus, change attitude, and adjust the approach in the way an organization operates. Not long ago, Mercedes-Benz was still a "German" company, General Electric was "American," and Sony was "Japanese," but today these companies are truly global. Years ago, a lot of U.S. multinational corporations had operations in Canada or perhaps Mexico, but not in many other countries. Now, U.S. firms such as Coca-Cola, Procter & Gamble, and Texas Instruments do most of their business and employ most of their workers outside the United States. Countless products of U.S. companies are made outside the country. Many non-U.S. companies make products here, such as Toyota American, which manufactures cars in Kentucky. Companies still regularly do business in Canada and Mexico, but many now have operations in Hong Kong, Singapore, Japan, the United Kingdom, France, Germany, and Southeast Asia, to name a few. More and more U.S. global corporations are doing business in former Eastern Bloc countries. Vietnam, a country with which the United States was at war throughout the 1960s until the mid-1970s, now has U.S. firms operating there. Stewart McCardle, vice president of global financial services for Weichert Relocation Resources Inc., said, "U.S. companies are placing employees throughout Africa, the Middle East and Eastern Europe. In South America, it's not just Brazil or Argentina, but also Chile and Colombia."[10]

Today, globalization is not limited to only large organizations. It is now important for both large and small firms. Going global can provide a company with an assortment of rewards. The major benefit is that having a global customer base provides some protection against domestic business cycles. Companies that export tend to be more profitable, better organized, and more competitive than are companies that are exclusively domestically focused.

Most companies initially become global without making substantial investments in foreign countries by exporting, licensing, or franchising. Ultimately, they may become a multinational, global, or transnational corporation.

Exporting

exporting

Selling abroad, either directly or indirectly, by retaining foreign agents and distributors.

Exporting entails selling abroad, either directly or indirectly, by retaining foreign agents and distributors. It is a way that many small businesses enter the global market. When deciding to enter the global arena, exporters need to identify and understand their target markets. Companies must determine whether the market or country needs their products or services, whether there are any import tariffs or quotas, and the local pricing structures. Also, exporters have to understand and manage other countries' cultures and governmental policies.[11]

Licensing

licensing

Arrangement whereby an organization grants a foreign firm the right to use intellectual properties such as patents, copyrights, manufacturing processes, or trade names for a specific period of time.

Licensing is an arrangement whereby an organization grants a foreign firm the right to use intellectual properties such as patents, copyrights, manufacturing processes, or trade names for a specific period of time. Licensing is usually limited to manufacturers. The use of a licensing arrangement is expanding in emerging markets.

Franchising

franchising

Option whereby the parent company grants another firm the right to do business in a prescribed manner.

Franchising is an option whereby the parent company grants another firm the right to do business in a prescribed manner. The growth of franchising in the world is phenomenal. Franchisees must follow stricter operational guidelines than do licensees. Fifteen years ago only the giants such as McDonalds were meaningfully engaged in international franchising. Today, among the top 200 franchisors in the United States, 32 percent of their units operate outside the United

multinational corporation (MNC)

Firm that is based in one country (the parent or home country) and produces goods or provides services in one or more foreign countries (host countries).

global corporation

Organization that has corporate units in a number of countries that are integrated to operate as one organization worldwide.

transnational corporation

Organization that moves work to the places with the talent to handle the job and the time to do it at the right cost.

States, a one-third jump in only 10 years.[12] High demand U.S. franchise categories include food and beverage, health and beauty, wellness and fitness, professional services, education, apparel/textile, and retail.[13] KFC saw the benefit of being an early entrant into China and has more than 3,000 KFCs located throughout China, making Yum! Brands the largest U.S. franchisor in that country.[14] Yum! Brands, also the parent company of Pizza Hut and Taco Bell, intends to open 80 percent of its 900 new restaurants in 2011 in emerging markets. Quizno's franchised for the first time in India. Naked Pizza of New Orleans recently opened its N K D Pizza in Dubai, United Arab Emirates.[15]

In determining whether international franchising is justified, the company must evaluate the amount of time, effort, risk, and legal proceedings related to selling a franchise internationally. It also must determine whether the product is valued in the targeted country. Also, the unique culture of the country should be a part of the decision-making process. Most franchise companies have to bend and change to the cultural experiences of each individual country. Many countries such as Australia, Brazil, China, France, Indonesia, Italy, Japan, Malaysia, Mexico, Russia, South Korea, Spain, and Venezuela have their own specific regulations.[16] Most U.S. companies rely heavily on contractual relationships; however, in many other countries, people conduct business based on relationships first rather than relying on a contract. For example, in countries such as Singapore, Australia, and the United Kingdom, it is best to focus on the specifics of the contract and provide detailed information when negotiating with prospects or their attorneys. In most Latin American countries, the Middle East, and China, it is very important to first build a solid relationship with the investor.[17]

Multinational Corporation

Companies can vary greatly in their degree of global involvement. A **multinational corporation (MNC)** is a firm that is based in one country (the parent or home country) and produces goods or provides services in one or more foreign countries (host countries). A multinational corporation directs manufacturing and marketing operations in several countries; these operations are coordinated by a parent company, usually based in the firm's home country.

Global Corporation

A **global corporation** is an organization that has corporate units in a number of countries that are integrated to operate as one organization worldwide. The global corporation operates as if the entire world were one entity. Global corporations sell essentially the same products throughout the world with components that may be made and/or designed in different countries. Expectations are that as the world becomes more globally open, the globalization of corporations will become much more commonplace. Not many years ago Procter & Gamble was primarily a U.S. business investing heavily in food brands. Now it is a truly global corporation with more than 300 brands in over 180 countries crossing the Americas, Europe, the Middle East and Africa, and Asia.[18] Its corporate leaders are an extremely diverse group, representing many cultures and backgrounds. Another global company, Johnson & Johnson has more than 115,000 employees in 250 businesses in 70 countries.[19]

Transnational Corporation

Today, global corporations are transforming themselves into transnationals. A **transnational corporation** moves work to the places with the talent to handle the job and the time to do it at the right cost. William J. Amelio, the CEO of Lenovo, the world's third-largest computer maker, calls his global workforce strategy "worldsourcing." Lenovo has executive offices in five cities worldwide and organizes its workforce around hubs of expertise, such as hardware designers in Japan and marketers in India. "You operate as if there's just one time zone," Amelio says. "And you're always on."[20]

The importance of human resource management in the global environment is illustrated by the fact that the Human Resource Certification Institute now has an international component. The Global Professional in Human Resources certification focuses on strategic HR management, global talent acquisition and mobility, global compensation and benefits, organizational effectiveness, talent development, workforce relations, and risk management.[21]

Global Strategic Human Resource Management

The world is experiencing an increasing global workforce. Global human resource problems and opportunities are enormous and are expanding. Individuals dealing with global human resource matters face a multitude of challenges beyond that of their domestic counterparts. These considerations range from cultural to political barriers to international aspects such as compensation. Before upper management decides on a global move, it is vitally important that the critical nature of human resource issues be considered. Companies that engage in the global economy place even greater emphasis on strategic HR.

Culture differences are often the biggest barrier to doing business in the world market. The functional areas associated with effective global human resource management are similar to the ones they experience domestically, as shown in Figure 14-1. Although the five functions are the same, the global external environmental factors may significantly impact the manner in which they are implemented. Sound global human resource management practices are required for successful performance in each area. As with domestic human resources, the functional areas are not separate and distinct, but are highly interrelated.

OBJECTIVE 14.3

Explain global staffing.

Global Staffing

Companies must choose from various types of global staff members and may use specific approaches to global staffing. Global staff members may be selected from among three different types: expatriates, host-country nationals, and third-country nationals.

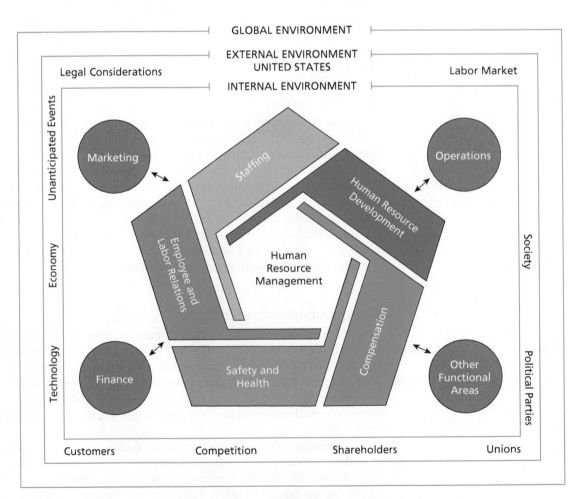

FIGURE 14-1

Environment of Global Human Resource Management

Global Issues Confronting Women

Sexual harassment is only one concern facing women in the global environment. According to a recent United Nations study entitled *Women, the United Nations Entity for Gender Equality and the Empowerment of Women,* some countries do not provide women equal access to jobs because they are barred from working in the same industries as men or are forbidden to work at night. The report further estimates 603 million women live in countries where domestic violence is not considered a crime.[22]

The global assignment of women and members of racial/ethnic minorities can involve cultural and legal issues. Regrettably, female talent is underutilized in emerging countries. This may be partly explained by family-related constraints and pressures, as well as work-related issues that combine to force women to either settle for dead-end jobs or leave the workforce. For example, in Saudi Arabia, women are not permitted to drive.[23] In China, there is a social stigma attached to women who use professional help or who place their parents in assisted-living facilities. Often global careers are affected when a worker decides to return to China to take care of her family. In the United Arab Emirates, a single woman cannot board a plane or stay in a hotel unless a male relative is willing to accompany her. In many emerging markets, workplace bias seems to escalate for young mothers. In India, a woman returning from a global assignment often is given less-challenging roles or projects or receives lower performance ratings.[24]

There are also some positive trends that have emerged regarding women working the global environment. According to a recent study, nearly three million female university graduates enter the Chinese workforce each year. Of the total Graduate Management Admission Test applicants, 40 percent are male and 60 percent are female. The study also discovered that 76 percent of Chinese women aspire to top-level positions compared to only 52 percent in the United States.[25]

Economic growth in the BRIC countries of Brazil, Russia, India, China and in the United Arab Emirates far outpaces growth in developed nations. Women are rapidly moving into the management ranks. In 2009, women accounted for about 40 percent of the Brazilian labor force, but held 45 percent of managerial jobs and 30 percent of executive positions. China has the highest female labor-force participation rate of all BRIC nations, with 75 percent of women ages 15 to 65 in the workforce. Ninety-one percent of Chinese companies have senior female leaders, and women hold 32 percent of all senior management positions. But, these women also confront problems of gender bias, significant elder care responsibilities, and long workweeks.[26]

American workers employed by American-controlled businesses operating overseas are still protected under the American employment laws. Women currently make up nearly 25 percent of expatriates, which is up from 14 percent not long ago.[27] Unfortunately, these gains in female expatriate participation rates have not been equally distributed worldwide. The gender gaps still exist in the Middle East, South Asia, and parts of Africa.[28] There are some countries in which the sexist culture is so ingrained that women would have extreme difficulty participating on equal footing with the majority population in the workforce. In fact, there are some cultures today that will not accept a woman as a boss.

| OBJECTIVE **14.4**
Explain some global issues confronting women.

expatriate
Employee who is not a citizen of the country in which a firm's operations are located, but is a citizen of the country in which the organization is headquartered.

host-country national (HCN)
Employee who is a citizen of the country where the subsidiary is located.

third-country national (TCN)
Citizen of one country, working in a second country, and employed by an organization headquartered in a third country.

Expatriate

An **expatriate** is an employee who is not a citizen of the country in which the firm operations are located, but is a citizen of the country in which the organization is headquartered. The U.S. expatriate population has grown rapidly largely because of the large numbers of workers who are being sent to China and India.

Host-country National

A **host-country national (HCN)** is an employee who is a citizen of the country where the subsidiary is located. An example would be a U.S. citizen working for a Japanese company in the United States. Normally, the bulk of employees in international businesses will be host-country nationals. Companies that are staffed by locals not only are typically less expensive, but also offer advantages from a cultural and business standpoint. In most industries, host-country nationals comprise more than 98 percent of the workforce in the foreign operations of North American and Western European multinational companies. Halliburton is a leading energy services company headquartered in the United States with 60,000 employees working in 80 countries, and speaking 200 languages. Halliburton's workforce, including managers, is overwhelmingly made up of citizens of the host country.[29] Hiring local people and operating the company like local companies whenever possible is good business. The ultimate goal of most foreign operations is to turn over control to local management.

Third-country national

A **third-country national (TCN)** is a citizen of one country, working in a second country, and employed by an organization headquartered in a third country. An example would be an Italian citizen working for a French company in Germany.

Approaches to Global Staffing

Using the three basic types of global staff, there are four major approaches to global staffing: ethnocentric, polycentric, regiocentric, and geocentric staffing. These approaches reflect how the organization develops its human resource policies and the preferred types of employees for different positions.

ethnocentric staffing

Staffing approach in which companies primarily hire expatriates to staff higher-level foreign positions.

ETHNOCENTRIC STAFFING With **ethnocentric staffing**, companies primarily hire expatriates to staff higher-level foreign positions. This would be the case with Rich Products Corporation, based in Buffalo, New York, with $2.6 billion in annual sales. Rich sells food products in 73 countries and employs 7,300 workers worldwide. Judy Campbell, vice president, international human resources, said, "Our strategy has always been to focus on local talent development. We have never had more than six expats in any of our international locations."[30] This strategy assumes that home-office perspectives and issues should take precedence over local perspectives and issues and that expatriates will be more effective in representing the views of the home office. The corporate human resources department is primarily concerned with selecting and training managers for foreign assignments, developing appropriate compensation packages, and handling adjustment issues when managers return home. Generally, expatriates are used to ensure that foreign operations are linked effectively with parent corporations.

polycentric staffing

Staffing approach in which host-country nationals are used throughout the organization, from top to bottom.

POLYCENTRIC STAFFING When host-country nationals are used throughout the organization, from top to bottom, it is referred to as **polycentric staffing**. In developed countries such as Japan, Canada, and the United Kingdom, there has been more reliance on local executives and less on traditional expatriate management. The ultimate goal of most foreign operations is to turn over control to local management. The use of the polycentric staffing model is based on the assumption that host-country nationals are better equipped to deal with local market conditions. Organizations that use this approach will usually have a fully functioning human resource department in each foreign subsidiary responsible for managing all local human resource issues. Corporate human resource managers focus primarily on coordinating relevant activities with their counterparts in each foreign operation. Most global employees are usually host-country nationals, because this helps to clearly establish that the company is making a commitment to the host country and not just setting up a foreign operation. Host-country nationals often have much more thorough knowledge of the culture, the politics, and the laws of the locale, as well as how business is done. There is no standard format in the selection of host-country nationals.

regiocentric staffing

Staffing approach that is similar to the polycentric staffing approach, but regional groups of subsidiaries reflecting the organization's strategy and structure work as a unit.

REGIOCENTRIC STAFFING **Regiocentric staffing** is similar to the polycentric approach, but regional groups of subsidiaries reflecting the organization's strategy and structure work as a unit. There is some degree of autonomy in regional decision making, and promotions are possible within the region but rare from the region to headquarters. Each region develops a common set of employment practices.

geocentric staffing

Staffing approach that uses a worldwide integrated business strategy.

GEOCENTRIC STAFFING **Geocentric staffing** is a staffing approach that uses a worldwide integrated business strategy. The firm attempts to always hire the best person available for a position, regardless of where that individual comes from. The geocentric staffing model is most likely to be adopted and used by truly global firms. Usually, the corporate human resource function in geocentric companies is the most complicated, since every aspect of HR must be dealt with in the global environment.

Recruiting Host-country Nationals

One of the biggest mistakes that can be made in the multinational arena is to assume that the recruiting approaches that work in the parent company will also be effective in recruiting host-country nationals. For example, an error that many recruiters make is believing that all countries in Europe are similar or the same. Thinking that Italy is similar to France simply because the countries are close to each other is like believing that the United States is similar to Mexico because they are neighbors in North America. The use of technology in global recruiting also varies considerably. For example, although Scandinavian companies in Norway, Sweden, and Denmark were amongst the first to promote Internet use for recruiting, recruiters in France, Italy, and much of southern Europe do not use it as much.[31]

HR Web Wisdom

Worldwide ERC: The Workforce Mobility Association

http://www.worldwideerc.org/ about_us

Association for professionals who oversee, manage, or support U.S. domestic and international employee transfers.

Selecting Expatriates

Expatriates are often selected from those already within the organization, and the process involves four distinct stages: self-selection, creating a candidate pool, technical skills assessment, and making a mutual decision.

In stage one, self-selection, candidates determine whether they are right for a global assignment, whether their spouses and children are interested in relocating internationally, and whether this is the best time for a move. In the case of self-selection, the candidates assess themselves on all of the relevant dimensions for a job and then decide whether to pursue a global assignment. The self-assessment extends to the entire family. One survey found that 55 percent of employees facing dual-career issues are less likely to put themselves forward as a candidate for a global assignment.[32] When candidates are selected for expatriate assignments, spouses, partners, and entire families also need to be "selected." Basically, candidates must decide whether to go to the next step in the selection process.

Stage two involves creating a candidate database organized according to the firm's staffing needs. Included in the database is information such as the year the employee is available to go overseas, the languages the employee speaks, the countries the employee prefers, and the jobs for which the employee is qualified.

Stage three involves scanning the database for all possible candidates for a given global assignment; then the list is forwarded to the assigning department. There, each candidate is assessed on technical and managerial readiness relative to the needs of the assignment. In the final stage, one person is identified as an acceptable candidate based on his or her technical or managerial readiness and is tentatively selected.

If the decision is made to employ expatriates, certain selection criteria should be carefully considered in stages two and three. It takes a special blend of person to add up to an outstanding expat who can be productive and accepted in an unfamiliar setting. Expatriate selection criteria should include cultural adaptability, strong communication skills, technical competence, professional or operational expertise, global experience, country-specific experience, interpersonal skills, language skills, family flexibility, and country- or region-specific considerations. However, according to one survey by Cartus, a workforce development provider, when considering employees for international assignments, 72 percent of companies chose technical competence and 65 percent chose job experience.[33]

Background Investigation

Conducting a background investigation on potential employees is especially important in the global environment. According to the HireRight study, 25 percent of global companies either conduct employee screening or have plans to start, an increase from 11 percent in 2009.[34] Conducting background investigations when working in the global environment is equally, or even more, important, but differences across cultures and countries often put up barriers. Each country has its own laws, customs, and procedures for background screenings. For instance, Japanese law covers a person working at the Tokyo office of a U.S.-based company and includes privacy statutes that prohibit criminal checks on Japanese citizens. The United Kingdom does not allow third parties such as background-checking firms to have direct access to criminal records held by local police. Instead, the job applicant and the recruiting organization must sign and submit a formal request to a specific agency responsible for handling criminal records. It can take up to 40 business days to get information back. HireRight, a pre-employment screening company in Irvine, California, tells the story of a person who had been in the United States for two years and had applied for a job with a multinational firm. There were no gaps in the individual's employment history that would suggest he had ever been in jail. However, further checking revealed that he had been convicted of murder in his home country and in accord with a practice that was legal at the time, had paid a proxy to serve his prison term while he remained free and in the workforce.[35]

OBJECTIVE **14.5**

Describe global human resource development.

Global Human Resource Development

Some training and development professionals believe that training and development strategies that work for a U.S. audience can be equally effective abroad. Unfortunately, nothing could be further from the truth. Global training and development is needed because people, jobs, and organizations are often quite different. Next, various aspects of global HR development will be discussed.

FIGURE 14-2
The Expatriate Preparation and Development Program

Expatriate Preparation and Development

Prior to Departure: Orientation and Training	During Assignment: Continual Development	Near Completion: Repatriation Orientation Training
Language Culture History Local Customs Living Conditions	Expanding Skills Career Planning Home-Country Development	U.S. Lifestyle U.S. Workplace U.S. Employees

Expatriate Training and Development

The training of employees going on a global assignment has often been bleak, but appears to be improving. The development process should start as soon as workers are selected—definitely before they begin the global assignment. Organizations are recognizing that expatriate employees and their families face special situations and pressure that training and development activities must prepare them to deal with. Employees and their families must have an effective orientation program and a readjustment-training program. In addition, the employee must have a program of continual development. Figure 14-2 illustrates the ideal expatriate preparation and development program, which includes pre-move orientation and training, continual development, and repatriation orientation and training.

Pre-move Orientation and Training

Pre-move orientation and training of expatriate employees and their families are essential before the global assignment begins. The pre-move orientation needs to be aggressively undertaken so that the expatriate understands cultural dos and don'ts and is immersed in the language. Obviously providing an expatriate a cultural "dummies" guide and a basic phrasebook for speaking the language is not enough. Continuing employee development, in which the employee's global skills are fitted into career planning and corporate development programs, makes the eventual transition to the host home country less disruptive. Marc Sokol, senior vice president at Personnel Decisions International, said, "The cost of failure is very high. If you leave it to self-study, then you're rolling the dice."[36]

Many organizations have established a formal *buddy system* to alleviate the stress new expatriates and their families normally endure and to reduce the time it takes for expatriates to operate at peak productivity. Buddies often inform expatriates of host-office norms and politics, invite them into their homes, introduce them to friends and networks, and help bolster their credibility in the office.

Continual Development: Online Assistance and Training

Companies now offer online assistance and training in areas such as career services, cross-cultural training, and employee assistance programs. The Internet offers global employees assistance 24 hours a day, seven days a week. Technology is a timesaving and cost-effective solution for the stress experienced by employees who are on assignment or doing business travel. With a satellite phone individuals can communicate with one another in undeveloped countries. The distance problems from headquarters cannot be overcome without e-mail and voice mail, but for some issues Skype can be used if there is an Internet connection. Satellite phones throughout the world can also have Internet access, but the price goes up because additional hardware is required. Even if the assignment is a short-term business trip, technology can be used to provide ongoing contact and support with the home country. For example, online career services can give expatriates and their spouses the opportunity to upgrade skills while on assignment.

Repatriation Orientation and Training

Orientation and training are also necessary prior to **repatriation**, which is the process of bringing expatriates home. Repatriation is often the weak link in global human resource management.

HR Web Wisdom

Cartus
http://www.cartus.com/

Global mobility and workforce development support to organizations worldwide.

repatriation
Process of bringing expatriates home.

Returning expatriates have not always had a pleasant experience. Even though a company may spend considerable money in sending managers overseas, too many returning managers report dissatisfaction with the process.[37] Many companies do not specify in advance how the international experience will fit into an employee's career progression. In fact, numerous expatriates were not even guaranteed a job upon their return.[38] Further, expats often come home to a company that has undergone significant change from such events as mergers, acquisitions, reorganizations, and workforce contraction or expansion, which can create an unfamiliar environment.[39]

International businesses spend upward of $1 to $2 million per expatriate manager during a four-year period only to have 20 to 50 percent resign within a year of their return.[40] Reasons given for leaving include they were not being properly prepared to return to their work and were not able to use skills they learned abroad. Employers should make every effort to find a place in the organization that will use the expat's experience gained during the assignment. Also, the returning expat should be given a job with at least the same degree of responsibility and authority.

To counter the challenges of repatriation, firms need to have a formal in-house repatriation program in place. A dialogue regarding expectations and career planning upon return will help to manage expectations. Also, the exchange should continue after the employee has returned home. In addition, acknowledgment and recognition of the significant overseas contribution is a courtesy that the returning employee has earned and richly deserves. Ideally, there should be a clear career path or position identified for the expatriate employee upon his or her return. An effective repatriation training program should support the assignees in defining their new or strengthened skills and knowledge and instruct them on how to posture themselves in the corporate environment to which they have returned.

Global E-learning

The recent recession has made organizations more aware of the cost benefits generated by e-learning.[41] Globalization has created a special need for e-learning, and companies are embracing it to train the global workforce. In the past, a training program for a *Fortune* 200 company in the Far East would likely cost between $250,000 and $500,000 for travel and related expenses. Many believe that live, instructor-led training is still more effective, but the question that must be asked is, "how much more effective?" E-learning allows companies to keep the money and still receive a good training product. The Towards Maturity 2010–2011 Benchmark Survey predicts that at least 25 percent of multinational companies are introducing mobile-device learning, online learning tools, virtual classrooms, podcasting, and social learning tools to support trainers.[42]

The most obvious deterrent to any global e-learning implementation is the failure to recognize the impact of cultural differences on the program's success.[43] Not analyzing the culture or failing to recognize important cultural differences can seriously damage success. One study found that only 25 percent of e-learning implementation plans addressed cultural differences that affect management. Cultural accessibility is required so all learners are able to achieve the same learning outcomes by putting the same amount of effort. A problem that evolves in implementing global e-learning is that the e-learning program is embedded with the culture of the person(s) who developed the program.[44]

Research showed that 91 percent of employees of global corporations said that English is "required" or "important" in their jobs, and that the need is increasing dramatically. Eighty-nine percent of employees said they are more likely to climb the corporate ladder if they can communicate in English. Many companies offer courses only in English or in English and one other language, usually Spanish. An English-only focus works for firms that routinely conduct their business all over the world in English. But others need courses in more than one language. Companies that want to offer courses in several languages usually turn to translators. Financial services provider GE Capital relies on translation companies to offer Web-based courses in English, French, German, and Japanese.[45]

Hilton's team members are scattered the world over. In a sector that sees high turnover rates, it is also hard to imagine that a classroom trainer could keep up with the demands of hundreds of new workers requiring training. Hilton, along with many multinational companies, realized that it could save money through online courses. Hilton first introduced e-learning when the company launched its Hilton University with 60 generic business skills programs and 21 finance programs. Over the years, Hilton put in place an additional 40 business skills courses and significantly increased the number of generic online courses offered. Hilton came a long way in a short period, from 5,000 course completions after the first year to over 40,000 completions in the third year.[46]

Virtual Teams in a Global Environment

Virtual teams are becoming commonplace in many global organizations. In today's workplace it is not surprising to have as many as 50 percent of employees working on virtual teams.[47] Intel Corporation conducted a study that revealed that approximately two-thirds of their employees collaborated with team members located at different sites and in different regions.[48] With virtual teams, team members do not have to meet face-to-face to be effective, thereby eliminating "dead time" caused by traveling. These teams operate across boundaries of time and geography and have become a necessity of everyday working life.

Virtual teams enable companies to accomplish things more quickly and efficiently. The times when virtual team members are in one place are few, especially when members are located across the globe. This often makes global teams more difficult to manage effectively. Communication is the key to keeping teams working effectively together.[49]

Some of the difficulties that virtual teams confront with regard to communication are discussed next. Without face-to-face communication, team members often do not feel as connected or committed to the team. The virtual work environment does not provide opportunities to build trust that come from close proximity.[50] Although meeting face-to-face requires time and expense, virtual teams that invest in one or two such meetings per year perform better overall than those that do not.[51] Obviously face-to-face communication is best for providing feedback followed by video, telephone, instant messaging, e-mail, and bulletin boards. E-mail and bulletin boards are generally best for tasks that require little collaboration such as information sharing. When teams need to solve complex problems or make decisions, technology such as videoconferencing or telepresence can be a valuable asset.[52]

Communication problems between team members appear to be directly proportional to the number of time zones that separate them. An effective virtual leader rotates the time frames when conference calls for team meetings are going to be held so that the same people are not always inconvenienced. If it is only a couple of zones, teammates will be in their offices earlier or later than one another, but their workdays still overlap enough to allow phone calls. If the distance stretches from 9 to 12 time zones, workdays do not overlap at all, and e-mail and voice mail must be used.[53] There is also the language problem to contend with. Since English is becoming the world language, those for whom English is a second language may be at a disadvantage. Many Asians are concerned with saving face if they do not understand something. They may be hesitant to ask questions that would reveal their ignorance, thus widening the communication gap. On the other hand, those who are fluent only in English may be at a disadvantage when working with their international colleagues who move easily between their native languages, English, French, and Mandarin.[54]

There are some general rules to follow in selecting virtual team members. Chad Thompson, Aon Hewitt's senior consultant with the talent and rewards practice, believes that the best virtual workers are those who thrive on interdependent working relationships. He also believes that employees who do not mind or who like ambiguity in their job responsibilities and who have strong communication skills also tend to succeed in virtual work environments. Workers who have been labeled as "lone wolves" usually do not function well in a virtual team because they do not collaborate well.[55]

Virtual team members do not have the luxury of getting together over lunch or just communicating informally in the office. To overcome this lack of informal getting to know each other, Facebook (featuring pictures and profiles of team members), a discussion board, a team calendar, or a chat room might be beneficial. Team members can then connect with each other in ways other than meetings and establish a stronger group bond.[56]

OBJECTIVE 14.6

Explain global compensation.

Global Compensation

Companies that are successful in the global environment align their human resource programs in support of their strategic business plans. A major component is the manner in which the human resource total compensation program supports the way the business is structured, organized, and operated both globally and regionally.

Compensation for Host-country Nationals

Certainly, in compensation-related matters, organizations should think globally but act locally. The realities of global business—in which each country has its own culture and different service expectations—must be reflected in the way employees are serviced.[57] Brad Boyson, head of HR and corporate services for Hamptons MENA, a property company with operations throughout the Middle East, believes that prudent HR professionals should "benchmark on local conditions and add as needed."[58]

One reason that organizations relocate to other areas of the world is probably the high-wage pressures in the home country that threaten their ability to compete on a global basis. Globally, the question of what constitutes a fair day's pay is not as complicated as it is in the United States; normally, it is slightly above the prevailing wage rates in the area. The same is often true of benefits and nonfinancial rewards. Variations in laws, living costs, tax policies, and other factors all must be considered when a company is establishing global compensation packages. For example, Puerto Rico has laws requiring the paying of severance pay and a Christmas bonus. Employers in Nigeria are required to provide a life insurance policy for employees at a rate of three times their salary. In Italy, a mandatory benefit is paid when an employee leaves an organization, regardless of whether this is due to resignation, termination, or retirement. In Belgium, employers offering a defined contribution pension scheme must provide a guaranteed investment return of 3.25 percent.[59]

Some countries have employment laws that feature specific criteria for terminations, including those related to layoffs, shutdowns, mergers and acquisitions, and discharge for cause. Other termination laws call for notice periods, severance requirements, payout of paid time off and incentive compensation, benefits continuation, and employee consent and grievance procedures.[60]

The company will want to create a precise picture of employment and working conditions to establish appropriate practices in each country. Some of the factors that should be considered include minimum-wage requirements, which often differ from country to country and even from city to city within a country; working-time information, such as annual holidays, vacation time and pay, paid personal days, standard weekly working hours, probation periods, and overtime restrictions and payments; and hiring and termination rules and regulations covering severance practices.

Culture often plays a part in determining compensation. North American compensation practices encourage individualism and high performance; continental European programs typically emphasize social responsibility; the traditional Japanese approach considers age and company service as primary determinants of compensation. In other countries, there is no guarantee that additional compensation will ensure additional output. In mainland China, workers who are paid by the hour often do not work hard. Under the communist system, working harder than anyone else did not result in additional pay. Therefore, there was no reason to do so. It has been found that, in some countries, additional pay has resulted in employees' working less. As soon as employees have earned enough to satisfy their needs, time spent with family or on other noncompany activities is perceived as more valuable than additional cash. In former communist countries, people were used to a system in which pay and performance were not related. Under the old system, good employees were paid the same as poor performers. With the collapse of the Iron Curtain, the idea that pay and performance should be related is now making its way into people's minds.

In countries such as France and Greece, where the best graduates often choose government positions with secure paychecks for life, it is quite difficult to attract good employees with pay schemes that include high bonuses for achieving specific objectives. In places such as Hong Kong, where people value risk and are motivated by personal financial gains, employees who have achieved a significant professional result expect a financial form of recognition (raise, bonus, or commission) within a matter of weeks. They are likely to look for another employer if they have to wait until their next annual performance review. Whereas people in the United States derive great status from high pay, nations in large parts of Europe and Asia shun conspicuous wealth. In Italy, where teamwork is more valued than individual initiative, sales incentives for top sales professionals working in small teams can be demotivational. The recipient of a large award may feel awkward when receiving larger than a fair share of the reward pie.

Because of these and other cultural differences, it is difficult to design a global, one-size-fits-all pay scheme that attracts the best talent in all countries. In particular, pay-for-performance schemes often need to be adapted to local preferences, depending on whether income security or higher risks and returns are preferred.

Expatriate Compensation

Expatriate compensation provides exceptional challenges compared to home-country employment, such as developing packages that are reasonably cost-effective while still attractive and motivating. For expatriate managers and professionals, the situation is more complex than simply paying at or slightly above local host-country compensation rates. The largest expatriate costs historically have included overall remuneration, housing, cost-of-living allowances, and physical relocation. Because of the cost associated with moving a manager overseas, some firms are using shorter periods, often done far earlier in a manager's career, to give workers global involvement without moving the entire family.[61] Regarding tax-equalization payments, U.S. citizens living overseas can exclude up to $92,900 of gross income earned abroad.[62] Also, credits against U.S. income taxes are given for a portion of the foreign income taxes paid by U.S. expatriates beyond the $92,900 level.

In the past few years, additional challenges have hit companies as they have attempted to go global. First, the devaluation of the U.S. dollar has had a major impact on expat compensation. Also, there have been changes to the U.S. tax code that affect expatriate lifestyle. These challenges come at a time when global business is expanding. Meeting these challenges will affect how effectively the United States competes in the global market. In the past expats regularly received a premium for taking an overseas assignment. Today, overseas jobs with rich expat packages are becoming less prevalent.[63]

OBJECTIVE **14.7**

Describe global safety and health.

Global Safety and Health

Special needs are often encountered when global safety and health issues are encountered. Global health care provider CIGNA International has teamed up with CIGNA Behavioral Health to offer employee assistance programs (EAPs) for expatriate employees of multinational firms. The EAP allows CIGNA International participants to access a multilingual support and counseling network. Employees and their dependents can receive assistance through telephone or personal visits for a wide range of behavioral health and work–life concerns. The program is designed to help employees better manage stress and anxiety, depression, and substance abuse, as well as to help them lead healthy lifestyles.

Specific to global assignments are emergency evacuation services and global security protection. An international firm was preparing to evacuate 15 expatriate employees and dependents from a country that had suffered an earthquake. When it came time to meet at the departure point, 25 people showed up. Those arranging for the evacuation had not known that two technical teams were in the country supporting clients at the time.

Often, evacuation and care of injured employees is done through private companies. Medical emergencies are frightening under any circumstances, but when an employee becomes sick or injured abroad, it can be a traumatic experience. If the travelers are assigned to more remote or less developed areas, companies should be aware that in many medical facilities needles are often reused, equipment is not properly used, and there is a lack of basic medical supplies. Also, employees and their families living abroad must constantly be aware of security issues. Many firms provide bodyguards who escort executives everywhere. Some firms even have disaster plans to deal with evacuating expatriates if natural disasters, civil conflicts, or wars occur.

Global companies continue to face global safety risks. That is one of the lessons learned after the 1984 disaster in Bhopal, India, affected Union Carbide's worldwide operations. The Bhopal disaster was the worst industrial disaster in history. It was caused by the accidental release of 40 metric tons of methyl isocyanate (MIC) from a Union Carbide India, Limited (UCIL), pesticide plant located in the heart of the city of Bhopal, in the Indian state of Madhya Pradesh. UCIL was a joint venture between Union Carbide and a consortium of Indian investors. The accident in the early hours produced heavier-than-air toxic MIC gas, which rolled along the ground through the surrounding streets, killing thousands outright and injuring anywhere from

150,000 to 600,000 others, at least 15,000 of whom died later from their injuries. Some sources give much higher fatality figures.[64]

Health and safety professionals with international experience say one of the most important trends sweeping through successful multinational companies is the shift to a single safety management system that applies to all their operations throughout the world. Although the example of Bhopal revealed the risks of safety failures, experts emphasize that taking a global approach to safety and health is not only about avoiding problems. It also opens up a wealth of opportunities to improve performance. Although events on the scale of Bhopal are rare, many companies have discovered that the way they treat their workers anywhere on the planet can pose a risk to their corporate reputation.

Employers should also be concerned with health issues for host-country nationals. In many instances, employee health has deteriorated because of an increase in chronic disease and lifestyle-related health issues, not only in developed countries, but also in emerging economies such as Mexico, China, and India. Twenty years ago, less than 10 percent of Mexican adults were obese; today, 68 percent are overweight and the problem is becoming increasingly widespread in younger people. It is estimated that 57.2 percent of the Indian population will have diabetes by 2025. China and the Philippines are troubled by inconsistent health care, especially among the poor.[65]

Global Employee and Labor Relations

OBJECTIVE 14.8
Explain global employee and labor relations.

Obviously, the strength and nature of unions differ from country to country, with unions ranging from nonexistent to relatively strong. In fact, unionism in private companies is a declining phenomenon in nearly all developed countries.[66] Codetermination, which requires firms to have union or worker representatives on their boards of directors, is very common in European countries. Even though they face global competition, unions in several European countries have resisted changing their laws and removing government protections. Laws make it hard to fire workers, so companies are reluctant to hire. Generous and lengthy unemployment benefits discourage the jobless from seeking new work. Motorola paid a net pretax charge of about $83 million in related severance fees for jobs cut in Germany. Wage bargaining remains centralized, and companies have little flexibility to fashion contracts that fit their needs. High payroll taxes raise labor costs, and their laws mandating cumbersome layoff procedures increase the cost of the product.

On the other hand, in some South American countries, such as Chile, collective bargaining for textile workers, miners, and carpenters is prohibited. And unions are generally allowed only in companies of 25 workers or more. This practice has encouraged businesses to split into small companies to avoid collective bargaining, leaving workers on their own.

ETHICAL DILEMMA

Mordita

Your company, a distributor of heavy mining equipment, wants to trade in the Mexican market where cash under the table, *mordita* (a little bit), is part of doing business. This payoff practice is so ingrained in the Mexican culture that a business virtually cannot open a Mexican operation without going along. You have observed many companies that did not pay and they failed to enter the Mexican market, as well as those that paid and entered the market, and overall, did fairly well. You can continue to raise your stature with mining companies, farmers, and contractors, and encourage them to lobby the government to freely open the market, or you can pay the bribe.

What would you do?
What factor(s) in this ethical dilemma might influence a person to make a less-than-ethical decision?

OBJECTIVE **14.9**

Describe legal and political factors affecting global human resource management.

Global Legal and Political Factors

The growing complexity of legal compliance in the global environment is one of the most important trends affecting global business. Managers working for global businesses have to contend with a growing tide of employment legislation that cuts across national boundaries. Legal and political forces are unique to each country, and sometimes, the laws of one contradict those of another. For instance, the French authorities acknowledge that their data-protection laws are in direct conflict with the U.S. Sarbanes–Oxley Act, but they insist that multinationals comply with French law. Further, the nature and stability of political and legal systems vary across the globe. U.S. firms enjoy relatively stable legal and political systems, and the same is true in many of the developed countries. In other nations, however, the legal and political systems are much less stable. Some governments are subject to coups, dictatorial rule, and corruption, which can substantially alter both the business and legal environments. Legal systems can also become unstable, with contracts suddenly becoming unenforceable because of internal politics.

HR regulations and laws vary greatly among countries. In the United States, United Kingdom, and Canada the list of hiring standards to avoid is quite lengthy and precise. In India, it is legal for an advertisement for an Indian airline flight attendant to read: "18–27 years old, different height minimums for males and females, status unmarried, unblemished complexion and good eyesight."[67] As previously mentioned, merely conducting a background check is different from one country to another. In many Western European countries, laws on labor unions and employment make it difficult to lay off employees. Because of political and legal differences, it is essential that a comprehensive review of the political and legal environment of the host country is conducted before beginning global operations.

Some have asked the question, "Does operating under local laws and customs free a company of all ethical considerations?" Google certainly understands the problems that can occur when attempting to go global. To do business in China, Google had to submit its search results to government censorship, an undesirable concession. Still, company leaders felt the benefits to the Chinese people would exceed the evils of the censored results and went ahead with it. But after repeated squabbling with the Chinese government and evidence of hacking into the Gmail accounts of dissidents in late 2009 and in March 2010, Google removed its search engine from China.[68] Each company will have to evaluate what it would do in instances such as Google encountered.

Americans may encounter laws that are routinely ignored by host countries, creating somewhat of a dilemma. For example, the laws in some countries that require a minimum age for factory workers are often not enforced. The U.S. Department of Labor report revealed continued child labor abuses in the apparel and textile industries.

Also affecting the environment in which global companies operate are certain tariffs and quotas that can greatly impact business profitability. **Tariffs** are taxes collected on goods that are shipped across national boundaries. For example, in 2005, Mexico imposed a tariff on U.S. exports because Congress had not repealed the Byrd amendment, formally known as the Continued Dumping and Subsidy Offset Act of 2000. Mexico imposed tariffs of $20.9 million in three product categories, including a 30 percent duty on dairy products, including baby formula, a 20 percent duty on wine, and a 9 percent duty on candy and chewing gum.[69] Recently the United States ordered an additional tariff on Chinese tires of 35 percent the first year, 30 percent the second, and 25 percent the third, on top of the 4 percent tariff the United States traditionally levies. The union said that more than 5,000 tire workers lost their jobs between 2004 and 2008 because of Chinese tire imports, with another 3,000 poised to lose their jobs.[70] In 2010, U.S.–China trade relations heated again, this time over chicken. China, the largest market for U.S. chicken exports, planned to impose anti-dumping tariffs of up to 105.4 percent on U.S. broiler chicken imports saying that the poultry products were dumped at unfair prices onto the China market, causing "substantial damage" to domestic chicken producers.[71] There is much talk about eliminating tariffs around the world, but actions directed at eliminating them have been limited. In 2012, the import tariffs and tax credits that had long sheltered ethanol distilled from corn in the United States from the ethanol made from Brazilian sugarcane were removed.[72] **Quotas** are policies that limit the number or value of goods that can be imported across national boundaries. The amount of textiles that can be imported to the United States is often limited by quotas.

tariffs
Taxes collected on goods that are shipped across national boundaries.

quotas
Policies that limit the number or value of goods that can be imported across national boundaries.

NAFTA and CAFTA

The North American Free Trade Agreement (NAFTA) between Canada, Mexico, and the United States facilitated the movement of goods across boundaries within North America. Although no agreement is perfect, NAFTA has opened markets and established a record of growth and success that could prove key to a strong recovery.[73] It forms a free-trade zone of over 400 million people with a combined gross domestic profit of about $12 trillion dollars. In 2010, Canada purchased $248.2 billion from the United States and Mexico purchased $163.3 billion. In 2010, U.S. exports to NAFTA were $411.5 billion, up 23.4 percent from the prior year.

Labor relations took a major step forward, with a side agreement on labor designed to protect workers in all three countries from the effects of competitive economic pressures. NAFTA established a Commission for Labor Cooperation with offices in each country, which is governed by a council made up of labor ministers of Canada, Mexico, and the United States. Each country is accountable for complying with its own labor laws when dealing with occupational safety and health; child labor; migrant workers; human resource development; labor statistics; work benefits; social programs for workers; productivity improvements; labor management relations; employment standards; the equality of men and women in the workplace; and forms of cooperation among workers, management, and government. A country that consistently fails to enforce its own labor laws could be fined up to $20 million per violation. There are also a number of principles identifying broad areas of common agreement to protect the rights and interests of each workforce. Since NAFTA was implemented, trade between the United States, Canada, and Mexico has grown dramatically as all three countries have seen increased volumes of trade.[74] Even so, the calls to renegotiate the treaty are growing more intense as the economic condition of the member countries worsens.[75]

CAFTA, the Central American Free Trade Agreement, was ratified by America's Congress after a long political battle and signed into law in 2005. If increases like those that occurred in Mexico in the wake of the North American Free Trade Agreement (NAFTA) take place, it would provide a huge economic boost for a region whose infrastructure remains startlingly basic.[76] However, there are those who believe that CAFTA has failed to live up to expectations. There are claims of fraud from textile executives who are calling on Congress and the administration to overhaul the textile enforcement division of U.S. Customs & Border Protection and crack down on what they claim are soaring levels of fraud.[77]

OBJECTIVE 14.10

Describe possible advantages and disadvantages related to globalization for small and medium-sized businesses.

Globalization for Small to Medium-Sized Businesses

International sales have become a vital and growing part of the market for small to medium-sized businesses.[78] A recent study found that nearly a quarter of U.S. small firms receive some sales from overseas, and another 6 percent is expect to join their ranks for a combined total of approximately one million SMB owners who engage in international sales in the near future.[79] Globalization, the Internet, and e-commerce have made it easier than ever for small businesses to reach the 95 percent of consumers that do not live in the United States. Exporting gives small businesses the opportunities to tap into new markets, increase sales, generate economies of scale, and improve inventory management, as well as help maintain American competitiveness and create jobs.

The United States has a goal of doubling exports in five years, from $1.57 trillion in 2009 to $3.14 trillion in 2014. This growth is projected to create two million new jobs.[80] To achieve this goal, the SBA has programs available to help small business customers expand into exporting. In 2009, SBA supported about 1,500 export loans to small business, totaling more than $580 million, and generating more than $1.6 billion in sales. Export loan providers include the following:[81]

- *Export Working Capital Loans* are short-term loans of 12 months or less. These loans provide a line of credit for suppliers, inventory, or production of goods. As a result of the Small Business Jobs Act, the SBA guarantee on these loans is 90 percent, with the maximum size of the loan being $5 million.
- *Export Express Loans* help small businesses that need capital fast to take advantage of a possible overseas sale. They can help cover marketing materials, translation, or travel costs for a trade mission. These loans can get approval by the SBA within 36 hours. The Small

Business Jobs Act increased loan sizes up $500,000 and are 90 percent guaranteed up to $350,000. There is also a 75 percent guarantee for loans larger than $350,000.

- *International Trade Loans* help businesses invest in real estate and working capital to support exporting over the long term. These loans can be used for expansion, renovation, and modernization of facilities, or in some cases refinancing existing loans. Usually, these loans are needed when a few big orders from abroad start to flow in, and the business needs to expand to a larger location or buy equipment to meet demand. International Trade Loans can be for up to $5 million. They carry a 90 percent guarantee, and maturity is usually 10 to 15 years for machinery or 25 years for real estate.[82]

There are numerous examples where the SBA has been helpful. An Export Working Capital Loan helped Nidek Medical Products, Inc., a manufacturer of medical nebulizers and oxygen concentrators for 25 years with 40 employees. The company was focusing largely on international sales and had established distribution warehouses in South America and Europe. But carrying the receivables for export sales had created a cash crunch and put the company's finances in jeopardy. With assistance from the SBA, the company received a $1.3 million Export Working Capital Loan that solved its cash flow difficulties.

The move into global markets can be intimidating for leaders of smaller businesses, but HR professionals in these companies can help. They can learn more about the cultural and human capital factors that will have the biggest effect on new international initiatives. They can work with government and business groups to navigate the legal and bureaucratic environments that can make it difficult for businesses to get started in new markets.[83]

MyManagementLab

Go to **mymanagementlab.com** to complete the problems marked with this icon ⭐.

Summary

1. *Describe the impact of global bribery in the international arena.* The United States is rigorously enforcing the Foreign Corrupt Practices Act (FCPA), which prohibits U.S. firms from bribing foreign officials. However, countries other than the United States face far fewer constraints when dealing with bribery. Not having the ability to use bribery as a tool of doing business has been costly for American companies.

2. *Describe the evolution of global business and global strategic human resource management.* Most companies initially become global without making substantial investments in foreign countries by exporting, licensing, or franchising. A multinational corporation is a firm that is based in one country (the parent or home country) and produces goods or provides services in one or more foreign countries (host countries). A global corporation has corporate units in a number of countries that are integrated to operate as one organization worldwide. A transnational corporation moves work to the places with the talent to handle the job and the time to do it at the right cost.

   The world is experiencing an increasing global workforce. Global human resource problems and opportunities are enormous and are expanding. Individuals dealing with global human resource matters face a multitude of challenges beyond that of their domestic counterparts.

3. *Explain global staffing.* Companies must choose from various types of global staff members and may use specific approaches to global staffing. Global staff members may be selected from among three different types: expatriates, host-country nationals, and third-country nationals. There are four major approaches to global staffing: ethnocentric, polycentric, regiocentric, and geocentric staffing.

4. *Explain some global issues confronting women.* The global assignment of women and members of racial/ethnic minorities can involve cultural and legal issues. Regrettably, female talent is underutilized in emerging countries. Part of the reason is that family-related pulls and work-related pushes combine to force women to either settle for dead-end jobs or leave the workforce.

5. *Describe global human resource development.* Some training and development professionals believe that training and consulting principles and strategies that work for a U.S. audience can be equally effective abroad. Nothing could be further from the truth. Global training and development is needed because people, jobs, and organizations are often quite different. The ideal expatriate preparation and development program includes pre-move orientation and training, continual development, and repatriation orientation and training.

6. *Explain global compensation.* Globally, the question of what constitutes a fair day's pay for host-country nationals is not as complicated as it is in the United States; normally, it is slightly above the prevailing wage rates in the area. The same is often true of benefits and nonfinancial rewards.

Expatriate compensation provides exceptional challenges compared to home-country employment, such as developing packages that are reasonably cost-effective while still attractive and motivating. For expatriate managers and professionals, the situation is more complex than simply paying at or slightly above local host-country compensation rates.

7. *Describe global safety and health.* U.S.-based global operations are often safer and healthier than host-country operations, but frequently not as safe as similar operations in the United States.

8. *Explain global employee and labor relations.* The strength and nature of unions differ from country to country, with unions ranging from nonexistent to relatively strong.

9. *Describe legal and political factors affecting global human resource management.* Legal and political forces are unique for each country. The growing complexity of legal compliance in the global environment is one of the most important trends affecting global business. Managers working for global businesses have to contend with a growing tide of employment legislation that cuts across national boundaries.

10. *Describe possible advantages and disadvantages related to globalization for small and medium-sized businesses.* There has been a growing push among business organizations and the government to help small and medium-sized businesses increase their exports.

Key Terms

exporting   360
licensing   360
franchising   360
multinational corporation (MNC)   361
global corporation   361
transnational corporation   361

expatriate   363
host-country national (HCN)   363
third-country national (TCN)   363
ethnocentric staffing   364
polycentric staffing   364

regiocentric staffing   364
geocentric staffing   364
repatriation   366
tariffs   372
quotas   372

Exercises

1. Other than technical competency for the job, what characteristics do you believe that a person should possess for a global job in the following countries?
   a. plant manager in Great Britain
   b. engineer in Saudi Arabia
   c. plant manager in Mexico

2. What obstacles might have to be overcome to open a global organization for the following?
   a. Coca-Cola in China
   b. McDonald's in Colombia
   c. Ford manufacturing in Thailand

Questions for Review

1. What impact has the Foreign Corrupt Practices Act had on conducting business globally?
2. How has global business evolved?
3. Define the following terms:
   (a) exporting
   (b) licensing
   (c) franchising
   (d) multinational corporation
   (e) global corporations
   (f) transnational corporation
4. What are some global issues confronting women?
5. What are the various types of global staff members?
6. What is the general process for selecting expatriates?
7. Why is pre-move orientation and training of expatriates so important?

8. Why is repatriation orientation and training needed?
9. What is the importance of e-learning in the global environment?
10. What difficulties do virtual teams have in the global environment?
11. What is meant by the statement with reference to compensation for host-country nationals, "Organizations should think globally but act locally"?
12. What has been the status of expatriate compensation in recent years?
13. What are factors to consider in global health and safety?
14. What are some problems and opportunities related to small and medium-sized businesses in the global environment?

INCIDENT 1 The Overseas Transfer

In college, Pat Marek majored in industrial management and was considered by his teachers and peers to be a good all-around student. Pat not only took the required courses in business, but also learned French as a minor. After graduation, Pat took an entry-level management training position with Tuborg International, a multinational corporation with offices and factories in numerous countries, including the United States. His first assignment was in a plant in Chicago. His supervisors quickly identified Pat for his ability to get the job done and still maintain good rapport with subordinates, peers, and superiors. In only three years, Pat had advanced from a manager trainee to the position of assistant plant superintendent.

After two years in this position, he was called into the plant manager's office one day and told that he had been identified as ready for a foreign assignment. The move would mean a promotion. The assignment was for a plant in Haiti, a predominantly French-speaking country; but Pat wasn't worried about living and working there. He was excited and wasted no time in making the necessary preparations for the new assignment.

Prior to arriving at the plant in Haiti, Pat took considerable time to review his French textbook exercises. He was surprised at how quickly the language came back to him. He thought that there wouldn't be any major difficulties in making the transition from Chicago to Haiti. However, Pat found, on arrival, that the community where the plant was located did not speak the pure French that he had learned. There were many expressions that meant one thing to Pat but had an entirely different meaning to the employees of the plant.

When meeting with several of the employees a week after arriving, one of the workers said something to him that Pat interpreted as uncomplimentary. Actually, the employee had greeted him with a rather risqué expression but in a different tone than Pat had heard before. All of the other employees interpreted the expression to be merely a friendly greeting. Pat's disgust registered in his face.

As the days went by, this type of misunderstanding occurred a few more times, until the employees began to limit their conversation with him. In only one month, Pat managed virtually to isolate himself from the workers within the plant. He became disillusioned and thought about asking to be relieved from the assignment.

Questions

1. What problems had Pat not anticipated when he took the assignment?
2. How could the company have assisted Pat to reduce the difficulties that he confronted?
3. Do you believe the situation that Pat confronted is typical of an American going to a foreign assignment? Discuss.

INCIDENT 2 Was There Enough Preparation?

"Hi, Sam. How are the preparations going for your assignment in Japan?"

"Well, Elvis, I really feel prepared for the assignment, and the high level of apprehension I first experienced is gone."

"What exactly did the preparation program involve, Sam?"

"The experience was really exhaustive. First, I spent a good deal of time in a comprehensive orientation and training program. The program covered training and familiarization in the language, culture, history, living conditions, and local customs of Japan. Then, to make the transition back to home easier and better for my career, I have developed a plan with my boss that includes several trips back here to remain a key part of this operation. Also, my career development training will include the same training as the other managers in the home office. Finally, I was completely briefed on repatriation orientation and training that I would experience when I returned. Also, I was fully briefed on the compensation package, which appears to be fairly generous."

"That is great, Sam. Have you found a place to live yet?"

"Not yet, Elvis, but my wife and children are leaving in three days to meet with the company's relocation person to consider the various possibilities."

"How did the family like the orientation training, Sam?"

"Well, my wife ordered some Japanese language tapes, and I think she read all of the information that was covered in the class. She and the children will be fine because they have time to adapt; they don't have to hit the ground running like I do."

Questions

1. Do you believe that Sam's family is adequately prepared for the move to Japan? Why or why not?
2. Should the company's orientation program have included training for Sam's family? Discuss.
3. Is repatriation orientation and training necessary for Sam's family on their return to the United States?

MyManagementLab

Go to **mymanagementlab.com** for Auto-graded writing questions as well as the following Assisted-graded writing questions:

14-1. What are the approaches to global staffing?

14-2. What are some global employee and labor relations problems?

14-3. Mymanagementlab Only – comprehensive writing assignment for this chapter.

Notes

1. "Ungreasing the Wheels," *Economist* 393 (November 21, 2009): 68–69.
2. Wendy Wysong, "New Attention on FCPA Investigations," *Financial Executive* 25 (October 2009): 52–54.
3. Arielle Bikard, "IBM and Johnson & Johnson Settle FCPA Allegations," *Compliance Week* 8 (May 2011): 10.
4. Cathleen Flahardy, "FCPA Fallout," *Inside Counsel* 21 (January 2010): 15.
5. "Avon Fires Four in Bribery Probe," *Women's Wear Daily* 201 (May 5, 2011): 2.
6. Matt Birk, "Prescription for FCPA Compliance," *Internal Auditor* 67 (February 2010): 53–57.
7. Gail Dutton, "Do the Right Thing," *Entrepreneur* 36 (May 2008): 92.
8. Charles Odell and Cheryl Spielman, "Global Positioning: Managing the Far-Reaching Risks of an International Assignment Program," *Benefits Quarterly* 25 (2009 Fourth Quarter): 23–29.
9. Brian Shappell, "Lost (or Gained) in Translation," *Business Credit* 114 (January 2012): 36–39.
10. Eric Krell, "Be Global Risk Manager," *HR Magazine* 57 (March 2012): 81–84.
11. Jaime Santiago, "Exporting, Anyone?" *Caribbean Business* 39 (April 28, 2011): 21.
12. "Perspectives in International Franchising," *Franchising World* 43 (March 2011): 8–10.
13. Kristin Houston, "U.S. Commercial Service to Franchisors: Seize the Trends and Grow Globally," *Franchising World* 43 (March 2011): 15–17.
14. Philip F. Zeidman and David Hood, "What Do Troubled International Markets Mean to Franchise Expansion?" *Franchising World* 44 (January 2012): 51–53.
15. Ron Ruggless, "Global Growth with Local Help," *Nation's Restaurant News* 45 (February 21, 2011): 1–10.
16. Margaret McEntire, "Best Practices for International Franchising: Be Aware of Cultural Differences," *Franchising World* 43 (March 2011): 29.
17. Bachir Mihoubi, "Dealing with the Complexities of International Expansion," *Franchising World* 43 (March 2011): 11–14.
18. "Personal Care: Company Spotlight: Procter & Gamble," *MarketWatch: Global Round-up* 9 (March 2010): 112–118.
19. Debi O'Donovan, "Johnson and Johnson Takes World View on Compensation," *Employee Benefits* (June 2011): 7.
20. Jena McGregor and Steve Hamm, "Managing the Global Workforce," *BusinessWeek* (January 28, 2008): 34–35.
21. http://www.hrci.org/HRCertification.aspx?id=67
22. Susan R. Heyman, "Working Women around the World Lack Basic Workplace Protections, United Nations Reports," *SHRM Online* (July 26, 2011).
23. Jesse Elliston, "The 2011 Global Women's Progress Report," *Newsweek* 158 (September 26, 2011): 27–29.
24. Sylvia Ann Hewlett and Ripa Rashid, "The Battle for Female Talent in Emerging Markets," *Harvard Business Review* 88 (May 2010): 101–106.
25. Ann Pace, "Chinese Women Flood the Global Talent Ranks," *T+D* 65 (June 2011): 20.
26. Alice Andors, "Hidden in Plain Sight," *HR Magazine* 57 (January 2012): 34–35.
27. Shirley Puccino, "Worldwide Practices and Trends in Expatriate Compensation and Benefits," *Benefits & Compensation Digest* 44 (January 2007): 34–38.

28. Isobel Coleman, "The Global Glass Ceiling," *Foreign Affairs* 89 (May/June 2010): 13–20.
29. Cindy Bigner, "Halliburton Finds the Best Talent in Every Country and Culture," *Profiles in Diversity Journal* 13 (May/June 2011): 47.
30. Fay Hansen, "Looking South," *Workforce Management* 87 (April 21, 2008): 21–26.
31. Jeremy Eeskanazi, "When in Rome, Recruit Like the Romans Do: An Environmental Scan of the European Recruiting Landscape," *Journal of Corporate Recruiting Leadership* 5 (June 2010): 3–9.
32. Lorraine Bello and Galen Tinder, "Dual Career Implications on Workforce Mobility: The Evolution of the Relocating Spouse/Partner," *Benefits & Compensation Digest* 46 (September 2009): 36–39.
33. Ann Pace, "Training for the Leap Overseas," *T+D* 63 (August 2009): 18.
34. "Addressing 5 Gaps in Investigative Screening Programs," *Security Director's Report* 10 (October 2010): 4–6.
35. Pamela Babcock, "Foreign Assignments," *HR Magazine* 50 (October 2005): 91–98.
36. Michael Laff, "Offshore Acclimation," *T+D* 63 (May 2009): 22–23.
37. Avan R. Jassawalla and Hermant C. Sashittal, "Thinking Strategically About Integrating Repatriated Managers in MNCs," *Human Resource Management* 48 (September/October 2009): 769–792.
38. Michelle V. Rafter, "Return Trip for Expats," *Workforce Management* 88 (March 16, 2009): 1–3.
39. Alice Andors, "Happy Returns," *HR Magazine* 55 (March 2010): 61–63.
40. Mishra Jitendra, "Repatriation," *Advances in Management* 4 (January 2011): 7–19.
41. Eddie Kikelly, "A Rapid Evolution," *e.learning age* (June 2010): 14–15.
42. Armin Hopp, "Soft Steps Towards Digital Learning," *Training Journal* (January 2012): 51–54.
43. Andrea Edmundson, "When Cultural Values Interfere with Globalized E-learning," *MultiLingual* 21 (June 2010): 28–30.
44. Andrea Edmundson, "Culturally Accessible E-learning: An Overdue Global Business Imperative," *T+D* 63 (April 2009): 40–45.
45. Deepak Desai, "Globalization and the English Skills Gap," *Chief Learning Officer* 7 (June 2008): 62–63.
46. Hanif Sazen, "Keeping It Fresh," *e.learning age* (June 2005): 28–29.
47. "Virtual Team Failure 6 Common Missteps that Threaten Your Team's Success," *Communication Briefings* 30 (February 2011): 5–6.
48. Jay F. Nunamaker, Jr., Bruce A. Reinig, and Robert O. Briggs, "Principles for Effective Virtual Teamwork," *Communications of the ACM* 52 (April 2009): 113–117.
49. Lara Schlenkrich and Christopher Upfold, "A Guideline for Virtual Team Managers: The Key to Effective Social Interaction and Communication," *Electronic Journal of Information Systems Evaluation* 12 (2009): 109–118.
50. Marissa Garff, "The Virtual Reality," *T+D* 65 (August 2011): 22.
51. "Virtual Team Failure 6 Common Missteps that Threaten Your Team's Success," *Communication Briefings* 30 (February 2011): 5–6.

52. Darleen DeRosa, "Hello, Is Anybody Out There? Six Steps to High-Impact V-Meetings," *T+D* 65 (August 2011): 28–29.

53. "Leading the Virtual Team," *Associations Now* (May 2008): 18.

54. Elliott Masie, "A Global Learning Language," *Chief Learning Officer* 11 (January 2012): 10.

55. Bill Leonard, "Managing Virtual Teams," *HR Magazine* 56 (June 2011): 38–42.

56. Billie Williamson, "Managing Virtually: First, Get Dressed," *BusinessWeek Online* (June 17, 2009): 19.

57. Jeff Miller, "The Touchstones of Successful Global Benefits Outsourcing," *Benefits Quarterly* (2011 Second Quarter): 24–27.

58. David Tobenkin, "Learn the Landscape," *HR Magazine* 56 (May 2011): 51–54.

59. Vicki Taylor, "Benefits around the World," *Employee Benefits* (February 2006): Special Section, 8–9.

60. Yvette Lee, Lesa Albright, and Ruhal Dooley, "Tele-terminating, Terminating Employees Abroad, Recruiting Diversity," *HR Magazine* 55 (June 2010): 31–32.

61. Siegfried Russwurm, Luis Hernández, Susan Chambers, and Keumyong Chung, "Developing Your Global Know-How," *Harvard Business Review* 89 (March 2011): 436–433.

62. http://www.irs.gov/publications/p54/ch04.html#en_US_publink100047498

63. Hashi Syedain, "From Expats to Global Citizens," *People Management* (January 2012): 22–26.

64. http://en.wikipedia.org/wiki/Bhopal_disaster, February 14, 2010.

65. Randall Stram, "Globally, Wellness Programs Lead to Healthier Employees," *Benefits Magazine* 48 (March 2011): 22–25.

66. Samuel Estreicher, "'Think Global, Act Local': Employee Representation in a World of Global Labor and Product Market Competition," *Labor Lawyer* 24 (Winter 2009): 253–265.

67. Kathryn Tyler, "What Are Global Cultural Competencies?" *HR Magazine* 56 (May 2011): 44–46.

68. Steven Levy, "Google and Its Ordeal in China," *Fortune* 163 (May 2, 2011): 94–100.

69. "Mexico Hits U.S. Exports with Tariffs in Retaliation for Byrd Amendment," *Metal Center News* 45 (September 2005): 71.

70. Miles Moore, "WTO to Probe China Tire Tariffs," *Rubber & Plastics News* 39 (January 25, 2010): 3.

71. "Chicken Tariffs Escalate US–China Controversy," *Journal of Commerce* 11 (February 15, 2010): 8.

72. "Brazilian Brew," *Economist* 401 (January, 7 2012): 57.

73. Andrea MacDonald, "NAFTA: A Delicate Balance," *World Trade* 22 (October 2009): 30–33.

74. Adrienne Selko, "NAFTA: Learning to Love Thy Neighbor," *Industry Week* 258 (February 2009): 38–41.

75. Denise Bedell, "Revisiting NAFTA," *Global Finance* 23 (March 2009): 22–24.

76. "Nothing's Free in This World," *Economist* 376 (August 6, 2005): 30.

77. Kristi Ellis, "Textile Execs Claim CAFTA Fraud," *Women's Wear Daily* 197 (June 19, 2009): 128.

78. Graziella Sicoli, "Evolving Dynamics in the Process of Business Internationalization," *Global Journal of Business Research* 6 (2012): 117–124.

79. "International Small Businesses Need Facebook, Twitter," *Channel Insider* (June 23, 2011): 1.

80. http://www.sba.gov/administrator/7390/6086

81. http://sba.gov/aboutsba/sbaprograms/internationaltrade/index.htm

82. http://www.sba.gov/content/international-trade-loan-fact-sheet-small-businesses

83. Jennifer Schramm, "Think Globally," *HR Magazine* 56 (June 2011): 56.

Glossary

Active job seekers: Individuals committed to finding another job whether presently employed or not.

Adverse impact: Concept established by the *Uniform Guidelines;* it occurs if women and minorities are not hired at the rate of at least 80 percent of the best-achieving group.

Affirmative action: Stipulated by Executive Order 11246, it requires employers to take positive steps to ensure employment of applicants and treatment of employees during employment without regard to race, creed, color, or national origin.

Affirmative action program (AAP): Approach developed by organizations with government contracts to demonstrate that workers are employed in proportion to their representation in the firm's relevant labor market.

Agency shop: Labor agreement provision requiring, as a condition of employment, that each nonunion member of a bargaining unit pay the union the equivalent of membership dues as a service charge in return for the union acting as the bargaining agent.

Alcoholism: Medical disease characterized by uncontrolled and compulsive drinking that interferes with normal living patterns.

AllianceQ: Group of Fortune 500 companies, along with over 3,000 small and medium-sized companies, that have collaborated to create a pool of job candidates.

Alternative dispute resolution (ADR): Procedure whereby the employee and the company agree ahead of time that any problems will be addressed by an agreed-upon means.

American Federation of Labor and Congress of Industrial Organizations (AFL-CIO): Central trade union federation in the United States.

Applicant pool: Number of qualified applicants recruited for a particular job.

Apprenticeship training: Training method that combines classroom instruction with on-the-job training.

Arbitration: Process in which a dispute is submitted to an impartial third party for a binding decision; an arbitrator basically acts as a judge and jury.

Assessment center: Selection technique that requires individuals to perform activities similar to those they might encounter in an actual job.

Attitude survey: Survey that seeks input from employees to determine their feelings about topics such as the work they perform, their supervisor, their work environment, flexibility in the workplace, opportunities for advancement, training and development opportunities, and the firm's compensation system.

Authorization card: Document indicating that an employee wants to be represented by a labor organization in collective bargaining.

Availability forecast: Determination of whether the firm will be able to secure employees with the necessary skills, and from what sources.

Baby boomers: People born just after World War II through the mid-1960s.

Bargaining unit: Group of employees, not necessarily union members, recognized by an employer or certified by an administrative agency as appropriate for representation by a labor organization for purposes of collective bargaining.

Beachhead demands: Demands that the union does not expect management to meet when they are first made.

Behavior modeling: T&D method that permits a person to learn by copying or replicating behaviors of others to show managers how to handle various situations.

Behavioral interview: Structured interview where applicants are asked to relate actual incidents from their past relevant to the target job.

Behaviorally anchored rating scale (BARS) method: Performance appraisal method that combines elements of the traditional rating scale and critical incident methods; various performance levels are shown along a scale with each described in terms of an employee's specific job behavior.

Benchmarking: Process of monitoring and measuring a firm's internal processes, such as operations, and then comparing the data with information from companies that excel in those areas.

Benefits (indirect financial compensation): All financial rewards that are not included in direct financial compensation (indirect financial compensation).

Blended training: The use of multiple training methods to deliver T&D.

Board interview: An interview approach in which several of the firm's representatives interview a candidate at the same time.

Bonus: One-time annual financial award, based on productivity that is not added to base pay.

Bottom-up forecast: Forecasting method in which each successive level in the organization, starting with the lowest, forecasts its requirements, ultimately providing an aggregate forecast of employees needed.

Boycott: Agreement by union members to refuse to use or buy the firm's products.

Broadbanding: Compensation technique that collapses many pay grades (salary grades) into a few wide bands to improve organizational effectiveness.

Burnout: Incapacitating condition in which individuals lose a sense of the basic purpose and fulfillment of their work.

Business games: T&D method that permits participants to assume roles such as president, controller, or marketing vice president of two or more similar hypothetical organizations and compete against each other by manipulating selected factors in a particular business situation.

Card check: Organizing approach by labor in which employees sign a nonsecret card of support if they want unionization, and if 50 percent of the workforce plus one worker sign a card, the union is formed.

Career: General course that a person chooses to pursue throughout his or her working life.

Career development: Formal approach used by the organization to ensure that people with the proper qualifications and experiences are available when needed.

Career path: A flexible line of movement through which a person may travel during his or her work life.

Career planning: Ongoing process whereby an individual sets career goals and identifies the means to achieve them.

Career security: Requires developing marketable skills and expertise that help ensure employment within a range of careers.

Caregiver (family responsibility) discrimination: Discrimination against employees based on their obligations to care for family members.

Carpal tunnel syndrome (CTS): Common repetitive stress injury caused by pressure on the median nerve that occurs as a result of a narrowing of the passageway that houses the nerve.

Case study: T&D method in which trainees are expected to study the information provided in the case and make decisions based on it.

Cash balance plan: Retirement plan with elements of both defined benefit and defined contribution plans.

Central tendency error: Evaluation appraisal error that occurs when employees are incorrectly rated near the average or middle of a scale.

Change to Win Coalition: Union federation consisting of seven unions that broke from the AFL-CIO and formally launched a rival labor federation representing about 6 million workers in 2005.

Checkoff of dues: Agreement by which a company agrees to withhold union dues from members' paychecks and to forward the money directly to the union.

Classification method: Job evaluation method in which classes or grades are defined to describe a group of jobs.

Clawback policy: Allows the company to recover compensation if subsequent review indicates that payments were not calculated accurately or performance goals were not met.

Closed shop: Arrangement making union membership a prerequisite for employment.

Coaching: Often considered a responsibility of the immediate boss, who provides assistance, much like a mentor, but the primary focus is about performance.

Cognitive aptitude tests: Tests that determine general reasoning ability, memory, vocabulary, verbal fluency, and numerical ability.

Collective bargaining: Performance of the mutual obligation of the employer and the representative of the employees to meet at reasonable times and confer in good faith with respect to wages, hours, and other terms and conditions of employment, or the negotiation of an agreement, or any question arising thereunder, and the execution of a written contract incorporating any agreement reached if requested by either party; such obligation does not compel either party to agree to a proposal or require the making of a concession.

Committee on Political Education (COPE): Political arm of the AFL-CIO.

Comparable worth: Determination of the values of dissimilar jobs (such as company nurse and welder) by comparing them under some form of job evaluation, and the assignment of pay rates according to their evaluated worth.

Compensation: Total of all rewards provided employees in return for their services.

Compensation policy: Policies that provide general guidelines for making compensation decisions.

Compensation survey: A means of obtaining data regarding what other firms are paying for specific jobs or job classes within a given labor market.

Competency-based pay: Compensation plan that rewards employees for the capabilities they attain.

Compressed workweek: Any arrangement of work hours that permits employees to fulfill their work obligation in fewer days than the typical five-day workweek.

Consumer-driven health care plan: Gives each employee a set amount of money annually with which to purchase health care coverage that involves high-deductible insurance coverage combined with a tax-advantaged account such as a health saving account, health reimbursement accounts, and flexible saving account.

Construct validity: Test validation method that determines whether a test measures certain constructs, or traits, that job analysis finds to be important in performing a job.

Content validity: Test validation method whereby a person performs certain tasks that are actually required by the job or completes a paper-and-pencil test that measures relevant job knowledge.

Contingent workers: Described as the "disposable American workforce" by a former secretary of labor, have a nontraditional relationship with the worksite employer, and work as part-timers, temporaries, or independent contractors.

Corporate career Web sites: Job sites accessible from a company home page that list available company positions and provide a way for applicants to apply for specific jobs.

Corporate culture: System of shared values, beliefs, and habits within an organization that interacts with the formal structure to produce behavioral norms.

Corporate social responsibility (CSR): Implied, enforced, or felt obligation of managers, acting in their official capacity, to serve or protect the interests of groups other than themselves.

Corporate university: T&D delivery system provided under the umbrella of the organization.

Cost-of-living allowance (COLA): Escalator clause in a labor agreement that automatically increases wages as the U.S. Bureau of Labor Statistics cost-of-living index rises.

Country's culture: Set of values, symbols, beliefs, languages, and norms that guide human behavior within the country.

Craft union: Bargaining unit, such as the Carpenters and Joiners Union, which is typically composed of members of a particular trade or skill in a specific locality.

Criterion-related validity: Test validation method that compares the scores on selection tests to some aspect of job performance determined, for example, by performance appraisal.

Critical incident method: Performance appraisal method that requires keeping written records of highly favorable and unfavorable employee work actions.

Customized benefit plan: Benefit plan that permits employees to make yearly selections to largely determine their benefit package by choosing between taxable cash and numerous benefits.

Decertification: Reverse of the process that employees must follow to be recognized as an official bargaining unit.

Defined benefit plan: Retirement plan that provides the participant with a fixed benefit upon retirement.

Defined contribution plan: Retirement plan that requires specific contributions by an employer to a retirement or savings fund established for the employee.

Demotion: Process of moving a worker to a lower level of duties and responsibilities, which typically involves a reduction in pay.

Development: Learning that goes beyond today's job and has a more long-term focus.

Direct financial compensation: Pay that a person receives in the form of wages, salary, commissions, and bonuses.

Disciplinary action: Invoking a penalty against an employee who fails to meet established standards.

Disciplinary action without punishment: Process in which a worker is given time off with pay to think about whether he or she wants to follow the rules and continue working for the company.

Discipline: State of employee self-control and orderly conduct that indicates the extent of genuine teamwork within an organization.

Discretionary benefits: Benefit payments made as a result of unilateral management decisions in nonunion firms and from labor–management negotiations in unionized firms.

Disparate treatment: Occurs when an employer treats some employees less favorably than others because of race, religion, sex, national origin, or age.

Diversity: Any perceived difference among people: age, race, religion, functional specialty, profession, sexual orientation, geographic origin, lifestyle, tenure with the organization or position, and any other perceived difference.

Diversity management: Ensuring that factors are in place to provide for and encourage the continued development of a diverse workforce by melding actual and perceived differences among workers to achieve maximum productivity.

Downsizing: Reverse of a company growing; it suggests a one-time change in the organization and the number of people employed (also known as restructuring or rightsizing).

Dual-career family: A situation in which both husband and wife have jobs and family responsibilities.

Dual-career path: Career path that recognizes that technical specialists can and should be allowed to contribute their expertise to a company without having to become managers.

E-learning: T&D method for online instruction using technology-based methods such as the Internet, intranet, and CD-ROM.

Emotional intelligence (EQ): Ability to recognize and manage emotions.

Employee assistance program (EAP): Comprehensive approach that many organizations have taken to deal with burnout, alcohol and drug abuse, and other emotional disturbances.

Employee engagement: Level of commitment workers make to their employer, seen in their willingness to stay at the firm and to go beyond the call of duty.

Employee equity: Equity that exists when individuals performing similar jobs for the same firm receive pay according to factors unique to the employee, such as performance level or seniority.

Employee referral: An employee of the company recommends a friend or associate as a possible member of the company; this continues to be the way that top performers are identified.

Employee requisition: Document that specifies job title, department, the date the employee is needed for work, and other details.

Employee self-service (ESS): Processes that automate transactions that previously were labor intensive for both employees and HR professionals.

Employee stock option plan (ESOP): Plan in which a firm contributes stock shares to a trust, which then allocates the stock to participating employee accounts according to employee earnings.

Employer branding: Firm's corporate image or culture created to attract and retain the type of employees the firm is seeking.

Employment at will: Unwritten contract created when an employee agrees to work for an employer but no agreement exists as to how long the parties expect the employment to last.

Employment interview: Goal-oriented conversation in which an interviewer and an applicant exchange information.

Equity theory: Motivation theory that people assess their performance and attitudes by comparing both their contribution to work and the benefits they derive from it to the contributions and benefits of comparison others whom they select—and who in reality may or may not be like them.

Ergonomics: Process of designing the workplace to support the capabilities of people and job or task demands.

Essay method: Performance appraisal method in which the rater writes a brief narrative describing the employee's performance.

Ethics: Discipline dealing with what is good and bad, or right and wrong, or with moral duty and obligation.

Ethnocentric staffing: Staffing approach in which companies primarily hire expatriates to staff higher-level foreign positions.

Event recruiting: Recruiters going to events being attended by individuals the company is seeking.

Exclusive provider organization (EPO): Managed-care health organization that offers a smaller preferred provider network and usually provides few, if any, benefits when an out-of-network provider is used.

Executive: A top-level manager who reports directly to a corporation's chief executive officer (CEO) or to the head of a major division.

Executive order (EO): Directive issued by the president that has the force and effect of law enacted by Congress as it applies to federal agencies and federal contractors.

Exempt employees: Employees categorized as executive, administrative, professional, or outside salespersons.

Exit interview: Means of revealing the real reasons employees leave their jobs; it is conducted before an employee departs the company and provides information on how to correct the causes of discontent and reduce turnover.

Expatriate: Employee who is not a citizen of the country in which the firm operations are located, but is a citizen of the country in which the organization is headquartered.

Exporting: Selling abroad, either directly or indirectly, by retaining foreign agents and distributors.

External environment: Factors outside an organization's boundaries that affect a firm's human resources makeup.

External equity: Equity that exists when a firm's employees receive pay comparable to workers who perform similar jobs in other firms.

Factor comparison method: Job evaluation method that assumes there are five universal factors consisting of mental requirements, skills, physical requirements, responsibilities, and working conditions; the evaluator makes decisions on these factors independently.

Final-offer arbitration: An arbitration procedure used in the public sector whereby the arbitrator selects one party's offer either as a package or issue-by-issue selection.

Financial equity: Perception of fair pay treatment for employees.

Flexible spending account (FSA): Benefit plan established by employers that allows employees to deposit a certain portion of their salary into an account (before paying income taxes) to be used for eligible expenses.

Flextime: Practice of permitting employees to choose their own working hours, within certain limitations.

Flooding the community: Process of the union inundating communities with organizers to target a particular business in an organizing attempt.

Forced distribution method: Performance appraisal method in which the rater is required to assign individuals in a work group to a limited number of categories, similar to a normal frequency distribution.

401(k) plan: Defined contribution plan in which employees may defer income up to a maximum amount allowed.

Franchising: Option whereby the parent company grants another firm the right to do business in a prescribed manner.

Free agents: People who take charge of all or part of their careers by being their own bosses or by working for others in ways that fit their particular needs or wants.

Gainsharing: Plans designed to bind employees to the firm's productivity and provide an incentive payment based on improved company performance.

General duty clause: As used by OSHA, employers are required to furnish, to each employee, a place of employment that is free from recognizable hazards that are causing, or likely to cause, death or serious harm to the employee.

Generalist: A person who may be an executive and performs tasks in a variety of HR-related areas.

Generation X: Label affixed to the 40 million American workers born between the mid-1960s and late 1970s.

Generation Y: Comprises people born between the late 1970s and mid-1990s.

Generation Z or Digital Natives: Internet-assimilated children born between 1995 and 2009.

Genetic tests: Tests given to identify predisposition to inherited diseases, including cancer, heart disease, neurological disorders, and congenital diseases.

Geocentric staffing: Staffing approach that uses a worldwide integrated business strategy.

Glass ceiling: Invisible barrier in organizations that impedes women and minorities from career advancement.

Global corporation: Organization that has corporate units in a number of countries that are integrated to operate as one organization worldwide.

Golden parachute contract: Perquisite that protects executives in the event that another company acquires their firm or the executive is forced to leave the firm for other reasons.

Graphoanalysis: Use of handwriting analysis as a selection factor.

Grievance: Employee's dissatisfaction or feeling of personal injustice relating to his or her employment.

Grievance procedure: Formal, systematic process that permits employees to express complaints without jeopardizing their jobs.

Group interview: Meeting in which several job applicants interact in the presence of one or more company representatives.

Halo error: Evaluation error that occurs when a manager generalizes one positive performance feature or incident to all aspects of employee performance, resulting in a higher rating.

Hay Group Guide Chart-Profile Method (Hay Plan): Refined version of the point method used by approximately 8,000 public and private-sector organizations worldwide to evaluate clerical, trade, technical, professional, managerial and/or executive level jobs.

Hazard pay: Additional pay provided to employees who work under extremely dangerous conditions.

Health: Employees' freedom from physical or emotional illness.

Health maintenance organization (HMO): Managed-care health organization that covers all services for a fixed fee but exercises control over which doctors and health facilities a member may use.

Health reimbursement accounts (HRAs): Allows an employer to set aside funds to reimburse medical expenses paid by participating employees.

Health savings accounts (HAS): Tax-free health spending and savings accounts available to individuals and families who have qualified high-deductible health insurance policies as determined by IRS regulation.

Horn error: Evaluation error that occurs when a manager generalizes one negative performance feature or incident to all aspects of employee performance, resulting in a lower rating.

Host-country national (HCN): Employee who is a citizen of the country where the subsidiary is located.

Human capital metrics: Measures of HR performance.

Human resource development (HRD): Major HRM function consisting not only of training and development but also of individual career planning and development activities, organization development, and performance management and appraisal.

Human resource ethics: Application of ethical principles to human resource relationships and activities.

Human resource information system (HRIS): Any organized approach for obtaining relevant and timely information on which to base human resource decisions.

Human resource management (HRM): Utilization of individuals to achieve organizational objectives.

Human resource manager: Individual who normally acts in an advisory or staff capacity, working with other managers to help them deal with human resource matters.

Human resource planning: Systematic process of matching the internal and external supply of people with job openings anticipated in the organization over a specified period of time.

HR outsourcing (HRO): Process of hiring external HR professionals to do the HR work that was previously done internally.

In-basket training: T&D method in which the participant is asked to establish priorities for and then handle a number of business papers, e-mail messages, memoranda, reports, and telephone messages that would typically cross a manager's desk.

Indirect financial compensation (benefits): All financial rewards that are not included in direct financial compensation.

Industrial union: Bargaining unit that generally consists of all the workers in a particular plant or group of plants.

Interest arbitration: Arbitration that involves disputes over the terms of proposed collective bargaining agreements.

Internal employee relations: Those human resource management activities associated with the movement of employees within the organization.

Internal equity: Equity that exists when employees receive pay according to the relative value of their jobs within the same organization.

Internet recruiter: Person whose primary responsibility is to use the Internet in the recruitment process (also called cyber recruiter).

Internship: Special form of recruitment that involves placing a student in a temporary job with no obligation either by the company to hire the student permanently or by the student to accept a permanent position with the firm following graduation.

Job: Group of tasks that must be performed for an organization to achieve its goals.

Job analysis: Systematic process of determining the skills, duties, and knowledge required for performing jobs in an organization.

Job bidding: Procedure that permits employees who believe that they possess the required qualifications to apply for a posted position.

Job description: Document that provides information regarding the essential tasks, duties, and responsibilities of a job.

Job design: Process of determining the specific tasks to be performed, the methods used in performing these tasks, and how the job relates to other work in an organization.

Job enlargement: Increasing the number of tasks a worker performs, with all of the tasks at the same level of responsibility.

Job enrichment: Changes in the content and level of responsibility of a job so as to provide greater challenges to the worker.

Job evaluation: Process that determines the relative value of one job in relation to another.

Job evaluation ranking method: Job evaluation method in which the raters examine the description of each job being evaluated and arrange the jobs in order according to their value to the company.

Job fair: Recruiting method engaged in by a single employer or group of employers to attract a large number of applicants to one location for interviews.

Job hazard analysis (JHA): Multistep process designed to study and analyze a task or job and then break down that task into steps that provide a means of eliminating associated hazards.

Job-knowledge tests: Tests designed to measure a candidate's knowledge of the duties of the job for which he or she is applying.

Job posting: Procedure for informing employees that job openings exist.

Job pricing: Placing a dollar value on the job's worth.

Job rotation: Moves employees from one job to another to broaden their experience.

Job security: Implies security in one job, often with one company.

Job sharing: Two part-time people split the duties of one job in some agreed-on manner and are paid according to their contributions.

Job specification: A document that outlines the minimum acceptable qualifications a person should possess to perform a particular job.

.Jobs: Network of employment Web sites where any company can list job openings for free.

Just-in-time training: Training provided anytime, anywhere in the world when it is needed.

Keyword résumé: Résumé that contains an adequate description of the job seeker's characteristics and industry-specific experience presented in keyword terms in order to accommodate the computer search process.

Keywords: Words or phrases that are used to search databases for résumés that match.

Labor market: Potential employees located within the geographic area from which employees are recruited.

Lateral skill path: Career path that allows for lateral moves within the firm, taken to permit an employee to become revitalized and find new challenges.

Learning organization: Firm that recognizes the critical importance of continuous performance-related T&D and takes appropriate action.

Leniency: Giving an undeserved high performance appraisal rating to an employee.

Licensing: Arrangement whereby an organization grants a foreign firm the right to use intellectual properties such as patents, copyrights, manufacturing processes, or trade names for a specific period of time.

Likes and dislikes survey: Procedure that helps individuals in recognizing restrictions they place on themselves.

Line managers: Individuals directly involved in accomplishing the primary purpose of the organization.

Local union: Basic element in the structure of the U.S. labor movement.

Lockout: Management keeps employees out of the workplace and runs the operation with management personnel and/or replacements.

Maintenance of membership: Employees who are members of the union at the time the labor agreement is signed or who later voluntarily join must continue their memberships until the termination of the agreement as a condition of employment.

Management development: Consists of all learning experiences provided by an organization resulting in upgrading skills and knowledge required in current and future managerial positions.

Manager self-service (MSS): The use of software and the corporate network to automate paper-based human resource processes that require a manager's approval, record-keeping or input, and processes that support the manager's job.

Mandatory bargaining issues: Bargaining issues that fall within the definition of wages, hours, and other terms and conditions of employment.

Market (going) rate: Average pay that most employers provide for a similar job in a particular area or industry.

Mediation: Neutral third party enters the negotiations and attempts to facilitate a resolution to a labor dispute when a bargaining impasse has occurred.

Mentoring: Approach to advising, coaching, and nurturing for creating a practical relationship to enhance individual career, personal, and professional growth and development.

Merit pay: Pay increase added to employees' base pay based on their level of performance.

Mission: Unit's continuing purpose, or reason for being.

Mobile learning: Any learning that takes place via mobile or portable devices such as cell phones, personal digital assistants, tablets, media players, and e-readers.

Multinational corporation: Firm that is based in one country (the parent or home country) and produces goods or provides services in one or more foreign countries (host countries).

Musculoskeletal disorders (MSDs): Conditions that affect the body's muscles, joints, tendons, ligaments, and nerves.

NACElink Network: An alliance among the National Association of Colleges and Employers, DirectEmployers Association, and Symplicity Corporation; a national recruiting network and suite of Web-based recruiting and career services automation tools serving the needs of colleges, employers, and job candidates.

National union: Organization composed of local unions, which it charters.

Negligent hiring: Liability a company incurs when it fails to conduct a reasonable investigation of an applicant's background, and then assigns a potentially dangerous person to a position where he or she can inflict harm.

Negligent retention: Liability an employer may incur when a company keeps persons on the payroll whose records indicate strong potential for wrongdoing and fails to take steps to defuse a possible violent situation.

Network career path: Method of career progression that contains both a vertical sequence of jobs and a series of horizontal opportunities.

Niche sites: Web sites that cater to highly specialized job markets such as a particular profession, industry, education, location, or any combination of these specialties.

Nonfinancial compensation: Satisfaction that a person receives from the job itself or from the psychological and/or physical environment in which the person works.

Norm: Frame of reference for comparing an applicant's performance with that of others.

Objectivity: Condition that is achieved when everyone scoring a given test obtains the same results.

Offboarding: Facilitates employee departure from the company by assisting the completion of exit tasks, including exit interviews, forms completion, the return of company property, and ensuring that employees receive the appropriate extended benefits.

Offshoring: Migration of all or a significant part of the development, maintenance, and delivery of services to a vendor located in another country.

Ombudsperson: Complaint officer with access to top management who hears employee complaints, investigates, and recommends appropriate action.

Online higher education: Educational opportunities including degree and training programs that are delivered, either entirely or partially, via the Internet.

Onshoring: Moving jobs not to another country but to lower-cost American cities.

On-the-job-training (OJT): An informal T&D method that permits an employee to learn job tasks by actually performing them.

Open shop: Employment on equal terms to union members and nonmembers alike.

Organization development (OD): Planned and systematic attempts to change the organization, typically to a more behavioral environment.

Organizational fit: Management's perception of the degree to which the prospective employee will fit in with the firm's culture or value system.

Orientation: Initial T&D effort for new employees that informs them about the company, the job, and the work group.

Outplacement: A procedure whereby laid-off employees are given assistance in finding employment elsewhere.

Outsourcing: Process of hiring an external provider to do the work that was previously done internally.

Paid time off (PTO): Means of dealing with the problem of unscheduled absences by providing a certain number of days each year that employees can use for any purpose.

Passive job seekers: Potential job candidates, who are typically employed, satisfied with their employer, and content in their current role but if the right opportunity came along, they might like to learn more.

Pay followers: Companies that choose to pay below the going rate because of a poor financial condition or a belief that they do not require highly capable employees.

Pay grade: Grouping of similar jobs to simplify pricing jobs.

Pay leaders: Organizations that pay higher wages and salaries than competing firms.

Pay range: Minimum and maximum pay rate with enough variance between the two to allow for a significant pay difference.

Performance appraisal (PA): Formal system of review and evaluation of individual or team task performance.

Performance management (PM): Goal-oriented process directed toward ensuring that organizational processes are in place to maximize the productivity of employees, teams, and ultimately, the organization.

Permissive bargaining issues: Issues may be raised, but neither side may insist that they be bargained over.

Perquisites (perks): Special benefits provided by a firm to a small group of key executives and designed to give the executives something extra.

Personality tests: Self-reported measures of traits, temperaments, or dispositions.

Piecework: Incentive pay plan in which employees are paid for each unit they produce.

Phased retirement: Any arrangement that allows people to move from full-time work to retirement in steps.

Point method: Job evaluation method where the raters assign numerical values to specific job factors, such as knowledge required, and the sum of these values provides a quantitative assessment of a job's relative worth.

Point-of-service (POS): Managed-care health organization that requires a primary care physician and referrals to see specialists, as with HMOs, but permits out-of-network health care access.

Polycentric staffing: Staffing approach in which host-country nationals are used throughout the organization, from top to bottom.

Position: Collection of tasks and responsibilities performed by one person.

Postexit questionnaire: Questionnaire sent to former employees several weeks after they leave the organization to determine the real reason they left.

Preferred provider organization (PPO): Managed-care health organization in which incentives are provided to members to use services within the system; out-of-network providers may be utilized at greater cost.

Premium pay: Compensation paid to employees for working long periods of time or working under dangerous or undesirable conditions.

Profession: Vocation characterized by the existence of a common body of knowledge and a procedure for certifying members.

Professional employer organization (PEO): A company that leases employees to other businesses.

Profit sharing: Compensation plans that result in the distribution of a predetermined percentage of the firm's profits to employees.

Progressive disciplinary action: Approach to disciplinary action designed to ensure that the minimum penalty appropriate to the offense is imposed.

Prohibited bargaining issues: Issues that are statutorily outlawed from collective bargaining.

Project labor agreement: Prehire collective bargaining agreement between construction firm owners and one or more labor organizations establishing the terms and conditions of employment for a specific construction project.

Promotion: Movement of a person to a higher-level position in an organization.

Promotion from within (PFW): Policy of filling vacancies above entry-level positions with current employees.

Psychomotor abilities tests: Tests that measure strength, coordination, and dexterity.

Public awareness campaigns: Labor maneuvers that do not coincide with a strike or organizing campaign to pressure an employer for better wages, benefits, and the like.

Quality circles: Groups of employees who voluntarily meet regularly with their supervisors to discuss problems, investigate causes, recommend solutions, and take corrective action when authorized to do so.

Quotas: Policies that limit the number or value of goods that can be imported across national boundaries.

Ranking method: Performance appraisal method in which the rater ranks all employees from a group in order of overall performance.

Rating scales method: Performance appraisal method that rates employees according to defined factors.

Realistic job preview (RJP): Method of conveying both positive and negative job information to the applicant in an unbiased manner.

Recruitment: Process of attracting individuals on a timely basis, in sufficient numbers, and with appropriate qualifications to apply for jobs with an organization.

Recruitment methods: Specific means used to attract potential employees to the firm.

Recruitment sources: Where qualified candidates are located.

Reengineering: Fundamental rethinking and radical redesign of business processes to achieve dramatic improvements in critical, contemporary measures of performance such as cost, quality, service, and speed.

Reference checks: Validations from individuals who know the applicant that provide additional insight into the information furnished by the applicant and allow verification of its accuracy.

Regiocentric staffing: Staffing approach that is similar to the polycentric staffing approach, but regional groups of subsidiaries reflecting the organization's strategy and structure work as a unit.

Reliability: Extent to which a selection test provides consistent results.

Relocation benefits: Company-paid shipment of household goods and temporary living expenses, covering all or a portion of the real estate costs associated with buying a new home and selling the previously occupied home.

Repatriation: Process of bringing expatriates home.

Requirements forecast: Determining the number, skill, and location of employees the organization will need at future dates in order to meet its goals.

Reshoring: Reverse of offshoring and involves bringing work back to the United States.

Resilience: Ability to bounce back and adapt in a positive manner to difficult situations.

Results-based system: Performance appraisal method in which the manager and subordinate jointly agree on objectives for the next appraisal period; in the past a form of management by objectives.

Résumé: Goal-directed summary of a person's experience, education, and training developed for use in the selection process.

Reverse mentoring: A process in which older employees learn from younger ones.

Right-to-work laws: Laws that prohibit management and unions from entering into agreements requiring union membership as a condition of employment.

Rights arbitration: Arbitration involving disputes over the interpretation and application of the various provisions of an existing contract.

Role-playing: T&D method in which participants are required to respond to specific problems they may encounter in their jobs by acting out real-world situations.

Sabbaticals: Temporary leaves of absence from an organization, usually at reduced pay.

Safety: Protection of employees from injuries caused by work-related accidents.

Salary compression: Situation that occurs when less experienced employees are paid as much as or more than employees who have been with the organization a long time due to a gradual increase in starting salaries and limited salary adjustment for long-term employees.

Say on pay: Provision that gives shareholders in all but the smallest companies an advisory vote on executive pay.

Scanlon plan: Gainsharing plan that provides a financial reward to employees for savings in labor costs resulting from their suggestions.

Secondary boycott: Union attempt to encourage third parties (such as suppliers and customers) to stop doing business with a firm; declared illegal by the Taft–Hartley Act.

Selection: Process of choosing from a group of applicants the individual best suited for a particular position and the organization.

Selection ratio: Number of people hired for a particular job compared to the number of qualified individuals in the applicant pool.

Self-assessment: Process of learning about oneself.

Seniority: Length of time an employee has been associated with the company, division, department, or job.

Severance pay: Compensation designed to assist laid-off employees as they search for new employment.

Shared service center (SSC): A center that takes routine, transaction-based activities dispersed throughout the organization and consolidates them in one place (also known as a center of expertise).

Shareholders: Owners of a corporation.

Shift differential: Additional money paid to employees for the inconvenience of working less-desirable hours.

Simulators: T&D delivery system comprised of devices or programs that replicate actual job demands.

Situational interview: Gives interviewers better insight into how candidates would perform in the work environment by creating hypothetical situations candidates would be likely to encounter on the job and asking them how they would handle them.

Skill-based pay: System that compensates employees for their job-related skills and knowledge, not for their job titles.

Social audit: Systematic assessment of a company's activities in terms of its social impact.

Specialist: Individual who may be a human resource executive, a human resource manager, or a nonmanager, and who is typically concerned with only one of the five functional areas of human resource management.

Spot bonus: Relatively small monetary gift provided employees for outstanding work or effort during a reasonably short period of time.

Staffing: Process through which an organization ensures that it always has the proper number of employees with the appropriate skills in the right jobs, at the right time, to achieve organizational objectives.

Standardization: Uniformity of the procedures and conditions related to administering tests.

Stock option plan: Incentive plan in which executives can buy a specified amount of stock in their company in the future at or below the current market price.

Strategic planning: Process by which top management determines overall organizational purposes and objectives and how they are achieved.

Strength/weakness balance sheet: A self-evaluation procedure, developed originally by Benjamin Franklin, that assists people in becoming aware of their strengths and weaknesses.

Stress: Body's nonspecific reaction to any demand made on it.

Stress interview: Form of interview in which the interviewer intentionally creates anxiety.

Strictness: Being unduly critical of an employee's work performance.

Strike: Action by union members who refuse to work in order to exert pressure on management in negotiations.

Structured interview: Interview in which the interviewer asks each applicant for a particular job the same series of job-related questions.

Substance abuse: Use of illegal substances or the misuse of controlled substances such as alcohol and drugs.

Succession planning: Process of ensuring that qualified persons are available to assume key managerial positions once the positions are vacant.

Survey feedback: Organization development method of basing change efforts on the systematic collection and measurement of subordinate's attitudes through anonymous questionnaires.

Talent management: Strategic endeavor to optimize the use of human capital, which enables an organization to drive short- and long-term results by building culture, engagement, capability, and capacity through integrated talent acquisition, development, and deployment processes that are aligned to business goals.

Tariffs: Taxes collected on goods that are shipped across national boundaries.

Team building: Conscious effort to develop effective work groups and cooperative skills throughout the organization.

Team equity: Equity that is achieved when teams are rewarded based on their group's productivity.

Telecommuting: Work arrangement whereby employees, called "teleworkers" or "telecommuters," are able to remain at home (or otherwise away from the office) and perform their work using computers and other electronic devices that connect them with their offices.

Termination: Most severe penalty that an organization can impose on an employee.

Third-country national (TCN): Citizen of one country, working in a second country, and employed by an organization headquartered in a third country.

360-degree feedback evaluation method: Popular performance appraisal method that involves evaluation input from multiple levels within the firm as well as external sources.

Traditional career path: Employee progresses vertically upward in the organization from one specific job to the next.

Training: Activities designed to provide learners with the knowledge and skills needed for their present jobs.

Training and development (T&D): Heart of a continuous effort designed to improve employee competency and organizational performance.

Transfer: Lateral movement of a worker within an organization.

Transnational corporation: Moves work to the places with the talent to handle the job and the time to do it at the right cost.

Two-tier wage system: A wage structure where newly hired workers are paid less than current employees for performing the same or similar jobs.

Unemployment compensation: Provides workers whose jobs have been terminated through no fault of their own monetary payments for up to 26 weeks or until they find a new job.

Uniform Guidelines: Provide a single set of principles that were designed to assist employers, labor organizations, employment agencies, and licensing and certification boards in complying with federal prohibitions against employment practices that discriminate on the basis of race, color, religion, sex, and national origin.

Union: Employees who have joined together for the purpose of dealing with their employer.

Union salting: Process of training union organizers to apply for jobs at a company and, once hired, working to unionize employees.

Union shop: Requirement that all employees become members of the union after a specified period of employment (the legal minimum is 30 days) or after a union-shop provision has been negotiated.

Unstructured interview: Interview in which the job applicant is asked probing, open-ended questions.

Validity: Extent to which a test measures what it claims to measure.

Vestibule system: T&D delivery system that takes place away from the production area on equipment that closely resembles equipment actually used on the job.

Virtual job fair: Online recruiting method engaged in by a single employer or group of employers to attract a large number of applicants.

Vocational interest tests: Tests that indicate the occupation a person is most interested in and the one likely to provide satisfaction.

Voluntary benefits: Benefits which are 100 percent paid by the employee but the employer typically pays the administrative cost.

Wage curve: Fitting of plotted points to create a smooth progression between pay grades (also known as the pay curve).

Workers' compensation: Provides a degree of financial protection for employees who incur expenses resulting from job-related accidents or illnesses.

Work standards method: Performance appraisal method that compares each employee's performance to a predetermined standard or expected level of output.

Workplace bullying: Acts of continual hostile conduct that deliberately hurt another person emotionally, verbally, or physically.

Workplace violence: Physical assault, threatening behavior, verbal abuse, hostility, or harassment directed toward employees at work or on duty.

Work-sample tests: Tests that require an applicant to perform a task or set of tasks representative of the job.

Zero-base forecast: Forecasting method that uses the organization's current level of employment as the starting point for determining future staffing needs.

Name Index

Company Index

Subject Index